Discrete Mathematics:

APPLIED ALGEBRA FOR COMPUTER AND INFORMATION SCIENCE

LEONARD S. BOBROW

University of Massachusetts, Amherst, Massachusetts

MICHAEL A. ARBIB

University of Massachusetts, Amherst, Massachusetts

HEMISPHERE PUBLISHING CORPORATION

1025 Vermont Ave., N.W. — Washington, D.C. 20005

Washington   London

W. B. Saunders Company: West Washington Square
Philadelphia, Pa. 19105

12 Dyott Street
London, WCIA 1DB

833 Oxford Street
Toronto, Ontario M8Z 5T9, Canada

Discrete Mathematics   ISBN 0-7216-1768-9

Last Digit is the Print Number   9   8   7   6   5   4   3   2   1

For
OUR PARENTS

Preface

Where calculus and differential equations have long provided the key mathematical tools for physics, chemistry, and engineering, algebra and discrete mathematics provide many of the tools of computer science, coding and information theory, and systems engineering. The aim of this book is to provide material for courses at the senior and first-year graduate levels which develop these algebraic tools and show how they may be applied, be they courses in Mathematics, Computer and Information Science, Electrical Engineering, or elsewhere. The first chapter is designed to make the book accessible to a reader with little background beyond high school algebra; the ninth and last chapter presents an exposition of the latest research in algebraic automata theory. Yet the intervening material is so designed as to carry the hard-working reader right through from the elements to the abstract theory.

This book has grown out of a specific need—to provide a text for a two-semester core course in fundamental concepts of Computer and Information Science—but has been so written (as we shall show in more detail below) that selected chapters may serve as the text for a one-semester course in any of the following courses: Modern Algebra with Applications; An Introduction to Automata Theory; Coding and Information Theory; and Algebraic Automata Theory. We have used material from the book in the classroom for the core course, for Introduction to Automata Theory, and for Coding and Information Theory, and we have used this experience to devise expository and motivational material omitted from comparable texts. Moreover, each author has carefully revised, expanded, and sometimes changed beyond recognition the sections drafted by the other author to make sure the material is accessible to readers who are new to the various fields of application that they present.

We now turn to an analysis of the individual chapters, after which we indicate how they may be grouped to form material for a variety of courses:

Chapter 1, "A Working Vocabulary," is our response to the discovery that all too many engineers and computer scientists complete their undergraduate careers with no mathematics beyond elementary calculus, and no appreciation of the definition-theorem-proof-corollary approach to mathematics. Chapter 1 is designed not only to provide the usual summary of basic concepts of sets, functions, graphs, and trees, but also to provide a careful exposition of such ideas as axiomatic methods, definitions and proofs by induction, *reductio ad absurdum,* etc. Thus, this chapter may be omitted by readers with a course in formal mathematics behind them, but may require two or three weeks of careful classroom exposure for students whose background is weak. It is because the latter class is so large that we have deemed it inappropriate to relegate this material to an appendix.

Chapter 2, "Automata and Semigroups I," shows how concepts from set theory and graph theory may be used to formalize the properties of certain types of finite-state information processors and how proof by induction can establish such properties; stresses how naturally semigroups, monoids, and groups arise in the study of such machines; studies how simple Boolean logic can be used to build such machines from specified components; introduces the concept of an equivalence relation (many students find this concept confusing, and so great care has been taken with motivation here); and shows how Cantor's diagonal argument illuminates the computing ability of finite-state machines. Chapter 2 closes by showing the powerful role of equivalence relations in specifying the construction of machines with specified behavior.

Chapter 3, "Computability," introduces the Turing machine as the general-purpose computer that can do everything any computer can do, if suitably programmed, and shows that there are problems which no Turing machine, and hence no computer, can solve. In particular, we construct a universal Turing machine and prove the unsolvability of the halting problem for Turing machines. We build on this result in Chapter 4 to give an informal proof of Gödel's Incompleteness Theorem. Finally, we present a general framework which embraces Turing machines, parallel computers, and tessellation automata, and we give an informal account of how self-reproducing machines may be embedded in such tessellations.

Chapter 4, "Language Theory," starts with an exposition of that class of formal languages, the context-free languages, which has to date been most associated with the specification of programming systems. We then analyze the deciding, accepting, and generating powers of various machines, placing the context-free languages in a hierarchy that runs from the regular sets associated with finite-state machines, through the context-free and context-sensitive languages, to the recursive and recursively enumerable sets associated with Turing machines. We then introduce tree automata, and see how the tree automata which check strings for membership in a language may be simulated by pushdown automata. Finally, we build on the experience gained in verifying properties by induction on the height of trees to verify the correctness of a simple compiler.

As its title suggests, Chapter 5, "Automata and Semigroups II," continues the work of Chapter 2, but now develops a great deal of modern algebra, introducing homomorphisms, direct products, subsemigroups, submonoids, and (normal) subgroups, developing important properties, and applying them to such topics in automata theory as machine decomposition and network complexity theory. Finally, in a section which may be omitted at a first reading, we show how Ω-algebras provide a unified setting for semigroups, monoids, and groups, and relate them to the tree automata of Chapter 4.

Chapter 6, "Applied Probability Theory," introduces three chapters related to coding and information theory. After providing an exposition of basic notions of discrete probability theory, we introduce Hartley's measure of information and study its role in coding theorems for noiseless and noisy channels (Shannon's Theorem). We close by introducing Markov chains and by studying basic properties of stochastic automata.

Chapter 7, "Linear Machines and Codes," introduces the algebraic concepts of ring, field, module, and vector space, relates matrices to linear machines, and then, in another section which may be omitted at first reading, ties these concepts back to the Ω-algebras of Chapter 5. We then see how these algebraic notions are applied in the study of group codes and linear machines, closing with a study of the fate of our Chapter 2 construction of automata with specified behavior in case the automata are linear.

Chapter 8, "Algebraic Coding Theory," builds on our Chapter 7 study of group codes. We study important general properties of principal ideal rings and their modules, and then use the cases in which the ring is a polynomial ring to establish important properties of cyclic and BCH codes.

Chapter 9, "Machines in a Category," is something of an indulgence on Arbib's part, providing an exposition of his recent research with Ernest Manes on a general theory of machines broad enough to include the ordinary automata of Chapter 2, the tree automata of Chapter 4, and the linear machines of Chapter 7. Thanks to Bobrow's efforts in recasting the original draft, the more adventurous reader may find our introduction to the modern algebraic theory of categories surprisingly comprehensible, and gain some genuine aesthetic pleasure from seeing how economically and elegantly the general definitions subsume the particular cases.

In developing a new curriculum in Computer and Information Science at the University of Massachusetts, we designed four core courses on the Fundamentals of Computation; of Computing Systems; of Cybernetics; and of Information. The first seven chapters of the present book constitute the text for the courses on Computation and Information. For the reader acquainted with *Curriculum '68: Recommendations for Academic Programs in Computer Science,* a report of the ACM curriculum committee on computer science, *Comm. ACM, 11* (1968) 151–197, it may suffice to say that we use our two-semester sequence to provide many topics from B3: Introduction to Discrete Structures; I6: Switching Theory; and I7: Sequential Machines; to introduce the elementary portions of A1: Formal Languages and Syntactic Analysis and A7: Theory of Computability; as well as to introduce discrete probability theory and its application in coding and information theory. Naturally, not all topics in the *Curriculum '68* courses listed above can be touched upon in two semesters. For example, we defer logic (other than the elements used in switching theory) until the discussion of mechanical theorem-proving in our artificial intelligence course, and offer a course in combinatorics to deal with those combinatorial aspects of discrete mathematics which do not fit into the present volume. We believe that the arrangement of material in our two core courses enables the student to gain perspectives and to see relationships which are obscured by the more fragmented approach of *Curriculum '68*. In addition, of course, the design of our core gives the student far more flexibility in creating a program of study, since it reduces by almost a third the number of courses required to gain a basic working vocabulary in theoretical aspects of Computer and Information Science.

With this as background, let us give suggested breakdowns of the courses listed above into chapters of this book, and then briefly discuss the scope of each chapter:

Core Courses in Computer and Information Science

Course A: 1. A Working Vocabulary
2. Automata and Semigroups I
3. Computability
4. Language Theory
Course B: 5. Automata and Semigroups II (except 5-6)
6. Applied Probability Theory
7. Linear Machines and Codes (except 7-2)

The next four courses all require that the reader have some facility with the basic set-theoretic concepts and the proof techniques developed in Chapter 1:

Modern Algebra with Applications

2. Automata and Semigroups I (except 2-3)
5. Automata and Semigroups II
7. Linear Machines and Codes
8. Algebraic Coding Theory

Coding and Information Theory

6. Applied Probability Theory (except 6-5)
2-1, 2-2, and 2-3. Some concepts of automata and semigroups
7. Linear Machines and Codes (except 7-5)
8. Algebraic Coding Theory

Introduction to Automata Theory

2. Automata and Semigroups I
3. Computability
4. Language Theory
5-5. Network Complexity Theory (with patch-in of elementary group theory)
6-1. (First half) Basic Notions of Discrete Probability Theory
6-5. Markov Chains and Stochastic Automata

Algebraic Automata Theory

(Prerequisite: Equivalent of 2-1, 2-2, and 2-3; and some linear algebra.)
2-5. Building Automata with Specified Behavior
4-1 and 4-3. Context-Free Languages and Tree Automata
5. Automata and Semigroups II
7. Linear Machines and Codes
9. Machines in a Category

Great care has been taken to design the sections so that all the above courses, and many yet to be dreamed of, can be taught without referring to omitted sections, save that Chapter 1 provides a standard reference source for elementary concepts and definitions.

The book may be used with its companion volume, "System Theory: A Unified State-Space Approach to Continuous and Discrete Systems" by L. Padulo and M. A. Arbib, as the text for a four-semester Junior-Senior course in Applied Mathematics which presents both modern algebra and advanced calculus together with their application in the Computer, Information, and System Sciences.

LEONARD S. BOBROW
MICHAEL A. ARBIB

Contents

Chapter 9

CHAPTER 1

A Working Vocabulary

This chapter is meant to serve three purposes:

1) To introduce the reader with little background in algebra to the ideas of precise definitions and careful formal proofs.

2) To develop formally certain properties of various number systems and to list others in order to provide a source of examples for the theory and applications developed in subsequent chapters.

3) To summarize the basic concepts of sets, functions, graphs, and trees to provide a convenient reference, and to make the subsequent chapters as independent as possible.

When using this book as a text, this chapter should be skimmed quickly if the students already have a reasonable familiarity with the "lemma-theorem-proof-corollary" approach to algebra. In fact, it could even be assigned as home reading during the first week of the course, since it is designed to remind the reader of material with which he is probably familiar, placing the material in appropriate perspective for use in the rest of this book. However, many students have calculus as their only mathematical background for a course such as this, and *for them it is vitally necessary to go over a large part of this chapter very carefully* in class so that they know how to rephrase familiar statements in this "new language" before they must use it to talk of new concepts. Even such simple concepts as "proof by induction" or "Cartesian product of sets" appear strange against the (clearly defective!) background of the usual calculus course.

We thus recommend the following classroom use of this chapter *for students with a weak background in algebra:*

1

1. Discuss key concepts of Section 1–1 in class. It is most important that students get a feel for the distinction between intuition and formal proof, and that the concepts of inductive definition and inductive proof become natural to them.

2. Assign a few exercises from Section 1–2, stress a few key definitions in class, but reserve most of the material as a reference source, with pieces to be worked into later lectures as required.

3. The points made in Section 1–3 are sufficiently important that it is probably worth working through the proof of Theorem 2 in class, emphasizing which technique is used in which part. It may be useful, two weeks later, to ask the students to give a similar analysis of a proof encountered in the main body of the text.

4. Discuss key concepts of Section 1–4 briefly in class. The only point that really needs stressing here is that when we have many different notations (e.g., $\frac{1}{2}$, $\frac{2}{4}$, $\frac{3}{6}$, $\frac{117}{234}$) for the same thing, we must check that our operations really manipulate the thing itself, and will not yield different results if we denote the thing in different ways.

5. Section 1–5 does not need explicit discussion. The definition of a labelled graph may best be noted when discussing state graphs in Section 2–1, while the discussion of rooted trees is best reserved until they are actually used.

The material can then be covered in four to six lectures. We stress that, for students who have taken an introductory course in linear or modern algebra, little or no class time need be spent on Chapter 1 before proceeding to subsequent chapters.

1–1   N and Proof by Induction

To survive in a changing world, one must be able to generalize: to apply the fruits of one's past experience to new and superficially different situations. The key to this is the ability to notice, and make use of, similarities of a subtle kind in apparently different circumstances. Mathematicians have refined this ability in what is called the *axiomatic method*. This method reached its first flowering in the work of Euclid, who observed that one could write down a few "self-evident truths" about the properties of lines and points and angles, and from these *axioms* deduce subtle geometrical properties by pure logic alone. However, where Euclid thought his axioms described the essence of a single reality—the space in which we live—the last hundred years has seen the axiomatic method developed into a far more flexible tool. Axioms are no longer thought of as being the "self-evident truths" of any one system. Rather, they are thought of as a list of important properties which may be possessed by many systems. For example, the "group axioms" we shall introduce (using the mathematician's special sense of "group") in Section 2–2 are shared by such diverse systems as the set of all integers under addition, the collection of motions of a rigid body through space, and the dynamics of what may be called reversible automata. Thus, when we prove that some statement may be deduced from a given set of axioms, we are guaranteeing that all systems which share the properties captured by the axioms must also share the properties captured by such a statement.

Thus, a methodology we shall apply again and again will be to examine a number of examples which interest us in order to abstract from them a number of properties which interest us. These properties may then be captured in a formal definition, such as, "A *group* is a collection of such-and-such which obey the axioms so-and-so." The art, of course, is to abstract the really crucial properties from the examples so that the theorems we deduce do express things we want to know about structures which share those axioms.

To make this discussion concrete, and to give the reader a better feel for the axiomatic method, we now show that three apparently trivial axioms capture enough of the properties of the set of **non-negative integers** (also called the **natural numbers**)

$$\mathbf{N} = \{0, 1, 2, 3, \ldots\}$$

to allow us to define addition and multiplication, among other operations, and to prove such facts as that $(m + n)p = mp + np$ for all natural numbers m, n, and p.

We start by observing that **N** contains 0, and all—and only—those other numbers that can be obtained from 0 by repeatedly passing to the next number. Let us use σ to denote the **successor function** which replaces n by its successor—so that $\sigma(0) = 1$, $\sigma(1) = 2$, . . . , $\sigma(3759) = 3760$, and so on, where, for each n in **N**, $\sigma(n)$ denotes the result of operating upon n with the function σ.

We may think of σ as given by a means for generating, from each number name, another name that has not been used before. If we use ordinary base 10 notation to name numbers, then σ operates as follows:

1. If the rightmost digit d of the decimal notation for n is not 9, then replace d by its successor, using the table

d	0	1	2	3	4	5	6	7	8
$\sigma(d)$	1	2	3	4	5	6	7	8	9

Then the resultant string of symbols is the decimal notation for $\sigma(n)$.

2. If the rightmost digit d of the decimal notation for n is 9, but there is a digit not equal to 9 in the notation, let d_1 be the rightmost such digit. Change all the 9's to the right of d_1 to 0 and change d_1 to $\sigma(d_1)$ to obtain the decimal notation for $\sigma(n)$.

3. If the decimal notation for n is a string of 9's, change each 9 to a 0, and precede the resultant string of 0's by a 1 to obtain the decimal notation for $\sigma(n)$.

Example 1

Using $n_1 \overset{\sigma}{\mapsto} n_2$ as shorthand notation for "σ transforms n_1 into n_2" we can show the following examples of applying rules 1, 2, and 3 respectively:

$$1993 \overset{\sigma}{\mapsto} 1994$$
$$2199 \overset{\sigma}{\mapsto} 2200$$
$$999 \overset{\sigma}{\mapsto} 1000 \qquad\qquad \Diamond$$

[We use the symbol $\Diamond$ to denote the end of an example.]

The crucial properties of the non-negative integers are captured in three simple statements about the function σ first set forth by the Italian logician G. Peano.

The Peano Axioms

The set **N** contains an element 0, and is equipped with a function which assigns a number $\sigma(n)$ to each number n in such a way that the following properties hold:

N1. For no n in **N** does $\sigma(n) = 0$ (0 is the first member of **N**).
N2. If $m \neq n$, then $\sigma(m) \neq \sigma(n)$ (Distinct numbers have distinct successors).
N3. If a subset S of **N** contains 0, and contains $\sigma(n)$ for each n in S, then in fact S is precisely **N**.

To understand the Peano axioms somewhat better, let us represent **N** by the array shown in Figure 1–1, in which we use a circle to represent each number, and draw an arrow from each number to its successor.

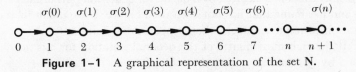

Figure 1–1 A graphical representation of the set **N**.

Axiom N1 tells us that the structure has a first member. Without it we could

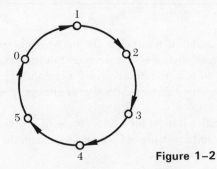

Figure 1–2

get structures like that shown in Figure 1–2, which has no first element but does satisfy both N2 and N3.

Axiom N2 rules out structures like that shown in Figure 1–3, in which Axioms N1 and N3 are satisfied, but 3 and 6 have the same successor.

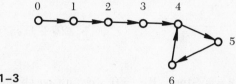

Figure 1–3

Finally, N3 ensures that every element can be reached from 0 by taking enough steps, and thus rules out "multi-track" structures such as that shown in Figure 1–4. This obeys N1 and N2 but fails to obey N3, since no "hatted" element is "reachable" from 0.

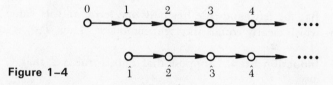

Figure 1–4

What we have just shown is that the three axioms, N1, N2, and N3, are *independent*. For each pair of axioms we have exhibited a **model,** i.e., a structure which has the properties described by those two axioms, and for which the other axiom is false. Thus, no axiom can be deduced from the other two. In other words, we really need all three axioms; none of the three is superfluous. A whole area of mathematics, called **model theory,** is devoted to showing that a set of axioms is **consistent** (i.e., free from contradictions) and **independent** (i.e., no axiom is superfluous). Consistency always holds if we write down axioms to describe properties of some actual model; but if we write down properties of several different structures to see what happens when we put them together, we do have to check for consistency, usually by exhibiting a model which possesses all the properties.

An important concept throughout our studies will be definition and proof by **INDUCTION:** N3 tells us that we may deduce that a property of numbers—let us call it $P(n)$—is true of all natural numbers if we can carry out the two following steps:

i. **The Basis Step:** Prove that $P(0)$ is true.
ii. **The Induction Step:** Verify that whenever $P(n)$ is true for any n, then $P(\sigma(n))$ must also be true.

For, if S is the subset of **N** for which $P(n)$ is true, N3 clearly guarantees that S is in fact all of **N.** Proofs which break down into these two steps are called **proofs by induction.** Of course, we have to conjecture that $P(n)$ is indeed true for all n before we try to prove it!

Example 2†

Let $P(n)$ be the statement, "the sum of the first $(n + 1)$ odd numbers equals $(n + 1)^2$," or, in symbols, $P(n)$ is shorthand for the statement

$$\sum_{k=0}^{n} (2k + 1) = (n + 1)^2$$

Basis Step. If $n = 0$, we must check that

$$\sum_{k=0}^{0} (2k + 1) = (0 + 1)^2$$

But the left-hand side has only one term, and its value is $[2 \cdot 0 + 1] = 1$, which clearly equals the right hand side. Thus, $P(0)$ is indeed true.

Induction Step. Suppose that $P(n)$ is true, i.e., that

$$\sum_{k=0}^{n} (2k + 1) = (n + 1)^2$$

Can we then deduce that $P(\sigma(n))$ must also be true?

We compute $\sum_{k=0}^{n+1} (2k + 1)$:

$$\sum_{k=0}^{n+1} (2k + 1) = \sum_{k=0}^{n} (2k + 1) + (2(n + 1) + 1) \text{ by definition of summation}$$

$$= (n + 1)^2 + (2(n + 1) + 1) \quad \text{by our induction hypothesis that } P(n) \text{ is true}$$

$$= ((n + 1) + 1)^2 \text{ by the binomial theorem:}$$
$$(a + b)^2 = a^2 + 2ab + b^2$$

$$= (\sigma(n) + 1)^2, \text{ as was to be proved}$$

---

†In this example, and in Exercise 3, we shall use familiar properties of numbers. However, henceforth we shall take care to show that properties we use can be developed from the Peano axioms.

Thus, $P(\sigma(n))$ is indeed true whenever $P(n)$ is true. Thus $P(n)$ is true for all n, by N3.   ◊

Besides serving to verify the truth of properties of the integers, N3—which is often referred to as the **induction axiom**—allows us to define a numerical function f (i.e., a rule which transforms each natural number n into "another"† number $f(n)$) in two stages as follows:

Basis Step.   Specify $f(0)$.

Induction Step.   Provide a rule $\mathcal{R}$ which, given any n and the already computed value of $f(n)$, will enable us to determine $f(\sigma(n))$. Symbolically, $\mathcal{R}$ is a rule such that for all values of n we have

$$f(\sigma(n)) = \mathcal{R}(f(n), n)$$

Then to compute $f(n)$ for any particular n, we first obtain $f(0)$ from the basis step; then we use the induction step to compute $f(1)$ from $f(0)$, then again use the induction step to compute $f(2)$ from $f(1)$, and so on, until we use the induction step for the last time, finally to obtain $f(n) = f(\sigma(n-1))$ from $f(n-1)$. [Of course, if the n of current interest were 0, then the basis step alone would suffice.]

For an inductive definition to be really interesting, $\mathcal{R}$ is usually in some sense "simpler" than f. If the rule for $\mathcal{R}$ is of the form "given $f(n)$ and n, ignore $f(n)$, form $\sigma(n)$ from n, and then form $f(\sigma(n))$ from n," nothing has been gained. The definitions we are about to give are all "interesting" in the sense that f is genuinely more complex than $\mathcal{R}$—we form addition from σ, multiplication from addition, and so forth. In our study of partial recursive functions in Section 3-1, we shall see the role played by definition by induction in building up all effectively computable functions from a starting collection of functions which are very simple indeed.

Let us give some examples, and then see how an inductive definition of f can yield a "flow diagram" for computing it.

Example 3

Define the function f by the induction scheme:

$$f(0) = 5$$
$$f(\sigma(n)) = \sigma(f(n))$$

---

†We put the word "another" in quotes because we do not exclude the possibility that $f(n)$ might equal n. For example, if f transforms n into n^2, then we have $f(1) = 1$ for this particular choice of the rule f.

We calculate $f(1)$, $f(2)$, $f(3)$, and $f(4)$ as follows:

$$f(1) = f(\sigma(0)) = \sigma(f(0)) = \sigma(5) = 6$$
$$f(2) = f(\sigma(1)) = \sigma(f(1)) = \sigma(6) = 7$$
$$f(3) = f(\sigma(2)) = \sigma(f(2)) = \sigma(7) = 8$$
$$f(4) = f(\sigma(3)) = \sigma(f(3)) = \sigma(8) = 9 \qquad \diamond$$

In setting up a mathematical theory, our task is to provide formalized concepts which capture essential properties of interest to us. In picturesque language we might imagine the series of natural numbers arising from the invention of new names to describe the number of stones in a pile: 0 is the name used in talking of an empty pile; and $\sigma(n)$ is the name we are to use in talking of the pile that results from adding a single stone to the pile that we have already agreed to characterize as containing n stones.

Now we might want to introduce the notation $n + m$ to describe the number of stones in a pile obtained by combining two piles, the first of which contains n stones and the second of which contains m stones. Note that if we fix the number of stones in the second pile to be m, we have m stones in the combined pile when there are 0 stones in the first pile; and that, again keeping m fixed, if we increase the number of stones in the first pile by one then we increase the number of stones in the combined pile by one. We thus feel that we can capture all the properties of addition within our formalization by identifying $n + m$ with the value $\sigma^m(n)$ of the function σ^m whose inductive definition is as follows:

Basis Step. $\sigma^m(0) = m$

(1)

Induction Step. $\sigma^m(\sigma(n)) = \sigma(\sigma^m(n))$

Example 4

Let us use the formula (1) to compute $\sigma^4(3)$

Basis Step. $\sigma^4(0) = 4$

Induction Step 1. $\sigma^4(1) = \sigma^4(\sigma(0)) = \sigma(\sigma^4(0)) = \sigma(4) = 5$

Induction Step 2. $\sigma^4(2) = \sigma(5) = 6$

Induction Step 3. $\sigma^4(3) = \sigma(6) = 7$

Thus, with 3 iterations of the induction step we find that $3 + 4$ does indeed equal 7. $\qquad \diamond$

In our formal theory, then, we are going to mean $\sigma^m(n)$ whenever we write $n + m$. But now a little care is required, for within our formal theory we may only make use of properties of $\sigma^m(n)$ that follow from the inductive definition of σ^m and from the stipulated properties N1 to N3 of the natural numbers. For example, we shall have to prove below that with our definition of addition, we do indeed have the property that $\sigma(n) = n + 1$. Again, while our experience with piles of stones suggests that the number of stones in the combination of two piles will not depend upon which pile we choose as our first pile, it still requires formal proof to check that we have actually captured this property in our formalization. The word "commute" means "exchange" or "interchange," and we shall thus speak of this result as the **commutative law** for addition. As an exercise in proofs by induction, let us check that it is indeed true that $\sigma^m(n) = \sigma^n(m)$ for all natural numbers m and n, as well as deducing other properties of σ^m along the way. To the reader who objects, "Well, it's so obvious that $m + n = n + m$ that it's a waste of time to prove it," we can only reply that it is a good idea to get used to formal proofs now, while we have plenty of intuition to help us understand what we are doing. Later on we shall have to use such proof techniques to prove the properties of structures for which intuition may be misleading, and rigorous constructions from the axioms become absolutely essential. For now, let us state and verify some properties of natural numbers which are "obvious" from the motivation of combining piles of stones, but which require proof by induction within our formal framework:

PROPERTY 1

For all natural numbers n,

$$n + 0 = n = 0 + n$$

that is, $\sigma^0(n) = n = \sigma^n(0)$.

Proof

That $\sigma^n(0) = n$ is just the basis step of our definition of σ^n, and thus needs no further proof. However, to verify that $\sigma^0(n) = n$ for all n, we must proceed by induction on n.

Basis Step. $\sigma^0(0) = 0$ by the basis step of the definition of σ^0.

Induction Step.   Suppose we have that $\sigma^0(n) = n$. We must deduce from this that $\sigma^0(\sigma(n)) = \sigma(n)$. But

$\sigma^0(\sigma(n)) = \sigma(\sigma^0(n))$ by the induction step of the definition
of σ^0 (i.e., σ^m with $m = 0$).

$= \sigma(n)$ by our current hypothesis on n.

Thus we are done, and $\sigma^0(n) = n$ for all n.   □

[We use the symbol □ to indicate that no further proof will be given.]

To derive our next property, we must now prove a **lemma**—in other words, a "little" theorem which has little interest of its own, but provides a useful tool for the proof of other theorems:

LEMMA 1

For all natural numbers n and m,

$$\sigma^{\sigma(n)}(m) = \sigma(\sigma^n(m))$$

that is, $m + \sigma(n) = \sigma(m + n)$

Proof

We proceed by induction on m.

Basis Step. For all n, $\sigma^{\sigma(n)}(0) = \sigma(n)$ by the basis step of the
definition of $\sigma^{\sigma(n)}$

$= \sigma(\sigma^n(0))$ by the basis step of the
definition of σ^n

Induction Step. Suppose m is such that $\sigma^{\sigma(n)}(m) = \sigma(\sigma^n(m))$ for every n. We must deduce from this that $\sigma^{\sigma(n)}(\sigma(m)) = \sigma(\sigma^n(\sigma(m)))$ for every n. But

$\sigma^{\sigma(n)}(\sigma(m)) = \sigma(\sigma^{\sigma(n)}(m))$ by the induction step of the
definition of $\sigma^{\sigma(n)}$
$= \sigma(\sigma(\sigma^n(m)))$ by our crucial hypothesis on m
$= \sigma(\sigma^n(\sigma(m)))$ by the induction step of the
definition of σ^n

Thus we are done, and $\sigma^{\sigma(n)}(m) = \sigma(\sigma^n(m))$ for all m and n.   □

Now, Property 1 told us that $\sigma^0(m) = m$ for all m; and since $1 = \sigma(0)$, we can now deduce from Lemma 1 that

$$\sigma^1(m) = \sigma^{\sigma(0)}(m) = \sigma(\sigma^0(m)) = \sigma(m)$$

for all m. In other words, we really are justified in using the notations $m + 1$ (that is, $\sigma^1(m)$) and $\sigma(m)$ interchangeably. This is hardly a surprising result, but it is another check that we do seem to have formalized addition in the right way.

[*A short sermon:* Lewis Carroll had Humpty Dumpty remark in a rather scornful tone that "When *I* use a word, it means just what I choose it to mean—neither more nor less." The mathematician feels the same way about his symbols. In Property 1 we proved that $\sigma^0(n) = n$ for all *n*—and yet we now claim that we proved that $\sigma^0(m) = m$ for all *m*! This freedom to use different labels is a very important one to the mathematician. The convention that the mathematician follows is this: If, in a given paragraph (statement), one does not say how one is using a symbol, then it is to be used as it was last used. For example, in this book we shall never use **N** to denote anything but the set of non-negative integers. But if one assigns a symbol anew in that paragraph, then its prior meaning is to be ignored, and the new convention is to be followed until (if ever) yet another assignment is made. Similarly, a computer programmer may use a certain register in the computer's memory to store a customer's bank balance during one part of the execution of the program—but once one passes to that part of the program which stores, say, another customer's social security number in that register, it is futile to regard the address of the register as still being a "reference to" or "symbol for" the first customer's bank balance.]

PROPERTY 2

For all natural numbers *m* and *n*,

$$m + n = n + m$$

that is,

$$\sigma^n(m) = \sigma^m(n)$$

Proof

We shall proceed by induction on *n*.

Basis Step.   That $m + 0 = 0 + m$ for all *m* has already been verified as Property 1.

Induction Step.   Suppose, then, that *n* is such that $m + n = n + m$ for all *m*. We must verify that $m + \sigma(n) = \sigma(n) + m$ is also true for all *m*. But

$$
\begin{aligned}
\sigma(n) + m &= \sigma^m(\sigma(n)) && \text{by our convention as to how we have} \\
&&& \text{formalized addition} \\
&= \sigma(\sigma^m(n)) && \text{by the induction step of the definition} \\
&&& \text{of } \sigma^m \\
&= \sigma(\sigma^n(m)) && \text{by our current hypothesis on } n. \\
&= \sigma^{\sigma(n)}(m) && \text{by Lemma 1}
\end{aligned}
$$

Thus we are done, and for every *n*, we have that $n + m = m + n$ for every *m*. $\qquad\square$

PROPERTY 3

For all natural numbers m, n, and p,

$$(m + n) + p = m + (n + p)$$

Proof

Left as an exercise. [Hint: Use induction on n, making use of Lemma 1 several times.] □

So much for addition and its properties. We shall shortly undertake a similar analysis of multiplication. But now, with the example of addition before us, let us see how the inductive definition:

Basis Step: $f(0)$ is given
Induction Step: Compute $f(n + 1)$ from $f(n)$ by the rule

$$f(n + 1) = \Re(f(n), n)$$

can be turned into a program for computing any desired value of f. We simply set up three registers, one of which holds the n for which we require $f(n)$, one of which contains k (the last integer for which we have so far evaluated f), and one of which contains y, which is the result of that latest evaluation. We start with $k = 0$, and thus with $y = f(0)$; we then keep increasing k by 1, and updating y by the induction step, until k reaches the given value n, at which time y is the desired value $f(n)$. This process is shown in the flow diagram of Figure 1–5.

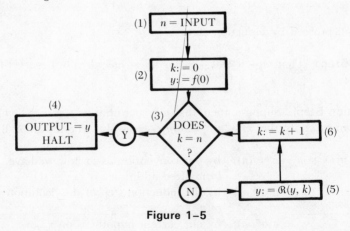

Figure 1–5

A few words of explanation to the reader unacquainted with flow diagrams:

We start at box (1), which tells us that the current input provides the value of n to be used in our computation. Box (2) tells us that we must initially set k to 0 and set y to $f(0)$. Box (3) tells us to find out whether the present value of k is equal to n. If the answer is yes (Y), we go to box (4), which tells us to print out the current value of y as our output, and halt—the computation is complete. But if the answer is no (N), we may not halt yet, but instead must go to box (5) and then to box (6). The lines in these boxes are not (patently false!) equations, but instead are instructions which are to be interpreted as follows:

> $y := \Re(y, k)$: form the *new* value of y by using rule $\Re$ to operate upon the *old* values of y and k. The new value of y replaces the old value of y, which is discarded.
>
> $k := k + 1$: form the *new* value of k by adding 1 to the *old* value of k. The new value of k replaces the old value of k, which is discarded.

In other words, the combined effect of boxes (5) and (6) is indeed to decree that $f(k + 1) = \Re(f(k), k)$ for the k with which we entered box (5). After we have completed these two replacements, the flow diagram sends us back to box (3) to find out whether k is now big enough. If not, the cycle repeats until it is (and this must take us through the cycle n times—why?) at which time we exit through (4) with the desired $f(n)$ as our output.

When we actually *do* mathematics, we have to pursue false leads, sketch out arguments, come back later to fill in missing details, and so on. When we *communicate* mathematics, we simply present the shortest path that we can find to replace our original meanderings. In the next example, then, we present a discursive exposition of how one might hit upon the right definition of a function, and contrast it to the polished definition that we can then extract from the original, relatively messy version. Readers with little experience in this sort of mathematics should not be discouraged if their initial solutions to the exercises are far messier than even the first part of the next example. But they should always try to rewrite the solution in a more elegant form before passing on to the next exercise. If this two-stage approach is assiduously followed, generating elegant proofs will become so habitual that the first stage may eventually be omitted for all save lengthy or tricky problems. Clearly, we shall usually give only the elegant proofs in what follows; the reader, in studying such a proof, should always ask himself the question, "Now, how would *I* have discovered a proof like that?" And, every now and again, the result of such reflection will be the discovery of a *better* proof, and that is very satisfying indeed!

Example 5

For the set **N** of natural numbers, consider the function s_n which subtracts n from a given number m if in fact $m \geq n$ (m is greater than or equal to n), but yields 0 if not. We write $s_n(m) = m \div n$.

This is a tough one, for we have to break this definition down into a series of intermediates. To see the problem we start naively: The obvious candidate for the basis step is $s_n(0) = 0$. But suppose we have computed $s_4(3) = 0$ and use an induction step to get $s_4(4) = 0$. How can this induction step then again use 0 (which is $s_4(4)$) to now get 1 (which is $s_4(5)$)? Somewhat bruised, we try a different tack, and instead of computing $s_n(m)$ by induction on m, we first try to define the function $f : m \mapsto m \div n$ (read: the function f which replaces m by $m - n$ if $m \geq n$, and which replaces m by 0 if $m < n$) by induction on n as follows:

$$f(0) = m \div 0 = m$$
$$f(\sigma(n)) = m \div \sigma(n) = (m \div n) \div 1$$

The reader should convince himself of the truth of the last equation. This last equation is of the right form, save for one problem—it requires us to be able to compute the function $g : r \mapsto r \div 1$ (which is the function which decreases a number by 1 unless that number is 0, in which case the result is also 0). But the definition of this function is simplicity itself:

$$g(0) = 0 \div 1 = 0$$
$$g(\sigma(n)) = \sigma(n) \div 1 = n$$

Thus, we see that the definition of s_n is broken into three stages:

I. Define $g : r \mapsto r \div 1$ by
$$g(0) = 0 \div 1 = 0$$
$$g(\sigma(n)) = \sigma(n) \div 1 = n$$

Axiom N3 assures us that $r \div 1$ is then defined for all $r \in \mathbf{N}$.

II. Define $f : n \mapsto m \div n$ by
$$f(0) = m \div 0 = m$$
$$f(\sigma(n)) = m \div \sigma(n) = (m \div n) \div 1$$

For any given $n \in \mathbf{N}$, Axiom N3 then assures us, that $m \div n$ is defined for all $n \in \mathbf{N}$.

III. Define s_n by $s_n(m) = m \div n$ for each $m \in \mathbf{N}$. We don't need to use Axiom N3 in III, for we already learned at stage II that we could define $m \div n$ for any pair of integers m and n.   ◊

Example 6

Computing $n \div 1$ is easy:

$$0 \div 1 = 0; \; 1 \div 1 = \sigma(0) \div 1 = 0; \; 2 \div 1 = \sigma(1) \div 1 = 1;$$
$$3 \div 1 = \sigma(2) \div 1 = 2, \text{ etc.}$$

To compute $s_4(2)$, we must compute $2 \div 4$ by induction on n in $2 \div n$. We have:

$$2 \div 0 = 2$$
$$2 \div 1 = 2 \div \sigma(0) = (2 \div 0) \div 1 = 2 \div 1 = 1$$
$$2 \div 2 = 2 \div \sigma(1) = (2 \div 1) \div 1 = 1 \div 1 = 0$$
$$2 \div 3 = 0 \div 1 = 0$$
$$2 \div 4 = 0 \div 1 = 0 \qquad\qquad \Diamond$$

It is worth noting that in our intuitive discussion of how to set up $m \div n$ we used the concepts of inequality and of subtraction, saying that $m \div n$ was $m - n$ if $m \geq n$, but that it was 0 if $m \leq n$. However, in our formal definition no use was made of these concepts. In Section 1-4, we shall formally define unlimited subtraction $m - n$ of arbitrary (negative or non-negative) integers in terms of our present formal notion of the limited subtraction $m \div n$ of non-negative integers. Here let us give the *formal* definition of the relation of inequality in terms of our formalized concept of limited subtraction:

Let m and n be two natural numbers.

> If $m \div n = 0$, we may write $m \leq n$.
>
> If $n \div m \neq 0$, we may write $m < n$.
>
> If $n \leq m$, we may write $m \geq n$.
>
> If $n < m$, we may write $m > n$.

The next property of the natural numbers is "not quite as good" as the corresponding property of **Z**, the set of all (negative as well as non-negative) integers which we shall study in Section 1-3, so let us call this "provisional" version which holds in **N** by the name 4**N**, rather than 4. Similarly, the ninth property of **N** listed below will be called 9**N**.

PROPERTY 4N

For all natural numbers m and n,

$$(m + n) \div n = m$$

Proof

We proceed by induction on n.

Basis Step. $\quad (m + 0) \doteq 0 = m \doteq 0$ for all $m \in \mathbf{N}$ by Property 1

$$= m \qquad \text{by the basis step in the}$$
$$\text{definition of } n \mapsto m \doteq n$$

Induction Step. We must show that if n is such that $(m + n) \doteq n = m$ *for all values of* m then $(m + \sigma(n)) \doteq \sigma(n) = m$ also for all values of m. But

$$(m + \sigma(n)) \doteq \sigma(n) = [(m + \sigma(n)) \doteq n] \doteq 1 \qquad \text{by the induction step}$$
$$\text{of the definition of}$$
$$n \mapsto m \doteq n$$
$$= [\sigma(m + n) \doteq n] \doteq 1 \qquad \text{by Lemma 1}$$
$$= [\sigma(n + m) \doteq n] \doteq 1 \qquad \text{by Property 2} \qquad (2)$$
$$= [(n + \sigma(m)) \doteq n] \doteq 1 \qquad \text{by Lemma 1}$$
$$= [(\sigma(m) + n) \doteq n] \doteq 1 \qquad \text{by Property 2}$$
$$= \sigma(m) \doteq 1 \qquad \text{by our current hypothesis} \qquad (3)$$
$$\text{on } n$$
$$= m \qquad \text{by the induction step of}$$
$$\text{our definition of } r \doteq 1$$

Thus we are done, and for every n in $\mathbf{N}$ it is true that $(m + n) \doteq n = m$ for every m in $\mathbf{N}$. $\qquad\qquad\qquad\qquad\qquad\qquad\qquad\qquad\qquad\qquad\qquad \square$

Two comments are in order about the proof. Henceforth we shall assume the use of Properties 1 to 4 to be so standard that we may omit steps such as the three equations marked (2) above, and simply substitute $\sigma(m) + n$ for $m + \sigma(n)$ without explicit justification. Secondly, note that we made use of the fact that our induction hypothesis stated that for the given n, $(m + n) \doteq n = m$ *for all* m, so that in equation (3) we could use this equality with the m under explicit consideration replaced by its successor, $\sigma(m)$.

Let us now sketch the results of formalizing **multiplication**. Our motivation this time is that $m \cdot n$ is to be the number of stones obtained by compiling n piles, each of which contains m stones. If there are no piles, there are clearly no stones ($m \cdot 0 = 0$); while if we add an extra pile at the start, we add m stones to the final total ($m \cdot (n + 1) = (m \cdot n) + m$). Thus, it seems reasonable to formalize multiplication in terms of the function p_m whose inductive *definition* is as follows:

Basis Step. $\quad p_m(0) = 0$

Induction Step. $\quad p_m(\sigma(n)) = \sigma^m(p_m(n))$

We shall indeed henceforth mean $p_m(n)$ whenever we write $m \cdot n$.

Let us apply this scheme to evaluate $p_3(4) = 3 \cdot 4$:

Basis Step. $p_3(0) = 0$
Induction Step 1. $p_3(1) = \sigma^3(p_3(0)) = 0 + 3 = 3$
Induction Step 2. $p_3(2) = 3 + 3 = 6$
Induction Step 3. $p_3(3) = 6 + 3 = 9$
Induction Step 4. $p_3(4) = 9 + 3 = 12$

It is clear that, continuing in this way, we can multiply any number n by 3, simply by adding n 3's together.

As with addition, so with multiplication must we check that our formalization has captured the essential properties that our intuition demands. Here is a list of properties that do indeed follow from our definition of p_m, and from the postulated properties N1 to N3 of **N**:

PROPERTY 5

For all $n \in$ **N,**

$$n \cdot 1 = n = 1 \cdot n$$

that is, $$p_n(1) = n = p_1(n)$$

PROPERTY 6

For all pairs of natural numbers m and n,

$$m \cdot n = n \cdot m$$

that is, $$p_m(n) = p_n(m)$$

PROPERTY 7

For all m, n, and p in **N,**

$$(m \cdot n) \cdot p = m \cdot (n \cdot p)$$

PROPERTY 8

For all natural numbers m, n, and p,

$$m \cdot (n + p) = (m \cdot n) + (m \cdot p)$$

PROPERTY 9N

For all m, n, and $p \in \mathbf{N}$,

$$\text{if } m \cdot n = m \cdot p \text{ and } m \neq 0, \text{ then } n = p$$

Example 7

We will show that Properties 1, 4**N**, and 8 imply that we must have for all n

that $$n \cdot 0 = 0$$

By Property 1, we have that $0 = 0 + 0$. Thus,

$$n \cdot 0 = n \cdot (0 + 0)$$
$$= n \cdot 0 + n \cdot 0 \quad \text{by Property 8}$$

But, again by Property 1, $n \cdot 0 = 0 + n \cdot 0$

Thus, $$0 + n \cdot 0 = n \cdot 0 + n \cdot 0$$

and so $$(0 + n \cdot 0) \doteq (n \cdot 0) = (n \cdot 0 + n \cdot 0) \doteq (n \cdot 0)$$

Hence, by Property 4**N** we deduce that

$$0 = n \cdot 0 \qquad\qquad \Diamond$$

We leave the proofs of Properties 5 through 8 as exercises for the reader, and simply show—once these earlier properties have been verified—that we can deduce Property 9**N**.

Proof of Property 9**N**

We proceed by induction on n. (The reader may wish to see whether or not he can get a better proof by induction on m.)

Basis Step.   We must show that 0 is such that for all $m \neq 0$, the only p which yields $m \cdot 0 = m \cdot p$ is 0. But this is immediate from the fact that our definition of multiplication ensures that $m \cdot p$ cannot be 0 unless either m or p is 0. [Exercise: Verify that this is indeed true. Hint: Remember N1.]

Induction Step.   Suppose that n is such that for all $m \neq 0$, the only p which yields $m \cdot n = m \cdot p$ is n itself. We must show that this implies the same property of $\sigma(n)$. But if

$$m \cdot \sigma(n) = m \cdot p$$

then

$$m \cdot n + m = m \cdot p$$

and so

$$(m \cdot n + m) \doteq m = m \cdot p \doteq m,$$

or

$$m \cdot n = m \cdot p \doteq m$$

$$= m \cdot (p \doteq 1)$$

By our current hypothesis on n, it follows that $n = p \doteq 1$, and so $\sigma(n) = p$ [see Exericse 11]. □

In this section we have determined that our formal framework allows us to capture many of the properties of natural numbers, and of functions for combining them, that we would want any theory to embrace. In Section 1–3 we shall show how to formalize the set **Z** of all (negative as well as non-negative) integers, and the set **Q** of rational numbers. However, it would be pointless to spell out at great length the formal verification of their properties as we have done here. Our lengthy exposition in this section was not so much to prove Properties 1 through 9, for we assume that every reader is more than familiar with them (at least as soon as he learns the notation $\doteq$), but rather to use the discussion to give the reader a feel for the techniques of formal definition and rigorous mathematical proof by induction that will play so important a role in the study of discrete structures and new applications that will occupy us in subsequent chapters.

EXERCISES FOR SECTION 1–1

1. Give the construction analogous to that preceding Example 1 for numbers in binary notation. The same number may have different names.

2. Show that if a system satisfies Axiom N3 it cannot have two distinct elements 0 and $0'$ whereby it satisfies Axiom N3. [Hint: Consider the set S whose single element is $0'$.]

3. Prove by induction that $\sum\limits_{k=0}^{n} k = n(n+1)/2$. (Compare Example 2.)

4. Verify that for any pair of natural numbers n and m:
  (i) If $m < n$ or $m = n$, then $m \leq n$.
 (ii) If $m \leq n$, then $m < n$ or $m = n$. [This is the *converse* of (i).]
(iii) One and only one of the following three cases can hold: $m < n$, $m = n$, or $m > n$.

5. Provide the basis step and induction step for an inductive definition of the function e_m which assigns to any natural number n the number m^n. In other words, write down $e_m(0)$, and specify $e_m(\sigma_{(n)})$ in terms of $e_m(n)$ and n. Use this procedure to compute $e_6(3)$.

6. Note that $(n + 1)! = (n + 1) \cdot (n!)$ to define $n \mapsto n!$ inductively in terms of p_m for various m. Use your definition to evaluate 6!.

7. Verify Property 5.
8. Verify Property 6.
9. Verify Property 7.
10. Verify Property 8.
11. Verify that **(i)** $m \cdot p \doteq m = m \cdot (p \doteq 1)$
        (ii) If $n = p \doteq 1$, then $\sigma(n) = p$, if $p \neq 0$.
        (iii) So long as p is not 0, if $m \neq 0$ and $m \cdot \sigma(n) = m \cdot p$, show that $n = p \doteq 1$.

1–2 Sets and Functions

Our discussion of the set of natural numbers in Section 1–1 has implicitly used a certain amount of set theory, and our purpose in this section is to make that theory explicit in introducing the reader to the basic terminology of sets and functions that will be used again and again throughout this volume.

A **set** is a collection of objects or abstract entities. We use the notation $x \in X$ to denote the fact that the object x **belongs** to the set X. We shall also read $x \in X$ as saying that x is an **element** of the set X. If x does *not* belong to X, we may write $x \notin X$.

If we know that a set X contains precisely the elements $a_1, a_2, \ldots, a_n$, we shall denote this fact by writing $X = \{a_1, a_2, \ldots, a_n\}$. For example, the set A of all natural numbers less than 5 may be written as $A = \{0, 1, 2, 3, 4\}$. We can also extend this notation to infinite sets, as made clear by the example

$$\mathbf{N} = \{0, 1, 2, 3, \ldots.\}$$

of the natural numbers studied in the previous section. It is worth stressing that a set is characterized purely by the elements which belong to it, and *not* by the order in which they are listed or by whether or not elements are repeated. [Later we shall introduce the notion of *sequence*, in which order *is* important.] Thus, we can equally well represent $\mathbf{N}$ by the less usual display

$$\mathbf{N} = \{1, 0, 3, 2, 5, 4, 7, 6, \ldots\}$$

and the above set A also equals

$$\{4, 3, 4, 2, 1, 1, 3, 2, 0\}$$

Of course, a set need not be a set of numbers—consider the set of all faithful husbands.

Warning. Do not confuse $\{a\}$, the set with only one member, namely a, and a, the element itself. For example, $0 \in \{0\}$ is true, but $0 = \{0\}$ is false, while $0 \in 0$ is false but $0 = 0$ is true. Again, the set $\{\{a, b\}\}$ has only one element, namely the set $\{a, b\}$; while this latter set has two elements, namely a and b.

Having said that a set is a collection of elements, it may seem paradoxical to speak of a set with *no* elements. However, it does prove convenient to accept the **empty set** as a legitimate set. We denote it by $\emptyset$. Thus, for example,

$$\text{the set of odd numbers divisible by } 2 = \emptyset$$

and

$$\text{the set of all 4-meter-tall humans} = \emptyset$$

and

$$\text{the set of all real unicorns} = \emptyset$$

Sometimes it is convenient to describe a set not by enumerating its elements, but rather by specifying a property characteristic of all elements of the set. Thus, we use

$$\{x \mid P(x)\}$$

to denote the set of all those x's for which the statement $P(x)$ is true. For example, we can represent the set of positive integers as

$$\mathbf{Z}_+ = \{x \mid x \in \mathbf{N} \text{ and } x > 0\}$$

and the set A given above by

$$A = \{x \mid x \in \mathbf{N} \text{ and } x < 5\}$$

We say that a set S' is a **subset** of a set S just in case every element of S' is also contained in S. We then write $S' \subset S$, and we may say that S' is **contained** in S or that S **contains** S'. The empty set is a subset of every set, while any set is a subset of itself: $\emptyset \subset A \subset A$ for all sets A.

Given any set S, we use $\mathcal{P}(S)$ or 2^S to denote the set of all subsets of S:

$$\mathcal{P}(S) = 2^S = \{S' \mid S' \subset S\}$$

We call 2^S the **power set** of S.

Example 1

Let us list all the subsets of $S = \{a, b, c\}$.

The power set of S is

$$2^S = \{\emptyset, \{a\}, \{b\}, \{c\}, \{a, c\}, \{b, c\}, \{a, b\}, S\}$$

Note that S has 3 elements, while its 2^S has 2^3 elements.   ◊

Example 2

Let A, B, and C be sets. We will prove that if $A \subset B$ and $B \subset C$, then $A \subset C$. This property is called the **transitive law** of containment.

First let $a \in A$. Since $A \subset B$, then $a \in B$. However, since $B \subset C$, it must then follow that $a \in C$. Hence, $A \subset C$, since every a in A is also in C.   ◊

We say that two sets A and B are **equal** just in case they have the same elements. We denote the equality of sets by $A = B$. Thus, $A = B$ if and only if $A \subset B$ and $B \subset A$. If $A \subset B$ and $A \neq B$, we say that A is a **proper subset** of B.

Now let us study several ways in which we can combine old sets to form new ones:

The **union** of two sets A and B, written $A \cup B$, is the set of all elements each of which is in either A or B or both, i.e.,

$$A \cup B = \{x \mid x \in A \text{ or } x \in B\}$$

More generally, if we have any **family** of sets $\{A_\alpha \mid \alpha \in I\}$ (i.e., we pick any set I of "indexes" and then have one set A_α indexed by each $\alpha \in I$), then their **union**, denoted $\bigcup_{\alpha \in I} A_\alpha$, is the set of all elements which belong to A_α for at least one $\alpha \in I$.

The **intersection** of A and B, written $A \cap B$, is the set of all elements each of which is in both A and B, i.e.,

$$A \cap B = \{x \mid x \in A \text{ and } x \in B\}$$

More generally, the **intersection** of a family of sets $\{A_\alpha \mid \alpha \in I\}$, denoted $\bigcap_{\alpha \in I} A_\alpha$, is the set of all elements which belong to each A_α for every $\alpha \in I$.

Example 3

$\varnothing \cup A = A$

$\varnothing \cap A = \varnothing$

$\{1, 2, 3\} \cup \{3, 4, 5\} = \{1, 2, 3, 4, 5\}$

$\{1, 2, 3\} \cap \{3, 4, 5\} = \{3\}$

For all sets A and S, if $A \subset S$ then $A \cap S = A$

For all sets A and B, $(A \cap B) \subset A \subset (A \cup B)$

Incidentally, the simple example $\{1, 2\} \cap \{3, 4\} = \varnothing$ makes it clear why we include $\varnothing$ among our legitimate sets.   ◊

In studying various properties of unions and intersections of sets, a pictorial device is often of help. If S is a set and A and B are subsets of S, we may represent the elements of S as all the points of a rectangle, and the subsets A and B as all the points of certain regions within the rectangle. One such representation is shown in Figure 1–6. Such an illustration is referred to as a **Venn diagram.** In this particular Venn diagram, no point in the region

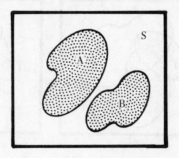

Figure 1–6

marked A is also in the region marked B. In other words, $A \cap B = \varnothing$, in which case we say that the sets A and B are **disjoint** or **mutually exclusive.** An example of the case $A \cap B \neq \varnothing$ is shown in Figure 1–7. The densest region there represents the subset $A \cap B$.

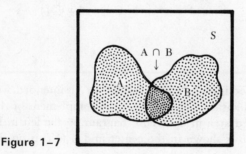

Figure 1–7

Example 4

The following is a list of statements which can easily be visualized with the aid of Venn diagrams:

I. $A \cup B = B \cup A$
II. $(A \cup B) \cup C = A \cup (B \cup C)$
III. $A \cap B = B \cap A$
IV. $(A \cap B) \cap C = A \cap (B \cap C)$

As a consequence of II and IV, we can omit parentheses to write $A \cup B \cup C$ and $A \cap B \cap C$ unambiguously. In general, however, parentheses cannot be ignored. For example, if we write $A \cup B \cap C$, we cannot be sure whether we mean $A \cup (B \cap C)$ or $(A \cup B) \cap C$; that these need not be equal can be seen from Figure 1–8, in which $A \cup (B \cap C)$ is shown shaded on the left, while $(A \cup B) \cap C$ is shown shaded on the right. Do note, however, that $(A \cup B) \cap C \subset A \cup (B \cap C)$. ◊

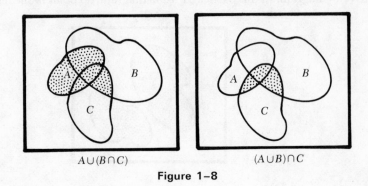

$$A \cup (B \cap C) \qquad\qquad (A \cup B) \cap C$$

Figure 1–8

Suppose that S is a set and A is a subset of S. Then the **complement** of A in S, denoted $S \backslash A$, is the set of all the elements in S which are not in A, i.e.,

$$S \backslash A = \{x \mid x \in S \text{ and } x \notin A\}$$

Example 5

If it is understood from the context which set S is intended, we shall abbreviate $S \backslash A$ to $\bar{A}$, and speak of it simply as the complement of A.

The shaded area in the Venn diagram on the left in Figure 1–9 shows $\bar{A}$, while $\overline{A \cup B}$ is shown in the center and $\overline{A \cap B}$ is on the right. ◊

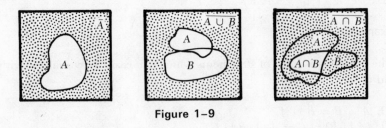

Figure 1–9

Three obvious consequences of the definition of the complement are:

1. $A \cap \bar{A} = \varnothing$
2. If $A \subset S$, then $A \cup \bar{A} = S$
3. If $B = \bar{A}$, then $\bar{B} = A$; that is, $A = \bar{\bar{A}}$

More generally, we shall use the notation $A \setminus B$ for $\{x \mid x \in A$ and $x \notin B\}$ even if B is *not* a subset of A. We shall then refer to $A \setminus B$ as the **difference** of A and B.

Example 6

Suppose that A and B are subsets of S. We will now prove that $B = (A \cap B) \cup (\bar{A} \cap B)$.

Proof

We have $B = S \cap B$ since $B \subset S$

$\qquad\quad = (A \cup \bar{A}) \cap B$ since $A \cup \bar{A} = S$

$\qquad\quad = (A \cap B) \cup (\bar{A} \cap B)$ since $\cap$ is distributive over $\cup$ (Exercise 2) $\square$

One more way of generating new sets from old ones is that used in analytic geometry, where we characterize each point of the plane by an ordered pair of real numbers, the first of which is the x-coordinate (or x_1-coordinate), and the second of which is the y-coordinate (or x_2-coordinate). Thus, the usual plane may be given coordinates as the direct product (or Cartesian product, in honor of Descartes' invention of analytic geometry) $\mathbf{R} \times \mathbf{R}$ (where $\mathbf{R}$ is the set of real numbers; see Section 1–4) as soon as we make the following general definition:

Given any two sets A and B, their **Cartesian product** $A \times B$ is the set of all ordered pairs whose first element is from A and whose second is from B; symbolically,

$$A \times B = \{(a, b) \mid a \in A \text{ and } b \in B\}$$

In general, given n sets $A_1, A_2, \ldots, A_n$, their Cartesian product is the set

$$A_1 \times A_2 \times \cdots \times A_n = \{(a_1, a_2, \ldots, a_n) \mid a_i \in A_i \text{ for } i = 1, 2, \ldots, n\}$$

Note that two ordered pairs are equal only if their corresponding elements are equal: $(a, b) = (c, d) \Leftrightarrow a = c$ and $b = d$. This is different from equality of sets, where order is immaterial:

$$\{a, b\} = \{c, d\} \text{ if either } a = c \text{ and } b = d, \text{ or } a = d \text{ and } b = c$$

Example 7

Suppose $A = \{0, 1\}$ and $B = \{a, b, c\}$. Then

$$A \times B = \{(0, a), (0, b), (0, c), (1, a), (1, b), (1, c)\}$$
$$A \times A = \{(0, 0), (0, 1), (1, 0), (1, 1)\}$$
$$B \times B = \{(a, a), (a, b), (a, c), (b, a), (b, b), (b, c),$$
$$(c, a), (c, b), (c, c)\} \qquad\qquad \Diamond$$

We now should have some feel for sets, and for the elementary operations of set union, set intersection, set difference, and the direct product of sets. With this as background, we may now see how points of a set X may be *mapped* onto points of a set Y (think of X as a region of the Earth and Y as a page of an atlas to get a feel for the terminology):

A **map** (or **mapping** or **function**) f from a set X to a set Y is an assignment, to each element x of X, of a unique corresponding element y of Y. We write $f : X \to Y$ or $X \xrightarrow{f} Y$ to denote that f takes elements from the set X (the **domain** of f) to yield elements in the set Y (the **codomain** of f). We write $x \mapsto f(x)$ (note that we use a different arrow) to show the effect of f upon individual elements.

We say that two functions $f : X \to Y$ and $f' : X' \to Y'$ are **equal** if $X = X'$, $Y = Y'$, and $f(x) = f'(x)$ for all $x \in X$.

Given any two sets X and Y, we may use either of two notations, Y^X or $[X \to Y]$, to denote the set of all maps from X into Y. Thus, $f : X \to Y$ and $X \xrightarrow{f} Y$ and $f \in Y^X$ and $f \in [X \to Y]$ are four notations for the same thing. The notation $[X \to Y]$ is in one sense the most natural for the mapping set, but the following lemma shows why the notation Y^X is also natural.

LEMMA 1

If X and Y are finite sets with $|X| = m$ and $|Y| = n$ (i.e., X has m elements and Y has n elements), then

$$|Y^X| = n^m$$

Proof

Let us write X as $\{x_1, x_2, \ldots, x_m\}$. Then, in defining any function f, we must choose each of $f(x_1), f(x_2), \ldots, f(x_m)$. In choosing $f(x_1)$ we are at liberty to choose any of the n distinct elements of Y, and we have the same choice for each of the $f(x)$. Thus, in defining f we must make m choices, each from n elements, so clearly there are a total of n^m possible functions from X to Y.

□

Example 8

X and Y may be the same, as in the function which transforms an integer into its negative:

$$\mathbf{Z} \to \mathbf{Z} : x \mapsto -x \qquad (\mathbf{Z} \text{ is the set of all integers})$$

(In this case, we've ignored naming the function.)   ◊

Example 9

Two functions may look the same when we look at what they do to individual elements, yet be different because they have different domains. Consider

$$f_1 : \mathbf{Z} \times \mathbf{Z} \to \mathbf{Z} : (m, n) \mapsto m + n$$
$$f_2 : \mathbf{Q} \times \mathbf{Q} \to \mathbf{Q} : (m, n) \mapsto m + n \qquad (\mathbf{Q} \text{ is the set of all rational numbers})$$

Both functions add numbers. But we shall see in Section 1–4 that a "program" for f_2 is quite different from one for f_1, and in fact f_2 uses f_1 as a "subroutine":

$$f_2\left(\frac{p}{q}, \frac{r}{s}\right) = \frac{f_1(ps, qr)}{qs}$$

This is unavoidable because f_2 can operate on a far larger domain than can f_1.   ◊

Example 10

Given a set X, the **identity function** id_X is the mapping $id_X : X \to X$ defined by $id_X(x) = x \in X$. If $X \subset Y$, then the **inclusion function** i_X is the mapping $i_X : X \to Y$ defined by $i_X(x) = x \in Y$. *Although these functions may appear to be the same, they are not, since their codomains are different.* This convention seems artificial at first sight, but turns out to be crucial in careful treatments of many parts of modern mathematics.   ◊

Example 11

Not every element of the codomain need be an "image." Consider

$$f : \mathbf{Z} \to \mathbf{Z} : x \mapsto x^2$$

Then an element of the codomain is not an $f(x)$ unless it is positive and a perfect square.   ◊

Example 12

Although specifying x uniquely specifies $f(x)$ (for a given map f), it is by no means true that a given "image" need have a unique "source." Consider

$$f:\mathbf{N} \rightarrow \mathbf{N}:x \mapsto x \div 1$$

Both $f(1)$ and $f(0)$ equal 0.   ◊

Example 13

Just as a computer programmer may write a program only to find that it will not properly process all possible data, so may we specify a transformation rule only to find that the domain is not what we originally thought it to be. For example, considering the central role of the multiplicative inverse in the theory of rational numbers, we might consider the "function"

$$\mathbf{Q} \rightarrow \mathbf{Q}:x \mapsto x^{-1}$$

(recall that $\mathbf{Q}$ is the set of rationals) as a natural object for our study. However, we see that we are mistaken when we recall that a rational number can have a multiplicative inverse only if it is nonzero. Thus, the above prescription for a function is invalid (i.e., there is no such function), and what we really meant to study is the "genuine" function

$$\mathbf{Q}\backslash\{0\} \rightarrow \mathbf{Q}\backslash\{0\}:x \mapsto x^{-1}$$ ◊

In our study of computable functions, we shall often be interested in partial functions. For example, if we specify $f(n)$ by the rule, "Compute upon n using a certain computer program Pr_1 until the computer stops. The computer output is then the value $f(n)$," then there may only be certain values of n, say $n \in d(f) \subset \mathbf{N}$, for which the computer actually halts. For all $n \in \mathbf{N}\backslash d(f)$, the program Pr_1 enters an endless loop, for example. In other words, when we say that $f:\mathbf{N} \rightarrow \mathbf{N}$, say, is a **partial** function, we mean that there is a subset $d(f) \subset \mathbf{N}$ for which $f:d(f) \rightarrow \mathbf{N}$ is a function in the usual mathematical sense of the word. If $d(f) = \mathbf{N}$, we say that f is **total.** Thus, a partial function $f:\mathbf{N} \rightarrow \mathbf{N}$ may be total, in which case it is just an ordinary function.

As our example of a map from some land to an atlas indicates, the concept of mapping is far broader than the concept of a numerical function. For example, let B be the set of books that have a page 17 which is not blank, let C be the set of all finite sequences made up from symbols used in such books, and define

$$f:B \to C:b \mapsto \text{the string of symbols on the left hand}$$
$$\text{margin of page 17 of } b$$

The reader may concoct similarly implausible or plausible examples.

Example 9 stressed the virtue of making explicit the sets whose elements a function is to transform. We should also emphasize the virtue of the $\mapsto$ notation by noting that it distinguishes among the three functions

$$\mathbf{N} \times \mathbf{N} \to \mathbf{N}:(m, n) \mapsto m \dot{-} n$$
$$\mathbf{N} \to \mathbf{N}:m \mapsto m \dot{-} n$$
$$\mathbf{N} \to \mathbf{N}:n \mapsto m \dot{-} n$$

which in a sloppier notation might all be referred to ambiguously as "the function $m \dot{-} n$."

If $f:X_1 \times X_2 \to Y$, we write $f(x_1, x_2)$ rather than $f((x_1, x_2))$. The notation $f(\cdot, x_2)$ will denote the function $X_1 \to Y$ which maps x_1 to $f(x_1, x_2)$. Thus, we have just distinguished $m \dot{-} n$, $(\cdot) \dot{-} n$, and $m \dot{-} (\cdot)$.

A **sequence** is just a function from the natural numbers $f:\mathbf{N} \to X$. If $f(n) = x_n$, we call it the nth **term** [or $(n + 1)$st symbol] of the sequence, and often write

$$f = (x_0, x_1, x_2, \ldots, x_n, \ldots)$$

A **finite** sequence of **length** $m \in \mathbf{N}$ is a map $f:\{0, 1, 2, \ldots, m - 1\} \to X$. If $m = 0$, we denote by Λ the unique sequence of length 0, $\{\Lambda\} = X^\circ$, which has $|X|^0$ elements.

Example 14

The function $f:\mathbf{N} \to \mathbf{N}:n \mapsto n^2$ is the sequence

$$f = (0, 1, 4, 9, 16, 25, 36, 49, \ldots)$$

The function $f:\mathbf{N} \to \mathbf{Z}:n \mapsto (-2)^n$ is the sequence

$$f = (1, -2, 4, -8, 16, -32, 64, \ldots)$$

The function $f:\{0, 1, 2, 3, 4, 5, 6\} \to \mathbf{Q}:n \mapsto -1/(n + 1)$ is the finite sequence

$$f = (-1, -\tfrac{1}{2}, -\tfrac{1}{3}, -\tfrac{1}{4}, -\tfrac{1}{5}, -\tfrac{1}{6}, -\tfrac{1}{7}) \qquad \Diamond$$

We now present certain terminology that proves useful in the study of functions. If $f: A \to B$, then for $a \in A$ we call $f(a)$ the **image** of a. For $A' \subset A$, we denote by $f(A')$ the **set** $\{b \mid b \in B$ and $b = f(a)$ for some $a \in A'\}$ and call $f(A')$ the **image** of A'. For $B' \subset B$, we call the set $\{a \mid a \in A$ and $f(a) \in B'\}$ the **inverse image** of B', and denote it by $f^{-1}(B')$. These sets are shown in Figure 1–10.

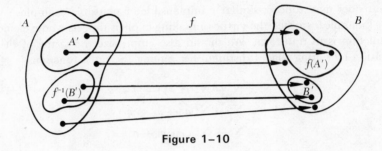

Figure 1–10

Warning. Do not let the notation $f^{-1}(B')$ lead you to believe that we are here trying to define a function from B to A called f^{-1}. In general, this cannot be done.

Example 15

Let A be the set of points in the left-hand column of Figure 1–11, and B the set of points in the right-hand column; for each $a \in A$, we draw an arrow from a to $f_1(a)$. Then $f_1(\{a_1, a_2\}) = \{b_2, b_3\}$ is the image of $A' = \{a_1, a_2\} \subset A$, while $f_1^{-1}(\{b_2, b_3\}) = \{a_1, a_2, a_3\}$ is the inverse image of $B' = \{b_2, b_3\} \subset B$. Thus, $B' = f_1(A')$ does *not* imply that $A' = f_1^{-1}(B')$. However, it is always true that $A' \subset f^{-1}(f(A'))$ for any $f: A \to B$ and any $A' \subset A$. $\Diamond$

We say that a function $X \to Y$ is **onto** or **surjective** if every element of Y is the image of at least one element of X. We sometimes write $f: X \twoheadrightarrow Y$ as an abbreviation for "$f: X \to Y$ is surjective." Thus, we have that

$$X \xrightarrow{f} Y \Leftrightarrow f(X) = Y,$$

where the symbol $\Leftrightarrow$ means "if and only if".

Clearly, f_2 and f_4 of Figure 1–11 are surjective, but neither f_1 nor f_3 is. We say that a function $f: X \to Y$ is **one-to-one** or **injective** if no two distinct elements of X have equal images in Y. We sometimes write $f: X \rightarrowtail Y$ as an abbreviation for "$f: X \to Y$ is injective." Thus:

$$f: X \rightarrowtail Y \Leftrightarrow [\text{for all } x, x' \text{ in } X: f(x) = f(x') \Rightarrow x = x']$$

Clearly, f_1 and f_2 are not injective, but f_3 and f_4 are. We say that a function

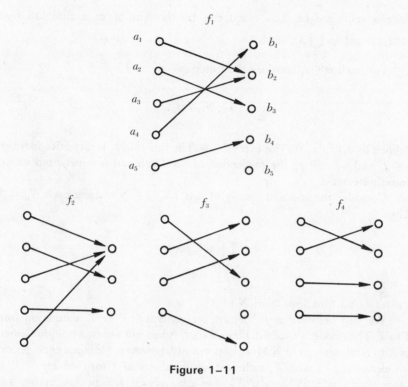

Figure 1–11

is **bijective** if it is both injective and surjective. Hence f_4 is the only bijective function of those shown in Figure 1–11.

If a function $f: X \to Y$ is bijective, we say that there is a one-to-one (1:1) correspondence between X and Y. If $f(x) = y$, then we say that x corresponds to y (written $x \leftrightarrow y$). Two sets X and Y are said to **have the same cardinal number,** written $|X| = |Y|$, if there exists a bijection $f: X \to Y$. Consequently, two finite sets with the same cardinal number contain exactly the same number of elements. We shall develop this notion in more detail in Section 2–3.

Let $F = \{A_\alpha \mid \alpha \in I\}$ be a family of sets indexed by the set I. Let $A = \bigcup_{\alpha \in I} A_\alpha$. Then the Cartesian product of the family F of sets is the set Φ of all functions $f: I \to A$ such that $f(\alpha) \in A_\alpha$ for every $\alpha \in I$. We denote Φ by

$$\Phi = \prod_{\alpha \in I} A_\alpha$$

Note that this is a set which is bijective with that of the usual definition of a Cartesian product (see p. 25) if I is finite:

$$A_1 \times A_2 \times \cdots \times A_n = \{(a_1, a_2, \ldots, a_n) \mid a_j \in A_j \text{ for } j = 1, 2, \ldots, n\}$$

since a sequence $(a_1, a_2, \ldots, a_n)$ can be thought of as a function from $\{1, 2, \ldots, n\}$ to $\bigcup_{\alpha \in I} A_\alpha$.

For each $\alpha \in I$, consider the function

$$p_\alpha : \Phi \to A_\alpha$$

defined by $p_\alpha(f) = f(\alpha)$ for every $f \in \Phi$. The function p_α is surjective for every $\alpha \in I$, and we call p_α the **projection** of the Cartesian product onto its αth **coordinate set** A_α.

Consider the indexed family of sets $\{X_n \mid n \in \mathbf{N}\}$ where each $X_n = X$. Then

$$\prod_{n \in \mathbf{N}} X_n = X^{\mathbf{N}},$$

the set of all functions from $\mathbf{N}$ to X.

We said before that f^{-1} is not, for general $f: X \to Y$, a function from Y to X. The reason is twofold. First of all, f^{-1} does not assign a unique element in X to each element in Y. More importantly, however, f^{-1} is not even defined for elements of Y and X; rather, it sends subsets of Y into subsets of X. In other words, $f^{-1}: \mathcal{P}(Y) \to \mathcal{P}(X)$. For example, if f is not surjective, and $B' \cap f(A) = \varnothing$, then $f^{-1}(B') = \varnothing$.

If $f: X \to Y$ is bijective, then for each $y \in Y$ there exists one and only one $x \in X$ such that $f(x) = y$. Thus, $f^{-1}(\{y\}) = \{x\}$. Under this circumstance, we may consider f^{-1} to be a function from Y into X. This mapping is also a bijection. For example, the identity function $id_X : X \to X : x \mapsto x$ is a bijection and $id_X^{-1} = id_X$.

Suppose we fix a set X, and consider subsets of X. For each subset $A \subset X$ we define its **characteristic** function

$$\chi_A : X \to \{0, 1\}$$

by the rule

$$\chi_A(x) = \begin{cases} 1 \text{ if } x \in A \\ 0 \text{ if } x \notin A \end{cases}$$

Conversely, given any function $f \in \{0, 1\}^X$, we may associate with it the set $f^{-1}(1)$, and then see that $f = \chi_{f^{-1}\{1\}}$. (Why?) We have thus proved the following result.

LEMMA 2

The map

$$\mathcal{P}(X) \rightarrow \{0, 1\}^X : A \rightarrow \chi_A$$

is a bijection (a one-to-one correspondence) between subsets of X and characteristic functions on X.   □

If $f : X \rightarrow Y$ we may read this as "X is mapped by f into Y" and denote it by $X \xrightarrow{f} Y$. If we should have both $X \xrightarrow{f} Y$ and $Y \xrightarrow{g} Z$, we may denote this by the diagram $X \xrightarrow{f} Y \xrightarrow{g} Z$. If this case holds (i.e., the domain of g equals the codomain of f), we say that f and g are **composable,** and define their composition $g \circ f$ to be the function $g \circ f : X \rightarrow Z$ whose assignments are made according to the equation

$$[g \circ f](x) = g[f(x)].$$

We thus know that if $X \xrightarrow{f} Y$, $Y \xrightarrow{g} Z$, and $Z \xrightarrow{h} W$, then

$$h \circ (g \circ f) = (h \circ g) \circ f : X \rightarrow W : x \mapsto h(g(f(x)))$$

Moreover, if id_X is the identity map $X \rightarrow X : x \mapsto x$ and id_Y is the identity map $Y \rightarrow Y : y \mapsto y$, then $f \circ id_X = f = id_Y \circ f$.

We say that the diagram

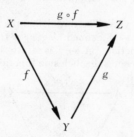

is **commutative,** or **commutes,** for no matter what path we follow from one point to another, so long as we move in the direction of the arrows and apply the stated function at each transition, we shall apply the same overall mapping. Thus, in mapping X into Z in the above diagram, it is immaterial to the overall result whether we map directly from X to Z via $g \circ f$, or whether we first map X into Y via f, and then map the result from Y to Z via g.

We shall find many occasions in the ensuing theory where we will find the proof of theorems reducing to "diagram-chasing," i.e., drawing up a mapping diagram, and then checking paths to verify commutativity.

EXERCISES FOR SECTION 1-2

1.   Prove that for all sets A, B, and C we have
(i) $A \cup B = B \cup A$
(ii) $(A \cup B) \cup C = A \cup (B \cup C)$
(iii) $A \cap B = B \cap A$
(iv) $(A \cap B) \cap C = A \cap (B \cap C)$
2.   Draw Venn diagrams to see the following distributive laws.
(a) $A \cup (B \cap C) = (A \cup B) \cap (A \cup C)$ [We say that $\cup$ is **distributive** over $\cap$.]
(b) $A \cap (B \cup C) = (A \cap B) \cup (A \cap C)$ [We say that $\cap$ is distributive over $\cup$.]
Provide logical proofs of the two equalities.
3.   Prove that $A \setminus B = A \setminus (A \cap B)$.
4.   The following two statements are known as **DeMorgan's Laws:**

$$\overline{A \cup B} = \overline{A} \cap \overline{B}$$
$$\overline{A \cap B} = \overline{A} \cup \overline{B}$$

Demonstrate these laws by using Venn diagrams.
5.   Use distributivity (Exercise 2) to prove that if A and B are subsets of S, then $A \cup B = A \cup (\overline{A} \cap B)$.
6.   Specify a function resulting in the following sequences:
(a) $f = (1, 3, 5, 7, 9, 11, 13, \ldots)$
(b) $f = (\frac{1}{4}, 1, 9, 4, 4, \frac{25}{4}, 9, 49, 4, 16, \ldots)$
7.   Give an example to show that, in general, $A' \neq f^{-1}(f(A'))$.
8.   In the functions listed in Examples 8 through 14, which are injective, which are surjective, and which are bijective?
9.   Let $X = \{a, b, c\}$ and $Y = \{0, 1\}$. Enumerate the $2^3 = 8$ possible functions from X to Y.
10.   Let $f : X \to Y$ and $A \subset X$. Then we define the **restriction** of f to A, denoted $f|A$, to be the function $g : A \to Y$ defined by $g(a) = f(a)$ for each $a \in A$.

If $g = f|A$, then the function $f : X \to Y$ is said to be an **extension** of g over the set X. Thus, if $i_A : A \to X$ denotes the inclusion function, we know that the diagram

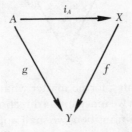

is commutative.

Let $A = \{1\}$, $X = \{1, 2\}$, $Y = \{1, 2, 3\}$, and define $g : A \to Y$ by $g(1) = 3$. How many different functions $f : X \to Y$ exist, such that $f|A = g$?
11.   We have defined the product of two sets

$$A \times B = \{(a, b) \mid a \in A \text{ and } b \in B\}$$

and have equipped it with two projection maps

$$p_1 : A \times B \to A : (a, b) \mapsto a$$
$$p_2 : A \times B \to B : (a, b) \mapsto b$$

Suppose, now, that we are given a set C equipped with two maps, $p_1' : C \to A$ and $p_2' : C \to B$. Can we find a map $C \xrightarrow{p} A \times B$ such that the following diagram commutes?

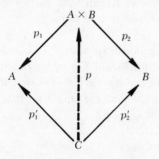

From $p_1 \circ p = p'_1$ we deduce that $p(c) = (p'_1(c), ?)$.
From $p_2 \circ p = p'_2$ we deduce that $p(c) = (?, p'_2(c))$.
Thus, the only possible choice for p is $p(c) = (p_1'(c), p_2'(c))$, and it is clear that the choice works.

Suppose, now, that we reverse all the arrows to get the following diagram.

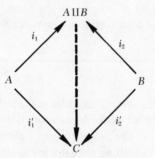

Take $A \amalg B$ to be the **disjoint union** (or **coproduct**) of A and B, where we tag elements of A and B to avoid overlap when we take the union:

$$A \amalg B = \{(a, 1) \,|\, a \in A\} \cup \{(b, 2) \,|\, b \in B\}$$

and define $A \xrightarrow{i_1} A \amalg B : a \mapsto (a, 1)$ and $B \xrightarrow{i_2} A \amalg B : b \mapsto (b, 2)$. Verify that for each pair of maps $A \xrightarrow{i_1'} C$ and $B \xrightarrow{i_2'} C$ there is a unique map $A \amalg B \xrightarrow{i} C$ which makes our second diagram commute.

1-3   Proof Techniques

Throughout this book, we will be called upon to prove a host of statements (in the form of lemmas, theorems, corollaries, properties, and so forth). It seems useful, then, to present a brief exposition here of a number of the most useful proof techniques.

Proof by Induction

From Section 1-1, the reader should have digested the concept of proof by induction rather completely. Recall that to prove a property $P(i)$ of the natural numbers, we proceed in two steps:

I. *The Basis Step:* We demonstrate that $P(i)$ is true for $i = 0$. (If we wish to prove that $P(i)$ holds for all $i \geq m$, we begin with $i = m$.)

II. *The Induction Step:* We assume that $P(i)$ is true for $i = n$, and under this assumption demonstrate that $P(i)$ must be true for $i = n + 1$.

Proof by Exhaustion of Cases

A proof may be performed by demonstrating the validity of a statement for all possible cases. For example, in proving a property to hold for all integers we might, as exemplified in the proof of Theorem 2 below, give three proofs showing that the property holds for all integers of the form $3m$, for all integers of the form $3m + 1$, and for all integers of the form $3m + 2$. Since all integers are of one of these three forms, this exhausts all possible cases.

Proof by Contradiction

The next proof technique we will consider is that of **proof by contradiction.** It is also called **reductio ad absurdum:** reduction to an absurdity. In this method, we begin by using the property that a given statement is either true or false, but not both. We assume that the given statement is false, and then use definitions and facts (whether obvious or previously proven) to develop some statement which contradicts that which we know to be factual. Since the contradiction was developed by assuming that the given statement was false and by using only known truths, it must be that our original assumption was incorrect. This then proves that the original statement is true.

At first sight, proof by contradiction may not appear to be very significant, but it is often the easiest and best proof technique. Let us now give a classical *reductio ad absurdum*:

We say that a number $p \in \mathbf{N}$ is **prime** if $p \neq 1$, and if it is impossible to express p as a product $m \cdot n$ of natural numbers neither of which is p. It can then easily be shown (we omit the proof as being beside the point) that every number is divisible by a prime—if $n \in \mathbf{N}$, there exists a prime p and an $m \in \mathbf{N}$ such that $n = p \cdot m$. Of course, if n is prime, then $n = p$ and $m = 1$.

Thus, 2, 3, and 5 are prime, but $4 = 2 \cdot 2$ and $6 = 2 \cdot 3$ are not. We owe to Euclid the theorem that **N** contains infinitely many primes:

THEOREM 1

There is an infinity of primes in **N**.

Proof

Suppose, by way of contradiction, that there is a finite set

$$\{p_1, p_2, \ldots, p_m\} \subset \mathbf{N}$$

which contains all prime numbers, with $p_1 = 2 < p_2 = 3 < p_3 = 5 < \cdots < p_{m-1} < p_m$. Form the product of these primes and add 1 to obtain

$$r = p_1 \cdot p_2 \ldots \cdot p_m + 1$$

Now r must be divisible by a prime: $r = p \cdot m$ for some prime p. But p cannot be one of $p_1, \ldots, p_m$ since each of these leaves a remainder of 1 when divided into r. Hence there is a prime p not in our original list, *contradicting our assumption* that the number of primes is finite. But if the number of primes is not finite, then it must be infinite, and so our theorem is seen to be true.

□

Necessary Conditions

When a statement A implies a statement B, we say that B is a **necessary condition** for A. This is simply because it is "necessary" for B to be true when A is true. There is more than one form in which a necessary condition can be cast. For example, we can write:

  (i) A is true implies B is true.
 (ii) If A is true, then B is true.
(iii) A can be true only if B is true.
 (iv) A necessary condition for A to be true is that B is true.
  (v) It is necessary that B be true in order for A to be true.

The above five statements are equivalent, and can all be symbolized mathematically by $A \Rightarrow B$. To prove necessity, we simply start with A (the hypothesis) and present a series of supported statements until we conclude B (possibly by employing methods of contradiction).

Note that if $A \Rightarrow B$, it is *not* necessarily true that $B \Rightarrow A$ (which is the **converse** of $A \Rightarrow B$.) For example, suppose we take $\mathbf{Z}$ to be the set $\{\ldots, -3, -2, -1, 0, 1, 2, 3, \ldots\}$ of all integers, be they negative, zero, or positive; and then consider the two statements:

$$A_n = n \in \mathbf{Z} \text{ with } 0 \le n \le 2; \text{ and}$$
$$B_n = n \in \mathbf{Z} \text{ with } n^2 \le 4$$

Then we have $A_n \Rightarrow B_n$, but we do not have $B_n \Rightarrow A_n$. Taking $n = -1$, we see a case in which B_n holds but A_n does not hold, thus showing that A_n cannot be a necessary condition for B_n.

If we denote the negation of A by $\bar{A}$ (so that A is false means $\bar{A}$ is true; and A is true means $\bar{A}$ is false), then it is useful to note that: To prove $A \Rightarrow B$ is equivalent to proving its **contrapositive** $\bar{B} \Rightarrow \bar{A}$. To say that whenever A is true, then B must be true, is just to deny that B can be false when A is true; in other words, it is to say that whenever B is false then A is false; i.e., that $\bar{B} \Rightarrow \bar{A}$. We shall apply this technique in the second half of our proof of Theorem 2.

Sufficient Conditions

We previously mentioned that for the case $A \Rightarrow B$, we refer to B as a necessary condition for A. In a similar vein, we say that A is a **sufficient condition** for B. This is due to the fact that the truth of A is "sufficient" for us to conclude the truth of B. Since the statement of a necessary condition can take many forms, it's quite clear that the same is true for the statement of a sufficient condition. In fact, the three statements (i) to (iii) given above constitute valid ways of saying that A is a sufficient condition for B. To be explicit, we would rewrite statements (iv) and (v) to the equivalent forms:

(iv') A sufficient condition for B to be true is that A is true.

(v') For B to be true, it is sufficient that A is true.

Necessary and Sufficient Conditions

We now discuss the most interesting case: That for which not only $A \Rightarrow B$, but in which we also have the converse, $B \Rightarrow A$ (B implies A) or $A \Leftarrow B$ (A is implied by B). We symbolize this situation by $A \Leftrightarrow B$. In words, we may say:

(a) A is true if and only if B is true.
(b) A necessary and sufficient condition that A be true is that B be true (or vice versa).

If one statement is both a necessary and sufficient condition for another, then the statements are equivalent even though they may be worded in completely different ways. Often it is more convenient to work with a necessary and sufficient condition of some property rather than directly with the original definition. Under this circumstance, we may wish to think of the condition as an alternative definition. Even in many definitions themselves, authors (including ourselves) will sometimes use the term "if and only if," although technically it is somewhat redundant.

Throughout the book we will either spell out "if and only if," shorten it to "iff," or use the symbol $\Leftrightarrow$ when dealing with necessary and sufficient conditions.

Finally, to prove $A \Leftrightarrow B$ (i.e., a necessary and sufficient condition), we must actually complete two proofs (the order is irrelevant): We must prove both $A \Rightarrow B$ and its converse $B \Rightarrow A$.

For some proofs, once it is demonstrated that $A \Rightarrow B$, it is just a matter of working backwards to show that $B \Rightarrow A$. Unfortunately, for a substantial number of proofs, it is impossible to proceed in this manner, and a completely different approach is required.

We close this section by proving a simple "if and only if" theorem, whose proof demonstrates most of the points we have made above.

THEOREM 2

A number is a multiple of 3 if and only if the sum of the digits in its decimal representation is a multiple of 3.

It turns out that the proof of this theorem will be easier if we first prove a lemma.

LEMMA 3

Let $\langle n \rangle$ denote the decimal representation of the number $n \in \mathbf{N}$, and let $r(n)$ equal the sum of the digits in $\langle n \rangle$. Then $r(n + 3)$ differs from $r(n)$ by a multiple of 3.

Proof

We prove the result by exhausting two cases:

 (I) The last digit d of $\langle n \rangle$ is 0, 1, 2, 3, 4, 5 or 6. In this case we form $\langle n + 3 \rangle$ by changing d to $d + 3$. Thus, $r(n + 3) = r(n) + 3$, satisfying the claim of the lemma.

(II) The last digit d of $\langle n \rangle$ is 7, 8, or 9. In that case we form $\langle n + 3 \rangle$ from the string $\langle n \rangle = d_m \, d_{m-1} \ldots d_1 \, d \; (m \geq 0)$ of digits by the following rule, which exhausts three possible subcases:

(1) If $d_1 \neq 9$, set $\langle n + 3 \rangle = d_m \, d_{m-1} \ldots (d_1 + 1)(d - 7)$. If $m = 0$, this rule changes d to $1(d - 7)$. Then $r(n + 3) = 1 + r(n) - 7 = r(n) - 6$, satisfying the claim of the lemma.

(2) If $\langle n \rangle = d_m \, d_{m-1} \ldots d_{k+2} \, d_{k+1} 9 \ldots 9 \, d$ (where $1 \leq k \leq m$), set $\langle n + 3 \rangle = d_m \, d_{m-1} \ldots d_{k+2}(d_{k+1} + 1)0 \ldots 0(d - 7)$. Then $r(n + 3) = r(n) - 9k - 6$, satisfying the claim of the lemma.

(3) If $\langle n \rangle = 9 \ldots 9 \, d$, set $\langle n + 3 \rangle = 10 \ldots 0(d - 7)$. Then $r(n + 3) = r(n) - 9m - 6$, satisfying the claim of the lemma.

Having verified the lemma for all subcases, we have proved it to be true.   □

With this lemma we have an immediate **corollary**—a result which follows so easily that it is almost part of the original result:

COROLLARY 4

If $n = 3m$, then $r(n)$ is a multiple of 3.

If $n = 3m + 1$, then $r(n)$ is of the form $3k + 1$.

If $n = 3m + 2$, then $r(n)$ is of the form $3k + 2$.

Proof

The proof is by induction on m for each of the three cases. However, it is so obvious from the lemma that we do not bother to write it out.   □

Finally, we come to the proof of Theorem 2, which uses the corollary just given.

Proof of Theorem 2

(i) n is a multiple of $3 \Rightarrow r(n)$ is a multiple of 3. This is immediate from the first clause of the corollary to the lemma.

(ii) $r(n)$ is a multiple of $3 \Rightarrow n$ is a multiple of 3.

We prove this by proving the contrapositive: n is not a multiple of $3 \Rightarrow r(n)$ is not a multiple of 3. But there are only two subcases, $n = 3m + 1$ and $n = 3m + 2$, and the truth of these two cases is provided by the second and third clauses of the corollary to the lemma.   □

With this example before him, the reader should be able to see where we use induction, proof by contradiction, exhaustion of cases, and proof of the contrapositive in the development of the major proof, even when we are not so self-conscious in the exposition of our proof techniques.

1–4   Other Number Systems

Having gained a feel for the use of the axiomatic method and proof by induction in Section 1–1, and for the basic terminology of sets and functions in Section 1–2; and having introduced some useful proof techniques in Section 1–3, we now turn to a brief study of some elementary properties of four number systems: the set **Z** of all integers, the set **Q** of all rational numbers, the set **R** of all real numbers, and the set **C** of all complex numbers.

The Set **Z** of Integers

The reader will have noticed that when working with **N** (in Section 1–1), we could form successors (going from n to $n + 1$) indefinitely, but that, wherever we started, we could only form predecessors (going from n to $n \doteq 1$) a finite number of times before we got stuck at zero. Referring to Figure 1–12, this may be expressed in geometric terms by saying we could move arbitrarily many steps to the right, but not so to the left.

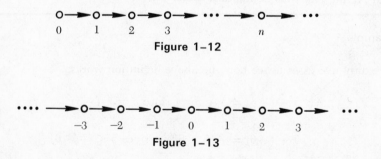

Figure 1–12

Figure 1–13

This suggests forming a new set by adding points "to the left of" 0 as in Figure 1–13. We label the point n steps "to the left of" 0 by $-n$, and agree that -0 is the same as 0:

$$0 = -0$$

In this way we come to study the set **Z** of all integers

$$\mathbf{Z} = \{\ldots, -3, -2, -1, 0, 1, 2, 3, \ldots\}$$

If we let $\mathbf{Z}_+ = \{1, 2, 3, \ldots\}$, the set of **positive** integers, and $\mathbf{Z}_- = \{-1, -2, -3, \ldots\}$, the set of **negative** integers,† then $\mathbf{Z} = \mathbf{Z}_- \cup \{0\} \cup \mathbf{Z}_+$, the union of $\mathbf{Z}_-$, $\{0\}$, and $\mathbf{Z}_+$. Also, by definition, $\mathbf{Z} = \mathbf{Z}_- \cup \mathbf{N}$.

We start our discussion of functions of integers by defining the negative of an integer $n \in \mathbf{Z}$ by the exhaustion of three possible cases.

$$-(n) = \begin{cases} -n \text{ if } n \in \mathbf{Z}_+ \\ 0 \text{ if } n = 0 \\ m \text{ if } n = -m \in \mathbf{Z}_- \end{cases}$$

We then define the absolute value of an integer n to be n if $n \in \mathbf{N}$, but $-n$ if $n \in \mathbf{Z}_-$. In symbols,

$$|n| = \begin{cases} n \text{ if } n \in \mathbf{N} \\ -n \text{ if } n \in \mathbf{Z}_- \end{cases}$$

Now let us see how we can use our knowledge of functions defined on $\mathbf{N}$ to define corresponding functions on $\mathbf{Z}$. We first define

$$m + n = \begin{cases} m + n \text{ if } m, n \in \mathbf{N} \\ [m \div (-n)] \text{ if } m \in \mathbf{N}, n \in \mathbf{Z}_- \text{ and } m \geq -n \\ -[(-n) \div m] \text{ if } m \in \mathbf{N}, n \in \mathbf{Z}_- \text{ and } m \leq -n \\ -[(-m) + (-n)] \text{ if } m \in \mathbf{Z}_- \end{cases}$$

The fourth formula reduces the case $m \in \mathbf{Z}_-$ to a case involving $-m$, which is in $\mathbf{N}$, and can thus be handled under one of the first three cases.

Example 1

We study five cases to see how the above definition works:

$$5 + (-3) = 5 \div 3 \qquad \text{since } 5 \geq -(-3)$$
$$= 2$$
$$5 + (-6) = -[6 \div 5] \qquad \text{since } 5 \leq -(-6)$$
$$= -1$$
$$(-2) + (-3) = -[2 + 3] = -5$$
$$(-5) + 3 = -[5 + (-3)] = -2$$
$$(-5) + 6 = -[5 + (-6)] = -(-1) = 1 \qquad \qquad \Diamond$$

It is now easy to define "unrestricted" subtraction by the formula

$$m - n = m + (-n)$$

---

†Note: The order does not matter in listing the elements of a set.

We can then define the predecessor p for any n in $\mathbf{Z}$ by $p(n) = n - 1$, and the successor σ for any n in $\mathbf{Z}$ by $\sigma(n) = n + 1$.

We now define multiplication by:

$$m \cdot n = \begin{cases} m \cdot n \text{ if } m \in \mathbf{N}, n \in \mathbf{N} \\ -[m \cdot (-n)] \text{ if } m \in \mathbf{N}, n \in \mathbf{Z}_- \\ -[(-m) \cdot n] \text{ if } m \in \mathbf{Z}_-, n \in \mathbf{N} \\ (-m) \cdot (-n) \text{ if } m \in \mathbf{Z}_-, n \in \mathbf{Z}_- \end{cases}$$

Here we treat separately four cases that among them exhaust all possible pairs of integers.

Just as for the natural numbers, so must we now check a few basic properties of these functions as defined for all integers. Again, they are all properties that we know so well that they hardly require checking; and again the point is to see that these properties follow from our definitions, and not from some "magical" properties of numbers that we have not yet written down. We shall not spell out the proofs of all of these properties, but just give a few, hoping that our intuition about numbers will allow us to assimilate the proof techniques and allow us to build up a new, more abstract intuition, which will come in handy when we explore the algebraic properties of such new structures as groups, rings, and fields.

PROPERTY 1

For all integers n,

$$n + 0 = n = 0 + n \qquad \text{(0 is the **identity** for +)}$$

Proof

We already know from Section 1–1 that this statement is true provided that n is nonnegative. Thus, our only task here is to further prove that $n + 0 = n = 0 + n$ for $n \in \mathbf{Z}_-$. From the fourth line of our definition of addition, we deduce that

$$\begin{aligned} (-m) + 0 &= -((-(-m)) + (-0)) \\ &= -(m + 0) \qquad \text{since } -(-m) = m \text{ and } -0 = 0 \\ &\qquad\qquad\qquad \text{by definition of the } - \text{ operation} \\ &= -m \qquad\qquad \text{since } m \in \mathbf{N} \text{ assures us that} \\ &\qquad\qquad\qquad m + 0 = m \end{aligned}$$

From the third line of our definition of addition we deduce that

$$0 + (-m) = -((-(-m)) \div 0)$$
$$= -(m \div 0)$$
$$= -m$$

Thus, whether n be positive, negative or zero, it is indeed the case that

$$n + 0 = n = 0 + n \qquad \qquad \square$$

PROPERTY 2

For all pairs of integers m and n,

$$m + n = n + m \qquad (+ \text{ is } \textbf{commutative})$$

We have already verified this for m and n in **N**, and need only check that this allows us to handle the equality for the other three cases in the definition of addition. This is left to the reader as an exercise. Similarly, we can prove the following properties (3 through 8) of **Z**, but there would seem little value in explicitly presenting the proofs here. A few of the more instructive ones are left as exercises for the reader:

PROPERTY 3

For all integers m, n, and p,

$$(m + n) + p = m + (n + p) \qquad (+ \text{ is } \textbf{associative})$$

PROPERTY 4

For all integers n,

$$n + (-n) = 0 = (-n) + n \qquad (-n \text{ is the } \textbf{inverse} \text{ of } n \text{ under } +)$$

PROPERTY 5

For all integers n,

$$n \cdot 1 = 1 \cdot n = n \qquad (1 \text{ is the } \textbf{identity} \text{ for } \cdot)$$

PROPERTY 6

For all pairs of integers m and n,

$$m \cdot n = n \cdot m \qquad (\cdot \text{ is } \textbf{commutative})$$

PROPERTY 7

For all integers m, n, and p,

$$(m \cdot n) \cdot p = m \cdot (n \cdot p) \qquad (\cdot \text{ is } \textbf{associative})$$

PROPERTY 8

For all integers m, n, and p,

$$m \cdot (n + p) = (m \cdot n) + (m \cdot p) \qquad (\cdot \textbf{ distributes} \text{ over } +)$$

[Note: From this moment on, in many cases we will denote the product $m \cdot n$ by mn, simply because of laziness.]

The next property of the integers is not "quite as good" as the corresponding property of $\mathbf{Q}$, the set of all rational numbers, so let us call this "provisional" version which holds in $\mathbf{Z}$ by the name 9$\mathbf{Z}$ rather than 9:

PROPERTY 9**Z**

For all integers m, n, and p, if $mn = mp$ and $m \neq 0$, then $n = p$.

Proof

If $mn = mp$, then $mn + m(-n) = mp + m(-n)$. By Property 8,

$$m(n + (-n)) = m(p + (-n))$$

By analogy with Example 7 of Section 1–1 (p. 18), we can use Properties 1, 4, and 8 to show that $m \cdot 0 = 0$. We then use Property 4 and the definition of "unrestricted" subtraction to write

$$m \cdot (p - n) = 0.$$

If we can demonstrate that $p - n = 0$, it follows that $p = n$. (Why is this so?) Thus, to conclude the proof, we must verify that if $m \neq 0$, then

$$ms = 0 \text{ implies } s = 0$$

If $m \in \mathbf{Z}_+$, this is clear from the inductive definition of $p_m : s \mapsto ms$; on the other hand, if $m = -t$ where $t \in \mathbf{Z}_+$, then the statement reduces to the previous case by noting that $(-t)s = -(ts) = 0$ is equivalent to saying that $ts = 0$ whenever $s = 0$.   □

Note that in proving property 9Z we could make use of the function $m - n$, whereas in proving property 9N we had to make more cumbersome use of $m \dotminus n$.

The Set **Q** of Rational Numbers

If the need to form unlimited predecessors justified the introduction of the negative integers, then it is the need to divide that justifies the introduction of the **rational numbers**—those numbers which can be represented as *ratios* of the form p/q, with $p \in \mathbf{Z}, q \in \mathbf{Z}_+$. Returning to our number line of Figure 1–13, we feel it to be geometrically plausible to be able to divide each interval into q equal parts, and then use $\dfrac{p}{q}$ to denote the point we obtain by moving p of these $\dfrac{1}{q}$-steps to the right of 0 if p is positive, and $-p$ of these steps to the left of 0 if p is negative (see Figure 1–14 for the case $q = 3$).

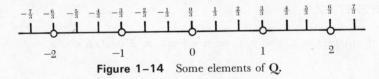

Figure 1–14   Some elements of **Q**.

In going from **N** to **Z** we had a minor problem: -0 was an extra label for 0. In forming the rationals we have a far worse problem, for if $\dfrac{p}{q}$ labels a point, then clearly $\dfrac{kp}{kq}$ must label the same point for any $k \in \mathbf{Z}_+$.

For example:

$$\frac{1}{2} = \frac{2}{4} = \frac{3}{6} = \frac{4}{8}, \text{ etc.}$$

We thus denote by $\mathbf{Q}$ the set of all symbols $\dfrac{p}{q}$ with $p \in \mathbf{Z}$ and $q \in \mathbf{Z}_+$ with the understanding that two **rationals** $\dfrac{p}{q}$ and $\dfrac{r}{s}$ (with $q, s \in \mathbf{Z}_+$, and $p, r \in \mathbf{Z}$) are **equal** (i.e., are to be treated the same and so may be substituted for one another in the course of proofs about rational numbers) whenever the equality

$$ps = rq$$

of products of integers holds.

We **embed** the integers in the rationals by **identifying** the integer n with the rational $\dfrac{n}{1}$. Note that distinct integers yield distinct rationals, since $\dfrac{m}{1} = \dfrac{n}{1}$ is equivalent to stating that $m \cdot 1 = n \cdot 1$ by definition of equality in $\mathbf{Q}$; and, by Property 5 of the integers, this means that $m = n$.

Now we use the availability of various functions in $\mathbf{Z}$ to define their extension to $\mathbf{Q}$. Note that in each case we must check two things:

(i) That the definition reduces to the old definition when we use the rational form $\dfrac{n}{1}$ of an integer n, etc.

(ii) That the definition depends on the rational number and not on the particular representation $\dfrac{p}{q}$ chosen to write it down. For example, the "function"

$$\frac{p}{q} \mapsto p$$

which transforms a representation of a ratio into its numerator is *not* a function of rational numbers, since it gives different results when applied to $\dfrac{1}{2}$ and $\dfrac{2}{4}$, even though these denote the same number. However, the function

$$\frac{p}{q} \mapsto \frac{2p}{q}$$

is legitimate, since if $\dfrac{p}{q} = \dfrac{r}{s}$ (i.e., $ps = rq$), then we must have $\dfrac{2p}{q} = \dfrac{2r}{s}$ [since it is certainly then the case, recalling Property 8 of the integers, that

$(2p)s = 2(ps) = 2(rq) = (2r)q]$. A function that is independent of representation in this way is termed **well-defined**.

Addition. We define $\dfrac{p}{q} + \dfrac{r}{s} = \dfrac{ps + rq}{qs}$.

(i) Consistency with old definition:

$$\frac{m}{1} + \frac{n}{1} = \frac{m \cdot 1 + n \cdot 1}{1 \cdot 1} = \frac{m + n}{1} \text{ as required}$$

(ii) Independence of choice of representation:

Suppose that $\dfrac{p}{q} = \dfrac{p'}{q'}$ and $\dfrac{r}{s} = \dfrac{r'}{s'}$ so that $pq' = p'q$ and $rs' = r's$.

Then

$$\frac{p}{q} + \frac{r}{s} = \frac{ps + rq}{qs} = \frac{(p'r'q's')(ps + rq)}{(p'r'q's')qs} \qquad \text{(Why?)}$$

$$= \frac{(p's')(pq')(r's) + (rs')(p'q)(r'q')}{(p'q)(r's)q's'}$$

$$= \frac{(p's')(pq')(rs') + (rs')(pq')(r'q')}{(pq')(rs')q's'}$$

$$\text{since } pq' = p'q \text{ and } rs' = r's$$

$$= \frac{(pq'rs')(p's' + r'q')}{(pq'rs')q's'}$$

$$= \frac{p's' + r'q'}{q's'}$$

$$= \frac{p'}{q'} + \frac{r'}{s'}$$

Note: The above proof breaks down if p' or r' is 0. So let us check the case $p' = 0$. Then, since q and q' both belong to $\mathbf{Z}_+$, the equality $pq' = p'q$ implies that $p = 0$. So we have

$$\frac{p}{q} + \frac{r}{s} = \frac{0 \cdot s + rq}{qs} = \frac{rq}{qs} = \frac{qr}{qs} = \frac{r}{s}$$

and this certainly equals $\dfrac{0}{q'} + \dfrac{r}{s}$. We thus not only have checked that addition is well-defined, but have shown that Property 1 ($n + 0 = n = n + 0$) holds for all rationals n, as well as for all integers. The reader may check that Properties 2 and 3 are also preserved.

Negative. We define $-\left(\dfrac{p}{q}\right)$ to be $\dfrac{-p}{q}$. Clearly $-\left(\dfrac{m}{1}\right) = \left(\dfrac{-m}{1}\right)$ so that we have consistency, while if $\dfrac{p}{q} = \dfrac{p'}{q'}$, it is trivial to check that $\dfrac{-p}{q} = \dfrac{-p'}{q'}$, so the negative is well-defined. We now verify Property 4:

$$\left(\frac{p}{q}\right) + \left(-\left(\frac{p}{q}\right)\right) = \frac{p}{q} + \frac{-p}{q}$$

$$= \frac{pq + (-p \cdot q)}{q^2}$$

$$= \frac{pq + (-(pq))}{q^2}$$

$$= \frac{0}{q^2}$$

$$= 0$$

Subtraction. $x - y = x + (-y)$. Since we build this from functions that are consistent and well-defined, it is automatic that this too is consistent and well-defined.

Multiplication. $\left(\dfrac{p}{q}\right)\left(\dfrac{r}{s}\right) = \dfrac{pr}{qs}$

Consistency: $\left(\dfrac{m}{1}\right)\left(\dfrac{n}{1}\right) = \dfrac{mn}{1 \cdot 1} = \dfrac{mn}{1}$ as required

Well-definedness: If $\dfrac{p}{q} = \dfrac{p'}{q'}$ and $\dfrac{r}{s} = \dfrac{r'}{s'}$ then

$$\left(\frac{p}{q}\right)\left(\frac{r}{s}\right) = \frac{pr}{qs} = \frac{pq'rs'}{qsq's'} = \frac{p'qr's}{qsq's'} = \frac{p'r'}{q's'} = \left(\frac{p'}{q'}\right)\left(\frac{r'}{s'}\right)$$

[The reader should make sure that he understands the justification for each of the above equalities.]

Let's check Properties 5 and 6. The reader may then check Properties 7, 8, and 9Z as an exercise.

Property 5: $\left(\dfrac{p}{q}\right) \cdot 1 = \left(\dfrac{p}{q}\right) \cdot \left(\dfrac{1}{1}\right) = \dfrac{p \cdot 1}{q \cdot 1} = \dfrac{p}{q}$

Similarly,
$$1 \cdot \left(\frac{p}{q}\right) = \frac{p}{q}$$

Property 6: $\left(\dfrac{p}{q}\right) \cdot \left(\dfrac{r}{s}\right) = \left(\dfrac{pr}{qs}\right) = \left(\dfrac{rp}{sq}\right) = \left(\dfrac{r}{s}\right)\left(\dfrac{p}{q}\right)$

Note that in verifying each property for $\mathbf{Q}$ we made crucial use of the corresponding property for $\mathbf{Z}$.

With this as background, we are now able to give the *raison d'être* for the rationals—the availability of division.

Division. $\left(\dfrac{p}{q}\right) / \left(\dfrac{r}{s}\right) = \dfrac{ps}{rq}$ and is defined only for the case $\dfrac{r}{s} \neq 0$ (i.e., only for the case $r \neq 0$).

Consistency: Here consistency is a little different, since we did not define division on the integers. So we check consistency of notation:

$$m/n = \left(\frac{m}{1}\right) / \left(\frac{n}{1}\right) = \frac{m \cdot 1}{n \cdot 1} = \frac{m}{n}, \qquad \text{as it should be!}$$

Well-definedness: If $\dfrac{p}{q} = \dfrac{p'}{q'}$ and $\dfrac{r}{s} = \dfrac{r'}{s'}$ then

$$\left(\frac{p}{q}\right) / \left(\frac{r}{s}\right) = \frac{ps}{rq} = \frac{pq's}{rq'q} = \frac{p'qs}{rq'q} = \frac{p's}{rq'}$$

$$= \frac{p'r's}{r'rq'} = \frac{p'rs'}{r'rq'} = \frac{p's'}{r'q'} = \left(\frac{p'}{q'}\right) / \left(\frac{r'}{s'}\right)$$

In particular, we use the notation $\left(\dfrac{p}{q}\right)^{-1}$ for $1/\left(\dfrac{p}{q}\right) = \dfrac{q}{p}$, and call it the **inverse** of $\dfrac{p}{q}$ with respect to multiplication. We may now note the additional property which distinguishes the rationals from the integers:

PROPERTY 9

For all rationals $x \neq 0$, there exists a rational x^{-1} such that $x \cdot x^{-1} = x^{-1} \cdot x = 1$ (x^{-1} is the *inverse* of x under $\cdot$).

In fact, Property 9 implies Property 9Z: If m, n, and p are rationals with $m \neq 0$ and $mn = mp$, then

$$(m^{-1})(mn) = (m^{-1})(mp)$$

But then $(m^{-1}m)n = (m^{-1}m)p$

Thus $1 \cdot n = 1 \cdot p$

and so $n = p$ as desired.   □

The Set **R** of Real Numbers

We now shall develop an even larger class of numbers which includes the rational numbers as a proper subset.

Consider the isosceles right-angled triangle shown in Figure 1–15. Suppose that the length of the two equal sides is 1 and the length of the hypotenuse is x. By the Theorem of Pythagoras we know that

$$x^2 = 1^2 + 1^2$$

We may ask whether or not x is rational; i.e., is there a rational number x such that $x^2 = 1^2 + 1^2 = 2$? We will now demonstrate that the answer is

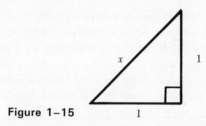

Figure 1–15

no. We will prove this by *reductio ad absurdum:* we assume that such a number exists and develop a contradiction, to deduce that our assumption was invalid.

THEOREM 1

There is no rational number x such that $x^2 = 2$.

Proof

Assume that x is a rational number with $x^2 = 2$. We can express x as p/q, where there is no positive integer $r > 1$ that divides both p and q (such an r can be "cancelled"). Since $(p/q)^2 = 2$, we have $p^2/q^2 = 2$, whence $p^2 = 2q^2$. Thus, p^2 is an even number. Since the square of an odd number is odd,† p must be an even number, say $p = 2s$. We then have $(2s)^2 = 2q^2$ so that

---

†Note that we are not going to derive from scratch all the properties of the numbers we use. Thus we do not define "odd" or "even," for example.

$2^2 s^2 = 2q^2$, whence $2s^2 = q^2$. Since q^2 is even, q must be even. Thus, the positive integer $r = 2$ divides both p and q—which is a contradiction to our assumption that p and q are not divisible by the same positive integer $r > 1$. Hence, there do not exist integers p and q such that $(p/q)^2 = 2$. $\square$

Since the length x of the hypotenuse of Figure 1–15 cannot be a ratio of integers, it is said to be **irrational.** We denote this particular irrational number by $\sqrt{2}$.

Note that although $\sqrt{2}$ is not rational, we can certainly approximate it with arbitrary accuracy by rational numbers. For example,

$$\left(\frac{14}{10}\right)^2 = 1.96$$

$$\left(\frac{141}{100}\right)^2 = 1.9881$$

$$\left(\frac{1414}{1000}\right)^2 = 1.999396$$

Continuing in this manner, we may approximate $\sqrt{2}$ more and more accurately. However, as we have seen, we will never be able to find a rational number which equals $\sqrt{2}$. In summary, although $\sqrt{2}$ is irrational, there exists a sequence of rational numbers $x_1, x_2, x_3, \ldots, x_n, \ldots$ such that for n large enough, x_n^2 comes arbitrarily close to 2. In other words, given any positive rational number ε (no matter how small), there exists an integer N (perhaps very large) such that for $n > N$ we have $|2 - x_n^2| < \varepsilon$.

Having assimilated the point that if we allow decimal expansions (such as the 1.414 ... which expresses $\sqrt{2}$) of the form

$$b_k \cdots b_3 b_2 b_1 b_0 \cdot a_1 a_2 a_3 a_4 \cdots a_n \cdots$$

which continue indefinitely to the right, then we may obtain irrational numbers, the reader may use his geometric intuition to define $r + r'$, $-(r)$, $r \cdot r'$, r/r', etc., for the set **R** of real numbers so defined, and pass on to the next subsection. However, those readers who enjoy going into mathematical details may wish to see how we may formally introduce real numbers in terms of certain special sequences of rationals, called Cauchy sequences.

Suppose that $x_1, x_2, x_3, \ldots, x_n, \ldots$ is a sequence such that x_n^2 gets closer to 2 as n gets larger. Then "fluctuations" in the sequence get smaller as n gets larger. More formally, we have the following.

THEOREM 2

Suppose that $x_1, x_2, x_3, \ldots, x_n, \ldots$ is a sequence of rational numbers such that for any rational number $\varepsilon > 0$ there exists an integer N such that

$|2 - x_n^2| < \varepsilon$ for any $n > N$. Then for any rational number $\delta > 0$ there exists an integer M such that $|x_p - x_q| < \delta$ for $p, q > M$.

Proof

$$|x_p - x_q| = \left| (x_p - x_q) \frac{x_p + x_q}{x_p + x_q} \right|$$

$$= \left| \frac{x_p^2 - x_q^2}{x_p + x_q} \right|$$

$$= \frac{|x_p^2 - x_q^2|}{|x_p + x_q|}$$

$$= \frac{|-2 + x_p^2 + 2 - x_q^2|}{|x_p + x_q|}$$

However, since $|a + b| \le |a| + |b|$,

$$|x_p - x_q| \le \frac{|-2 + x_p^2| + |2 - x_q^2|}{|x_p + x_q|}$$

$$\le \frac{|2 - x_p^2| + |2 - x_q^2|}{|x_p + x_q|}$$

Since for any rational number $\varepsilon > 0$ there exists an integer N_ε such that $|2 - x_n^2| < \varepsilon$ for $n > N_\varepsilon$, given any rational number $\delta > 0$, let us choose $M \ge N_\delta$. We then have

$$|x_p - x_q| < \frac{\delta + \delta}{|x_p + x_q|}$$

$$< \delta.$$

assuming, as is reasonable, that $x_p > 1$ and $x_q > 1$ for $p, q \ge N_\delta$. $\qquad \square$

The sequence $x_1, x_2, x_3, \ldots, x_n, \ldots$ previously given is an example of what is known as a Cauchy sequence.

DEFINITION 1

A sequence $x_1, x_2, x_3, \ldots, x_n, \ldots$ of rational numbers is called a **Cauchy sequence** if for every rational number $\delta > 0$ there exists an integer M such that $|x_p - x_q| < \delta$ for all integers $p, q > M$. $\qquad \bigcirc$

[The symbol $\bigcirc$ is used to indicate the end of a definition.]

As for the sequence $x_1, x_2, x_3, \ldots, x_n, \ldots$ given in the last theorem, we saw that this sequence approximates $\sqrt{2}$. This is an example of the fact that a Cauchy sequence of rational numbers can approximate an irrational number. However, Cauchy sequences may also approximate rational numbers.

In general, there are many ways of approximating a given number. For example, the rational number 12/99 may be approximated by either of following two Cauchy sequences:

$$0.1, \ 0.121, \ 0.12121, \ 0.1212121, \ \ldots$$

and

$$0.12, \ 0.1212, \ 0.121212, \ 0.12121212, \ \ldots$$

However, if we interweave these two sequences, we obtain

$$0.1, \ 0.12, \ 0.121, \ 0.1212, \ 0.12121, \ 0.121212, \ \ldots$$

which is also a Cauchy sequence that approximates 12/99.

DEFINITION 2

We say that two Cauchy sequences $x_1, x_2, x_3, \ldots x_n, \ldots$ and $y_1, y_2, y_3, \ldots,$ $y_n, \ldots$ of rational numbers are **co-Cauchy** if $x_1, y_1, x_2, y_2, \ldots, x_n, y_n, \ldots$ is a Cauchy sequence.   ○

Intuitively, two sequences are co-Cauchy whenever they are getting close to the same (rational or irrational) real number. Thus, just as we viewed a rational number as an expression of the form $\dfrac{p}{q}$, and then decreed that $\dfrac{p}{q}$ and $\dfrac{r}{s}$ represent the same rational number so long as $ps = rq$, so now do we view a real number $r \in \mathbf{R}$ as a Cauchy sequence of rational numbers, decreeing that two Cauchy sequences represent the same real number if and only if they are co-Cauchy. To make this statement less formidable, we note that every decimal number

$$b_k \ldots b_1 b_0 \cdot a_1 a_2 a_3 \ldots a_n \ldots \tag{1}$$

yields the Cauchy sequence

$$\begin{aligned}
x_1 &= b_k \ldots b_1 b_0 \cdot a_1 \\
x_2 &= b_k \ldots b_1 b_0 \cdot a_1 a_2 \\
x_3 &= b_k \ldots b_1 b_0 \cdot a_1 a_2 a_3
\end{aligned} \tag{2}$$

and so on, so that if $\varepsilon > 10^{-N}$, we have that $|x_m - x_n| < \varepsilon$ for $m, n > N$.

Conversely (and this is harder—we leave the proof only to the more enterprising reader), every Cauchy sequence of rational numbers is co-Cauchy with a Cauchy sequence of the form (2) for some decimal number (1). Thus, our usual interpretation of **R** as the set of decimal numbers of the form (1) is well-founded. Finally, note that our usual convention that, for example, 0.9999 . . . and 1.0000 . . . represent the same real number follows from the fact that their Cauchy sequences are co-Cauchy:

$$0.9, \ 1.0, \ 0.99, \ 1.00, \ 0.999, \ 1.000, \ 0.9999, \ 1.0000, \ . \ . \ .$$

is clearly a Cauchy sequence, with $|x_m - x_n| < 10^{-k}$ for $m, n \geq 2k + 1$.

As a consequence of our definition, we see that any rational number r may be regarded as the real number defined by the Cauchy sequence r, $r, r, \ . \ . \ . \ , r, \ . \ . \ .$. Furthermore, distinct rationals r and r' yield distinct reals, for were this not so, the sequence $r, r', r, r', r, r', \ . \ . \ .$ would be Cauchy, which is impossible since $|r - r'|$ cannot be made arbitrarily small.

We are now in a position to define our arithmetic functions for real numbers.

DEFINITION 3

If $\alpha = (a_1, a_2, a_3, \ . \ . \ . \ , a_n, \ . \ . \ .)$ and $\beta = (b_1, b_2, b_3, \ . \ . \ . \ , b_n, \ . \ . \ .)$, are Cauchy sequences, we define the following:

I. $\alpha + \beta = (a_1 + b_1, a_2 + b_2, a_3 + b_3, \ . \ . \ . \ , a_n + b_n, \ . \ . \ .)$
II. $\alpha \cdot \beta = \ \ (a_1 b_1, a_2 b_2, a_3 b_3, \ . \ . \ . \ , a_n b_n, \ . \ . \ .)$
III. $-\alpha = \ \ (-a_1, -a_2, -a_3, \ . \ . \ . \ , -a_n, \ . \ . \ .)$
IV. $1/\alpha = \ \ (1/a_1, 1/a_2, 1/a_3, \ . \ . \ . \ , 1/a_n, \ . \ . \ .)$
   provided that $a_i \neq 0$ for $i = 1, 2, 3, \ . \ . \ . \ , n, \ . \ . \ .$ $\bigcirc$

It is not difficult to verify that the real numbers satisfy Properties 1 to 9 given for **Q** in the previous subsection.

The Set **C** of Complex Numbers

Now suppose we consider $\mathbf{R}^2 = \mathbf{R} \times \mathbf{R}$ as given the usual Cartesian representation of the plane, so that $e_1 = (1, 0)$ and $e_2 = (0, 1)$ are to be thought of as unit vectors at right angles to one another. Now let us introduce two transformations of $\mathbf{R}^2$ into itself—the identity transformation I which leaves each vector x unchanged, and the transformation J which rotates a vector anticlockwise through $90°$. The reader can verify the following formulas from Figure 1–16:

$$I(x_1, x_2) = (x_1, x_2)$$
$$J(x_1, x_2) = (-x_2, x_1)$$

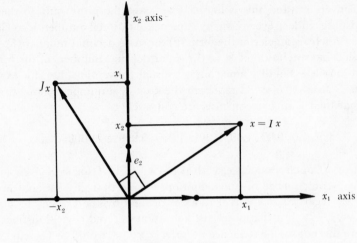

Figure 1–16

The expression $a_1I + a_2J$ then denotes the operation which sends the vector (x_1, x_2) to the vector $a_1(x_1, x_2) + a_2(-x_2, x_1) = (a_1x_1 - a_2x_2, a_1x_2 + a_2x_1)$.

Now suppose we operate upon this vector with $b_1I + b_2J$. Then

$$(b_1I + b_2J)(x_1,x_2) = (b_1(a_1x_1 - a_2x_2) - b_2(a_1x_2 + a_2x_1), b_1(a_1x_2 + a_2x_1)$$
$$+ b_2(a_1x_1 - a_2x_2))$$
$$= ((b_1a_1 - b_2a_2)x_1 - (b_1a_2 + b_2a_1)x_2, (b_1a_1 - b_2a_2)x_2$$
$$+ (b_1a_2 + b_2a_1)x_1)$$

Thus,

$$(b_1I + b_2J)(a_1I + a_2J) = (b_1a_1 - b_2a_2)I + (b_1a_2 + b_2a_1)J$$

In particular, setting $b_1 = a_1 = 0$ and $b_2 = a_2 = 1$, we see that

$$J^2 = -I$$

and we find that the collection of all **operators** $a_1I + a_2J$, for $(a_1a_2) \in \mathbf{R}^2$, is "identical" to the set $\mathbf{C}$ of all **complex numbers** $a_1 + a_2i$, while each a_1 in $\mathbf{R}$ may be identified with $a_1 + 0i$ in $\mathbf{C}$. We thus have the definitions

$$(b_1 + b_2i) + (a_1 + a_2i) = (b_1 + a_1) + (b_2 + a_2)i$$
$$(b_1 + b_2i) \cdot (a_1 + a_2i) = (b_1a_1 - b_2a_2) + (b_1a_2 + b_2a_1)i$$

which are consistent with the definitions in $\mathbf{R}$ when we identify b_1 with $b_1 + 0i$ and a_1 with $a_1 + 0i$.

Note that each operator $a_1I + a_2J$ has an additive inverse

$$(a_1I + a_2J) + ((-a_1)I + (-a_2)J) = 0$$

and a multiplicative inverse (as long as one of a_1 and a_2 is nonzero)

$$(a_1 I + a_2 J)\left(\frac{a_1}{a_1^2 + a_2^2} I + \frac{-a_2}{a_1^2 + a_2^2} J\right) = I$$

Also, we see that each complex number has an additive inverse

$$(a_1 + a_2 i) + ((-a_1) + (-a_2)i) = 0$$

and a multiplicative inverse

$$(a_1 + a_2 i) \cdot \left(\frac{a_1}{a_1^2 + a_2^2} + \frac{-a_2}{a_1^2 + a_2^2} i\right) = 1$$

It is left to the reader to verify, then, that $\mathbf{C}$ shares Properties 1 through 9 with $\mathbf{Q}$ and $\mathbf{R}$. The extra property that $\mathbf{C}$ has beyond $\mathbf{Q}$ and $\mathbf{R}$ is that, whatever elements $a_n, a_{n-1}, \ldots, a_2, a_1, a_0$ we pick from $\mathbf{C}$, there always exists a complex number x in $\mathbf{C}$ such that

$$a_n x^n + a_{n-1} x^{n-1} + \cdots + a_2 x^2 + a_1 x + a_0 = 0$$

The proof of this property is complex, and would take us beyond the scope of this volume. Of course, it is not true for the reals: Taking $a_2 = 1$, $a_1 = 0$, and $a_0 = 1$ we have

$$x^2 + 1 = 0$$

which is satisfied by no x in $\mathbf{R}$, but is satisfied for both $x = i$ and $x = -i$ in $\mathbf{C}$.

EXERCISES FOR SECTION 1–4

1. Show that Property 2 of $\mathbf{N}$ enables us to prove Property 2 of $\mathbf{Z}$.
2. Show that Property 4 of $\mathbf{Z}$ implies Property 4N of $\mathbf{N}$.
3. Verify Property 4 for $\mathbf{Z}$.
4. Verify Property 5 for $\mathbf{Z}$.
5. Verify Property 8 for $\mathbf{Z}$.
6. Verify that Properties 1, 4, and 8 imply that $n \cdot 0 = 0$ for any n in $\mathbf{Z}$.
7. Verify Property 2 for $\mathbf{Q}$.
8. Verify Property 3 for $\mathbf{Q}$.
9. Verify Property 7 for $\mathbf{Q}$.
10. Verify Property 8 for $\mathbf{Q}$.
11. Verify Property 9Z for $\mathbf{Q}$.
12. Given that the Cauchy sequences $x_1, x_2, x_3, \ldots, x_n, \ldots$ and $y_1, y_2, y_3, \ldots, y_n, \ldots$ of rational numbers approximate the same number, verify that $x_1, x_2, x_3, \ldots, x_n, \ldots$ and $x_1, y_1, x_2, y_2, \ldots, x_n, y_n, \ldots$ approximate the same number.
13. Show that each of the four sequences of Definition 3 is a Cauchy sequence, save that when $\alpha = 0$, the sequence $1/\alpha$ is *not* Cauchy.

14. Show that arithmetic for real numbers does not depend upon the particular choice of approximating sequences for α and β. For example, prove that if α and α' are co-Cauchy, and β and β' are co-Cauchy, then $\alpha + \beta$ and $\alpha' + \beta'$ are co-Cauchy.

1–5 Graphs and Trees

The reader is probably most familiar with the word "graph" in the sense of a graph (or plot) of a real function $f: \mathbf{R} \to \mathbf{R}$, as shown for $f(x) = x^2$ in Figure 1–17. In this case, our graph is the locus of the point having the coordinates $(x, f(x))$, where $f(x) = x^2$. However, we shall now introduce an entirely different notion of a graph, and briefly discuss some related concepts.

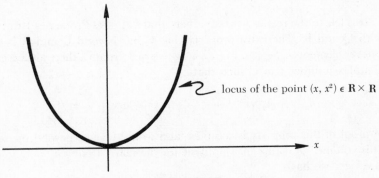

locus of the point $(x, x^2) \in \mathbf{R} \times \mathbf{R}$

Figure 1–17

The first paper on graph theory, appearing in 1736, was written by the Swiss mathematician Leonhard Euler (1707–1783). This paper began with a discussion of a problem which arose in Königsberg, East Prussia (now Kaliningrad, Lithuania, U.S.S.R.). An aerial view (from a balloon?) of a portion of the city is depicted in Figure 1–18.

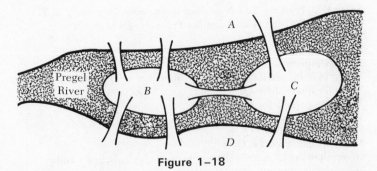

Figure 1–18

Within the city, there were two islands in the Pregel River, connected to the mainland and each other by seven bridges, as can be seen in Figure 1–18.

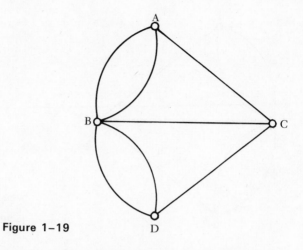

Figure 1-19

But, was it possible to walk across every bridge once and only once? In order to answer this burning question, known as the Königsberg Bridge Problem, Euler schematically represented the land areas as points and the bridges as lines connecting the points, as shown in Figure 1-19. The resulting inter-connection of points and lines is an example of a graph. (The formal defini-tion is given below.) By establishing a few of the basic properties of graphs, Euler was able to deduce that it was impossible to cross each bridge only once, thereby solving the Königsberg Bridge Problem.

More formally, we now have the following:

DEFINITION 1

A **graph** $G = (V, E)$ is a pair of sets: (1) a set V of points called **vertices** or **nodes,** and (2) a set E of lines called **edges,** where each edge can be represented by an unordered pair of vertices. (More than one edge can be represented by the same pair of vertices.)   ○

If both V and E are finite sets, then G is a **finite graph.** (Our primary interest in graphs in this book will be with the finite case.)

Example 1

Figure 1-20 shows the graph of the Königsberg Bridge Problem in which the vertices and edges have been labelled with the elements of the sets $V = \{v_1, v_2, v_3, v_4\}$ and $E = \{e_1, e_2, e_3, e_4, e_5, e_6, e_7\}$, respectively. For this graph we can represent e_1 by either (v_1, v_2) or (v_2, v_1). The same may be said for e_2, even though $e_1 \neq e_2$.   ◊

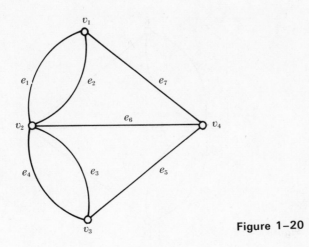

Figure 1–20

An edge e_i, which is represented by (v_j, v_k), is said to be **incident** at vertex v_j and vertex v_k. A graph $G' = (V', E')$ is a **subgraph** of $G = (V, E)$ if $V' \subset V$, $E' \subset E$, and all the incidence relationships of G are preserved.

Example 2

For the graph G shown in Figure 1-20, the sets $V' = \{v_1, v_3, v_4\}$ and $E' = \{e_5, e_7\}$ form a subgraph of the given graph G. However, the sets $V'' = \{v_1, v_3, v_4\}$ and $E'' = \{e_5, e_6, e_7\}$ do not form a subgraph of G, since e_6 is incident at v_2 and v_4 in G and $v_2 \notin V''$.   ◊

Given a graph $G = (V, E)$, consider a sequence of vertices in V and distinct edges in E

$$v_{i_1}, e_{i_1}, v_{i_2}, e_{i_2}, v_{i_3}, \ldots, v_{i_{n-1}}, e_{i_{n-1}}, v_{i_n}$$

such that e_{i_j} is incident at v_{i_j} and $v_{i_{j+1}}$ for $j = 1, 2, \ldots, n - 1$. If all the vertices in the sequence are also distinct, then the subgraph $(\{v_{i_1}, v_{i_2}, \ldots, v_{i_n}\}$, $\{e_{i_1}, e_{i_2}, \ldots, e_{i_{n-1}}\})$ is a **path** of G; while if all the vertices except the first and last are distinct, the subgraph is a **circuit** (or **cycle**) of G.

Example 3

For the graph in Figure 1-20, the sequence

$$v_1, e_1, v_2, e_3, v_3, e_5, v_4$$

corresponds to a path, while the sequence

$$v_1, e_1, v_2, e_3, v_3, e_5, v_4, e_7, v_1$$

corresponds to a circuit. The sequence

$$v_1, e_1, v_2, e_3, v_3, e_5, v_4, e_6, v_2$$

does not correspond to either a path or a circuit. ◊

A graph in which there exists a path between every pair of vertices is said to be **connected.** A connected graph that contains no circuits is called a **tree.** An edge of a tree is referred to as a **branch.**

Example 4

Clearly, the graph $G = (V, E)$ in Figure 1–20 is connected and is not a tree. However, this graph contains many trees as subgraphs, a few of which are

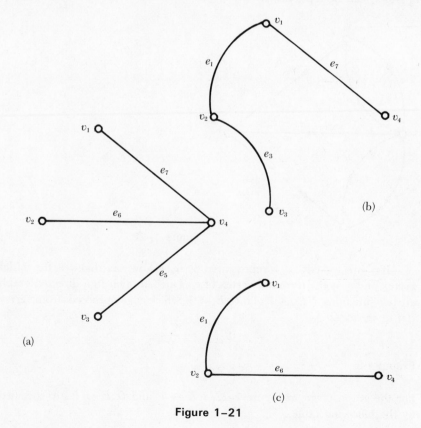

Figure 1–21

shown in Figure 1–21. Since they contain all the vertices of G, the subgraphs in Figures 1–21(a) and (b) are called **spanning trees.** The concept of a tree, and especially the rooted trees of Definition 2 on page 64, will be very important to us in this book.   ◊

Suppose we take a graph and place an arrowhead on each edge. (The location of the arrowhead on the branch is immaterial.) The result is called a directed graph. Formally, the definition of a directed graph is the same as for an undirected graph, with the exception that each edge can be represented by only one ordered pair of vertices. The definitions of an edge incident to a vertex and of a subgraph remain unchanged.

Example 5

The directed graph in Figure 1–22 was obtained from the graph in Figure 1–20 by arbitrarily placing arrowheads on the edges. For this directed graph, e_1 can be represented only by (v_1, v_2) and e_2 only by (v_2, v_1). However, both e_3 and e_4 can be represented by (v_3, v_4).   ◊

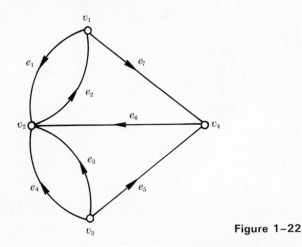

Figure 1–22

If a directed edge e_i is represented by (v_j, v_k), we say that v_j is the **initial vertex** and v_k is the **terminal vertex** of e_i. Thus, implicit in a directed graph are two functions, $I: E \to V$ and $O: E \to V$, where edge e proceeds from vertex $I(e)$ to vertex $O(e)$.

Example 6

For the graph given in Figure 1–22, $I: E \to V$ and $O: E \to V$ are specified by the following table.

e	e_1	e_2	e_3	e_4	e_5	e_6	e_7
$I(e)$	v_1	v_2	v_3	v_3	v_3	v_4	v_1
$O(e)$	v_2	v_1	v_2	v_2	v_4	v_2	v_4

◇

We say that a directed graph is **labelled** if each vertex and each edge bears a **label;** i.e., if we have a set A of labels and a labelling map $V \cup E \to A$ which assigns a label from A to each edge and each vertex.

The study of both pure and applied graph theory has grown quickly over the last dozen years or so, as evidenced by the increase in the amount of literature in the field (see list of references). A major reason has been the solution of a number of discrete problems (mainly in electrical engineering and operations research) by means of graph theoretic techniques. Furthermore, the range of applications is widening at an increasing pace. For example, in the computer area, graph theory has seen success with the problem of diagnosis. However, it is expected that computer oriented applications of graph theory will grow at an enormous rate in the coming decade. As far as this book is concerned, though, our discussion of graph theory has been limited to only those concepts that we directly use in it. For example, we shall turn to the labelled graphs which represent finite automata in Section 2–1. In the rest of this section, we study a special class of finite directed trees—the **rooted** trees—which will be of use in many places, such as our study of formal languages in Chapter 4, and of coding theory in Chapter 6.

We now want to emphasize those finite labelled graphs which have the form of **trees,** as shown in Figure 1–23. If we say that a vertex v of the directed

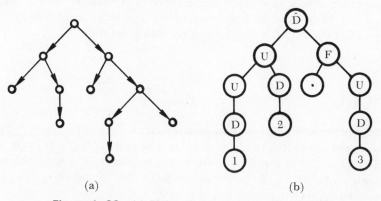

(a)   (b)

Figure 1–23 (a) Unlabelled rooted tree; (b) labelled tree.

graph (V, E) is a **predecessor** of the vertex v', and that v' is a **successor** of v, and if there exists an edge e with $I(e) = v$ and $O(e) = v'$, we may characterize a rooted tree as a graph of the following kind.

DEFINITION 2

A directed graph (V, E) is a **rooted tree** if it satisfies the following conditions:

(i) There is exactly one vertex with no predecessor (the **root** of the tree).
(ii) Every other vertex has exactly one predecessor.
(iii) The successors of each vertex are ordered (in the sense, for example, that moving from left to right places an ordering on the successors of each node of the trees of Figure 1–24).

We say that a vertex of a rooted tree is **maximal** if it has no successors.

○

It will prove convenient to ignore arrowheads on branches and to have a standard way of **addressing** the vertices of a rooted tree by strings of natural numbers. (We use $\mathbf{N}^*$ to denote the set of all such strings, and use Λ to denote the "empty string.")

PROCEDURE

Let us be given a rooted tree (V, E).

Stage 0. Label the root of the tree by the empty string Λ from $\mathbf{N}^*$.

Stage n + 1. Let $v_1, \ldots, v_k$ be the vertices labelled at stage n which are not maximal. For each j, let w_j be the string from $\mathbf{N}^*$ used to label v_j, and let $v_{j0}, \ldots, v_{jl}$ ($l \geq 0$) be the $l + 1$ successors of v_j in their prescribed order. Then we label each v_{ji} ($0 \leq i \leq l$) with the string $w_j i$ from $\mathbf{N}^*$.

Example 7

The above procedure yields the addresses shown on the tree in Figure 1–24. Note how appropriate the term "address" is. The address $x_1 x_2 \ldots x_n$ tells us precisely how to get to the node: start at Λ, take the $(x_1 + 1)$st branch to get to node x_1, follow $n - 2$ further instructions to get to node $x_1 x_2 \ldots x_{n-1}$, then take the $(x_n + 1)$st branch to get to node $x_1 x_2 \ldots x_n$.   ◊

Henceforth in this volume *we shall only consider finite rooted trees, and call them trees, for short.* Note that a nonempty finite subset T of $\mathbf{N}^*$ is the set of all addresses obtained from some tree by the above procedure iff it satisfies the following two conditions: If $wx \in T$, with $w \in \mathbf{N}^*$ and $x \in \mathbf{N}$, then

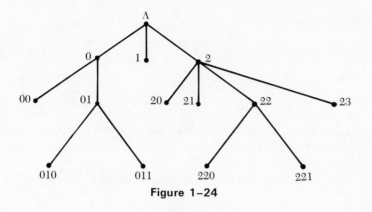

Figure 1–24

$$w \in T \tag{Ti}$$

$$wy \in T \text{ for all } y \in \mathbf{N} \text{ with } 0 \leq y \leq x. \tag{Tii}$$

Note also that the vertex labelled w is a predecessor of the vertex labelled w' iff $w' = wx$ for some $x \in \mathbf{N}$. Thus, in what follows we shall find it convenient to identify trees with subsets T of $\mathbf{N}^*$ which satisfy conditions (Ti) and (Tii); it is not necessary to specify the edges explicitly, since they can be recovered from the addresses of the vertices by the following procedure:

Given a tree $T \subset \mathbf{N}^*$, the edge set is the subset $E = \{(w, w') \mid w' = wx$ for some $x \in \mathbf{N}\}$ of $T \times T$, and we define $I : E \to T : (w, w') \mapsto w$ and $O : E \to T : (w, w') \mapsto w'$. *Note:* If a node w has more than ten incident branches, we must use a notation which distinguishes $(w, 10)$, the eleventh successor of w, from $(w, 1, 0)$, the first successor of the second successor of w. However, in most cases we can use the simple notation $w10$ without fear of ambiguity, and so we only write $x_1 x_2 \ldots x_n$ in the more cumbersome form $(x_1, \ldots, x_n)$ when doubt is likely to arise.

Given a tree $T \subset \mathbf{N}^*$, we define the **height** of T to be the length of the longest string in T. For example, a longest string in Figure 1–24 is 221, and so the height of that tree is 3.

Now let us define mathematically the *frontier* of a tree in the sense of the maximal nodes (i.e., $w \in T$ for which $w0 \notin T$) arranged from left to right. Given two nodes w, w' in the tree $T \subset \mathbf{N}^*$, it is clear that w is to the left of w' whenever, when we trace the paths to w and w' at the point $\hat{w}$ at which they diverge, the branch leading to w is to the left of the branch leading to w'.

DEFINITION 3

Given two nodes w, w' of the tree $T \subset \mathbf{N}^*$, we say that w **is to the left of** w' (denoted $w \prec w'$) iff there exists $\hat{w}$ in $\mathbf{N}^*$, $x < y$ where $x, y \in \mathbf{N}$, and w_1,

w_2 in $\mathbf{N}^*$ such that

$$w = \hat{w}xw_1 \quad \text{and} \quad w' = \hat{w}yw_2. \qquad \bigcirc$$

Example 8

In the tree of Figure 1–24, $20 \prec 221$ since we may take $\hat{w} = 2$, $x = 0$, $y = 2$, $w_1 = \Lambda$, $w_2 = 1$ to obtain

$$20 = \hat{w}xw_1 \prec \hat{w}yw_2 = 221$$

from the above definition. Similarly, $220 \prec 23$. $\qquad \Diamond$

DEFINITION 4

The **frontier** of a tree $T \subset \mathbf{N}^*$ is the sequence $(w_1, w_2, \dots, w_k)$ of all maximal nodes of T arranged in ascending order with respect to $\prec$. $\qquad \bigcirc$

Example 9

The frontier of the tree of Figure 1–24 is

$$(00, 010, 011, 1, 20, 21, 220, 221, 23) \qquad \Diamond$$

To close our formal definitions, we define a labelled tree:

DEFINITION 5

Let A be any set. Then an A-**labelled tree** (A-**tree**, for short) is a tree $T \subset \mathbf{N}^*$ together with a function $h: T \to A$. We call $h(w)$ the label of node w (adopting the abbreviation "node w" for "the node whose address is w"). $\qquad \bigcirc$

Example 10

The labelled tree of Figure 1–23(b) is an A-tree for the set $A = \{\hat{D}, U, F, D, \cdot, 1, 2, 3\}$ and is specified by the function $h: T \to A$ which has

$$h(\Lambda) = \hat{D}; \; h(0) = U, \, h(1) = F, \dots, h(1100) = 3. \qquad \Diamond$$

Further Reading for Chapter 1

The basic elements of set theory, of the inductive definition of the integers, and of the various number systems have been told so many times that it is hard to select a few books from the many available. An exceptionally well written modern presentation, which treats these ideas at textbook length, is provided by Eisenberg [1971]. Standard chapter-or-two treatments may be found in such modern algebra texts as Hollister [1972] and Johnson [1966]; and in such applied algebra texts as Birkhoff and Bartee [1970] and Berztiss [1971]. For more of such notations of logic hinted at in Section 1–1 as consistency and independence, see Enderton [1972]. Graph theory, with varying degrees of application, is treated by Busacker and Saaty [1965], Frank and Frisch [1971], and Harary [1969].

A. T. BERZTISS [1971] *Data Structures: Theory and Practice,* New York: Academic Press.

G. BIRKHOFF and T. C. BARTEE [1969] *Modern Applied Algebra,* New York: McGraw-Hill.

R. G. BUSACKER and T. SAATY [1965] *Finite Graphs and Networks,* New York: McGraw-Hill.

M. EISENBERG [1971] *Axiomatic Theory of Sets and Classes,* New York: Holt, Rinehart and Winston.

H. B. ENDERTON [1972] *A Mathematical Introduction to Logic,* New York: Academic Press.

H. FRANK and I. T. FRISCH [1971] *Communication, Transmission and Transportation Networks,* Reading, Mass.: Addison-Wesley.

F. HARARY [1969] *Graph Theory,* Reading, Mass.: Addison-Wesley.

H. A. HOLLISTER [1972] *Modern Algebra: A First Course,* New York: Harper and Row.

R. E. JOHNSON [1966] *University Algebra,* Englewood Cliffs, N.J.: Prentice Hall.

CHAPTER 2

Automata and Semigroups I

The purpose of this chapter is to introduce the reader to a number of basic concepts in computer science, while at the same time providing a grounding in key notions of algebra. In the first section we give a leisurely introduction to the notion of an automaton (in the guise commonly described as a finite-state sequential machine), motivate the notion with some simple circuitry, introduce the notion of a state graph, and give the reader some practice in the process whereby one passes from intuition to algebraic formalization. Building upon Section 2–1, we provide in Section 2–2 the basic algebraic concepts of semigroups, monoids, and groups. Then, in Section 2–3, we reinforce the circuitry examples of Section 2–1 by showing how any automaton may be built using appropriate switching elements. Some simple aspects of propositional logic are introduced along the way. Then, in Section 2–4, we introduce one of the most powerful techniques in all of algebra, that of the equivalence relation. Once mastered, this concept seems so simple that it is easy to forget how hard students find it at first, and thus we have taken some pains to provide an intuitive language of "barrels" which will make the basic definitions more comprehensible, and then illustrate the notion with a wide variety of applications ranging from the decomposition theory of automata to Cantor's theorem that the real numbers are not denumerable. Then, in Section 2–5, we give one of the most important applications of equivalence relations, showing how to build automata with specified behavior, as well as developing the reachability and observability theory of machines.

2–1   Automata and State Graphs

In this section we give the reader a concrete feel for the basic notions of sets and functions by showing how naturally they let us formalize the description of simple machines such as might be used as units in the hardware of a digital computer. Since the emphasis in this section is on providing practice in algebraic thinking, the more sophisticated reader may wish simply to read the definitions, Example 1, the theorems, and their proofs to extract the information he needs for later sections.

To introduce our study of automata, let us specify a machine which *counts modulo 10* and then see how it may be modified to serve as a component of a machine which counts modulo 1000. Along the way we shall see how machines may be specified verbally, or by means of a directed graph called a *state diagram,* or with mathematical precision in terms of three sets and two functions.

First we must formalize the notion of **counting modulo** m for any integer $m \geq 1$. To this end, we introduce the notation $\mathbf{Z}_m$ for the set $\{0, 1, 2, \ldots, m - 1\}$. Thus, in particular, we have $\mathbf{Z}_1 = \{0\}$, $\mathbf{Z}_2 = \{0, 1\}$, while $\mathbf{Z}_{10} = \{0, 1, 2, 3, 4, 5, 6, 7, 8, 9\}$. Now if we think of forming repeatedly the successor function of numbers written in decimal notation, we see that the last digit is always an element of $\mathbf{Z}_{10}$, and is incremented by the function

$$\sigma(n) = \begin{cases} 0 & \text{if } n = 9 \\ n + 1 & \text{if } 0 \leq n < 9 \end{cases}$$

and it is natural to think of this σ as a **successor function** for $\mathbf{Z}_{10}$.

More generally, the successor function $\sigma : \mathbf{Z} \to \mathbf{Z} : n \mapsto n + 1$ yields for each integer $m \geq 1$ a well-defined successor function

$$\sigma : \mathbf{Z}_m \to \mathbf{Z}_m : n \mapsto \begin{cases} 0 & \text{if } n = m - 1 \\ n + 1 & \text{if } 0 \leq n < m - 1 \end{cases}$$

so that where by *counting* we mean "repeatedly applying σ to elements of $\mathbf{Z}$" (and thus chasing through 0, 1, 2, 3, . . .), by *counting modulo m* we shall mean "repeatedly applying σ to elements of $\mathbf{Z}_m$" (and thus chasing through 0, 1, 2, 3, . . . , $m - 1$, 0, 1, 2, . . .). Note that whereas our counting in $\mathbf{Z}$ never repeats itself, our counting modulo m is cyclical, returning to 0 every m steps. Figure 2–1, in which $\mathbf{Z}$ is wrapped around a helix, shows graphically how the endless $\mathbf{Z}$-counting yields cyclical $\mathbf{Z}_m$-counting for the case $m = 4$.

For us, then, a **counter modulo** m will be a device with m *states* (we shall call them 0, 1, . . . , $m - 1$) and two *inputs* (we shall call them 0 and 1), which counts modulo m the number of 1-inputs. In other words, we demand that if the system receives input 0 it does not change state; but that if it is in state q and receives input 1, then its next state will be $q + 1$ (where the addition is, of course, modulo m).

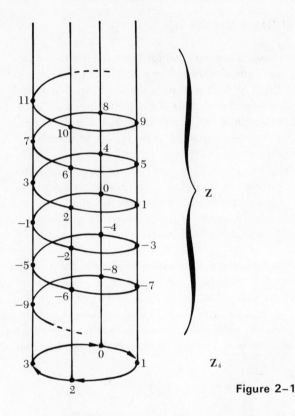

Figure 2–1

This device (let us denote it as C_m) can also be described by a directed graph **(state diagram)** in which we have one node for each state; and we have one edge directed away from each state-node for each input, an edge being directed toward the node of the state to which that input sends the given state. We draw the state diagram of C_{10} explicitly in Figure 2–2. As long as we supply 1's at the input, we keep counting around the loop modulo 10; when 0's come in, we stop counting until the 1's resume. Thus C_{10} "remembers" how many 1's have been applied at the input since it was last in its zero state; but since its "memory" is "limited," it can only tell us the low-order digit of the base 10 expansion of (i.e., the ordinary numerical notation for) the number.

To reinforce our understanding of machine design, we show how C_{10} must be modified so that three copies of the modified machine may be interconnected as in Figure 2–3 to yield a machine which counts modulo 1000. Here, C_{10}^3 keeps track of the hundreds, C_{10}^2 keeps track of the tens, and C_{10}^1 keeps track of the units.

C_{10}^1 will clearly work satisfactorily as far as keeping track of the units is concerned; counting modulo 10 and providing the units digit of a count modulo 1000 are just the same task. But C_{10}^2 can only do its task correctly if it receives a 1-input each time C_{10}^1 completes a cycle through all 10 digits. Thus, we must modify C_{10} so that it will produce an output of 1 whenever

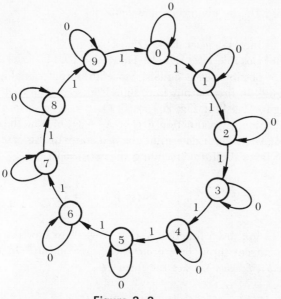

Figure 2–2

it has completed a cycle. But C_{10} completes a cycle each time it receives an input of 1 when it is in state 9. Thus, we want the output to be 1 for the state-input pair $(9, 1)$, and the output to be 0 for all other state-input pairs.

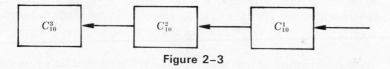

Figure 2–3

In addition to the output of 0 or 1 which C_{10}^1 needs to supply C_{10}^2 (and which C_{10}^2 in turn needs to supply C_{10}^3), we must also have an output line which communicates the current state of the machine "to the outside world." Thus, our modified version of C_{10} (call it D_{10}) suitable for incorporation into the modulo 1000 counter will have the form shown in Figure 2–4.

(to outside world)

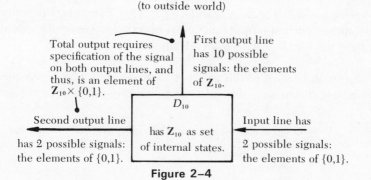

Total output requires specification of the signal on both output lines, and thus, is an element of $\mathbf{Z}_{10} \times \{0,1\}$.

First output line has 10 possible signals: the elements of $\mathbf{Z}_{10}$.

Second output line has 2 possible signals: the elements of $\{0,1\}$.

D_{10} has $\mathbf{Z}_{10}$ as set of internal states.

Input line has 2 possible signals: the elements of $\{0,1\}$.

Figure 2–4

We specify D_{10} by giving five particulars:

(i) A set Q of internal *states:* Here $Q = \mathbf{Z}_{10}$.

(ii) A set X of possible *input* signals: Here $X = \{0, 1\}$.

(iii) A set Y of possible *output* signals: Since an output signal is the ordered pair (signal on first output line, signal on second output line), we see from Figure 2–4 that $Y = \mathbf{Z}_{10} \times \{0, 1\}$.

(iv) A specification, by a function $\delta: Q \times X \to Q$, of how the current state and the current input determine the *next* state. In this case the *next-state function* δ takes the form (recalling that $\sigma(9) = 0$)

$$\delta: \mathbf{Z}_{10} \times \{0, 1\} \to \mathbf{Z}_{10} \qquad \text{where } \delta(k, x) = \begin{cases} k & \text{if } x = 0 \\ \sigma(k) & \text{if } x = 1 \end{cases}$$

(v) A specification, by a function $\lambda: Q \times X \to Y$, of how the current state and the current input determine the *current* output.* In this case the *current-output function* λ takes the form

$$\lambda: \mathbf{Z}_{10} \times \{0, 1\} \to \mathbf{Z}_{10} \times \{0, 1\}: (k, x) \mapsto (k, y),$$
$$\text{where } y = \begin{cases} 1 & \text{if } k = 9 \text{ and } x = 1 \\ 0 & \text{otherwise} \end{cases}$$

since, when the current state is k, we want the first output line simply to signal the state k irrespective of the input x; while the second output line should signal 1, rather than 0, whenever D_{10} is about to complete a cycle of counting, i.e., when $k = 9$ and $x = 1$.

With this specific discussion of D_{10}, the reader should be prepared to accept the value of the following general definition:

DEFINITION 1

An **automaton** (or **machine**) is specified by a quintuple $M = (Q, X, Y, \delta, \lambda)$ where Q, X, and Y are sets (called the sets of **states, inputs,** and **outputs,** respectively), and $\delta: Q \times X \to Q$ and $\lambda: Q \times X \to Y$ are functions (called the **next-state** and **current-output** functions, respectively). We say the automaton is **finite** if the sets X, Y, and Q are all finite.   ○

Our interpretation of this abstract construct is as follows: We imagine that we have chosen some time scale such that the successive units count off

---

*Other models would specify the *next* output, but the current model better fits our present application.

the successive periods at which we may apply inputs to our system. Then the force of the specification $(Q, X, Y, \delta, \lambda)$ is that, if at time t we find the machine in state $q(t) \in Q$ and apply input $x(t) \in X$, then the immediate output $y(t) \in Y$ and the next state $q(t + 1) \in Q$ will satisfy the equations

$$\delta(q(t), x(t)) = q(t + 1)$$
$$\lambda(q(t), x(t)) = y(t)$$

To the finite automaton $M = (Q, X, Y, \delta, \lambda)$ we associate the labelled directed graph [called the **state diagram** or **state graph**] which has one vertex q for each state of M, and one edge (q, x) for each state-input signal pair of M. We have that $I(q, x) = q$ while $O(q, x) = \delta(q, x)$. We label each edge (q, x) with the compound symbol $x/\lambda(q, x)$, which indicates both the input and the output associated with the transition that that edge represents.

Example 1

Consider the automaton represented by the state diagram shown in Figure 2–5.

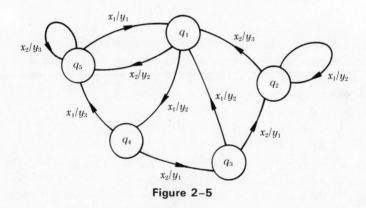

Figure 2–5

In this graph, an edge directed from q_i to q_j having the label x_a/y_b indicates that when the automaton is in state q_i, an input of x_a will produce the current output y_b and will result in the next state being q_j.

For this automaton we have the sets:

$$Q = \{q_1, q_2, q_3, q_4, q_5\}$$
$$X = \{x_1, x_2\}$$
$$Y = \{y_1, y_2, y_3\}$$

and the functions δ and λ given by:

$$\delta(q_1, x_1) = q_4 \qquad \lambda(q_1, x_1) = y_2$$
$$\delta(q_1, x_2) = q_5 \qquad \lambda(q_1, x_2) = y_2$$
$$\delta(q_2, x_1) = q_2 \qquad \lambda(q_2, x_1) = y_2$$
$$\delta(q_2, x_2) = q_1, \text{ etc.} \qquad \lambda(q_2, x_2) = y_3, \text{ etc.} \qquad \Diamond$$

Now, one of the key notions we are trying to convey in this book is that algebra is as much a language as a collection of definitions and theorems. Thus, it is important that the reader realize that our above formalization of the notion of machine is but one of many. The reader should gain some confidence that, faced with some new situation, he would be able to provide his own formalization. To further this feeling, let us now give another formalization of the notion of a machine. Rather than proceed as quickly as possible, we shall take the opportunity to increase the reader's facility with commutative diagrams.

What would it mean to say that the output of our machine $(Q, X, Y, \delta, \lambda)$ depended only on the state of the machine? Simply that for each $q \in Q$, and any pair of inputs $x, x' \in X$ we have that

$$\lambda(q, x) = \lambda(q, x') \tag{1}$$

for this says that, as soon as we know q, the current input is of no further use in determining the output. In fact, we can then define a function $\beta : Q \to Y$ by taking $\beta(q)$ to be simply $\lambda(q, x_0)$ for some arbitrarily chosen $x_0 \in X$, since equation (1) then assures us that

$$\lambda(q, x) = \beta(q) \qquad \text{for all } q \in Q \text{ and all } x \in X \tag{2}$$

Now remember that two functions are equal iff they have both the same domain and codomain, and if each transforms elements of their common domain in the same way. Can we rephrase equation (2), an equality of elements of Y, in terms of an equality of functions? The answer is yes, but to get it we should first introduce the notion of a **projection**. For any pair of sets A and B we can define the projections p_1 and p_2 of $A \times B$ onto A and B, respectively, as follows:

$$p_1 : A \times B \to A : (a, b) \mapsto a$$
$$p_2 : A \times B \to B : (a, b) \mapsto b.$$

As we see from Figure 2–6, this captures the usual notion of projection onto the axes that we have in coordinate (Euclidean) geometry.

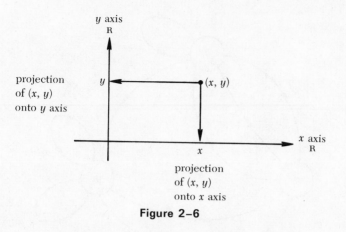

Figure 2–6

Using, in particular, the projection $p_1 : Q \times X \to Q$, we recognize that $\beta(q) = \beta[p_1(q, x)] = (\beta \circ p_1)(q, x)$; so that the equality (2) can simply be rewritten in the language of function equality as:

$$\beta \circ p_1 = \lambda : Q \times X \to Y \tag{3}$$

Recalling our discussion of commutative diagrams in Section 1–2, we see that (3) can in turn be rephrased by saying:

The diagram

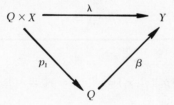

$$\tag{4}$$

commutes.

Example 2

Consider the automaton whose state diagram is Figure 2–7, so that we have:

$$\delta(q_1, x_1) = q_1 \qquad \lambda(q_1, x_1) = y_1$$
$$\delta(q_1, x_2) = q_2, \text{ etc.} \qquad \lambda(q_1, x_2) = y_1, \text{ etc.}$$

By inspection of λ, we see that:

$$\lambda(q_1, x_1) = \lambda(q_1, x_2) = \lambda(q_1, x_3) = y_1$$
$$\lambda(q_2, x_1) = \lambda(q_2, x_2) = \lambda(q_2, x_3) = y_2$$
$$\lambda(q_3, x_1) = \lambda(q_3, x_2) = \lambda(q_3, x_3) = y_1$$

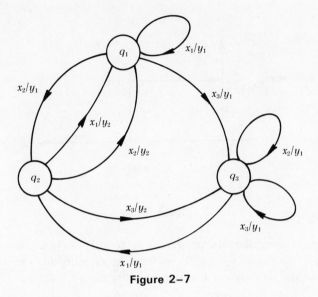

Figure 2–7

Clearly, then, we see that the output of the machine is independent of the input. Hence, we define the function $\beta : Q \to Y$ as follows:

$$\beta(q_1) = y_1$$
$$\beta(q_2) = y_2$$
$$\beta(q_3) = y_1$$

Thus, for example, we see that

$$[\beta \circ p_1](q_1, x_1) = \beta(q_1) = y_1 = \lambda(q_1, x_1)$$

and we may use the **state-output graph** shown in Figure 2–8 to represent the machine. This has the same underlying graph as Figure 2–7, but is differently

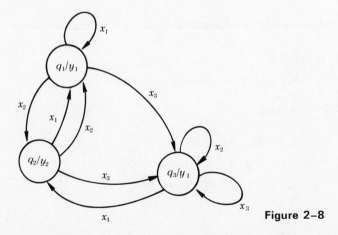

Figure 2–8

labelled: node q is now labelled by $q/\beta(q)$, while the edge (q, x) from q to $\delta(q, x)$ is simply labelled by x.   ◊

With this observation we are ready to define a *state-output machine*, that is, one whose current output depends only on its current state.

DEFINITION 2

An automaton $(Q, X, Y, \delta, \lambda)$ is said to be a **state-output automaton** if there exists a function $\beta : Q \to Y$ such that the diagram

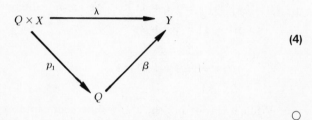

(4)

commutes.   ○

We have taken pains to show the reader how the equalities (1) and (2) can be transmuted into the commutative diagram (4). However, it should be noted that (with practice) the diagram becomes an aid to intuition, rather than an escape from it. For we can interpret (4) directly by saying that "to compute the output (i.e., to follow λ from $Q \times X$ to Y) we may just as well throw away the input (follow p_1 from $Q \times X$ to Q) and then just look at the state to compute the output (follow β from Q to Y)." In other words, it is often easier to chase arrows around a diagram like (4) than to disentangle an equation like (2) which makes explicit the fates of the elements of the various sets involved.

Actually, when talking of state-output automata, we shall usually mention β explicitly and ignore λ. Thus, in what follows, a state-output automaton will be a quintuple (Q, X, Y, δ, β) with the interpretation that $\delta(q(t), x(t)) = q(t + 1)$ while $\beta(q(t)) = y(t)$.

Having thrown away the ability to consult the input in determining the output, it might seem that state-output machines are more limited than other automata. However, we can in fact show that *any* automaton M can be simulated by a *state-output* machine $\hat{M}$ if we are prepared to pay a price; namely, that $\hat{M}$ may have more states than M, and will always be one step behind M. In other words, we are claiming that to each state q of M there corresponds a state $k(q)$ of $\hat{M}$ such that the string of outputs we get by feeding a given string of inputs into M started in state q and into $\hat{M}$ started in state $\hat{q}$ will be just the same, save for a unit delay in the output of $\hat{M}$. This result is formalized in Theorem 1, after introducing the notation of Definitions 3 and 4. However, the reader who is not yet completely at home with algebraic formulae may appreciate the following exposition of the "genesis" of such formalizations.

Our above statement relating M and $\widehat{M}$ is somewhat imprecise, so we use our notation to rephrase it with a little more precision in the following statement: To each automaton $M = (Q, X, Y, \delta, \lambda)$ there corresponds a state-output automaton $\widehat{M} = (\widehat{Q}, X, Y, \widehat{\delta}, \beta)$ and an injection $k: Q \hookrightarrow \widehat{Q}$ such that if we start M in state $q(t)$ at time t and apply inputs $x(t), x(t + 1), \ldots,$ $x(t + \tau)$ to receive outputs $y(t), y(t + 1), \ldots, y(t + \tau)$ at the indicated times; and if we start $\widehat{M}$ in state $k(q(t))$ at time t and apply the same inputs $x(t),$ $x(t + 1), \ldots, x(t + \tau)$ to receive outputs $\widehat{y}(t), \widehat{y}(t + 1), \ldots, \widehat{y}(t + \tau),$ $\widehat{y}(t + \tau + 1)$ at the indicated times, then we shall have the following equalities:

$$y(t) = \widehat{y}(t + 1) \qquad \text{[We are not interested in } \widehat{y}(t).]$$
$$y(t + 1) = \widehat{y}(t + 2)$$
$$\vdots$$
$$y(t + \tau) = \widehat{y}(t + \tau + 1).$$

While it is true that the above statement captures formally the meaning of the statement which preceeded it, it must be confessed that it does so in a rather messy way. In understanding why it is messy, in appreciating why we proceed as we do in cleaning it up, and in noting how much more elegant the final statement of the theorem is, we shall have added a great deal to our feel for the virtues of the algebraic approach.

What we clearly need are (i) a good way to talk about sequences and (ii) a compact way of describing how our machines process strings of inputs.

DEFINITION 3

For any set X, we let X^* denote the set of all finite sequences of elements of X. A typical element of X^* would thus be $w = x_{i_1} x_{i_2} \ldots x_{i_n}$ comprising n elements, in order, from X. We say that such a string has *length* n, and write $\ell(w) = n$. We shall find it convenient to include in X^* the **empty string** of length 0; but shall denote it by Λ, rather than simply leaving a possibly ambiguous blank.

Given two sequences $w_1 = x_{i_1} x_{i_2} \ldots x_{i_n}$ and $w_2 = x_{j_1} x_{j_2} \ldots x_{j_m}$, we define their **concatenation** $w_1 \cdot w_2$ to be the string of w_1 followed by the string of w_2; i.e.,

$$w_1 \cdot w_2 = x_{i_1} x_{i_2} \ldots x_{i_n} x_{j_1} x_{j_2} \ldots x_{j_m} \in X^*$$

We shall also decree that $w_1 \cdot \Lambda = w_1 = \Lambda \cdot w_1$.

We shall use X^+ to denote $X^* \backslash \{\Lambda\}$, that is, the set of all finite nonempty sequences of elements from X.   ○

We obviously have $\ell(w_1 \cdot w_2) = \ell(w_1) + \ell(w_2)$ for all $w_1, w_2 \in X^*$, and it is also clear that for all strings w_1, w_2, w_3 in X^* we have

$$(w_1 \cdot w_2) \cdot w_3 = w_1 \cdot (w_2 \cdot w_3)$$

[We may paraphrase this by saying that concatenation is associative and has identity Λ; in the next section we shall see that this makes X^* a *monoid* under concatenation. We shall also see that X^+ is a *semigroup*, but not a monoid, under concatenation.]

Example 3

Typical strings of $\{0, 1\}^*$ are: Λ, 0, 1, 00, 01, 10, 11, . . . , 101001110, etc. We have that $01 \cdot \Lambda = 01$ and $\Lambda \cdot 11 = 11$, and

$$\begin{aligned}(110 \cdot 01) \cdot 1101 &= 11001 \cdot 1101\\ &= 110011101\\ &= 110 \cdot (011101)\\ &= 110 \cdot (01 \cdot 1101).\end{aligned} \qquad \Diamond$$

We should now like to extend $\delta : Q \times X \to Q$ to a map $\delta^* : Q \times X^* \to Q$ with the following interpretation: If $M = (Q, X, Y, \delta, \lambda)$ is in state $q \in Q$ at time t, and receives the input string $x(t)x(t + 1) \ldots x(t + \tau)$ in X^*, then its state at time $t + \tau + 1$ should be $\delta^*(q, x(t)x(t + 1) \ldots x(t + \tau))$.

We proceed by induction:

If w is of length 0, so that $w = \Lambda$, "applying" w should not change the state. We thus want $\delta^*(q, \Lambda) = q$ for all $q \in Q$.

Now suppose that we know $\delta(q, w)$ for all w of length n. Any $\hat{w}$ of length $n + 1$ can be written $\hat{w} = wx$, where w is of length n and $x \in X$. But then, as is clear from Figure 2–9, we should define $\delta^*(q, wx)$ to be $\delta(\delta^*(q, w), x)$.

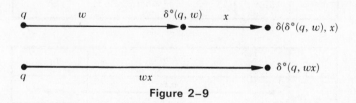

Figure 2–9

Thus, we make the following definition:

DEFINITION 4

Given any function $\delta : Q \times X \to Q$ we define its **X^*-extension** to be the unique map $\delta^* : Q \times X^* \to Q$ satisfying the following induction scheme:

Basis Step. $\delta^*(q, \Lambda) = q$ for all $q \in Q$.

Induction Step. $\delta^*(q, wx) = \delta(\delta^*(q, w), x)$ for all $q \in Q$, $w \in X^*$, and $x \in X$.

◯

Note that δ and δ^* agree for sequences of length 1, since if $x \in X$, we have

$$
\begin{aligned}
\delta^*(q, x) &= \delta^*(q, \Lambda x) && \text{since } x = \Lambda x \\
&= \delta(\delta^*(q, \Lambda), x) && \text{by the induction step} \\
&= \delta(q, x) && \text{by the basis step}
\end{aligned}
$$

We should also note (Exercise 3) that

$$\delta^*(q, w'w) = \delta^*[\delta^*(q, w'), w]$$

for all w, w' in X^* and q in Q.

Armed with the ability to go from δ to δ^*, let us now return to the problem of restating our theorem.

If we start M in state q at time t and apply the input string wx with $w \in X^*$ and $x \in X$, then at time $t + l(w)$ the machine will be in state $\delta^*(q, w)$, will read in input x, and will thus emit output $\lambda(\delta^*(q, w), x)$.

If we start $\hat{M}$ in state $\hat{q}$ at time t and apply the input string wx, then at time $t + l(wx) = [t + l(w)] + 1$ the machine will be in state $\hat{\delta}^*(\hat{q}, wx)$ [extending $\hat{\delta}$ just as we extended δ] and will thus emit $\beta(\hat{\delta}^*(\hat{q}, wx))$.

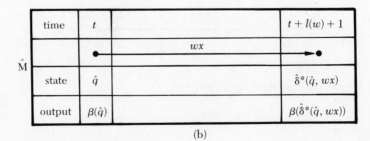

(a)

(b)

Figure 2–10 In (a), x' is the first symbol of w. Why can we not fill in the square marked? in part (a)?

We summarize the last two paragraphs by the tables shown in Figure 2–10.

Thus our theorem, even to the specification of the unit delay in the output of $\widehat{M}$ relative to the corresponding output of M, may be recast into the following compact algebraic form.

THEOREM 1

To each automaton $M = (Q, X, Y, \delta, \lambda)$ there corresponds a state-output automaton $\widehat{M} = (\widehat{Q}, X, Y, \widehat{\delta}, \beta)$ and an injection $k: Q \hookrightarrow \widehat{Q}$ such that

$$\lambda[\delta^*(q, w), x] = \beta[\widehat{\delta}^*(k(q), wx)] \text{ for all } q \in Q , w \in X^* \text{ and } x \in X. \quad \text{(5)}$$

Intuitive Proof of Theorem 1

Let $\widehat{M}$ differ from M only in that it has an extra register to store, for use at time $t + 1$, the output that M would have emitted at time t. Then $\widehat{M}$ can produce its outputs by consulting this register, and so is a state-output machine, even if M was not. We now turn to a formal proof (but see Exercise 6).

Formal Proof of Theorem 1

Given $M = (Q, X, Y, \delta, \lambda)$ we define $\widehat{M} = (\widehat{Q}, X, Y, \widehat{\delta}, \beta)$ as follows:

We set
$$\widehat{Q} = Q \times Y$$
$$\widehat{\delta}: \widehat{Q} \times X \to \widehat{Q}: ([q, y], x) \mapsto [\delta(q, x), \lambda(q, x)]$$
$$\beta: \widehat{Q} \to Y: [q, y] \mapsto y$$

and, having fixed upon any one element y_0 of Y, we define the map

$$k: Q \to \widehat{Q}: q \mapsto [q, y_0]$$

We must now check that, with this choice of $\widehat{Q}, \widehat{\delta}, \beta$, and k, we do indeed have that

$$\lambda(\delta^*(q, w), x) = \beta(\widehat{\delta}^*(k(q), wx)) \quad \text{(6)}$$

for all $q \in Q$, $w \in X^*$, and $x \in X$. To prove this it will be convenient (we shall see why below) to verify an even stronger result, namely that

$$\lambda(\delta^*(q, w), x) = \beta(\widehat{\delta}^*([q, y], wx)) \quad \text{(7)}$$

for all $q \in Q$, $y \in Y$, $w \in X^*$, and $x \in X$. (Note that we recapture (6) from (7) by taking $y = y_0$.) We do this by induction on the length of w:

Basis Step. If $w = \Lambda$, we have that (7) holds since

$$\lambda(\delta^*(q, \Lambda), x) = \lambda(q, x)$$

while

$$
\begin{aligned}
\beta(\widehat{\delta}^*([q,y], \Lambda x)) &= \beta(\widehat{\delta}^*([q,y], x)) && \text{since } \Lambda \text{ is the empty string} \\
&= \beta([\delta(q, x), \lambda(q, x)]) && \text{by the definition of } \widehat{\delta} \\
&= \lambda(q, x) && \text{by the definition of } \beta.
\end{aligned}
$$

Induction Step. Suppose that (7) holds for $w = w_1$, and all $q \in Q$, $y \in Y$, and $x \in X$. We must deduce that for any x_1 in X, we must then have that (7) also holds for $w = x_1 w_1$, and all $q \in Q$, $y \in Y$, and $x \in X$. Now

$$
\begin{aligned}
\beta(\widehat{\delta}^*([q,y], x_1 w_1 x)) &= \beta(\widehat{\delta}^*(\widehat{\delta}([q,y], x_1), w_1 x)) \\
&= \beta(\widehat{\delta}^*([\delta(q, x_1), \lambda(q, x_1)]), w_1 x) \\
&\qquad \text{by the definition of } \widehat{\delta}, \\
&\qquad \text{so that } [\delta(q, x_1), \lambda(q, x_1)] \\
&\qquad \text{is in } \widehat{Q}. \\
&= \lambda(\delta^*(\delta(q, x_1), w_1), x) \\
&\qquad \text{since (7) holds for } w = w_1, \\
&\qquad \text{for any state, even } \delta(q, x_1), \\
&\qquad \textit{and for any output, even } \lambda(q, x_1). \\
&\qquad \text{The reader will now see why we had} \\
&\qquad \text{to replace (6) by (7) to make our} \\
&\qquad \text{inductive proof go through.} \\
&= \lambda(\delta^*(q, x_1 w_1), x) \\
&\qquad \text{by Exercise 3.}
\end{aligned}
$$

Thus (7) does indeed hold for $x_1 w_1$ if it holds for w_1; and we are done. $\square$

Example 4

For the automaton M shown in Figure 2–11, a corresponding state-output automaton $\widehat{M}$ in which we have $\beta([q_i, y_j]) = y_j$ for $i = 1, 2, 3$ and $j = 1, 2$ is given in Figure 2–12. For this example, let us consider the following input string:

$$w = x_1 x_2 x_1 x_1 x_2 x_2 x_1 x_2 x_1$$

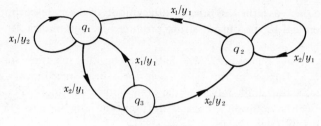

Figure 2-11

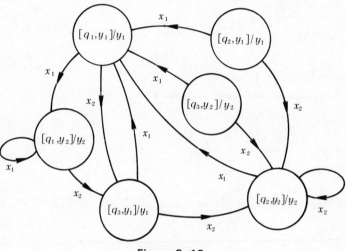

Figure 2-12

If M is in state q_1 when this input string is applied, the result is represented below:

output: y_2 y_1 y_1 y_2 y_1 y_2 y_1 y_1 y_1

next state: q_1 q_1 q_3 q_1 q_1 q_3 q_2 q_1 q_3 q_1

Now if $\widehat{M}$ is in state $[q_1, y_1]$ when the same input string is applied, we get:

next state: $[q_1,y_1][q_1,y_2][q_3,y_1][q_1,y_1][q_1,y_2][q_3,y_1][q_2,y_2][q_1,y_1][q_3,y_1][q_1,y_1]$

while if $\widehat{M}$ is in state $[q_1, y_2]$ when the input is applied, we get:

next state: $[q_1,y_2][q_1,y_2][q_3,y_1][q_1,y_1][q_1,y_2][q_3,y_1][q_2,y_2][q_1,y_1][q_3,y_1][q_1,y_1]$

Thus, in either case, the last nine output symbols of the state-output machine $\widehat{M}$ are identical to the output string produced by automaton M.   ◊

Buoyed by Theorem 1, we shall not consider machines of the type $(Q, X, Y, \delta, \lambda)$ further in this book (save for a brief mention at the end of Section 2–3), but shall only consider state-output machines. For such machines we want a notation to capture the input-output characteristics we have just studied in Theorem 1.

If we start a machine $M = (Q, X, Y, \delta, \beta)$ in state q and read in the input string $w \in X^*$, then M will go to state $\delta^*(q, w)$, where its output will be $\beta(\delta^*(q, w))$. (See Figure 2–13, which is a recasting of Figure 2–10(b).)

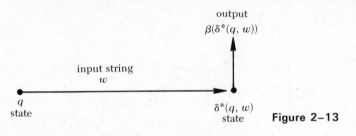

Figure 2–13

DEFINITION 5

For any state q of a state-output machine $M = (Q, X, Y, \delta, \beta)$, we call the function

$$M_q : X^* \to Y : w \mapsto \beta(\delta^*(q, w))$$

the **response function** or the **behavior of M started in state** q. Thus $M_q(w)$ is the output of M after starting in state q and reading in the input string w.   ○

Parenthetically, we should note that it is easy to construct from M_q the function $\widetilde{M}_q : X^* \to Y^*$ which gives as $\widetilde{M}_q(w)$ the entire sequence of outputs emitted by M, when started in state q, in response to w. We form $\widetilde{M}_q$ as follows:

Basis Step. $\widetilde{M}_q(\Lambda) = \beta(q)$.

Induction Step. $\widetilde{M}_q(wx) = \widetilde{M}_q(w) \cdot M_q(wx)$ for w in X^*, x in X. Thus in general we have

$$\widetilde{M}_q(x_1 \ldots x_n) = M_q(\Lambda)M_q(x_1)M_q(x_1x_2) \ldots M_q(x_1 \ldots x_n).$$

Conversely, then, given $\widetilde{M}_q$ we may recapture M_q by defining $M_q(w)$ in Y to be the last symbol of the string $\widetilde{M}_q(w)$ from Y^*.

Example 5

For M, the simple 2-state machine of Figure 2–14, we may tabulate the first few values of M_{q_1} and $\widetilde{M}_{q_1}$ as follows:

w	$M_{q_1}(w)$	$\widetilde{M}_{q_1}(w)$
Λ	0	0
0	0	00
1	1	01
00	0	000
01	1	001
010	0	0010

◊

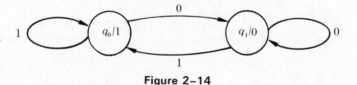

Figure 2–14

DEFINITION 6

We call *any* function $f: X^* \to Y$ a **behavior**. The **realization problem** is then to find, given a behavior f, a machine (state-output automaton) M and a state q of M such that

$$M_q = f: X^* \to Y.$$

The pair (M, q), said to be an "initialized" machine, is then called a **realization** of f.   ○

In Section 2–4, we shall prove that most behaviors $f: X^* \to Y$ do not have finite-state realizations, but in Section 2–5 we shall provide general methods for building, for *any* behavior, a realization which is in some sense minimal. In particular, then, we can build a realization of f with the smallest number of states if any finite-state M exists for which $f = M_q$ for some state q.

EXERCISES FOR SECTION 2–1

1. Show that three copies of D_{10}, if interconnected as shown in Figure 2–15, do indeed yield a system which counts modulo 1000. Letting k_3 denote the current state

output of overall system

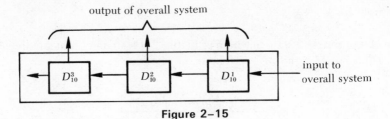

input to overall system

Figure 2–15

of the left-most machine, k_2 denoting the state of the middle machine, and k_1 denoting the state of the right-most machine, and letting k_i' be the state which succeeds $k_i (i = 1, 2, 3)$, carry out the verification in five stages:

(i) If input is 0, show that no state changes.

(ii) If input is 1, show that:

    (a) If $k_1 \neq 9$, then $k_3' = k_3$, $k_2' = k_2$ and $k_1' = k_1 + 1$.

    (b) If $k_1 = 9$ but $k_2 \neq 9$, then $k_3' = k_3$, $k_2' = k_2 + 1$, $k_1' = 0$.

    (c) If $k_1 = k_2 = 9$ but $k_3 \neq 9$, then $k_3' = k_3 + 1$, and $k_1' = k_2' = 0$.

    (d) If $k_1 = k_2 = k_3 = 9$, then $k_1' = k_2' = k_3' = 0$.

2. Write out Q, X, Y, δ, and λ for the machines of Figures 2–16 and 2–17. If a machine is a state-output automaton, specify β and draw its state-output graph.

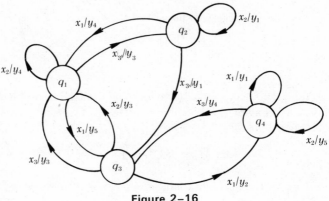

Figure 2–16

3. Prove, by induction on the length of w, that $\delta^*(q, w'w) = \delta^*[\delta^*(q, w'), w]$ for all w, w' in X^* and q in Q.

4. Determine $\delta^*: \mathbf{Z}_{10} \times \{0, 1\}^* \to \mathbf{Z}_{10}$ for our modulo-10 counter D_{10}.

5. Find a state-output machine $\hat{M}$ which corresponds to the automaton M of Figure 2–18. Apply various input strings to M and $\hat{M}$ and check that both automata yield the same output strings.

6. The sceptical reader may ask, "Since the informal proof of Theorem 1 is so patently correct, why bother to do all the hard work of a formal proof?" A partial answer is given by the fact that we had almost finished the formal proof before we realized that an induction on (7), rather than on (6), was necessary to make the proof go through. A fuller answer is given by the fact that the process of formalization forces us to take account of details that easily pass unnoticed in the informal proof. To make this point, consider the following alternative informal "proof":

Alternative "Proof": Let $\hat{M}$ differ from M only in that it has an extra register to store, for use at time $t + 1$, the input that M received at time t. Then $\hat{M}$ can

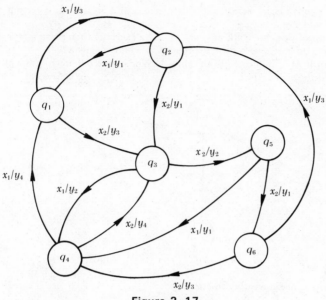

Figure 2–17

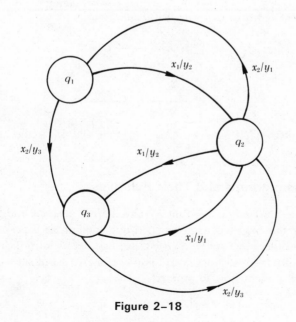

Figure 2–18

produce its outputs by consulting this register, and so is a state-output machine, even if M was not.

This proof does *not* work as it stands. The exercise, then, is to *modify* it in such a way that you can give a formal proof of it which *does* work.

7.   For the M of Figure 2–19, compute M_{q_0} for strings of length ≤ 3, and compute $\tilde{M}_{q_2}$ for strings of length 2.

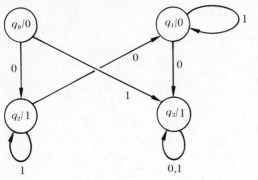

Figure 2–19

8.   Suppose we have the functions

$$f : A \to B$$

and

$$g : C \to D$$

Then it is natural to define a function called $f \times g$ for which

$$f \times g : A \times C \to B \times D : (a, c) \mapsto (f(a), g(c))$$

for all $a \in A$ and $c \in C$. As an exercise in writing down commutative diagrams, verify that (6) may be rewritten as saying that the diagram

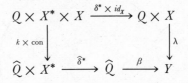

commutes, where $X^* \times X \xrightarrow{\text{con}} X^* : (w, x) \mapsto wx$ and id_X is the identity map $X \to X : x \mapsto x$.

2–2   Semigroups and Their Relatives

Having hinted in Section 2–1 that X^* and X^+ are a *monoid* and a *semigroup*, respectively, the time has come to spell out what these concepts are, and proceed from there to a study of *groups*. But first, let us introduce a notation for **powers of sets** (as distinct from the power-set, or set of subsets, of a set). For $n \geq 1$, it is clear how to proceed:

For $n = 1$, we set $S^1 = S$.

For $n > 1$, we set $S^n = S^{n-1} \times S$.   **(1)**

It is thus clear that S^n may be thought of as the set of all sequences of S of length n (if in doubt, verify by induction). It thus seems reasonable to have S^0 consist of one element, the unique "sequence" of length 0. If we write $S^0 = \{\Lambda\}$, then there is clearly a bijection $S \to S^0 \times S: s \mapsto (\Lambda, s)$, and so we may use our inductive formula (1) even for $n = 1$. The point of this paragraph is to note that an element of S may be identified with a function from S^0 to S, by identifying $f(\Lambda)$ with the function $f: S^0 \to S$.

Thus, specifying a constant in S may also be regarded as specifying a **nullary operator** $S^0 \to S$, i.e., an operator which assigns an element of S to each choice of *no* elements in S. In the same terminology, a **unary operator** on S is a map $S^1 \to S$ which assigns an element of S to each choice of *one* element in S; a **binary operator** on S is a map $S^2 \to S$ which assigns an element of S to each choice of *two* elements in S; and, in general, an **n-ary operator** on S is a map $S^n \to S$ which assigns an element of S to each choice of n elements in S.

Example 1

Suppose $S = \{a, b, c\}$. Then $S^0 = \{\Lambda\}$ and there are three nullary operators f_1, f_2, f_3 from S^0 to S:

$$f_1: S^0 \to S: \Lambda \mapsto a$$
$$f_2: S^0 \to S: \Lambda \mapsto b$$
$$f_3: S^0 \to S: \Lambda \mapsto c$$

There are $3^3 = 27$ unary operators (count them) from $S^1 \to S$. An example of one is given by $f_4: S^1 \to S$, where

$$f_4: (\Lambda, a) \mapsto b \qquad \text{or} \qquad f_4: a \mapsto b$$
$$f_4: (\Lambda, b) \mapsto c \qquad \text{or} \qquad f_4: b \mapsto c$$
$$f_4: (\Lambda, c) \mapsto b \qquad \text{or} \qquad f_4: c \mapsto b$$

Since $|S| = 3$ and $|S^2| = 3^2 = 9$, there are $3^9 = 2673$ binary operators from S^2 to S. One example is $f_5: S^2 \to S$ given by the table of Figure 2–20, in which $f(x, y)$ appears in row x and column y.   ◊

f_5	a	b	c
a	c	b	b
b	a	b	a
c	a	c	b

Figure 2–20

With this terminology, we may now comfortably define semigroups, monoids, and groups, providing examples of each concept in turn.

DEFINITION 1a

A **semigroup** is a pair (S, m), where S is a set and m is a binary operator on S which is **associative**, i.e.,

$$m(m(s_1, s_2), s_3) = m(s_1, m(s_2, s_3)) \quad \text{for all } s_1, s_2, s_3, \text{ in } S.$$

We sometimes say that S is a semigroup *with respect to m*. $\bigcirc$

Example 2

(i) $(X^+,$ concatenation$)$ is a semigroup. [Since we usually only consider concatenation when combining strings of X^* or X^+, we shall usually omit explicit mention of concatenation, and say "X^* is a semigroup" and "X^+ is a semigroup" without risk of ambiguity.]

(ii) $(\mathbf{N}, +)$ and $(\mathbf{N}, \cdot)$ [where $\cdot$ is ordinary multiplication] are both semigroups. [Note that here we have two different *semigroups* with the same *underlying set*, so that we cannot omit mention of the operation without risking ambiguity.]

(iii) $(\mathbf{Z}, -)$ [where $- : \mathbf{Z} \times \mathbf{Z} \to \mathbf{Z} : (m, n) \mapsto m - n$] is *not* a semigroup since $a - (b - c) \neq (a - b) - c$ unless $c = 0$.

(iv) $(\mathbf{N}, \max)$ [where $\max(m, n)$ is the larger of m and n] is a semigroup since $\max(m, \max(n, p)) = \max(\max(m, n), p) = $ the largest of m, n, and p. $\Diamond$

DEFINITION 2a

A **monoid** is a triple $(S, m, 1)$, where (S, m) is a semigroup and $1 \in S$ is a nullary operator which is an **identity** for m, i.e.,

$$m(1, s) = s = m(s, 1) \quad \text{for all } s \in S.$$ $\bigcirc$

Example 3

(i) X^+ cannot be made into a monoid since $\ell(ww') > \ell(w)$ for all w, w' in X^+ (thus ruling out $ww' = w$ for any w, w' in X^+). However, $(X^*,$ concatenation, $\Lambda)$ is a monoid, since $w \cdot \Lambda = w = \Lambda \cdot w$ for all w in X^*. X^* is called **the free monoid generated by** X.

(ii) $(\mathbf{N}, +, 0)$ is a monoid since $n + 0 = n = 0 + n$ for all $n \in \mathbf{N}$, but $(\mathbf{Z}_+, +)$ cannot be made into a monoid since $n + n' > n$ for all $n, n' \in \mathbf{Z}_+$.

(iii) $(\mathbf{N}, \cdot, 1)$ is a monoid since $n \cdot 1 = n = 1 \cdot n$ for all $n \in \mathbf{N}$.

(iv) $(\mathbf{N}, \max, 0)$ is a monoid since $\max(n, 0) = n = \max(0, n)$ for all $n \geq 0$. However, $(\mathbf{Z}, \max)$ cannot be made into a monoid, unless we add to $\mathbf{Z}$ the point $(-\infty)$.   ◊

DEFINITION 3a

A **group** is a quadruple $(S, m, 1, i)$, where $(S, m, 1)$ is a monoid and i is a unary operator which is an **inverse** for m with respect to 1, i.e.,

$$m(s, i(s)) = 1 = m(i(s), s) \quad \text{for all } s \in S.$$ ○

Before giving examples of groups, let us "unpack" Definition 3a to obtain the definition of a group which the reader is more likely to find elsewhere in the literature.

DEFINITION 3b

A **group** is a set S together with a binary operation $S \times S \to S : (s_1, s_2) \mapsto s_1 \cdot s_2$ such that:

(1) The operation is associative; i.e., $(s_1 \cdot s_2) \cdot s_3 = s_1 \cdot (s_2 \cdot s_3)$ for all $s_1, s_2, s_3 \in S$.

(2) There is an identity $1 \in S$ such that $1 \cdot s = s = s \cdot 1$ for all $s \in S$.

(3) Each element $s \in S$ has an inverse $s^{-1} \in S$ such that

$$s \cdot s^{-1} = 1 = s^{-1} \cdot s.$$ ○

Example 4

(i) $(\mathbf{Z}, +, 0, -)$ is a group, where $-$ is here the unary operator $\mathbf{Z} \to \mathbf{Z} : n \mapsto -n$, since $n + (-n) = 0 = (-n) + n$. Recall that we invented the integers precisely because $(\mathbf{N}, +, 0)$ could *not* be made into a group without augmenting $\mathbf{N}$.

(ii) There is no function $i : X^* \to X^*$ for which $(X^*, \text{concatenation}, \Lambda, i)$ is a group, since the inequality $l(ww') \geq l(w)$ rules out the possibility that $w \cdot w' = \Lambda$ for any w' unless $w = \Lambda$.

(iii) $(\mathbf{Q}\backslash\{0\}, \cdot, 1, ^{-1})$ where $^{-1} : \mathbf{Q}\backslash\{0\} \to \mathbf{Q}\backslash\{0\} : \dfrac{p}{q} \mapsto \dfrac{q}{p}$ is a group. Recall that we invented the rationals precisely because $(\mathbf{Z}\backslash\{0\}, \cdot, 1)$ could *not* be made into a group without augmenting the integers.

(iv) The rigid body motions of the plane form the underlying set of a group. (How?)   ◊

From this point, let us use the following convention. When speaking of semigroups, monoids, and groups in general terms, we will refer to the underlying set as S, denote the binary operation by $\cdot$, and represent an identity by 1 and an inverse of an element $s \in S$ by s^{-1}. In specific cases, we will indicate the customary notation if it is different from the general. Consequently, we may rewrite our previous definitions in the following form:

DEFINITION 1b

A **semigroup** is a pair $(S, \cdot)$, where S is a set and $\cdot$ is a binary operator on S such that

$$(s_1 \cdot s_2) \cdot s_3 = s_1 \cdot (s_2 \cdot s_3) \quad \text{for all } s_1, s_2, s_3 \in S,$$

i.e., the binary operator $\cdot$ is associative.

We may say that S is a semigroup under $\cdot$, and if it is obvious what the binary operation is, we may simply say that S is a semigroup.   O

DEFINITION 2b

A **monoid** is a triple $(S, \cdot, 1)$, where $(S, \cdot)$ is a semigroup and where 1 is an element in S such that

$$1 \cdot s = s = s \cdot 1 \quad \text{for all } s \in S$$

i.e., the element $1 \in S$ is an identity for $(S, \cdot)$.

Again, when there is no possibility of ambiguity, we may say that S is a monoid.   O

DEFINITION 3c

A **group** is a quadruple $(S, \cdot, 1, {}^{-1})$, where $(S, \cdot, 1)$ is a monoid and for each $s \in S$ there exists an element $s^{-1} \in S$ such that

$$s \cdot s^{-1} = 1 = s^{-1} \cdot s,$$

i.e., the element $s^{-1} \in S$ is an inverse of $s \in S$.   O

As previously indicated, under the proper circumstances, we may simply say that S is a group.

We note that $(\mathbf{N}, +)$ and $(\mathbf{Z}, +)$ are *commutative,* or *abelian,* in the sense of Definition 4:

DEFINITION 4

We say that a binary operation $S \times S \to S:(s_1, s_2) \mapsto s_1 \cdot s_2$ is **commutative, or abelian***, if

$$s_1 \cdot s_2 = s_2 \cdot s_1 \quad \text{for all } s_1, s_2 \text{ in } S.$$

We say that semigroup, monoid, or group is *commutative* or *abelian* if its binary operation is. ○

If a group is commutative, it is usual to write $s_1 + s_2$ for $s_1 \cdot s_2$; 0 for 1; and $(-s)$ for s^{-1}. With this convention, Definition 3b yields:

DEFINITION 3d

An **abelian group** is a set S together with a binary operation $S \times S \to S:(s_1, s_2) \mapsto s_1 + s_2$ such that:

(0) The operation is commutative: $s_1 + s_2 = s_2 + s_1$ for all s_1, s_2 in S.
(1) The operation is associative: $(s_1 + s_2) + s_3 = s_1 + (s_2 + s_3)$ for all s_1, s_2, s_3 in S.
(2) There is an additive identity 0 in S: $s + 0 = s$ for all s in S.
(3) Each element s in S has an additive inverse $(-s)$ in S such that $s + (-s) = 0$. ○

In a very precise sense, we shall see that a group $(S, \cdot, 1, ^{-1})$ is completely determined by its underlying semigroup $(S, \cdot)$. Before proving this, let us refine our terminology for talking about identities and inverses.

DEFINITION 5

Let $m: S \times S \to S$ be *any* binary operation. Then an element e of S is called a **left identity for** m if $m(e, s) = s$ for all s in S; a **right identity for** m if $m(s, e) = s$ for all s in S; and a (two-sided) **identity for** m if it is both a left and a right identity for m, i.e., $m(e, s) = s = m(s, e)$ for all s in S. ○

---

*Named for the Norwegian mathematician Niels H. Abel (1802–1829).

Example 5

The operation $\mathbf{N} \times \mathbf{N} \to \mathbf{N}:(m, n) \mapsto m - n$ has right identity 0 (since $m - 0 = m$ for all m in $\mathbf{N}$) but no left identity (since if $e - n = n$ for all n in $\mathbf{N}$, we would have that $e = 2n$ for all n in N; and that is ridiculous!).

$\diamond$

LEMMA 1

If $m:S \times S \to S$ has a left identity e and a right identity e', then they are equal, and so $e = e'$ is an identity for m.

Proof

Since $m(e, s') = s'$ for all s' in S; and since $m(s, e') = s$ for all s in S, we may set $s' = e'$ and $s = e$ to deduce that

$$e' = m(e, e') = e.$$ $\square$

In particular, if e and e' are both identities for m, then they must be equal. Since this is true for any $m:S \times S \to S$, it must certainly be true for the associative $\cdot:S \times S \to S$ of a semigroup, and we deduce the following:

COROLLARY 2

Suppose $(S, \cdot, 1)$ and $(S, \cdot, 1')$ are two monoids with the same underlying semigroup $(S, \cdot)$. Then $1 = 1'$ and the two monoids are identical. $\square$

We thus see that if a semigroup $(S, \cdot)$ has an identity 1, then that identity is unique and we may, without ambiguity, speak of $(S, \cdot)$ [or even of S, when $\cdot$ is understood] as a monoid, meaning of course the monoid $(S, \cdot, 1)$. Let us see how we can turn any semigroup S (with $\cdot$ understood) into a monoid S^1:

If S is already a monoid in the above sense, we are done, and $S^1 = S$ [i.e., we take the monoid $(S, \cdot, 1)$ with underlying set (also called the **carrier**) $S = S^1$].

However, if S is not a monoid, we adjoin to the set S a new element, which we shall denote by 1, and use S^1 to denote the augmented set $S \cup \{1\}$. We then extend $\cdot$ from $S \times S \to S$ to $S^1 \times S^1 \to S^1$ by defining

$$s_1 \cdot s_2 = \begin{cases} s_1 \cdot s_2 \text{ as already defined, if } s_1, s_2 \in S \\ s_1 \quad \text{if } s_2 = 1 \\ s_2 \quad \text{if } s_1 = 1 \end{cases}$$

We must check that the extended operation is associative, i.e., that

$$s_1 \cdot (s_2 \cdot s_3) = (s_1 \cdot s_2) \cdot s_3$$

for all $s_1, s_2, s_3 \in S^1$. Now if s_1, s_2, s_3 all lie in S, this equation holds by the associativity of $\cdot$ on S. Thus it only remains to check that the equation holds when at least one s_j is 1. We check this for the case $s_1 = 1$; the reader should check the other cases for himself. Clearly, we have that

$$1 \cdot (s_2 \cdot s_3) = s_2 \cdot s_3 = (1 \cdot s_2) \cdot s_3$$

by twice making use of our decree that $1 \cdot s = s$ for all $s \in S^1$.

Finally, it is clear that 1 is an identity for S^1:

$$s \cdot 1 = s = 1 \cdot s \text{ for all } s \in S^1$$

Thus $(S^1, \cdot, 1)$ is a monoid as required.

We have seen that if the multiplication of a semigroup $(S, \cdot)$ admits an identity, then that identity is unique, so $(S, \cdot)$ then determines a unique monoid $(S^1, \cdot, 1)$. To obtain the corresponding result for groups we must do for inverses what we have just done for identities:

DEFINITION 6

Let $m: S \times S \to S$ be any binary operation with (left or right or two-sided) identity 1. Given $s \in S$, an element s' of S is called a **left inverse of** s **with respect to** m if $m(s', s) = 1$; a **right inverse of** s **with respect to** m if $m(s, s') = 1$; and a **two-sided inverse of** s **with respect to** m if it is both a left and a right inverse of s, so that $m(s', s) = 1 = m(s, s')$.   ○

Example 6

Given the right identity 0 for $\mathbf{N} \times \mathbf{N} \to \mathbf{N} : (m, n) \mapsto m - n$, we see that each element n has itself as a two-sided inverse (since $n - n = 0$).   ◊

LEMMA 3

Let $(S, \cdot, 1)$ be a monoid. Then if s in S has left inverse s' and right inverse s'', they are equal; and so $s' = s''$ is an inverse for s.

Proof

$$
\begin{aligned}
s' &= s' \cdot 1 && \text{since 1 is the identity} \\
&= s' \cdot (s \cdot s'') && \text{since } s'' \text{ is a right inverse} \\
&= (s' \cdot s) \cdot s'' && \text{by associativity} \\
&= 1 \cdot s'' && \text{since } s' \text{ is a left inverse} \\
&= s''
\end{aligned}
$$

□

We have already seen that if the multiplication of a semigroup $(S, \cdot)$ admits an identity 1, then that identity is unique. We now see further that if $(S, \cdot)$ admits inverses for each s in S, then they are unique for each s in S.

COROLLARY 4

Suppose $(S, \cdot, 1, ^{-1})$ and $(S, \cdot, 1', {}^{(-1)'})$ are two groups with the same underlying semigroup $(S, \cdot)$. Then $1 = 1'$ and ${}^{(-1)'} = {}^{-1}: S \to S$, and the two groups are identical. $\square$

Consequently, we may say that 1 is *the* identity of the group, and for each $s \in S$, s^{-1} is *the* inverse of s.

For further exercise in the above sort of manipulation, we verify that, for $(S, \cdot)$ to determine a group, it is sufficient that it have a left identity and left inverses. The reader should note that this is a surprisingly stronger result than our last lemma.

LEMMA 5

Let $(S, \cdot)$ be a semigroup with left identity 1, that is,

$$1 \cdot s = s \quad \text{for all } s \in S$$

and a function $^{-1}: S \to S: s \mapsto s^{-1}$ such that s^{-1} is a left inverse of s for each s in S, that is,

$$s^{-1} \cdot s = 1 \quad \text{for all } s \in S.$$

Then $(S, \cdot, 1, ^{-1})$ is a group.

Proof

We first prove that the left inverse of s is also a right inverse, i.e., that

$$s \cdot s^{-1} = 1 \quad \text{for all } s \in S.$$

Given s with left inverse s^{-1}, let $s_1 = (s^{-1})^{-1}$ be the left inverse of s^{-1}, so that $s_1 \cdot s^{-1} = 1$. Then we have

$$
\begin{aligned}
s \cdot s^{-1} &= 1 \cdot (s \cdot s^{-1}) && \text{since 1 is a left identity} \\
&= (s_1 \cdot s^{-1}) \cdot (s \cdot s^{-1}) && \text{since } s_1 \text{ is a left inverse of } s^{-1} \\
&= s_1 \cdot [s^{-1} \cdot (s \cdot s^{-1})] && \text{by associativity} \\
&= s_1 \cdot [(s^{-1} \cdot s) \cdot s^{-1}] && \text{by associativity} \\
&= s_1 \cdot [1 \cdot s^{-1}] && \text{since } s^{-1} \text{ is a left inverse of } s \\
&= s_1 \cdot s^{-1} && \text{since 1 is a left identity} \\
&= 1 && \text{since } s_1 \text{ is a left inverse of } s^{-1}
\end{aligned}
$$

Hence, s^{-1} is a right inverse of S.

We will now prove that 1 is also a right identity for $(s, \cdot)$, i.e.,

$$s \cdot 1 = s \quad \text{for all } s \in S.$$

We have

$$
\begin{aligned}
s \cdot 1 &= s \cdot (s^{-1} \cdot s) && \text{since } s^{-1} \text{ is a left inverse of } s \\
&= (s \cdot s^{-1}) \cdot s && \text{by associativity} \\
&= 1 \cdot s && \text{since } s^{-1} \text{ is a right inverse of } s \\
&= s && \text{since } 1 \text{ is a left identity.}
\end{aligned}
$$

Hence, 1 is a right identity. □

To conclude this section, let us see how we may associate an automaton with any semigroup (and thus with any monoid or group):

Given a semigroup S, then **the machine of S** is

$$M(S) = (S, S, S, \delta_S, id_S)$$

which has S for its state, input, and output sets; has multiplication in S

$$\delta_S : S \times S \to S : (s, s') \mapsto s \cdot s'$$

for its next-state function (an input updates the state by multiplying it on the right); and has the identity function of S

$$id_S : S \to S : s \mapsto s$$

as its output function, so that, at any time, the output and state are identical. The situation is represented by Figure 2–21, in which the state and output of the system are s, the input to the system is s', and the next state of the system (indicated following the /) is $s \cdot s'$.

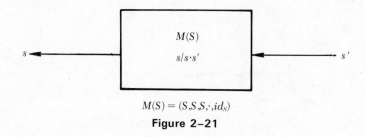

$$M(S) = (S, S, S, \cdot, id_S)$$

Figure 2–21

EXERCISES FOR SECTION 2-2

1. Given $|S| = m$, how many n-ary operators are there?

2. Which operations of Examples 2 and 4 are commutative? If an operation is not commutative, give an explicit example of an s_1 and s_2 such that $s_1 \cdot s_2 \neq s_2 \cdot s_1$.

3.   Suppose S is a monoid with identity 1. Adjoin a new element I to S to form $S^I = S \cup \{I\}$, and extend $\cdot$ to $S^I \times S^I \to S^I$ by

$$s_1 \cdot s_2 = \begin{cases} s_1 \cdot s_2 & \text{if } s_1, s_2 \in S \\ s_1 & \text{if } s_2 = I \\ s_2 & \text{if } s_1 = I \end{cases}$$

Prove that $(S^I, \cdot, I)$ is a monoid. Why is 1 not an identity for S^I?

4.   Suppose S is a group. If $s_1, s_2 \in S$, prove that

$$(s_1 \cdot s_2)^{-1} = s_2^{-1} \cdot s_1^{-1}$$

5.   Let $s \in S$, where S is a group. Prove that

$$(s^{-1})^{-1} = s$$

6.   Prove that, if an element s' of S has a right inverse, then the next state function induced by input s'

$$\delta_S(\cdot, s'): S \to S: s \mapsto s \cdot s'$$

is an injection. Prove that if s' has a left inverse, then $\delta_S(\cdot, s')$ is a surjection. Deduce that, if S is a group, then every map $\delta_S(\cdot, s)$, for s' in S, must be a bijection.

2-3   Automata and Switching Circuits†

We now turn our attention to the task of simulating automata by means of networks composed of simple logical elements, which we shall call **modules.** A typical module, as shown in Figure 2–22, has a finite number of input lines and a single output line. If at any moment each line (both input and output) is capable of carrying any one element of $\mathbf{Z}_m$ as a signal, we call the module an m-**module.** In this section we shall concentrate on the simulation of finite-state automata by networks composed of binary modules, i.e., 2-modules.

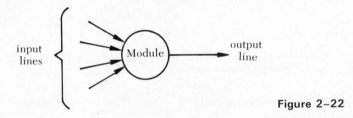

Figure 2–22

We will now specify the circuitry we shall use to build finite automata using simple binary modules. Suppose we make the convenient mathematical fiction that the modules are of two kinds:

---

†The reader uninterested in, or previously acquainted with, switching theory may pass immediately to Section 2–4 without loss of continuity.

(i) **Pure unit delays:** 2-modules with one input line and one output line such that x_t, the input at time t, is precisely y_{t+1}, the output at time $t + 1$. This element is shown in Figure 2–23.

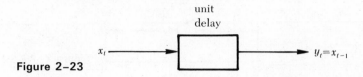

unit
delay

x_t ⟶ ⟶ $y_t = x_{t-1}$

Figure 2–23

(ii) **Delayless switching functions:** 2-modules for which y_t, the output at time t, is $f(x_1, x_2, \ldots, x_n)_t$, some specified function of $x_1, x_2, \ldots, x_n$, the inputs at time t. Such an element is shown in Figure 2–24. (In Section 2–4, Example 15, we shall see that such functions form what is called a *Boolean algebra*.) As was done in Figure 2–24, it is often convenient to drop the indication of time dependence from the input and output labellings.

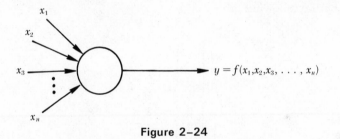

x_1
x_2
x_3 ⟶ ⟶ $y = f(x_1, x_2, x_3, \ldots, x_n)$
x_n

Figure 2–24

Constructing a network of modules requires some care, as we will demonstrate with an example: First let us define a single-input delayless binary module as shown in the following table:

x	y
0	1
1	0

We say that y is the **complement** of x, and we denote this by $y = \bar{x}$. We refer to such an element as a **NOT gate** (or **inverter**) and represent it as shown in Figure 2–25. If we arbitrarily connect the output of an inverter to its input,

Figure 2–25 x ⟶ ▷○ ⟶ $y = \bar{x}$

we obtain the network of Figure 2–26. In this case, the formation of a loop from the output to the input results in both the output and the input being the same, i.e., $\bar{x} = x$. Clearly, this is contradictory. For this reason, situations like this must be avoided when forming networks.

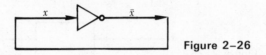

Figure 2–26

Circuits with one or more loops (e.g., Figure 2–26), however, can be converted into well-behaved networks by inserting a delay element into each loop.

We say that a network is **combinational** (or **combinatorial**) if it contains only delayless elements and is free of loops. Clearly then, the input at time t to such a network uniquely specifies the output at time t.

We have already introduced the NOT gate. We now shall introduce two more delayless binary modules. The first is a two-input **OR gate.** If x_1 and x_2 are the inputs to this gate, then we denote the output by $y = x_1 \vee x_2$ and define y by the following table:

x_1	x_2	$x_1 \vee x_2$
0	0	0
0	1	1
1	0	1
1	1	1

Thus, the output of such a gate is $x_1 \vee x_2 = 1$ if either $x_1 = 1$ OR $x_2 = 1$ OR both. The representation of an OR gate is shown in Figure 2–27.

OR gate

Figure 2–27

The second element is a two-input **AND gate** whose output is $y = x_1 \wedge x_2$, where y is specified by the following table:

x_1	x_2	$x_1 \wedge x_2$
0	0	0
0	1	0
1	0	0
1	1	1

Therefore, we see that the output of such a gate is $x_1 \wedge x_2 = 1$ only if both $x_1 = 1$ AND $x_2 = 1$. An AND gate is represented as shown in Figure 2–28.

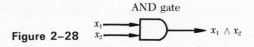

AND gate

Figure 2–28

We will shortly show that every binary function $f: \{0, 1\}^n \to \{0, 1\}^p$ can be realized by a combinational network containing only AND, OR, and NOT gates. First, however, let us present a few examples.

Example 1

Let us realize the function

$$f: \{0, 1\}^2 \to \{0, 1\} : (x_1, x_2) \mapsto f(x_1, x_2)$$

specified by the table

x_1	x_2	$f(x_1, x_2)$
0	0	0
0	1	1
1	0	1
1	1	0

Thus, we see that $f(x_1, x_2) = 1$ if either $x_1 = 0$ ($\bar{x}_1 = 1$) AND $x_2 = 1$; OR, $x_1 = 1$ AND $x_2 = 0$ ($\bar{x}_2 = 1$). Expressing this algebraically, we have

$$f(x_1, x_2) = (\bar{x}_1 \wedge x_2) \vee (x_1 \wedge \bar{x}_2)$$

A combinational network containing only AND, OR, and NOT gates which realizes this function is shown in Figure 2–29.   ◊

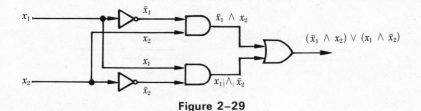

Figure 2–29

The astute reader has probably noticed that the function given in the last example actually specifies modulo 2 addition. Thus, Figure 2–29 is a network realization of a two-input modulo 2 adder constructed from AND, OR, and NOT gates.

Because of its frequent appearance, a modulo 2 adder is given its own symbol, which is shown in Figure 2–30.

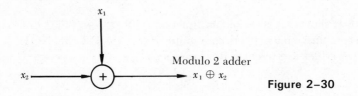

Modulo 2 adder
$x_1 \oplus x_2$

Figure 2–30

The two-input modulo 2 adder is also referred to as an **EXCLUSIVE-OR gate** since the output equals 1 if either $x_1 = 1$ OR $x_2 = 1$, but *not* both.

Now let us consider the functions $f_1(x_1, x_2, x_3) = (x_1 \vee x_2) \vee x_3$ and $f_2(x_1, x_2, x_3) = x_1 \vee (x_2 \vee x_3)$. As shown below, it is a simple matter of enumeration to verify that $f_1(x_1, x_2, x_3) = f_2(x_1, x_2, x_3)$:

x_1	x_2	x_3	$x_1 \vee x_2$	$f_1(x_1, x_2, x_3)$	x_1	x_2	x_3	$x_2 \vee x_3$	$f_2(x_1, x_2, x_3)$
0	0	0	0	0	0	0	0	0	0
0	0	1	0	1	0	0	1	1	1
0	1	0	1	1	0	1	0	1	1
0	1	1	1	1	0	1	1	1	1
1	0	0	1	1	1	0	0	0	1
1	0	1	1	1	1	0	1	1	1
1	1	0	1	1	1	1	0	1	1
1	1	1	1	1	1	1	1	1	1

Thus, we see that $\vee$ is associative and we may write $x_1 \vee x_2 \vee x_3$ unambiguously. We leave it as an exercise for the reader to convince himself that $\wedge$ is also associative, and as a result, writing $x_1 \wedge x_2 \wedge x_3$ results in no confusion.

As a consequence of associativity, let us specify three-input AND gates, as well as three-input OR gates, and represent them as shown in Figure 2–31.

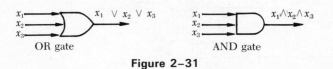

OR gate   AND gate

Figure 2–31

Clearly, each such gate may be constructed from a pair of two-input gates of the same type. It should also be fairly obvious how our previous discussion can be extended in order to specify n-input OR and AND gates.

Example 2

Let us realize the function specified by the following table:

x_1	x_2	$f(x_1, x_2)$
0	0	1
0	1	1
1	0	1
1	1	0

From inspection of this table we write

$$f(x_1, x_2) = (\bar{x}_1 \wedge \bar{x}_2) \vee (\bar{x}_1 \wedge x_2) \vee (x_1 \wedge \bar{x}_2)$$

and the corresponding realization is shown in Figure 2–32. (See Exercise 2.)

◊

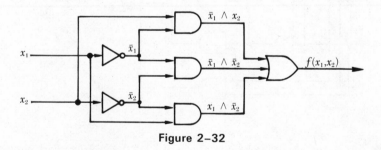

Figure 2–32

Let us consider one more example of this type:

Example 3

We will realize the function

$$f:\{0, 1\}^3 \to \{0, 1\}:(x_1, x_2, x_3) \mapsto f(x_1, x_2, x_3)$$

specified by the table

x_1	x_2	x_3	$f(x_1, x_2, x_3)$
0	0	0	0
0	0	1	1
0	1	0	1
0	1	1	0
1	0	0	1
1	0	1	0
1	1	0	0
1	1	1	1

using only AND, OR, and NOT gates. From inspection of the table we write

$$f(x_1, x_2, x_3) = (\bar{x}_1 \wedge \bar{x}_2 \wedge x_3) \vee (\bar{x}_1 \wedge x_2 \wedge \bar{x}_3)$$
$$\vee (x_1 \wedge \bar{x}_2 \wedge \bar{x}_3) \vee (x_1 \wedge x_2 \wedge x_3).$$

From this expression we easily obtain the network shown in Figure 2–33.

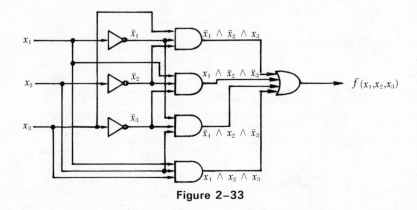

Figure 2–33

Note. If we re-inspect the table above, we see that the network shown in Figure 2–33 realizes a three-input modulo 2 adder. ◊

Before turning to the demonstration that any combinational circuit can be built from AND, OR, and NOT gates, let us briefly study *threshold logic units*.

DEFINITION 1

A binary module with n input lines and function $f: \{0, 1\}^n \rightarrow \{0, 1\}$ is said to be a **threshold logic unit** if associated with the ith input line there is a real number w_i called the **weight** of line i (for $i = 1, 2, \ldots, n$) and if associated with the whole module is a real number θ called the **threshold** such that the output of the module is 1 iff the weighted sum of its input reaches or exceeds the threshold:

$$f(x_1, \ldots, x_n) = 1 \Leftrightarrow \sum_{i=1}^{n} w_i x_i \geq \theta \qquad \qquad \bigcirc$$

Example 4

We show that AND, OR, and NOT gates can each be realized as threshold logic units:

Take $n = 2$, $w_1 = w_2 = 1$ and $\theta = 2$; then

$$w_1 x_1 + w_2 x_2 \geq \theta \Leftrightarrow x_1 + x_2 \geq 2 \Leftrightarrow x_1 \wedge x_2 = 1.$$

Take $n = 2$, $w_1 = w_2 = 1$ and $\theta = 1$; then

$$w_1 x_1 + w_2 x_2 \geq \theta \Leftrightarrow x_1 + x_2 \geq 1 \Leftrightarrow x_1 \vee x_2 = 1.$$

Take $n = 1$, $w_1 = -1$, $\theta = 0$; then

$$w_1 x_1 \geq \theta \Leftrightarrow -x_1 \geq 0 \Leftrightarrow x_1 = 0 \Leftrightarrow \bar{x}_1 = 1. \qquad \Diamond$$

Example 5

The EXCLUSIVE-OR gate is not realizable as a threshold logic unit, since to say

$$w_1 x_1 + w_2 x_2 \geq \theta \Leftrightarrow x_1 \oplus x_2 = 1$$

is to say that (see Figure 2–34) there is a line $w_1 x_1 + w_2 x_2 = \theta$ such that

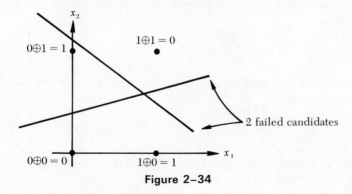

Figure 2–34

the points $(0, 0)$ and $(1, 1)$ are on one side, while $(1, 0)$ and $(0, 1)$ are on the other. But this is clearly impossible. ◊

We shall return to this last example in Section 5–5 when we explore the limits of the pattern recognition networks known as Perceptrons. We shall also study a pattern recognition system based on a threshold logic unit at the end of Section 6–1.

A form of threshold logic unit was introduced by McCulloch and Pitts in 1943 as an idealization of brain cells, or neurons. The units are thus often called **McCulloch-Pitts neurons.** An input to a neuron is called **excitatory** if $w_1 > 0$, and **inhibitory** if $w_1 < 0$. Our theorem below that every combinational circuit can be built from AND, OR, and NOT gates may thus also be taken as a proof that it may be built from idealized neurons. It is to that proof that we now turn.

Let us first reconsider one of our previous examples. For the table

x_1	x_2	$f(x_1, x_2)$
0	0	0
0	1	1
1	0	1
1	1	0

we saw that $f(x_1, x_2) = (\bar{x}_1 \wedge x_2) \vee (x_1 \wedge \bar{x}_2)$. More formally, from the table let us write the expression

$$f(x_1, x_2) = (f(0, 0) \wedge x_1^0 \wedge x_2^0) \vee (f(0, 1) \wedge x_1^0 \wedge x_2^1)$$
$$\vee (f(1, 0) \wedge x_1^1 \wedge x_2^0) \vee (f(1, 1) \wedge x_1^1 \wedge x_2^1)$$
$$= \bigvee_{\substack{\alpha_1 = 0 \text{ or } 1 \\ \alpha_2 = 0 \text{ or } 1}} (f(\alpha_1, \alpha_2) \wedge x_1^{\alpha_1} \wedge x_2^{\alpha_2})$$

If we define $x^0 = \bar{x}$ and $x^1 = x$, then this expression is called the **disjunctive normal form** of $f(x_1, x_2)$. Substituting the actual values for $f(\alpha_1, \alpha_2)$, we have that

$$f(x_1, x_2) = (0 \wedge \bar{x}_1 \wedge \bar{x}_2) \vee (1 \wedge \bar{x}_1 \wedge x_2) \vee (1 \wedge x_1 \wedge \bar{x}_2) \vee (0 \wedge x_1 \wedge x_2)$$

and since $0 \wedge x = 0$ and $1 \wedge x = x$ (verify with a table) the disjunctive normal form becomes

$$f(x_1, x_2) = (\bar{x}_1 \wedge x_2) \vee (x_1 \wedge \bar{x}_2).$$

Thus, we see that we had originally expressed $f(x_1, x_2)$ in disjunctive normal form.

We now formalize the previous discussion.

THEOREM 1

Let $f: \{0, 1\}^n \to \{0, 1\}$ be an arbitrary binary function of n variables. Then, if we let $x^0 = \bar{x}$ and $x^1 = x$, we can write f in the disjunctive normal form:

$$f(x_1, x_2, \ldots, x_n) = \bigvee_{\substack{\alpha_1 = 0 \, \text{or} \, 1 \\ \alpha_2 = 0 \, \text{or} \, 1 \\ \vdots \\ \alpha_n = 0 \, \text{or} \, 1}} (f(\alpha_1, \alpha_2, \ldots, \alpha_n) \wedge x_1^{\alpha_1} \wedge x_2^{\alpha_2} \wedge \cdots \wedge x_n^{\alpha_n})$$

$$= \bigvee_{\substack{\text{those} \, \alpha_j = 0 \, \text{or} \, 1 \\ \text{such that} \\ f(\alpha_1, \alpha_2, \ldots, \alpha_n) = 1}} (x_1^{\alpha_1} \wedge x_2^{\alpha_2} \wedge \cdots \wedge x_n^{\alpha_n})$$

Proof

First note that

$$x^0 = 1(\bar{x} = 1) \text{ iff } x = 0$$

and

$$x^1 = 1(x = 1) \text{ iff } x = 1$$

Thus, we have that

$$x^\alpha = 1 \text{ iff } x = \alpha$$

This implies that

$$x_1^{\alpha_1} \wedge x_2^{\alpha_2} \wedge \cdots \wedge x_n^{\alpha_n} = 1 \text{ iff } x_j = \alpha_j \text{ for all } j = 1, 2, \ldots, n.$$

Hence, we have that

$$\bigvee_{\substack{\alpha_1 = 0 \, \text{or} \, 1 \\ \alpha_2 = 0 \, \text{or} \, 1 \\ \vdots \\ \alpha_n = 0 \, \text{or} \, 1}} (f(\alpha_1, \alpha_2, \ldots, \alpha_n) \wedge x_1^{\alpha_1} \wedge x_2^{\alpha_2} \wedge \cdots \wedge x_n^{\alpha_n})$$

$$= \left[\bigvee_{\substack{x_j \neq \alpha_j \\ \text{for some} \\ j = 1, 2, \ldots, n}} (f(\alpha_1, \alpha_2, \ldots, \alpha_n) \wedge x_1^{\alpha_1} \wedge x_2^{\alpha_2} \wedge \cdots \wedge x_n^{\alpha_n}) \right]$$

$$\vee [f(x_1, x_2, \ldots, x_n) \wedge x_1^{x_1} \wedge x_2^{x_2} \wedge \cdots \wedge x_n^{x_n}]$$

$$= \left[\bigvee_{\substack{x_j \neq \alpha_j \\ \text{for some} \\ j = 1,2,\ldots,n}} (f(\alpha_1, \alpha_2, \ldots, \alpha_n) \wedge 0 \right] \vee f(x_1, x_2, \ldots, x_n)$$

$$= 0 \vee f(x_1, x_2, \ldots, x_n)$$
$$= f(x_1, x_2, \ldots, x_n), \text{ as was to be shown.} \qquad \square$$

The fact that we can write an arbitrary function $f\colon \{0, 1\}^n \to \{0, 1\}$ in disjunctive normal form establishes the fact that we can realize f using only AND, OR, and NOT gates. Since we can write

$$f(x_1, x_2, \ldots, x_n) = \bigvee_{\substack{\text{those } \alpha_j = 0 \text{ or } 1 \\ \text{such that} \\ f(\alpha_1, \alpha_2, \ldots, \alpha_n) = 1}} (x_1^{\alpha_1} \wedge x_2^{\alpha_2} \wedge \cdots \wedge x_n^{\alpha_n})$$

such a realization takes the form of the network shown in Figure 2–35.

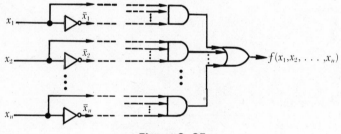

Figure 2–35

Let us note that a function realization of the form shown in Figure 2–35 is "a" realization, and not necessarily the "best" realization. The problem of finding the most desirable network which realizes a function is fundamental to switching theory. For an in-depth discussion on this topic, the reader is referred to one of the numerous books on switching theory.

We have shown that any binary function $f\colon \{0, 1\}^n \to \{0, 1\}$ can be realized by a network using only AND, OR, and NOT gates. As a consequence of this, we now have our desired result.

COROLLARY 2

For every function $g\colon \{0, 1\}^n \to \{0, 1\}^m$, there exists a combinational network consisting only of AND, OR, and NOT gates such that an input of $(x_1, x_2, \ldots, x_n)$ at time t yields an output of $g(x_1, x_2, \ldots, x_n)$ at time t. $\quad \square$

As a demonstration of this corollary, let us work an example.

Example 6

Suppose $g:\{0,1\}^2 \to \{0,1\}^2:(x_1,x_2) \mapsto (g_1(x_1,x_2),g_2(x_1,x_2))$ is specified by the following table:

x_1	x_2	$g_1(x_1,x_2)$	$g_2(x_1,x_2)$
0	0	1	0
0	1	0	0
1	0	0	1
1	1	1	0

We may then write

$$g_1(x_1,x_2) = (\overline{x}_1 \wedge \overline{x}_2) \vee (x_1 \wedge x_2)$$
$$g_2(x_1,x_2) = x_1 \wedge \overline{x}_2.$$

Therefore, a combinational network realizing g is given in Figure 2–36. $\Diamond$

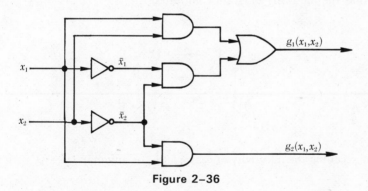

Figure 2–36

In Exercises 1 and 3, the reader is asked to demonstrate that an AND gate, an OR gate, and a NOT gate can all be realized using either only NOR gates or only NAND gates. It is for this reason that we may now conclude that we can realize any function $g:\{0,1\}^n \to \{0,1\}^m$ by a combinational network consisting entirely of either NOR gates or NAND gates.

Let us now return to our problem of automaton simulation by giving a formal definition of simulation and then working an example. Following this, we will establish a general simulation procedure.

Given the two machines M and M' as shown in Figure 2–37, our notion of simulation is to say that M *simulates* M' if M can process strings just as M' does, provided we can encode the input, decode the output, and start in an appropriate state. We will require both the encoder and decoder to

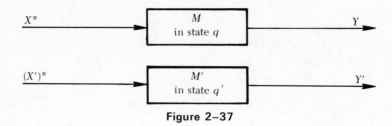

Figure 2–37

be memoryless (i.e., to operate symbol by symbol) in order to force M to do all the computational work involving memory.

There are many ways of formalizing the relationship just expressed, but here we shall give one of the simplest (and also one of the strongest).

DEFINITION 2

We say of two automata $M = (Q, X, Y, \delta, \lambda)$ and $M' = (Q', X', Y', \delta', \lambda')$ that M **simulates** M' if there exist maps $h_1 : X' \to X$, $h_2 : Q' \hookrightarrow Q$ and $h_3 : Y \to Y'$ such that the following diagram commutes:

$$
\begin{array}{ccc}
Q' \times X' & \xrightarrow{\ \delta' \times \lambda'\ } & Q' \times Y' \\
{\scriptstyle h_2 \times h_1} \big\downarrow & & \big\uparrow {\scriptstyle h_4 \times h_3} \\
Q \times X & \xrightarrow{\ \delta \times \lambda\ } & Q \times Y
\end{array}
$$

where, recalling the injectivity of h_2, we let h_4 be any map $Q \to Q'$ such that

$$h_4(h_2(q')) = q' \text{ for each } q' \in Q'.$$

Hence, we have Figure 2–38.   ○

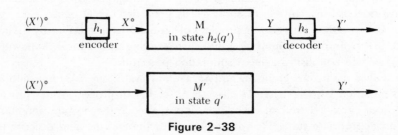

Figure 2–38

Example 7

Let us simulate the machine $(Q', X', Y', \delta', \lambda')$ given in Figure 2–39. Since we want to simulate this automaton with binary modules, we must represent Q', X', Y', δ', and λ' with binary entities.

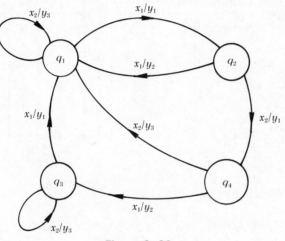

Figure 2–39

First, because there are two inputs, we can take $X = \{0, 1\}$. Therefore, let us define the function $h_1 : X' \rightarrow X = \{0, 1\}$ by

$$h_1(x_1) = 0$$
$$h_1(x_2) = 1$$

Since the machine to be simulated has four states, we may use the elements of $\{0, 1\}^2$ as states. Thus, let us define the function $h_2 : Q' \rightarrow Q = \{0, 1\}^2$ arbitrarily as

$$h_2(q_1) = (0, 0)$$
$$h_2(q_2) = (0, 1)$$
$$h_2(q_3) = (1, 0)$$
$$h_2(q_4) = (1, 1)$$

Finally, because there are three outputs, we may define $h_3 : Y = \{0, 1\}^2 \rightarrow Y'$ by

$$h_3(0, 0) = y_1$$
$$h_3(0, 1) = y_2$$
$$h_3(1, 0) = y_3$$

$h_3(1, 1)$ may be defined arbitrarily, since we shall not use it. We may now write the behavior of the machine in tabular form:

Present State	Input	Output	Next State		Present State (s_1, s_2)		Input i	Output (u_1, u_2)		Next State (t_1, t_2)	
q_1	x_1	y_1	q_2	$\Rightarrow$	0	0	0	0	0	0	1
q_1	x_2	y_3	q_1		0	0	1	1	0	0	0
q_2	x_1	y_2	q_1		0	1	0	0	1	0	0
q_2	x_2	y_1	q_4		0	1	1	0	0	1	1
q_3	x_1	y_1	q_1		1	0	0	0	0	0	0
q_3	x_2	y_3	q_3		1	0	1	1	0	1	0
q_4	x_1	y_2	q_3		1	1	0	0	1	1	0
q_4	x_2	y_3	q_1		1	1	1	1	0	0	0

From the second table, we can write

$$u_1 = (\overline{s_1} \wedge \overline{s_2} \wedge i) \vee (s_1 \wedge \overline{s_2} \wedge i) \vee (s_1 \wedge s_2 \wedge i)$$
$$u_2 = (\overline{s_1} \wedge s_2 \wedge i) \vee (s_1 \wedge s_2 \wedge \overline{i})$$
$$t_1 = (\overline{s_1} \wedge s_2 \wedge i) \vee (s_1 \wedge \overline{s_2} \wedge i) \vee (s_1 \wedge s_2 \wedge \overline{i})$$
$$t_2 = (\overline{s_1} \wedge \overline{s_2} \wedge \overline{i}) \vee (\overline{s_1} \wedge s_2 \wedge i)$$

Since the next state (t_1, t_2) will become the present state (s_1, s_2) one unit of time later, we place t_1 and t_2 at the inputs of unit delay elements. Thus, the outputs of the delays are s_1 and s_2, respectively. Hence, a realization of $(Q', X', Y', \delta', \lambda')$ is shown in Figure 2–40. $\lozenge$

We may now always simulate a finite automation $M' = (Q', X', Y', \delta', \beta')$ as follows:

(i) Choose integers r, n, and p such that

$$2^r \geq |Q'|$$
$$2^n \geq |X'|$$
$$2^p \geq |Y'|$$

and arbitrarily define the injections

$$h_1 : X' \to \{0, 1\}^n$$
$$h_2 : Q' \to \{0, 1\}^r$$

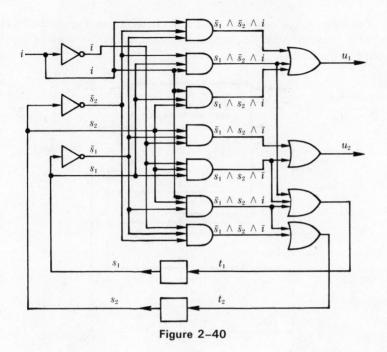

Figure 2–40

and the surjection

$$h_3 \colon \{0, 1\}^p \to Y'$$

(ii) We construct the combinational network which realizes the function

$$g \colon \{0, 1\}^{r+n} \to \{0, 1\}^{p+r}$$

defined by

$$g(s_1, s_2, \ldots, s_r, i_1, i_2, \ldots, i_n) = (u_1, u_2, \ldots, u_p, t_1, t_2, \ldots, t_r)$$

which is such that whenever

$$(s_1, s_2, \ldots, s_r) \text{ encodes } q \in Q'$$

and

$$(i_1, i_2, \ldots, i_n) \text{ encodes } x \in X'$$

then

$$(u_1, u_2, \ldots, u_p) \text{ decodes as } \lambda'(q, x) \in Y'$$

and

$$(t_1, t_2, \ldots, t_r) \text{ encodes } \delta'(q, x)$$

(iii) Insert r unit delays to which $t_1, t_2, \ldots, t_r$ are the inputs and from which $s_1, s_2, \ldots, s_r$ are the respective outputs.

The form of the resulting simulation is shown in Figure 2–41. Thus, any finite automaton may be simulated by a modular network of the form shown in Figure 2–41.

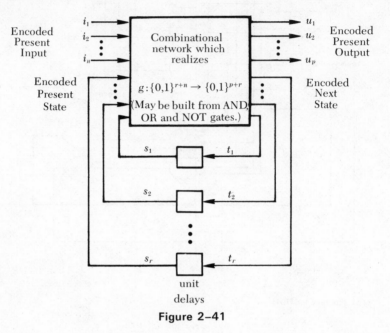

Figure 2–41

EXERCISES FOR SECTION 2–3

1.   Let us realize the function specified by the following table:

x_1	x_2	$f(x_1, x_2)$
0	0	1
0	1	0
1	0	0
1	1	0

We therefore have that $f(x_1, x_2) = 1$ provided that $x_1 = 0$ $(\bar{x}_1 = 1)$ AND $x_2 = 0$ $(\bar{x}_2 = 1)$. Thus, we write

$$f(x_1, x_2) = \bar{x}_1 \wedge \bar{x}_2$$

and this function can be realized by the network shown in Figure 2–42.

Although the combinational network of Figure 2–42 realizes the function $f(x_1, x_2) = \bar{x}_1 \wedge \bar{x}_2$, such a realization is by no means unique. To confirm this state-

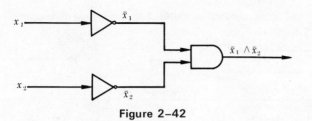

Figure 2–42

ment, we could have realized the same function merely by inverting the output of an OR gate, since

x_1	x_2	$x_1 \vee x_2$	$\overline{x_1 \vee x_2}$
0	0	0	1
0	1	1	0
1	0	1	0
1	1	1	0

Thus, we see that

$$\overline{x}_1 \wedge \overline{x}_2 = \overline{x_1 \vee x_2}$$

This is called **DeMorgan's law.** Consequently, an alternative realization of the function is shown in Figure 2–43. It is conveniently symbolized as shown in Figure

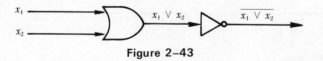

Figure 2–43

2–44, and is referred to as a **NOR gate** (a reverse contraction of **OR-NOT** gate).

NOR gate

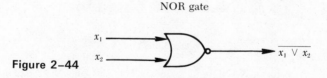

Figure 2–44

Construct tables to verify that:
(a)   the NOR network in Figure 2–45 realizes a NOT gate.

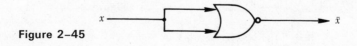

Figure 2–45

(b) the NOR network in Figure 2–46 realizes an OR gate.

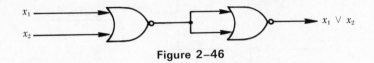

Figure 2–46

(c) the NOR network in Figure 2–47 realizes an AND gate.

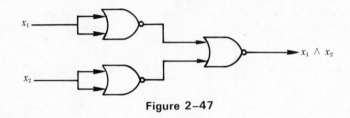

Figure 2–47

2. Returning to Example 2, note that we have that

$$(\bar{x}_1 \wedge \bar{x}_2) \vee (\bar{x}_1 \wedge x_2) \vee (x_1 \wedge \bar{x}_2) = \overline{x_1 \wedge x_2}.$$

Thus, a much simpler realization of $f(x_1, x_2)$ is shown in Figure 2–48. This network,

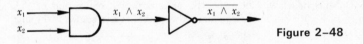

Figure 2–48

like the NOR gate, is rather important. It is therefore symbolized as shown in Figure 2–49, and is referred to as a **NAND gate** (a reverse contraction of **AND-NOT** gate).

NAND gate

Figure 2–49

Use the alternative form of DeMorgan's law

$$\overline{x_1 \wedge x_2} = \bar{x}_1 \vee \bar{x}_2$$

to realize a NAND gate by using only OR and NOT gates.

3. Construct tables to verify that:
(a) the NAND network in Figure 2–50 realizes a NOT gate.

Figure 2–50

(b) the NAND network in Figure 2–51 realizes an OR gate.

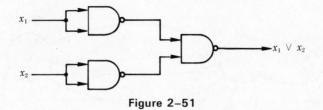

Figure 2–51

(c)   the NAND network in Figure 2–52 realizes an AND gate.

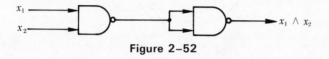

Figure 2–52

4.   Given the arbitrary binary function $f:\{0, 1\}^n \to \{0, 1\}$, prove that f can be written in the so-called **conjunctive normal form:**

$$f(x_1, x_2, \ldots, x_n) = \bigwedge_{\substack{\alpha_1 = 0 \text{ or } 1 \\ \alpha_2 = 0 \text{ or } 1 \\ \vdots \\ \alpha_n = 0 \text{ or } 1}} (f(\bar{\alpha}_1, \bar{\alpha}_2, \ldots, \bar{\alpha}_n) \vee x_1^{\alpha_1} \vee x_2^{\alpha_2} \vee \cdots \vee x_n^{\alpha_n})$$

$$= \bigwedge_{\substack{\text{those } \alpha_j = 0 \text{ or } 1 \\ \text{such that} \\ f(\bar{\alpha}_1, \bar{\alpha}_2, \ldots, \bar{\alpha}_n) = 0}} (x_1^{\alpha_1} \vee x_2^{\alpha_2} \vee \cdots \vee x_n^{\alpha_n})$$

5.   Find a network realization of the function $g:\{0, 1\}^3 \to \{0, 1\}^2$ specified by the following table:

x_1	x_2	x_3	$g_1(x_1, x_2, x_3)$	$g_2(x_1, x_2, x_3)$
0	0	0	0	0
0	0	1	1	0
0	1	0	1	0
0	1	1	0	1
1	0	0	1	0
1	0	1	0	1
1	1	0	0	1
1	1	1	1	0

6.   Simulate the automaton shown in Figure 2–53.

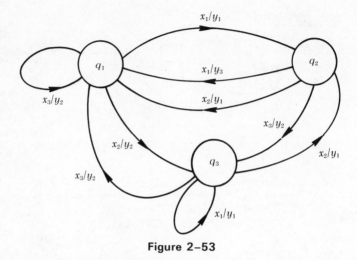

Figure 2–53

2–4   Equivalence Relations

In this section we complement our discussion of sets and functions of Section 1–2 by introducing the formal notion of a *relation*. In particular, we shall be interested in what are called *equivalence relations,* and shall find that these provide important new insights into the structures $\mathbf{Z}_m$ that we encountered while counting modulo m in Section 2–1.

Given a set of people, we might state for two individuals a and b that "a is the father of b," or "a is the daughter of b" or "a is a sibling of the maternal grandfather of b." In the general context of our algebraic investigations, given two sets A and B, by a **relation** from A to B we shall mean a specification for each $a \in A$ and $b \in B$ of whether or not they are related in a given way.

For example, $\leq$ is the relation from $\mathbf{N}$ to $\mathbf{N}$ (we may also speak of it as a **binary** relation on $\mathbf{N}$ to indicate that two terms are involved) such that $m \leq n$ if and only if the number m is no larger than the number n, or in fact, $m \leq n$ iff $m \doteq n = 0$.

Let us give four equivalent formalizations, then, for the notion of a relation from A to B.

DEFINITION 1(i)

A **relation** R from A to B is a subset of $A \times B$. We write aRb, and say that a is R-related to b, whenever $(a, b) \in R$. ○

Example 1

The relation $\leq$ is given by

$$\leq \; = \{(m,n) \,|\, m \in \mathbf{N}, \, n \in \mathbf{N} \text{ and } m \doteq n = 0\} \subset \mathbf{N} \times \mathbf{N} \qquad ◊$$

DEFINITION 1(ii)

A **relation** R from A to B is a function $A \times B \to \{0, 1\}$. We write aRb, and say that a is R-related to b, whenever $R(a, b) = 1$.   ○

Example 2

The relation $\leq$ is given by $\leq : \mathbf{N} \times \mathbf{N} \to \{0, 1\} : (m, n) \mapsto 1 \dot{-} (m \dot{-} n)$. [Check that this works.]   ◊

The equivalence of the characterizations (i) and (ii) follows from our observation in Section 1–5 that we may characterize a subset by its characteristic function. Our next equivalent definition turns our attention from the question "Given a and b, are they related?" to "Given a, to what is it related?":

DEFINITION 1(iii)

A **relation** R from A to B is a function $A \to \mathcal{P}(B)$. We write aRb, and say that a is R-related to b, whenever $b \in R(a)$.   ○

Example 3

The relation $\leq$ is given by $\leq : \mathbf{N} \to \mathcal{P}(\mathbf{N}) : n \mapsto \{n, n + 1, n + 2, n + 3, \ldots\}$.   ◊

We recapture the subset characterization (i) from $R : A \to \mathcal{P}(B)$ by forming the subset $\{(a, b) \mid b \in R(a)\}$ of $A \times B$. Conversely, given $R \subset A \times B$, we may recapture the function characterization (iii) by forming the function $A \to \mathcal{P}(B) : a \mapsto \{b \mid (a, b) \in R\}$.

Finally, if we are interested in the relatives of a subset A' of A rather than those of an individual $a \in A$, we may transform $R : A \to \mathcal{P}(B)$ into a function $\widehat{R} : \mathcal{P}(A) \to \mathcal{P}(B)$ by the simple rule

$$\widehat{R}(A') = \bigcup_{a \in A'} R(a)$$

i.e., $\widehat{R}(A')$ is just the set of all R-relatives of "people" in A'. The construction makes it clear that $\widehat{R}$ has a special property, namely that for every family $\{A_\alpha\}_{\alpha \in I}$ of subsets of A, we have the equality

$$\widehat{R}\left(\bigcup_{\alpha \in I} A_\alpha\right) = \bigcup_{\alpha \in I} \widehat{R}(A_\alpha).$$

We then say that $\widehat{R}$ is **completely additive.** Given a completely additive $\widehat{R}$, we may recapture R simply by setting

$$R(a) = \widehat{R}(\{a\})$$

Thus, a relation may also be characterized as follows:

DEFINITION 1(iv)

A **relation** R from A to B is a completely additive function $\mathcal{P}(A) \to \mathcal{P}(B)$. We write aRb, and say that a is R-related to b, whenever $b \in R(\{a\})$.   ○

Having seen four different ways of defining relations, we now turn to the study of two special types of relations: the *partial orderings* (of which $\leq$ on **N** is an example) and the *equivalence relations* (of which $=$ on **N** is a [rather dull] example).

Consider the set of all integers **Z.** Let R be the subset $\leq$, where $\leq = \{(x,y) \mid x,y \in \mathbf{Z}$ and x is less than or equal to $y\} \subset \mathbf{Z} \times \mathbf{Z}$. Then **Z** together with $\leq$ is a partially ordered set, in that it satisfies the three conditions of the following definition:

DEFINITION 2

A set S together with a binary relation R is called a **partially ordered set** if the following three laws are satisfied.

I. Reflexivity: xRx for all $x \in S$.
II. Antisymmetry: If xRy and yRx, then $x = y$ for all $x,y \in S$.
III. Transitivity: If xRy and yRz, then xRz for all $x,y,z \in S$.   ○

A more illuminating example, which points up that the ordering need only be partial, is the set of all the subsets of a set S under set inclusion. The binary relation is $R = \{(X, Y) \mid X, Y \in \mathcal{P}(S)$ and X is a subset of $Y\}$. This relation is denoted by $\subset$. Clearly, $X \subset X$ and by definition if $X \subset Y$ and $Y \subset X$, then $X = Y$. Furthermore, if $X \subset Y$ and $Y \subset Z$, then $X \subset Z$. Thus, $\mathcal{P}(S)$ along with $\subset$ is a partially ordered set. However, unlike the corresponding case for the integers, it may well be that neither $X \subset Y$ nor $Y \subset X$. Under these circumstances, we say that X and Y are **incomparable.**

Another concept of fundamental importance in mathematics is that of *equivalence.* For intuition here, think of sorting apples into barrels, and write $a \equiv b$ if and only if a and b are placed in the same barrel:

DEFINITION 3

A binary relation $\equiv$ on a set S is called an **equivalence relation** if the following three conditions are satisfied:

I. Reflexivity: $x \equiv x$ for all $x \in S$.
II. Symmetry: $x \equiv y \Rightarrow y \equiv x$ for all $x, y, \in S$.
III. Transitivity: $s \equiv y$ and $y \equiv z \Rightarrow x \equiv z$ for all $x, y, z \in S$.

If $x \equiv y$, we say that x is **equivalent** to y. $\bigcirc$

An equivalence relation on the set of rational numbers $\mathbf{Q}$ is given by $\{(p/q, r/s) \mid ps = rq\}$. This particular equivalence relation is denoted by $=$. (Do not confuse $=$ when it is used with numbers and when it is used with sets. They are not the same.) Thus, we can write $\frac{1}{2} = \frac{25}{50}$, $\frac{2}{5} = \frac{8}{20}$, etc.

Example 4

Let us verify that the binary relation on $\mathbf{Z}$ given by $\equiv = \{(x,y) \mid x, y \in \mathbf{Z}$ and $x - y$ is even$\}$ is an equivalence relation. (An alternative way of specifying this relation is to say: $x \equiv y$ if and only if $x - y$ is even.)

I. For any $x \in \mathbf{Z}$, we have $x - x = 0$ which is even. Hence, $x \equiv x$ and reflexivity holds.
II. Suppose $x \equiv y$. Then $x - y$ is even. But $y - x = -(x - y)$, which is also even. Thus, $y \equiv x$, and the symmetry condition is satisfied.
III. Let $x \equiv y$ and $y \equiv z$. Then $x - y$ and $y - z$ are both even. Since the sum of two even numbers is even, $(x - y) + (y - z) = x - z$ is even. Hence, $x \equiv z$ and we have demonstrated transitivity. $\Diamond$

Example 5

Suppose that $\equiv$ is an equivalence relation on S. By symmetry we know that for all $x, y \in S$ if $x \equiv y$, then $y \equiv x$. By transitivity, however, if $x \equiv y$ and $y \equiv x$, then $x \equiv x$ which suggests reflexivity. In the definition of an equivalence relation, if II and III imply I, condition I would be superfluous. Why then is I not implied by II and III? The answer is the following:

Condition I states that $x \equiv x$ *for all* $x \in S$. In order for II and III to imply I, it must be true that for every $x \in S$ there exists some $y \in S$ such that $x \equiv y$. However, in general, the existence of at least one such $y \in S$ is not guaranteed. $\Diamond$

Suppose S is a set and $x \in S$. Then the subset $[x]_\equiv = \{y \mid y \in S$ and $y \equiv x\}$ is called the **equivalence class** of x **modulo** $\equiv$. It is the "barrel" containing x.

Note that according to this definition, we may represent an equivalence class by any one of its members. That is, if x and x' are in the same equivalence class of S modulo $\equiv$, then $x \equiv x'$ so that $y \equiv x$ iff $y \equiv x'$. ($y \equiv x$ and $x \equiv x' \Rightarrow y \equiv x'$. Conversely, $y \equiv x'$, $x \equiv x'$, and hence, $x' \equiv x \Rightarrow y \equiv x$.) Thus,

$$[x]_\equiv = \{y \mid y \in S \text{ and } y \equiv x\}$$
$$= \{y \mid y \in S \text{ and } y \equiv x'\}$$
$$= [x']_\equiv.$$

Example 6

Consider the equivalence relation $\equiv$ on $\mathbf{Z}$ given by $x \equiv y$ if and only if $x - y$ is even. Then the equivalence class of 0 modulo $\equiv$ is

$$[0]_\equiv = \{0, 2, -2, 4, -4, 6, -6, \dots\} = \text{the set } \mathbf{Z}_e \text{ of even integers,}$$

while the equivalence class of 1 modulo $\equiv$ is

$$[1]_\equiv = \{1, -1, 3, -3, 5, -5, 7, -7, \dots\} = \text{the set } \mathbf{Z}_o \text{ of odd integers.}$$

Since $x' \in [x]_\equiv$ iff $x' \equiv x$ iff $[x']_\equiv = [x]_\equiv$ we have that

$$[0]_\equiv = [2]_\equiv = [-2]_\equiv = [4]_\equiv = [-4]_\equiv = \cdots$$

and similarly

$$[1]_\equiv = [-1]_\equiv = [3]_\equiv = [-3]_\equiv = \cdots.$$

Thus, we see that for this equivalence relation there are only two equivalence classes, each of which can be represented by any element in the class, and there is no overlap between these classes. Note well, then, that there may be infinitely many distinct labels for equivalence classes (in this case there are as many labels as there are elements of $\mathbf{Z}$) and yet only two distinct classes (in this case $[0]_\equiv$ and $[1]_\equiv$). $\Diamond$

The equivalence relation $\sim_m$ on $\mathbf{Z}$ given by

$$x \sim_m y \Leftrightarrow x - y \text{ is a multiple of the integer } m$$

yields the following equivalence classes of $\mathbf{Z}$ modulo $\sim_m$:

$$[0]_m = \{0, m, -m, 2m, -2m, \ldots\} \text{ (abbreviating } [x]_{\sim_m} \text{ to } [x]_m)$$
$$[1]_m = \{1, m + 1, -m + 1, 2m + 1, -2m + 1, \ldots\}$$
$$[2]_m = \{2, m + 2, -m + 2, 2m + 2, -2m + 2, \ldots\}$$
$$\vdots$$
$$[m - 1]_m = \{m - 1, 2m - 1, -1, 4m - 2, -m - 1, \ldots\}$$

and, in fact, two positive integers are in the same equivalence class of **Z** modulo m if and only if when divided by m they have the same remainder.

The observant reader will note that we have one equivalence class of **Z** modulo m for each element of the set

$$\mathbf{Z}_m = \{0, 1, \ldots, m - 1\}$$

which introduced our study of automata in Section 2–1. In fact, we have a bijection given by

$$[k]_m \leftrightarrow k \text{ for } 0 \le k \le m - 1.$$

Henceforth, then, we shall use $\mathbf{Z}_m$ also as a denotation for the collection of equivalence classes of integers modulo m. The reader should have no trouble in telling from the context when k denotes k as an element of **Z** for unbounded counting, and when k denotes an element of $\mathbf{Z}_m$, so that as one of only m different "barrels," it can only enable us to count modulo m. We usually refer to $\mathbf{Z}_m$ as the **set of integers modulo** m.

DEFINITION 4

Given a set S and an equivalence relation $\equiv$ on S, then the set whose elements are the equivalence classes of S modulo $\equiv$ is denoted by $S/\equiv$. We refer to $S/\equiv$ as the **factor set** of S (with respect to $\equiv$). Thus,

$$S/\equiv \; = \{[x]_\equiv \,|\, x \in S\}$$

where the equivalence class $[x]_\equiv = \{y \,|\, y \in S \text{ and } y \equiv x\}$. ○

For "$x \sim_2 y \Leftrightarrow x - y$ is even" and "$x \sim_m y \Leftrightarrow x - y$ is a multiple of m," we have

$$\mathbf{Z}_2 = \mathbf{Z}/\sim_2 = \{[0]_2, [1]_2\} \quad \text{and}$$
$$\mathbf{Z}_m = \mathbf{Z}/\sim_m = \{[0]_m, [1]_m, [2]_m, \ldots, [m - 1]_m\}, \text{ respectively.}$$

For the former, it may have been noted that $[0]_2 \cup [1]_2 = \mathbf{Z}$ and $[0]_2 \cap [1]_2 = \varnothing$. Also, for the latter, $[0]_m \cup [1]_m \cup [2]_m \cup \cdots \cup [m - 1]_m = \mathbf{Z}$

and $[i]_m \cap [j]_m = \emptyset$ for $i, j = 0, 1, 2, \ldots, m - 1$ and $i \neq j$. In other words, for both these examples, the equivalence classes form a *partition* of S, defined as follows:

DEFINITION 5

Suppose S is a set and $\{S_\alpha \,|\, \alpha \in I\}$ is a family of subsets of S. If the subsets are pair-wise disjoint, i.e., if

$$S_i \cap S_j = \emptyset \text{ for } i \neq j \text{ in } I$$

and if

$$\bigcup_{\alpha \in I} S_\alpha = S,$$

then we say that the subsets are a **partition** P of S, and each S_k is called a **block** of P. ○

LEMMA 1

If $\equiv$ is an equivalence relation on S, then the equivalence classes of S modulo $\equiv$ form a partition of S.

(Note: For the sake of convenience, instead of $[x]_{\equiv}$, we will denote the equivalence class containing x by $[x]$.)

Proof

First we pick a representative x_i from each distinct equivalence class. Thus $[x_i] \neq [x_j]$ for $i \neq j$, but each $[x]$ is $[x_i]$ for some i. We must show that the family $\{[x_i]\}_{i \in I}$ so obtained is a partition. Clearly

$$\bigcup_{i \in I} [x_i] = S$$

since each x in S is in $[x]$, and each $[x]$ is an $[x_i]$ for some $i \in I$. Thus, to complete our proof, we must show that

$$[x_i] \cap [x_j] = \emptyset \text{ for } i \neq j$$

To turn this around, we shall show that if $[x_i] \cap [x_j] \neq \emptyset$, then it must follow that $[x_i] = [x_j]$. If $w \in [x_i] \cap [x_j]$, then $w \equiv x_i$ and $w \equiv x_j$, so we must have, by an earlier observation, that $[w] = [x_i]$ and $[w] = [x_j]$. Hence $[x_i] = [x_j]$.

□

Since the equivalence classes of S modulo $\equiv$ (which are the elements of $S/\equiv$) partition S, we call $S/\equiv$ the partition of S **induced** by the equivalence relation $\equiv$.

Given a set S and an equivalence relation $\equiv$ on S, we have formed the set $S/\equiv$ whose elements are the equivalence classes modulo $\equiv$. It is only natural, therefore, to define a function $\eta_\equiv : S \to S/\equiv$ which sends each element in S to the equivalence class which contains that element; i.e., $\eta_\equiv : x \mapsto [x]_\equiv$. Clearly, $\eta_\equiv$ is a surjection, and consequently, we call $\eta_\equiv$ the **canonical surjection** of S onto the factor set $S/\equiv$.

Example 7

Let the relation $\sim$ on $\mathbf{Z} \times \mathbf{Z}_+$ (from $\mathbf{Z} \times \mathbf{Z}_+$ to $\mathbf{Z} \times \mathbf{Z}_+$) be defined by

$$(p, q) \sim (r, s) \Leftrightarrow ps = rq$$

We check that $\sim$ is an equivalence relation:

Reflexivity: $pq = pq$, and so $(p, q) \sim (p, q)$.

Symmetry: If $ps = rq$, then certainly $rq = ps$ and thus

$$(p, q) \sim (r, s) \Rightarrow (r, s) \sim (p, q)$$

Transitivity: If $ps = rq$ and $rt = vs$, then

$$(pt) \cdot s = (ps) \cdot t = (rq) \cdot t = (rt) \cdot q = (vs) \cdot q = (vq) \cdot s$$

and thus $pt = vq$ since $s \neq 0$. Hence, $(p, q) \sim (r, s)$ and $(r, s) \sim (v, t) \Rightarrow (p, q) \sim (v, t)$.   ◊

The reader will now recognize that our construction of the rational numbers in Section 1–3 simply characterized a rational number as an equivalence class modulo $\sim$:

$$\mathbf{Q} = (\mathbf{Z} \times \mathbf{Z}_+)/\sim$$

We have seen that an equivalence relation induces a partition of a set. Let us investigate the converse by means of the following.

Example 8

Suppose $S = \{1, 2, 3, \ldots, 21\}$ has the partition P with the blocks

$$S_1 = \{1, 3, 5, 7, 9, 10\}$$
$$S_2 = \{2, 4, 6, 8, 11\}$$
$$S_3 = \{12, 13, 14, 15, 16, 17, 18\}$$
$$S_4 = \{19, 20, 21\}$$

Let us define a binary relation R on S by the following:
If $x \in S$ and $y \in S$, then xRy if and only if x and y are in the same block of P. Clearly, R is reflexive, symmetric, and transitive. Thus, this relation, denoted by $\equiv_P$, is an equivalence relation.   ◊

We now conclude that for every partition P of a set S there is an equivalence relation $\equiv_P$ defined by:

$$x \equiv_P y \text{ if and only if } x \text{ and } y \text{ are in the same block of } P.$$

Furthermore, P is the partition of S induced by the equivalence relation $\equiv_P$.

We now turn to a study of the circumstances under which a function $f: X \to Y$ can yield a corresponding function $X/\equiv \;\to\; Y/\sim$ on factor sets. We start with two examples:

Recalling our discussion of functions, let us define the following two assignments which are intended to be from **Q** to **Q**:

$$\frac{p}{q} \mapsto 2p$$

$$\left(\frac{p}{q}, \frac{r}{s}\right) \mapsto \frac{ps + rq}{qs}$$

The first "function" is not well-defined as a function of rational numbers, for we have that $\frac{1}{2} = \frac{2}{4}$, but the assignment takes $\frac{1}{2}$ to 2 and $\frac{2}{4}$ to 4. In other words, the first assignment really depends upon the *ordered pair* (p, q) and *not* on the *rational number* $\frac{p}{q}$ which it represents.

On the other hand, the second assignment is well-defined as a function of rational numbers, for whenever we have $\frac{p}{q} = \frac{p'}{q'}, \frac{r}{s} = \frac{r'}{s'}$ it follows that $\dfrac{ps + rq}{qs} = \dfrac{p's' + r'q'}{q's'}$. This function corresponds to addition of rational numbers.

Our purpose, now that we have the general definition of an equivalence relation, is to understand the general concept of which the above discussion is a particular case. We do this first pictorially, and then give a formal description of the process thus well-defined.

Suppose that we have two sets X and Y, with an equivalence relation $\equiv$ on X, and an equivalence relation $\sim$ on Y. We may think of $\equiv$ as placing the elements of X in one set of barrels (with $x \in [x]_\equiv$); and of $\sim$ as placing the elements of Y in another set of barrels (with $y \in [y]_\sim$).

Given $f_1 : X \to Y$ as shown in Figure 2–54, the barrel of origin does *not* uniquely determine the barrel of destination. For example, x_3 and x_4 are both in A_2 but $f_1(x_3) \in B_1$ while $f_1(x_4) \in B_2$. Thus, the map $f_1 : X \to Y$ may *not* be thought of as a function from $X/\equiv$ to $Y/\sim$.

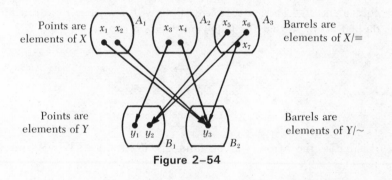

Figure 2–54

Given $f_2 : X \to Y$ as shown in Figure 2–55, the barrel of origin *does* uniquely determine the barrel of destination. Whenever two points x and x' are in the same barrel of $X/\equiv$, then their image $f_2(x)$ and $f_2(x')$ are in the same barrel of $Y/\sim$. Thus, the map $f_2 : X \to Y$ may be thought of as a function $\widehat{f_2}$ from $X/\equiv$ to $Y/\sim$, with $\widehat{f_2}(A_1) = B_1$, $\widehat{f_2}(A_2) = B_1$ and $\widehat{f_2}(A_3) = B_2$.

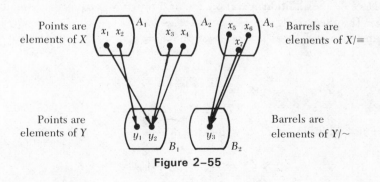

Figure 2–55

The intuition that the reader may have gained from studying Figures 2-54 and 2-55 may then be formalized in the following definition:

DEFINITION 6

We say that the equivalences $\equiv$ and $\sim$ are **compatible** with $f: X \to Y$ if and only if we have for all x and x' in X that

$$x \equiv x' \Rightarrow f(x) \sim f(x') \tag{1}$$

We may then define the **factored map** $\widehat{f}: X/\equiv \to Y/\sim$ by the formula

$$\widehat{f}([x]_{\equiv}) = [f(x)]_{\sim} \tag{2} \quad \bigcirc$$

In the language of commutative diagrams, we are simply saying that the equivalences $\equiv$ and $\sim$ are compatible with f whenever we can fill in the dashed arrow so that the following diagram commutes:

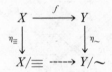

in which case the arrow will be uniquely determined (Why?) and will equal $\widehat{f}$.

Example 9

It is clear how to extend the above concept to a function of several variables. Let us exemplify this by considering the fate of addition $\mathbf{Z} \times \mathbf{Z} \to \mathbf{Z}: (x, x') \mapsto x + x'$ under two different equivalence relations:

(i) Does $+$, the addition operation, factor through $\sim_m$, equivalence modulo m? In other words, if $x \sim_m x_1$ and $x' \sim_m x'_1$, is $x + x' \sim_m x_1 + x'_1$? The answer is yes, for if $x = x_1 + km$ and $x' = x'_1 + k'm (k, k' \in \mathbf{Z})$, then

$$\begin{aligned} x + x' &= x_1 + km + x'_1 + k'm \\ &= (x_1 + x'_1) + (k + k')m \\ &\sim_m x_1 + x'_1. \end{aligned}$$

Thus, addition on $\mathbf{Z}_m$ is well-defined by

$$+ : \mathbf{Z}_m \times \mathbf{Z}_m \to \mathbf{Z}_m : ([x]_m, [x']_m) \mapsto [x + x']_m.$$

(ii) Let A be the set of all integers greater than 1, and let $\equiv$ be the equivalence relation

$x \equiv x'$ iff x and x' are either both prime or both composite

Thus, $A/\equiv$ has two equivalence classes; $[2]_\equiv$, the class of all prime numbers, and $[4]_\equiv$, the class of all composite numbers. However, addition is not well-defined on $A/\equiv$, for $2 \equiv 3$ and $5 \equiv 7$ but $2 + 5 = 7$, a prime, and so is not equivalent to $3 + 7 = 10$, a composite.   ◊

To provide a little vocabulary which is related to the relations studied so far in this section, we now introduce the notions of a *lattice* and a *Boolean algebra* and relate them to switching and automata theory.

DEFINITION 7

A **lattice** is a set L, together with two binary operations $\wedge$(meet) and $\vee$(join) such that

(L1) $x \wedge y = y \wedge x$; $x \vee y = y \vee x$ (commutativity)
(L2) $x \wedge (y \wedge z) = (x \wedge y) \wedge z$; $(x \vee y) \vee z = x \vee (y \vee z)$
                                                                 (associativity)
(L3) $x \wedge (x \vee y) = x$; $x \vee (x \wedge y) = x$ (the absorption laws)

hold for all x, y, and z in L.   ○

Example 10

Let $\mathcal{P}(S)$ be the set of all subsets of the set S. Then $[\mathcal{P}(S), \cap, \cup]$ is a lattice, with intersection for meet and union for join, since $X \cap Y = Y \cap X$, $X \cup Y = Y \cup X, \ldots, X \cup (X \cap Y) = X$.   ◊

Example 11

Let $\mathbf{Z}$ be the integers. Then $[\mathbf{Z}, \min, \max]$ is a lattice, with maximum for the join and minimum for the meet, since $\min(x, y) = \min(y, x), \ldots,$ $\max(x, \min(x, y)) = x$.   ◊

LEMMA 2

The absorption laws (L3) imply that $x \wedge x = x$ and $x \vee x = x$ for all x in X.

Proof

Since the roles of $\vee$ and $\wedge$ are clearly symmetrical, we need only verify that $x \wedge x = x$. To do this, set $y = x \wedge x$ in $x \wedge (x \vee y) = x$ to get

$$x \wedge (x \vee (x \wedge x)) = x.$$

But $x \vee (x \wedge x) = x$ on taking $y = x$ in $x \vee (x \wedge y) = x$. Thus $x \wedge x = x$, as required. □

DEFINITION 8

The collection $[B, \wedge, \vee, ', 0, 1]$, where $[B, \wedge, \vee]$ is a lattice, $x \mapsto x'$ is a unary operation on B, and 0 and 1 are constants in B, is called a **Boolean algebra** if and only if it satisfies the following laws:

(B1) $x \wedge (y \vee z) = (x \wedge y) \vee (x \wedge z)$; $x \vee (y \wedge z) = (x \vee y) \wedge (x \vee z)$

(distributivity)

(B2) $x \wedge 0 = 0$; $x \vee 0 = x$; $x \wedge 1 = x$; $x \vee 1 = 1$

(bounds)

(B3) $x \wedge x' = 0$; $x \vee x' = 1$ (complements)

(B4) $(x')' = x$ (involution)

(B5) $(x \wedge y)' = x' \vee y'$; $(x \vee y)' = x' \wedge y'$ (de Morgan) ○

Example 12

We have already seen that $[\mathcal{P}(S), \wedge, \vee]$ is a lattice. If we take $X' = S \backslash X$ for $X \subset S$; $0 = \varnothing$ and $1 = S$, then we do indeed satisfy laws B1 through B5. For example, $X \wedge 0 = X \cap \varnothing = \varnothing = 0$; and de Morgan's laws are just the de Morgan's laws of Section 1–2.   ◊

Example 13

$[\mathbf{Z}, \max, \min]$ *cannot* be made into a Boolean algebra, since if n were the choice for the zero, the fact that $\min(n, n - 1) = n - 1$ would contradict B2. If we adjoin $-\infty$ as the zero, and $+\infty$ as the one, then $[\mathbf{Z}, \max, \min,$

$-\infty, +\infty]$ satisfies B1 and B2. However, there is no element $n' \in \mathbf{Z} \cup \{-\infty, +\infty\}$ which satisfies $\max(n, n') = +\infty$ and $\min(n, n') = -\infty$, so that B3 is doomed to failure. ◊

Example 14

(This is the classic example due to George Boole, who started the whole subject of Boolean algebra which now fills volumes): Let

$$B = \{0, 1\} \text{ with } \wedge = \min, \vee = \max, 0' = 1 \text{ and } 1' = 0.$$

Then $[B, \vee, \wedge]$ is clearly a lattice, and we can in fact check all the laws B1 through B5. For example, $\min(x, 0) = 0$, $\max(x, 1) = 1$ whether x be 0 or 1; and $(0')' = 1' = 0$ and $(1')' = 1$. Writing down the explicit tables below, we see that $\wedge$ is indeed the AND of our switching circuits of Section 2–3, while $\vee$ is OR and $'$ is NOT. Thus, this Boolean algebra is sometimes referred to as the **switching algebra.**

Min	0	1
0	0	0
1	0	1

Max	0	1
0	0	1
1	1	1

x	x'
0	1
1	0

◊

In the light of these last comments, it is of interest to view Example 12 in relation to switching theory.

Example 15

Consider the set $\mathfrak{F}_n$ of all switching functions in n variables; i.e., the collection of all functions $\{0, 1\}^n \to \{0, 1\}$. Since each function f is a characteristic function, we have that the map

$$f \mapsto \operatorname{supp}(f) = \{(x_1, \ldots, x_n) \mid f(x_1, \ldots, x_n) = 1\}$$

is a bijection between $\mathfrak{F}_n$ and $\mathcal{P}(\{0, 1\}^n)$. Referring to Example 12, we may turn $\mathfrak{F}_n$ into a Boolean algebra by setting

$$f_1 \wedge f_2 = f_1 \text{ AND } f_2; f_1 \vee f_2 = f_1 \text{ OR } f_2, \text{ and } f_1' = \overline{f_1}$$

since we have

$$\operatorname{supp}(f_1 \text{ AND } f_2) = \operatorname{supp}(f_1) \cap \operatorname{supp}(f_2)$$
$$\operatorname{supp}(f_1 \text{ OR } f_2) = \operatorname{supp}(f_1) \cup \operatorname{supp}(f_2)$$
$$\operatorname{supp}(\overline{f}) = \{0, 1\}^n \backslash \operatorname{supp}(f).$$

◊

Having related switching theory to Boolean algebra, let us now relate automata theory to lattices. We start by showing that the equivalence relations on a set form a lattice, and then relate this lattice to series and parallel composition of automata.

DEFINITION 9

Let E_1 and E_2 be equivalence relations on a set S. Then we define two new relations on S by the rules:

$$x(E_1 \cdot E_2)\widehat{x} \Longleftrightarrow xE_1\widehat{x} \text{ and } xE_2\widehat{x}$$

$$x(E_1 + E_2)\widehat{x} \Longleftrightarrow x = \widehat{x} \text{ or there exists a sequence}$$
$$x_1, \ldots, x_n (n \geq 2) \text{ of elements of } S, \text{ and}$$
$$j_1, \ldots, j_{n-1} \text{ of elements of } \{1, 2\} \text{ such}$$
$$\text{that } x = x_1 E_{j_1} x_2 E_{j_2} \ldots E_{j_{n-1}} x_n = \widehat{x}$$

Then $E_1 \cdot E_2$ and $E_1 + E_2$ are both equivalence relations and we have the result:

LEMMA 3

Let $\mathcal{E}(S)$ be the set of equivalence relations on S. Then $(\mathcal{E}(S), \cdot, +)$ is a lattice.

Proof

(L1) is obvious. We prove that $E_1 \cdot (E_1 + E_2) = E_1$ to give the flavor of the other verifications:

Certainly $xE_1\widehat{x} \Longrightarrow x(E_1 + E_2)\widehat{x}$.

Thus $[xE_1\widehat{x} \text{ and } x(E_1 + E_2)\widehat{x}] \Longleftrightarrow x_1 E_1\widehat{x}$, as was to be shown.   □

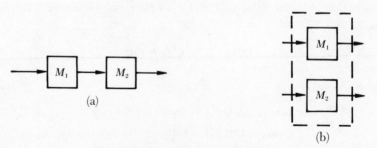

Figure 2–56   (a) Series; (b) parallel.

We now state the definition of series and parallel composition of machines, being motivated by Figure 2–56.

DEFINITION 10

Let $M_1 = (Q_1, X_1, Y_1, \delta_1, \beta_1)$ and $M_2 = (Q_2, X_2, Y_2, \delta_2, \beta_2)$ be two automata.

(a) If $Y_1 = X_2$, we define their **series composition** to be the machine

$$M_3 = (Q_1 \times Q_2, X_1, Y_2, \delta_3, \beta_3)$$

where $\qquad \delta_3((q_1, q_2), x_1) = (\delta_1(q_1, x_1), \delta_2(q_2, \beta_1(q_1))$

and $\qquad \beta_3(q_1, q_2) = \beta_2(q_2)$

(b) Regardless of Y_1 and X_2, we define their **parallel composition** to be the machine

$$M_4 = (Q_1 \times Q_2, X_1 \times X_2, Y_1 \times Y_2, \delta_4, \beta_4)$$

where $\quad \delta_4((q_1, q_2), (x_1, x_2)) = (\delta_1(q_1, x_1), \delta_2(q_2, x_2))$

and $\qquad \beta_4(q_1, q_2) = (\beta_1(q_1), \beta_2(q_2))$ $\qquad\qquad\qquad$ ○

DEFINITION 11

We say that an equivalence relation E on the state set Q of an automaton $M = (Q, X, Y, \delta, \beta)$ has the **substitution property** if E is compatible with $\delta(\cdot, x): Q \to Q$ for each x in X, that is, if $qE\widehat{q}$ then $\delta(q, x)E\,\delta(\widehat{q}, x)$ for each x in X. $\qquad\qquad\qquad$ ○

Let us see how this definition relates to series and parallel composition:

Example 16

Let us take $M_1 = M_2 = M(\mathbf{Z}_2)$, so that both have $X = Y = Q = \{0, 1\}$, $\delta(q, x) = q \oplus x$, and $\beta(q) = q$. Then δ_3 for the series connection is specified by the display

q \ x	0	1
00	00	10
01	01	11
10	11	01
11	10	00

Note that the equivalence relation E_1 with partition $(\{00, 01\}, \{10, 11\})$ corresponding to states of M_1 has the substitution property.

For the parallel connection, δ_4 is specified by the display

q \ x	00	01	10	11
00	00	01	10	11
01	01	00	11	10
10	10	11	00	01
11	11	10	01	00

In this case, not only does E_1 have the substitution property, but so does E_2, whose partition is $(\{00, 10\}, \{01, 11\})$ corresponding to states of M_2. Note that $E_1 \cdot E_2 = 0$, the equivalence relation $x0\widehat{x} \Leftrightarrow x = \widehat{x}$. ◊

This correspondence between states of component machines and blocks of a partition with the substitution property holds in general, since the following results are obvious by inspection.

PROPOSITION 4

Let M_3 be the series composition of M_1 and M_2, as in Definition 10a. Then the equivalence relation on Q_3 defined by

$$(q_1, q_2)E_1(\widehat{q}_1, \widehat{q}_2) \Leftrightarrow q_1 = \widehat{q}_1$$

satisfies the substitution property. □

PROPOSITION 5

Let M_4 be the parallel composition of M_1 and M_2, as in Definition 10b. Then the equivalence relations on Q_4 defined by

$$(q_1, q_2)E_1(\widehat{q}_1, \widehat{q}_2) \Leftrightarrow q_1 = \widehat{q}_1$$

and
$$(q_1, q_2)E_2(\widehat{q}_1, \widehat{q}_2) \Leftrightarrow q_2 = \widehat{q}_2$$

both have the substitution property, and, moreover, satisfy $E_1 \cdot E_2 = 0$. □

To conclude this section we turn to one of the most famous equivalence relations, that which tells us when two sets may be thought of as having the same number of elements, and relate one of its properties to the automata theory of Section 2–1.

DEFINITION 12

Two sets X and Y **have the same cardinal number** if and only if there is
a bijection $f: X \to Y$, and we write $|X| = |Y|$.   ○

The property of having the same cardinal number (i.e., two sets are
related if and only if $|X| = |Y|$) is indeed an equivalence relation:

Reflexivity: $|X| = |X|$ since the identity function id_X is a bijection.

Symmetry: $|X| = |Y| \Rightarrow |Y| = |X|$ since whenever $f: X \to Y$ is a bijec-
tion, its inverse $f^{-1}: Y \to X$ is defined and is a bijection, too.

Transitivity: $|X| = |Y|$ and $|Y| = |Z| \Rightarrow |X| = |Z|$ since whenever
$f: X \to Y$ and $g: Y \to Z$ are bijections, so is their composition $g \circ f: X \to Z$.

We often refer to the equivalence class of a set under this relation as the
cardinal number of the class, and denote this by $|X|$.

Consider the list of sets:

$$[0] = \varnothing$$
$$[1] = \{0\}$$
$$[2] = \{0, 1\}$$
$$\vdots$$
$$[n] = [n - 1] \cup \{n - 1\} \qquad n \in \mathbf{N}$$

We say that a set X is **finite** iff $|X| = |[n]|$ for some $n \in \mathbf{N}$; and it is clear
that this is consistent with our usual usage of writing $|X| = n$, and saying
that X has n elements. We say that X is **infinite** if it is not finite. The amazing
thing about Definition 12 is that it gives us a theory of infinite numbers,
as well as our familiar theory of finite integers. We owe this theory to Georg
Cantor, who showed that not all infinities are the same. In Theorem 6, we
shall present his famous diagonal argument, which shows that the cardinality
of the real numbers is essentially larger than the cardinality of the integers,
and then deduce that, for given finite sets X and Y, most behaviors $f: X^* \to Y$
(Section 2–1) do not have finite-state realizations.

Clearly $\mathbf{N}$ is infinite, and we use the symbol $\aleph_0$ (read: aleph-null) to
denote $|\mathbf{N}|$. Surprisingly, our intuition with finite sets can be dangerously
misleading when we come to consider infinite sets; an infinite set A may be
a *proper* subset of an infinite set B and yet have the *same* cardinality as B.
For example, $|\mathbf{N}| = |\mathbf{Z}|$, since the map $h: \mathbf{N} \to \mathbf{Z}$ for which

$$h(m) = \begin{cases} n & \text{if } m = 2n \\ -n & \text{if } m = 2n - 1 \end{cases}$$

is clearly a bijection. (What is its inverse?)

Perhaps even more surprisingly, $|\mathbf{Q}| = \aleph_0$, as can be seen from the possibility of indefinitely continuing the following display of Figure 2–57.

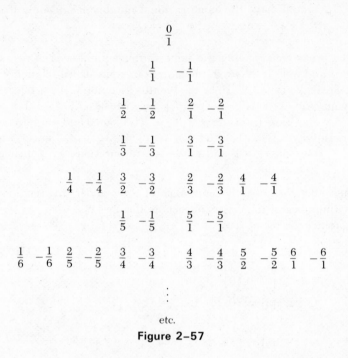

etc.

Figure 2–57

The ith row of this display consists of all the rational numbers of the form a/b or $-a/b$, where the integers $a > 0$ and $b > 0$ have no common factors greater than 1 and $a + b = i$. Clearly, such a display enumerates all the rational numbers without repetition. In fact, Figure 2–58 is a schematic flow diagram for generating the above display and its continuation. (We say that m and n are **coprime** or **relatively prime** if their largest common factor is 1.)

The above examples may make one suspect that all infinite sets have cardinality $\aleph_0$. In fact, this is not so, as Cantor first showed by essentially the following "diagonal" argument:

THEOREM 6

The cardinality $c = |\mathbf{R}|$ of the real numbers is strictly greater than the cardinality $\aleph_0$ of the natural numbers.

Proof

Suppose that we have any map $\mathbf{N} \to \mathbf{R}$ of the natural numbers into the reals. We prove that it cannot be onto (and thus certainly cannot be a bijection)

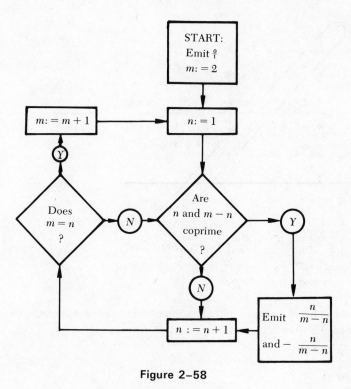

Figure 2–58

to deduce that $|\mathbf{R}|$, even though infinite, cannot equal $\aleph_0$. In fact, we prove an even stronger result; that no map $k:\mathbf{N} \to (0, 1)$ can map $\mathbf{N}$ onto the set of real numbers $\{x \in \mathbf{R} \,|\, 0 < x < 1\}$ bounded by 0 and 1. Suppose that

$$k(n) = 0 \cdot k_{n0}k_{n1}k_{n2} \ldots k_{nn} \ldots$$

where $0 \le k_{nj} \le 9$ is the jth digit of the decimal expansion of $k(n)$. Then we may construct the real number

$$r = 0.r_1r_2r_3 \ldots r_n \ldots$$

by the rule
$$r_n = \begin{cases} 1 \text{ if } k_{nn} \ne 1 \\ 2 \text{ if } k_{nn} = 1 \end{cases}$$

That is, r is formed from the diagonal of the array of Figure 2–59 by altering its digits according to the above rule.

But this real number cannot equal $k(n)$ for any n, since r differs from $k(n)$ in (at least) the digit r_n of its decimal expansion. Thus $r \notin k(\mathbf{N})$, and so k

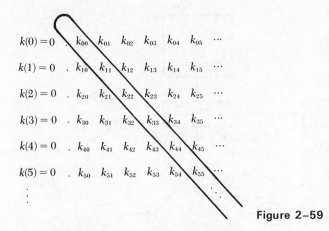

Figure 2–59

is not onto. But since k was *any* map $\mathbf{N} \to (0, 1)$, it follows that there can be *no* bijection $\mathbf{N} \to \mathbf{R}$. Thus, $|\mathbf{R}| \neq \aleph_0$, and so we introduce the new symbol c to denote the cardinality of $\mathbf{R}$. $\square$

As our first application of the above technique to automata theory, we return to the behaviors of Definition 2–1–6 to prove:

THEOREM 7

For given finite sets X and Y, most behaviors $f\colon X^* \to Y$ do not have finite-state realizations, in the precise sense that the set of behaviors has cardinality c, while the set of essentially distinct realizations only has cardinality $\aleph_0$.

Proof

Let w_0, w_1, w_2, w_3, . . . be any enumeration of X^*, i.e., $w_i \in X^*$ for $i = 0$, 1, 2, . . . (Exercise 12). Any function $f\colon X^* \to Y$ may then be uniquely represented by the infinite sequence

$$f(w_0)f(w_1)f(w_2)f(w_3) \cdot \cdot \cdot$$

of elements of Y. If $Y = \{ y_1, y_2, \ldots, y_{N'} \}$, we may regard these sequences as radix-N' expansions of real numbers between 0 and 1. Every real number thus yields one (or two—why and when?) behavior(s), and it is therefore clear that the set of behaviors has cardinality c.

On the other hand, consider any machine $M = \{ Q, X, Y, \delta, \beta \}$. Clearly, the way we name the states does not affect the behavior of the machine, and so we shall always label the state set of an n-state M as $\{ q_0, q_1, \ldots, q_{n-1} \}$, with M_{q_0} being the behavior of interest to us.

Now list the n-state machines (Exercise 13) in any convenient order as

$$M^{n1}, M^{n2}, M^{n3}, \ldots, M^{n\alpha_n}$$

Then clearly the sequence

1-state machines   2-state machines

$$\overbrace{M^{11}, M^{12}, \ldots, M^{1\alpha_1}}, \ \overbrace{M^{21}, M^{22}, \ldots, M^{2\alpha_2}},$$

3-state machines $\ldots$ n-state machines

$$\overbrace{M^{31}, M^{32}, \ldots, M^{3\alpha_3}}, \ldots, \overbrace{M^{n1}, M^{n2}, \ldots, M^{n\alpha_n}}, \ldots$$

gives us an enumeration of all the finite-state machines with input set X and output set Y. Thus, the set of all machines has cardinality $\aleph_0$, and the map

$$\text{finite-state machines} \to \text{behaviors}: (M, q_0) \mapsto M_{q_0}$$

cannot be onto; and, in fact, it follows that most behaviors $f: X^* \to Y$ do not have finite-state realizations, i.e., are not of the form M_{q_0} for any finite state M. However, we shall see in the next section that every behavior does have a realization, even though that realization will usually have an infinite set of states. □

One of the most important applications of diagonal arguments in the theory of computation is in showing that there is no effective procedure for telling, given an arbitrary Turing machine (computer) Z and an arbitrary input string w, whether or not Z ever *halts* for input data w. Thus, after our study of realization, we shall turn in Chapter 3 to a general overview of the concept of computation, and of equivalences between different modes of computation, which will provide a setting for the theory of Turing machines.

EXERCISES FOR SECTION 2–4

1.   Let R be the binary relation on **Q** given by $R = \mathbf{Z} \times \mathbf{Z}_+$. Which of the following are true?
   (a) $3R6$
   (b) $(-3)R6$
   (c) $(-3)R(-6)$
   (d) $(1/2)R5$
   (e) $(1/3)R(1/3)$
2.   Let R be the binary relation on **Q** given by

$$R = \{(p/q, r/s) \mid p, r \in \mathbf{Z}; \ q, s \in \mathbf{Z}_+ \text{ and } ps = rq\}$$

or, in other words, by

$$R = \{(p/q, r/s) \mid p/q \in \mathbf{Q}, \ r/s \in \mathbf{Q}, \ \text{and} \ p/q = r/s\}$$

Which of the following are true?
(a) $(2/1)R(10/5)$
(b) $(3/4)R(6/9)$
(c) $(-7/8)R(7/8)$

3. Let R be the binary relation on $\mathbf{Q}$ given by the function $R: \mathbf{Q} \times \mathbf{Q} \to \{0, 1\}$ defined as

$$R(p/q, r/s) = \begin{cases} 0 \ \text{if} \ ps - rq \neq 0 \\ 1 \ \text{if} \ ps - rq = 0 \end{cases}$$

Which of the following are true?
(a) $(2/1)R(10/5)$
(b) $(3/4)R(6/9)$
(c) $(-7/8)R(7/8)$

4. Let R be the binary relation on $\mathbf{Q}$ given by $R: \mathbf{Q} \to \mathcal{P}(\mathbf{Q}): p/q \mapsto \{mp/q \mid m \in \mathbf{Z}\}$.

Which of the following are true?
(a) $(6/1)R(10/1)$
(b) $(6/1)R(0/1)$
(c) $(1/2)R(10/2)$
(d) $(1/2)R(5/1)$
(e) $(2/3)R(-2/3)$

5. Determine whether or not the binary relation on $\mathbf{Z}$ given by $R = \{(x, y) \mid x, y \in \mathbf{Z}$ and $x - y$ is odd$\}$ is an equivalence relation.

6. Prove for any fixed $m \in \mathbf{Z}$ that the binary relation on $\mathbf{Z}$ given by $\sim_m = \{(x, y) \mid x, y \in \mathbf{Z}$ and $x - y$ is a multiple of $m\}$ is an equivalence relation.

7. For the equivalence relation on $\mathbf{Q}$ given by

$$\equiv \ = \{(p/q, r/s) \mid p, r \in \mathbf{Z}; \ q, s \in \mathbf{Z}_+ \ \text{and} \ pr = qs\},$$

enumerate the following equivalence classes modulo $\equiv$.
(a) $[1/3]_\equiv$
(b) $[-2/5]_\equiv$
(c) $[4/12]_\equiv$

8. Suppose that $x \sim_5 y$ if and only if $x - y$ is a multiple of 5. List the equivalence classes of $\mathbf{Z}$ modulo $\sim_5$.

9. What are the elements of the sets
(a) $\mathbf{Z}/\sim_0$?
(b) $\mathbf{Z}/\sim_1$?

10. For $\mathbf{Z}_m$, prove that $x \sim_m y$ if and only if there exists some $k \in \mathbf{Z}$ such that $y = x + km$.

11. Give a flow diagram for enumerating $\mathbf{N}^2 = \mathbf{N} \times \mathbf{N}$. Then prove by induction that $|\mathbf{N}^n| = \aleph_0$ for every $n \in \mathbf{Z}_+$.

12. Prove that if $X = \{x_1, x_2, \ldots, x_N\}$, then the map

$$X^* \to \mathbf{N} : x_{i_m} x_{i_{m-1}} \cdots x_{i_1} \mapsto \sum_{j=1}^{m} i_j \cdot N^{j-1}$$

(which we decree to send Λ to 0) is a bijection. Thus, for finite X, we have $|X^*| = \aleph_0$.

13.   Verify that there are "only" $\alpha_n = (n^N \cdot N')^n$ machines with $Q = \{q_0, \ldots, q_{n-1}\}$, $X = \{x_1, x_2, \ldots, x_N\}$ and $Y = \{y_1, \ldots, y_{N'}\}$.

14.   Verify B1, B3, and B5 for the 2-element Boolean algebra of Example 14.

15.   Prove that the set of all equivalence relations with the substitution property on the state set of an automaton forms a lattice under $\cdot$ and $+$.

2-5   Building Automata with Specified Behavior

One of the most important problems in computer science is to go from the description of a problem to the description of a program for solving it. Moreover, the approach of computer science is not to seek *ad hoc* solutions to individual problems as they arise, but rather to seek general "recipes" or **algorithms** for solving all of a large class of problems. In this section we shall consider the problem of defining the state set and dynamics of automata with specified input-output behavior, just as in Section 4–5 we shall study **compilers** which can take any program written in one programming language and transform it into an equivalent program in another language.

Let us start by recalling the general realization problem, illustrate how it may be solved in an *ad hoc* manner in three specific examples, and then adumbrate the general solution.

In Section 2–1 we saw how to associate (Definition 5) with any machine M and state q the function $M_q : X^* \to Y : w \mapsto \beta[\delta^*(q, w)]$, so that $M_q(w)$ is the output emitted by M after reading string w, if started in state q. We then stated (Definition 6) the **realization problem** to be: Given any behavior (i.e., any function $f : X^* \to Y$), find a machine (state-output automaton) M and a state q of M such that $M_q = f : X^* \to Y$. The "initialized" machine (M, q) is then called a **realization** of f.

We shall see that every $f : X^* \to Y$ has a realization, even though we know (Theorem 2–4–7) that, even if X and Y are both finite sets, most behaviors do not have a *finite-state* realization. However, before proceeding to the general theory, we give three examples in which finite-state realizations are possible, with an *ad hoc* construction in each case.

Example 1

The behavior $f_1 : \{0, 1\}^* \to \{0, 1\}$ is defined by

$$f_1(w) = \begin{cases} 1 & \text{if } w = w'001 \text{ for some } w' \in X^* \\ 0 & \text{if not} \end{cases}$$

To solve this problem, we shall directly construct a machine using the switching circuitry introduced in Section 2–3. Clearly, all our machine has to do is remember the last 3-element substring of its input string, and then emit an output 1 whenever that substring is 001. To store the last three digits, we simply connect three delay elements in series, as shown in Figure 2–60.

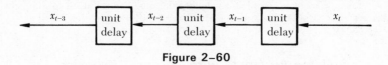

Figure 2–60

Since we would like to produce an output of 1 when $x_{t-3} = 0$ AND $x_{t-2} = 0$ AND $x_{t-1} = 1$, we may write

$$y = \bar{x}_{t-3} \wedge \bar{x}_{t-2} \wedge x_{t-1}$$

and the network for the machine is shown in Figure 2–61.

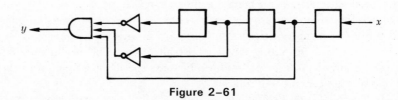

Figure 2–61

Note: A circuit of this type is usually referred to as a **shift register.** [We shall study *linear* shift registers in Section 7–4, and study their use in coding theory in Chapter 8.]

If we label the state in which $x_{t-3} = i$, $x_{t-2} = j$ and $x_{t-1} = k$ as ijk, we may note that this machine M_1 has the state-output graph of Figure 2–62.

We have specified machine M^1, but have yet to specify the q for which $M_q^1 = f_1$. Note that $M_q^1(w) = f_1(w)$ for *any* q so long as $\ell(w) \geq 3$. The problem is to choose an initial state which does not yield spurious 1 outputs for w with $\ell(w) \leq 2$. For this reason 000 is unsatisfactory, since $M_{000}^1(1) = 1$ whereas $f_1(1) = 0$. In fact, there are only two acceptable choices:

$$f_1 = M_{100}^1 = M_{111}^1 \qquad\qquad \Diamond$$

Example 2

The behavior $f_2 : \{0, 1\}^* \to \{0, 1\}$ is defined by

$$f_2(w) = \begin{cases} 1 \text{ if } w = w'11 \text{ for some } w' \text{ in } X^* \\ 0 \text{ if not} \end{cases}$$

This time we proceed directly to construct a state graph for the desired machine M^2. A little thought shows that only three states are required:

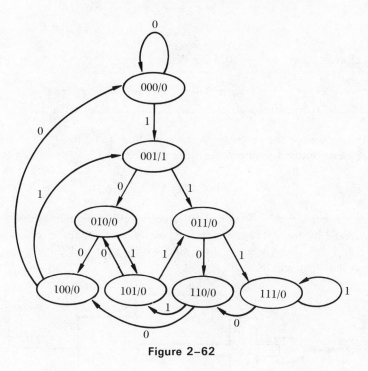

Figure 2–62

q_0—the initial state which records that either we have just started or we have just seen a 0.

q_1—the state which records that we have only seen a single 1 since the last 0 (or since we started).

q_2—the "accepting" state with output 1 which records that the last two inputs were both 1's.

The appropriate relations between these states are then shown in the state graph of Figure 2–63, and we see that $f_2 = M_{q_0}^2$.   ◊

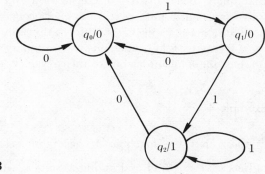

Figure 2–63

Example 3

The behavior $f_3 : \{0, 1\}^* \rightarrow \{0, 1\}$ is defined by

$$f_3(w) = \begin{cases} 1 \text{ if } w = w'001 \text{ or } w'11 \text{ for some } w' \text{ in } X^* \\ 0 \text{ if not} \end{cases}$$

In this case, we use the machine M^1 we have built to realize f_1, the machine M^2 we have built to realize f_2, and the fact that

$$f_3(w) = f_1(w) \lor f_2(w)$$

(where we recall that $x_1 \lor x_2 = 1$ iff either x_1 OR x_2 equals 1) to see that f_3 is realized by state $(111, q_0)$ of M^3, where M^3 is the parallel composition of M^1 and M^2 with common input and with output fed through an OR gate, as shown in Figure 2–64. ◊

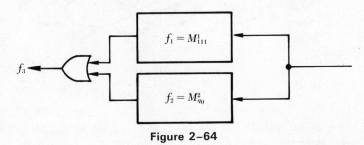

Figure 2–64

We have thus seen three methods for building realizations; by the switching circuit methods of Section 2–3, by the construction of a minimal state graph, and by parallel composition (as further discussed in Section 5–2) of simpler machines which are "already available." In the rest of this section we shall concentrate on finding general procedures for passing from f to a minimal realization of f, i.e., an **initialized machine** (M, q) such that $M_q = f$ while M has, in a sense we shall make precise, "as few states as possible."

In Theorem 2–4–3 we gave a general set-theoretic argument which shows that "most" behaviors $X^* \rightarrow Y$, even for a *fixed* finite X and Y, do not have finite-state realizations. Here, let us give a concrete example by showing that no finite-state machine can multiply arbitrarily large numbers in the sense that, given the n low-order bits of two binary numbers, the machine will produce the n low-order bits of their product as an output string.

Example 4

Suppose that the machine M has input set $X = \left\{ \begin{pmatrix} 0 \\ 0 \end{pmatrix}, \begin{pmatrix} 0 \\ 1 \end{pmatrix}, \begin{pmatrix} 1 \\ 0 \end{pmatrix}, \begin{pmatrix} 1 \\ 1 \end{pmatrix} \right\}$, output set $Y = \{0, 1\}$ and an initial state q_0 with the behavior $f_m : X^* \rightarrow Y$

defined by

$$f_m\left(\binom{x_1}{x_1'}\binom{x_2}{x_2'}\cdots\binom{x_n}{x_n'}\right) = \text{the coefficient of } 2^{n-1} \text{ in the product}$$

$$\text{of } \sum_{j=1}^{n} x_j 2^{j-1} \text{ and } \sum_{k=1}^{n} x_k' 2^{k-1}$$

$$\left(\text{We call } x_1 x_2 \ldots x_n \text{ the "reversed binary string" encoding of } \sum_{j=1}^{n} x_j 2^{j-1}.\right)$$

We will show that, no matter how large an integer N we choose, M has at least N states. Noting, for any j, that $0^N 10^j$ is a reversed binary string encoding of the number 2^N, we see that we must have

$$M_{q_0}\left(\binom{0}{0}^N\binom{1}{1}\binom{0}{0}^j\right) = \begin{cases} 1 \text{ if } j = N \\ 0 \text{ if not} \end{cases}$$

since this is to be the coefficient of 2^{N+j} in the product 2^{2N} of 2^N and 2^N, which has the reversed binary string $0^{2N}1$.

Now let $q^{(j)} = \delta^*\left(q_0, \binom{0}{0}^N\binom{1}{1}\binom{0}{0}^j\right)$. We see from Figure 2–65 that,

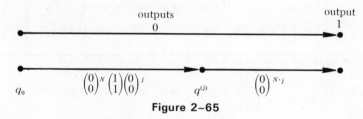

Figure 2–65

for each $j < N$, each $q^{(j)}$ has the property that

$$M_{q^{(j)}}\left(\binom{0}{0}^k\right) = \begin{cases} 1 \text{ if } k = N - j \\ 0 \text{ if not} \end{cases}$$

Since for $j = 0, 1, 2, \ldots, N$ each $q^{(j)}$ has a distinct response function, we conclude that the states $q^{(j)}$ are all distinct, and thus M has at least N states. But our choice of N was arbitrary, and so we conclude that M—and thus *any* realization of f_m—has an infinite set of states.   ◊

Having seen that our quest for a minimal realization may not always end in a finite-state realization, let us now embark on that quest by studying the **state-merging technique,** which converts any realization into a minimal realization. When we have mastered this technique, we shall see how we may find a realization "for free" (albeit an uneconomical one), and then see how the latter procedure may be combined with state-merging into a streamlined process for finding the minimal realization directly.

Example 5

Suppose we are given the machine M of Figure 2–66. We may note that if we start in state q_0 or q_1, we stay in $\{q_0, q_1\}$ so long as all inputs are 0, while

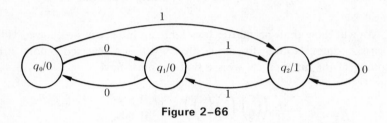

Figure 2–66

a 1 flips us into $\{q_2\}$. Conversely, if we start in q_2, we do not return to $\{q_0, q_1\}$ until an input 1 is received. Thus, we see that

$$\delta^*(q_0, w) = q_2 \text{ iff } w \text{ contains an odd number of 1's}$$
$$\delta^*(q_1, w) = q_2 \text{ iff } w \text{ contains an odd number of 1's}$$
$$\delta^*(q_2, w) = q_2 \text{ iff } w \text{ contains an even number of 1's}$$

and since q_2 is the only state with output 1, we deduce that

$$M_{q_0}(w) = \begin{cases} 1 \text{ if } w \text{ contains an odd number of 1's} \\ 0 \text{ if not} \end{cases}$$
$$M_{q_1} = M_{q_0}$$
$$M_{q_2} = 1 - M_{q_0}$$

Thus, although M has three states, it only has two distinct behaviors. This suggests that we can obtain a minimal machine by merging states with the same behavior. If we merge q_0 and q_1 into a single state q_0, and relabel q_2 as $\widehat{q}_2$, then M collapses into the 2-state machine $\widehat{M}$ of Figure 2–67, where

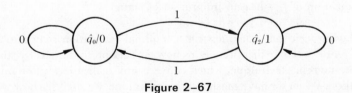

Figure 2–67

we note that every output and state-transition is consistent with the merging of q_0 and q_1 in M. ◊

In fact, the method always works—given any machine M, we can always form a new machine, called the *reduced form of M,* which exhibits exactly the same behaviors as M, but has only one state for each distinct behavior.

THEOREM 1 (THE STATE-MERGING THEOREM)

Given a machine $M = (Q, X, Y, \delta, \beta)$, we define its **reduced state set** to be

$$\widehat{Q} = Q/\sim$$

where $\sim$ is the **indistinguishability relation** on Q defined by $q_1 \sim q_2 \Leftrightarrow M_{q_1} = M_{q_2}$. Then $\sim$ is compatible with both δ and β, so that we may define

$$\widehat{\delta}:\widehat{Q} \times X \to \widehat{Q}:([q], x) \mapsto [\delta(q, x)]$$
$$\widehat{\beta}:\widehat{Q} \to Y:[q] \mapsto \beta(q)$$

to obtain $\widehat{M} = (\widehat{Q}, X, Y, \widehat{\delta}, \widehat{\beta})$, called the **reduced form** of M, which has the property that $\widehat{M}_{[q]} = M_q$ for each q in Q; and thus, no two states of $\widehat{M}$ are indistinguishable.

Proof

(i) It is immediately proved that $\sim$ is an equivalence relation:
  I. $M_q = M_q$
  II. $M_{q_1} = M_{q_2} \Rightarrow M_{q_2} = M_{q_1}$
  III. $M_{q_1} = M_{q_2}$ and $M_{q_2} = M_{q_3} \Rightarrow M_{q_1} = M_{q_3}$
  Thus, $\widehat{Q} = Q/\sim$ is indeed well-defined and has one element $[q]$ for each distinct collection of states indistinguishable from a given state:

$$[q_1] = [q_2] \Leftrightarrow M_{q_1} = M_{q_2}$$

(ii) To see that $\sim$ is compatible with δ, we must show that for all q_1, q_2 in Q, and all x in X, we have that $q_1 \sim q_2 \Rightarrow \delta(q_1, x) \sim \delta(q_2, x)$; that is,

$$M_{q_1} = M_{q_2} \Rightarrow M_{\delta(q_1,x)} = M_{\delta(q_2,x)}$$

But

$$M_{\delta(q_1,x)}(w') = M_{q_1}(xw')$$

so that

$$M_{q_1} = M_{q_2} \Rightarrow M_{q_1}(w) = M_{q_2}(w) \text{ for all } w \text{ in } X^*.$$

Hence,

$$M_{q_1}(xw') = M_{q_2}(xw') \text{ for all } w' \text{ in } X^*$$
$$\Rightarrow M_{\delta(q_1,x)}(w') = M_{\delta(q_2,x)}(w') \text{ for all } w' \text{ in } X^*$$
$$\Rightarrow M_{\delta(q_1,x)} = M_{\delta(q_2,x)}$$

Thus, we can indeed define the function $\widehat{\delta}:\widehat{Q} \times X \to \widehat{Q}$ by

$$\widehat{\delta}([q], x) = [\delta(q, x)]$$

(iii) To see that $\sim$ is compatible with β, we simply note that

$$[q_1] = [q_2] \Rightarrow M_{q_1} = M_{q_2} \Rightarrow M_{q_1}(\Lambda) = M_{q_2}(\Lambda) \Rightarrow \beta(q_1) = \beta(q_2)$$

Thus, we can indeed define the function $\widehat{\beta}:\widehat{Q} \to Y$ by

$$\widehat{\beta}([q]) = \beta(q)$$

(iv) We next show that $\widehat{M}_{[q]} = M_q$ for each q in Q. We proceed by proving that $\widehat{M}_{[q]}(w) = M_q(w)$, for all w in X^*, by induction on the length of w.

Basis Step.

$$\widehat{M}_{[q]}(\Lambda) = \widehat{\beta}([q]) \text{ by definition of } \widehat{M}_{[q]}$$
$$= \beta(q) \quad \text{by (iii)}$$
$$= M_q(\Lambda) \text{ by definition of } M_q$$

Induction Step. A little subtlety is required here. To deduce that $M_{[q]}(xw) = M_q(xw)$ for a *given* q in Q and any x in X, we assume as our induction hypothesis that it has already been established that $\widehat{M}_{[q']}(w) = M_{q'}(w)$ for *all* q' in Q. The confirmation of the induction step is then immediate, on taking $q' = \delta(q, x)$, as follows:

$$\widehat{M}_{[q]}(xw) = \widehat{M}_{\delta([q],x)}(w) = \widehat{M}_{[\delta(q,x)]}(w) = \widehat{M}_{[q']}(w) = M_{q'}(w)$$
$$= M_{\delta(q,x)}(w) = M_q(xw)$$

(v) Finally, we must check that no two states of $\widehat{M}$ are indistinguishable. But this is immediate, for if $\widehat{M}_{[q_1]} = \widehat{M}_{[q_2]}$, then (iv) tells us that $M_{q_1} = M_{q_2}$, so that we have $[q_1] = [q_2]$; i.e., states of $\widehat{M}$ cannot be indistinguishable unless they are the same. □

The reader should check that Theorem 1 does indeed yield the passage from M to $\widehat{M}$ in Example 5.

In fact, Theorem 1 is not as informative as it could be. Thus, we make the following definition:

DEFINITION 1

A machine $M = (Q, X, Y, \delta, \beta)$ is **observable** if no two distinct states are indistinguishable, i.e., if

$$M_q = M_{q'} \Leftrightarrow q = q' \text{ for all } q, q' \text{ in } Q \qquad \bigcirc$$

Then Theorem 1 asserts that the reduced form of a machine is observable. But, in fact, the state-merging procedure has the stronger property that it *preserves state transitions,* for, by the definition of $\widehat{\delta}$, we have

$$\widehat{\delta}([q], x) = [\delta(q, x)]$$

This property of the map $q \mapsto [q]$ is sufficiently important to be enshrined in the general notion of a *dynamorphism.*

DEFINITION 2

A map $h: Q \to Q'$ from the state set Q of one machine $M = (Q, X, Y, \delta, \beta)$ to the state set Q' of a machine $M' = (Q', X, Y', \delta', \beta')$ is said to be a **dynamorphism** if it preserves state-transitions; i.e., if

$$\delta'(h(q), x) = h(\delta(q, x)) \quad \text{for all } q \text{ in } Q, x \text{ in } X$$

[The word dynamorphism is a contraction for "dynamic homomorphism"— we only demand that h respect the dynamics induced by the action of X, without regard for outputs.] If, moreover, $Y = Y'$ and we have

$$\beta'(h(q)) = \beta(q) \text{ for all } q \text{ in } Q,$$

then we call h an **(i/o)-homomorphism** (i/o is short for input-output). $\bigcirc$

We can now restate Theorem 1 in the more informative form of the next corollary.

COROLLARY 2

Given any machine $M = (Q, X, Y, \delta, \beta)$, its reduced form $\widehat{M} = (\widehat{Q}, X, Y, \widehat{\delta}, \widehat{\beta})$ is observable, and the map $q \mapsto [q]$ is an (i/o)-homomorphism from M to $\widehat{M}$. $\square$

The reader should also note (Exercise 4) the following useful fact.

LEMMA 3

If h is an (i/o)-homomorphism from M to M', then $M_q = M'_{h(q)}$ for all states q of M. $\quad\square$

An important notion which complements that of observability (are two states doing the same job?) is that of reachability (can every state get to do its job?):

DEFINITION 3

We say state q_2 is **reachable from** state q_1 of machine M if and only if for at least one w in X^* we have

$$\delta^*(q_1, w) = q_2$$

Furthermore, we say that the initialized machine (M, q_0) is **reachable** if and only if all states of M are reachable from q_0. $\quad\bigcirc$

Dynamorphisms preserve reachability of pairs of states:

LEMMA 4

If h is a dynamorphism from M to M', and if q_2 is reachable from q_1 in M, so that $\delta^*(q_1, w) = q_2$ for some w in X^*, then $(\delta')^*(h(q_1), w) = h(q_2)$, and so $h(q_2)$ is reachable from $h(q_1)$. In particular, if h is a surjection and if (M, q_0) is reachable, then for $h(q_0) = q'_0$, (M', q'_0) must be reachable, too (Exercise 5). $\quad\square$

Since the map $q \mapsto [q]$ of state-merging is clearly a surjection, we now deduce:

COROLLARY 5

If the machine (M, q_0) is reachable, then so is its reduced form. $\quad\square$

Given any *initialized* machine (M, q_0), we may form

$$M^{(q_0)} = (r(q_0), X, Y, \delta_1, \beta_1)$$

where $r(q_0)$ is the set of all states reachable from q_0;

$$\delta_1(q, x) = \delta(q, x) \quad \text{for all } q \text{ in } r(q_0) \text{ and } x \text{ in } X$$

and

$$\beta_1(q) = \beta(q) \quad \text{for all } q \text{ in } r(q_0)$$

[Why must $\delta_1(q, x)$ be in $r(q_0)$?] We define the **minimized form** of (M, q_0) to be the reduced form of $M^{(q_0)}$, and Corollaries 2 and 5 then yield:

COROLLARY 6

The minimized form of any machine is reachable and observable.   ☐

The above discussion holds whether or not the machines are finite-state. Let us now see how the reduction process for *any* machine can be replaced by a process of successive approximations; and let us see that if $\widehat{Q}$ is a finite set for which we can guarantee that $|\widehat{Q}| \leq N$, then this series of approximations will successfully terminate in at most N steps.

To go from Q to $\widehat{Q}$, we merge states which are completely indistinguishable. To obtain our kth approximation Q_k of $\widehat{Q}$, we only merge those states which cannot be distinguished in "experiments" of length $\leq k$ steps:

Given $M = (Q, X, Y, \delta, \beta)$, we say that two states q_1 and q_2 of Q are **k-indistinguishable,** written $q_1 \sim_k q_2$, iff $M_{q_1}(w) = M_{q_2}(w)$ for all w in X^* of length at most k.

Thus $q_1 \sim_0 q_2$ iff $\beta(q_1) = \beta(q_2)$, while for all integers $k \leq k'$ we have that

$$q_1 \sim_{k'} q_2 \Longrightarrow q_1 \sim_k q_2$$

Setting $Q_k = Q/\sim_k$ for each k in $\mathbf{N}$, with $[q]_k = \{q' | q' \sim_k q\}$, we thus have a well-defined surjection

$$Q_{k'} \twoheadrightarrow Q_k : [q]_{k'} \mapsto [q]_k \text{ whenever } k' \geq k$$

LEMMA 7

$$q_1 \sim_{k+1} q_2 \Leftrightarrow [q_1 \sim_k q_2 \text{ and, for all } x \text{ in } X, \delta(q_1, x) \sim_k \delta(q_2, x)]$$

Proof

$$q_1 \sim_{k+1} q_2 \Leftrightarrow M_{q_1}(w) = M_{q_2}(w) \text{ for all } \ell(w) \leq k + 1$$
$$\Leftrightarrow M_{q_1}(w') = M_{q_2}(w') \text{ and } M_{q_1}(xw') = M_{q_2}(xw')$$
$$\text{for all } x \text{ in } X \text{ and all } \ell(w') \leq k$$
$$\Leftrightarrow q_1 \sim_k q_2 \text{ and, for all } x \text{ in } X, \delta(q_1, x) \sim_k \delta(q_2, x) \qquad ☐$$

LEMMA 8

If $Q_j = Q_{j+1}$, then $Q_j = Q_k$ for all $k \geq j$, and thus $Q_j = \widehat{Q}$.

Proof

Clearly, it suffices to prove that $Q_j = Q_{j+1} \Rightarrow Q_{j+1} = Q_{j+2}$. But if we have $q_1 \sim_j q_2 \Leftrightarrow q_1 \sim_{j+1} q_2$ for *all* q_1 and q_2 in Q, it is immediate from Lemma 7 that $q_1 \sim_{j+1} q_2 \Leftrightarrow q_1 \sim_{j+2} q_2$.   □

LEMMA 9

Suppose that $|\widehat{Q}| \leq N$, where $N \geq 2$. Then $Q_{N-2} = \widehat{Q}$.

Proof

Let j be the largest integer such that $Q_j \neq Q_{j-1}$. Then by Lemma 8, $Q_j = \widehat{Q}$. We will show that $j \leq N - 2$.

If $Q_1 \neq Q_0$, then $|Q_1| \geq |Q_0| + 1$. Proceeding in this way, if $Q_j \neq Q_{j-1}$, then

$$|Q_j| \geq |Q_{j-1}| + 1 \geq |Q_0| + j$$

Since $N \geq |\widehat{Q}| \geq |Q_j|$, we have that

$$N \geq |Q_0| + j$$

or

$$j \leq N - |Q_0|.$$

If $|Q_0| = 1$, then all the states yield the same output and they must all be indistinguishable. Thus, $Q_0 = \widehat{Q}$. If $|Q_0| > 1$, then $j \leq N - 2$.   □

Thus we now have the following informal description of an algorithm for state-merging, which is guaranteed to terminate by Step $N - 2$ if $|\widehat{Q}| \leq N$.

Step 0: Form Q_0 by putting all the states q with the same $\beta(q)$ into the same "barrel." If Q_0 is not "equal" to Q, go to Step 1. If it is "equal", $\widehat{Q} = Q_0$.

Step n + 1: Let $S_1, \ldots, S_k$ be the "barrels" of Q_n. Subdivide each S_j by putting into separate "barrels" any states q_1 and q_2 for which there exists an x in X with $\delta(q_1, x) \in S_\ell$, $\delta(q_2, x) \in S_k$ for $\ell \neq k$. If no S_j is subdivided in this process, stop, with $\widehat{Q} = Q_n$. If at least one S_j is subdivided, the resulting set of "barrels" forms Q_{n+1}. Go to Step $n + 2$.

The above theory tells us, then, that if f has a minimal realization with at most N states, we can obtain it from any other realization in at most $N-2$ iterations of the state-merging algorithm. However, we have yet to show that, given $f:X^* \to Y$, there is a "sneaky" way to get a realization of f. It is so easy to obtain that we shall call it the **free** realization, and denote it F^f. (We shall see that the word "free" has a deeper mathematical interpretation when we study machines in a category in Chapter 9.) The machine F^f simply stores whatever sequence has been applied since it was in its initial state and then operates upon the current sequence with f to obtain its current output; i.e.,

$$F^f = (X^*, X, Y, \mathrm{conc}, f)$$

has the next-state function

$$\mathrm{conc}:X^* \times X \to X^*:(w, x) \mapsto wx$$

and output function

$$f:X^* \to Y$$

Clearly

$$\mathrm{conc}^*:X^* \times X^* \to X^*:(w, w') \mapsto ww'$$

and thus

$$F^f_w(w') = f(\mathrm{conc}^*(w, w')) = f(ww')$$

In particular, $F^f_\Lambda(w') = f(\Lambda w') = f(w')$, so that (F^f, Λ) is indeed a realization (albeit an infinite one) of f.

Example 6

Given the behavior $f:\{0, 1\}^* \to \{0, 1\}$ where

$$f(w) = \begin{cases} 1 & \text{if } w \text{ contains an odd number of 1's} \\ 0 & \text{if not} \end{cases}$$

then a portion of the free realization F^f is shown in Figure 2–68.   ◊

Let us now see how we can apply our state-merging techniques to F^f to obtain the minimal realization of f, which will be denoted by M_f.

We first introduce the notation L_w for the function

$$L_w:X^* \to X^*:w' \mapsto ww'$$

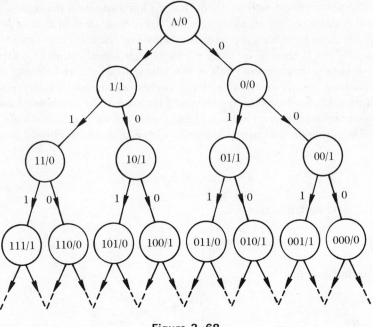

Figure 2–68

of Left concatenation by w. Then we have that

$$F_w^f(w') = f(ww') = f \circ L_w(w')$$

Thus, two input strings w_1 and w_2 lead F^f from Λ to indistinguishable states if and only if we have the functional equality:

$$f \circ L_{w_1} = f \circ L_{w_2}$$

Let us, then, use E_f to denote the **indistinguishability relation** on F^f defined by:

$$w_1 E_f w_2 \Leftrightarrow f \circ L_{w_1} = f \circ L_{w_2}$$

It can be shown that F_f is an equivalence relation (Exercise 9). We call E_f the **Nerode equivalence** of $f : X^* \to Y$, after the American mathematical logician Anil Nerode, who was one of its co-discoverers.

The general state-merging theorem applied to the free realization F^f yields the following reduced form M_f as our minimal realization of f:

$$M_f = (Q_f, X, Y, \delta_f, \beta_f)$$

where the states of M_f are functions, that is,

$$Q_f = \{g \,|\, g = f \circ L_w \text{ for some } w \in X^*\}$$

since $Q_f = X^*/E_f$ under the bijection $f \circ L_w \leftrightarrow [w]$; and

$$\delta_f : Q_f \times X \to Q_f : (g, x) \mapsto g \circ L_x$$

since $([w], x) \mapsto [wx]$ so that

$$(f \circ L_w, x) \mapsto f \circ L_{wx} = (f \circ L_w) \circ L_x;$$

and

$$\beta_f : Q_f \to Y : g \mapsto g(\Lambda)$$

since

$$[w] \mapsto f(w) = f \circ L_w(\Lambda)$$

Clearly

$$\delta_f^*(g, w') = g \circ L_{w'}$$

and so

$$\begin{aligned}(M_f)_g(w') &= \beta_f(\delta_f^*(g, w')) \\ &= g \circ L_{w'}(\Lambda) \\ &= g(w')\end{aligned}$$

In other words, we have identified each state of M_f with its behavior, and have included one distinct state for every distinct behavior of a state reachable from a state with behavior f. Since F^f is reachable, and M_f was obtained from F^f by state-merging, M_f is the minimized form of F^f and so is reachable and observable. In fact (M_f, f) is the **minimal realization** in that it is the *unique* minimized realization of f, up to the relabelling of states, as follows from the more general lemma:

LEMMA 10

Let (M, q_0) and (M', q_0') be two reachable and observable machines for which $M_{q_0} = M'_{q_0'}$. Then there exists a *unique* dynamorphism h from M to M' such that $h(q_0) = q_0'$. Moreover, h is an (i/o)-homomorphism and a bijection.

Proof

To prove this, we start by seeing what properties h must have, if it exists, and then use these properties to construct it. If h were to satisfy the properties of the lemma, we would have

$$h(q_0) = q_0' \text{ and } h(\delta^*(q_0, w)) = (\delta')^*(q_0', w) \text{ for all } w \text{ in } X^* \tag{1}$$

Let us check that this in fact defines a map from Q to Q':

$$\delta^*(q_0, w_1) = \delta^*(q_0, w_2) \Rightarrow M_{q_0} \circ L_{w_1} = M_{q_0} \circ L_{w_2} \text{ by definition of } M_{q_0} \circ L_w$$
$$\Rightarrow M'_{q'_0} \circ L_{w_1} = M'_{q'_0} \circ L_{w_2} \text{ since } M_{q_0} = M'_{q'_0}$$
$$\Rightarrow (\delta')^*(q'_0, w_1) = (\delta')^*(q'_0, w_2)$$
$$\text{since } M \text{ is observable}$$

Thus (1) defines a unique dynamorphism, and this is the h of our lemma. The above implications, or the explicit display

$$\beta'[h(\delta^*(q_0, w)] = M'_{q'_0}(w) = M_{q_0}(w) = \beta[\delta^*(q_0, w)],$$

show that it is also an (i/o)-homomorphism. $\square$

We may summarize our investigation, then, by the following useful result (where, for practice in change of notation, we represent states by equivalence classes of E_f rather than by response functions—an exercise in just the sort of relabelling of states represented in the last lemma).

THEOREM 11

Given any behavior $f: X^* \rightarrow Y$, form the system

$$M_f = (Q_f, X, Y, \delta_f, \beta_f)$$

where

$$Q_f = X^*/E_f \text{ (with } w_1 E_f w_2 \Leftrightarrow f \circ L_{w_1} = f \circ L_{w_2})$$
$$\delta_f: Q_f \times X \rightarrow Q_f: ([w], x) \mapsto [wx]; \text{ and}$$
$$\beta_f: Q_f \rightarrow Y: [w] \mapsto f(w)$$

Then the initialized machine $(M_f, [\Lambda])$ is a *minimal realization* of f in that it is reachable and observable, and differs from the minimized form of any other realization of f only by the relabelling of states. $\square$

COROLLARY 12

If f has a finite-state realization, then (M_f, f) is a finite-state realization, and has the smallest number of states of any realization of f. $\square$

Example 7

As a reminder that Theorem 11 is not restricted to finite-state realizations of f, let us determine the equivalence classes of E_{f_m} for the infinite-state realization of the multiplication function f_m of Example 4:

$$f_m\left(\begin{pmatrix} x_1 \\ x_1' \end{pmatrix} \cdots \begin{pmatrix} x_n \\ x_n' \end{pmatrix}\right) = \text{the coefficient of } 2^{n-1} \text{ in the product of}$$

$$\sum_{j=1}^{n} x_j 2^{j-1} \text{ and } \sum_{k=1}^{n} x_k' 2^{k-1}$$

Now, by definition of f_m,

$$w_1 E_{f_m} w_2 \Leftrightarrow f \circ L_{w_1} = f \circ L_{w_2}$$

$$\Leftrightarrow \text{ for all numbers of the form } \left(r \cdot 2^n + \sum_{j=1}^{n} x_j 2^{j-1}\right) \text{ and}$$

$$\left(r' \cdot 2^n + \sum_{k=1}^{n} x_k' 2^{k-1}\right) \text{ the coefficient of every } 2^m$$

(for $m \geq n$) is the same, irrespective of whether it is

w_1 or w_2 that equals $\begin{pmatrix} x_1 \\ x_1' \end{pmatrix} \cdots \begin{pmatrix} x_n \\ x_n' \end{pmatrix}$

But it is clear (consider numbers of the form $(2^l + k_1) \cdot k_2$ for fixed k_1 and k_2 and increasingly large l) that the last condition can only be met if $w_1 = w_2$. Hence, in this case we actually have X^* itself as our reduced state set.   ◊

We now have an abstract description of the machine M_f. The question then arises as to whether or not we may actually construct this machine. We already know that if $|Q_f| \leq N$, then our state-merging technique will terminate in at most $N - 2$ iterations. However, at least the first step of the state-merging algorithm requires that we examine all the states of the given machine, and this is not helpful when, as is the case with F^f, the given machine has an infinite state set. Our next task, then, is to show that *if we do in fact know that* $|Q_f| \leq N$, we need only examine a finite subset of the states of F^f (i.e., a finite subset of X^*) in order to obtain M_f.

First, we consider *any* machine $M = (Q, X, Y, \delta, \beta)$, and define

$$S^q = \{\delta^*(q, w) \,|\, w \text{ in } X^*\}$$

to be the set of all states of M *reachable* from q. Then define

$$S^q_k = \{\delta^*(q, w) \,|\, w \text{ in } X^* \text{ and } l(w) \leq k\}$$

to be the set of all states reachable from q in at most k steps. Clearly, we have the following chain of inclusions:

$$\{q\} = S^q_0 \subset S^q_1 \subset S^q_2 \subset \ldots \subset S^q_k \subset \ldots \subset S^q$$

with

$$S^q = \bigcup_{k \geq 0} S^q{}_k$$

Now, just as in our discussion of state-merging, we obtain termination lemmas.

LEMMA 13

If $S^q{}_j = S^q{}_{j+1}$, then $S^q{}_j = S^q{}_k$ for all $k \geq j$, and thus $S^q{}_j = S^q$.

Proof

Suppose that $S^q{}_j = S^q{}_{j+1}$, and that $q_1 \in S^q{}_{j+2}$.
Then $q_1 = \delta^*(q, wx)$ where $\ell(w) = j + 1$ and $x \in X$
$\qquad = \delta(\delta^*(q, w), x)$.
But $\delta^*(q, w) \in S^q{}_{j+1}$ and thus $\delta^*(q, w)$ equals some $q' \in S^q{}_j$, by assumption.
Therefore, $q_1 = \delta(q', x)$ and so is in $S^q{}_{j+1}$, and thus in $S^q{}_j$. $\qquad\square$

COROLLARY 14

If $|S^q| \leq N$, then $S^q{}_{N-1} = S^q$.

Proof

See Exercise 11. $\qquad\square$

Of course, for an infinite machine it need never happen that $S^q{}_j = S^q{}_{j+1}$, as shown in the following example.

Example 8

Consider the machine with $X = \{0, 1\}$, with infinite state set $Q = \mathbf{N}$ (we omit outputs, since our interest here is in reachability), and with next-state function $\delta : \mathbf{N} \times \{0, 1\} \to \mathbf{N}$ defined by

$$\delta(n, 0) = n$$
$$\delta(n, 1) = n + 1$$

In other words, this is the counter for $\mathbf{N}$ corresponding to the modulo m counters for $\mathbf{Z}_m$ that introduced our study of automata in Section 2–1. It is clear that for this machine

$$S^0 = \mathbf{N}$$

while

$$S^0_k = \{0, 1, 2, \ldots, k\} \text{ for all } k$$

so that

$$S^0_k \neq S^0_{k'} \text{ for any } k \neq k'$$

Note, too, that $S^n \neq \mathbf{N}$ for any $n \neq 0$, since 0 is reachable from no other state. ◊

Putting Lemma 13 together with Lemma 8 and Theorem 11 on state-merging, we have the following satisfying result.

THEOREM 15

Let $f: X^* \to Y$ be any behavior. Let us define the k-indistinguishability relation of X^* by

$$w_1 E^k_f w_2 \Leftrightarrow f(w_1 w) = f(w_2 w) \text{ for all } w \text{ in } X^* \text{ of length at most } k$$

and the k-reachable set of M_f by

$$S^f_k = \{[w] \mid \ell(w) \leq k\} \subset Q_f$$

Then if $S^f_p = S^f_{p+1}$ we have $S^f_p = Q_f$; and if $E^u_f = E^{u+1}_f$ we have $E^u_f = E_f$. Hence, if p and u are such that

$$S^f_p = S^f_{p+1} \text{ and } E^u_f = E^{u+1}_f$$

we deduce that

$$Q_f = \{w \in X^* \mid \ell(w) \leq p\}/E^u_f \qquad \square$$

In particular, our estimates of p and u for a finite-state realization of f yield:

COROLLARY 16

If $|Q_f| \leq N$, then

$$Q_f = \{w \in X^* \mid \ell(w) \leq N - 1\}/E^{N-2}_f \qquad \square$$

In Section 7–5, we shall derive a similar result for linear machines. But now we turn to an example of the use of Corollary 16.

Example 9

Suppose that we wish to construct M_f for the parity function $f: \{0, 1\}^* \rightarrow \{0, 1\}$ defined by

$$f(w) = \begin{cases} 1 \text{ if } w \text{ contains an even number of 1's} \\ 0 \text{ if not} \end{cases}$$

and that we are assured that $|Q_f| \leq 3$. Then the only states of F^f we need to merge are those of length $\leq N - 1 = 2$; and we need only test them with sequences of length not greater than $N - 2 = 1$. Thus we tabulate $F_w^f(w') = f(ww')$ for $\ell(w) \leq 2$ and $\ell(w') \leq 1$ and obtain the following table of $f(ww')$:

w \ w'	Λ	0	1
Λ	1	1	0
0	1	1	0
1	0	0	1
00	1	1	0
01	0	0	1
10	0	0	1
11	1	1	0

We conclude that M_f has only two states, $[\Lambda]$ and $[1]$, with outputs 1 and 0, respectively. Noting that

$$[\Lambda 0] = [0] = [\Lambda]$$
$$[\Lambda 1] = [1]$$
$$[10] = [1]$$
$$[11] = [\Lambda]$$

we obtain for f the usual state-diagram of Figure 2–69. ◊

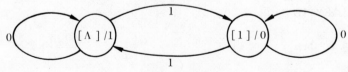

Figure 2–69

In summary, then, we have seen two ways of describing initialized machines:

Internal-State Descriptions: $M = (Q, X, Y, \delta : Q \times X \to X, \beta : Q \to Y)$ together with the initial state q in Q.

External Descriptions: $f : X^* \to Y$.

Let us now write:

Int = the set of all initialized internal-state descriptions (M, q)

Ext = the set of all external descriptions f

Then we have described two functions:

The Behavior Function $\mathcal{B} : Int \to Ext : (M, q) \mapsto M_q = \beta(\delta^*(q, \cdot))$

The Realization Function $\mathcal{R} : Ext \to Int : f \mapsto (M(f) = (Q_f, X, Y, \delta_f, \beta_f), f)$

We may note that $\mathcal{B}\mathcal{R}(f) = \mathcal{B}(M(f), f) = M(f)_f = f$ so that

$$\mathcal{B}\mathcal{R} : Ext \to Ext \text{ is the identity function on external descriptions}$$

while $\mathcal{R}\mathcal{B}(M, q) = \mathcal{R}(M_q) = (M(M_q), M_q)$ which is the reduced form of M, when restricted to those states reachable from q. Thus

$$\mathcal{R}\mathcal{B} : Int \to Int \text{ is the minimized form function on internal-state descriptions.}$$

EXERCISES FOR SECTION 2–5

1.   The construction of Example 1 uses three delay elements to achieve a realization of f_1 in state-output form. Modify the construction to show how only two delay elements are required if the output may depend directly on the current input.

2.   **(i)**   Use the method of Example 2 to find a realization of the f_1 of Example 1 with as few states as possible.

   (ii)   Construct a shift-register state output realization of the f_2 of Example 2.

3.   For the machine M shown in Figure 2–70, determine whether or not there exists a $q_0 \in Q = \{q_1, q_2, q_3, q_4, q_5, q_6, q_7\}$ such that (M, q_0) is a reachable initialized machine.

4.   Let h be an (i/o)-homomorphism from M to M', where both have input set X. Then prove, by induction on the length of w, that $\beta(\delta^*(q, w)) = \beta'((\delta')^*(h(q, w))$ for all w in X^* and all states q of M.

5.   Given machines $M = (Q, X, Y, \delta, \beta)$ and $M' = (Q', X, Y', \delta', \beta')$, suppose that the surjection $h : Q \to Q'$ is a dynamorphism such that $h(q_0) = q_0'$. Prove that if (M, q_0) is reachable, then (M', q_0') is also reachable.

6.   For the machine M shown in Figure 2–70, recall the definition following Corollary 5, and determine the state graph of

   (a) $M^{(q_1)}$
   (b) $M^{(q_3)}$
   (c) $M^{(q_4)}$
   (d) $M^{(q_6)}$

7.   Draw a flow diagram implementing the state-merging algorithm. [You may assume that subroutines are available for β and δ.]

8.   Check your "program" for Exercise 7 by hand-simulating its effect on the machine given in Figure 2–70.

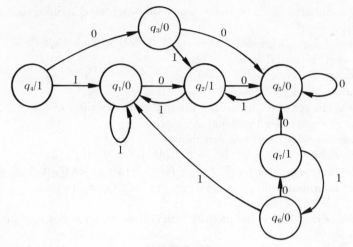

Figure 2–70

9. Verify that E_f is an equivalence relation.
10. Show that for *any* machine M, any state q of M, and any w in X^*, we have the equality

$$M_{\delta(q,w)} = M_q \circ L_w$$

11. Prove Corollary 14.

Further Reading for Chapter 2

M. A. Arbib [1969] Theories of Abstract Automata. Englewood Cliffs, N.J.: Prentice-Hall.

E. Engeler [1973] Introduction to the Theory of Computation, New York: Academic Press.

M. A. Harrison [1965] Introduction to Switching and Automata Theory, New York: McGraw-Hill.

J. Hartmanis and R. E. Stearns [1966] Algebraic Theory of Sequential Machines, Englewood Cliffs, N.J.: Prentice-Hall.

M. Minsky [1967] Computation: Finite and Infinite Machines, Englewood Cliffs, N.J.: Prentice-Hall.

CHAPTER 3

Computability

In this relatively short chapter, we develop little in the way of new algebraic ideas, but rather concentrate on some of the fundamental concepts of computability. [This chapter may in fact be omitted by the reader interested only in the more algebraic phases of discrete mathematics—our only use of it elsewhere is in the discussion of recursive and recursively enumerable sets, and of Gödel's Theorem, in Section 4–2.] In particular, we explore some of the formalizations of the notion of an "effectively computable function"—namely, a function which can be computed by some idealized computing machine which is free from all limitations of time or memory. In particular, we introduce the collection of Turing machines, which we believe to be such that, for any effectively computable function, there exists a Turing machine which computes it. We also introduce another class of functions, namely the partial recursive functions, which are built up by a number of operations including an operation of recursion similar to the definition by induction studied in Section 1–1. We observe, while leaving some of the details as exercises for Section 3–3, that a function is computable by a Turing machine if and only if it is a partial recursive function, thus increasing our belief in the assertion that the effectively computable functions are precisely those which can be computed by Turing machines. In Section 3–2 we prove a result—which comes as no surprise to the experienced programmer—that there is a universal Turing machine, namely one that can compute any effectively computable function, so long as it is appropriately programmed. However, what may come as more of a surprise is that we can find functions of genuine interest to the computer scientist which are not effectively computable—such as the function which, given the description of a Turing machine and the data which are to be fed to it, will determine whether or not the machine will ever halt when fed that data. In Section 4–2, we shall

163

apply this result—the unsolvability of the halting problem—to outline Gödel's incompleteness theorem that any really rich formalization of mathematics which meets certain requirements about the effectiveness of the means of deduction will not be adequate to provide formal proofs of *all* the true statements which may be formalized in its language. Finally, in Section 3–3 we provide a very general language for describing computations, which can be seen as a clear generalization of our discussion of Turing machines in Section 3–1, and yet which is sufficiently broad to encompass such highly parallel computations as those of cellular automata. In particular, we give a brief, informal discussion of the ways in which self-reproducing automata have been embedded in cellular arrays.

3–1   Turing Machines and Partial Recursive Functions

An intuitive picture of a *Turing* machine* is given in Figure 3–1: the machine has a finite piece of tape on which is written a string of symbols, one per square, with one of the admissible tape symbols being simply a blank. At

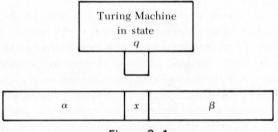

Figure 3–1

any time the machine, being in some state q, scans the symbol x on a given square of the tape; and on the basis of the particular state-symbol pair (q, x), takes the following steps: (1) the machine replaces x by a symbol x' (x' may equal x, of course, or may be the blank); (2) it changes state from q to q' (again q' may equal q); and (3) it moves L (one square left on the tape), R (one square right), or N (not at all). The machine stops when (and if) it reaches a state-symbol pair (q, x) which determines that q' is just q, that x' is just x, and that the machine does not move. Finally, we decree that whenever the machine reaches the end of its tape, a blank square will be adjoined to that end.

The machine computes a function $f: w \mapsto f(w)$ as follows: The initial data are encoded as a string w of tape symbols, and the machine is placed in a designated initial state scanning the left-most square of the encoding. The machine then proceeds to print symbols, change state, and move on the tape. If and when the machine stops, the result of the computation $f(w)$ may be decoded from the tape at that time.

*Named for the British mathematician Alan M. Turing.

The function computed by a Turing machine will thus be partial in the sense that it may not be defined for all possible input tapes. However, recall from our background discussion that we do *not* imply that a function cannot be total if we say that it is partial. Rather, we use the word "partial" to remind ourselves that no guarantee of totality has been made. We shall see that for some Turing machines, we can prove that they compute total functions; for others we can prove they do not, while in yet other cases—and this is a profound result—the question of totality cannot be settled by any effective procedure.

Let us now express the above concepts in precise mathematical language:

DEFINITION 1

A **Turing machine** Z is a quadruple

$$Z = (Q, X_b, P, q_0)$$

where

> Q is a finite set called the set of **states,**
> $X_b = X \cup \{b\}$ is a finite set (where $b \notin X$ symbolizes the blank) called the set of **tape symbols** or **input alphabet,**
> $P: Q \times X_b \to Q \times X_b \times \{L, N, R\}$ is the **local transition function,** and
> $q_0 \in Q$ is the **initial state.**   ○

As we can see from Figure 3–1, the tape of Z at any time may be described by a string of tape symbols of length at least one (α and β may both be empty strings); but we must always have at least one symbol, namely the x (and this x may well be the blank b) under current scan. Thus, we may represent the set of tapes which Z may encounter by the set X_b^+ of nonempty strings on X_b.

We also see that we can completely represent the total state of the machine at any time by specifying four things: (1) the symbol-string α to the left of the scanned square, (2) the state q of the control box, (3) the symbol x under scan, and (4) the symbol-string β to the right of the scanned square. Now if we assume that we use different symbols to denote states and tape symbols, so that $Q \cap X = \varnothing$, then given the string

$$\alpha q x \beta \tag{1}$$

we may uniquely recapture α, q, x and β. Note that expression (1) is *not* a string on the set of tape symbols, but is a string on the larger alphabet $Q \cup X_b$. Thus, $\alpha q x \beta \in (Q \cup X_b)^+$. In fact, we can be more precise, for we may write

$$\alpha q x \beta \in X_b^* Q X_b^+$$

where

$$X_b^* Q X_b^+ = \{w_1 w_2 w_3 \mid w_1 \in X_b^*, w_2 \in Q, w_3 \in X_b^+\} \subset (Q \cup X_b)^+$$

We call each string (1) an **instantaneous description** (ID) of Z, and denote the set of IDs of Z by $\mathfrak{D}_Z$.

We may now define how the IDs of Z change under a single application of the local transition function P. Cases (i) and (ii) below simply handle the "splicing on" of blank squares when Z reaches the end of its tape.

DEFINITION 2

The **next-ID function** $\delta_Z : \mathfrak{D}_Z \rightarrow \mathfrak{D}_Z : \alpha q x \beta \mapsto \delta_Z(\alpha q x \beta)$ of the Turing machine Z is defined by the following scheme:

(i) $\delta_Z(q\beta) = \delta_Z(bq\beta)$ for all q in Q, β in X_b^+.
(ii) $\delta_Z(\alpha q x) = \delta_Z(\alpha q x b)$ for all α in X_b^*, q in Q, x in X_b.
(iii) For all β and γ in X_b^*, x_1 and x in X_b, and q in Q, we define

$$\delta_Z(\gamma x_1 q x \beta) = \begin{cases} \gamma q' x_1 x' \beta & \text{if } P(q, x) = (q', x', L) \\ \gamma x_1 q' x' \beta & \text{if } P(q, x) = (q', x', N) \\ \gamma x_1 x' q' \beta & \text{if } P(q, x) = (q', x', R) \end{cases} \qquad \bigcirc$$

We have said that Z stops when it reaches a (q, x) configuration for which $P(q, x) = (q, x, N)$. We can capture this concept by saying:

DEFINITION 3

An ID w is **terminal** if $\delta_Z(w) = w$. $\qquad \bigcirc$

Example 1

Suppose we are given the Turing machine $Z = (Q, X_b, P, q_0)$, where

$$Q = \{q_0, q_1, q_2\}$$
$$X_b = \{0, 1, b\}$$

and P is given by:

$$P(q_0, 0) = P(q_0, b) = (q_1, 0, L)$$
$$P(q_0, 1) = (q_1, 1, R)$$
$$P(q_1, 0) = (q_1, b, R)$$
$$P(q_1, 1) = P(q_2, b) = (q_2, 0, N)$$

$$P(q_1, b) = (q_2, 1, L)$$
$$P(q_2, 0) = (q_0, 0, L)$$
$$P(q_2, 1) = (q_2, 1, N)$$

Let us describe the behavior of this machine when the input tape reads 1001 with the machine initially scanning the second 0. As a consequence of our definition of δ_Z, we obtain the following list of IDs:

1	0	q_0	0	1
1	q_1	0	0	1
1	b	q_1	0	1
1	b	b	q_1	1
1	b	b	q_2	0
1	b	q_0	b	0
1	q_1	b	0	0
q_2	1	1	0	0

where the last ID is terminal. Alternatively, if the initial ID is 0 1 q_0 1, the result is

0	1	q_0	1	
0	1	1	q_1	b
0	1	q_2	1	1

(where the b is spliced on)

and 0 1 q_2 1 1 is terminal. Thus, for these two initial IDs, the Turing machine eventually stops.   ◊

Now, the idea of a *computation* is to set Z up in some ID, say w_0, and then let Z run until it reaches a terminal configuration; if no terminal condition is reached, then we do not obtain a computation. More formally:

DEFINITION 4

A **computation** of Z is a finite sequence

$$w_0, w_1, \ldots, w_n$$

of IDs such that for $j = 0, 1, 2, \ldots, n - 1$, $w_{j+1} = \delta_Z(w_j) \neq w_j$ while w_n is terminal.   ○

Note that given w_0, there may be no computation of which it is the first ID, because w_0 may send Z into a runaway condition which never terminates. However, if w_0 is the first term of a computation, it is clear that it is the first term of exactly one computation. Thus, we can make the following definition (where $d(\delta_Z^*)$ is the domain of definition of the partial function δ_Z^*):

DEFINITION 5

The **global transition function** $\delta_Z^*: \mathfrak{D}_Z \to \mathfrak{D}_Z$ of the Turing machine Z is the partial function for which:

(i) $d(\delta_Z^*) = \{w \in \mathfrak{D}_Z \,|\, \text{there exists a computation of } Z \text{ with first term } w\}$
(ii) if $w \in d(\delta_Z^*)$, then $\delta_Z^*(w)$ is the terminal ID of the computation whose first term is w. $\qquad\bigcirc$

It will prove important to define δ_Z^* somewhat more formally below. However, let us first complete our description of the function computed by a Turing machine and give some examples.

Given a string θ of X_b^+, we place Z in state q_0 scanning the left-most square of θ; thus, our initial ID is $q_0\theta$. We then run the machine, starting with the ID $q_0\theta$, until it stops, if indeed it does. If the machine halts, then we simply read the tape contents $\alpha x\beta$ from the terminal ID $\alpha q x\beta = \delta_Z^*(q_0\theta)$ to obtain our result.

Thus, if we let $h_1: X_b^+ \to \mathfrak{D}_Z$ be the encoding function $h_1: \theta \mapsto q_0\theta$ and let $h_2: \mathfrak{D}_Z \to \mathfrak{D}_Z$ be the decoding function $h_2: \alpha q x\beta \mapsto \alpha x\beta$,† we have the simple definition which follows:

DEFINITION 6

The **function computed by the Turing machine** Z is the partial function $F_Z^b: X_b^+ \to X_b^+$ defined by the following commutative diagram:

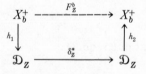

Thus, $F_Z^b(\theta)$ is obtained by deleting the state symbol from $\delta_Z^*(q_0\theta)$, if the latter is defined, and is otherwise undefined. $\qquad\bigcirc$

---

†The reader familiar with Section 5–1 may recognize that h_2 is the restriction to $\mathfrak{D}_Z$ of the homomorphism $h: (Q \cup X_b)^* \to X_b^*$ defined by $h(q) = \Lambda$, $h(x) = x$ for q in Q, x in X_b.

Example 2

For the Turing machine given in Example 1, let us determine $F_Z^b(1001)$. We do this by establishing the computation:

$$
\begin{array}{ccccc}
q_0 & 1 & 0 & 0 & 1 \\
1 & q_1 & 0 & 0 & 1 \\
1 & b & q_1 & 0 & 1 \\
1 & b & b & q_1 & 1 \\
1 & b & b & q_2 & 0 \\
1 & b & q_0 & b & 0 \\
1 & q_1 & b & 0 & 0 \\
q_2 & 1 & 1 & 0 & 0
\end{array}
$$

Thus, $F_Z^b(1001) = 1100$.   ◊

We shall now use the function $\delta_Z^* : \mathfrak{D}_Z \to \mathfrak{D}_Z$ to define a new function from $(X^*)^n$ to X^*. We take an element of $(X^*)^n$, say $(w_1, w_2, \ldots, w_n)$, and form the string $w_1 b w_2 \ldots b w_n \in X_b^+$, which yields the ID $q_0 w_1 b w_2 b \ldots b w_n \in \mathfrak{D}_Z$. The computation resulting from this ID, if it exists, consists of strings of X^* separated by blanks, and one state symbol. We decode this ID by a function $h_3 : \mathfrak{D}_Z \to X^*$ which takes the concatenation of the two strings in X^* which are separated by the state symbol. There is one exception: if the machine halts scanning a blank, the image is Λ. For example, if $X = \{0, 1\}$ and $n = 3$, then

$$
\begin{array}{l}
h_3(1 \quad 0 \quad q \quad 1 \quad 1) = 1011 \\
h_3(1 \quad b \quad 0 \quad 1 \quad q \quad 1 \quad b \quad b \quad 1) = 011 \\
h_3(1 \quad b \quad 1 \quad b \quad b \quad 0 \quad 1 \quad q \quad 0 \quad b \quad 0) = 010 \\
h_3(1 \quad 0 \quad b \quad 1 \quad 1 \quad q \quad 1 \quad 0 \quad 0 \quad b \quad 1) = 11100 \\
h_3(1 \quad 1 \quad b \quad q \quad 1 \quad 0 \quad b \quad 1) = \Lambda 10 = 10 \\
h_3(0 \quad 1 \quad b \quad 1 \quad 0 \quad q \quad b \quad 1 \quad 0) = \Lambda
\end{array}
$$

More formally, we have the following:

DEFINITION 7

The function

$$
F_Z^n : (X^*)^n \to X^*
$$

called the **n-ary function** of Z, is defined as follows: We define the function $h_3: \mathfrak{D}_Z \to X^*$ by the rule

$$h_3(\alpha q x \beta) = \begin{cases} \Lambda & \text{if } x = b \\ \alpha_2 x \beta_1 & \text{if } x \neq b, \text{ if } \alpha = \alpha_1 \alpha_2 \text{ with } \alpha_1 \in \{\Lambda\} \cup X_b^* b \\ & \text{and } \alpha_2 \in X^*, \text{ and if } \beta = \beta_1 \beta_2 \text{ with } \beta_1 \in X^* \text{ and} \\ & \beta_2 \in \{\Lambda\} \cup b X_b^* \end{cases}$$

Then

$$F_Z^n : (X^*)^n \to X^* : (w_1, w_2, \ldots, w_n) \mapsto h_3[\delta_Z^*(w_1 b w_2 b \ldots b w_n)] \qquad \bigcirc$$

DEFINITION 8

A function $f: (X^*)^n \to X^*$ is said to be **(partial) TM-computable** if there exists a Turing machine (TM) Z such that $f = F_Z^n$. We say that f is **total** if it is defined for all the elements of $(X^*)^n$. $\qquad \bigcirc$

Note: The word "partial" should remind us that the function need not be defined for all its values. We use the word "total" if we wish to emphasize that a function is always defined. We reiterate that a partial function does *not* have to be sometimes undefined. As mathematicians find it convenient to consider linear problems as a *subclass* of nonlinear problems, so do we find it convenient to consider the total functions as a subclass of the partial functions. Note, too, the result of Exercise 3.

In turning to examples, we shall find it convenient to represent the local transition function by a list of quintuples, with one quintuple $qxx'Mq'$ for each $(q, x) \in Q \times X_b$ such that $P(q, x) = (q', x', M) \neq (q, x, N)$. Thus, if $(q, x) \in Q \times X_b$ heads no quintuple in the list, (q, x) is a **halting configuration**.

Example 3

For the Turing machine of Example 1, we can represent the local transition function by the following list of quintuples:

$$
\begin{array}{ccccc}
q_0 & 0 & 0 & L & q_1 \\
q_0 & 1 & 1 & R & q_1 \\
q_0 & b & 0 & L & q_1 \\
q_1 & 0 & b & R & q_1 \\
q_1 & 1 & 0 & N & q_2
\end{array}
$$

$$
\begin{array}{ccccc}
q_1 & b & 1 & L & q_2 \\
q_2 & 0 & 0 & L & q_0 \\
q_2 & b & 0 & N & q_2
\end{array}
$$

Since none of the above quintuples begins with $q_2 1$, then $(q_2, 1)$ is a halting configuration.   ◊

Example 4

We now give an example of building a Turing machine to do a specific task. Let us construct a Z with input alphabet $X_b = \{0, 1, b\}$ and states $\{q_0, q_1, q_2, q_3, q_4, q_5, q_6, q_7, q_8, q_s\}$, where b is the blank and q_s is a **stop state;** i.e., no quintuple starts with q_s. We define the machine Z in terms of its 1-ary function's behavior on strings which contain no blanks (i.e., $w \in \{0, 1\}^*$) as follows:

$$
F_Z^1(w) = \begin{cases} 1 \text{ if } w = 0^r 1 0^r \text{ for some } r \in \mathbf{N} \\ 0 \text{ if not} \end{cases}
$$

One way to obtain this result is to place w on the tape of Z, and to have Z start at the left-most symbol of w. (If $w = \Lambda$, then Z reads b.) Then Z goes back and forth from one end of the string to the other blanking out 0's at each end in pairs (i.e., when a 0 at the left end is blanked, a 0 at the right end must also be blanked) until the resulting string does not contain a 0 at both ends. (For the special case that w consists entirely of 0's, b replaces w.) The following are four examples showing successive snapshots taken of the tape each time a 0 has been blanked according to the above reduction (a blank being left blank):

(i) 0011000	(ii) 0010	(iii) 0010100	(iv) 0001000
011000	010	010100	001000
01100	01	01010	00100
1100		1010	0100
110		101	010
			10
			1

After Z has completed the reduction, it tests the resulting string. If the string is $w' = 1$, then Z halts, since the 1 on the tape is the correct value of $F_Z^1(w)$. If $w' \neq 1$, then Z blanks out w' and prints a 0, and then halts.

Having explained the operation of Z, we invite the reader to check the detailed operation of the quintuples which follow:

I. If the string is 0^m, $m \geq 0$, go to q_8 (see **IV** below), and the output is 0. In any case, delete left-most 0.

$$
\begin{array}{ccccc}
q_0 & b & b & N & q_8 \\
q_0 & 0 & b & R & q_1 \\
q_1 & 0 & 0 & R & q_1 \\
q_1 & b & b & L & q_8 \\
\end{array}
$$

II. If not, go to end of string.

$$
\begin{array}{ccccc}
q_1 & 1 & 1 & R & q_2 \\
q_2 & 0 & 0 & R & q_2 \\
q_2 & 1 & 1 & R & q_2 \\
q_2 & b & b & L & q_3 \\
\end{array}
$$

III. If there is a 0 at right-most end, delete it, return to left-most end, and repeat process.

$$
\begin{array}{ccccc}
q_3 & 0 & b & L & q_4 \\
q_4 & 0 & 0 & L & q_4 \\
q_4 & 1 & 1 & L & q_4 \\
q_4 & b & b & R & q_0 \\
\end{array}
$$

IV. If there is no 0 at right-most end, go to state q_8, and halt with 0 on tape.

$$
\begin{array}{ccccc}
q_3 & 1 & b & L & q_8 \\
q_8 & 0 & b & L & q_8 \\
q_8 & 1 & b & L & q_8 \\
q_8 & b & 0 & N & q_s \\
\end{array}
$$

V. If the 1 at left-most end is the whole string, halt; if not, go to q_6 and halt with 0 on tape.

$$
\begin{array}{ccccc}
q_0 & 1 & 1 & R & q_5 \\
q_5 & b & b & L & q_s \\
q_5 & 0 & 0 & L & q_6 \\
q_5 & 1 & 1 & L & q_6 \\
q_6 & 1 & 0 & R & q_7 \\
q_7 & 1 & b & R & q_7 \\
q_7 & 0 & b & R & q_7 \\
\end{array}
$$

(if we stop while scanning b then $F^1_Z(w) = \Lambda$)

◊

Example 5

This example indicates that we *may* interpret the string processing of a Turing machine as numerical processing.

Encode the number m as $\langle m \rangle$, **the 2-adic encoding** of m, a string of 1's and 2's, where $i_j \in \{1, 2\}$ and

$$\langle m \rangle = i_1 \ldots i_n \Leftrightarrow m = \sum_{j=1}^{n} i_j 2^{n-j} = i_1 2^{n-1} + i_2 2^{n-2} + \cdots + i_{n-1} 2^1 + i_n 2^0$$

For instance,

$$\langle 7 \rangle = 111$$

and

$$\langle 19 \rangle = 1211$$

Note that we do not use the usual binary encoding since it does not provide a unique string for each number; e.g., $001 = 01 = 1$ in binary. Note also that $\langle 0 \rangle$ is the empty string.

We begin by encoding 14 and 38 for the purpose of helping us to establish a description of how to form $\langle 2m \rangle$ from $\langle m \rangle$. We then describe a Turing machine (with $X_b = \{1, 2, b\}$) which, if started in state q_0 while scanning the left-most square of a tape with just $\langle m \rangle$ written on it, will eventually halt with $\langle 2m \rangle$ on its tape.

Firstly,

$$7 = 1 \cdot 2^2 + 1 \cdot 2^1 + 1 \cdot 2^0 \Rightarrow \langle 7 \rangle = 111$$

so

$$14 = 2 \cdot 7 = 2 \cdot 2^2 + 2 \cdot 2^1 + 2 \cdot 2^0 \Rightarrow \langle 14 \rangle = 222$$

Secondly,

$$19 = 1 \cdot 2^3 + 2 \cdot 2^2 + 1 \cdot 2^1 + 1 \cdot 2^0 \Rightarrow \langle 19 \rangle = 1211$$

so

$$38 = 2 \cdot 19 = 2 \cdot 2^3 + 2(2 \cdot 2^2) + 2 \cdot 2^1 + 2 \cdot 2^0$$
$$= 1 \cdot 2^4 + 2 \cdot 2^3 + 0 \cdot 2^2 + 2 \cdot 2^1 + 2 \cdot 2^0$$
$$= 1 \cdot 2^4 + 1 \cdot 2^3 + 2 \cdot 2^2 + 2 \cdot 2^1 + 2 \cdot 2^0 \Rightarrow \langle 38 \rangle = 11222$$

This suggests the following:

Since $\langle m_1 \rangle 0$ is an illegal expression for $\langle 2m \rangle$, we change the 0 to a 2 by "borrowing" a 1 from the next digit to the left. If that digit is a 2, we change it to 1 and stop. If it is a 1, we cannot write 0, so we replace it by a 2, and repeat the process. If the string $\langle m_1 \rangle$ consists of all 1's, we conclude this process by blanking the left-most 1.

Using the fact (Exercise 6) that $\langle 2m \rangle = \langle m - 1 \rangle 2$, we see that multiplication by 2, apart from placing a 2 on the right, is just simply subtraction of 1 from $\langle m \rangle$. Hence, multiplication by 2 can be performed by the Turing machine described by the following list of quintuples:

$$
\begin{array}{ccccc}
q_0 & 1 & 1 & R & q_0 \\
q_0 & 2 & 2 & R & q_0 \\
q_0 & b & 2 & L & q_1 \\
q_1 & 1 & 2 & L & q_1 \\
q_1 & 2 & 1 & N & q_s \\
q_1 & b & b & R & q_2 \\
q_2 & 2 & b & R & q_s
\end{array}
$$

If we indicate the symbol being scanned by an arrow, in multiplying 7 by 2, our machine behaves as follows:

$$
\begin{array}{cccccccccc}
q_0 & q_0 & q_0 & q_0 & q_1 & q_1 & q_1 & q_1 & q_2 & q_s \\
\downarrow & \downarrow & \downarrow & \downarrow & \downarrow & \downarrow & \downarrow & \downarrow & \downarrow & \downarrow \\
111, & 111, & 111, & 111b, & 1112, & 1122, & 1222, & b2222, & 2222, & 222
\end{array}
$$

In multiplying 19 by 2, we get the sequence:

$$
\begin{array}{ccccccccc}
q_0 & q_0 & q_0 & q_0 & q_0 & q_1 & q_1 & q_1 & q_s \\
\downarrow & \downarrow & \downarrow & \downarrow & \downarrow & \downarrow & \downarrow & \downarrow & \downarrow \\
1211, & 1211, & 1211, & 1211, & 1211b, & 12112, & 12122, & 12222, & 11222
\end{array}
$$

Note that the above described machine handles $m = 0$ ($\langle m \rangle$ = the empty string) correctly. (Verify this!)

An alternative approach in constructing a machine that multiplies by 2 is actually to implement bit-by-bit addition. In this arithmetic, we may carry 0, 1, or 2; and we need only observe the rules:

$$
1 + 1 = 2
$$
$$
2 + 2 = 2 \text{ carry } 1
$$
$$
1 + 1 + 1 = 1 \text{ carry } 1
$$
$$
1 + 2 + 2 = 1 \text{ carry } 2
$$
$$
2 + 1 + 1 = 2 \text{ carry } 1
$$
$$
2 + 2 + 2 = 2 \text{ carry } 2
$$

Then our multiply machine is to have five states: q_0, q_1, q_2, q_3, and q_s. The machine starts in state q_0 on the left-most square and proceeds according to the quintuples:

$$
\begin{array}{ccccc}
q_0 & 1 & 1 & R & q_0 \\
q_0 & 2 & 2 & R & q_0 \\
q_0 & b & b & L & q_1 \\
q_1 & b & b & R & q_s \\
q_1 & 1 & 2 & L & q_1 \\
q_1 & 2 & 2 & L & q_2 \\
q_2 & b & 1 & N & q_s \\
q_2 & 1 & 1 & L & q_2 \\
q_2 & 2 & 1 & L & q_3 \\
q_3 & b & 2 & N & q_s \\
q_3 & 1 & 2 & L & q_2 \\
q_3 & 2 & 2 & L & q_3
\end{array}
$$

Thus, in multiplying 7 by 2, we have:

$$
\begin{array}{ccccccccc}
q_0 & q_0 & q_0 & q_0 & q_1 & q_1 & q_1 & q_1 & q_s \\
\downarrow & \downarrow & \downarrow & \downarrow & \downarrow & \downarrow & \downarrow & \downarrow & \downarrow \\
111, & 111, & 111, & 111b, & 111, & 112, & 122, & b222, & 222
\end{array}
$$

Multiplying 19 by 2, we have:

$$
\begin{array}{cccccc}
q_0 & q_0 & q_0 & q_0 & q_0 & q_1 \\
\downarrow & \downarrow & \downarrow & \downarrow & \downarrow & \downarrow \\
1211, & 1211, & 1211, & 1211, & 1211b, & 1211,
\end{array}
$$

$$
\begin{array}{ccccc}
q_1 & q_1 & q_2 & q_2 & q_s \\
\downarrow & \downarrow & \downarrow & \downarrow & \downarrow \\
1212, & 1222, & 1222, & b1222, & 11222
\end{array} \quad \lozenge
$$

Let us now briefly formalize our definition of the global transition function. First we define $\widehat{\delta}_Z : \mathfrak{D}_Z \times \mathbf{N} \to \mathfrak{D}_Z$ in such a way that $\widehat{\delta}_Z(w, n)$ is the ID obtained from w by n applications of δ_Z. Clearly, then, $\widehat{\delta}_Z$ may be defined by the recursion scheme:

$$
\begin{aligned}
\widehat{\delta}_Z(w, 0) &= w \\
\widehat{\delta}_Z(w, n + 1) &= \delta_Z(\widehat{\delta}_Z(w, n))
\end{aligned}
\tag{2}
$$

Next, let $p_Z : \mathfrak{D}_Z \to \mathbf{N}$ be a function which tells us whether or not a string is a terminal ID for Z. So we define

$$
p_Z(w) = \begin{cases} 0 \text{ if } \delta_Z(w) = w \\ 1 \text{ if not} \end{cases}
$$

Then, let us define $\eta_Z : \mathfrak{D}_Z \to \mathbf{N}$, the (clearly partial) function which tells us how many steps are required to reach a terminal ID, by applying the *minimum function* μ_n to p_Z:

$$\eta_Z(w) = \mu_n[p_Z(\widehat{\delta}_Z(w, n)) = 0] \tag{3}$$

i.e., $\eta_Z(w)$ is the least n, if one such exists, for which $\widehat{\delta}_Z(w, n)$ is terminal; it is otherwise undefined.

Then it should be clear that δ_Z^* is defined by the following equation:

$$\delta_Z^*(w) = \widehat{\delta}_Z(w, \eta_Z(w))$$

Thus, given the relatively simple functions δ_Z and the ability to test for equality of strings, we can build up δ_Z^* by the three operations of recursion (which was used in (2)), and of composition and minimization (both of which were used in (3)). This suggests that *all* TM-computable functions can be built up from a simple basis set of functions by repeated application of these three operations. Let us make, then, the following definitions.

DEFINITION 9

The **primitive recursive** and **partial recursive** functions $(X^*)^n \to X^*$ are defined as follows: We first define three types of basis functions:

(i) For each $x \in X$, $L_x : X^* \to X^*$ is the **left successor** $w \mapsto xw$.
(ii) For each $n \in \mathbf{N}$, $U^n : (X^*)^n \to X^* : (w_1, \ldots, w_n) \mapsto \Lambda$ is the function which replaces n arguments by the **unit** Λ.
(iii) For each $n \in \mathbf{N}$, and $1 \leq j \leq n$, $\Pi^n_j : (X^*)^n \to X^* : (w_1, \ldots, w_n) \mapsto w_j$ is the function which **projects** the jth of n arguments.

We next define three operations:

(a) **Composition** is the operation which, when applied to the partial functions $h : (X^*)^m \to X^*$ and $g_j : (X^*)^n \to X^*$ for $1 \leq j \leq m$, yields the function $f : (X^*)^n \to X^*$ defined by

$$f(w_1, \ldots, w_n) = h(g(w_1, \ldots, w_n), \ldots, g_m(w_1, \ldots, w_n))$$

(b) **Recursion** is the operation which, when applied to the functions $g : (X^*)^{n-1} \to X^*$ and $h_x : (X^*)^{n+1} \to X^*$, of which there is one for each $x \in X$, yields the function $f : (X^*)^n \to X^*$ defined *recursively* by

$$f(\Lambda, w_2, \ldots, w_n) = g(w_2, \ldots, w_n)$$
$$f(xw, w_2, \ldots, w_n) = h_x(f(w, w_2, \ldots, w_n), w, w_2, \ldots, w_n) \text{ for } x \in X$$

(c) **Minimization** in $\{x\}^*$, where x is an element of X, is the operation which, when applied to $g:(X^*)^n \to X^*$, yields the function $f:(X^*)^{n-1} \to X^*$ defined by

$$f(w_1, \ldots, w_{n-1}) = \mu_x w[g(w_1, \ldots, w_{n-1}, w) = 1]$$

the string x^k for which k is the smallest integer such that $g(w_1, \ldots, w_{n-1}, x^k) = 1$, while $g(w_1, \ldots, w_{n-1}, x^l)$ is defined, but non-null, for $0 \le l < k$.

We then say that a function is **primitive recursive** if it can be built up from the functions (i), (ii), and (iii) by a finite number of applications of the operations of composition and recursion; and is **partial recursive** if it can be built up from the functions (i), (ii), and (iii) by a finite number of applications of the operations of composition, recursion, *and* minimization.

○

The reader may find it instructive to compare this inductive definition of two families of functions with the inductive definition of the family of regular sets that we give in Section 4-2.

It is possible to show that p_Z and δ_Z, as defined above, are primitive recursive (on X_b) for any machine Z. It then follows that $\widehat{\delta}_Z$ is *primitive recursive* and that δ_Z^* is thus *partial recursive*. Using the methods of Section 3-3, the following result can in fact be shown (though we do *not* provide the proof here).

THEOREM 1

A function $f:(X^*)^n \to X^*$ is TM-computable iff it is partial recursive.   □

It is results of this kind that confirm the widely held belief (known as **Turing's hypothesis** or **Church's thesis**) that a function can be effectively computed by any means whatsoever only if it can be computed by a Turing machine. Thus when, in the next section, we show that no Turing machine can solve a problem, we convince ourselves that there is *no effective procedure* at all for solving it.

EXERCISES FOR SECTION 3-1

1. For the Turing machine given in Example 1, the following inputs will result in the machine halting:

(a)	1	b	q_0	0	
(b)	1	b	q_0	b	0
(c)	1	0	q_0	b	1
(d)	1	1	q_0	b	1

(e)	1	1	q_0	0	1
(f)	1	q_0	1	0	
(g)	1	q_0	1	0	1

In each case find the corresponding terminal ID by determining the corresponding computation.

2.   For the Turing machine given in Example 1, determine $F_Z^b(1000)$.

3.   Construct a Turing machine Z such that F_Z^2 is a total TM-computable function, but such that F_Z^b is *not* always defined. [Hint: Let Z move right until it meets the second blank. If, on moving right one more square, it finds a blank, it stops; if not, it goes into an endless loop.]

4.   In Example 4, why do we need the quintuple q_5 b b L q_s?

5.   Write an alternative program for a TM which computes the same function as in Example 4, but which will halt with output 0 if after its first scan it finds that there is not exactly one 1 on its tape.

6.   With reference to Example 5, prove that $\langle 2m \rangle = \langle m - 1 \rangle 2$.

7.   Using the techniques of the last part of Example 5, describe a Turing machine which, if started in state q_0 while scanning the left-most symbol of the string $\langle m \rangle b \langle n \rangle$, will finally halt with the string $\langle m + n \rangle$ on the tape.

8.   Find a Turing machine Z with input alphabet $X_b = \{0, 1, 2, b\}$ such that

$$F_Z(x) = \begin{cases} 1 \text{ if } x \text{ is a string of } n^2 \text{ ones, for some } n \\ 0 \text{ if } x \text{ is a string of } m \text{ ones, } m \neq n^2 \text{ for any } n \end{cases}$$

and we shall not worry about the value for strings not in $\{1\}^*$. [Hint: If we note the equalities $(n + 1)^2 = n^2 + 2n + 1$ and $2n + 1 = (2(n - 1) + 1) + 2$, we can find a machine with 12 states which will do this task. A better trick, or slicker programming, may well lower this figure.]

3-2   Universality and the Halting Problem

A familiar concept in computer science is that once a computer, say M, is sufficiently "general-purpose," a program written for any other machine may be recoded to yield a program for M which will compute the same function. We shall take a careful look at such a process of translation when we study how to prove the correctness of a compiler in Section 4-5. Here we present a 1936 result due to A. M. Turing that antedates the digital computer by almost a decade and yet conveys the essential idea of our opening sentence: namely, that there exists a Turing machine U which is universal, in the sense that the behavior of any other machine Z may be encoded as a string $e(Z)$ such that U will process the w of any string of the form $e(Z), w$ just as w would be processed by Z; diagramatically, we mean

$$w \underset{Z}{\mapsto} w' \Rightarrow (e(Z), w) \underset{U}{\mapsto} e(Z), w'$$

Before constructing our universal machine U, we build upon the examples which extended our feel for the utility of lists of quintuples for describing

Turing machines to show how to enumerate these lists, and in an effective way, so that given an integer k we may effectively find our kth TM; and given a TM, we may effectively find k, its position in the enumeration. (This is essentially the same problem as that of enumerating finite automata which was discussed in Section 2–4.)

Let us always encode the states of a TM as $q_0, q_1, \ldots, q_{p-1}$ and the inputs as $x_0, x_1, \ldots, x_{n-1}$ (with $x_0 = b$) and call the maximum of p and n the **degree** of the TM. Note that there are only finitely many TMs of a given degree.

We represent a TM of degree d by the ordered list of its quintuples, where the ordering is such that $q_i x_j \ldots$ precedes $q_i x_k \ldots$ if $j < k$, and $q_i \ldots$ precedes $q_j \ldots$ if $i < j$. We may then arrange the TMs of degree d in "dictionary" order by considering the list of their quintuples as words formed from an appropriate alphabet. (Recall that halting configurations have no quintuple representations.)

Finally, by placing first the TMs of degree 1, then those of degree 2, and so on, we obtain an **effective enumeration** (quite obviously infinite)

$$Z_1, Z_2, Z_3, \ldots, Z_k, Z_{k+1}, \ldots$$

in which every Turing machine (each represented by its list of quintuples) appears.

Here we have used the notion of effective enumeration in only the informal sense. However, the clever reader may note that if we identify a TM with its list of quintuples as printed in some finite alphabet, then it is possible to design a TM which can go from a list of quintuples to the number n (in binary notation, say) that encodes it; and, conversely, to design another TM which can convert n into the list of quintuples that it encodes. To this end, we shall now give a more explicit scheme for effectively enumerating the Turing machines.

Let us encode x_j as the string $x\langle j\rangle_{10}$, where $\langle j\rangle_{10}$ is the number j written out in base ten with the highest order digit nonzero (save that $\langle 0\rangle_{10} = 0$). Similarly, encode q_k as $q\langle k\rangle_{10}$. A typical quintuple might then be encoded as $q1x7x13Lq2$. [Recall that this represents $P(q_1, x_7) = (q_2, x_{13}, L)$.]

We then replace a list of quintuples by the string of encoded quintuples so arranged that the quintuple beginning $q_i x_j$ precedes the quintuple beginning $q_k x_\ell$ if $i < k$, or if $i = k$ but $j < \ell$, successive quintuples being separated by semicolons. For instance, the list

$$
\begin{array}{ccccc}
q_0 & x_1 & x_2 & L & q_0 \\
q_0 & x_2 & x_1 & R & q_1 \\
q_1 & x_0 & x_2 & N & q_2 \\
q_1 & x_2 & x_2 & R & q_1
\end{array}
$$

is encoded by the string:

$$q0x1x2Lq0;q0x2x1Rq1;q1x0x2Nq2;q1x2x2R1 \tag{1}$$

Now notice that the only symbols we use in such an encoding are elements of the set $\{0, 1, 2, 3, 4, 5, 6, 7, 8, 9, q, x, R, L, N, ;\}$. Since there are 16 symbols in this set, we may regard the string (1) of quintuples as a single number written in base 16.

Thus, we have given an effective procedure for going from a Turing machine (once we have labelled the inputs and states appropriately) to a single base 16 number. Given a Turing machine Z, we shall call the number so obtained its **description number**, $DN(Z)$.

Now we must verify that we can reverse the process. It should be clear that most numbers written in base 16 cannot be obtained as description numbers of Turing machines. Thus, let us associate *every* number which is not of the form $DN(Z)$ with the trivial machine Z_{ϕ}, which has one input and one state, and which just sits there; its list of quintuples is empty.

Now, given a number to radix 16, we scan it from left to right. If it does not break up into a sequence of quintuples, arranged in proper order and separated by semicolons, we stop with Z_{ϕ} as the result of our computation. If the decoded number does break up into a sequence of quintuples (arranged in proper order and separated by semicolons), our output is the Turing machine Z described by the corresponding list of quintuples. Furthermore, if p is the largest index j of an x_j in that list, and n is the largest index k of a q_k in that list, then Z has input alphabet $\{x_0, \ldots, x_p\}$ and state set $\{q_0, \ldots, q_n\}$. (Remember, there are no quintuples representing halting configurations.)

Thus, we have an effective procedure for retrieving Z from the number $DN(Z)$.

We have specified two distinct ways of enumerating all the Turing machines as a sequence

$$Z_1, Z_2, Z_3, \ldots, Z_k, \ldots$$

such that given Z we can effectively find that k for which $Z = Z_k$, and such that given k we can effectively find Z_k.

There are many other such effective enumerations;† different ones are more convenient for different purposes. However, we shall find that for general theoretical enquiries, all these enumerations are equally effective (!); and that for nearly all our studies, it will suffice to know that an enumeration is effective, without bothering to mention the specific details of the encoding of TMs (lists of quintuples) as numbers.

---

† We may equally well effectively enumerate the TMs with a fixed tape alphabet $X_b = X \cup \{b\}$.

We shall now show how numerical functions may be computed by Turing machines. We shall say the string $x_1 \ldots x_n \in \{1, 2, \ldots, r\}^*$ is the **r-adic encoding** of $m \in \mathbf{N}$ (and write $\langle m \rangle_r = x_n \ldots x_1$) iff $m = \sum_{j=1}^{n} x_j r^{j-1}$; and so $\langle 0 \rangle_r = \Lambda$. Compare this with the **r-ary encoding**: $\langle m \rangle'_r = x_n \ldots x_1$ with each $x_j \in \{0, 1, \ldots, r-1\}$ iff $m = \sum_{j=1}^{n} x_j r^{j-1}$, and $\langle 0 \rangle'_r = 0 = 00 = 00 \ldots 0$. Note that the 1-adic encoding of $n \in \mathbf{N}$ is a string of n 1's, but there is no such thing as a 1-ary encoding.

DEFINITION 1

A numerical function $f: \mathbf{N}^n \to \mathbf{N}$ is **TM-computable to radix r** iff there exists a Turing machine Z with alphabet $\{b, 1, 2, \ldots, r\}$ such that

$$F_Z^n(\langle m_1 \rangle_r, \ldots, \langle m_n \rangle_r) = \langle f(m_1, \ldots, m_n) \rangle_r$$

where it is understood that if either side of the equation is undefined, then both sides are.   ○

In fact, it can be shown that a numerical function f is TM-computable to radix r $(r \geq 1)$ iff it is TM-computable to radix 1. Thus we may drop the qualifying phrase "to radix r" and simply speak of a numerical function as TM-computable. It may be shown that the choice of an encoding of numbers is irrelevant so long as it is effective; for instance, it may be proved that a numerical function f is (partial) TM-computable iff there exists a TM Z such that

$$f(n) = \text{the number of 1's in the string } F_Z^b(b^n 1)$$

To foreshadow our study of the halting problem, we provide a result that relates our enumeration of Turing machines to our discussion of numerical functions.

THEOREM 1

There is no total TM-computable numerical function g which enumerates the total recursive functions in the sense that the partial TM-computable function h is total iff h equals the function $F_{g(n)}^1$ computed by $Z_{g(n)}$ for some n.

Proof Outline

In this proof we shall make use of the notion that, if we can outline an effective procedure for computing a function, then in fact it is TM-computable. The reader who feels that this is unreasonable may return and fill in the details after our discussion of the halting problem.

Let us interpret each F_n^1 (i.e., $F_{Z_n}^1$) as a numerical function computed to a suitable radix. If g is a total TM-computable function, then the following is an effective procedure for computing a *total* numerical function: given n, compute $g(n)$, then find $Z_{g(n)}$ and use it to compute $F_{g(n)}^1(n)$, and then add one to this result.

Thus, if $F_{g(n)}^1$ is *total* for every n, then we conclude that

$$h(n) = F_{g(n)}^1(n) + 1$$

is a total TM-computable function. But it cannot equal $F_{g(n_0)}^1$ for any n_0, for then we would have the contradiction $h(n_0) = F_{g(n_0)}^1(n_0) = F_{g(n_0)}^1(n_0) + 1$. Thus, we conclude that for any total TM-computable numerical function g, the enumeration $F_{g(0)}^1, F_{g(1)}^1, F_{g(2)}^1, \ldots$ cannot contain all (and only) the total functions. $\square$

We now turn to the universal TM U. Firstly, we will show that there is no loss of generality in simulating machines having only the two symbols, say b and 1, in their input alphabet. Secondly, we will outline a Universal machine $\widehat{U}$ which uses three tape heads to accomplish its task. Finally we will show that $\widehat{U}$ may be replaced by a single-headed U, albeit at a great reduction in computation speed.

Our first stage is a simple one. If we replace each symbol of a large tape alphabet by a distinct string of m symbols from $\{1, b\}^m$, we may simulate our original machine Z by a new machine $\widehat{Z}$ which simulates a single move of Z in at most $3m - 2$ moves according to the scheme shown in Figure 3–2.

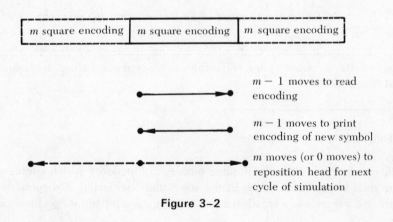

| m square encoding | m square encoding | m square encoding |

$m - 1$ moves to read encoding

$m - 1$ moves to print encoding of new symbol

m moves (or 0 moves) to reposition head for next cycle of simulation

Figure 3–2

Let us now state this result formally, and then provide a careful proof for the case $m = 2$.

THEOREM 2

Given any Turing machine $Z = (Q, X_b, P, q_0)$ and any injective encoding $h: X_b \to \{1, b\}^m$, there exists a Turing machine

$$\hat{Z} = (\hat{Q}, \{1\}_b, \hat{P}, \hat{q}_0)$$

which simulates Z in a precise sense as follows: there exists an encoding $h': Q \to \hat{Q}$ of states of Z such that for every ID $\alpha q \beta$ of Z we may obtain the encoding of its successor in $3m - 2$ steps by the use of $\hat{Z}$; that is

$$\delta_Z(\alpha q \beta) = \alpha' q' \beta' \implies \delta_{\hat{Z}}^{3m-2}(h(\alpha)h'(q)h(\beta)) = h(\alpha')h'(q')h(\beta')$$

Proof

Let us consider the case $m = 2$. Thus, assume we have $X = \{b, x_1, x_2, x_3\}$ and the bijection h given by $h(b) = bb$, $h(x_1) = b1$, $h(x_2) = 1b$, $h(x_3) = 11$.
 We set

$$\hat{Q} = Q \times \{0, 1, 2, 3\} \times \{b, 1\} \times \{L, R, N\}$$

and define the function

$$h': Q \to \hat{Q}: q \mapsto (q, 0, b, N)$$

The cycle of simulation by $\hat{Z}$ of the action of q upon symbol x in Z proceeds in four steps. In each step, we use the components of the quadruples as indicators as follows: (state of Z, stage of simulation cycle, Z'—symbol to be remembered, direction in which Z is to move next).

(i) In state $(q, 0, b, N)$ read the first symbol of $h(x)$, say it is x, and store it as the third component of the state (i.e., change b to $\tilde{x}$). Update the counter from 0 to 1. The result is $(q, 1, \tilde{x}, N)$. Move right one square.

(ii) In state $(q, 1, \tilde{x}, N)$ read the second symbol of $h(x)$. This, together with $\tilde{x}$, determines x completely. (Recall that q and x determine the quintuple $qxq'x'M$ of Z whose action is to be simulated.) Change q to q', update the counter from 1 to 2, print the second symbol of $h(x')$ and store its first symbol (say it is $\hat{x}$) in the third component of the state, and store M (where $M \in \{L, R, N\}$) in the fourth component of the state. Move left one square.

(iii) In state $(q', 2, \widehat{x}, M)$ print $\widehat{x}$, go to state $(q', 3, b, M)$, and move 2 squares M.

(iv) In state $(q', 3, b, M)$, go to state $(q', 0, b, N)$ and move 2 squares M. $\square$

The reader should make sure he has understood this construction by applying it to the special case of a 3-state Turing machine with $m = 2$ and checking that a simple computation proceeds as desired.

We now show how any Turing machine Z with a 2-symbol alphabet can be simulated by a Turing machine $\widehat{U}$ which has three heads with which it can scan the three tracks of a tape, as shown in Figure 3–3.

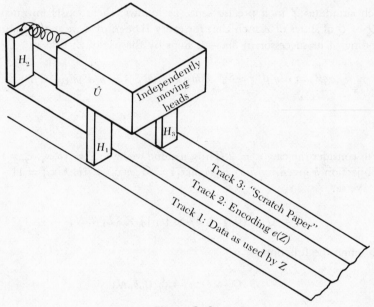

Figure 3–3

The idea is that H_1 sits on the first track of tape just the way that the head of Z sits on its binary tape. $\widehat{U}$ then consults the quintuples of Z, using H_2 to read their encoding on track 2, to command H_1 what to print and how to move; it uses H_3 on track 3 for the subsidiary computations required to reposition H_2 to scan the correct quintuple encoding at the next cycle of the simulation.

Although the details can be filled in in many ways, they are not very illuminating, and so will be omitted. The reader may find a complete and elegant characterization of a Universal Turing machine in Chapters 6 and 7 of Marvin Minsky's book entitled "Computation: Finite and Infinite Machines." Here let us content ourselves with indicating how a multi-head machine can be reduced to a single head machine.

Suppose that we have a machine with p heads scanning a single tape on which are printed symbols from the alphabet X_b. Then at any time the control box will be in a state q of Q, and will receive as input the p symbols scanned by its heads, i.e., an element of $(X_b)^p$. The output of the control unit is an element of $((X_b)^p \times M) \cup \{\text{halt}\}$, where $M = \{I \mid I$ is a possible instruction to the heads to move at most distance $1\}$ (where we use the metric

$$|x - x'| = \sum_{i=1}^{l} |x_i - x'_i| \text{ on the } l\text{-dimensional tape}).$$

Thus, the Turing machine is specified as usual by quintuples

$$q_i x_j x_k I q_l$$

with the sole difference that the x's and I's are "vectors," and that we must employ a convention for use if two heads try to print different symbols on a single "square." A computation of such a machine starts with the assignment of a state to the control unit, of non-blank symbols to a finite number of "squares," and of positions for all the heads; and it then proceeds in the usual fashion, stopping when and only when no quintuple beginning with $q_i x_j$ is applicable.

Our task is to show that any such computation can be simulated, in a suitable sense, on an "ordinary" Turing machine (i.e., with $p = 1$) such that the number of steps required for such a simulation is bounded.

LEMMA 3 (REDUCTION OF HEADS)

If a generalized Turing machine $\widehat{Z}$ has p scanners on a single 1-dimensional tape, then it may be simulated by an ordinary TM Z in such a way that a single step of $\widehat{Z}$, when its tape is n squares long, may be simulated by Z in at most $2n + 2p$ steps.

Proof

Let our p-head machine $\widehat{Z}$ have alphabet X_b. We simulate it with a 1-head machine Z with alphabet $(X_b \times S_p) \cup \{*\}$, where S_p is the set of all subsets of $\{1, 2, \ldots, p\}$, and $*$ will mark the left-hand end of the tape. (Why don't we need a marker at both ends?) We write x for $(x, \varnothing)$.

If $\widehat{Z}$ has the non-blank tape

$$x_1 x_2 \ldots x_m$$

with head j scanning x_{i_j}, we let Z have its head scan the left-most square of

$$(x_1, \mathfrak{X}_1)(x_2, \mathfrak{X}_2) \ldots (x_m, \mathfrak{X}_m)$$

where
$$\mathcal{H}_k = \{\, j \mid k = i_j \,\}$$

Thus we encode

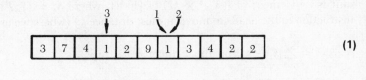

$$\begin{array}{|c|c|c|c|c|c|c|c|c|c|c|} \hline 3 & 7 & 4 & 1 & 2 & 9 & 1 & 3 & 4 & 2 & 2 \\ \hline \end{array}$$ **(1)**

by

$$\downarrow$$
$$*\quad 3\quad 7\quad 4\quad (1, \{3\})\quad 2\quad 9\quad (1, \{1, 2\})\quad 3\quad 4\quad 2\quad 2$$

Thus, the head information is encoded on the tape. It is now necessary to design the logic so that this information is updated after each cycle of the simulation. The control box of Z contains p registers which are to contain the p scanned symbols of $\widehat{Z}$.

In a simulation, Z moves ↓ right from * until it has filled all p registers. It then "knows" the new settings required, and moves ↓ left, changing squares appropriately, until it has returned to * (which may have to be displaced one square left).

If the right-most square in which the second symbol is non-null is n squares to the right of *, then the simulation will take at most $2n + 2p$ steps, the extra $2p$ steps being required to simulate the worst possible repositioning of heads.   □

Another mode of simulation requires only p extra symbols $S_1, \ldots, S_p$, encoding (1) by

$$3\quad 7\quad 4\quad S_3\quad 1\quad 2\quad 9\quad S_1\quad S_2\quad 1\quad 3\quad 4\quad 2\quad 2$$

or with *no* extra symbols encoding (1) as†

$$b\quad 3\quad b\quad 7\quad b\quad 4\quad 3\quad 1\quad b\quad 2\quad b\quad 9\quad 6\quad 3\quad b\quad 4\quad b\quad 2\quad b\quad 2$$

We chose a method which seemed easy to describe and which can be further reduced with our knowledge of alphabet reduction.

We have thus established, in outline, the following result:

THEOREM 4 (THE UNIVERSAL TURING MACHINE)

There exists a Turing machine U which is universal in the sense that

$$F_U(DN(Z), w) = DN(Z), F_Z(w)$$

---

†Here we use the encoding:

$\varnothing$	$\{1\}$	$\{2\}$	$\{3\}$	$\{2, 3\}$	$\{1, 3\}$	$\{1, 2\}$	$\{1, 2, 3\}$
↕	↕	↕	↕	↕	↕	↕	↕
b	1	2	3	4	5	6	7

for every TM Z, and every w for which $F_Z(w)$ is defined (for suitable binary encodings of the expressions on each side of the equality).   □

Having demonstrated the power and flexibility of effective computation, as captured in Turing machines, we now show that even this power and flexibility has limits.

A very practical question for the computer scientist is: "Will this program process data in the way intended?" Even more fundamental, perhaps, than determining whether or not a program is correct is telling whether or not it will terminate at all, let alone with the right answer. Rephrasing the last question in terms of Turing machines, then, we have:

THE HALTING PROBLEM

Given a Turing machine Z_n, and a data string w, is $F_{Z_n}(w)$ defined? That is, does Z_n ever halt if started in its q_0 state scanning the left-most square of w?

It would be pleasant if we could find some universal halting tester which, when given a number n and a string w, could effectively tell us whether or not the machine Z_n will ever halt if its input data is w. However, our next theorem will tell us that no such machine exists. Before we give the formal proof that *no* effective procedure can solve the halting problem, let us see why the *obvious* procedure fails. Let us simply take the Universal machine U and run it on the tape $(e(Z_n), w)$. When it halts, control is transferred to a subroutine that prints out a 1 to signify that the computation of Z_n on w does indeed halt. But when can control be transferred to a subroutine that prints a 0 to signify that Z_n never halts with data w? After a billion years of simulation by U, are we to conclude that Z_n will *never* halt on w, or that, with the passage of another eon or two, computation will clearly halt? This approach clearly fails. But to prove that *all* approaches fail is a far more subtle task, and to prove it we must use a descendant of the diagonal argument used by Cantor (cf. Section 2-4) to show that no enumeration could include all the real numbers.

THEOREM 5 (THE HALTING PROBLEM IS UNSOLVABLE)

There exists no Turing machine which can compute the function

$$F_H(n, w) = \begin{cases} 1 \text{ if } F_{Z_n}(w) \text{ is defined} \\ 0 \text{ if } F_{Z_n}(w) \text{ is undefined} \end{cases}$$

Proof

Let us henceforth write f_n for F_{Z_n}, and assume, by way of contradiction, that there does exist a k such that

$$f_k(n, m) = \begin{cases} 1 \text{ if } f_n(m) \text{ is defined} \\ 0 \text{ if } f_n(m) \text{ is undefined} \end{cases}$$

Let $\sigma(m, n)$ be the total effective function which, when given m and n, finds the encoding of the machine which will print $e(Z_m)$, n to the left of its data and then execute the universal program U. Thus

$$f_{\sigma(m,n)}(x) = f_m(n, x)$$

Making use of this machine, we can now build toward our contradiction by combining it with our hypothetical halting-problem solver Z_k to form a machine Z_γ which computes on data (n, x) as follows:

Compute $f_k(\sigma(n, n), x) = y$, say.
If $y = 0$ (i.e., $Z_{\sigma(n,n)}$ does not halt on x) print 1 as result.
If $y = 1$ (i.e., $Z_{\sigma(n,n)}$ does halt on x) compute $f_{\sigma(n,n)}(x) = z$, say.
    If $z = 0$, print 1 as result.
    If $z \neq 0$, print 0 as result.
Thus

$$f_\gamma(n, x) = \begin{cases} 1 \text{ if } f_{\sigma(n,n)}(x) \text{ is undefined or } 0 \\ 0 \text{ if } f_{\sigma(n,n)}(x) \text{ is defined but not } 0 \end{cases}$$

Note that our construction of f_γ is like a diagonal construction, in that we have made $f_\gamma(n, x)$ different from every $f_m(n, x)[= f_{\sigma(m,n)}(x)]$ for which $m = n$. We get a contradiction, then, by taking $m = n = \gamma$ and setting $s = \sigma(\gamma, \gamma)$:

$$\begin{aligned} f_s(x) &= f_{\sigma(\gamma,\gamma)}(x) \\ &= f_\gamma(\gamma, x) \text{ by definition of } \sigma \\ &= \begin{cases} 1 \text{ if } f_s(x) \text{ is undefined or } 0 \\ 0 \text{ if } f_s(x) \text{ is defined but not } 0 \end{cases} \end{aligned}$$

From this contradiction we deduce the impossibility of solving the halting problem with any Turing machine Z_k.   □

EXERCISES FOR SECTION 3–2

1.   Find the description number for the Turing machine given in Example 3–1–1, where the elements of X_b are $b = x_0$, $0 = x_1$, and $1 = x_2$.
2.   Prove (at least in outline) that it would not have mattered in the definition of TM-computability if we had used r-ary instead of r-adic encoding.

3.   Describe the Turing machine associated with each of the following base 16 numbers:

   (a) $q0x0x1Lq0;q0x1x2Rq1;q0x2x1Nq1;q1x0x0Lq1;q1x1x1Nq0;q1x2x2Lq0$
   (b) $q0x1;Rq1x;q2x1x0;Lq1x0Nx1$

3-3   Highly Parallel Machines

With the advent of integrated circuitry, there has been renewed interest in what have been called *iterative arrays,* or *tessellation automata,*† which are machines formed from regular arrays of quite complex machines, such as might be formed on a single semiconductor chip. Such arrays have also been of interest because of von Neumann's theory of self-reproducing automata. We start, then, by giving an informal account of von Neumann's theory. After this, we provide the formal definition of tessellation automata, and show how each Turing machine may be easily embedded in a one-dimensional tessellation. We close by providing a general model of parallel computation which subsumes the tessellation automata but which still only computes (cf. Section 3-1) partial recursive functions.

Von Neumann [1951] noted that when machines built other machines, there was a degradation in complexity (an assembly line is more complicated than what it produces), whereas the offspring of an animal seems generally to be at least as complex as the parent, with complexity increasing in the long range of evolution. Von Neumann asked whether there was an immutable difference here, or whether one could design "self-reproducing machines" which could produce other machines without a degradation in complexity. Such a question suggests that we study automata theory not just in terms of processing input sequences to yield outputs, but rather in terms of a more constructional approach in which we study how information can be read out and processed to control the growth and change in structure of an automaton.

Let us see, then, how we might describe, in relation to Turing machines, a complicated machine which can produce something as complicated as itself. We first observe that the question: "Is there a machine which, if set loose in a component-rich environment, will form components into a copy of itself?" can be made trivial, as in the "domino example" in Figure 3-4.

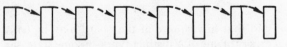

Figure 3-4   Trivial self-reproduction. A domino on edge is the basic component. We stand dominoes in a chain, as shown, and let the automaton we want to reproduce be a *falling* domino. A falling domino knocks down its neighbor, and thus "reproduces"—*falling* is propagated down the chain.

---

†A **tessella** is a small square piece of marble, say, out of which a mosaic pavement may be made. A **tessellation** is then such a mosaic. Replacing the tessella by automata, we form a tessellation automaton!

   Motivated by the fact that in human reproduction a single cell, containing a large but nonetheless finite number of ongoing chemical reactions, can develop into an aggregate with much greater capabilities, let us consider the following artificial, but at least automata-theoretic, question: "How, starting from one fixed kind of finite automaton as basic cell and given any Turing machine, can we design an automaton able to simulate that Turing machine, and which can also reproduce itself?" If the question is phrased in this way, we can avoid the domino objection. To complete the formalization of this (admittedly non-embryological) problem, consider an infinite "chess board," with each square either empty or containing a single component. Each component can be in one of various states, and we think of an organism as represented by a group of cells, collected together somewhere in the plane (see Figure 3–5). We are thus talking of regions in a tessellation automaton.

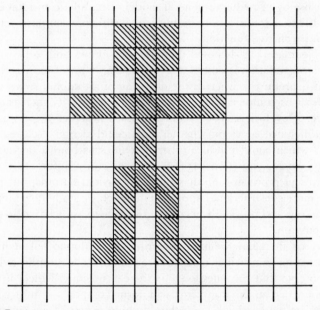

Figure 3–5   An "organism" of active (hatched) cells embedded in a chessboard array.

   We have said that any square of the board may be empty or contain some component, say of one of N distinct types, in some state, say q_i. However, we may lump these $N + 1$ alternatives into one super-component C, which has one more state than the total number of states of the N components. For mathematical purposes, it is easier to think of there being a copy of one fixed component in every cell, so that rather than study the kinematics of components moving around in the plane we look at a more tractable process of how an array, with the remaining cells in the passive state, passes information to compute, and to "construct" new configurations.

Von Neumann [1966] was able to show that with a 29-state "super-component" he could set up a simulation of a complex Turing-type machine which, besides being able to carry out computations on its tape, would also be able to "reproduce" itself. The 29 states would be seen as several states corresponding to an OR-gate, several states corresponding to an AND-gate, several states corresponding to different types of transmission line, and so forth. Von Neumann's proof was not completed at the time of his death, but the manuscript he left was edited by Arthur Burks, and has since been published as a book called *The Theory of Self-Reproducing Automata*. The proof is nearly 200 pages long. (This price we pay for simple components is a complex program. To take an analogy from computer programming, it's like trying to program in machine language, rather than in an appropriate high-level language. In biological terms, we might say that it's like trying to understand a complicated organism directly in terms of macromolecules, rather than via the intermediary of cellular structure.)

Turing's result that there exists a universal computing machine suggested to von Neumann that there might be a universal construction machine A, which, when furnished with the suitable description I_N of any appropriate automaton N, will construct a copy of N (see Figure 3-6).

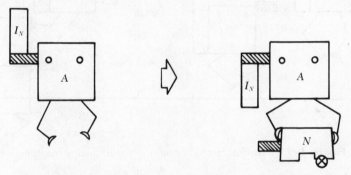

Figure 3-6   Fanciful description of universal constructor A.

In what follows, all automata for whose construction we use A will share with A the property of having a place where an instruction I can be inserted. We may thus talk of "inserting a given instruction I into a given automaton."

If the automaton A has description I_A inserted into it, it will proceed to construct a copy of A. However, A is *not* self-reproducing, for A with appended description I_A produces A without I_A—it is as if a cell had split in two with only one of the daughter cells containing the genetic message. Adding a description of I_A to I_A does not help—now $A + I_A + I_{I_A}$ produces $A + I_A$, and we seem to be in danger of an infinite regress. Such a consideration suggested to von Neumann that the correct strategy might involve "duplication of the genetic material." He thus introduced an automaton B (Figure 3-7) which can make a copy of any instruction I with which it is furnished—I being an aggregate of elementary parts, and B just being a

(I)   (II)

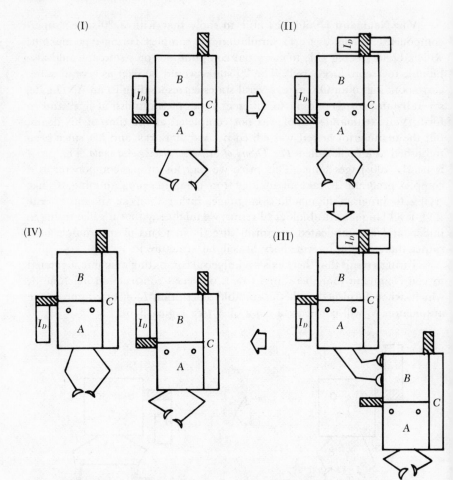

(IV)   (III)

Figure 3–7   Fanciful description of a self-reproducing machine.

"copier." Next, automaton C will insert the copy of I into the automaton constructed by A. Finally, C will separate this construction from the system $A + B + C$ and "turn it loose" as an independent entity.

Let us then denote the total aggregate $A + B + C$ of Figure 3–7 by D. In order to function, the aggregate D must have an instruction I inserted into A. Let I_D be the description of D, and let E be D with I_D inserted into A. Then E *is* self-reproductive and no vicious circle is involved, since D exists before we have to define the instruction I_D.

We thus see that once we can prove the existence of a universal constructor for automata constructed of a given set of components, the logic required to proceed to a self-reproducing automaton is very simple, though there is something somewhat whimsical in the idea of a universal constructor, as if a mother could have offspring of any species, depending only on the father.

Our concern now is to examine the difficulties involved in actually providing a universal constructor. Von Neumann did not do this in his 1951 original paper and the task involves over a hundred pages of his 1966 book. The problem is essentially this: A Turing machine is only required to carry out logical manipulations on its tape, sensing symbols, moving the tape, printing symbols, and carrying out elementary logical operations. A universal *computer* only has to carry out the same operations, but a universal *constructor* must also be able to recognize components, move them around, manipulate them, join them together. Thus, presumably, constructors of Turing machines require more components than do Turing machines themselves. We are immediately confronted with the possibility of another infinite regress! Given a set of components C_1, to construct machines which build all the automata made of components from C_1, we may need a bigger set of components C_2. To build all machines constructed of components C_2, we may need a larger set C_3 of components, and so on. The question is: "Is there a fixed point? Can we find a set of components C such that all automata built from components of C can be constructed by automata built from the same set C?" This may be called **the fixed point problem for components;** it is the fundamental problem in the theory of self-reproducing automata. Once we have found a set of components C from which, for each automaton A, there can be built an automaton $c(A)$ which constructs A, it turns out to be a fairly routine matter to prove the existence of a universal constructor. We then know from von Neumann that it is a simple matter to prove **the construction fixed point theorem,** namely that there exists a self-reproducing machine U which can construct a copy of U. There have been several procedures following on von Neumann's to exhibit a set of components which satisfies the component fixed point theorem. Von Neumann (1966) used 29-state components and gave an elaborate construction taking about 200 pages. James Thatcher (1965) used the same 29-state components as von Neumann, but gave a more elegant construction of perhaps half the length. E. F. Codd (1965), with remarkable ingenuity and interaction with a computer, showed that a construction similar to von Neumann's could go through using components with only eight states. Arbib (1966) showed that the construction could be done with great simplicity, in a matter of eight pages, if one allowed the use of much more complicated components (but no more complicated than the chips now available thanks to integrated circuitry).

Rather than detail these various structures here, we turn to a more formal presentation of tessellation automata, which, as we have already suggested in Figure 3-5, may be thought of as arrays of identical automata, with each automaton placed at a node of a graph which is infinite but extremely regular. We consider graphs whose vertices are the points with integer coordinates in some n-dimensional Euclidean space; i.e., we consider sets $\mathbf{Z}^n = \{(z_1, \ldots, z_n) | z_j \in \mathbf{Z}, 1 \leq j \leq n\}$, $\mathbf{Z}$ being the set of all integers. ($\mathbf{Z}^n$ may be replaced by any abelian group, but the easy generalization need not concern us here.) Then the edges are so disposed that any cell has the same edges—as far as *relative* position goes—that it would have anywhere in the graph.

DEFINITION 1

A **tessellation automaton** is given by the following specification:

(i) There is a graph G with a set of vertices $\mathbf{Z}^n$ for some n, and a finite subset $\langle g_1, \ldots, g_d \rangle$ of $\mathbf{Z}^n$ called the **template** such that an edge leads from z_1 to z_2 in G iff $z_1 - z_2$ is in the template.

(ii) At each vertex of G there is a copy of a given automaton which is of degree d in the sense that $M = (Q^d, QQ, \delta, id_Q)$; i.e., M has d input lines, each bearing a signal from q, so that if M is in state q at time t and receives input q_j on its jth input line, $1 \leq j \leq d$, then its output at t is q, while its state at time $t + 1$ is $\delta(q, (q_1, \ldots, q_d))$. The jth input to the automaton at z is supplied by the state of the automaton at $z + g_j$. We require that the automaton have a **quiescent state** q_0 such that a quiescent cell will remain quiescent if all its neighbors are quiescent:
$\delta(q_0, q_0, \ldots, q_0) = q_0$. ○

Thus, a linear array in which each cell receives inputs from its neighbors has the underlying graph $\mathbf{Z}$ with template $\langle -1, 1 \rangle$, while a two-dimensional array in which a cell receives inputs from the adjacent cells along the axis directions has $\mathbf{Z}^2$ with template $\langle (-1, 0), (0, 1), (1, 0), (0, -1) \rangle$.

It is usual to graph a tessellation with cells occupying squares rather than points; in Figure 3–8 we have sketched a fragment of a two-dimensional

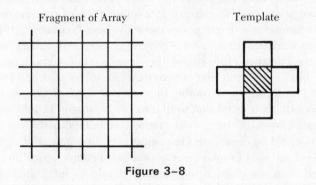

Fragment of Array   Template

Figure 3–8

array, and also shown the template for $\langle (-1, 0), (0, 1), (1, 0), (0, -1) \rangle$ which is such that if the cross-hatched square is placed over any cell, then the other cells of the template will be over the cells from which that cell receives its input.

Let us check our understanding of these ideas by observing the following trivial fact:

FACT 1

Given any Turing machine Z, there exists an automaton M_Z of degree 2 which, if inserted at the nodes of the tessellation $\{\mathbf{Z}, \langle -1, 1 \rangle\}$, will simulate Z.

Proof

We let M_Z have two halves—the top half corresponds to Z's control head, either in some state or unactivated, while the bottom half corresponds to a square of Z's tape, possibly blank. Then if at any time Z is in state q scanning x_j of the string $x_1 \ldots x_n$ of symbols, the tessellation will have all but n squares blank, and those will have $x_1, \ldots, x_n$ on their "tape halves" while all but the jth will have unactivated "state halves," the jth square having q in its state half, as shown in Figure 3–9.

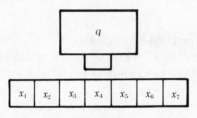

is simulated by

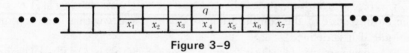

Figure 3–9

It is left as Exercise 1 to write out how a quintuple $qxx'mq'$ is to be reflected in the next-state function $\delta : \widehat{Q} \times \widehat{Q}^2 \to \widehat{Q}$, where $\widehat{Q} = Q \cup \{b\} \times X$ is the state set of M_Z. □

COROLLARY 2

Given a tessellation and an initial pattern, it is undecidable whether or not a "steady state" (i.e., no further change of state in any cell) will be reached.

Proof

Just consider the embedding of a Turing machine Z with an unsolvable halting problem (Theorem 3–2–5). The resultant tessellation will reach steady state if and only if Z halts computing when started from the ID corresponding to the initial pattern in the configuration.   □

To provide the promised general framework for the study of highly parallel computers, we start by introducing the notion of a recursive computer. On this basis, we can prove that various computer models compute only partial recursive functions. If at some time a computer has n registers, the jth of which contains the word w_j, we may represent the *complete state* of the computer by the string $w_1 b w_2 b \ldots b w_n$ in Y^*, where we assume that the spacing symbol b does not occur in any w_j. Now recall Definitions 3–1–2 through 3–1–6, which set forth Turing machine computations and the functions which they computed. With this in mind and the special interpretation of Y^* given above, the reader may find it easy to digest the following string of definitions:

DEFINITION 2

A **recursive computer** $\mathcal{C}$ on the alphabet Y is a partial recursive function $f_{\mathcal{C}} : Y^* \to Y^*$. We call $\widehat{Q} = Y^*$ the set of **complete states** for $\mathcal{C}$; and call $\xi \in \widehat{Q}$ a **halting state** if $f_{\mathcal{C}}(\xi) = \xi$. A **computation** for $\mathcal{C}$ is then any finite sequence

$$\xi_0, \xi_1, \xi_2, \ldots, \xi_n$$

of elements of $\widehat{Q}$ such that $\xi_{j+1} = f_{\mathcal{C}}(\xi_j) \neq \xi_j$ for $0 \leq j < n$, and, further, $\xi_n = f_{\mathcal{C}}(\xi_n)$ is a halting state. Given a state ξ of Q, we define $f_{\mathcal{C}}^*(\xi)$ to be the halting state of the computation of $\mathcal{C}$ which starts with ξ (and is thus unique, if it is defined).

A **program** Π for $\mathcal{C}$ is then a pair of maps $\alpha : (X^*)^M \to Q$ and $\beta : Q \to (X^*)^n$ which are partial recursive on $(X \cup Y)$. The (partial) function computed by $\mathcal{C}$ with program Π is then the function $\mathcal{C}_\Pi : (X^*)^m \to (X^*)^n$ defined by commutativity of the diagram

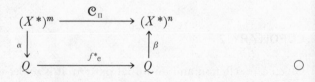

○

In other words, $\mathcal{C}_\Pi$ is the computation obtained (i) by using α to read the data and appropriate instructions into memory, and (ii) computing with $\mathcal{C}$ until the computation halts, whereupon (iii) β is used to read the result from the registers. In any case, it is then straightforward to verify (Exercise 2) the following theorem, which provides the framework for proving partial recursiveness of various computed functions.

THEOREM 3

If $\mathcal{C}$ is a recursive computer and Π is a program for $\mathcal{C}$, then the function $\mathcal{C}_\Pi$ is partial recursive. □

With this, we now turn to a more structured version of the recursive computer which is broad enough to encompass a host of parallel computer architectures, including the tessellation automata discussed above.

In specifying such a computer, we shall assume that there is an underlying graph $G = (V, E \subset V \times V)$, such that a register is located at each node in V. (Note that we no longer require G to be highly regular.) In many models it will be convenient to take V infinite, but to require that only finitely many registers are nonempty at any time. For example, many conventional computers can be subsumed in the case $G = (\mathbf{N}, \sigma)$ of an array of registers numbered 0, 1, 2, 3, . . . but with no *a priori* bound on the number of active registers. Again, tessellation automata correspond to the case in which $V = \mathbf{Z}^n$ and E is the neighborhood relation.

We next assume that the machine has associated with it a set B of possible values which may occur in its registers. Certain of these values may be decoded uniquely as operational or jumping commands. Let $B_1 \subset B$ be the set of "command values." We then define $\nu(v, b)$ to be the instruction encoded by value b if it occurs in register v. (The dependence of ν on v takes account of one type of relative addressing. It is straightforward to include index registers, too, but we shall not do it here.)

We postulate that the computer can execute any of a finite repertoire $g_1, \ldots, g_k$ of operations

$$g_j : B^{m_j} \to B^{n_j}$$

and

$$\bar{g}_1, \ldots, \bar{g}_l \text{ of jump instructions}$$

$$\bar{g}_j : B^{r_j} \to \text{finite subsets of } V$$

We then require that $\nu(v, b)$ for $b \in B_1$ have one of the following forms:

(i) an operation on a series of registers, $(v'_1, \ldots, v'_{n_j}) : = g_j(v_1, \ldots v_{m_j})$ with each v'_i and v_t in V; or

(ii) a jump instruction, $J_{\bar{g}_j}(v_1, \ldots v_{r_j})$ with each v_i in V; or

(iii) a pair of instructions, one of form (i) and one of form (ii).

We denote the set of such forms by $\mathcal{I}(g_1, \ldots, g_k; \bar{g}_1, \ldots, \bar{g}_l)$. Finally, we must adopt a convention as to what happens when several values are being simultaneously loaded into one register. We adopt, completely arbitrarily, the convention that it retains its old value. Putting all the pieces together, we obtain the following general definition:

DEFINITION 3

A **parallel stored program machine (PSPM)** is determined by a sextuple

$$M = [G = (V, E), B, \{g_1, \ldots, g_k\}, \{\overline{g}_1, \ldots, \overline{g}_\ell\}, B_1, \nu]$$

where $G = (V, E)$ is a directed graph, the **address structure** of M,

> B is the set of possible **register contents**,
> $\{g_1, \ldots, g_k\}$ is a set of **operation labels**,
> $\{\overline{g}_1, \ldots, \overline{g}_\ell\}$ is a set of **jump labels**,
> $B_1 \subset B$ is the set of **instruction encodings**; and
> $\nu \colon V \times B_1 \to \mathcal{I}(g_1, \ldots g_k; \ \overline{g}_1 \ldots \overline{g}_\ell)$ is the **instruction decoding function.** ○

If V is infinite, we shall distinguish a $b_0 \in B$ to represent "empty contents," and allow only finitely many registers to be "nonempty." A state of the recursive computer $\mathcal{C}_M$ associated with PSPM M is then given by specifying the contents of each register, and which registers are to be decoded for instruction execution. Thus, $\mathcal{C}_M$ has the state set $\widehat{Q}$, where

$$\widehat{Q} = \{(f, S) \mid \{v \mid f(v) \neq b_0\} \text{ is finite, and } S \text{ is finite}\} \subset B^V \times \mathcal{P}(V).$$

Given $\widehat{Q}$, we may form $\mathcal{C}_M$, on defining the next-state function δ_M by

$$\delta_M(q, S) = (q', S')$$

where (q', S') is defined as follows:
  (a) We decode $\nu(v, q(v))$ for each $v \in S$.
  (b) If decoding yields an operation of the form

$$(v'_1, \ldots, v'_{n_j}) \colon = g_j(v_1, \ldots, v_{m_j})$$

we then take $q'(v'_r)$, $1 \leq r \leq n_j$, to be the rth component of $g_j(q(v_1), \ldots q(v_{m_j}))$—save that, should another operation specify a different value for $q'(v'_r)$, we simply set $q'(v'_r) = q(v_r)$. In general, we set $q'(v) = q(v)$ unless a new value is specified in the above manner by some $\nu(v, q(v))$ for $v \in S$.
  (c) If decoding yields a jump of the form

$$J_{\overline{g}_j}(v_1, \ldots, v_{r_j})$$

we include each element of the finite set $\overline{g}_j(q(v_1), \ldots, q(v_{r_j}))$ in S'. If v is in S and $\nu(v, q(b))$ is a pure operation (i.e., of form (i)) then we also include

v in S'. S' contains all and only the elements of V specified in the preceding two sentences.

There is a genuine sense in which δ_M is a partial recursive function—so that $\mathcal{C}_M$ is indeed a recursive computer—so long as ν, the g_j's and the $\bar{g}_k$'s are partial recursive.

This formulation is very general. For example, it includes the tessellation automaton of Definition 1 on $\mathbf{Z}$ with neighborhood template $\{g_1, \ldots, g_d\}$ and transition function $\delta : Q^{n+1} \to Q$ on taking $B = Q$ and setting

$$\nu(v, b) = [v_1 := \delta(v, v + g_1, \ldots, v + g_n), J_{\bar{g}(v)}]$$

for all $v \in V$, all $b \in B$, where $J_{\bar{g}(v)} = \{v, v + g_1, \ldots, v + g_n\}$.

EXERCISES FOR SECTION 3–3

1.   Write out the prescription for quintuple implementation in the proof of Fact 1. [Hint: A cell does not change state unless it or an immediate neighbor has an activated "state half."]

2.   Emulate the discussion of equations (2) and (3) of Section 3–1 to prove Theorem 3 of Section 3–3.

3.   Prove Theorem 3–1–1.

Further Reading for Chapter 3

M. A. Arbib [1969] Theories of Abstract Automata, Englewood Cliffs, N.J.: Prentice-Hall.

A. W. Burks (Ed.) [1970] Essays on Cellular Automata, Urbana: University of Illinois Press.

M. Davis [1958] Computability and Unsolvability, New York: McGraw-Hill.

E. Engeler [1973] Introduction to the Theory of Computation, New York: Academic Press.

M. Minsky [1967] Computation: Finite and Infinite Machines, Englewood Cliffs, N.J.: Prentice-Hall.

H. Rogers, Jr. [1959] The Present Theory of Turing Machine Computability, New York: McGraw-Hill.

J. von Neumann [1966] Theory of Self-Reproducing Automata (edited and completed by A. W. Burks), Urbana: University of Illinois Press.

For more on Turing machines and partial recursive functions, see Arbib, Davis, Engeler, Minsky, and Rogers; for more on self-reproducing automata, see Arbib, Burks, and von Neumann.

CHAPTER 4

Language Theory

Since software is one of the two main interests of the computer scientist, and since programming languages are the heart of software, it comes as no surprise that language theory constitutes one of the crucial topics in the application of algebraic methods to computer and information science. In this chapter, we present many of the key concepts of language theory. One of the most important formalizations of programming languages has been that of the context-free language, such as in the Backus-Naur Form (BNF) used in the specification of ALGOL. Thus, we start our development by providing the theory of context-free languages in Section 4–1. However, it must be stressed that the context-free languages themselves provide but one of many formalizations of languages, and thus in Section 4–2 we turn to an overall perspective which places them in a hierarchy that starts with the regular sets (or finite-state languages) associated with finite automata, then moves on to the context-free languages, and then on to the context-sensitive languages, culminating in the recursive sets which are decided by Turing machines and, finally, the recursively enumerable sets which are accepted by Turing machines. Moreover, we shall relate Gödel's Incompleteness Theorem to the distinction between the recursive and the recursively enumerable sets.

In many texts on language, primary emphasis is placed upon the strings which constitute the language. However, a growing amount of research in computer science is based upon the realization that it is the derivation trees that constitute the fundamental structure of interest. Thus, in Section 4–3, we provide an introduction to tree automata—machines which can process the rooted trees which we introduced in Section 1–5. Then, in Section 4–4, we use the notation introduced by the Polish logicians to represent trees as strings, so that we may reveal pushdown automata as the machines which simulate tree automata when they process the strings which encode the trees. Our discussion of tree automata is not only valuable in relation to language theory, but will prove of importance in providing motivation for our study of universal algebras in Section 5-6.

Finally, in Section 4-5, we depart somewhat from our study of language theory, while still maintaining our interest in programming languages, by proving the correctness of a simple compiler. The crucial point about this section is that it reinforces our emphasis in Section 1-1 on the importance of induction as a proof technique. In this case we look at programs represented by trees, and, by a proof which uses induction on the height of the tree, prove that each tree program is correctly compiled.

4-1   Context-Free Languages

Noam Chomsky suggested the idea of a *context-free grammar* as an important *partial* specification of the syntax of natural languages. (The name is justified by the fact that replacement of grammatical symbols is not influenced by context, in contrast with the context-sensitive grammars we shall introduce in Section 4-2.) We shall provide one example of its use in a natural language, and then show how a context-free grammar has been used in specifying a fragment of the programming language ALGOL. In Section 4-2, we shall then formalize the ways in which machine computations may decide membership in, or accept or generate the members of, various formal languages before studying, in Section 4-3, context-free grammars in terms of tree-processing. Then, in Section 4-4, we shall study the Polish notation for representing trees, and we shall relate context-free grammars to pushdown automata.

Consider the following observations on English grammar:

(1) One of the possible forms of a legal *sentence* is a *noun phrase* followed by a *verb phrase*.
(2) One of the possible forms of a legal *noun phrase* is an *article* followed by a *noun*.
(3) One of the possible forms of a legal *verb phrase* is a *verb* followed by an *adverb*.
(4) *Sank* is a legal *verb*.
(5) *The* is a legal *article*.
(6) *Hippopotamus* is a legal *noun*.
(7) *Gracefully* is a legal *adverb*.

If we introduce the abbreviation "$A \mapsto BC\ldots$" for "one of the possible forms of a legal A is a B followed by a C followed by $\ldots$", and if we use the symbols S, VP, NP, Art, N, Adv, and V for sentence, verb phrase, noun phrase, article, noun, adverb and verb, respectively, then these seven fragments of English grammar may be succinctly presented as follows:

(1) S ⟼ NP VP
(2) NP ⟼ Art N
(3) VP ⟼ V Adv
(4) V ⟼ sank
(5) Art ⟼ the
(6) N ⟼ hippopotamus
(7) Adv ⟼ gracefully

A **legal derivation** is one in which we form a sentence by starting with the symbol S and replacing the grammatical **variables** as specified by one of the seven **production rules** given above, until finally we only have **terminals,** or words of English, and no further replacements are possible. In the present example, the productions are so limited that they can only produce one English sentence:

S ⟼ NP VP	by applying production (1)
⟼ Art N VP	by (2)
⟼ the N VP	by (5)
⟼ the hippopotamus VP	by (6)
⟼ the hippopotamus V Adv	by (3)
⟼ the hippopotamus sank Adv	by (4)
⟼ the hippopotamus sank gracefully	by (7)

In the above example, the order of applications could have been varied (write out a legal derivation in which the second production applied is (3)), but in each case the derivation would have corresponded to the same **derivation tree** (shown in Figure 4–1) in which we join a symbol to those symbols,

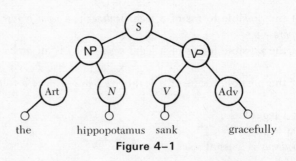

Figure 4–1

in correct order, by which it is replaced by the application of a production. In other words, the left-to-right ordering in our trees reflects the left-to-right ordering in our strings.

The particular sequence of string processing that we gave above to represent this tree is called the **leftmost derivation** since in it we have always applied our productions to the leftmost variable in the string at each stage.

In a moment we shall give a formal definition of the notion of context-free grammar we have just exemplified, and then provide an example which makes the important point that a finite set of productions can produce an infinite set of syntactically correct strings. But, first, a few comments: We may note that we have just described the process of **generating** a sentence. Equally, if not more, important in applications will be the inverse process of **parsing** a sentence, i.e., of finding whether there is any syntactically correct way of generating it.

In the rest of this chapter we shall concentrate on programming languages. Thus, before leaving the subject of natural languages, we should note that the context-free grammars we are studying here tell only part of the story of the syntax of natural languages. Another important function of English grammar, for example, is to let us recognize that "the hippopotamus is not sinking gracefully" can be thought of as obtained by first growing "the hippopotamus sinks gracefully" and then carrying out a "negation **transformation**" which inserts the word "not" and modifies the verb appropriately. Other transformations can change the tense of a verb, shift the voice of a sentence from active to passive, and so forth. The point remains that all these devices are *syntactic* in that they depend only upon the form of a sentence, and not upon its meaning, and are thus too restricted to give a fully satisfactory account of natural language.

DEFINITION 1

A **context-free grammar** is a quadruplet† $G = (X, V, P, S)$, where:

> X is a finite set called the set of **terminals**
> V is a finite set (with $X \cap V = \varnothing$) called the set of **variables**
> P is a finite subset of $V \times (X \cup V)^*$ called the set of **productions**
>> [We write $v \mapsto u$ if $v \in V$, $u \in (X \cup V)^*$, and $(v, u) \in P$]
> S is an element of V and is called the **starting symbol.**   ○

Example 1

Let us choose $X = \{a, b\}$ and $V = \{S\}$. Thus, $X \cup V = \{a, b, S\}$. We select the set of productions to be:

$$P = \{(S, ab), (S, aSb)\} \subset V \times (X \cup V)^*$$

---

†The reader will note the effects of a finite alphabet—graph theorists denote their graphs by G; for a linguist G denotes a grammar. Context will serve to indicate which discrete structure the current G denotes.

Hence, we may write the production as:

$$S \mapsto ab$$
$$S \mapsto aSb$$

Therefore, (X, V, P, S) is a context-free grammar. ◊

We say a string w *generates* a string w' if and only if we can transform w into w' by successive applications of the rules of P:

DEFINITION 2

Given two strings w, w' in $(X \cup V)^*$, we say:

(i) w **directly generates** w' (via G) [written $w \underset{G}{\Rightarrow} w'$] iff there exist $\tilde{w}$ and $\hat{w}$ in $(X \cup V)^*$ and (v, u) in P such that

$$w = \tilde{w}v\hat{w} \text{ and } w' = \tilde{w}u\hat{w}$$

i.e., iff w' can be obtained from w by a single application of a production from P.

(ii) w **generates** w' (via G) [written $w \underset{G}{\overset{*}{\Rightarrow}} w'$] iff $w = w'$, or there exists an $n \geq 2$ and strings $w_1, \ldots, w_n$ such that

$$w = w_1, w_j \underset{G}{\Rightarrow} w_{j+1} \text{ for } j = 1, 2, \ldots, n-1, \text{ and } w_n = w'$$

i.e., iff w' can be obtained from w by *zero* or more applications of productions from P. ○

Example 2

We select $X = \{a, b\}$ and $V = \{S, y, z\}$. Then $X \cup V = \{a, b, S, y, z\}$. If we choose the productions:

$$S \mapsto ay \qquad y \mapsto bzz \qquad z \mapsto ab$$
$$S \mapsto bz \qquad \qquad \qquad z \mapsto ba$$

the result is another context-free grammar,

$$(\{a, b\}, \{S, y, z\}, \{(S, ay), (S, bz), (y, bzz), (z, ab), (z, ba)\}, S)$$

Let $$w = abySbSzbaa$$

and $$w' = abybzbSzbaa$$

Then $w \underset{G}{\Rightarrow} w'$ since we can set

$$w = \widetilde{w}u\widehat{w} \quad \text{and} \quad w' = \widetilde{w}v\widehat{w}$$

where
$$\widetilde{w} = aby$$
$$v = S$$
$$\widehat{w} = bSzbaa$$
$$u = bz$$

and $(v, u) \in P$.

Similarly, if $w'' = abybbabayabbaa$, then we can find the strings w_1, w_2, w_3, w_4, w_5 such that

$$w_1 = w$$
$$w_2 = abybzbSzbaa \qquad (w = w_1 \underset{G}{\Rightarrow} w_2)$$
$$w_3 = abybbabSzbaa \qquad (w_2 \underset{G}{\Rightarrow} w_3)$$
$$w_4 = abybbabayzbaa \qquad (w_3 \Rightarrow w_4)$$
$$w_5 = abybbabayabbaa \qquad (w_4 \underset{G}{\Rightarrow} w_5)$$
$$w'' = w_5$$

Hence, $w \underset{G}{\overset{*}{\Rightarrow}} w''$. ◊

We then define $L(G)$ to be the set of terminal strings which S generates via G:

DEFINITION 3

Let G be a context-free grammar with starting symbol S. Then the **language** of G is denoted by $L(G)$ and is defined by

$$L(G) = \{w \in X^* \mid S \underset{G}{\overset{*}{\Rightarrow}} w\}.$$

We say a set $L \subset X^*$ is a **context-free language** if $L = L(G)$ for some context-free grammar G. ○

Example 3

Let us determine the language $L(G)$ of the context-free grammar G considered in Example 2. We have

$$S \underset{G}{\Rightarrow} ay \underset{G}{\Rightarrow} abzz \underset{G}{\Rightarrow} ababz \underset{G}{\Rightarrow} ababab$$

$$S \underset{G}{\Rightarrow} ay \underset{G}{\Rightarrow} abzz \underset{G}{\Rightarrow} ababz \underset{G}{\Rightarrow} ababba$$

$$S \underset{G}{\Rightarrow} ay \underset{G}{\Rightarrow} abzz \underset{G}{\Rightarrow} abbaz \underset{G}{\Rightarrow} abbaab$$

$$S \underset{G}{\Rightarrow} ay \underset{G}{\Rightarrow} abzz \underset{G}{\Rightarrow} abbaz \underset{G}{\Rightarrow} abbaba$$

$$S \underset{G}{\Rightarrow} bz \underset{G}{\Rightarrow} bab$$

$$S \underset{G}{\Rightarrow} bz \underset{G}{\Rightarrow} bba$$

Hence,

$$L(G) = \{bba, bab, abbaba, abbaab, ababba, ababab\},$$

and this language is finite. Note that the string *ababba* can be produced by the derivation tree shown in Figure 4–2. ◊

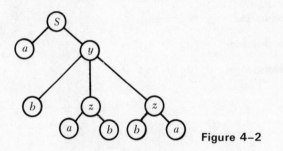

Figure 4–2

In developing the theory of context-free languages, it will often be convenient to make the requirement that no production has an empty right-hand side:

LEMMA 1

Let $G = (V, X, P, S)$ be a context-free grammar; and let G' be obtained from G by the following process:

(i) Set $j = 0$ and $P_0 = P$.

(ii) Set $V_{j+1} = \{v \in V | (v, \Lambda) \in P_j\}$ and $\hat{P}_j = P_j \backslash \{(v, \Lambda) | v \in V_{j+1}\}$.

(iii) Form P_{j+1} from $\hat{P}_j$ by replacing each (v, w) in $\hat{P}_j$ by the set of all $(v, \hat{w})$ for which $\hat{w}$ is obtained from w by deleting zero or more occurrences of variables which lie in V_{j+1}.

(iv) If $P_{j+1} = \widehat{P}_j$, then set $P' = \widehat{P}_j$ and go to step (v); otherwise, replace j by $j + 1$, and return to step (ii).

(v) Set $G' = (V, X, P', S)$.

Then no production of G' has an empty right-hand side, and $L(G') = L(G)\backslash\{\Lambda\}$.

Proof

Exercise 4. $\square$

Example 4

Let $X = \{a, b\}$, $V = \{S\}$, and $P = \{(S, \Lambda), (S, ab), (S, aSb)\}$. Then $V_1 = S$ and

$$\widehat{P}_0 = \{(S, ab), (S, aSb)\}$$
$$P_1 = \{(S, ab), (S, aSb), (S, ab)\} = \widehat{P}_0$$

Then $P' = \{(S, ab), (S, aSb)\}$ and we have

$$L(G') = \{a^n b^n \,|\, n \geq 1\} = \{a^n b^n \,|\, n \geq 0\}\backslash\{\Lambda\}$$
$$= L(G)\backslash\{\Lambda\} \qquad\qquad \Diamond$$

We now turn to an example, extracted from the syntax of the programming language ALGOL, of a context-free grammar which generates an infinite "language."

Example 5

We shall proceed in stages to introduce various aspects of the syntax of decimal number representations. At each stage, we shall present versions of the syntax in three ways, to help the reader gain familiarity with each: one in set-theoretic form, one in terms of the productions as introduced above, and one using the BNF (Backus-Naur Form) notation for productions introduced in specifying ALGOL.

A. Digits:

(i) Set Theory: $D = \{0, 1, 2, 3, 4, 5, 6, 7, 8, 9\}$

(ii) Productions: $D \mapsto 0$
$$D \mapsto 1$$
$$\vdots$$
$$D \mapsto 8$$
$$D \mapsto 9$$

(iii) ALGOL: ⟨digit⟩ :: = 0|1|2| ... |8|9

[Note that in ALGOL notation we use a symbol in brackets ⟨ ⟩ to denote a class, and symbols without brackets, such as 0 or 9, to indicate a terminal. The vertical bar "|" is shorthand for "or." We then read ⟨X⟩ :: = A|⟨B⟩C| ... as "something is an X if it is A, or a B followed by C or ...."]

B. Unsigned Integers:

(i) Set Theory: $U = D^+ = \{d_1 \ldots d_n \mid d_j \in D, \text{ for } j = 1, 2, \ldots, n\}$
Note that this implies† that

$$U = D \cup UD$$

i.e., an unsigned integer is either a single digit, or else a nonempty string of digits (which is thus another unsigned integer) followed by a digit. We may characterize U in production form as follows:

(ii) Productions $U \mapsto D$
$$U \mapsto UD \qquad \text{(and the productions for } D\text{)}$$

For example, the string 375 would be produced by the derivation tree given in Figure 4–3.

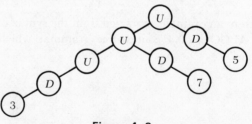

Figure 4–3

(iii) ALGOL: ⟨unsigned integer⟩ :: = ⟨digit⟩|⟨unsigned integer⟩⟨digit⟩

C. Decimal Fractions:

(i) Set Theory: $F = \{\cdot w \mid w \in U\} = \cdot U$
(ii) Productions: $F \mapsto \cdot U$ (and the productions for U)
(iii) ALGOL: ⟨decimal fraction⟩ :: = ·⟨unsigned integer⟩

---

†Recall that for any two sets A and B of strings, AB is the set of all concatenations of strings of the form $\{ab \mid a \in A, b \in B\}$.

D. Decimal Number

(i) Set Theory: $\widehat{D} = U \cup F \cup UF$
$$= \{w \,|\, w \in D^+\} \cup \{\cdot w \,|\, w \in D^+\} \cup$$
$$\{w \cdot w' \,|\, w, w' \in D^+\}$$

(ii) Productions: $\widehat{D} \mapsto U$
$\widehat{D} \mapsto F$ (and the productions for U and F)
$\widehat{D} \mapsto UF$

(iii) ALGOL: ⟨decimal number⟩ :: = ⟨unsigned integer⟩|⟨decimal fraction⟩|⟨unsigned integer⟩ ⟨decimal fraction⟩

For example, the derivation 3.141 may be represented by the tree shown in Figure 4–4, where the dotted outline indicates how we may read off the

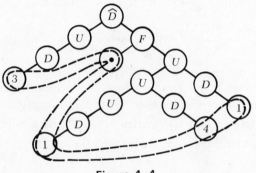

Figure 4–4

derived string by passing from left to right along the "frontier" of the tree. We shall formalize this notion of a derivation tree in Definition 6 below. A string belongs to the language iff it is the frontier of a valid derivation tree. Why could we *not* derive 3..141?

Let us just check that our specification of the decimal numbers can indeed be combined into a context-free grammar. In fact, they are specified by the grammar (V, X, P, S) if we take

$$V = \{D, U, F, \widehat{D}\}$$
$$X = \{\cdot, 0, 1, 2, 3, 4, 5, 6, 7, 8, 9\}$$
(note that $\cdot$ is one of our terminals)
$$S = \widehat{D}$$
$$P = \{D \mapsto 0, \ldots, D \mapsto 9, U \mapsto D, U \mapsto UD, F \mapsto \cdot U,$$
$$\widehat{D} \mapsto U, \widehat{D} \mapsto F, \widehat{D} \mapsto UF\} \qquad\qquad \lozenge$$

We have seen that the essence of a derivation is expressed in its derivation tree, and we shall take up the study of context-free grammars as tree-manipulating systems in Section 4–3. To simplify the discussion, we shall henceforth (save for Section 2) use Lemma 1 to justify *restricting our attention to productions with nonempty right hand sides*. We have also noted that many sequences of production applications can correspond to a single derivation tree, but that we can obtain a unique correspondence between derivation sequences and derivation trees of *terminal* strings (i.e., strings of X^+) by using left-most derivations, which we now formalize:

DEFINITION 4

Given two strings w, w' in $(X \cup V)^+$, we say that

(i) w **directly ℓ-generates** w' (via G) [written $w \underset{G}{\Rightarrow}_\ell w'$] iff there exists $\widetilde{w}$ in X^* and $\widehat{w}$ in $(X \cup V)^*$ and (v, u) in P such that

$$w = \widetilde{w} v \widehat{w} \quad \text{and} \quad w' = \widetilde{w} u \widehat{w}$$

That is, we use the condition $\widetilde{w}$ in X^* to force the variable v which we replace to be the leftmost variable in w, and include the possibility $\widetilde{w} = \Lambda$ to allow for the possibility that v is in fact the leftmost symbol of w.

(ii) w **ℓ-generates** w' (via G) [written $w \underset{G}{\overset{*}{\Rightarrow}}_\ell w'$] iff $w = w'$ or there exist an $n \geq 2$ and strings $w_1, \ldots, w_n$ such that

$$w = w_1, \ w_j \underset{G}{\Rightarrow}_\ell w_{j+1} \text{ for } j = 1, 2, \ldots, n - 1, \text{ and } w_n = w' \quad \bigcirc$$

Example 6

Returning to the unsigned integers, we note that

$$U \underset{G}{\Rightarrow} UD \underset{G}{\Rightarrow} U5 \underset{G}{\Rightarrow} D5 \underset{G}{\Rightarrow} 45$$

can be replaced by the ℓ-derivation

$$U \underset{G}{\Rightarrow}_\ell UD \underset{G}{\Rightarrow}_\ell DD \underset{G}{\Rightarrow}_\ell 4D \underset{G}{\Rightarrow}_\ell 45$$

but that

$$UDD \underset{G}{\Rightarrow} U4D \underset{G}{\Rightarrow} U45$$

cannot be replaced by a leftmost derivation since the leftmost variable is never replaced. $\Diamond$

However, we take the following truth to be self-evident:

FACT 2

Let $G = (X, V, P, S)$ by any context-free grammar, w any string in $(X \cup V)^+$, and w' any terminal string in the sense that $w' \in X^+$. Then

$$w \underset{G}{\overset{*}{\Rightarrow}} w' \Leftrightarrow w \underset{G}{\overset{*}{\Rightarrow}}_l w'$$

In particular,

$$L(G) = \{w \in X^+ \mid S \underset{G}{\overset{*}{\Rightarrow}}_l w\} \qquad \square$$

In many cases, one needs to know the syntax of an English sentence to interpret its meaning. Consider the headline that appeared in a Denver newspaper in the summer of 1966: "Lieutenant-Governor finally has paid secretary." Abbreviating this to "Lt. has paid secretary" for ease of analysis, we see that this sentence has the two quite distinct derivation trees shown in Figure 4–5, and the first yields a less flattering view of the lieuten-

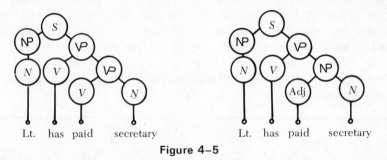

Figure 4–5

ant-governor than the second. In short, one cause of *ambiguity* in a language can be that a given terminal string has several distinct derivations, which lead to separate interpretations. This usually causes little harm in natural languages, where context serves, in most cases, to reduce the ambiguity. However, it will be intolerable in a programming language. Thus, it is often important to know whether or not a context-free grammar G is **unambiguous** in the technical sense: to each string of $L(G)$ there corresponds one and only one leftmost derivation (or, equivalently, one and only one derivation tree).

However, we shall not study ambiguity further in this introductory treatment.

We now make more explicit the way in which a context-free grammar sets forth rules for determining whether or not a tree represents a derivation which is valid with respect to that grammar. First, we must see what becomes of the labelled trees of Section 1–5 when we insist that a label can only occur on nodes with a specified number of successors.

DEFINITION 5

A **multigraded set** is a set Ω together with a **grading** function ν which assigns to each ω in Ω a **finite** subset $\nu(\omega)$ of $\mathbf{N}$ (i.e., $\nu : \Omega \to 2^{\mathbf{N}}$). We say ω has **arity** n (possibly among others) iff $n \in \nu(\omega)$. Let Ω be a multigraded set. Then an Ω-**labelled tree** (Ω-tree for short) is a tree $T \subset \mathbf{N}^*$ together with a function $h : T \to \Omega$ such that if w has n successors (i.e., $w0, w1, \ldots, w(n-1)$ are all in T but $wn \notin T$) then $n \in \nu(h(w))$. $\bigcirc$

Thus, we may either label vertices arbitrarily (in which case A is an arbitrary set) as in Section 1–5, or we may insist that the arity of a label must correspond to the number of successors of a vertex (in which case Ω is a graded set). If $\nu(\omega)$ has only one element n, we may write $\nu(\omega) = n$, rather than $\nu(\omega) = \{n\}$.

Example 7

Let $\Omega = \{0, 1, 2, 3, 4, 5, 6, 7, 8, 9, +, \times\}$ with $\nu(+) = \nu(\times) = 2$ and $\nu(\omega) = 0$ for all other $\omega \in \Omega$. Then clearly Ω can only label trees in which every non-maximal node has two successors (either $+$ or $\times$ labels each such node) while maximal nodes are labelled with digits. Thus the tree in Figure 4–6(a), which corresponds to the valid arithmetic expression $(2 \times 3) + (1 + (4 \times 0))$, is an Ω-tree while that in Figure 4–6(b), which corresponds to the invalid expression $(2 \times 3) + (+ + (4 \times 0))$, is not. $\Diamond$

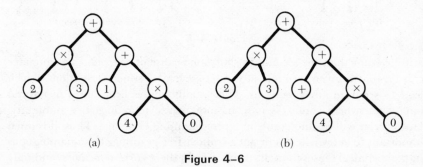

(a)   (b)

Figure 4–6

Example 8

We return to the grammar of Example 4 by which we characterized decimal numbers. It had the productions:

$$D \mapsto 0, \ldots, D \mapsto 9,\ U \mapsto D,\ U \mapsto UD,\ F \mapsto \cdot U,$$
$$\hat{D} \mapsto U,\ \hat{D} \mapsto F,\ \hat{D} \mapsto UF$$

We thus notice that in a valid derivation tree, D will always label a node of arity 1, 0 through 9 will always label nodes of arity 0, while F must always label a node of arity 2. However, U and $\widehat{D}$ can appear on nodes of arity 1 or 2. In this case, then, we take $\Omega = \{0, 1, 2, \ldots, 9, \cdot, D, U, F, \widehat{D}\}$ with

$$\nu(0) = \nu(1) = \cdots = \nu(9) = \nu(\cdot) = \{0\}$$
$$\nu(D) = \{1\}$$
$$\nu(F) = \{2\}$$
$$\nu(U) = \nu(\widehat{D}) = \{1, 2\}, \text{ the set of alternative arities.}$$

Then the tree shown in Figure 4–7 is an Ω-tree, although it is not a valid derivation tree.   ◊

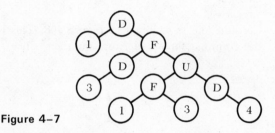

Figure 4–7

Note that in giving h we specify the domain T and the label $h(w)$ on each node $w \in T$, so that h really represents a labelled tree; $h(T)$, on the other hand, is just the set of labels which occur on the labelled tree h.

We may now generalize Example 8 as follows:

DEFINITION 6

Let $G = \{V, X, P, S\}$ be a context-free grammar. Then we define the multi-graded set Ω_G by taking $\Omega_G = V \cup X$, and then defining the grading function $\nu : \Omega_G \to \mathbf{N}$ by the rules:
(a) $\nu(x) = \{0\}$ for all $x \in X$
(b) $\nu(v) = \{n \mid \text{there exists a string } w \text{ of length } n \text{ such that } v \mapsto w \text{ is in } P\}$ ○

We may then say that Ω_G-tree is a *valid derivation tree* if its initial node Λ is labelled by S and the relation between each node and its successors is described by a production of P. Note that the definition of ν ensures that a maximal node is labelled with a terminal symbol; i.e., $0 \in \nu(\omega)$ iff $\omega \in X$.

DEFINITION 7

Let $G = \{V, X, P, S\}$ be a context-free grammar. We say that an Ω_G-tree $h: T \to \Omega_G$ is a **valid derivation tree** for the grammar G if it meets the two conditions:

(i) $h(\Lambda) = S$
(ii) If a node w has successors $w0, w1, \ldots, wn$, then

$$h(w) \mapsto h(w0)h(w1) \ldots h(wn)$$

is a production of P.   ○

Example 9

Consider the tree shown in Figure 4–8. This is a valid derivation tree for the grammar for our decimal numbers, since

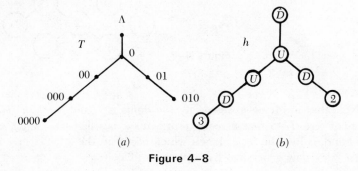

(a)   (b)
Figure 4–8

$\qquad h(\Lambda) = \widehat{D}$, and $\widehat{D}$ is the starting symbol of that grammar
$(h(\Lambda) \mapsto h(\Lambda 0)) = (\widehat{D} \mapsto U)$ is in P
$(h(0) \mapsto h(00)h(01)) = (U \mapsto UD)$ is in P
$(h(00) \mapsto h(000)) = (U \mapsto D)$ is in P
$(h(01) \mapsto h(010)) = (D \mapsto 2)$ is in P
$(h(000) \mapsto h(0000)) = (D \mapsto 3)$ is in P ◊

We have already defined (Section 1–5) the frontier of a tree to be the maximal nodes arranged from left to right. We may similarly define the frontier of a labelled tree to be the string obtained by concatenating the labels of the nodes on the frontier:

DEFINITION 8

Let $h: T \to \Omega$ be a labelled tree, and let $(w_1, \ldots, w_n)$ be the frontier of T. Then the **frontier** of h, denoted $fr(h)$, is the string $h(w_1) \ldots h(w_n)$ of Ω.

○

Example 10

The frontier of the Ω_G-tree of Figure 4–8 is the decimal number 32.   ◊

It should now be obvious that a string belongs to $L(G)$ iff it is the frontier of a valid derivation tree for G.

THEOREM 3

Let G be a context-free grammar, and let $T(G)$ be the set of valid derivation trees for G. Then

$$L(G) = fr(T(G))$$

where by $fr(T(G))$ we mean $\{ fr(h) | h \in T(G) \}$.   □

Note: The theorem asserts that a string of X^+ belongs to $L(G)$ iff there exists a valid derivation tree of which it is the frontier. It does *not* assert that if a string is the frontier of an invalid tree, it does not belong to $L(G)$; e.g., the valid string 32 is the frontier of the invalid tree given in Figure 4–9.

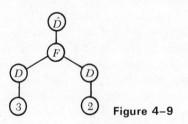

Figure 4–9

The theorem asserts, however, that a string does not belong to $L(G)$ if *every* Ω_G-tree of which it is the frontier is invalid. In Section 4–4, we shall discuss the problem of constructing a machine which will find a valid derivation tree, if one exists, which has a given string as its frontier—in other words, a machine for *parsing* strings.

EXERCISES FOR SECTION 4–1

1. Given the context-free grammar G defined by

$$X = \{a, b\}$$
$$V = \{S, y, z, \alpha\}$$
$$P = \{(S, yz), (S, b), (y, az), (y, \alpha), (z, b\alpha), (\alpha, a), (\alpha, ab)\}$$

determine $L(G)$ and give the derivation tree for each string in $L(G)$.

2. Construct derivation trees for the following decimal numbers:
- **(a)** 295
- **(b)** 47.385
- **(c)** .167

3. Show that the unsigned integers are also generated by the grammar obtained from that of Example 5 by deleting the variable F, deleting the production $F \mapsto \cdot U$, and replacing the productions $\widehat{D} \mapsto F$ and $\widehat{D} \mapsto UF$ by the productions $\widehat{D} \mapsto \cdot U$ and $\widehat{D} \mapsto U \cdot U$.

4. Verify that the process in Lemma 1 eventually terminates, and that $L(G') = L(G) \backslash \{\Lambda\}$.

4–2 Deciding, Accepting, and Generating†

In the last section, we saw how to generate languages—in the formal sense of a set of strings (a *language* on the *alphabet* X is then a subset L of X^*)—using context-free grammars. In this section, we place the context-free languages in a framework which includes languages processed by finite automata at the one end, and languages processed by Turing machines at the other end.

To start this review, let us note that we have, associated with each finite automaton M and state q of M, a *behavior* $M_q : X^* \to Y$ which tells us the output that will be emitted by M after processing an input string, having started in state q; and have associated with each Turing machine Z the *partial function* $F_Z^1 : X^* \to X^*$ which takes an input string and processes it until computation terminates (if it does) to give the result. This ties in with a perspective which views much of automata theory as the study of algorithmically specifiable partial functions $F : X^* \to Y^*$ which specify strings on the output alphabet Y for certain of the strings on the input alphabet X. [Much, but not all, of course. Exceptions are the tessellation automata of Section 3–3 and the tree automata that we shall study in the next section.] Let us then see how we can use any function $F : X^* \to Y^*$ to *decide* membership in a language; to *accept* those strings which belong to a language; or to *generate* a language (these processes may associate distinct languages with the given F). After defining the deciding, accepting and generating processes, we shall

---

†While the remainder of this chapter depends only upon Chapter 1, this section also makes use of concepts from Chapters 2 and 3.

see what they yield for F's associated with finite automata and with Turing machines, respectively, and then relate the context-free languages to the languages so defined.

DEFINITION 1

A subset L of X^* is **decidable** by $F:X^* \to W^*$ if there exist two distinct elements a and b of W^* such that

$$F(w) = \begin{cases} a \text{ if } w \in L \\ b \text{ if } w \notin L \end{cases} \qquad \bigcirc$$

Thus, if we can compute F effectively, we have an algorithm for deciding whether or not a string belongs to L, for Definition 1 guarantees that F is a total function which only takes the values a and b.

DEFINITION 2

A subset L of X^* is **acceptable** by $F:X^* \to W^*$ if there exists an element a of W^* such that

$$F(w) = a \Leftrightarrow w \in L \qquad \bigcirc$$

Thus, any set decidable by F is acceptable by F, though the converse need not be true. Note that, if F is *total* (i.e., defined for all w in X^*) then we may use F to decide whether or not a string belongs to L. However, if F is only partially defined, and we start computing $F(w)$ with some computer, then if after a period of time the computer has not halted, we may not be sure whether it will never halt, in which case w is not in L, or whether it will eventually halt, at which time we would see whether or not $F(w)$ was a in order to determine whether or not w was in L. Since (Section 3-2) there is no algorithm to tell whether or not a Turing machine will halt, it follows that there are sets acceptable by Turing machines which are not decidable by any effective procedure. We shall discuss this more formally in Theorem 11.

DEFINITION 3

A subset L of Y^* is **generable** by $F:X^* \to Y^*$ if and only if L is the empty set or is the image of F:

$$L = F(X^*) = \{F(w) \mid w \in X^*\} \qquad \bigcirc$$

Let us now see what these three definitions yield for finite automata and Turing machines. We shall then place the sets so defined in a general framework of grammatical description which includes the context-free languages.

DEFINITION 4

A subset L of X^* is a **finite-state language** (FSL) if it is accepted by a finite automaton response function $M_q : X^* \to Y$, i.e., there exists a finite automaton M, and a state q and output y of M, such that

$$L = M_q^{-1}(y) = \{w \in X^* \mid M_q(w) = y\}. \qquad \bigcirc$$

Example 1

From the familiar two-state machine of Figure 4–10, we may derive two finite-state languages:

$$M_{q_0}^{-1}(1) = M_{q_1}^{-1}(0) = \{w \in \{0,1\}^* \mid w \text{ contains an odd number of 1's}\}$$

and

$$M_{q_0}^{-1}(0) = M_{q_1}^{-1}(1) = \{w \in \{0,1\}^* \mid w \text{ contains an even number of 1's}\} \qquad \Diamond$$

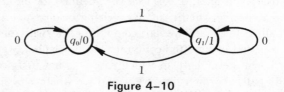

Figure 4–10

Now, a finite automaton response function is always total. Thus, it is to be expected that an FSL is decidable, and not just acceptable. All that is required is a change of output function to transform the machine M from an acceptor to a decider:

LEMMA 1

Let $M = (Q, X, Y, \delta, \beta)$ be a finite automaton. Let $L = M_q^{-1}(y)$ be an FSL, with $q \in Q$ and $y \in Y$. Pick any symbol $y' \neq y$. Then the automaton

$$M' = (Q, X, \{y, y'\}, \delta, \beta')$$

with $\beta':Q \rightarrow \{y,y'\}$ defined by

$$\beta'(q') = \begin{cases} y \text{ if } \beta(q') = y \\ y' \text{ if not} \end{cases}$$

is a decider for L:

$$M'_q(w) = \begin{cases} y \text{ if } w \in L \\ y' \text{ if } w \notin L \end{cases} \qquad \square$$

This clearly yields the following result:

THEOREM 2

A language $L \subset X^*$ is an FSL iff it is decidable by some finite automaton. $\square$

Turning now to generability, it is clear that the subsets of Y generated by the response functions M_q, for finite automata, are dull indeed, since they are simply the subsets of Y (Exercise 1). To restore some pizazz to the discussion of generability, then, we recall from Section 2-1 the notion of an extended response function:

$$\widetilde{M}_q : X^* \rightarrow Y^* : x_1 \ldots x_n \mapsto M_q(\Lambda)M_q(x_1)M_q(x_1 x_2) \ldots M_q(x_1 \ldots x_n).$$

Then in fact we have the following result:

THEOREM 3

A language $L \subset Y^*$ is an FSL if it is generable by some finite automaton M; i.e., if L is empty or if

$$L = \widetilde{M}_q(X^*)$$

for some state q of M.

Before proving Theorem 3, we introduce the important idea of a *non-deterministic machine*. This is a machine for which each input, rather than specifying (given the current state) precisely what the next state will be, instead specifies a *range* of *possible* next states. [This is in distinction to a stochastic machine (Section 6-5) in which each input determines a probability distribution on the next states.]

DEFINITION 5

A nondeterministic automaton

$$M = (Q, X, Y, \widehat{\delta}, \beta)$$

is specified by giving a state set Q, an input set X, an output set Y, an output function $\beta: Q \to Y$, and a nondeterministic next-state function

$$\widehat{\delta}: Q \times X \to \mathcal{P}(Q)$$

which assigns to each q in Q and x in X the subset $\widehat{\delta}(q, x)$ of Q of states which can possibly succeed q after application of input x. ○

Just as we extended $\delta: Q \times X \to Q$ to $\delta^*: Q \times X^* \to Q$, so may we extend $\widehat{\delta}: Q \times X \to \mathcal{P}(Q)$ to $\widehat{\delta}^*: Q \times X^* \to \mathcal{P}(Q)$ by the inductive definition:

$$\widehat{\delta}^*(q, \Lambda) = \{q\} \qquad \text{(Why } \{q\} \text{ and not } q?) \tag{1a}$$

while

$$\widehat{\delta}^*(q, wx) = \bigcup \{\widehat{\delta}(q', x) \mid q' \in \widehat{\delta}^*(q, w)\} \tag{1b}$$

Thus, $\widehat{\delta}^*(q, w)$ is the set of states in which M could possibly be after starting in state q and receiving input sequence w.

Example 2

A nondeterministic automaton may be described by a state diagram just as an ordinary automaton is—save that there may be zero, one, or more than one arrows issuing from a given state node and labelled with the same input. An example is the 3-state machine of Figure 4–11.

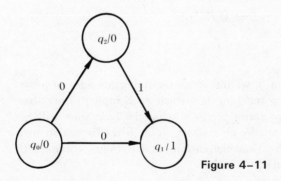

Figure 4–11

Here we have

$$\widehat{\delta}^*(q_0, \Lambda) = \{q_0\}$$
$$\widehat{\delta}^*(q_0, 0) = \{q_1, q_2\}$$
$$\widehat{\delta}^*(q_0, 1) = \varnothing$$
$$\widehat{\delta}^*(q_0, 00) = \varnothing$$
$$\widehat{\delta}^*(q_0, 01) = \{q_1\}$$

and $\widehat{\delta}^*(q_0, w) = \varnothing$ for all other w in $\{0, 1\}^*$.   ◊

We associate languages with nondeterministic finite-state automata (NFAs) by decreeing that for an NFA M, state q, and output y of M,

$$M_q^{-1}(y) = \{w \in X^* \,|\, \text{there exists } q' \text{ in } \widehat{\delta}^*(q, w) \text{ with } \beta(q') = y\}$$

It turns out that even this new definition does not let us escape the FSLs:

THEOREM 4

A language $L \subset X^*$ is an FSL iff it is $M_q^{-1}(y)$ for some NFA M.

Proof

The "only if" part is easy, for given a *deterministic* (i.e., ordinary) automaton M for which the finite-state language $L = M_q^{-1}(y)$, we may simply think of $M = (Q, X, Y, \delta, \beta)$ as being the NFA $\widehat{M} = (Q, X, Y, \widehat{\delta}, \beta)$ for which

$$\widehat{\delta}(q, x) = \{\delta(q, x)\}$$

to see that L also equals $\widehat{M}_q^{-1}(y)$, and so is accepted by an NFA.

The "if" part is somewhat more subtle, but in fact the strategy is fairly obvious from the definition of $\widehat{\delta}^*$ in equation (1)—we simply go from the nondeterministic machine M to a deterministic machine $\widetilde{M}$ which keeps track of all the states in which $\widetilde{M}$ could possibly be.

Let us be given, then, any nondeterministic machine

$$M = (Q, X, Y, \widehat{\delta}, \beta)$$

with specified initial state q and output y. We construct a deterministic automaton $\widehat{M}$ which accepts $M_q^{-1}(y)$ as follows. Pick any symbol $y' \neq y$. Then $\widehat{M}$ is the machine

$$\widehat{M} = (\mathcal{P}(Q), X, \{y, y'\}, \widetilde{\delta}, \widetilde{\beta})$$

whose individual states $\tilde{q} \in \mathcal{P}(Q)$ correspond to subsets of the state set Q of M, and for which $\tilde{\delta}$ and $\tilde{\beta}$ are defined as follows: For each $\tilde{q} \in \mathcal{P}(Q)$ and x in X, we set

$$\tilde{\delta}(\tilde{q}, x) = \bigcup_{q' \in \tilde{q}} \hat{\delta}(q', x)$$

while

$$\tilde{\beta}(\tilde{q}) = \begin{cases} y & \text{if there is a } q' \in \tilde{q} \text{ with } \beta(q) = y \\ y' & \text{if not} \end{cases}$$

It is then clear that

$$\hat{\delta}^*(\{q'\}, w) = \tilde{\delta}^*(q', w)$$

for each q' in Q and w in X^* (simply check the equations (1)) and it is then immediate from the definition of $M_q^{-1}(y)$ that

$$M_q^{-1}(y) = \hat{M}_{\{q\}}^{-1}(y)$$

But if M has a finite number n of states, then $\hat{M}$ has a finite number 2^n of states. Thus $M_q^{-1}(y)$, for our NFA M, is indeed an FSL. □

Example 3

For the machine M of Example 2, we have that

$$M_{q_0}^{-1}(1) = \{0, 01\}.$$

Applying the procedure of the above proof (taking $y = 1$ and $y' = 0$), we get the machine $\hat{M}$ shown in Figure 4–12, where we have only included the

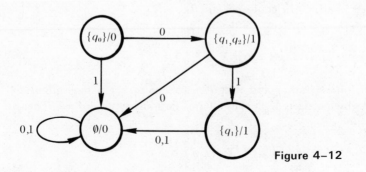

Figure 4–12

states reachable from the initial state $\{q_0\}$. We do indeed see that $\widehat{M}_{\overline{\{q_0\}}}^{-1}(1) = \{0, 01\}$, as desired. ◊

With this background we can return to the proof of Theorem 3, making use of our new knowledge that, in order to verify that a language is an FSL, it suffices to exhibit an NFA which accepts it.

Proof of Theorem 3

We must show that if $L = \widetilde{M}_q(X^*)$ for some FSA M, then L is an FSL. We define an NFA $\widehat{M} = (Q, Y, Y, \widehat{\delta}, \widehat{\beta})$ in terms of the FSA $M = (Q, X, Y, \delta, \beta)$ which accepts L by the rule

$$\widehat{\delta}(q', y) = \{\delta(q', x) \,|\, x \in X \text{ and } \beta[\delta(q', x)] = y\}$$

for each q' in Q and x in X. Then for each $\theta \in Y^*$ it is clear that

$$\widehat{\delta}^*(q', \theta) = \{\delta^*(q', w) \,|\, w \in X^* \text{ and } \widetilde{M}_{q'}(w) = \theta\}$$

Hence, if we set $\widehat{\beta}(q) = 1$ for all $q \in Q$, we have that

$$\begin{aligned}
\widehat{M}_q^{-1}(1) &= \{\theta \in Y^* \,|\, \widehat{\delta}^*(q, \theta) \neq \varnothing\} \\
&= \{\theta \in Y^* \,|\, \text{there exists } w \in X^* \text{ with } \widetilde{M}_q(w) = \theta\} \\
&= \widetilde{M}_q(X^*)
\end{aligned}$$

Since every language acceptable by a nondeterministic finite automaton is an FSL, we conclude that every set generable by a finite automaton must be an FSL. □

One of the questions often raised in language theory is: "Given a language or languages of a given type, and operations upon them, will the resultant languages be of the same type?" We now consider this in terms of three operations upon languages which, as we shall see (Theorem 7), preserve the property of being an FSL. But first let us note the following general fact:

FACT 5

Let $L \subset X^*$ be decidable by the function $F: X^* \to W^*$ with

$$F(w) = \begin{cases} a \text{ if } w \in L \\ b \text{ if } w \notin L \end{cases}$$

Then $\bar{L} = X^*\backslash L$ is also decidable by F.

Proof

We simply interchange the roles of a and b, and then have

$$F(w) = \begin{cases} b \text{ if } w \in \bar{L} \\ a \text{ if } w \notin \bar{L} \end{cases}$$

so that $\bar{L}$ is indeed decidable by F. $\qquad\qquad\square$

COROLLARY 6

If $L \subset X^*$ is an FSL, then so too is $\bar{L}$. $\qquad\qquad\square$

We now note three operations upon languages, not all of which are new:

DEFINITION 6

Given any two subsets L_1 and L_2 of X^*, we define three new sets by the following operations:

Union: $\qquad L_1 \cup L_2 = \{w \,|\, w \in L_1 \text{ or } w \in L_2\}$
Set Product: $\qquad L_1 \cdot L_2 = \{w \,|\, w = w_1 w_2 \text{ with } w_1 \in L_1 \text{ and } w_2 \in L_2\}$
Iteration: $\qquad L_1^* = \{w \,|\, \text{there exists } n \geq 0 \text{ and } w_1, \ldots, w_n \text{ in } L_1$
$\qquad\qquad\qquad\qquad \text{such that } w_1 \ldots w_n = w\}$ $\qquad\qquad\bigcirc$

[In algebraic language, L_1^* is called the monoid **generated** by L_1: it is the smallest subset of X^* which contains the identity Λ and is closed under concatenation (i.e., $\Lambda \in L_1^*$; and $w_1, w_2 \in L_1^* \Rightarrow w_1 w_2 \in L_1^*$).]

Note that, in case L_1 actually equals X, L_1^* does indeed equal X^* in the usual sense.

We say that a set A is **closed** under the operation $m : A \times A \times \cdots \times A \to A$ iff $m(a, a', \ldots, \tilde{a})$ is in A for all a in A, a' in A, ..., $\tilde{a}$ in A. Thus, to say that a family $\mathcal{L}$ of languages (i.e., a set of subsets of X^*) is **closed** under $\cup$, $\cdot$, and * is to say that $L_1 \cup L_2$, $L_1 \cdot L_2$, and L_1^* belong to $\mathcal{L}$ for any choice of L_1 and L_2 in $\mathcal{L}$. We then have the following **closure theorem:**

THEOREM 7

The family of FSLs on a given alphabet X is closed under $\cup$, $\cdot$, and *.

Proof

To say that L_1 and L_2 are FSLs is to say that we have two nondeterministic state graphs $G_j(j = 1, 2)$ with initial states q_{0j}, respectively, such that a string w in X^* belongs to L_j iff w labels at least one directed path in G_j which takes us from q_{0j} to a state-node labelled with output 1. Our theorem is proved if we can show how to manipulate these graphs to get graphs which define nondeterministic acceptors for $L_1 \cup L_2$, $L_1 \cdot L_2$, and L_1^*, and this we now do:

(i) $L_1 \cup L_2$ is accepted by the graph of Figure 4-13(a), in which there is one extra node q_0, and in which there is an edge labelled x from q_0 to node q' of G_j iff there is already an edge labelled x from q_{0j} to q' in G_j. If we label q_0 with a 1 whenever $\Lambda \in L_1 \cup L_2$, it is then clear that w labels a directed path from q_0 to a node labelled with a 1 iff $w \in L_1 \cup L_2$.

(ii) $L_1 \cdot L_2$ is accepted by the graph of Figure 4-13(b), in which there is an extra edge labelled x from state q in G_1 to state q_{02} in G_2 iff there is already an edge leading from q to a state of G_1 labelled with output 1. The states of G_2 then retain their original output labels, while the

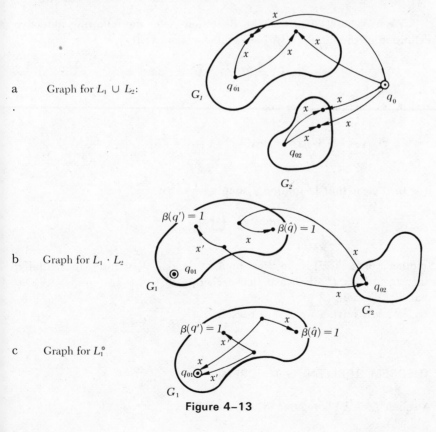

a   Graph for $L_1 \cup L_2$:

b   Graph for $L_1 \cdot L_2$

c   Graph for L_1°

Figure 4-13

states of G_1 are then all relabelled with output 0. A sequence w can then label a path from q_{01} to a state with output 1 iff it breaks into two parts, a part w_1 which leads in G_1 from q_{01} to a state originally labelled 1 in G_1 (but which in the new graph can also label a path to q_{02}), and a part w_2 which leads in G_2 from q_{02} to a state labelled 1; i.e., iff w is in $L_1 \cdot L_2$.

(iii) L_1^* is accepted by the graph of Figure 4–13(c) (Exercise 2).   □

Since every finite subset of X^* is an FSL (Exercise 3), we conclude that every set which can be built up from finite subsets of X^* by a finite number of applications of $\cup$, $\cdot$, and * must be an FSL. In fact, the converse is also true:

DEFINITION 7

A subset L of X^* is **regular** iff L is finite, or can be built up from finite subsets of X^* by a finite number of applications of the operations $\cup$, $\cdot$, and *.   ○

We may note, then, that this definition yields the following inductive definition of the family $\mathcal{R}(X)$ of regular sets on X: If

$$\mathcal{R}_0(X) = \{L \mid L \subset X^* \text{ is finite}\}$$

and if, for each $n \geq 1$, we take

$$\mathcal{R}_{n+1}(X) = \{L_1^* \mid L_1 \in \mathcal{R}_n(X)\} \cup \{L_1 \cup L_2 \mid L_1, L_2 \in \mathcal{R}_n(X)\}$$
$$\cup \{L_1 \cdot L_2 \mid L_1, L_2 \in \mathcal{R}_n(X)\}$$

it is then clear that Definition 7 simply says that

$$\mathcal{R}(X) = \bigcup_{n \geq 0} \mathcal{R}_n(X)$$

In other words, $\mathcal{R}(X)$ is the *closure* of $\mathcal{R}_0(X)$ under $\cup$, $\cdot$, and *. Incidentally, since $L_1 \cup L_1 = L_1$, it is clear that each $L_1 \in \mathcal{R}_n(X)$ is also in $\mathcal{R}_{n+1}(X)$, so that $\mathcal{R}_n(X) \subset \mathcal{R}_{n'}(X)$ for $n' \geq n$.

We now have a well-known result:

THEOREM 8 (KLEENE'S THEOREM)

A subset L of X^* is regular iff it is an FSL.

Proof

That every regular subset is an FSL we have already seen to be an immediate consequence of Theorem 7. It only remains to prove the converse.

Let L be an FSL, with $L = M_{q_1}^{-1}(y)$ for $M = (Q, X, Y, \delta, \beta)$, where we suppose that $Q = \{q_1, \ldots, q_n\}$. We then set

$$R_{ij} = \{w \mid \delta^*(q_i, w) = q_j\}$$

and it is then clear that

$$L = \bigcup \{R_{1j} \mid \beta(q_j) = 1\}$$

Hence, if we can prove that each R_{ij}, with $1 \leq i, j \leq n$, is regular, we can conclude that L, being a finite union of such sets, is itself regular.

To prove the regularity of the R_{ij}'s, we introduce the auxiliary sets

$$R_{ij}^k = \{w \mid w \text{ leads } M \text{ from } q_i \text{ to } q_j \text{ without passing through}$$
$$\text{any state other than } q_1, q_2, \ldots \text{ or } q_k \text{ in between}\}$$
$$= \{x_1 x_2 \ldots x_m \mid \delta^*(q_i, x_1 \ldots x_\ell) = q_r \text{ implies } 1 \leq r \leq k \text{ if}$$
$$1 \leq \ell < m, \text{ and } r = j \text{ if } \ell = m\}$$

We note immediately that $R_{ij}^0 = \{x \in X \mid \delta(q_i, x) = q_j\}$, which is finite and hence regular, while $R_{ij}^n = R_{ij}$. Hence, if we can prove, by induction on k, that each R_{ij}^k is regular, we are done. The basis step is secure, and it only remains to prove the validity of the induction step.

Suppose, then, that we know $R_{i'j'}^k$ to be regular for all i', j'. We must prove that each R_{ij}^{k+1} is also regular. Now, consider (referring to Figure 4–14)

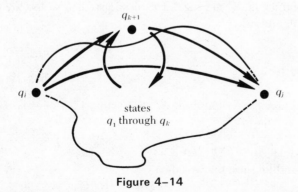

q_{k+1}

q_i

q_j

states
q_1 through q_k

Figure 4–14

some w in R_j^{k+1}. Either it never reaches q_{k+1}, or else it can be broken up into segments $w_1 w_2 \ldots w_m$, $m \geq 2$, where w_1 takes us from q_i to q_{k+1} via $\{q_1, \ldots, q_k\}$, and w_m takes us from q_{k+1} to q_j via $\{q_1, \ldots, q_k\}$, while each remaining w_ℓ (if $m > 2$) takes us from q_{k+1} back to q_{k+1} via $\{q_1, \ldots, q_k\}$. In short, we may write

$$R_{ij}^{k+1} = R_{i,k+1}^{k} \cdot (R_{k+1,k+1}^{k})^* \cdot R_{k+1,j}^{k} \cup R_{ij}^{k} \tag{2}$$

Since, by hypothesis, each of $A = R_{i,k+1}^{k}$, $B = R_{k+1,k+1}^{k}$, $C = R_{k+1,j}^{k}$, and $D = R_{ij}^{k}$ is regular, we deduce that $E = B^*$ is regular. Hence $F = A \cdot E$ is regular, and so $G = F \cdot C$ is regular, so that, finally,

$$R_{ij}^{k+1} = G \cup D$$

is regular. The regularity of L now follows. $\qquad\square$

As the reader may quickly convince himself by applying the induction formula (2) to the automaton of Example 3, the formula, while very helpful for gaining general insight, does not lend itself to ease of computation.

To close our discussion of FSLs, we note that every FSL may be described by a regular expression:

DEFINITION 8

Given an alphabet X, a **regular expression** on X is a string on the alphabet

$$\bar{X} = \{\cup, \cdot, *, (,), \bar{\Lambda}, \bar{\varnothing}\} \cup \{\bar{x}_i \mid x_i \in X\}$$

subject to the following rules:

(i) Each $\bar{x}_i$ is a regular expression, as is each of $\bar{\Lambda}$ and $\bar{\varnothing}$.
(ii) If w_1 and w_2 in $\bar{X}^*$ are regular expressions, then so too are $(w_1 \cup w_2)$, $(w_1 \cdot w_2)$, and w_1^*. $\qquad\bigcirc$

DEFINITION 9

For each regular expression w in $\bar{X}^*$, the **support** $|w|$ of w is the subset of X^* defined as follows:

(i) $|\bar{x}_i| = \{x_i\}$; $|\bar{\Lambda}| = \{\Lambda\}$; $|\bar{\varnothing}| = \varnothing$.
(ii) If $|w_1|$ and $|w_2|$ are known, then

$$|(w_1 \cup w_2)| = |w_1| \cup |w_2|$$
$$|(w_1 \cdot w_2)| = |w_1| \cdot |w_2|$$

and
$$|w_1^*| = |w_1|^*$$

$\qquad\bigcirc$

Given Theorem 8, it is then a simple matter to prove the following theorem:

THEOREM 9

$L \subset X^*$ is an FSL iff it is the support of some regular expression w on X. □

We now turn to the study of languages associated with Turing machine functions $F_Z^1 : X^* \to X^*$, that is, with partial recursive functions.

DEFINITION 10

The language $L \subset X^*$ is said to be **recursive** if and only if L is *decidable* by some recursive function g. ○

Since one can certainly program the function

$$\lambda_{ab} : X^* \to \{0, 1\}^* : w \mapsto \begin{cases} 1 \text{ if } w = a \\ 0 \text{ if } w = b \\ \Lambda \text{ if } w \notin \{a, b\} \end{cases}$$

we can always assume that such a g is replaced by $\lambda_{ab} \circ g$, where $g(w) = a$ if $a \in L$, and $g(w) = b$ if $b \notin L$. But this is just the characteristic function of L. Hence:

FACT 10

A subset L of X^* is a **recursive set** iff its characteristic function χ_L is effectively computable. □

Turning to acceptability, we find that—contrary to our experience in the finite-state case—a Turing machine acceptable set need not be Turing decidable:

Example 4

Let $H_Z \subset X^*$ be the set of strings for which the Turing machine Z halts. Let us modify the machine Z to yield the machine $\widehat{Z}$ that keeps endmarkers in place throughout its computation (Exercise 5) and, further, will erase its tape completely following arrival at a configuration in which Z would halt. In other words, if Z has no quintuple starting with $q'x'$, then $\widehat{Z}$ will have a quintuple

$$q'x'x'N\widehat{q}_L$$

which sends it the erasure subroutine

$$\widehat{q}_L xxL\widehat{q}_L \qquad \text{for } x \neq \$$$
$$\widehat{q}_L \$bR\widehat{q}_R$$
$$\widehat{q}_R xbR\widehat{q}_R \qquad \text{for } x \neq \text{¢}$$
$$\widehat{q}_R \text{ ¢ } bN\widehat{q}_S$$

where $\widehat{q}_L$, $\widehat{q}_R$, and $\widehat{q}_S$ are three new states; so that $\widehat{Z}$ moves left until it finds $\$$, and then moves right, erasing as it goes, until it finds ¢, which it then erases and halts. Then

$$F^1_{\widehat{Z}}(w) = \Lambda \Leftrightarrow w \in H_Z$$

and so H_Z is *acceptable* by the Turing machine $\widehat{Z}$.

Now, suppose that H_Z were decidable by some Turing machine. This would say that for any $w \in X^*$ we could effectively tell whether or not $w \in H_Z$; i.e., whether or not Z will ever halt given initial string w. But we know that no such procedure is in general available (the halting problem for Turing machines is unsolvable) and so we conclude that there exist sets H_Z which are *not* recursive. ◊

The above example, then, justifies a new definition:

DEFINITION 11

A subset L of X^* is **recursively enumerable** if it is acceptable by some partial recursive function f. ○

Also from Example 4, we immediately have:

THEOREM 11

There exist recursively enumerable sets which are not recursive. □

The name *recursively enumerable* follows from the fact (Theorem 12) that a set L is Turing acceptable iff it is Turing generable by some Z—for if we think of strings of X^* as numbers in $|X|$-adic encoding, we may think of the recursively enumerable set L as being *enumerated* by the recursive function F^1_Z:

$$L = \{F^1_Z(0), F^1_Z(1), F^1_Z(2), \ldots, F^1_Z(n), \ldots\} \tag{3}$$

Actually, there is a flaw in this argument. Try to spot it before we resolve it by Proposition 13.

THEOREM 12

Every recursively enumerable set is generable by some partial recursive function.

Proof

Suppose that L is the set of all w in X^* for which $g(w) = 1$, for some partial recursive function g. Consider, then, the function f defined by the rule

$$f(w) = \begin{cases} w & \text{if } g(w) = 1 \\ \text{undefined} & \text{if not.} \end{cases}$$

Then it is clear that f is a partial recursive function whose image is L:

$$w \in L \Leftrightarrow g(w) = 1 \Leftrightarrow w \in f(X^*). \qquad \square$$

The flaw in the discussion of (3) was that the above result may yield an F_Z^1 which is not total, and so we run the risk of the enumeration "sticking" at an n for which $F_Z^1(n)$ is not defined. The problem is removed by the following result:

PROPOSITION 13

Every nonempty recursively enumerable set is generable by some total recursive function.

Proof

Let $L = F_Z^1(X^*)$ and let $\hat{w}$ be any fixed element of L.

Let us enumerate the pairs of integers according to the tableau of Figure 4–15 so that $\zeta(0, 0) = 0$, $\zeta(1, 0) = 1$, $\zeta(0, 1) = 2$, ... ; and let us fix an enumeration $\{w_0, w_1, w_2, \ldots\}$ of X^*.

Then it is clear that the function h defined by the rule

$$h(n) = \begin{cases} F_Z^1(w_x) & \text{if } n = \zeta(x, y) \text{ and } Z \text{ halts computation within } y \\ & \text{steps when started with initial string } w_x \\ \hat{w} & \text{if not} \end{cases}$$

is a total recursive function whose range is L. $\qquad \square$

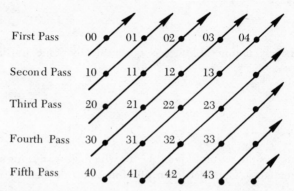

First Pass	00	01	02	03 04
Second Pass	10	11	12	13
Third Pass	20	21	22	23
Fourth Pass	30	31	32	33
Fifth Pass	40	41	42	43

Figure 4–15   We pass upward along successive diagonals to encounter every element of $\mathbf{N} \times \mathbf{N}$ in turn. Then $n = \zeta(x, y)$ if the pair (x, y) is the nth element in this enumeration.

We observed, following Definition 2, that any set decidable by an F is certainly acceptable by that F. Moreover, we noted in Fact 5 that if L is decidable by F, then so too is its complement $\overline{L} = X^* \backslash L$. Hence, if a set L is recursive, then so too is $\overline{L}$, and hence L and $\overline{L}$ are both recursively enumerable. In fact, the converse is also true:

THEOREM 14

A set L is recursive iff both L and $\overline{L}$ are recursively enumerable.

Proof

Suppose that, by grace of Proposition 13, we have two *total* recursive functions g_1 and g_2 such that

$$L = g_1(X^*) \qquad \text{and} \qquad \overline{L} = g_2(X^*).$$

Let us continue to use the enumeration $\{w_0, w_1, w_2, \ldots\}$ of X^*. Then Figure 4–16 exhibits an effective procedure for telling whether or not a particular w in X^* belongs to L, which is thus recursive. The procedure must eventually halt, since w lies either in L, in which case it must be $g_1(w_n)$ for some n, or in $\overline{L}$, in which case it must be $g_2(w_n)$ for some n. $\qquad \Box$

The fact that there exists a set which is recursively enumerable but not recursive may be considered an abstract form of the celebrated **incompleteness theorem** produced by **Gödel** in 1931, which showed that there were statements about the theory of numbers which could be expressed in the formal language

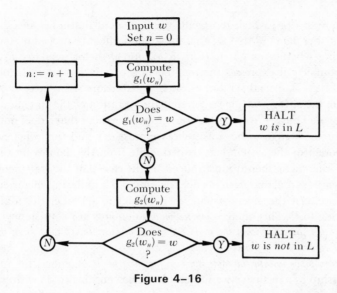

Figure 4–16

of Principia Mathematica and which were true, but which nonetheless did not follow as theorems from the axioms of Principia Mathematica. In other words, Gödel showed that there existed formal languages which could state many truths which were not deducible from the axioms of the given system.

Recall the basic idea of Euclidean geometry: from a small list of axioms summarizing the basic interrelationships between points and lines, we deduce, using simple rules of inference, a wide range of theorems expressing many complicated geometrical properties. The "Parallel Axiom" states that, given a point and a line, there is one and only one line passing through the given point parallel to the given line. For many centuries, geometers tried to deduce that statement from the other axioms, and it was only in the 19th century that this was proved to be impossible by showing that there existed geometrical systems in which this statement was false, even though in other systems this statement was true. The question that immediately arises, then, is whether for the augmented set of axioms there exist other truths which are not deducible, and so on, ad infinitum. Gödel's theorem tells us that there do, and our next task is to prove this: namely, that any axiomatic system in which we have effective means for deducing the implications of the axioms, and which is free of contradictions, either is limited in its expressive power, or else can express statements whose truth is not deducible from those axioms. To make life easy, we shall couch our discussion in informal terms. However, all the information necessary to construct a formal argument is provided.

We must first specify what we mean when we say that a system is consistent and not too limited in its expressive power. We shall say that a system is both *adequate* and *consistent* if, given any recursively enumerable set R and any integer n, there exists a string of symbols [which we shall abbreviate to $R(n)$] which represents the statement that n belongs to the set R. We further demand that we shall have some effective procedure for telling of a string whether or not it is an $R(n)$, and if so for what set R and for what number n it expresses the membership of n in the set R. In our logic we shall have a special symbol $\sim$ such that for any string α of symbols of the logic, the string $\sim\alpha$ shall represent the **negation** of the statement represented by α. Thus, $\sim R(n)$ shall represent the statement that n does not belong to R. For the system to be consistent, we must demand that whenever $R(n)$ is a theorem of the system (i.e., is deducible from the axioms by the given rules of inference), then it must indeed be the case that the statement which it represents is true, that is, that n does belong to R. Similarly, whenever $\sim R(n)$ is a theorem of the given system, then in fact it must be true that n does not belong to R. This, then, is *our notion of* **adequacy** *and* **consistency**—*namely that we can represent within the logic the notion of membership of a given number in a given recursively enumerable set, and that all the statements about such membership that we can prove within the logic must in fact be true.* Remember, the notion of membership in a recursively enumerable set has nothing to do with the given formal logic—it purely says that the device which generates the set will eventually generate the given number. Now we wish to show that **if a system is both adequate and consistent, then it must be incomplete**—in other words, if, without contradiction, it can represent any statement about membership of a number in a recursively enumerable set, then there must be true statements about such membership which are not theorems of the given system. We shall prove this by showing that *if every true statement were provable in the logic, then we could obtain a decision procedure for membership in recursively enumerable sets, which would imply the falsehood that every recursively enumerable set is recursive.* Thus, we wish to show that it is not the case that we can have a logical system such that for each recursively enumerable set R and number n, there is a string of symbols $R(n)$ with the property that $R(n)$ is a theorem if and only if n belongs to R, whereas $\sim R(n)$ is a theorem if and only if n does not belong to R.

The crucial point in proving this is the observation that *the theorems of any system which has effective means for deducing the implications of its axioms must form a recursively enumerable set.* To see this, consider how we prove a theorem. Any (hideously unabbreviated!) proof has several lines, the first of which is an axiom. The second line either is an axiom or is deducible from the first axiom by some rule of inference. And so it goes on. The nth line of any proof either is an axiom, or is deducible from some of the first $n - 1$ lines of the proof by one of the given rules of inference. It can be seen from this discussion that we may proceed to generate all the proofs of a system in the following effective way. First we write down all the proofs of length 1; in other words, we write down all the axioms. Then we write down in order all the proofs of length 2—namely, we look at each of the proofs of length 1 and then apply one rule of inference to get a proof of length 2. Similarly at the nth stage, having enumerated all the proofs of length $n - 1$, we may enumerate all the proofs of length n by taking each proof of length $n - 1$ in turn and applying the rules of inference to it in all possible ways. In this fashion we obtain a recursive enumeration of all the proofs within the logical system. But the theorems of the logical system are simply those strings of symbols which occur as the last lines of proofs in that logical system, and so our enumeration of the proofs of the system gives us an effective means for generating all the theorems of the system.

We shall now show that our logical system cannot be complete by showing that, if it were, we would have an effective means for telling of any number whether or not it belonged to a recursively enumerable set U for which there is no effective means for testing membership. Given any integer n, we can form the string $U(n)$ of symbols which represents the statement that n belongs to the set U. Then if the system is complete, either n does belong to U and $U(n)$ is a theorem of the system, or n does not belong to U and $\sim U(n)$ is a theorem of the system. Our effective, albeit hideously inefficient, method of determining whether or not n belongs to the set then follows immediately—we simply start generating the theorems of the system, one after another. If the system is complete, we are guaranteed that eventually either $U(n)$ or $\sim U(n)$ must be generated (and, since the system is consistent, only one of them will be generated). If it is $U(n)$ that eventually emerges, then we have determined that n does belong to the set U, whereas if $\sim U(n)$ emerges, at that stage we know that n does not belong to U. In other words, if we have an adequate consistent system which is complete, then we can effectively tell of a given number n whether or not it belongs to U. But this is impossible, and so we must conclude, with Gödel, that *every adequate consistent logical system must be incomplete*—in other words, there are true statements about arithmetic which are represented by strings of symbols which are not theorems of the given system.

Gödel's theorem thus says that, no matter how efficiently you try to axiomatize arithmetic, if that axiomatization allows one to generate effectively one after another the theorems of the system, then there are true statements which cannot be proved within the system. Note that if we find a statement which is true but whose representative is not provable within the system, and add it as a new axiom, then the new system is still subject to Gödel's theorem; the new system in turn is incapable of representing all truths as theorems. Thus, we deduce of any such system that there must be an infinity of true statements which are representable within the system but not provable within the system. In fact, it has been shown that there exist effective procedures for generating from each axiomatic system a new axiomatic system in which more truths about arithmetic are provable. There thus exist mechanical procedures for removing some of the limitations of any axiomatic system, but it is in the nature of things that no matter how many limitations we remove, an infinity still remain.

Having learned how to associate languages with machines, let us now gain a general perspective on the characterization of languages by *string manipulation systems.* We owe to Emil L. Post the general notion of productions. A k-antecedent **production** is of the form

$$g_{11}u_1^{(1)}g_{12}u_2^{(1)} \cdots g_{1m_1}u_{m_1}^{(1)}g_{1(m_1+1)}$$
$$\vdots \qquad \qquad \vdots$$
$$g_{k1}u_1^{(k)}g_{k2}u_2^{(k)} \cdots g_{km_k}u_{m_k}^{(k)}g_{k(m_k+1)}$$

produce

$$g_1u_1g_2u_2 \cdots g_mu_mg_{m+1}$$

We call each of the k strings preceding the word "produce" a **premiss** of the production, while the last line is called the **conclusion.** In this display, the g's represent specific strings including the null string, while the u's represent the operational variables of the production, and, in the application of the production, may be identified with arbitrary strings. These variables need not be distinct—equalities among them constrain our substitutions. We then add the restriction that each operational variable in the conclusion of the production is present in at least one of the premisses of the production, it having been understood that each premiss, and the conclusion, had at least one operational variable. This production corresponds to the rule of inference R for which $R(w_1, \ldots, w_k, w)$ is true iff there exist strings $h_j^{(i)}(1 \le i \le k;$ $1 \le j \le m_i + 1)$ [with $h_j^{(i)} = h_{j'}^{(i')}$ if $u_j^{(i)} = u_{j'}^{(i')}$] such that

$$w_i = g_{i1}h_1^{(i)}g_{i2}h_2^{(i)} \cdots g_{i(m_i+1)} \quad 1 \le i \le k$$

and
$$w = g_1h_1g_2h_2 \cdots g_mh_mg_{m+1}$$

where h_j is the $h_\ell^{(i)}$ such that u_j is the variable $u_\ell^{(i)}$.

Example 5

Consider the one-antecedent production

$$17R3Q \mapsto RR6Q$$

(where we replace "produce" by "$\mapsto$"). We may apply this to 1735, taking $R = \Lambda$, $Q = 5$ to yield 65. We may apply this to 17634362, either taking

$$R = 6, \; Q = 4362 \text{ to yield } 6664362; \text{ or taking}$$
$$R = 634, \; Q = 62 \text{ to yield } 634634662.$$

We cannot apply this to 39617, for instance.

For a 2-antecedent production, consider

$$R_13R_25 \text{ and } 6R_14 \quad \text{produce} \quad R_2.$$

Applying this to the set of strings $\{3435, 64, 634, 33175\}$ one may combine the third and fourth elements to yield 17; or combine the first and second to yield 43. ◊

DEFINITION 12

A **Post Generation System** is a quadruple $\mathcal{S} = (V, X, A, P)$, where

V is a finite set (the **variables**)
X is a finite set disjoint from V (the **terminal** symbols),
A is a finite subset of $(V \cup X)^*$ (the set of **axioms**), and
P is a set of **productions** whose fixed strings lie in $(V \cup X)^*$.   ○

A finite sequence of strings $w_1, w_2, \ldots, w_n$ is called a **proof** (of w_n) in $\mathcal{S}$ if, for each i $(1 \leq i \leq n)$, either

(1) w_i is an axiom in A; or
(2) there exist $j, \ldots, k < i$ such that $w_j, \ldots, w_k$ produce w_i by one of the productions in P.

We say that w is a **theorem**† of $\mathcal{S}$, or that w is **provable** in $\mathcal{S}$, if there is a proof of w in $\mathcal{S}$. We denote this by $\vdash_{\mathcal{S}} w$.

We shall say that a set is **generated** by $\mathcal{S}$, and call it $L(\mathcal{S})$, if it is the set of theorems of $\mathcal{S}$ which lie in X^*.

Given a set B, we write $B \vdash_{\mathcal{S}} w$ if there is a proof of w using the rules of inference of $\mathcal{S}$, and using B as the set of axioms. Then

$$L(\mathcal{S}) = \{w \in X^* | A \vdash_{\mathcal{S}} w\}.$$

DEFINITION 13

We shall say that a set of strings is **Post-generable** if there exists a Post Generation System $\mathcal{S}$ for which the given set equals $L(\mathcal{S})$.   ○

Given our general faith, engendered in Chapter 3, that any effective procedure can be simulated on a Turing machine, we would expect that any Post-generable set is recursively enumerable. This is indeed true, though the formal proof, while straightforward, is too tedious to present here.‡ Instead, we prove the converse: every recursively enumerable set is Post-generable.

---

† Cf. our informal discussion of what constitutes a theorem in our "proof" of Gödel's theorem above.

‡ Of course, we have already given an *informal* proof: In discussing Gödel's theorem, we noted that the theorems of any system which has effective means for deducing the implications of its axioms must form a recursively enumerable set.

In fact, we show that recursively enumerable sets can be generated by Post systems of a pleasingly simple form. We first define semi-Thue systems:

DEFINITION 14

A Post generation system is said to be a **semi-Thue**† system if each production is of the form

$$u_1 g u_2 \mapsto u_1 g' u_2$$

for suitable strings g and g'.   ○

We then have the promised characterization:

THEOREM 15

A set of strings is Post-generable using a semi-Thue system iff it is recursively enumerable.

Proof Outline

As we have already suggested, every semi-Thue generable set is recursively enumerable—one either believes this on general grounds, or else applies standard techniques for proving sets to be recursively enumerable.

Conversely, let the recursively enumerable set L be generated by the Turing machine Z which, for ease of exposition, we shall assume to halt when and only when it reaches state q_s.

We simulate Z by a semi-Thue system $\tau(Z)$ with alphabet $Q \cup X \cup \{h, k, k', k''\}$ [where we assume Q (the state set of Z) and X (the input set of Z) are disjoint, and that h and the k's are symbols in neither Q nor X] such that:

(1) $\tau(Z)$ has the single axiom hkh.
(2) There are productions to replace k by a string of $q_0 X^*$: a production $u_1 k u_2 \mapsto u_1 k x u_2$ for each $x \in X$, and a production $u_1 k u_2 \mapsto u_1 q_0 u_2$.
(3) Other productions of $\tau(Z)$ mimic the quintuples of Z; e.g., if $qxx'Lq'$ is a quintuple of Z, then

$$u_1 x_1 q x u_2 \mapsto u_1 q' x_1 x' u_2 \text{ (one for each } x_1 \text{ in } X)$$

---

†Pronounced "semi-two-way"—one is tempted to say "one-way." The Norwegian logician Thue introduced systems in which each production $u_1 g u_2 \mapsto u_1 g' u_2$ was coupled with the converse production $u_1 g' u_2 \mapsto u_1 g u_2$.

and

$$u_1 hqxu_2 \mapsto u_1 q'bx'u_2$$

are productions of $\tau(Z)$.

(4) Finally, there are productions which, for a string containing q_s, remove q_s and the h's (Exercise 8).

Thus, the only strings on X^* obtainable are those which we may find on the tape of Z at the end of a computation. □

Note that just as a Turing machine may never halt, so may a semi-Thue system produce an infinity of strings, none of which contain only "terminal" symbols—and thus generate the empty set.

Having seen that semi-Thue systems can be used to generate all recursively enumerable sets, we now study the restrictions on semi-Thue systems which yield context-sensitive, context-free, and finite-state languages. In Section 4–4 we shall show that the context-free languages are precisely the languages accepted by what we shall call nondeterministic pushdown automata. It can also be shown [Arbib, 1969, Section 5.4] that the context-sensitive languages are precisely the languages accepted by what are called nondeterministic linear-bounded automata.

We start by presenting a slight modification of semi-Thue systems in a vocabulary appropriate to their interpretation as grammars, in which there is only one axiom, and that comprises a one-element string. (We still use Λ to denote the empty word of length 0.)

DEFINITION 15

A **phrase-structure grammar** is a quadruple

$$G = (V, X, P, S)$$

where

(i) V is a finite nonempty set.

(ii) X is a finite nonempty set (with $X \cap V = \varnothing$), the set of **terminal symbols**.

(iii) P is a finite set of ordered pairs (u, v) with u in $(V \cup X)^* \backslash X^*$ and v in $(V \cup X)^*$. We usually write (u, v) as $u \mapsto v$ and call it a **production** or **rewriting rule** (note that v may be empty).

(iv) $S \in V$ is the **initial symbol**.

Given a grammar G, we write $y \Rightarrow z$, and say that y **directly generates** z, if y and z are words on V for which we can find u, u_1, u_2, and v such that (u, v) is in P and $y = u_1 u u_2$ and $z = u_1 v u_2$.

We use $\overset{*}{\Rightarrow}$ to denote the transitive closure of $\Rightarrow$. That is, if y and z are in V^*, then $y \overset{*}{\Rightarrow} z$ if $y = z$, or if there is a sequence $z_1, z_2, \ldots, z_k$ in V^* such that $y = z_1 \Rightarrow z_2 \Rightarrow z_3 \Rightarrow \cdots \Rightarrow z_{k-1} \Rightarrow z_k = z$. We call such a sequence $z_1, \ldots, z_k$ a **derivation** or **generation** of z from y (by the rules of the grammar G).

DEFINITION 16

$L \subset X^*$ is called a **phrase structure language** if there exists a phrase structure grammar $G = (V, X, P, S)$ such that

$$L = L(G) = \{w \in X^* | S \overset{*}{\Rightarrow} w\} \qquad \bigcirc$$

It follows from Theorem 15 that the phrase structure languages form the largest class of effectively generable subsets of X^* (Exercise 9).

Since we would like a computer to be able to tell whether or not a string of symbols constitutes a valid program, the class of phrase structure languages is thus too broad for it to serve as a model for programming languages. We next present a subfamily of the recursive sets to which we can give a grammar formulation.

DEFINITION 17

A **context-sensitive grammar** is a phrase structure grammar for which each production (u, v) satisfies the restriction on the length of the strings, $\ell(u) \leq \ell(v)$. L is a **context-sensitive language** if $L = L(G)$ for some context-sensitive grammar G. $\qquad \bigcirc$

FACT 16

No context-sensitive language contains Λ. $\qquad \square$

Example 6

We show that set $\{a^n b^n c^n | n \geq 1\}$ is context-sensitive. Let us use

$$V = \{S, S_1, B, B'\} \text{ with initial symbol } S, \text{ and}$$
$$X = \{a, b, c\}$$

and productions
$$\left.\begin{array}{l} S \mapsto aS_1B' \\ S \mapsto aB' \\ S_1 \mapsto aS_1B \\ S_1 \mapsto aB \end{array}\right\}$$
produce strings of the form
$a^nB^{n-1}B', \, n \geq 1$

$$\left.\begin{array}{l} B' \mapsto bc \\ Bb \mapsto bB \\ Bc \mapsto bcc \end{array}\right\}$$
convert $a^nB^{n-1}B'$
to $a^nb^nc^n$

Sample derivations:

(i) $S \Rightarrow aB' \Rightarrow abc.$

(ii) $S \Rightarrow aS_1B' \Rightarrow aaS_1BB' \Rightarrow aaaBBB' \Rightarrow aaaBBbc$
$\Rightarrow aaaBbBc \Rightarrow aaabBBc \Rightarrow aaabBbcc$
$\Rightarrow aaabbBcc \Rightarrow aaabbbccc$ ◊

To make clear the name "context-sensitive," consider a grammar which is context-sensitive in the strict sense that every production is of the form $\phi u\psi \mapsto \phi v\psi$ where $\phi \in (V \cup X)^*$, $\psi \in (V \cup X)^*$, $u \in V$, and $v \in (V \cup X)^+$ —i.e., each production replaces a single letter by a non-null string, but the replacement may depend on the context. Let us see that *any* context-sensitive production can be replaced by a series of strictly context-sensitive productions:

Given $x_1 \ldots x_n \mapsto x_1' \ldots x_m'$ with $m \geq n$, we introduce n new non-terminal symbols $A_n, \ldots, A_1$ and replace the above production by $2n$ strictly context-sensitive productions:

$$x_{n-1}x_n \mapsto x_{n-1}A_nx_{n+1}' \ldots x_m'$$
$$x_{j-1}x_jA_{j+1} \mapsto x_{j-1}A_jA_{j+1} \quad (1 < j < n)$$
$$A_{j-1}A_j \mapsto A_{j-1}x_j' \quad (1 < j \leq n)$$
$$x_1A_2 \mapsto A_1A_2$$
$$A_1 \mapsto x_1'$$

We now relate context-sensitive languages to the families of recursive and recursively enumerable sets.

THEOREM 17

Every context-sensitive language is a recursive set.

Proof Outline

Given v, we use the length condition to see that there are only finitely many derivations which yield distinct strings of length $\leq \ell(v)$, and we check all of these effectively to see if v is itself derivable. □

It is of interest to contrast this with the result of Exercise 10.

We may use a diagonal argument to show that a recursive set need not be context-sensitive:

THEOREM 18

There exist recursive sets which are not context-sensitive.

Proof

Let $G_1, G_2, \ldots$ be an effective enumeration of the context-sensitive grammars with terminal alphabet X. Enumerating the strings of X^* as $w_1, w_2, w_3, \ldots$ we may define a set $\widehat{L}$ by

$$w_n \in \widehat{L} \Leftrightarrow w_n \notin L(G_n)$$

Now $\widehat{L}$ is recursive, since we may effectively test whether or not w_n is generable by G_n. However, $\widehat{L}$ cannot be context-sensitive, for if $\widehat{L}$ equalled $L(G_m)$, say, we should have $w_m \in \widehat{S} \Leftrightarrow w_m \notin \widehat{S}$, a contradiction. □

The notion of context in this discussion refers to the context of a single letter. This motivates the definition of *context-free*, which we now restate:

DEFINITION 18

A **context-free (CF) grammar** is a phrase structure grammar in which each production $u \mapsto v$ has the property $\ell(u) = 1$; i.e., each rule has the form $u \mapsto v$ with $u \in V$, $v \in (V \cup X)^*$.

L is a **context-free language (CF language; CFL)** if $L = L(G)$ for some CF grammar G. ○

FACT 19

Λ may be in a CFL, but L context-free implies $L \backslash \{\Lambda\}$ context-sensitive. □

Example 7

If $X = \{a, b\}$, $V = \{S\}$, and $P = \{S \mapsto aSb, S \mapsto ab\}$, then $L(G) = \{a^n b^n \mid n \geq 1\}$, which is thus a CFL, although it is not regular (Definition 7).

Unfortunately, it is not usually possible to obtain so explicit a description of a language defined implicitly by a CF grammar.   ◊

By looking at derivations in terms of their trees, we may obtain the following result, known as the **pumping lemma** for context-free languages:

THEOREM 20

Let $G = (V, X, P, S)$ be a CF grammar. It is possible to determine two integers p and q such that every sentence z of $L(G)$ with $\ell(z) > p$ can be decomposed into the form $z = xuwvy$, where $u \neq \Lambda$ or $v \neq \Lambda$, $\ell(uwv) \leq q$ and $z_k = xu^k wv^k y \in L(G)$ for $k = 1, 2, \ldots$.

Proof

By Exercise 11, we may assume without loss of generality that $\ell(x) \geq 2$ whenever some $\xi \mapsto x$ is in P.

Let n be the number of symbols in V, and let p be the length of the longest string that can be derived with a tree of height at most n. Then every string z of length greater than p must have some symbol W of V occurring at least twice in a branch of its derivation tree, say $W \overset{*}{\Rightarrow} u'Wv' \overset{*}{\Rightarrow} uwv$ where $u' \overset{*}{\Rightarrow} u$, $W \overset{*}{\Rightarrow} w$, and $v' \overset{*}{\Rightarrow} v$. By our initial assumption, u or v is non-null. Thus $z = xuwvy$ and clearly $W \overset{*}{\Rightarrow} (u')^k W(v')^k \overset{*}{\Rightarrow} u^k wv^k$. So $z_k = xu^k wv^k y \in L(G)$. The bound q is obtained by noting that we may take $W \overset{*}{\Rightarrow} u'Wv' \Rightarrow uwv$ to have total branch length $\leq n + 1$.   □

FACT 21

The class of CFLs is not closed under intersection.

Proof

$L_1 = \{a^i b^j c^j \mid i, j \geq 1\}$ and $L_2 = \{a^i b^i c^j \mid i, j \geq 1\}$ are both CFLs, but $L_1 \cap L_2$ is not a CFL, by Exercise 13.   □

THEOREM 22

The class of CFLs is closed under the $\cup$, $\cdot$, and $*$ operations.

Proof

Given grammars for L_1 and L_2, replace them by grammars with disjoint sets of metalinguistic variables, to obtain

$$G_1 = (V^1, X, P_1, S_1) \quad \text{and} \quad G_2 = (V^2, X, P_2, S_2)$$

It is then easy to verify that G_3 is a grammar for $L_1 \cup L_2$, that G_4 is a grammar for $L_1 \cdot L_2$ and that G_5 is a grammar for L_1^*, where

$$G_3 = (V^1 \cup V^2 \cup \{S\}, X, P_1 \cup P_2 \cup \{S \mapsto S_1, S \mapsto S_2\}, S)$$
$$G_4 = (V^1 \cup V^2 \cup \{S\}, X, P_1 \cup P_2 \cup \{S \mapsto S_1 S_2\}, S)$$
$$G_5 = (V^1, X, P \cup \{S \mapsto \Lambda, S \mapsto S_1\}, S)$$

COROLLARY 23

The class of CFLs is not closed under complementation.

Proof

If it were, Theorem 22 would then imply that it was closed under intersection, contradicting Fact 21.   □

THEOREM 24

If L is a CFL and R is a regular set, then $L \cap R$ is also a CFL.

Proof

Let $R = M_{q_0}^{-1}(y)$ where $M = (Q, X, Y, \delta, \beta)$. Let $F = \{q \in Q \mid \beta(q) = y\}$. Let $G = (V, X, P, S)$ be a CF grammar for L. Let us introduce new auxiliary symbols (q, v, q') where each symbol is labelled by some $q \in Q$, $v \in V$, and $q' \in Q$.

Now let $\widehat{L}$ consist of all strings

$$(q_0, x_1, q_1)(q_1, x_2, q_2) \cdots (q_{n-1}, x_n, q_n)$$

such that $x_1 x_2 \ldots x_n \in L$ (so that each $x_j \in X$) and $q_n \in F$. Then $\widehat{L}$ is generated by the CF grammar $\widehat{G}$ with initial symbol $\widehat{S}$ and productions $\widehat{P}$:

$$\widehat{S} \mapsto (q_0, S, q) \text{ for each } q \in F$$

and

$$(p, \xi, q) \mapsto (p, v_1, q_1)(q_1, v_2, q_2) \cdots (q_{n-1}, v_n, q)$$

for each production $\xi \mapsto v_1 v_2 \ldots v_n$ of P, each $v_j \in V$, and *any* choice of q_1, $q_2, \ldots, q_{n-1}$. Now we adjoin to $\widehat{P}$ the productions

$$(p, v, q) \rightarrow v \text{ if } v \text{ is in } X \text{ and } \delta(p, v) = q.$$

These productions extract the string $x_1 \ldots x_n$ of X^* from the string (q_0, x_1, q_1) $\ldots (q_{n-1}, x_n, q_n)$ of $\widehat{L}$ whenever $\delta(q_0, x_1) = q_1, \ldots, \delta(q_{n-1}, x_n) = q_n$. Since $q_n \in F$, this says that we obtain $x_1 \ldots x_n$ iff it belongs not only to L but also to R. Thus, $L \cap R$ is a context-free language.   □

Example 8

Suppose L is context-free, and let L_n be the set of all words in L whose length is divisible by n. Then $L_n = L \cap R_n^*$, where R_n is the set of words of length n. Since R_n is finite, R_n^* is regular, and so L_n is a context-free language.   ◊

DEFINITION 19

For each a in X, let X_a be a finite nonempty set, and let $\tau(a)$ be a subset of X_a^*. We then extend τ to X^* by letting

$$\tau(\Lambda) = \{\Lambda\}, \tau(a_1 \ldots a_k) = \tau(a_1) \ldots \tau(a_k).$$

Such a τ is called a **substitution mapping**.   ○

If L is context-free and τ is an unrestricted substitution mapping, we cannot expect $\tau(L)$ to be context-free—just take $\tau(a)$ to be a non-context-free language, and set $L = \{a\}$ for a counter-example. However, if we confine each $\tau(a)$ to be a context-free set, we may prove the following result.

THEOREM 25 (THE SUBSTITUTION THEOREM)

If L is context-free and τ is a substitution mapping with $\tau(a)$ context-free for every a in X, then $\tau(L)$ is context-free.

Proof

This is an easy exercise (Exercise 15) of the type undertaken to prove Theorem 22.   □

COROLLARY 26

For every homomorphism $h: X^* \to Y^*$, for x in X (i.e., each $\tau(x)$ is a single element of Y^*) and every context-free $L \subset X^*$, we have that $h(L) \subset Y^*$ is also context-free.   □

We saw in Theorem 4 that the finite-state languages are those accepted by finite-state automata, whether these be deterministic or possibilistic (non-deterministic) in their operation. We may also characterize the regular sets as CFLs of a particular kind:

DEFINITION 21

A context-free grammar $G = (V, X, P, S)$ is said to be **right-linear** if each production in P is of the form $\xi \mapsto u$ or $\xi \mapsto u\alpha$, where u is in X^* and α is in V.   ○

We then have:

THEOREM 27

A set $R \subset X^*$ is regular iff there exists some right-linear grammar G such that $R = L(G)$.

Proof

Let $R = M_{q_0}^{-1}(y)$ with $F = \{q \in Q \mid \beta(q) = y\}$, and let

$$G = (V, X, P, S) \text{ where } V = Q \cup \{S\}$$

and let P contain

 (i) a production $\sigma \mapsto q_0$
 (ii) and for each $q, q' \in Q$ and $x \in X$ such that $\delta(q, x) = q$
    a production $q \mapsto xq'$
(iii) and for each q in F
    a production $q \mapsto \Lambda$.

Then $L(G) = R$. A somewhat modified reversal of this construction yields the converse.   □

Thus, the regular sets are all CFLs. However, not all CFLs are regular, an example of one which is not regular being $\{a^i b^i \mid i \geq 1\}$.

Recalling that $L^+ = \{x_1 \ldots x_n \mid n \geq 1 \text{ and } x_j \in L\}$, we may summarize the closure properties of the families of languages we have studied by Table 4–1.

Table 4-1.

				Closed Under			
		*	*Union*	*Inter-section*	*Complemen-tation*	*Intersection with a Regular Set*	*Substi-tution*
Family	Recursively Enumerable	Yes	Yes	Yes	No	Yes	Yes
	Recursive	Yes	Yes	Yes	Yes	Yes	Yes
	Context-Sensitive	Yes	Yes	Yes	?	Yes	Yes
	Context-Free	Yes	Yes	No	No	Yes	Yes
	Regular	Yes	Yes	Yes	Yes	Yes	Yes
	Finite	No	Yes	Yes	No	Yes	Yes

EXERCISES FOR SECTION 4-2

1.   Consider the automaton $M = (Q, X, Y, \delta, \beta)$ shown in Figure 4-17, in which we have left the outputs unspecified, but where the number of states exceeds the number of outputs, and where $X = \{x_1, \ldots, x_n\}$. Given any nonempty subset Y' of Y, assign outputs to the states in such a way that M_{q_0} generates the set Y'.

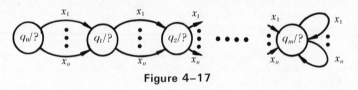

Figure 4-17

2.   Build upon part (ii) of the proof of Theorem 7 to provide an inductive proof of part (iii).

3.   Prove that every *finite* subset of X^* is an FSL, building upon the automaton shown in Figure 4-18, which accepts the set $\{\Lambda, 0, 01, 11, 010\}$.

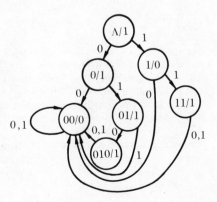

Figure 4-18

4.   Prove that the converse of Theorem 3 is false. [Hint: Consider the length of $\tilde{M}_q(w)$.]

5.   Given a Turing machine Z with tape alphabet X_b, which is always started in state q_0 scanning the leftmost square of a string from X^*, addition of the quintuples

$$\hat{q}_0 xxL\hat{q}_1$$
$$\hat{q}_1 b\$Rq_0$$

where $\hat{q}_0$ and $\hat{q}_1$ are new states, will cause it to place an endmarker \$ to the left of the string before starting its normal computation. The further quintuples

$$q_j\$bL\hat{q}_{2j}$$
$$\hat{q}_{2j} b\$Rq_j$$

where $\hat{q}_{2j}$ is a new state for each original state q_j of Z, will ensure that \$ is repositioned each time Z needs more work space to the left. Write out similar quintuples for placing and repositioning of an endmarker ¢ at the right-hand end of the string.

6.   Find a closed formula (by summing an arithmetic progression) for the $\zeta(x, y)$ of Figure 4–15.

7.   In the proof of Proposition 13, it is clear that every $h(n)$ is a w in L. Spell out why every w in L must be an $h(n)$.

8.   Complete steps (3) and (4) in the proof of Theorem 15.

9.   Prove that a set of words is a phrase structure language iff it is recursively enumerable. [Hint: This is almost a restatement of Theorem 15. How do we get around the restriction that if $u \mapsto v$ then $u \in (V \cup X)^* \backslash X^*$?]

10.   Use the proof of Theorem 15 to show that every recursively enumerable set is the homomorphic image (Section 5–1 defines this notion, but the exercise is intelligible without it) of a context-sensitive set, in that the map $h \mapsto \Lambda$, $x \mapsto x$, $q_s \mapsto \Lambda$ will convert a context-sensitive set on $X \cup \{q_s, h\}$ into a recursively enumerable set on X.

11.   Show that any context-free grammar G may be replaced by a context-free grammar G' in which every production $\xi \mapsto x$ has $\ell(x) \geq 2$; and such that $L(G) \backslash L(G')$ is a finite set, and $L(G') \subset L(G)$.

12.   Recall the number-theoretic result that $2^{p-1} \equiv 1 \pmod{p}$ for each prime $p > 2$. [This follows from the binomial expansion

$$(1 + 1)^p = 1 + p + \frac{p(p-1)}{2} + \cdots + p + 1$$

$$\equiv 2 \pmod{p}.]$$

Use this to show that the set of binary strings which are the *binary* expansions of prime numbers is not context-free (use Theorem 20).

13.   Use Theorem 20 to verify that $\{a^n b^n c^n \mid n \geq 1\}$, which (Example 6) is context-sensitive, is not a CFL. Show that $\{ww^R \mid w \in X^*\}$ is a CFL, whereas $\{ww \mid w \in X^*\}$ is context-sensitive but not a CFL.

14.   Mimic the proofs of Theorems 21 and 24 for context-*sensitive* languages.

15.   Prove Theorem 25.

16.   A **generalized sequential machine (gsm)** is a sextuple

$$M = (Q, X, Y, \delta, \lambda, q_0)$$

where Q, X, and Y are finite nonempty sets (the *states, inputs* and *outputs*)

$q_0 \in Q$ is the *start-state*

$\delta : Q \times X \to Q$ is the *next-state* function

$\lambda : Q \times X \to Y^*$ is the *output* function

Note that a single input may yield no output, a single output symbol, or a whole string. If $\lambda(Q \times X) \subset Y$, we obtain our familiar finite automata (also known as complete sequential machines, etc.). If M is a gsm, and $w \in X^*$, we define $M(w)$ indirectly by $M(\Lambda) = \Lambda$; $M(wx) = M(w)\lambda(\delta^*(q, w), x)$.

If L is CF, and M is a gsm, show that $M(L)$ is also a CFL. [Hint: Mimic the proof of Theorem 24. For example, let $f(w_1 w_2 \ldots w_k) = w_2 w_4 \ldots (w_i \in X)$. Clearly, f is a gsm mapping, and so $f(L)$ is a CFL, for any CFL L. Again, for each set of words L, let $\mathrm{Init}(L) = \{u \neq \Lambda \,|\, \text{there exists } w \text{ with } uw \text{ in } L\}$. For each a in X, set $\tau(a) = \{a, ac\}$ with $c \notin X$. Then $\tau(L) \cap X^* c X^*$ is still CF. Now, let S be the gsm which acts like an identity until it reaches a c, and then just "emits" Λ. Clearly $\mathrm{Init}(L) = S[\tau(L) \cap X^* c X^*]$ and so is a CFL.]

19. Let R be a regular subset of X^* and E be a symbol not in X. Construct a CF grammar G such that $L(G) = \{xEx^R \,|\, x \in R\}$, where x^R is the reversal of the string x. When is $L(G)$ regular?

20. Show that if L is CFL, so too is L^R.

21. For each entry in Table 4–1, identify where in the section its assertion is proved. If it is not proved here, supply the proof yourself.

4–3   Tree Automata

We now want to define automata which process trees in just the same way that our automata of Section 2–1 processed strings. (The very sophisticated reader will find the deep reason for this similarity in our study of machines in a category in Chapter 9.) We start with an example, then provide the general definition, and finally check that string processing is indeed a special case.

Example 1

A tree automaton for doing simple arithmetic:

Let Ω be the label set $\mathbf{N} \cup \{+, \times\}$, with arity $\nu(n) = 0$ for $n \in \mathbf{N}$ (see Definition 4–1–5), while $\nu(+) = \nu(\times) = 2$. A typical Ω-tree and its corresponding addresses are given in Figures 4–19(a) and 4–19(b), respectively. The job of our automaton is to "run up the tree," adding or multiplying as it goes. In this particular case, the $+$ sign at node 00 is to signal addition of the 1 at 000 and the 3 at 001 to yield the value 4 at 00. Similarly, $8 = 4 \times 2$ is obtained at node 01. Once these new values are available at 00 and 01, the $+$ sign at node 0 can signal the formation of $4 + 8 = 12$. The final result of the computation is then obtained as $12 + 3 = 15$ at node Λ.

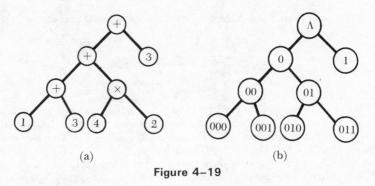

(a)   (b)

Figure 4–19

In ordinary automata theory, we may think of our "tree" as having the form shown in Figure 4–20, which corresponds to the string whose first element is the initial state, and whose remaining elements comprise the input string. When we process the string, we start in state q_0, and then sequentially convert inputs into states until we reach the final state at the end of the string.

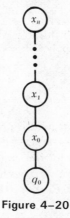

Figure 4–20

Similarly, in our arithmetic tree, we may think of the numbers on the terminal nodes as supplying a whole array of initial states, with the "inputs" + and × acting on *pairs* of states to yield a new state. We may then imagine our automaton working in parallel on the tree, evaluating the state at a node immediately after its successors have all been evaluated. We may now give a formal definition of a tree automaton for simple arithmetic which simply tells us, for each Ω-tree, the N-tree that results from evaluating every node. The automaton has

$$\text{input set } \Omega = \mathbf{N} \cup \{+, \times\} \qquad \text{(graded)}$$
$$\text{state set } \mathbf{N} \qquad \text{(ungraded)}$$

$$\text{transition functions: } \delta_n : \mathbf{N}^0 \to \mathbf{N} : \Lambda \mapsto n$$
$$\delta_+ : \mathbf{N}^2 \to \mathbf{N} : (n_1, n_2) \mapsto n_1 + n_2$$
$$\delta_\times : \mathbf{N}^2 \to \mathbf{N} : (n_1, n_2) \mapsto n_1 \cdot n_2$$

Then, given an Ω-tree $h: T \to \Omega$, the "run" of our arithmetic machine on h is simply the N-tree

$$\widehat{h}: T \to \mathbf{N}$$

which satisfies $\widehat{h}(w) = h(w)$ at the frontier, while

$h(w) = + \Rightarrow \widehat{h}(w) = \widehat{h}(w0) + \widehat{h}(w1)$: "input $+$" adds the states on its successor nodes

and

$h(w) = \times \Rightarrow \widehat{h}(w) = \widehat{h}(w0) \times \widehat{h}(w1)$: "input $\times$" multiplies the states on its successor nodes.

The *result* of the computation on h is then defined to be simply $\widehat{h}(\Lambda)$. $\Diamond$

We can now give a general definition of tree automata, based on Definition 4–1–5 of a multigraded set. First we define Ω-algebras:

DEFINITION 1

Let Ω be a multigraded set with arity function ν, so that $\nu(\omega)$ is a finite subset of $\mathbf{N}$ for each $\omega \in \Omega$. By an Ω-**algebra** $\mathcal{Q} = (Q, \delta)$ we mean a set Q, called the **carrier** of $\mathcal{Q}$, together with, for each $\omega \in \Omega$ and each $n \in \nu(\omega)$, a function

$$\delta_\omega^m: Q^m \to Q \qquad\qquad \bigcirc$$

In the tree automaton of Example 1 each ω only had one arity, and so we could abbreviate δ_n^0 to δ_n, δ_+^2 to δ_+, and $\delta_\times^2$ to $\delta_\times$ without ambiguity. [The reader of Section 5–6 will find that the above definition agrees with the definition given there in case each ω in Ω has only one arity.]

We may now define a tree automaton:

DEFINITION 2

A **tree automaton** is a quintuple

$$M = (Q, \Omega, Y, \delta, \beta)$$

where

Q is a set of **states**
Ω is a multigraded set of **inputs**
Y is a set of **outputs**

(Q, δ) is an **Ω-algebra,** and δ is called the **transition function** $\beta: Q \to Y$ is the **output function.**

An **input structure** for M is then simply an Ω-tree $h: T \to \Omega$. The **run** of M on h is then the Q-tree $\widehat{h}: T \to Q$ defined by:

(i) If w is a terminal node of T, then $\widehat{h}(w) = \delta^0_{h(w)}$.

(ii) If w has successors $h(w0), \ldots, h(w, n-1)$, then

$$\widehat{h}(w) = \delta^n_{h(w)}(\widehat{h}(w0), \ldots, \widehat{h}(w, n-1)).$$

The **evaluation** of h by M is then the output $\beta(\widehat{h}(\Lambda))$ of the state obtained at the Λ-node. $\bigcirc$

Let us see how an ordinary automaton (Section 2-1) starting in a specified initial state and processing strings to yield a final output may be regarded as a tree automaton. The intuition is provided by Figure 4–21, in

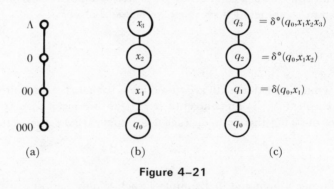

Figure 4–21

which (a) we first see a tree (a trunk?!) with its addresses, then (b) as an input structure, and then (c) after a run.

DEFINITION 3

Let $M = (Q, X, Y, \delta, \beta)$ be an ordinary automaton.

Let $\widehat{X}$ be the graded set $X \cup \{i\}$ with $\nu(x) = 1$ for each $x \in X$, while $\nu(i) = 0$; i is the label for the initial state component of the strings on which the tree automaton version of M is to run. [There is thus a bijection between $\widehat{X}$-trees and strings of the form w, with $w \in X^*$. Why?]

Then the tree-automaton of M started in initial state q_0 is

$$\widehat{M} = (Q, \widehat{X}, Y, \widehat{\delta}, \beta)$$

where $\widehat{\delta}^0_i = q_0$, and $\widehat{\delta}^1_x: Q \to Q: q \mapsto \delta(q, x)$ for each x in X. $\bigcirc$

In our arithmetic example, we took $Y = Q = \mathbf{N}$, and simply took $\beta = id_{\mathbf{N}}$. For a case in which $Y \neq Q$, we now construct a tree automaton for checking the validity of derivation trees for context-free grammars. We exemplify the process for our "decimal number" grammar, but give the general definition of a derivation-checker M_G for any context-free grammar.

Recall from Definition 4–1–6 that for each context-free grammar $G = (X, V, P, S)$ we may define the multigraded set $\Omega_G = V \cup X$ with grading function

$$\nu(x) = \{0\} \text{ for all } x \in X$$
$$\nu(v) = \{n \,|\, \text{there exists a string } w \text{ of}$$
$$\text{length } n \text{ with } (v, w) \in P\}$$

We then said that an Ω_G-tree $h \colon T \to \Omega_G$ was a valid derivation tree for G iff it met two conditions:

(i) $h(\Lambda) = S$
(ii) If a node w has successors $w0, w1, \ldots, wn$ then

$$h(w) \mapsto h(w0) \ldots h(wn)$$

is a production of P.

Now, the job of our automaton will be simply to chase up a derivation tree, seeing if each node corresponds to a valid production. If validity holds, the label on the node is left unchanged (though no longer graded, since it will then be considered as an element of Q_G rather than of Ω_G); but once an invalid production is encountered, the node is given the state R (for Reject) and this propagates up the tree. The output is 1 (for acceptance) if the run yields S at the Λ-node, and is otherwise 0. We illustrate this in Figures 4–22, 4–23, and 4–24 for the decimal number grammar.

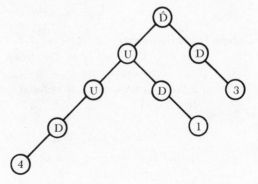

Figure 4–22 At each node, the production is correct, so input and state labels coincide. State label at node Λ is initial symbol $\hat{D}$, so output is 1.

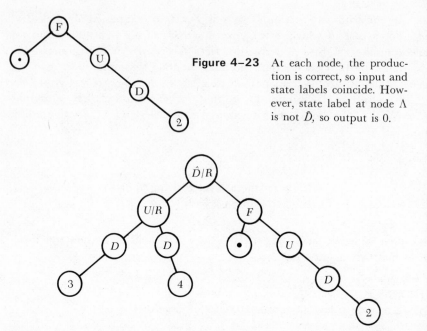

Figure 4–23   At each node, the production is correct, so input and state labels coincide. However, state label at node Λ is not $\hat{D}$, so output is 0.

Figure 4–24   All productions are correct, except $U \mapsto DD$. Thus, the state at node 0 becomes R. Then node Λ does not see the input structure $\hat{D} \mapsto UF$ (which is valid), but instead sees the state production $\hat{D} \mapsto RF$ which is invalid. Hence, state label at node Λ is R, and so the output is 0.

This then corresponds to the following general definition:

DEFINITION 4

Let $G = (X, V, P, S)$ be a context-free grammar. Then the **derivation-checker** for G is the tree automaton

$$M_G = (Q_G, \Omega_G, \{0, 1\}, \delta, \beta)$$

where Q_G is the (ungraded) state set $V \cup X \cup \{R\}$ (for some $R \notin V \cup X$)
Ω_G is $V \cup X$ graded as in Definition 4–1–6
$\{0, 1\}$ is the output set
δ is the transition function defined for each $\delta \in \Omega_G$ and each $\delta \in \nu(\omega)$ by:

    (i) If $\omega = x \in X$, then δ^0_ω is the constant x

    (ii) If $\omega = v \in V$, then $\delta^n_v : Q^n_G \to Q_G$ is defined by

$$\delta_v^n(q_1, q_2, \ldots, q_n) = \begin{cases} v & \text{if } v \mapsto q_1 \ldots q_n \text{ is in } P \\ R & \text{if not} \end{cases}$$

$\beta : Q_G \to \{0, 1\}$ is the output function defined by

$$\beta(q) = 1 \text{ iff } q = S. \qquad\qquad \bigcirc$$

Thus, tree automata play an important role in the theory of computation, both in checking the *syntax* of a grammar (the derivation-checker) and in providing the *semantics* (the arithmetic machine).

EXERCISES FOR SECTION 4-3

1. Prove that the evaluation of the $\hat{X}$-tree corresponding to w by $\hat{M}$ is precisely $M_{q_0}(w)$.

2. Let G be the context-free grammar

$$(\{a, b\}, \{S\}, \{S \mapsto ab, S \mapsto aSb\}, S)$$

(i) What is Ω_G?
(ii) What are the δ_ω^n's?
(iii) What is the run of M_G on each of the trees of Figure 4-25?

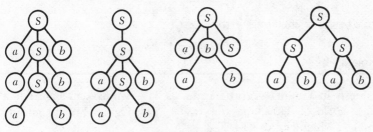

Figure 4-25

4-4   Polish Notation and Pushdown Automata

We have now seen that important aspects of the syntax and semantics of computation can be captured in terms of trees processing. However, most present-day computers process strings rather than trees. In this section, then, we introduce the Polish notation (named in honor of the Polish logician Łukasiewicz) for encoding trees as strings, and then show that pushdown automata are the appropriate sequential machines for processing these encodings in a way which simulates the processing of trees by tree automata. We then see how this yields a general (but relatively inefficient) procedure for parsing strings to see if they can be derived using a given context-free grammar.

DEFINITION 1

For an Ω-tree t, we call the string $e(t) \in \Omega^+$ the **Polish notation** for t, where e is defined for all Ω-trees by the following induction scheme:

Basis Step. Given a tree consisting of only a single node labelled α, encode it as α.

Induction Step. Given a tree of the form $(t_1, \ldots, t_n)\alpha$, i.e., of the form shown in Figure 4–26 (where each t_j is a tree, and need not comprise a single

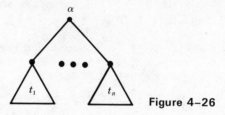

Figure 4–26

node), encode it as

$$e(t_1) \ldots e(t_n)\alpha$$

where $e(t_j)$ is the encoding of the tree t_j. ○

Example 1

The tree t_1 in Figure 4–27(a) encodes as $34+$ while t_2 in Figure 4–27(b) encodes as $76\times$. Thus, the tree $(t_1, t_2)+$ in Figure 4–27(c) encodes as $e(t_1)e(t_2)+$, which equals $34+76\times+$. ◊

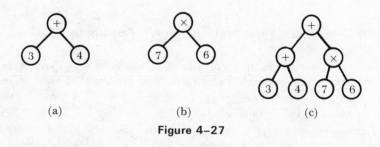

(a) (b) (c)

Figure 4–27

Actually, in making use of the encoding later, we shall find it essential to know how many successors each node has. For this reason we shall want to work with sets Ω for which each $\nu(\omega)$ has exactly one element. However, this entails no loss of generality, for we simply change our encoding procedure to read:

(i) Given a tree with a single node labelled α, encode it as α if $\nu(\alpha) = \{0\}$; encode it as α^0 if $|\nu(\alpha)| > 1$.

(ii) Set

$$e[(t_1, \ldots, t_n)\alpha] = \begin{cases} e(t_1) \ldots e(t_n)\alpha & \text{if } |\nu(\alpha)| = 1 \\ e(t_1) \ldots e(t_n)\alpha^n & \text{if } |\nu(\alpha)| > 1 \end{cases}$$

In other words, if $|\nu(\alpha)| > 1$ so that the arity of α is ambiguous, we introduce a new symbol α^n for each $n \in \nu(\alpha)$. Thus, in what follows, we may also assume a fixed arity for any operator symbol we encounter in a tree.

Example 2

We encode the tree in Figure 4-28 as $1DU^12DU^2 \cdot 3DU^1F\hat{D}^2$, where we note that only U and $\hat{D}$ need superscripts to make their arities unambiguous.

$\Diamond$

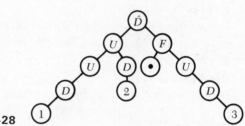

Figure 4–28

Example 3

We return to the tree shown in Figure 4–27(c) and its encoding $34 + 76 \times +$, and see how we can simulate on the string the evaluation that we can perform on the tree:

In each case, we must add 3 and 4 to get 7, multiply 7 and 6 to get 42, and then add 7 and 42 to get 49.

Let's see how we can do this by reading one symbol at a time from left to right on $34 + 76 \times +$. We do this by using a "pushdown stack" (see Figure 4–29) on which we may store a string of symbols, but can only read or write at the top. (For convenience we write the stack as a string, with the "top" symbol at the left.)

0. Start with empty stack   Stack = $[\Lambda]$
1. Read in first symbol, 3
   It is a number, so put it on top of stack   Stack = $[3]$
2. Read next symbol, 4
   It is a number, so put it on top of stack   Stack = $\begin{bmatrix} 4 \\ 3 \end{bmatrix}$

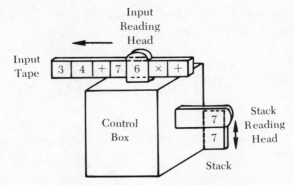

Figure 4–29   Pushdown automaton for evaluating arithmetic expressions. The input reading head reads the input tape from left to right; the stack reading head reads the top square of the stack, and may change it, remove several squares (the square below pops up to the top), or replace it by new squares (pushing the other squares down).

3. Read next symbol, +
   It is an operator, so pull last two symbols off stack, operate on them, and put result on top of stack

   Stack = $[7]$

4. Read next symbol, 7
   It is a number, so put it on top of stack

   Stack = $\begin{bmatrix} 7 \\ 7 \end{bmatrix}$

5. Read next symbol, 6

   (This is the stage of the computation shown in Figure 4–29: $34 + 7$ has already been read, and is on the input tape to the left of the reading head; 6 is now being read, while $\times +$ is to the right of the reading head, to be read later. The pushdown stack contains the two 7's that were there at the end of step 4.)

   It is a number, so put it on top of stack

   Stack = $\begin{bmatrix} 6 \\ 7 \\ 7 \end{bmatrix}$

6. Read next symbol, $\times$
   It is an operator, so pull last two symbols off stack, operate on them, and put result on top of stack

   Stack = $\begin{bmatrix} 42 \\ 7 \end{bmatrix}$

7. Read next symbol, +
   It is an operator, so pull last two symbols off stack, operate on them, and put result on top of stack

   Stack = $[49]$

We see that when this process has read the last symbol of the input string, it has on its pushdown stack a single number, which is the result of the computation.   ◊

We proceed from here in six stages:

(i) Give a formal definition of the automaton we have just described.
(ii) Prove that this automaton always correctly evaluates the encoding of an arithmetic tree.
(iii) Define the general notion of a pushdown automaton.
(iv) Define, for each tree automaton, a corresponding pushdown automaton.
(v) Generalize (ii) to prove that every tree automaton is correctly simulated by its corresponding pushdown automaton.
(vi) Apply the general result of (iv) and (v) to derivation-checkers to provide a general (though inefficient) parsing procedure for context-free languages.

STAGE (i)

The formal definition of the machine M_1 which evaluates encodings of arithmetic trees.

We are going to require our machine M_1 (shown performing a particular computation in Figure 4–29) to "look" only at the "top" symbol of its pushdown stack at each step. Thus, step 3 of Example 2, for example, will be broken down into two finer steps:

3.1 Read next symbol, $+$
It is an operator, so store it in control box.
Pull top symbol off stack, and store it in control box, too.

3.2 Pull top symbol off stack. Combine it with symbol in control box using the operator stored in the control box, and put result on top of stack. Empty control box.

Similarly, we break steps 6 and 7 into steps 6.1 and 6.2 and into steps 7.1 and 7.2, respectively.

We see that the states of the control box are going to be of the form Λ (nothing is being stored) or $(\circ, n)$ where $\circ$ is $+$ or $\times$, and n is the number pulled off the top of the stack. We then have the following prescription for the machine:

(a) If state of control box is Λ, and current input symbol is $n \in \mathbf{N}$, put n on top of the stack, leave state as Λ, and advance input tape one square. (This corresponds to steps 1, 2, 4, and 5 in Example 3.)

(b) If state of control box is Λ, current input symbol is $\circ \in \{+, \times\}$, and top symbol on stack is n, erase n from top of stack, change state to $(\circ, n)$, and advance input tape one square. (This corresponds to steps 3.1, 6.1, and 7.1.)

(c) If state of control box is $(\circ, n)$ and top symbol on stack is n', replace n' by $n \circ n'$ (i.e., $n + n'$ if $\circ$ is $+$; $n \times n'$ if $\circ$ is $\times$), change state to Λ, but do not advance input tape. (This corresponds to steps 3.2, 6.2, and 7.2.)

(d) In all other cases, halt.

We now rephrase the above in more formal terms: Our machine M_1 has:

> Input set $X = \mathbf{N} \cup \{+, \times\}$
>
> State set $Q = \{\Lambda\} \cup (\{+, \times\} \times \mathbf{N})$
>
> Pushdown set $Z = \mathbf{N}$
>
> Transition function $\delta : Q \times X \times Z \to Q \times Z^* \times \{0, 1\}$

where we interpret $\delta(q, x, z) = (q', w, m)$ to mean, "If the state of the control box is q, the current input symbol is x, and the top symbol on the stack is z, then change state to q', replace z by w, and advance the input tape m squares." Note that if $w = \Lambda$, then "replace z by w" simply means "erase z," while if $w = xz$, then "replace z by w" simply means "put x on top of z, atop the stack." Thus, the cases (a) through (d) above result in the following prescription for δ:

$$\delta(q, x, z) = \begin{cases} (\Lambda, xz, 1) & \text{if } q = \Lambda \text{ and } x \in \mathbf{N} & \text{(a)} \\ ((x, z), \Lambda, 1) & \text{if } q = \Lambda \text{ and } x \in \{+, \times\} & \text{(b)} \\ (\Lambda, n \circ z, 0) & \text{if } q = (\circ, n) & \text{(c)} \\ (q, z, 0) & \text{otherwise} & \text{(d)} \end{cases}$$

We now rework Example 2 to check this formalization. In each case we shall represent the current *total* state of M_1 by (w_1, q_1, w_2), where w_1 is that portion of the input tape yet to be read, q is the current *internal* state, and w_2 is the string on the pushdown stack. We call each such triple an *instantaneous description* (ID) for M_1. For typographical convenience we henceforth

write $\begin{bmatrix} n_1 \\ n_2 \\ \vdots \\ n_m \end{bmatrix}$ as $n_1 n_2 \ldots n_m$, so that the leftmost symbol of the string corresponds to the topmost symbol on the stack.

Example 4

We simply repeat the steps of Example 3, checking at each stage that δ yields the indicated transition.

Step 0: $(34 + 76 \times +, \Lambda, \Lambda)$ The whole input string is yet to
 be read, the internal state is Λ,
 and the stack is empty.
Step 1: $(4 + 76 \times +, \Lambda, 3)$ since $\delta(\Lambda, 3, \Lambda) = (\Lambda, 3, 1)$ by (a)
Step 2: $(+76 \times +, \Lambda, 43)$ since $\delta(\Lambda, 4, 3) = (\Lambda, 43, 1)$ by (a)
Step 3.1: $(76 \times +, (+, 4), 3)$ since $\delta(\Lambda, +, 4) = ((+, 4), \Lambda, 1)$ by (b)
Step 3.2: $(76 \times +, \Lambda, 7)$ since $\delta(7, (+, n), 3) = (\Lambda, 7, 0)$ by (c)

Rather than write out the complete justification for the remaining steps, we shall simply write out the remaining IDs, using $\theta_1 \vdash \theta_2$ to abbreviate "θ_1 is transformed into θ_2 by a single application of δ": $(76 \times +, \Lambda, 7) \vdash (6 \times +, \Lambda, 77) \vdash (\times +, \Lambda, 677) \vdash (+, (\times, 6), 77) \vdash (+, \overline{427}) \dagger \vdash (\Lambda, (+, 42), 7) \vdash (\Lambda, \Lambda, \overline{49})$.   ◊

STAGE (ii)

Prove that the above automaton M_1 correctly evaluates the encoding of any arithmetic tree.

 Let Ω_A (A for the Arithmetic label set) be the graded set $\mathbf{N} \cup \{+, \times\}$ with arity $\nu(n) = 0$ for $n \in \mathbf{N}$, and $\nu(+) = \nu(\times) = 2$. As before, we let e be the Polish notation encoding of Ω-trees, which is defined inductively by:

(a) For each tree t consisting of only a single node $t: \{\Lambda\} \to \mathbf{N}: \Lambda \mapsto n$, set $e(t) = \bar{n}$. (The bar is to meet the problem raised by the previous footnote.)
(b) For each tree $t = (t_1, t_2)\alpha$ we set $e(t) = e(t_1)e(t_2)\alpha$.

Our desired result then takes the following form:

THEOREM 1

Let $v(t)$ be the number obtained at node Λ as the result of the evaluation of the Ω_A-tree t by the arithmetic tree automaton defined in Example 4–3–1. Then if M_1 is started in state Λ with an empty stack, it will complete its computation on input tape $e(t)$ with the number $v(t)$ as the sole content of its pushdown stack.

---

†We use the bar over 42 so that $\overline{427}$ parses uniquely as $(42, 7)$ and cannot be confused with $(4, 2, 7)$, etc.

Proof

We simply use the definition of e to prove the theorem by induction; i.e., we first prove it for trees with a single node n, and then we verify that if it is true for t_1 and t_2 it must also be true for each $(t_1, t_2)\alpha$, where α equals $+$ or $\times$.

Basis Step. If the input tape consists of a single number n, then M_1 will simply print n on its stack and stop, as desired, since $(n, \Lambda, \Lambda) \vdash (\Lambda, \Lambda, n)$.

Induction Step. We note that, in the basis step, the machine would not have disturbed anything on the pushdown stack. We thus assume that we are given trees t_1 and t_2 such that, if M_1 starts with w on its stack and $e(t_i)$ as its input tape, it will complete its computation with $v(t_i)w$ on its stack. If we use $\theta_1 \vdash^* \theta_2$ to abbreviate "ID θ_1 is transformed into θ_2 by zero (i.e., $\theta_1 = \theta_2$), one (i.e., $\theta_1 \vdash \theta_2$), or more applications of δ", we can express this symbolically by $(e(t_i)w_1, \Lambda, w) \vdash^* (w_1, \Lambda, v(t_i)w)$ for $i = 1, 2$. But then our induction step proceeds smoothly:

Suppose M_1 starts with w on its stack and $e[(t_1, t_2)\alpha]w_1 = e(t_1)e(t_2)\alpha w_1$ on its input tape. After reading $e(t_1)$, it will then have $v(t_1)w$ on its stack and $e(t_2)\alpha w_1$ still on its input tape:

$$(e(t_1)e(t_2)\alpha w_1, \Lambda, w) \vdash^* (e(t_2)\alpha w_1, \Lambda, v(t_1)w)$$

After reading $e(t_2)$, it will then have $v(t_2)v(t_1)w$ on its tape:

$$(e(t_2)\alpha w_1, \Lambda, v(t_1)w) \vdash^* (\alpha w_1, \Lambda, v(t_2)v(t_1)w)$$

Reading α will cause it to read $v(t_2)$ off the stack:

$$(\alpha w_1, \Lambda, v(t_2)v(t_1)w) \vdash (w_1, (\alpha, v(t_2)), v(t_1)w)$$

and then read $v(t_1)$ off the stack and form $v(t_2)\alpha v(t_1)$, which is just $v[(t_1, t_2)\alpha]$, and place the result atop the stack:

$$(w_1, (\alpha, v(t_2)), v(t_1)w) \vdash (w_1, \Lambda, v(t_1)\alpha v(t_2)w)$$

to halt with $v[(t_1, t_2)\alpha]w$ on its stack, as was to be proved. □

Note that Theorem 1 only guarantees that M_1 will correctly process valid tree encodings, and promises nothing about its performance for other input strings.

STAGE (iii)

Define the general notion of a pushdown automaton.

We are simply going to mimic the construction of stage (i), save that we shall allow that a given (state, input, stack) configuration may have several (or one, or none) possible consequents. Our machine M_1 is special in that each configuration has a *unique* consequent, and it is thus an example of what is called a *deterministic* pushdown automaton.

DEFINITION 2

A **pushdown automaton (pda)** M is a quintuple

$$M = (Q, X, Z, \delta, q_0)$$

where

Q is a set of **states**
X is a set of **inputs**
Z is a set of **stack symbols**
$\delta: Q \times X \times Z \to$ finite subsets of $Q \times Z^* \times \{0, 1\}$
    is the **transition function**
q_0 in Q is the **initial state**

We say that M is **deterministic** if $\delta(q, x, z)$ has one element for $(q, x, z) \in Q \times X \times Z$.   ○

We interpret $(q', w, m) \in \delta(q, x, z)$ to mean, "If the state of the control box is q, the current input symbol is x, and the top symbol on the stack is z, then a possible move for M is to change state to q', replace z by the string w, and advance the input tape m squares." We formalize this interpretation as follows:

DEFINITION 3

An **instantaneous description** (ID) of a pda M is an element (θ, q, θ') from $X^* \times Q \times Z^*$, corresponding to

("yet to be read" input string θ, control box state q, stack string θ').   ○

Then δ yields the relation $\vdash_M$ of "one-step consequent" on IDs which is illustrated in Figure 4–30.

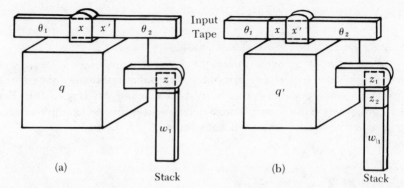

Input Tape

(a)

(b)

Stack

Stack

Figure 4–30 In (a) the pda is in state q, is scanning the x of the input tape $\theta_1 xx'\theta_2$, and is scanning the z atop its stack, which contains zw_1. This situation is described by the instantaneous configuration $(xx'\theta_2, q, zw_1)$—i.e., we only record that portion of the input tape which is yet to be read. If $(q', z_1 z_2, 1)$ is in $\delta(q, x, z)$, then in one step M can change internal state from q to q', replace z by $z_1 z_2$ atop the stack, and advance the input tape 1 square to the left, to pass from the situation shown in (a) to that shown in (b). We symbolize the relation between the two IDs of these configurations by writing

$$(xx'\theta_2, q, zw_1) \vdash_M (x'\theta_2, q', z_1 z_2 w_1)$$

DEFINITION 4

Let $(x\theta, q, z\hat{\theta})$ be an ID of M. Then we write

$$(x\tilde{\theta}, q, z\hat{\theta}) \vdash_M (\theta, q', \theta')$$

iff there exists $(q', w, 0)$ in $\delta(q, x, z)$ such that $(\theta, q', \theta') = (x\theta, q', w\hat{\theta})$ [$\theta = x\theta$ if we advance the input tape 0 squares while changing state to q' and replacing z by w atop the stack] or there exists $(q', w, 1)$ in $\delta(q, x, z)$ such that $(\theta, q', \theta') = (\tilde{\theta}, q', w\hat{\theta})$ [$\theta = \tilde{\theta}$ if we advance the input tape 1 square].

We define $\vdash_M^*$ to be the transitive closure of $\vdash_M$; in other words, $d \vdash_M^* d'$ iff $d = d'$ or iff there exist $d_1, d_2, \ldots, d_m (m \geq 2)$ such that

$$d = d_1 \vdash_M d_2 \vdash_M \cdots \vdash_M d_m = d'$$

The **result** $r_M(\theta)$ of the computation of pda M on input string θ in X^* is then defined to be the set of possible state-stack configurations which can result when M has read θ from initial state q_0 and a stack containing a single distinguished symbol z_0:

$$r_M(\theta) = \{(q, \theta') | (\theta, q_0, z_0) \vdash_M^* (\Lambda, q, \theta')\} \qquad \bigcirc$$

Note that, if M is deterministic, $r_M(\theta)$ will have at most one element for each θ in X^*. However, for a general pda, $r_M(\theta)$ may be empty, or may have many elements. The inport of Theorem 1 was that for the pda M_1 given above, if $q_0 = \Lambda$, then we know that the result of computing on the Polish notation of a tree t yields $v(t)z_0$ alone on the stack; i.e.,

$$r_{M_1}(e(t)) = \{(\Lambda, v(t)z_0)\} \text{ for each valid } \mathbf{N} \cup \{+, \times\}\text{-tree } t$$

Example 5

We present a deterministic pda M which will recognize the strings of the context-free language $\{a^n b^n \mid n \geq 1\}$ in the sense that

$$r_M(\theta) = (q_1, z_0) \Leftrightarrow \theta = a^n b^n \text{ for some } n \geq 1$$

This foreshadows the general result of Theorem 4 that every context-free language can be so associated with some (not necessarily deterministic) pda. The operation of M is simplicity itself: given a string of the form $a^m b^n \theta$, where $m, n \geq 0$ and θ is empty or starts with an a, it puts an a on the stack each time it reads an a from a^m; it then takes an a off the stack each time it reads a b from b^n. Formally, then M has

$$
\begin{array}{ll}
Q = \{q_0, q_1, q_2\} & \delta(q_0, a, z) = (q_0, az, 1) \\
X = \{a, b\} & \delta(q_0, b, a) = (q_1, \Lambda, 1) \\
Z = \{a, z_0\} & \delta(q_1, b, a) = (q_1, \Lambda, 1) \\
& \delta(q_1, x, z_0) = (q_2, z_0, 1) \\
& \delta(q_2, x, z) = (q_2, z, 0)
\end{array}
$$

For example, $(a^3 b^3, q_0, z_0) \vdash (a^2 b^3, q_0, az_0) \vdash (ab^3, q_0, a^2 z_0) \vdash (b^3, q_0, a^3 z_0)$
$\vdash (b^2, q_1, a^2 z_0) \vdash (b, q_1, az_0) \vdash (\Lambda, q_1, z_0)$. ◊

STAGE (iv)

Define, for each tree automaton, a corresponding pushdown automaton.

In this construction, we shall mimic the construction of stage (ii), but proceeding immediately to the formalism of stage (iii). Recall that we designed our encoding so that each symbol in the tree encoding had a unique arity. Then "input is a number" in stage (ii) corresponds to "$v(x) = 0$" in our general construction; while "input is an operator" becomes "$v(x) > 0$."

Let us then be given a tree automaton

$$M_T = (Q, \Omega, Y, \delta, \beta)$$

where, for simplicity, we shall assume that Ω already has $|v(\omega)| = 1$ for each $\omega \in \Omega$. Inputs for this automaton are Ω-trees. Inputs for our pda will then be encodings of such trees, and these are strings of symbols from Ω considered as an ungraded set.

Example 6

To motivate the construction which follows, suppose

$$\Omega = \{0, 1, \sim, +, m\}$$

where $\nu(0) = \nu(1) = \{0\}; \nu(\sim) = \{1\}, \nu(+) = \{2\}$ and $\nu(m) = \{3\}$. Suppose that our tree automaton M_T is such that

$$Q = \{0, 1\}$$
$$\delta_0 = 0; \delta_1 = 1$$
$$\delta_\sim(q) = \sim q \text{ where, as usual, } \sim 0 = 1 \text{ and } \sim 1 = 0$$
$$\delta_+(q_1, q_2) = q_1 \oplus q_2, \text{ addition modulo 2; and}$$
$$\delta_m(q_1, q_2, q_3) = 1 \text{ iff } q_2 = q_3 = 0.$$

Suppose we have designed a pda M_P which simulates M_T. Let us see how it might be expected to process the encoding of the Ω-tree of Figure 4–31.

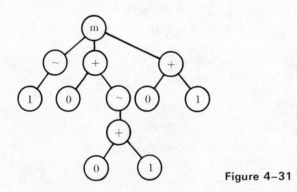

Figure 4–31

Then, copying Examples 3 and 4, we may break down the computation of M_P as follows. Step 12 proves to be the most interesting.

Step 0: Start in state Λ, with empty stack, and with the encoding of the tree on the tape. The initial ID is thus

$$\theta_0 = (1 \sim 001 + \sim + 01 + m, \Lambda, \Lambda)$$

Step 1: Transfer 1 atop the stack:

$$\theta_0 \vdash \theta_1 = (\sim 001 + \sim + 01 + m, \Lambda, 1)$$

Step 2: $\sim$ is a unary operator, and so can be used directly to transform the top symbol of the stack:

$$\theta_1 \vdash \theta_2 = (001 + \sim + 01 + m, \Lambda, 0)$$

Steps 3, 4, and 5: As in Step 1, each reads a symbol of the input tape and places it atop the stack:

$$\theta_2 \vdash \theta_3 \vdash \theta_4 \vdash \theta_5 = (+ \sim + 01 + m, \Lambda, 1000)$$

(Note the reversal of the order of consecutive input symbols when they are placed on the stack.)

Step 6: $+$ is a binary operator and so its action requires two substeps (compare Steps 3.1 and 3.2 of Example 3, and note that $0 \oplus 1 = 1$):

$$\theta_5 \vdash \theta_{6.1} = (\sim + 01 + m, (+, 1), 000) \vdash \theta_{6.2} = (\sim + 01 + m, \Lambda, 100)$$

Step 7: As in Step 2:

$$\theta_{6.2} \vdash \theta_7 = (+01 + m, \Lambda, 000)$$

Step 8: As in Step 6:

$$\theta_7 \vdash \theta_{8.2} = (01 + m, \Lambda, 00)$$

Steps 9 and 10: As in Step 1:

$$\theta_{8.2} \vdash \theta_9 \vdash \theta_{10} = (+m, \Lambda, 1000)$$

Step 11: As in Steps 6 and 8:

$$\theta_{10} \vdash \theta_{11.1} \vdash \theta_{11.2} = (m, \Lambda, 100)$$

Step 12: This is the really novel step. Since m has arity 3, it must act on the top *three* symbols on the stack. Since it can only read one symbol at a time, it must take three substeps to complete its task:

$$\theta_{11.2} = (m, \Lambda, 100) \vdash \theta_{12.1} = (\Lambda, (m, 1), 00)$$
$$\vdash \theta_{12.2} = (\Lambda, (m, 1, 0), 0)$$
$$\vdash \theta_{12.3} = (\Lambda, \Lambda, 0)$$

The reader should note here the force of our comment on Steps 3, 4, and 5. Looking at $\theta_{12.2}$, we are tempted to replace its $z = 0$ by $\delta_m(1, 0, 0)$, which is 1. However, since the order of constituents is reversed on the stack, we must replace its z with $\delta_m(0, 0, 1) = 0$, as indeed we have done in $\theta_{12.3}$.

The reader may wish to write down the δ corresponding to the above construction (Exercise 6).

Note that in this example the only states we ever encounter are $\Lambda, (+, 0)$, $(+, 1), (m, 0), (m, 1), (m, 0, 0), (m, 0, 1), (m, 1, 0)$, and $(m, 1, 1)$; i.e., the states other than Λ are all of the form

$$(\omega, z_1, \ldots, z_j)$$

where $\omega \in \Omega, z_1, \ldots, z_j$ are in Z (stack symbols), and $\nu(\omega) > j \geq 1.$ $\Diamond$

Building on Example 6, then, we see that where the control box of the machine of Stage (ii) had a state Λ, and a state $(\circ, m)$ for each operator $\circ$ of arity 2 and each $m \in \mathbf{N}$, the appropriate generalization is to have, in addition to Λ (which we now call q_0), a state $(\omega, z_1 \ldots z_j)$ for each operator ω of arity $m > 1$ and each string $z_1 \ldots z_j$ of stack symbols with $1 \leq j < m$. Step 2 of Example 6 indicates why we need no states corresponding to those ω which have $\nu(\omega) = 1$.

DEFINITION 4

Given the tree automaton $M_T = (Q, \Omega, Y, \delta, \beta)$, we then define the pda $M_P = s(M_T)$, called the **simulator** of M_T, as follows:

$$M_P = (\widehat{Q}, \widehat{X}, \widehat{Z}, \widehat{\delta}, q_0)$$

where $\widehat{Z}$, the set of pushdown symbols, is just the state set Q of the tree automaton M_T

$\widehat{Q}$, the set of states, is then $\{\Lambda\} \cup \{(\omega, z_1 \ldots z_j) \mid \nu(\omega) > j \geq 1$ and each z_i is in $\widehat{Z} = Q\}$

$\widehat{X}$, the set of inputs, is Ω, but ungraded

$\widehat{\delta}: \widehat{Q} \times \widehat{X} \times \widehat{Z} \to \widehat{Q} \times Z^* \times \{0, 1\}$ is the transition function given by the display (where the step number at the end of the line indicates a step at which this form of δ was used in Example 6):

$$\hat{\delta}(q, x, z) = \begin{cases} (q_0, \delta_x z, 1) \\ \qquad \text{if } q = q_0 \qquad\qquad \text{and } \nu(x) = 0 \qquad (\text{Step 1}) \\ (q_0, \delta_x(z), 1) \\ \qquad \text{if } q = q_0 \qquad\qquad \text{and } \nu(x) = 1 \qquad (\text{Step 2}) \\ ((x, z), \Lambda, 1) \\ \qquad \text{if } q = q_0 \qquad\qquad \text{and } \nu(x) > 1 \qquad (\text{Step 6.1}) \\ ((\omega, q_1, \dots, q_j z), \Lambda, 0) \\ \qquad \text{if } q = (\omega, q_1, \dots, q_j) \text{ and } \nu(\omega) > j + 1 \quad (\text{Step 12.2}) \\ (q_0, \delta_\omega(z, q_j, \dots, q_1), 0) \\ \qquad \text{if } q = (\omega, q_1, \dots, q_j) \text{ and } \nu(\omega) = j + 1 \quad (\text{Step 12.3}) \\ (q, z, 0) \\ \qquad\qquad \text{in every other case} \qquad\qquad\qquad\qquad\qquad\bigcirc \end{cases}$$

The last line just says, "If something has gone wrong, do not do anything more." The reader should check every line against Examples 4 and 6, taking especial note of our comment on Step 12 of Example 6, and of the commutativity of $+$ and $\times$ in Example 4, in comprehending the penultimate line of the definition of $\hat{\delta}$. However, the significance of all this will also be explained in the proof of the next theorem.

STAGE (v)

Generalize (ii) to prove that every tree automaton is correctly simulated by its corresponding pushdown automaton.

Hopefully, Example 6 has so well motivated our definition of the pda M_P which is called the simulator of the tree automaton M_T that our formal proof of Theorem 2 below, that M_P does indeed *correctly* simulate M_T, may add little to the reader's intuition, though it will help to increase his understanding of how to construct subtle proofs by induction. We thus suggest that at a first reading, or in an introductory course, the reader pass directly to the heuristic discussion which introduces Stage (vi). The more advanced reader will find that in Stage (v) we not only show that M_P will correctly simulate M_T, but also prove, in Theorem 3, that the computation of M_P on an input string w will have the two properties of never deleting all symbols from the stack, and of ending up with precisely one symbol on the stack, whenever w is the encoding of an Ω-tree.

Moving on, then, to the "second reading," we recall that, in the previous section, we defined the **run** of M_T on an Ω-tree $t: T \to \Omega$ to be the Q-tree $\hat{t}: T \to Q$ defined inductively by:

(i) $\hat{t}(w) = \delta_{t(w)}$ if $\nu(t(\omega)) = 0$

(ii) $\hat{t}(w) = \delta_{t(w)}(\hat{t}(w0), \dots, \hat{t}(w, n-1))$ if $\nu(t(\omega)) = n$ with $n > 0$.

We may now define the **result** of the run of M_T on t, denoted by $M_T(t)$, to be

$$M_T(t) = t(\Lambda)$$

and then the evaluation of the tree is $\beta[M_T(t)]$.

With this terminology, and the useful reminder of the inductive definition of a run on the tree, we may now use our terminology of Stage (iii) to state and prove our general theorem that M_P will process the encoding of t to end up with the result of the run of M_T on t as the sole content of its stack.

Let e be the Polish notation encoding of Ω-trees defined inductively by:

(a) For each tree $\omega: \{\Lambda\} \to \Omega : \Lambda \to \omega$, we set $e(\omega) = \omega$.
(b) For each tree $t = (t_1, \ldots, t_n)\omega$ (recall the notation of Definition 1), set
$e(t) = e(t_1) \ldots e(t_n)\omega$.

Then we may prove the following:

THEOREM 2

Let $M_T = (Q, \Omega, Y, \delta, \beta)$ be a tree automaton over the graded set Ω, and let $M_P = (\widehat{Q}, \widehat{X}, \widehat{Z}, \widehat{\delta}, q_0)$ be the simulator $s(M_T)$ of Definition 4.

Then for each Ω-tree t,

$$(e(t), q_0, \Lambda) \vdash^*_{M_P} (\Lambda, q_0, M_T(t))$$

Proof

As in the special case of Theorem 1, we prove our theorem by giving an inductive proof of the stronger assertion:

"For each Ω-tree t, for each input string θ in $\widehat{X}^*$, and for each stack string θ' in $\widehat{Z}^*$ we have $(e(t)\theta, q_0, \theta') \vdash^*_{M_P} (\theta, q_0, M_T(t)\theta')$."

Our Theorem 2 corresponds, then, to the special case of this assertion in which $\theta = \theta' = \Lambda$. Our basis step is to prove the assertion for each 1-node tree, while our induction step checks that its validity for $t_1, \ldots, t_n$ assures its validity for each tree $(t_1, \ldots, t_n)\omega$ with $\nu(\omega) = n$. The validity for all trees then follows by induction on the height of the tree (Section 1-5).

Basis Step. Let t be the one-node tree $t(\Lambda) = \omega$, with $e(t) = \omega$ and $M_T(t) = \delta_\omega$. Then, by the definition of $\widehat{\delta}$, we have

$$\widehat{\delta}(q_0, \omega, z) = (q_0, \delta_\omega z, 1)$$

Thus, by the definition of $\vdash_{M_P}$, we have, for all θ in $\widehat{X}^*$ and θ' in $\widehat{Z}^*$, that

$$(e(t)\theta, q_0, \theta') = (\omega\theta, q_0, \theta') \vdash_{M_P} (\theta, q_0, \delta_\omega \theta') = (\theta, q_0, M_T(t)\theta')$$

as was to be shown.

Induction Step. Assume that, for $1 \leq j \leq n$, it has been shown that

$$(e(t_j)\theta_j, q_0, \theta'_j) \vdash^*_{M_P} (\theta_j, q_0, M_T(t_j)\theta'_j) \tag{α_j}$$

for all θ_j in $\widehat{X}^*$ and all θ'_j in $\widehat{Z}^*$. Then we must deduce from this that, for all θ in $\widehat{X}^*$ and all θ' in $\widehat{Z}^*$ and all ω with $\nu(\omega) = n$, we have

$$(e((t_1, \ldots, t_n)\omega)\theta, q_0, \theta') \vdash^*_{M_P} (\theta, q_0, M_T((t_1, \ldots, t_n)\omega)\theta')$$

To do this, simply apply (α_j) for $j = 1, \ldots, n$ in turn, making appropriate choices of θ_j and θ'_j at each step:

We start with $e((t_1, \ldots, t_n)\omega)\theta = e(t_1) \ldots e(t_n)\omega\theta$ on the tape, and, by appealing to (α_1) through (α_n), we know that the effect of reading through each $e(t_j)$ will be to place $M_T(t_j)$ atop M_P's stack:

$$
\begin{aligned}
e((t_1, \ldots, t_n)\omega)&\theta, q_0, \theta') \\
&= (e(t_1) \ldots e(t_n)\omega\theta, q_0, \theta') \\
&\vdash^*_{M_P} (e(t_2) \ldots e(t_n)\omega\theta, q_0, M_T(t_1)\theta') \qquad \text{by } (\alpha_1) \\
&\quad \vdots \\
&\vdash^*_{M_P} (e(t_n)\omega\theta, q_0, M_T(t_{n-1}) \ldots M_T(t_1)\theta') \qquad \text{by } (\alpha_{n-1}) \\
&\vdash^*_{M_P} (\omega\theta, q_0, M_T(t_n) \ldots M_T(t_1)\theta') \qquad \text{by } (\alpha_n)
\end{aligned}
$$

Since ω is an n-ary operator, we must now load the *last* (noting the order reversal) $n - 1$ of its arguments into the control box before we can operate with δ_ω upon all of its arguments, and use the result to replace ω's *first* argument atop the stack. Continuing, then:

$$
\begin{aligned}
\omega\theta, q_0, M(t_n) &\ldots M(t_1)\theta') \\
&\vdash_M (\theta, (\omega, M_T(t_n)), M_T(t_{n-1}) \ldots M_T(t_1)\theta') \qquad \text{by definiton of } \widehat{\delta} \\
&\quad \vdots \\
&\vdash_M (\theta, (\omega, M_T(t_n), \ldots, M_T(t_2)), M_T(t_1)\theta') \qquad \text{by definition of } \widehat{\delta} \\
&\vdash_M (\theta, q_0, \delta_\omega(M_T(t_1), M_T(t_2), \ldots, M_T(t_n))\theta') \qquad \text{by definition of } \widehat{\delta} \\
&= (\theta, q_0, M_T((t_1, \ldots, t_n)\omega)\theta')
\end{aligned}
$$

Thus, we do indeed have that

$$(e(t)\theta, q_0, \theta') \vdash^*_{M_P} (\theta, q_0, M_T(t)\theta')$$

for $t = (t_1, \ldots, t_n)\omega$, as was to be shown. $\square$

We proved the above theorem on the assumption that the input string for $s(M_T)$ was indeed the encoding of an Ω-tree. In fact, the power of the pushdown stack concept is that it *forces* the input to be an Ω-tree, in the precise sense that the computation on input string w will never delete all symbols from the stack, and will end up with one symbol on the stack, if and only if w is an encoding of an Ω-tree.

THEOREM 3

Let $M_T = (Q, \Omega, Y, \delta, \beta)$ be a tree automaton, and let $M_P = (\widehat{Q}, \widehat{X}, \widehat{Z}, \widehat{\delta}, q_0)$ be the simulator $s(M_T)$. Let w in Ω^* have the property that when M_P computes upon w:

(i) $(w, q_0, \Lambda) \vdash^*_{M_P} (w', q', \Lambda)$ holds for no (w', q') in $\Omega^* \times Q$
                                except (w, q_0)
(ii) $(w, q_0, \Lambda) \vdash^*_{M_P} (\Lambda, q_0, q)$ holds for some q in $\widehat{Z} = Q$

Then w is the encoding $e(t)$ of some Ω-tree t.

Proof

Here is the intuition of the proof of this result: We only take symbols off the stack when we read an operator label ω of arity greater than 1. If condition (i) fails, ω has directed M_P to read some number of symbols (say m) off the stack, and so has arity $n > m$. This could never happen if the input were a valid tree encoding, and thus of the form $e(t_1) \ldots e(t_n)\omega\theta$. On the other hand, if (ii) fails, it says that the final ω of w does not pull enough symbols off the stack.

Then, let ω be the last symbol of an input string w which satisfies conditions (i) and (ii): We consider two cases, (I) $\nu(\omega) = 0$, and (II) $\nu(\omega) > 0$.

(I) If $\nu(\omega) = 0$, then M_P, in reading ω, must make a transition of the form

$$(\omega, q_0, \theta') \vdash_{M_P} (\Lambda, q_0, \omega\theta')$$

By (ii), we must have $\theta' = \Lambda$, and hence by (i) applied to $(w', q', \Lambda) = (\omega, q_0, \theta')$, we have $w' = w$, so that $w = \omega$ is indeed the encoding of a valid tree, namely the one-node tree $\Lambda \mapsto \omega$.

Conversely, if w is of length 1, so that $w = \omega$, it is clear that conditions (i) and (ii) are only satisfied if $\nu(\omega) = 0$.

(II) For the situation $\nu(\omega) > 0$, we study the case $\nu(\omega) > 1$, leaving the case $\nu(\omega) = 1$ as Exercise 8. Our proof will be by induction on the length of w. In other words, we assume that (i) and (ii) hold for any $\bar{w}$ of length less than that of w if and only if $\bar{w}$ is the encoding of an Ω-tree. We then study a $w = \bar{w}\omega$ for which conditions (i) and (ii) hold, and show that w encodes an Ω-tree.

Let $\nu(\omega) = n \geq 2$. Then, since (ii) tells us that a computation from $(\bar{w}\omega, q_0, \Lambda)$ will yield a single symbol on the stack, the definition of M_P assures us that there is a stack string $q_n \ldots q_1$ on which ω operates, so that

$$(\omega, q_0, q_n \ldots q_1) \vdash_{M_P}^* (\Lambda, q_0, \delta_\omega(q_1, \ldots, q_n))$$

For each q_j, then, we may fix the stage at which it was last printed. We write w_1 for the portion of w read until q_1 was last printed, and let w_j, $1 \leq j \leq n$, be the portion of w read between the last printing of q_{j-1} and the last printing of q_j. We claim that our induction hypothesis on $\bar{w}$'s shorter than w implies that each w_j is a valid tree encoding. To see this, consider the following sequence of IDs, whose existence is guaranteed by the way in which we defined the w_j's:

$$(w_1 w_2 \ldots w_n \omega, q_0, \Lambda) \vdash_{M_P}^* (w_2 \ldots w_n \omega, q_0, q_1)$$
$$\vdash_{M_P}^* (w_3 \ldots w_n \omega, q_0, q_2 q_1)$$
$$\vdots$$
$$\vdash_{M_P}^* (w_n \omega, q_0, q_{n-1} \ldots q_2 q_1)$$
$$\vdash_{M_P}^* (\omega, q_0, q_n \ldots q_1)$$
$$\vdash_{M_P}^* (\Lambda, q_0, \delta_\omega(q_1, \ldots, q_n))$$

Each w_j so defined must satisfy conditions (i) (since violating condition (i) would correspond to reading q_{j-1} off the stack) and (ii) (since this corresponds to the net effect of putting the single symbol q_j atop the stack). Hence, by our induction hypothesis, we have that each $w_j = e(t_j)$ for some Ω-tree t_j. But then

$$w = w_1 \ldots w_n \omega = e(t_1) \ldots e(t_n)\omega = e((t_1, \ldots, t_n)\omega)$$

and so w is also the encoding of a valid Ω-tree.   □

STAGE (vi)

Apply the general result of (iv) and (v) to derivation-checkers to provide a general (though inefficient) parsing procedure for context-free languages.

Again, the idea here is fairly simple, but the details may be omitted at a first reading. We saw in Section 4–3 that for each context-free grammar G there is a derivation-checker M_G, namely a tree automaton that can distinguish valid derivation trees for G from other Ω_G-trees. By Stage (v), it is then clear that we can build a pda, say M_{PG}, which can distinguish strings that are Polish notation for valid derivation trees of G from other strings on $(\Omega_G)^+$. Having written down the explicit description of an M_{PG} with the property that

$$(w, q_0, \Lambda) \vdash^*_{M_{PG}} (\Lambda, q_0, S) \text{ iff } w \text{ is the encoding of a valid}$$
$$\text{derivation tree for } G, \text{ so that}$$
$$w = e(t) \text{ with } t \in T(G)$$

we shall then so modify it that we obtain a *nondeterministic* pda M_{AG} with the property that it will end up in state q_0 with only S on its stack iff its input is a string of Ω_G^* which belongs to $L(G)$:

$$(w, q_0, \Lambda) \vdash^*_{M_{AG}} (\Lambda, q_0, S) \text{ iff } w \in L(G)$$

We call M_{AG} an **acceptor** for $L(G)$.

The *idea* is very simple. When fed a string w from Ω_G^+, the machine nondeterministically "inserts" nonterminals into the string, processing this augmented string just the way M_{PG} does. Then, if w belongs to $L(G)$, there is at least one way of augmenting w to obtain a valid derivation tree t whose frontier is w. Thus, it will certainly be the case that if w is in $L(G)$ then $(w, q_0, \Lambda) \vdash^*_{M_{AG}} (\Lambda, q_0, S)$. The hard part will be to prove the converse—namely, that if $(w, q_0, \Lambda) \vdash^*_{M_{AG}} (\Lambda, q_0, S)$ it is indeed necessary for w to belong to $L(G)$. With this description, the reader may decide whether or not to work the details which complete this section.

We start our formal development, then, by recalling the definition of a derivation-checker from Section 4–3, though we now employ the method introduced at the start of this section to ensure that each symbol of Ω_G has exactly one arity. For each variable v, we introduce a new variable v^n for each n which is the length of a w for which (v, w) is a production of G. Then let $\widehat{V}$ be the set of variables so obtained, and let Ω_G be $\widehat{V} \cup X$ with the obvious arity function. We may then repeat our old definition:

DEFINITION 5

The **derivation-checker** for $G = (X, V, P, S)$ is the tree automaton

$$M_G = (Q_G, \Omega_G, \{0, 1\}, \delta, \beta)$$

where

$$Q_G = V \cup X \cup \{R\}$$
$$\Omega_G \text{ is the graded set } \widehat{V} \cup X$$

δ is the transition function defined for each $\omega \in \Omega_G$ by
  (i) if $\omega = x \in X$, then δ_ω is the constant x
  (ii) if $\omega = v^n \in \widehat{V}$, then $\delta_{v^n}: Q_G^n \to Q_G$ is defined by

$$\delta_{v^n}(q_1, q_2, \ldots, q_n) = \begin{cases} v & \text{if } v \mapsto q_1 \ldots q_n \text{ is in } P \\ R & \text{if not} \end{cases}$$

$\beta: Q_G \to \{0, 1\}$ has $\beta(q) = 1$ iff $q = S$ ○

By the methods of Stage (iv), we may then immediately define the simulator of M_G:

DEFINITION 6

The deterministic pda

$$M_{PG} = (\widehat{Q}, \widehat{X}, \widehat{Z}, \widehat{\delta}, q_0)$$

which checks the validity of encodings of derivation trees is defined to have

$$\widehat{Q} = \{q_0\} \cup \{(v^n, q_1, \ldots, q_j) \mid v^n \in V, \text{ each } q_i \in Q_G, n > j \geq 1\}$$
$$\widehat{X} = \Omega_G \text{ ungraded} = \widehat{V} \cup X$$
$$\widehat{Z} = Q_G = V \cup X \cup \{R\}$$

while $\widehat{\delta}: \widehat{Q} \times \widehat{X} \times \widehat{Z} \to \widehat{Q} \times Z^* \times \{0, 1\}$ is given by

$$\widehat{\delta}(q, x, z) = \begin{cases} (q_0, xz, 1) & \text{if } q = q_0 \text{ and } x \in X \\ (q_0, v, 1) & \text{if } q = q_0 \text{ and} \\ & \quad x = v^1 \text{ and } v \mapsto z \text{ is in } P \\ (q_0, R, 1) & \text{if } q = q_0 \text{ and} \\ & \quad x = v^1 \text{ and } v \mapsto z \text{ is not in } P \\ ((v^n, z), \Lambda, 1) & \text{if } q = q_0 \text{ and } x = v^n \text{ with } n > 1 \\ ((v^n, q_1, \ldots, q_j, z), \Lambda, 0) & \text{if } q = (v^n, q_1, \ldots, q_j) \text{ and } j < n - 1 \\ (q_0, v, 0) & \text{if } q = (v^n, q_1, \ldots, q_{n-1}) \text{ and} \\ & \quad v \mapsto z q_{n-1} \ldots q_1 \text{ is in } P. \\ (q_0, R, 0) & \text{if } q = (v^n, q_1, \ldots, q_{n-1}) \text{ and} \\ & \quad v \mapsto z q_{n-1} \ldots q_1 \text{ is not in } P. \end{cases}$$

Our general theorem then assures us that, for each Ω_G-tree t,

$$(e(t), q_0, \Lambda) \vdash^*_{M_{PG}} (\Lambda, q_0, r(t))$$

where

$$r(t) = \begin{cases} S & \text{if } t \text{ is a valid derivation tree} \\ R & \text{if any node corresponds to an invalid production} \\ t(\Lambda) \notin \{R, S\} & \text{otherwise.} \end{cases} \qquad \bigcirc$$

To clarify the general description which follows of the acceptor M_{AG} for the language $L(G)$ of any context-free grammar G, we first present it for the grammar with productions $S \mapsto aSb$ and $S \mapsto ab$ which generates the language $\{a^n b^n \mid n \geq 1\}$. The reader may wish to compare it with the parsing procedure developed *ad hoc* for this language in Example 5, and draw his own conclusions. We shall comment upon the comparison after our proof of Theorem 4.

Example 7

First we follow Definition 6 to see how M_{PG} for the $\{S \mapsto ab, S \mapsto aSb\}$ grammar would process a tree encoding.

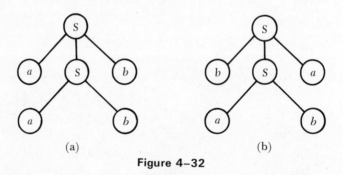

(a)   (b)

Figure 4–32

The tree of Figure 4–32(a) has the encoding $aabS^2bS^3$ and yields the computation

$$(aabS^2bS^3, q_0, \Lambda) \vdash (abS^2bS^3, q_0, a) \vdash (bS^2bS^3, q_0, aa)$$
$$\vdash (S^2bS^3, q_0, baa) \vdash (bS^3, (S^2, b), aa)$$
$$\vdash (bS^3, q_0, Sa) \qquad [\text{since } S \mapsto ab \text{ is valid}]$$
$$\vdash (S^3, q_0, bSa) \qquad \vdash (\Lambda, (S^3, b), Sa) \vdash (\Lambda, (S^3, b, S), a)$$
$$\vdash (\Lambda, q_0, S) \qquad [\text{since } S \mapsto aSb \text{ is valid}].$$

The tree of Figure 4–32(b) has the encoding $babS^2aS^3$ and yields the computation

$$(babS^2aS^3) \vdash^* (S^3, q_0, aSb) \quad \vdash (\Lambda, (S^3, a), Sb)$$

$$\vdash (\Lambda, (S^3, a, S), b) \vdash (\Lambda, q_0, R) \text{ [since } S \vdash bSa \text{ is not valid].}$$

Now, suppose we are given a string $aaabbb$. It is a string of $L(G)$ and has a derivation tree whose encoding is $aaabS^2bS^3bS^3$, obtained from $aaabbb$ by inserting S^2 and S^3 at appropriate places. On the other hand, $aabbb$ is not in $L(G)$, and so no matter how we insert S^2 and S^3, there is no way of obtaining the Polish notation for a valid derivation tree.

Suppose, then, that we modify M_{PG} to obtain a machine M_{AG} whose input alphabet contains only a and b, but which, in scanning an input tape from $\{a, b\}^+$, could nondeterministically insert an S^2 or an S^3 at any stage in the sense that its response to an a, say, when in state q_0 could be that appropriate to the a itself, or that which would be appropriate if an S^2 or an S^3 preceded it:

$$\bar{\delta}(q_0, a, z) = \{(q_0, az, 1), ((S^2, z), \Lambda, 1), ((S^3, z), \Lambda, 1)\}$$

while if it is in a state other than state q_0 it acts just as M_{AG} does. Thus, M_{AG} could yield the computation on ab

$$(ab, q_0, \Lambda) \vdash (b, q_0, a) \vdash (\Lambda, q_0, ba)$$

corresponding to M_{PG} acting on ab; and the computation

$$(ab, q_0, \Lambda) \vdash (b, q_0, a) \vdash (\Lambda, q_0, ba)$$

$$\vdash (\Lambda, (S^2, b), a) \vdash (\Lambda, q_0, S)$$

which terminates successfully, corresponding to the valid tree encoding abS^2 (the third $\vdash$ is "as if it had read an S^2"); and

$$(ab, q_0, \Lambda) \vdash (b, q_0, a) \vdash (b, (S^3, a), \Lambda) \vdash (b, (S^3, a), \Lambda)$$

a halting condition corresponding to the string aS^3b which does not encode a tree, let alone a valid derivation tree. ◊

The point, then, is that M_{AG}, if appropriately programmed, can yield a valid termination iff there is at least one way of inserting nonterminals into the string to yield the encoding of a valid derivation tree (i.e., iff the terminal string which served as input did indeed belong to $L(G)$).

We now give, for general G, the formal definition of M_{AG}, the pda which is an acceptor for $L(G)$, and then prove that it does indeed behave as advertised:

DEFINITION 7

Let $G = (X, V, P, S)$ be a context-free grammar. Then the **acceptor** for G is the pda

$$M_{AG} = (\widehat{Q}, X, \widehat{Z}, \widehat{\delta}, q_0)$$

where

$$\widehat{Q} \text{ and } \widehat{Z} \text{ are the same as for } M_{PG}$$

while

$$\widehat{\delta} : \widehat{Q} \times X \times \widehat{Z} \to \widehat{Q} \times \widehat{Z}^* \times \{0, 1\}$$

is given by the same definition as $\widehat{\delta}$ for M_{PG}, save that we no longer read elements of $\widehat{V}$ off the tape but instead nondeterministically insert them:

$$\widehat{\delta}(q_0, x, z) = \{(q_0, xz, 1)\} \cup \{(q_0, v, 0) | v^1 \in \widehat{V} \text{ and } v \mapsto z \text{ is in } P\}$$
$$\cup \{(q_0, R, 0) | v^1 \in \widehat{V} \text{ and } v \mapsto z \text{ is not in } P\}$$
$$\cup \{((v^n, z), \Lambda, 1) | v^n \in \widehat{V} \text{ and } n > 1\}$$

$$\widehat{\delta}((v_n, q_1, \ldots, q_j), x, z) = \begin{cases} \{((v^n, q_1, \ldots, q_j, z), \Lambda, 0)\} & \text{if } j < n - 1 \\ (q_0, v, 0) & \text{if } j = n - 1 \text{ and} \\ & v \mapsto zq_j \ldots q_1 \text{ is in } P \\ (q_0, R, 0) & \text{otherwise} \qquad \bigcirc \end{cases}$$

THEOREM 4

Let w be a string of X^*, and let the pda M_{AG} be the acceptor for the context-free grammar $G = (V, X, P, S)$. Then

$$w \in L(G) \Leftrightarrow (w, q_0, \Lambda) \vdash^*_{M_{AG}} (\Lambda, q_0, S)$$

Proof

The $\Rightarrow$ half of the proof is left as Exercise 11. To prove the converse, assume that $(w, q_0, \Lambda) \vdash^*_{M_{AG}} (\Lambda, q_0, S)$. Our task is to verify that $w \in L(G)$.

Let $d_1, \ldots, d_m$ be an actual sequence of IDs (there may be several) for which

$$(w, q_0, \Lambda) = d_1 \vdash_{M_{AG}} d_2 \vdash_{M_{AG}} \cdots \vdash_{M_{AG}} d_{m-1} \vdash_{M_{AG}} d_m = (\Lambda, q_0, S).$$

We shall show that M_{AG} behaves as if it were M_{PG} processing a string $\widehat{w}$, say, of Ω_G^*. The hard part will then be to verify that $\widehat{w}$ is $e(t)$ for some Ω_G-tree

t, for it will then be obvious that t is a valid derivation tree, and that w is the frontier of t, and hence is in $L(G)$.

We associate a string $\widehat{w}_j$ of Ω_G^* with each d_j inductively as follows:

Basis Step. $\widehat{w}_1 = \Lambda$

Induction Step. If d_{j+1} is obtained from d_j by choosing $(q_0, xz, 1)$ from $\delta(q_0, x, z)$ we set $\widehat{w}_{j+1} = \widehat{w}_j x$. If d_{j+1} is obtained from d_j by choosing $(q_0, v, 0)$ or $(q_0, R, 0)$ from $\widehat{\delta}(q_0, x, z)$ we set $\widehat{w}_{j+1} = \widehat{w}_j v^1$. If d_{j+1} is obtained from d_j by choosing $((v^n, z), \Lambda, 1)$ from $\widehat{\delta}(q_0, x, z)$ we set $\widehat{w}_{j+1} = \widehat{w}_j v^n$. If none of these cases apply, we set $\widehat{w}_{j+1} = \widehat{w}_j$.

It should then be obvious (the reader should provide the formal inductive proof as an exercise) that the definition of the d_j's and hence of the $\widehat{w}_j$'s, is such that

$$(\widehat{w}_m, q_0, \Lambda) \vdash^*_{M_{PG}} (\Lambda, q_0, S) \tag{1}$$

It should also be obvious (Exercise 12) that if $\widehat{w}_m$ is $e(t)$ for some Ω_G-tree t, then $w = fr(t)$. Relation (1) then implies that t is a valid derivation tree for G, and hence w is an element of $L(G)$. Thus, it only remains to prove that $\widehat{w}_m$ is indeed the encoding of some Ω_G-tree. But this follows from Theorem 3, and we are done. $\qquad \square$

Specially worthy of note in the above proof is that if w is valid, then any computation $d_1, \ldots, d_m$ that gets us from (w, q_0, Λ) to (Λ, q_0, S) actually lets us read off a derivation which yields w. Any such procedure for going from a string of $L(G)$ to a derivation tree for that string is called a **parsing procedure**. The above procedure, being completely general, does not make use of the special structures of any particular grammar G. This accounts for the greater efficiency of the parser of Example 5 relative to that outlined in Example 7. An active area of research consists of finding more efficient general procedures, and finding useful subclasses of the context-free languages for which yet better procedures exist. This is developed in the field of **syntactic analysis**.

EXERCISES FOR SECTION 4-4

1. Let $t = (t_1, \ldots, t_n)\alpha$. Recalling that t is a map from a subset of $\mathbf{N}^*$ to some label set, prove that $t(x - 1, w) = t_x(w)$ for each $x \in \{1, \ldots, n\}$ and each w in $\mathbf{N}^*$ such that xw is a node of t.

2. **(i)** Encode the tree of Figure 4-33.

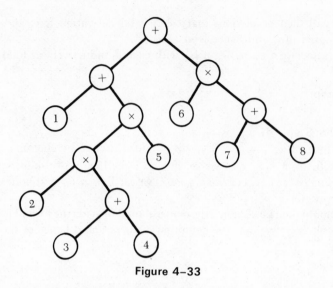

Figure 4–33

(ii) Decode $35 + 39 \times + 27 + \times 34 + \times$.

3. For the tree whose Polish notation is $27 + 1 \times 23 + +$, describe how M_1 processes it using the format of Example 3; then transcribe the computation using the $\vdash$ notation as in the latter half of Example 4, taking care to specify for each $\vdash$ whether (a), (b), (c), or (d) justified the corresponding use of δ.

4. Check the proof of Theorem 1 by seeing what M_1 does when started in state Λ with $23 + 14 \times +$ on its input tape, and $(1, 3, 7)$ on its stack. What happens if we add $+ \times +$ at the end of the input string?

5. Trace the computations of the pda M of Example 5 on the input strings a^3b^2, a^3b^4, a^3b^3ab, and $baba$.

6. In the situation of Example 6:

(i) Write down the explicit formulae for θ_3, θ_4, $\theta_{8.1}$, θ_9 and $\theta_{11.1}$.

(ii) Write down the formal definition of the deterministic

$$\delta : Q \times \{0, 1, \sim, +, m\} \times \{0, 1\} \to Q \times \{\Lambda, 0, 1\} \times \{0, 1\}$$

for that machine.

7. In proving the induction step of Theorem 2, we assumed $n > 1$. Supply the missing proof for the case $n = 1$.

8. Write out the case $\nu(\omega) = 1$ for the proof of Theorem 3.

9. Apply the argument in the proof of Theorem 3 to the string

$$21 + 37 + 47 \times + + 93 \times \times$$

to inductively decompose it to obtain the encoded tree. See what happens to $37 + 2 \times +$ and $37 + 2 \times 3 + 1$.

10. Write out the formulation, according to Definition 5, of the derivation-checker for our decimal number grammar.

11. Verify that M_{AG} does indeed process strings of $L(G)$ appropriately—the $\Rightarrow$ half of Theorem 4:

Let w be in $L(G)$ so that there exists a tree t with frontier w for which

$$(e(t), q_0, \Lambda) \vdash^*_{M_{PG}} (\Lambda, q_0, S)$$

Use this fact to prove that

$$(w, q_0, \Lambda) \vdash^*_{M_{AG}} (\Lambda, q_0, S)$$

12.   Provide the formal inductions mentioned in the proof of Theorem 4.

13.   Give efficient *ad hoc* parsing procedures for the unsigned number grammar; and then construct, by way of contrast, M_{AG} for this G. Run both automata on $3 \cdot 1 \cdot 6$ and $3 \cdot 16$.

4-5   Proving the Correctness of a Compiler

An area of growing interest to computer scientists is that of **proving assertions about programs.** Can we prove that a program really yields the computation of a desired function? Can we prove that a compiler correctly translates programs from one programming language into another? Of course, much of our study has the flavor of such questions. The theorems of the last section about the behavior of M_{PG} and M_{AG} are very much examples of assertions about programs, as are the statements of Section 3-1 relating Turing-computable functions and partial recursive functions. However, it seems worthwhile to focus explicit attention on the fact that one can prove assertions about programs, and we do so in this section by giving a general discussion of syntax, semantics, and compilers, and then go on to prove (by techniques akin to those of the previous section) that a certain compiler does indeed perform correctly.

We have seen that both strings and trees may provide the input structures for certain types of automata. In general, other types of **data structures** may also be used. Thus, quite apart from saying *how* a computer works, we must specify *what* it works with. The *what* comprises the *syntax,* and the *how* comprises the *semantics.*

The **syntax** is then specified by three sets of data structures:

$\mathfrak{X}$: the set of **input** structures

$\mathfrak{P}$: the set of **program** structures

$\mathfrak{Y}$: the set of **output** structures

Specifying the syntax, then, specifies whether or not a given structure may in fact serve as a valid input, program, or output structure. For example, in our study of tree automata over an algebra Ω, the valid input structures were the Ω-trees.

However, a given symbol may be interpreted in many ways; for example, a $+$ may represent addition modulo 2, addition of integers, or some quite arbitrary operation. In other words, the syntax gives no indication of what a data structure *means.* For this we need to specify how programs act on inputs to yield outputs. Any such *interpretation* of the structures is called a *semantics* and specifies an abstract computer. The semantics may be specified in many ways. We shall adopt one of the form, "Load program and data, compute until halting, print out result." The reader may wish to write down an alternative form, "Load program and start computing, reading input and printing output during computation as commanded by the program." However, the simpler version will suffice for our present purposes. It resembles the recursive computer format of Section 3–3.

DEFINITION 1

A **semantics** $\mathfrak{M}$ (of a restricted form) for the syntax $(\mathfrak{X}, \mathcal{P}, \mathcal{Y})$ is given by

$\mathcal{Q}$: a set of **machine configurations**

$m: \mathfrak{X} \times \mathcal{P} \to \mathcal{Q}$, the **loading function**

$\delta: \mathcal{Q} \to \mathcal{Q}$, the **configuration transition function**

$\beta: \mathcal{Q} \to \mathcal{Y}$, the **readout function**

Then (the resemblance to our discussion of Turing machine computations in Section 3–1 is intentional) a **computation** of $\mathfrak{M}$ is a sequence of elements

$$q_1, q_2, \cdots, q_n$$

from $\mathcal{Q}$, such that $\delta(q_j) = q_{j+1} \neq q_j$ for $1 \leq j < n$

$$\text{while } \delta(q_n) = q_n$$

We define $\delta^*(q_1)$ to be q_n if there is such a computation; and let it be undefined if no (finite) computation of $\mathfrak{M}$ with initial configuration q_1 exists. Then each **program** $\pi \in \mathcal{P}$ induces, via the semantics

$$\mathfrak{M} = (\mathcal{Q}, m, \delta, \beta)$$

the function

$$f_{\pi}^{\mathfrak{M}}: \mathfrak{X} \to \mathcal{Y}: x \to \beta[\delta^*(m(x, \pi))]$$

i.e., we read in the data x and the program π via m, compute with δ until termination, and then read out the result via β.   ○

Now, a common situation is that in which the machine (semantics)

$$\mathfrak{M} = (\mathcal{Q}, m, \delta, \beta)$$

does not physically exist, although it has proven very convenient actually to write data and programs in terms of the syntax $(\mathfrak{X}, \mathcal{P}, \mathcal{Y})$ for which $\mathfrak{M}$ was designed (though not built).

Suppose, however, that we have available a physical machine described by the semantics

$$\mathfrak{M}_1 = (\mathcal{Q}_1, m_1, \delta_1, \beta_1)$$

which will efficiently process data and programs in terms of the syntax $(\mathfrak{X}_1, \mathcal{P}_1, \mathcal{Y}_1)$. It would then be very useful if we could recode our input and output structures from $\mathfrak{X}$ to $\mathfrak{X}_1$ and from $\mathcal{Y}$ to $\mathcal{Y}_1$, and also translate our programs from $\mathcal{P}$ to $\mathcal{P}_1$ in such a way that $\mathfrak{M}_1$ will process the recoded input and program to provide the encoding of the result which $\mathfrak{M}$ would have produced (had it been physically operative) from the original input and program.

Putting all this in a rather abstract way, then, we may make the following definition:

DEFINITION 2

Let $\mathfrak{M} = (\mathcal{Q}, m, \delta, \beta)$ and $\mathfrak{M}_1 = (\mathcal{Q}_1, m_1, \delta_1, \beta_1)$ be two semantics with respective syntaxes $(\mathfrak{X}, \mathcal{P}, \mathcal{Y})$ and $(\mathfrak{X}_1, \mathcal{Y}_1, \mathcal{P}_1)$. Then **a compiler from $\mathfrak{M}$ to $\mathfrak{M}_1$** is a trio of maps

$$C = (e_1 : \mathfrak{X} \to \mathfrak{X}_1, c : \mathcal{P} \to \mathcal{P}_1, e_2 : \mathcal{Y} \to \mathcal{Y}_1).$$

We say that the compiler C is **correct** if and only if the following diagram commutes:

(1)

○

Note that it is immediate from diagram (1) that if two compilers (e_1, c, e_2) and (e_1', c', e_2') are correct, then so is their composite $(e_1' \circ e_1, c' \circ c, e_2' \circ e_2)$:

In a sense, then, our theorem about the passage from tree automata to the pushdown automata which simulate them is a proof about correctness of compilers. Before giving another example of such a proof, though, we should note a certain ambiguity in our terminology. In building a "real-world" compiler, there is not only the problem of specifying e_1, c, and e_2, but there is also the task of writing a program so that compilation may be done automatically on some convenient computer (possibly $\mathfrak{M}_1$). Because of this, there will not only be the problem of proving (e_1, c, e_2) correct in our present sense, but also the task of proving that the "implementation" does indeed compute e_1 and c correctly. We shall only present an example for the first half, since the techniques for the second half should by then be familiar.

Our example is going to involve a variation on the arithmetic tree automaton of Section 4–3, and we shall specify a compiler which replaces a tree computation by a computation on a simple, relatively conventional, serial computer.

Our *programs* will be trees in which some of the maximal nodes are replaced by *variable* symbols from the list $\{x_1, x_2, x_3, \ldots\}$. An *input* for such a program will be a string of numbers, the jth of which is to replace x_j in the program. A *computation* then provides the run of the arithmetic machine on the resultant tree, and the output is to be the value that is thus placed on the Λ-node.

Let us then formalize the syntax $(\mathfrak{X}, \mathcal{P}, \mathcal{Y})$ of this system:

$\mathfrak{X}$, the set of input structures, is $\mathbf{N}^*$

$\mathcal{P}$, the set of program structures, is just the set of $\overline{\Omega}$-trees, where

$$\overline{\Omega} = \mathbf{N} \cup \{x_n \mid n \in \mathbf{N}\} \cup \{+, \times\}$$

with arity function $\nu(n) = \nu(x_n) = 0$ for each $n \in \mathbf{N}$, $\nu(+) = \nu(\times) = 2$.

$\mathcal{Y}$, the set of output structures, is $\mathbf{N} \cup \{R\}$. (We shall need a reject state R to handle the case in which the input fails to specify values for all the variables which appear in the program).

If π is the program shown in Figure 4–34, then the corresponding function is $f_\pi^{\mathfrak{M}} : \mathfrak{X} \to \mathcal{Y} : (x_1, x_2) \mapsto (x_1 + 1)(x_1 + 3) + x_2(x_1 + 3) = (x_1 + 3)(x_1 + x_2 + 1)$.

We must next specify the semantics $(\mathcal{Q}, m, \delta, \beta)$ of the system, following the scheme suggested in Figure 4–34. $\mathcal{Q}$ is the set of $\overline{\overline{\Omega}}$-trees, where $\overline{\overline{\Omega}}$ is the multigraded set

$$\overline{\overline{\Omega}} = \mathbf{N} \cup R \cup \{+, \times\}$$

with arity function $\nu(n) = \nu(R) = \{0, 2\}$, $\nu(+) = \nu(\times) = 2$.

$m : \mathfrak{X} \times \mathcal{P} \to \mathcal{Q}$ replaces the number string $(n_1, n_2, \ldots, n_k)$ and the $\overline{\Omega}$-tree t by the $\overline{\overline{\Omega}}$-tree $\overline{t}$, which is just t with each variable x_j replaced by n_j if $j \leq k$, and replaced by R if $j > k$ (Figure 4–34(b)).

$\delta : \mathcal{Q} \to \mathcal{Q}$ is the state-transition operator which (as illustrated in Figure

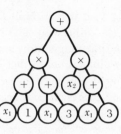

Figure 4–34(a)
A program for $\mathfrak{M}$.

Input Structure
$(2,5) \in \mathfrak{X} = N^\circ$

Data Structure
The $\overline{\overline{\Omega}}$-tree of Figure 4–34(a)

$\left.\begin{array}{l}\end{array}\right\}$

$m: \mathfrak{X} \times \mathcal{P} \to 2$

Replace x_1 by 2,
and x_2 by 5

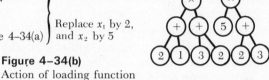

Figure 4–34(b)
Action of loading function

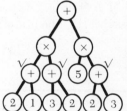

δ acts on q_0 by
evaluating all those

$\Longmapsto$

nodes (marked $\vee$) which
are not yet eval-
uated but which
have had all successors
evaluated

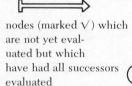

$q_1 \mapsto q_2 = \delta(q_1)$

$\Longmapsto$

$q_2 \mapsto q_3$

$\Longmapsto$

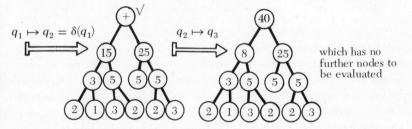

which has no
further nodes to
be evaluated

Figure 4–34(c)　Evaluation of an $\overline{\overline{\Omega}}$-tree by repeated application of δ.

4–34(c)) at each application evaluates one node higher along each
tree path, changing $\overline{t}: T \to \overline{\overline{\Omega}}$ to the tree $\delta(\overline{t}): T \to \overline{\overline{\Omega}}$ for which

$$\delta(\overline{t})(w) = \begin{cases} \overline{t}(w0)\overline{t}(w1) & \text{if } \overline{t}(w) = \circ \in \{+, \times\} \\ & \text{and } \overline{t}(w0) \text{ and } \overline{t}(w1) \text{ are in } \mathbf{N} \\ R & \text{if either } \overline{t}(w0) \text{ or } \overline{t}(w1) \text{ is } R \\ \overline{t}(w) & \text{otherwise} \end{cases}$$

$$\beta: \mathcal{Q} \to \mathcal{Y}: \bar{t} \mapsto \begin{cases} \bar{t}(\Lambda) & \text{if it is in } \mathbf{N} \cup R \\ R & \text{otherwise} \end{cases}$$

that is, the output map simply reads the label off the Λ-node of $\bar{t}$ if $\bar{t}$ is completely evaluated, and otherwise yields R.

It is clear that if any node of $m(w, \pi)$ is an R, then $f_\pi^{\mathfrak{M}}(w)$ will be R, but that otherwise $f_\pi^{\mathfrak{M}}(w)$ will be precisely the evaluation of the tree $m(w, \pi)$.

Our next job is to specify the syntax and semantics of our serial computer. We shall then specify our compiler and prove it to be correct.

As before, the input structures will be a string of numbers, and the output will be a number, but the programs will no longer be trees, but instead will be sequences of instructions of the following kinds:

$li(\alpha)$: **load** the number α **into** the accumulator
$sto(x)$: **store** the contents of the accumulator at address x
$ld(x)$: **load** the accumulator with the contents of address x
$ad(x)$: **add** the contents of address x to the contents of the accumulator
$mp(x)$: **multiply** the contents of the accumulator by the contents of address x

Putting this into symbols, we are saying that the syntax for our serial computer will be $(\mathfrak{X}, \mathcal{P}_1, \mathcal{Y})$ where $\mathfrak{X} = \mathbf{N}^*$ and $\mathcal{Y} = \mathbf{N} \cup \{R\}$ as before. We specify $\mathcal{P}_1$ to be the set of all strings on the alphabet (i.e., the instruction set):

$$\mathcal{I} = \{li(\alpha) \,|\, \alpha \in \mathbf{N}\} \cup \{sto(x), ld(x), ad(x), mp(x) \,|\, x \in \mathbf{N}\}$$

We may now specify the semantics $(\mathcal{Q}_1, m_1, \delta_1, \beta_1)$ of the system.

We think of the machine as having an infinite collection of registers

$$\ldots, r_{-n}, \ldots, r_{-1}, r_0, r_1, r_2, \ldots, r_m, \ldots$$

though in fact (compare the idea of a "potentially" infinite tape for a Turing machine) only finitely many are to be nonempty at any time. We use R to denote the contents of an empty register. These registers are to be used in the manner suggested by Figure 4–35: the program is loaded, in order, into the negative-numbered registers $r_{-1}, r_{-2}, r_{-3}, \ldots$; the accumulator is r_0; and the input data are stored, in order, in the even-numbered registers $r_2, r_4, r_6, \ldots$. This leaves the odd-numbered registers $r_1, r_3, r_5 \ldots$ available for the storage of working data.

Thus, each register contains either a number $n \in \mathbf{N}$ or an instruction $i \in \mathcal{I}$, or is empty (contains R). To specify the state of the machine, then, we must specify the contents of each register. We do this by specifying a function $q: \mathbf{Z} \to \mathbf{N} \cup \mathcal{I} \cup \{R\}$ which satisfies the three conditions:

(i) The program is in negatively numbered registers: $n < 0 \Rightarrow q(n) \in \mathcal{I} \cup \{R\}$

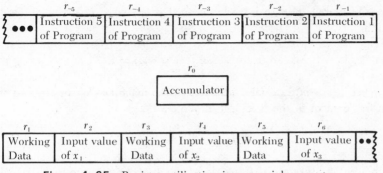

r_{-5}	r_{-4}	r_{-3}	r_{-2}	r_{-1}
Instruction 5 of Program	Instruction 4 of Program	Instruction 3 of Program	Instruction 2 of Program	Instruction 1 of Program

r_0

Accumulator

r_1	r_2	r_3	r_4	r_5	r_6	
Working Data	Input value of x_1	Working Data	Input value of x_2	Working Data	Input value of x_3	

Figure 4-35   Register utilization in our serial computer.

(ii) The input and working data are in the accumulator and the positively
     numbered registers: $n \geq 0 \Rightarrow q(n) \in \mathbf{N} \cup \{R\}$
(iii) Only finitely many registers are nonempty: $\{n \mid q(n) \neq R\}$ is finite.

We let $\mathcal{Q}_2$ denote the set of all functions q satisfying these three conditions.
To complete the specification of the state of our serial computer we must
specify which instruction, say the mth, is to be executed next (note that it
is stored in register r_{-m}). Putting this together, then, we find that our serial
computer has the state set

$$\mathcal{Q}_1 = \mathbf{N} \times \mathcal{Q}_2$$

where we make the interpretation that $(m, q) \in \mathbf{N} \times \mathcal{Q}_2$ denotes the state in
which the machine is now to execute the instruction $q(-m)$ of the program
$q(-1)q(-2) \ldots q(-k)$, using the number $q(0)$ as accumulator contents, and
with storage register values $q(1)$, $q(2)$, ... R corresponds to an empty
register.

   With this interpretation, the definition of m_1, δ_1, and β_1 are immediate:
$m_1 \colon \mathcal{X} \times \mathcal{P}_1 \to \mathcal{Q}_1$ sends the data string $n_1 \ldots n_k$ and the instruction string
$i_1 \ldots i_\ell$ to the state $(1, q) = m_1(n_1 \ldots n_k, i_1 \ldots i_\ell)$, where the 1 tells the
machine to execute the 1st instruction of the program, and where

$$q(z) = \begin{cases} i_{-z} & \text{if } -\ell \leq z \leq -1\text{: store the program in negatively} \\ & \qquad\qquad\qquad\qquad\text{numbered registers} \\ n_z & \text{if } 1 \leq z \leq k\text{:} \qquad\text{store the input data in even} \\ & \qquad\qquad\qquad\qquad\text{positively numbered registers} \\ R & \text{otherwise:} \qquad\text{leave registers empty unless} \\ & \qquad\qquad\qquad\qquad\text{their contents are specified by the program} \\ & \qquad\qquad\qquad\qquad\text{or input data} \end{cases}$$

The state-transition function $\delta \colon \mathcal{Q}_1 \to \mathcal{Q}_1$ is then the operator which, given
(m, q), looks at the mth instruction, namely $q(-m)$, and then executes it. Of

course, if there is no mth instruction, so that $q(-m) = R$, the machine does nothing:

$$\delta_1(m, q) = (m, q) \text{ if } q(-m) = R$$

However, if $q(-m)$ is a valid instruction, the machine executes it, and then transfers control to the next instruction, so that

$$\delta_1(m, q) = (m + 1, q')$$

where $q'(n) = q(n)$ for $n < 0$ (we do not change the program registers) while for $n \geq 0$

$$q'(n) = \begin{cases} \text{if } n = 0 \text{ then } \alpha; \text{ else } q(n) & \text{when } q(-m) = li(\alpha), \\ & \text{since } r_0 \text{ is the} \\ & \text{accumulator} \\ \text{if } n = x \text{ then } q(0); \text{ else } q(n) & \text{when } q(-m) = sto(x), \\ & \text{since } q(0) \text{ is the} \\ & \text{current content of the} \\ & \text{accumulator} \\ \text{if } n = 0 \text{ then } q(x); \text{ else } q(n) & \text{when } q(-m) = ld(x) \\ \text{if } n = 0 \text{ then } q(0) + q(x); \text{ else } q(n) & \text{when } q(-m) = ad(x), \\ & \text{since the content of} \\ & r_x \text{ is to be added to} \\ & \text{the accumulator} \\ & \text{content} \\ \text{if } n = 0 \text{ then } q(0) \times q(x); \text{ else } q(n) & \text{when } q(-m) = mp(x) \end{cases}$$

Of course, we make the convention that $a + b = R$ and $a \times b = R$ if either a or b is R. Finally, we decree that the output map just reads out the contents of the accumulator:

$$\beta : \mathcal{Q}_1 \to \mathcal{Y} : (m, q) \mapsto q(0)$$

Now that we have specified the syntax $(\mathcal{X}, \mathcal{P}_1, \mathcal{Y})$ and semantics $(\mathcal{Q}_1, m_1, \delta_1, \beta_1)$ of our serial computer, we now want to specify our compiler by giving the functions $e_1 : \mathcal{X} \to \mathcal{X}$, $c : \mathcal{P} \to \mathcal{P}_1$ and $e_2 : \mathcal{Y} \to \mathcal{Y}$ which comprise our compiler.

Since the input and output structures for $\mathfrak{M}_1$ and $\mathfrak{M}_2$ are the same, we shall take our input and output encodings to be simply the identity functions, $i_1 = id_{\mathcal{X}}$ and $e_2 = id_{\mathcal{Y}}$, respectively. However, it will require more work to define the way in which c compiles tree programs π in $\mathcal{P}$ to serial programs. Once we have made this definition, we can then turn to the task of confirming that the compiler (e_1, c, e_2) so defined is indeed correct.

Since the programs of $\mathcal{P}$ are trees, we shall define our function $c : \mathcal{P} \to \mathcal{P}_1$

inductively, first for one-node trees, and then for trees of the form $(t_1, t_2)+$ and $(t_1, t_2)\times$.

Basis Step. If t is a one-node $\overline{\Omega}$-tree, then that node is labelled either with an n or with an x_n.

If $t = n$, we set $c(t) = li(n)$ (load n into the accumulator)

If $t = x_n$, we set $c(t) = ld(2n)$ (load the content of register $2n$ into the accumulator)

Let us immediately verify that this basis step, at least, is correct, by comparing $f_t^{\mathfrak{M}}$ (the computation of our tree automaton $\mathfrak{M}$ for program t) and $f_{c(t)}^{\mathfrak{M}_1}$ (the computation of our serial computer $\mathfrak{M}_1$ on the compiled program $c(t)$) for the two basic cases, $t = n$ and $t = x_n$:

$$f_n^{\mathfrak{M}}(w) = n \text{ while } f_{c(n)}^{\mathfrak{M}_1}(w) = n \text{ as well.}$$

$$f_{x_n}^{\mathfrak{M}}(w) = \begin{cases} k & \text{if } w \text{ is of length} \geq n \text{ with } n\text{th number equal to } k \\ R & \text{if } w \text{ is not of length} \geq n \end{cases}$$

and clearly the same is true of $f_{c(x_n)}^{\mathfrak{M}_1}$, since we load the nth letter of w into register $2n$ [which will thus contain R if $\ell(w) < n$], and then load the contents of register $2n$ into the accumulator, where it may be read out as required.

Now suppose we have a program $c(t_1)$ which will form $f_{t_1}^{\mathfrak{M}}(w)$ in the accumulator of $\mathfrak{M}_1$, and a program $c(t_2)$ which will form $f_{t_2}^{\mathfrak{M}}(w)$ in the accumulator of $\mathfrak{M}_1$. Suppose we now want to compute $f_{(t_1,t_2)+}^{\mathfrak{M}}(w)$. The obvious strategy is to use $c(t_1)$ to compute $f_{t_1}^{\mathfrak{M}}(w)$, execute $sto(n)$ to place it in some convenient place, then execute $c(t_2)$ to place $f_{t_2}^{\mathfrak{M}}(w)$ in the accumulator, and then finally execute $ad(n)$ (for the same n) to get $f_{t_1}^{\mathfrak{M}}(w) + f_{t_2}^{\mathfrak{M}}(w)$ in the accumulator, as desired. The only catch is to choose n so that $f_{t_1}^{\mathfrak{M}}(w)$ is not destroyed during the execution of $c(t_2)$. If we know that $k(t_2)$ is a value of k such that $c(t_2)$ contains no instruction of the form $sto(k')$ for $k' > k$, it is then clear that we may take $n = k + 2$ without fear of overwriting, as schematized in Figure 4–36. Note that in our basis step, we may then take

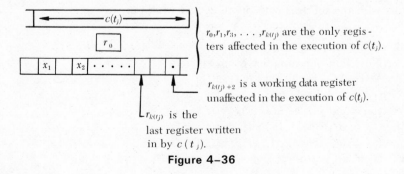

$r_0, r_1, r_3, \ldots, r_{k(t_j)}$ are the only registers affected in the execution of $c(t_j)$.

$r_{k(t_j)+2}$ is a working data register unaffected in the execution of $c(t_j)$.

$r_{k(t_j)}$ is the last register written in by $c(t_j)$.

Figure 4–36

$k(n) = k(x_n) = -1$. With this we have motivated our induction step:

Induction Step. Let t_1 and t_2 be $\overline{\Omega}$-trees for which $c(t_1)$, $c(t_2)$ in $\mathcal{P}_1$ and $k(t_1)$, $k(t_2)$ in $\mathbf{N}$ have already been defined. Then we set

$$c((t_1, t_2)+) = c(t_1), sto(k(t_2) + 2), c(t_2), ad(k(t_2) + 2)$$

which evaluates t_1, places the result in $r_{k(t_2)+2}$, evaluates t_2, and then adds the result to the evaluation of t_1; and set

$$c((t_1, t_2)\times) = c(t_1), sto(k(t_2) + 2), c(t_2), mp(k(t_2) + 2)$$

which evaluates t_1, places the result in $r_{k(t_2)+2}$, evaluates t_2, and then multiplies the result by the evaluation of t_1, as required. It is clear that we may take

$$k((t_1, t_2)+) = k((t_1, t_2)\times) = \max(k(t_1), k(t_2) + 2).$$

Before proving our compiler correct, we see what it does to the program shown in Figure 4–37, where, for ease of notation, we have placed in paren-

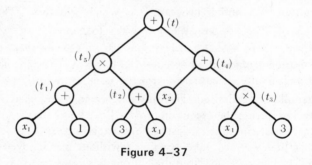

Figure 4–37

theses next to each node a label for the subtree whose root is that node. We start with the subtrees with depth 2, and work our way up:

I. $c(t_1) = ld(2)\ sto(1)\ li(1)\ ad(1)\ ;k(t_1) = 1$
   [Note that our compiler is not efficient.
   We could compile t_1 as $li(1)ad(2)$.]
   $c(t_2) = li(3)\ sto(1)\ ld(2)\ ad(1);\ k(t_2) = 1$
   $c(t_3) = ld(2)\ sto(1)\ li(3)\ ad(1);\ k(t_3) = 1$
II. $c(t_5) = c(t_1)\ sto(3)\ c(t_2)\ mp(3);\ k(t_2) = 3$
   $c(t_4) = ld(4)\ sto(3)\ c(t_3)\ ad(3);\ k(t_2) = 3$
III. $c(t) = c(t_5)\ sto(5)\ c(t_4)\ ad(5);\ k(t) = 5.$

Putting this all together, we then have (adding square brackets for clarity) that

$$c(t) = [ld(2)\ sto(1)\ li(1)\ ad(1)\ sto(3)\ li(3)$$
$$sto(1)\ ld(2)\ ad(1)\ mp(3)]\ sto(5)\ [ld(4)\ sto(3)$$
$$ld(2)\ sto(1)\ li(3)\ ad(1)\ ad(3)]\ ad(5).$$

We may now prove the correctness of the compiler so defined:

THEOREM 1

The compiler $(id_{\mathfrak{X}}, c, id_{\mathfrak{Y}})$ is correct in that

$$f_t^{\mathfrak{M}}(w) = f_{c(t)}^{\mathfrak{M}_1}(w)$$

for all w in $\mathfrak{X}$ and all t in $\mathcal{P}$.

Proof

As usual, the trick is to find the correct slight strengthening of the theorem, and then prove it by an easy induction on π. A little thought shows that the correct statement to prove inductively is:

(A): "Let $c(t) = i_1 \ldots i_m$. Let q be an element of $\mathcal{Q}_2$ such that $c(t)$ is loaded not in standard position, but in the m registers $r_{-p}, r_{-p-1}, \ldots, r_{-p-m+1}$; such that some data string $n_1 n_2 \ldots n_k$ has been correctly loaded into registers $r_2, r_4, \ldots, r_{2k}$. Thus $q(-p) = i_1$, $q(-p - 1) = i_2$, $\ldots$, $q(-p - m + 1) = i_m$; and $w = n_1 n_2 \ldots n_k$ from $\mathbf{N}^*$ has $q(2j) = n_j$ for $1 \le j \le k$, while $q(2j) = R$ for $n \ge k$.

Then our claim is that, in m steps, $\mathfrak{M}_1$ will execute $c(t)$, and will not disturb registers r_k which are not working data registers with $k < k(t)$. More formally, then, we assert that applying δ_1 m times to the state (p, q) of $\mathcal{Q}_1$ will yield the state $(p + m, q')$ where q' has $q'(0) = f_t^{\mathfrak{M}}(w)$, while $q'(n) \ne q(n)$ cannot occur for nonzero n unless $n = 2k' + 1$ for some $0 \le 2k' + 1 < k(t)$."

We note that our theorem follows immediately from (A) on taking $p = 1$ and $q(n) = R$ for $n < -m$.

Basis Step.   In case t is n or x_n, so that $c(t)$ is $li(n)$ or $ld(2n)$, respectively, while $k(t)$ is -1, the claim (A) is immediately true.

Induction Step.   We consider the case of $(t_1, t_2)+$, leaving $(t_1, t_2)\times$ to the mental substitutions of the reader:

Let (A) hold for $(t_1, c(t_1), k(t_1))$ and $(t_2, c(t_2), k(t_2))$, where the length of $c(t_j)$ is m_j. We must check, then, that (A) holds for $t = (t_1, t_2)+$ so that $c(t) = [c(t_1), sto(k(t_2) + 2), c(t_2), ad(k(t_2) + 2)]$, and $k(t) = \max (k(t_1), k(t_2) + 2)$ so that the encoding $c(t)$ has length $m = m_1 + m_2 + 2$. Then let (p, q) be an element of $\mathcal{Q}_1$ which satisfies the premiss of condition (A). Then:

(i) (p, q) satisfies (A) for t_1. Thus, applying $\delta_1 \, m_1$ times to (p, q) yields state $(p + m_1, q')$ where q' has $q'(0) = f_{t_1}^{\mathfrak{M}}(w)$, while $q'(n) \neq q(n)$ cannot occur for nonzero n unless $n = 2k' + 1$ for some $0 \leq 2k' + 1 < k(t_1)$.

(ii) Applying δ_1 once to $(p + m_1, q')$ yields the execution of $sto(k(t_2) + 2)$ to yield $(p + m_1 + 1, q'')$ where $q''(n) = q'(n)$ save for $n = k(t_2) + 2$, where $q''(n) = q'(0) = f_{t_1}^{\mathfrak{M}}(w)$.

(iii) $(p + m_1 + 1, q'')$ satisfies (A) for t_2. Thus, applying $\delta_1 \, m_2$ times to $(p + m_1 + 1, q'')$ yields state $(p + m_1 + m_2 + 1, q''')$ where $q'''(0) = f_{t_2}^{\mathfrak{M}}(w)$, while $q'''(n) \neq q''(n)$ cannot occur for nonzero n unless $n = 2k' + 1$ for some $0 \leq 2k' + 1 < k(t_2)$. In particular, $q'''(k(t_2) + 2) = q''(k(t_2) + 2) = f_{t_1}^{\mathfrak{M}}(w)$.

(iv) Applying δ_1 once to $(p + m_1 + m_2 + 1, q''')$ yields the execution of $ad(k(t_2) + 2)$ to yield $(p + m, \hat{q})$ where $\hat{q}(n) = q'''(n)$ save for $n = 0$, where $\hat{q}(0) = q'''(0) + q'''(k(t_2) + 2) = f_{t_2}^{\mathfrak{M}}(w) + f_{t_1}^{\mathfrak{M}}(w) = f_{(t_1, t_2)+}^{\mathfrak{M}}(w)$.

Putting (i) through (iv) together, we see that (A) does indeed hold for $(t_1, t_2)+$. $\qquad\qquad\qquad\qquad\qquad\qquad\qquad\qquad\qquad\qquad\quad \square$

EXERCISE FOR SECTION 4-5

1. Verify that $f_t^{\mathfrak{M}}(1, 2) = f_{c(t)}^{\mathfrak{M}1}(1, 2)$.

FURTHER READING FOR CHAPTER 4

Proceedings of the Association of Computing Machinery Conference on Proving Assertions about Programs, SIGPLAN Notices (Association for Computing Machinery) 1972, 7(1).

A. V. Aho and J. D. Ullman [1973] The Theory of Passing, Translation and Compiling (2 volumes), Englewood Cliffs, N.J.: Prentice-Hall.

M. A. Arbib [1969] Theories of Abstract Automata, Englewood Cliffs, N.J.: Prentice-Hall.

E. Engeler [1973] Introduction to the Theory of Computation, New York: Academic Press.

S. Ginsburg [1966] The Mathematical Theory of Context-Free Languages, New York: McGraw-Hill.

J. E. Hopcroft and J. D. Ullman [1969] Formal Languages and their Relation to Automata, Reading, Mass.: Addison-Wesley.

R. Y. Kain [1972] Automata Theory: Machines and Languages, New York: McGraw-Hill.

CHAPTER 5

Automata and Semigroups II

In the last two chapters we have developed important areas of Computer and Information Science—the theories of computability and of formal languages—which apply a number of the basic concepts of Chapter 1, but add little to our store of algebraic knowledge. In this chapter, then, we return to our development of algebraic concepts by providing much of the basic theory of semigroups, monoids, and groups, providing a number of important applications of this theory, and finally placing the theory in the general setting of universal algebras.

In Section 5-1, we introduce the crucial notion of a homomorphism, a structure-preserving map from one semigroup (or monoid or group) to another. In particular, we shall be interested in the homomorphism which sends the monoid of input strings of an automaton to the monoid of transformations which those strings can effect upon the state set of the machine. We shall then look at collections of transformations which form a group—each member of the group then being called a permutation. In Section 5-2, we shall consider the direct product as a way of forming new semigroups (or monoids or groups) from old ones, and shall see how this relates to the decomposition theory of machines which we touched on briefly in Section 2-4. Again, in Section 5-3, we shall see the way in which we can "pull out" smaller semigroups from a given group, and shall also study submonoids and subgroups. In 5-4, we shall note with particular interest the *normal* subgroups, which have properties of special importance in applications, as we shall illustrate with a further development of the approach to machine decomposition initiated in Section 5-2.

293

In Section 5–5, we show how group theory may be applied in two different theories of the complexity of finite networks—in one theory we look at networks in which the components have limited complexity, and then seek to understand how many layers of computing elements are required for the computation of a given function; in the other theory we take a network of a fixed layered structure, and ask what complexity of the components is requisite for appropriate function.

Finally, in Section 5–6, we introduce the notion of a universal algebra, and find that homomorphisms, direct products, and subalgebras can all be treated very naturally in this general setting, thus unifying and simplifying our understanding of the theory that has gone before.

5–1   Homomorphisms, Machine Monoids, and Permutations

In this section we study one way of building new structures from old—namely by "lumping together" elements of the old structure into "barrels" which form the elements of the new structure.

To start off our study, consider $\mathbf{Z}_m$, the integers modulo m. This is obtained from $\mathbf{Z}$ by lumping together those elements which differ by a multiple of m:

$$\mathbf{Z}_m = \mathbf{Z}/\sim_m \text{ where } n_1 \sim_m n_2 \text{ iff } n_1 - n_2 \text{ is a multiple of } m$$

We saw in Section 2–4 that $\sim_m$ had the pleasant property that it was compatible with addition:

$$n_1 \sim_m n_1' \text{ and } n_2 \sim_m n_2' \Rightarrow n_1 + n_2 \sim_m n_1' + n_2'$$

and this enabled us to define addition on $\mathbf{Z}_m$ by the rule

$$+ : \mathbf{Z}_m \times \mathbf{Z}_m \to \mathbf{Z}_m : ([n_1]_m, [n_2]_m) \mapsto [n_1 + n_2]_m$$

i.e.,

$$[n_1]_m + [n_2]_m \overset{\Delta}{=} [n_1 + n_2]_m$$

We know that addition on $\mathbf{Z}$ is associative. Let us check that addition on $\mathbf{Z}_m$ is also associative:

$$\begin{aligned}
([n_1]_m + [n_2]_m) + [n_3]_m &= [n_1 + n_2]_m + [n_3]_m \\
&= [(n_1 + n_2) + n_3]_m \\
&= [n_1 + (n_2 + n_3)]_m \\
&= [n_1]_m + [n_2 + n_3]_m \\
&= [n_1]_m + ([n_2]_m + [n_3]_m)
\end{aligned}$$

Consider another case. We know that $(\mathbf{Z}, \cdot)$ is also a semigroup, where $\cdot$ is numerical multiplication; and it was left as an exercise for the reader in Section 2–4 to verify that $\sim_m$ is also compatible with $\cdot$, so that multiplication may also be well-defined on $\mathbf{Z}_m$ by the equation

$$[n_1]_m \cdot [n_2]_m \overset{\Delta}{=} [n_1 \cdot n_2]_m$$

It is also clear (simply by changing $+$ to $\cdot$ in the above proof of associativity for addition) that $(\mathbf{Z}_m, \cdot)$ is then a semigroup as is $(\mathbf{Z}_m, +)$.

Thus in both cases, we started with a semigroup $(\mathbf{Z}, \circ)$ (where $\circ$ was either $+$ or $\cdot$) and an equivalence relation $\sim_m$ which was compatible with $\circ$; and in both cases, this enabled us to define $\circ$ on $\mathbf{Z}_m = \mathbf{Z}/\sim_m$, and we then were able to show that $(\mathbf{Z}_m, \circ)$ must also be a semigroup.

Our success in getting the above result for either choice of associative binary operation on $\mathbf{Z}$ encourages us to conjecture that the following general result is true: "Let $(S, \cdot)$ be a semigroup, and let $\equiv$ be an equivalence relation on S which is compatible with $\cdot$. Then we may define $\cdot$ on $S/\equiv$ and then deduce that $(S/\equiv, \cdot)$ is a semigroup." That this is indeed so follows from the next definition and theorem:

DEFINITION 1

Let $(S, \cdot)$ be a semigroup, and let $\equiv$ be an equivalence relation on S. We say that $\equiv$ is a **congruence** on $(S, \cdot)$ iff it is compatible with $\cdot$, i.e., iff

$$s_1 \equiv s_1' \text{ and } s_2 \equiv s_2' \Rightarrow s_1 \cdot s_2 \equiv s_1' \cdot s_2' \text{ for all } s_1, s_2, s_1', s_2' \in S$$

Thus, if $\equiv$ is a congruence on $(S, \cdot)$ we may define $\cdot$ as a binary operator on $S/\equiv$ by the equation

$$[s_1] \cdot [s_2] \overset{\Delta}{=} [s_1 \cdot s_2] \quad \text{for all } [s_1], [s_2] \in S/\equiv$$

(where we use $[s]$ as shorthand for $[s]_\equiv = \{s' \mid s \equiv s'\}$).   ○

Our conjecture then takes shape as the following:

THEOREM 1

If $\equiv$ is a congruence on the semigroup $(S, \cdot)$, then $(S/\equiv, \cdot)$ is also a semigroup.

Proof

We simply mimic our previous argument for $(\mathbf{Z}, +)$ to check that $\cdot$ is indeed associative on $S/\equiv$:

$$
\begin{aligned}
([s_1] \cdot [s_2]) \cdot [s_3] &= [s_1 \cdot s_2] \cdot [s_3] \\
&= [(s_1 \cdot s_2) \cdot s_3] \\
&= [s_1 \cdot (s_2 \cdot s_3)] \text{ by associativity in } S \\
&= [s_1] \cdot [s_2 \cdot s_3] \\
&= [s_1] \cdot ([s_2] \cdot [s_3]) \qquad \qquad \square
\end{aligned}
$$

Example 1

Note that not every equivalence relation yields a congruence. For example, let $A = \{n \,|\, n \in \mathbf{N} \text{ and } n \geq 2\}$ and let $(A, +)$ be the semigroup in which $+$ is addition restricted to elements of A. Then we may define an equivalence relation $\sim$ on A by

$$
x \sim y \Leftrightarrow x \text{ and } y \text{ are both prime or both composite}
$$

However $\sim$ is *not* a congruence on $(A, +)$ since $2 \sim 2$ and $2 \sim 3$, but $2 + 2$ is *not* equivalent to $2 + 3$, since 4 is composite while 5 is prime. $\Diamond$

We have already seen that the semigroup $(\mathbf{Z}, +)$ yields a semigroup $(\mathbf{Z}_m, +)$. Let us now see that $(\mathbf{Z}, +, 0)$ yields a monoid $(\mathbf{Z}_m, +, [0]_m)$. To do this we must simply check that $[0]_m$ is an identity for $+$ on $\mathbf{Z}_m$:

$$
\begin{aligned}
[0]_m + [n]_m &= [0 + n]_m \\
&= [n]_m = [n + 0]_m \qquad \text{since } 0 + n = n = n + 0 \\
&= [n]_m + [0]_m
\end{aligned}
$$

From this we may clearly jump to the general result:

DEFINITION 2

Let $(S, \cdot, 1)$ be a monoid, and let $\equiv$ be an equivalence relation on S. Then we say that $\equiv$ is a **congruence** on $(S, \cdot, 1)$ if it is a congruence on $(S, \cdot)$.
$\bigcirc$

THEOREM 2

Let $\equiv$ be a congruence on the monoid $(S, \cdot, 1)$. Then $(S/\equiv, \cdot, [1])$ is also a monoid.

Proof

Given the previous theorem, it only remains to check that $[1]$ is an identity for $\cdot$ on $S/\!\equiv$:

$$[s] \cdot [1] = [s \cdot 1] = [s] = [1 \cdot s] = [1] \cdot [s] \qquad \square$$

As an immediate consequence of this result we can, of course, deduce that $(\mathbf{Z}_m, \cdot, [1]_m)$ is also a monoid. Before moving on from monoids to groups, let us just introduce one more piece of terminology:

DEFINITION 3

If $\equiv$ is a congruence on the semigroup $(S, \cdot)$ then we call $(S/\!\equiv, \cdot)$ the **factor semigroup** [of $(S, \cdot)$ with respect to $\equiv$].

If $\equiv$ is a congruence on the monoid $(S, \cdot, 1)$ we call $(S/\!\equiv, \cdot, [1])$ the **factor monoid** [of $(S, \cdot, 1)$ with respect to $\equiv$]. ○

To move on to groups, we note that $(\mathbf{Z}, +, 0, -)$ is a group (where $-$ denotes the unary operator $n \mapsto -n$) and that $\sim_m$ is compatible with $-$.

$$n_1 \sim_m n_2 \Rightarrow n_1 = n_2 + km \text{ for some } k \in \mathbf{Z}$$
$$\Rightarrow -n_1 = -n_2 + (-k)m$$
$$\Rightarrow -n_1 \sim_m -n_2$$

Thus we may define $-$ on $\mathbf{Z}_m$ by $-[n]_m = [-n]_m$.

The reader will not be surprised if we now claim that $(\mathbf{Z}_m, +, [0]_m, -)$ is also a group. To see that it is, we must simply check that $-[n]_m$ is the inverse of $[n]_m$ for each $n \in \mathbf{Z}$:

$$[n]_m + (-[n]_m) = [n]_m + [-n]_m = [n + (-n)]_m = [0]_m$$

and, similarly, $(-[n]_m) + [n]_m = [0]_m$ as desired.

Hopefully the reader will, by now, have sufficiently settled into the rhythm of things that he could have predicted the next definition and theorem.

DEFINITION 4

Let $(S, \cdot, 1, {}^{-1})$ be a group, and let $\equiv$ be an equivalence relation on S. We say that $\equiv$ is a **congruence** on $(S, \cdot, 1, {}^{-1})$ if it is compatible with both $\cdot$ and ${}^{-1}$, i.e., $s_1 \equiv s_2 \Rightarrow s_1^{-1} \equiv s_2^{-1}$. ○

Thus, we may not only define $\cdot$ on $S/\!\equiv$ by $[s_1] \cdot [s_2] = [s_1 \cdot s_2]$, but also define $^{-1}: S/\!\equiv \;\rightarrow\; S/\!\equiv :[s] \mapsto [s^{-1}]$, that is, $[s]^{-1} \stackrel{\Delta}{=} [s^{-1}]$. (See Exercise 1.)

THEOREM 3

Let $\equiv$ be a congruence on the group $(S, \cdot, 1, ^{-1})$. Then $(S/\!\equiv, \cdot, [1], ^{-1})$ is also a group [and we call it the **factor group** of $(S, \cdot, 1, ^{-1})$ with respect to $\equiv$]. ⊏

The next result tells us that we do not have to work as hard as we might have thought to check that the equivalence relation $\equiv$ on S is a group congruence. In fact, as soon as $\equiv$ is compatible with $\cdot$ it is *automatically* compatible with $^{-1}$.

THEOREM 4

Let $(S, \cdot, 1, ^{-1})$ be a group. Then $\equiv$ is a congruence on $(S, \cdot, 1, ^{-1})$ $\Leftarrow$ $\equiv$ is a congruence on $(S, \cdot)$.

Proof

Clearly, the only thing we have to prove is that any congruence $\equiv$ on $(S, \cdot)$ is compatible with $^{-1}$. But

$$s_1 \equiv s_2 \Rightarrow s_1^{-1} \cdot s_1 \equiv s_1^{-1} \cdot s_2$$
$$\Rightarrow s_2^{-1} = 1 \cdot s_2^{-1} = (s_1^{-1} \cdot s_1) \cdot s_2^{-1} \equiv (s_1^{-1} \cdot s_2) \cdot s_2^{-1}$$
$$= s_1^{-1} \cdot (s_2 \cdot s_2^{-1}) = s_1^{-1} \quad ⊏$$

We shall return to the study of congruences on groups in our discussion of normal subgroups in Section 5–4 and shall then consider congruences in a more general setting in Section 5–6. Before relating congruences to homomorphisms in this section, we first note a few further properties of the integers modulo m.

Henceforth we shall write $\mathbf{Z}_m = \{0, 1, 2, \ldots, m - 1\}$ rather than $\{[0]_m, [1]_m, \ldots, [m - 1]_m\}$, leaving it to the context to make it clear when 1 denotes an element of $\mathbf{Z}$ or of $\mathbf{Z}_2$ or of $\mathbf{Z}_3$, or of any other $\mathbf{Z}_m$. Secondly, we shall make statements like "the integers modulo m form a group under addition" in place of the more formal "$(\mathbf{Z}_m, +, 0, -)$ is a group."

The integers modulo 2 form a group under addition, with an addition table given by

+	0	1
0	0	1
1	1	0

while the addition table for the group of integers modulo 3 is

+	0	1	2
0	0	1	2
1	1	2	0
2	2	0	1

We have seen previously that the integers modulo m form a monoid under multiplication. But, is it also true that $\mathbf{Z}_m$ is a group under multiplication? To answer this question we must see if for each $[x]_m \in \mathbf{Z}_m$ there exists an inverse, i.e., a $[y]_m \in \mathbf{Z}_m$ such that

$$[x]_m \cdot [y]_m = [1]_m = [y]_m \cdot [x]_m$$

However, for any $[y]_m \in \mathbf{Z}_m$ we have

$$[0]_m \cdot [y]_m = [0 \cdot y]_m = [0]_m$$

and we see that $[0]_m$ does not have a multiplicative inverse. Thus, $\mathbf{Z}_m$ is not a group under multiplication. (Why doesn't this contradict Theorem 4?)

We may feel, therefore, that the elimination of $[0]_m$ from consideration will result in $\mathbf{Z}_m \backslash \{[0]_m\}$ being a group under multiplication. Evidence for such a conclusion is the multiplication table of the nonzero elements of $\mathbf{Z}_2$. That is

and we have a group (although trivial) under multiplication.

The next tantalizing bit of information appears when we look at the nonzero elements of $\mathbf{Z}_3$. Since

·	1	2
1	1	2
2	2	1

we have a group under multiplication.

Finally, however, our bubble is burst when we consider the nonzero elements of $\mathbf{Z}_4$. In this case multiplication is given by

·	1	2	3
1	1	2	3
2	2	0	2
3	3	2	1

Investigation of this table reveals that the axioms of a group are not satisfied. In the first place, multiplication is not even an operator on $\mathbf{Z}_4 \backslash \{0\}$, and secondly, the element 2 does not have a multiplicative inverse.

The attentive reader may, after examining Exercise 3, see a pattern emerge. $\mathbf{Z}_m \backslash \{0\}$ does yield a group under multiplication for $m = 2, 3, 5$, and 7, but does *not* yield such a group for $m = 4, 6$, or 8. The pattern does in fact hold in general, and we shall prove, in Section 7–1, that $\mathbf{Z}_m \backslash \{0\}$ yields a group under multiplication iff m is a prime number.

We now relate congruences to homomorphisms: Suppose S is a semigroup and $\equiv$ is an equivalence relation on S. Recall that the canonical surjection $\eta : S \to S/\equiv$ is the function

$$\eta : s \mapsto [s]_\equiv$$

Thus, for any $s_1, s_2 \in S$, we have that

$$\eta(s_1 \cdot s_2) = [s_1 \cdot s_2]_\equiv$$

However, if $\equiv$ is a congruence on S, then $S/\equiv$ is a semigroup under the operation

$$[s_1]_\equiv \cdot [s_2]_\equiv = [s_1 \cdot s_2]_\equiv$$

Under this circumstance, we see that η is a map from the semigroup S to the semigroup $S/\equiv$ such that

$$\eta(s_1 \cdot s_2) = [s_1 \cdot s_2]_\equiv = [s_1]_\equiv \cdot [s_2]_\equiv = \eta(s_1) \cdot \eta(s_2)$$

It is just this discussion that suggests the following definition.

DEFINITION 5

Suppose S and S' are semigroups. Then a function $f : S \to S'$ is a **semigroup homomorphism** if

$$f(s_1 \cdot s_2) = f(s_1) \cdot f(s_2)$$

for all $s_1, s_2 \in S$.   ○

Example 2

Let $(\mathbf{N}, +)$ be the semigroup of the natural numbers under addition, and let $(\mathbf{N}, \cdot)$ be the semigroup of the natural numbers under multiplication. Then he map $n \mapsto 2^n$ is a semigroup homomorphism $(\mathbf{N}, +) \rightarrow (\mathbf{N}, \cdot)$ since for ıll $n_1, n_2 \in \mathbf{N}$, we have

$$2^{n_1+n_2} = 2^{n_1} \cdot 2^{n_2}$$

.e., if we set $f(n) = 2^n$, then it is indeed true that

$$f(n_1 + n_2) = f(n_1) \cdot f(n_2) \qquad \Diamond$$

We may extend the definition of a homomorphism one step further by he following definition.

DEFINITION 6

Suppose S and S' are monoids. Then a semigroup homomorphism $f: S \rightarrow S'$ i.e., f respects the binary operators of S and S') is a **monoid homomorphism** f it also respects the nullary operators of S and S'; that is,

$$f(1) = 1'$$

where 1 and $1'$ are the identities of S and S', respectively. $\bigcirc$

Since S and S' are monoids, one might *erroneously* think that the condition hat $f(1) = 1'$ is superfluous, since

$$f(1) \cdot f(s) = f(1 \cdot s) = f(s) = 1' \cdot f(s) \qquad \text{(1)}$$

However, since monoids do not necessarily contain inverses, we cannot conclude that $f(1) \cdot f(s) = 1' \cdot f(s) \Rightarrow f(1) = 1'$. Hence, we must explicitly tate that $f(1) = 1'$. We have only proved in equation (1) that $f(1)$ is an identity for all of $f(S)$, not for all of S'; this is made explicit in Example 3.

Example 3

The map $f: (\mathbf{N}, +, 0) \rightarrow (\mathbf{Z}, +, 0): n \mapsto -n$ is a monoid homomorphism since for all $n_1, n_2 \in \mathbf{N}$ we have

$$f(n_1 + n_2) = -(n_1 + n_2) = (-n_1) + (-n_2) = f(n_1) + f(n_2)$$

ınd

$$f(0) = -0 = 0$$

Now, is the map $f:(\mathbf{Z}_-, \min, -1) \to (\mathbf{N}, \max, 0): n \mapsto -n$ a monoid homomorphism? To answer this question, we first note that for all $n_1, n_2 \in \mathbf{Z}_-$ we have that

$$f(\min[n_1, n_2]) = -(\min[n_1, n_2])$$
$$= \max[-n_1, -n_2] = \max[f(n_1), f(n_2)]$$

and f is a semigroup homomorphism. However, since

$$f(-1) = -(-1) = 1 \neq 0$$

we see that f is not a monoid homomorphism. The number 1 is the minimum of $f(\mathbf{Z}_-) = \mathbf{Z}_+$, but is *not* the minimum of $\mathbf{N}$. ◊

The most natural extension of the definition of a homomorphism to groups is given by the following:

DEFINITION 7

Suppose S and S' are groups. Then a monoid homomorphism $f:S \to S'$ is a **group homomorphism** if it also respects the unary operators of S and S', i.e.,

$$f(s^{-1}) = f(s)^{-1}$$

for all $s \in S$. ○

However, just as a semigroup congruence on a group is automatically a group congruence, so is a semigroup homomorphism from one group to another automatically a group homomorphism:

THEOREM 5

Suppose that S and S' are groups. Then a map $f:S \to S'$ is a group homomorphism if and only if it is a semigroup homomorphism, i.e.,

$$f(s \cdot s') = f(s) \cdot f(s')$$

for all $s, s' \in S$.

Proof

Clearly we need only check that, if f is a semigroup homomorphism, then (i) $f(1) = 1'$; and (ii) $f(s^{-1}) = f(s)^{-1}$ for each $s \in S$:

.) Since $f(1) = f(1 \cdot 1) = f(1) \cdot f(1)$
we have that $1' = f(1) \cdot f(1)^{-1} = [f(1) \cdot f(1)] \cdot f(1)^{-1}$
$$= f(1) \cdot [f(1) \cdot f(1)^{-1}] = f(1)$$

ii) $f(s^{-1}) \cdot f(s) = f(s^{-1} \cdot s) = f(1) = 1'$
$\therefore f(s^{-1}) = f(s)^{-1}$ □

Since a homomorphism is a function, and since we have classified
$_{\text{J}}$nctions as surjective (onto), injective (1:1), and bijective (onto and 1:1),
$_{\text{J}}$e may now classify (semigroup, monoid, and group) homomorphisms.

DEFINITION 8

$f:S \rightarrow S'$ is a (semigroup, monoid, or group) homomorphism, we say that
is:

> an **epimorphism** if f is surjective
>
> a **monomorphism** if f is injective
>
> an **isomorphism** if f is bijective.   ○

Example 4

Let us reconsider the semigroup homomorphism $f:(\mathbf{N}, +) \rightarrow (\mathbf{N}, \cdot):n \mapsto 2^n$.
Suppose $m \in \mathbf{N}$. If f is surjective, then there must exist some $n \in \mathbf{N}$ such that
$n = 2^n$. This, however, is not true in general, and so f is not surjective.
Now suppose

$$f(n_1) = f(n_2)$$

Then
$$2^{n_1} = 2^{n_2}$$

which implies

$$n_1 = n_2$$

Thus, f is injective.
Therefore, f is a monomorphism, but not an epimorphism, and hence,
not an isomorphism.   ◊

We may now make precise the conditions under which we may say that
certain groups are equivalent or have the same structure:

DEFINITION 9

If there exists an isomorphism $f:S \rightarrow S'$, we say that S and S' are **isomorphic**
or that S is **isomorphic** to S'. If S and S' are isomorphic, we write $S \cong S'$.
○

Thus, if S and S' are isomorphic, then they are essentially the same thing. The only distinction between the two is that the elements, and possibly the operations, have different names.

Example 5

$\mathbf{Z}_2$ under addition is isomorphic to $\mathbf{Z}_3 \setminus \{0\}$ under multiplication, since we have

+	0	1
0	0	1
1	1	0

·	1	2
1	1	2
2	2	1

i.e., the map $f : \mathbf{Z}_2 \to \mathbf{Z}_3 \setminus \{0\} : \begin{cases} 0 \mapsto 1 \\ 1 \mapsto 2 \end{cases}$ is a group isomorphism.

Actually, since any group with two elements is isomorphic to $\mathbf{Z}_2$ (why?) we may say that there is only one group with two elements, and that is $\mathbf{Z}_2$.
◇

To give an interestingly different example of homomorphisms, let us relate two monoids associated with the study of a **semiautomaton** (i.e., the **dynamics** of an automaton),

$$\delta : Q \times X \to Q$$

First, there is the monoid $(X^*, \cdot, \Lambda)$, where $\cdot$ denotes concatenation, and where Λ denotes the "empty word" of length 0.

Secondly, consider the set $F_R(Q)$ of all maps

$$f : Q \to Q : q \mapsto (q)f$$

where the subscript R tells us that we are to think of the maps as acting on the *right*. We define composition of these maps

$$F_R(Q) \times F_R(Q) \to F_R(Q) : (f, g) \mapsto f \diamond g$$

in such a way as to respect the direction of arrow chasing in the following commutative diagram:

$$Q \xrightarrow{f} Q$$

i.e., $(q)(f \diamond g) = ((q)f)g$ for all $q \in Q$.

We check that $\diamond$ is associative by chasing the following diagram, which shows that we may as well write $f \diamond g \diamond h$ for $f \diamond (g \diamond h) = (f \diamond g) \diamond h$:

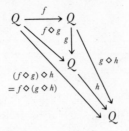

Finally, we note that the identity map on Q

$$id_Q : Q \rightarrow Q : q \mapsto q$$

is indeed an identity for the composition $\diamond$ on $F_R(Q)$

$$f \diamond id_Q = f = id_Q \diamond f \quad \text{for all } f \in F_R(Q)$$

Thus $(F_R(Q), \diamond, id_Q)$ is also a monoid.

Now we see how each semiautomaton $\delta : Q \times X \rightarrow Q$ induces a monoid homomorphism $X^* \rightarrow F_R(Q)$ (a formal proof follows shortly).

Remember that we could extend $\delta : Q + X \rightarrow Q$ to a map $\delta^* : Q \times X^* \rightarrow Q$ in such a way that $\delta^*(q, \Lambda) = q$; while

$$\delta^*(q, ww') = \delta^*(\delta^*(q, w), w') \quad \text{for all } q \in Q, \text{ and all } w, w' \in X^*$$

Thus, we may concatenate strings and apply the totality, or act with each string of the concatenation in order; the overall state transition is the same.

Thus, if we define the map (which acts on the right)

$$\delta_w^* : Q \rightarrow Q : q \mapsto \delta^*(q, w)$$

to be the function $\delta^*(\cdot, w)$, we see that δ_w^* is simply the state-transition function induced by application of the input string w—or induced by the **action of** w, for short. Pictorially, we have Figure 5-1.

Figure 5-1 $q \bullet \xrightarrow{\quad w \quad} (q)\delta_w^\circ = \delta^\circ(q, w)$

Example 6

Consider the δ shown in the state graph of Figure 5-2:

$$\delta(q_1, 0) = q_1; \; \delta(q_1, 1) = q_2; \; \delta(q_2, 0) = q_1; \; \delta(q_2, 1) = q_2$$

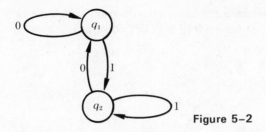

Figure 5-2

We may compute $\delta^*(q, 1101)$ for each q by following, in turn, the arrows marked 1, 1, 0, and 1, starting at q:

$$q_1 \overset{1}{\mapsto} q_2 \overset{1}{\mapsto} q_2 \overset{0}{\mapsto} q_1 \overset{1}{\mapsto} q_2 : \delta^*(q_1, 1101) = q_2$$

$$q_2 \overset{1}{\mapsto} q_2 \overset{1}{\mapsto} q_2 \overset{0}{\mapsto} q_1 \overset{1}{\mapsto} q_2 : \delta^*(q_2, 1101) = q_2$$

Thus $\delta^*_{1101} : Q \to Q$ is simply the map "reset to q_2."   ◊

The reader will find in Exercise 11 the equality $\delta^*_{1101101} = \delta^*_{1101} \diamond \delta^*_{101}$. This equality should be *expected* by the reader (why?). We reveal it now as a case of the following theorem:

THEOREM 6

For any semiautomaton $\delta : Q \times X \to Q$, the map

$$\delta^*_{\cdot} : X^* \to F_R(Q) : w \mapsto \delta^*_w$$

is a monoid homomorphism.

Proof

To verify that $\delta^*_{\cdot}$ is a homomorphism $(X^*, \cdot, \Lambda) \to (F_R(Q), \diamond, id_Q)$ we must simply verify that

(a) $\delta^*_{ww'} = \delta^*_w \diamond \delta^*_{w'}$ for all $w, w' \in X^*$ and that
(b) $\delta^*_\Lambda = id_Q$

To check (b) we simply recall that $\delta^*(q, \Lambda) = q$ for all $q \in Q$, for then

$$(q)\delta^*_\Lambda = \delta^*(q, \Lambda) = q = (q)id_Q \quad \text{for all } q \in Q$$

and so $\delta^*_\Lambda = id_Q$.

To check (a) we simply recall that $\delta^*(q, ww') = \delta^*(\delta^*(q, w), w')$ for all $q \in Q$, and all $w, w' \in X^*$. Then, for each $w, w' \in X^*$ we must have

$$\begin{aligned}
(q)\,\delta^*_{ww'} &= \delta^*(q, ww') = \delta^*(\delta^*(q, w), w') \\
&= \delta^*((q)\,\delta^*_w, w') \\
&= ((q)\,\delta^*_w)\,\delta^*_{w'} \\
&= (q)(\delta^*_w \diamond \delta^*_{w'}) \text{ for all } q \in Q
\end{aligned}$$

and so $\delta^*_{ww'} = \delta^*_w \diamond \delta^*_{w'}$. □

DEFINITION 10

The image $S_\delta = \{\delta^*_w \,|\, w \in X^*\}$ of X^* under δ^* yields a monoid $(S_\delta, \diamond, id_Q)$ under the right composition of $F_R(Q)$, called the **monoid of the dynamics (semiautomaton)** δ. (See Exercise 15.)   ○

In the 2-state machine of Example 6, we see that S_δ may indeed be a proper subset of $F_R(Q)$. $F_R(\{q_1, q_2\})$ has four members, as shown in Table 5-1, where $f_2 = id_Q$ since $(q)f_2 = (q)\,\delta^*_\Lambda = q$ for all $q \in Q$; while, in this case, $S_\delta = \{f_1, f_2, f_4\}$.

Table 5-1

f	$(q_1)f$	$(q_2)f$
f_1	q_1	q_1
f_2	q_1	q_2
f_3	q_2	q_1
f_4	q_2	q_2

Although we defined S_δ as the image of a homomorphism, we may also define it as a factor monoid of X^* as follows:

Define the relation $\equiv$ on X^* by

$$w \equiv w' \Leftrightarrow \delta^*(q, w) = \delta^*(q, w') \text{ for all } q \in Q$$

Then it is easy to check that $\equiv$ is an equivalence relation. In fact, it is a congruence, since $w_1 \equiv w'_1$ and $w_2 \equiv w'_2$ implies that

$$\begin{aligned}
\delta^*(q, w_1 w_2) &= \delta^*(\delta^*(q, w_1), w_2) \\
&= \delta^*(\delta^*(q, w'_1), w_2) \text{ since } w_1 \equiv w'_1 \\
&= \delta^*(\delta^*(q, w'_1), w'_2) \text{ since } w_2 \equiv w'_2 \\
&= \delta^*(q, w'_1 w'_2)
\end{aligned}$$

i.e., that $w_1 w_2 \equiv w'_1 w'_2$.

Thus, we may define the factor monoid with carrier $X^*/\equiv$. But since $w_1 \equiv w_2 \Leftrightarrow \delta^*_{w_1} = \delta^*_{w_2}$, it is clear that $X^*/\equiv$ and S_δ differ only in the labelling of their elements—in other words, they are isomorphic (Exercise 16).

In fact, for every homomorphism $f: S_1 \to S_2$ it is true that $f(S_1)$ is isomorphic to an appropriate factor structure $S_1/\equiv_f$, whether S_1 and S_2 both be semigroups, monoids, or groups. However, rather than prove these three theorems one-by-one here, we shall prove them in Section 5–6 in one fell swoop, using the language of Ω-algebras.

As an immediate application of this last observation, let us relate our present ideas to our study of finite-state languages (Definition 4–2–2) by means of the next theorem.

THEOREM 7

A subset L of X^* is an FSL (finite-state language) iff L is the union of equivalence classes of a finite congruence on X^*.

Proof

A finite congruence on X^* is given by a homomorphism

$$h: X^* \twoheadrightarrow S$$

of X^* onto a *finite* monoid S. If, then, $L = \{w \in X^* \mid h(w) \in R\}$ for some (finite) subset R of S, we note that it is accepted by the finite automaton

$$M = (S, X, \{0, 1\}, \delta, \beta)$$

with initial state e, the identity of S, when we define

$$\delta(s, x) = s \cdot h(x)$$

using multiplication in S, while

$$\beta = \chi_R : S \to \{0, 1\}$$

the characteristic function of R. Since h is a homomorphism, it is then clear that

$$\delta^*(e, w) = h(w)$$

and so $w \in M_e^{-1}(1) \Leftrightarrow \beta(h(w)) = 1 \Leftrightarrow h(w) \in R \Leftrightarrow w \in L$.

Conversely, let $\bar{M} = (Q, X, Y, \bar{\delta}, \bar{\beta})$ be a finite-state machine for which $L = \bar{M}_q^{-1}(y)$, and let

$$\eta : X^* \twoheadrightarrow S_\delta$$

be the canonical epimorphism of X^* onto the monoid of δ. Then, let

$$R = \{s \mid [w]_\delta = s \Rightarrow \bar{M}_q(w) = y\}$$

to deduce that $L = \eta^{-1}(R)$, a union of classes of a finite congruence on X^*.

$\square$

Recall from Section 2–2 that a semigroup $(S, \cdot)$ [or monoid $(S, \cdot, 1)$ or group $(S, \cdot, 1, ^{-1})$] is **commutative** or **abelian** iff we have

$$s_1 \cdot s_2 = s_2 \cdot s_1 \text{ for all } s_1, s_2 \text{ in } S$$

By contrast with $(\mathbf{Z}_m, +, 0, -)$, we now consider an important family of groups which are nonabelian, namely, for each set Q, the group of all permutations of Q (i.e., those elements of $F_R(Q)$ which permute the elements of Q, but do not merge any of them).

DEFINITION 11

A **permutation** of a set Q is simply a bijection $\sigma : Q \to Q$. We may thus regard each permutation as an element of the monoid $F_R(Q)$. $\bigcirc$

Example 7

If $X = \{x_0, x_1, x_2\}$, then the map σ_1 with $(x_0)\sigma_1 = x_1$, $(x_1)\sigma_1 = x_0$, and $(x_2)\sigma_1 = x_2$ is a permutation of X. $\Diamond$

To simplify our discussion of permutations of finite sets, let us replace any n-element set Q by the "canonical" n-element set

$$[n] = \{0, 1, 2, \ldots, n - 1\}$$

Then let us represent any permutation $\sigma : [n] \to [n]$ by the tableau

$$\sigma = \begin{pmatrix} 0 & 1 & \ldots & n - 1 \\ (0)\sigma & (1)\sigma & \ldots & (n - 1)\sigma \end{pmatrix}$$

With these replacements, the σ_1 of Example 7 takes the form

$$\sigma_1 = \begin{pmatrix} 0 & 1 & 2 \\ 1 & 0 & 2 \end{pmatrix}$$

In representing permutations in this manner, the description of the permutation is determined by the fact that the image of an element is written directly below that element, and has nothing to do with the order in which this information is presented. In other words, we have that

$$\sigma_1 = \begin{pmatrix} 0 & 1 & 2 \\ 1 & 0 & 2 \end{pmatrix} = \begin{pmatrix} 2 & 1 & 0 \\ 2 & 0 & 1 \end{pmatrix} = \begin{pmatrix} 1 & 0 & 2 \\ 0 & 1 & 2 \end{pmatrix}$$

Example 8

There are 6 permutations of [3]. These are:

$$\begin{pmatrix} 0 & 1 & 2 \\ 0 & 1 & 2 \end{pmatrix} \begin{pmatrix} 0 & 1 & 2 \\ 0 & 2 & 1 \end{pmatrix} \begin{pmatrix} 0 & 1 & 2 \\ 1 & 0 & 2 \end{pmatrix}$$

$$\begin{pmatrix} 0 & 1 & 2 \\ 1 & 2 & 0 \end{pmatrix} \begin{pmatrix} 0 & 1 & 2 \\ 2 & 0 & 1 \end{pmatrix} \begin{pmatrix} 0 & 1 & 2 \\ 2 & 1 & 0 \end{pmatrix}$$

$\Diamond$

We can form any permutation

$$\sigma = \begin{pmatrix} 0 & 1 & \dots & n-1 \\ (0)\sigma & (1)\sigma & \dots & (n-1)\sigma \end{pmatrix}$$

of $[n] = \{0, 1, \dots, n-1\}$ by choosing in turn:

(1) Any one of the n elements for $(0)\sigma$
(2) Any one of the $(n-1)$ remaining elements for $(1)\sigma$
(3) Any one of the $(n-2)$ remaining elements for $(2)\sigma$
$\vdots$
(n) The last remaining element for $(n-1)\sigma$

Thus, we see that we have

$$n(n-1)(n-2)\dots(1) = n!$$

possible permutations of $[n]$.

Given any two maps $\sigma_1 : Q \to Q$ and $\sigma_2 : Q \to Q$, we saw that we could form their *composite* $\sigma_1 \Diamond \sigma_2$ by the rule

$$(q)[\sigma_1 \Diamond \sigma_2] = [(q)\sigma_1]\sigma_2$$

It is easy to see (Exercise 14) that the composite of two permutations is again a permutation.

Example 9

For $Q = [4]$, let

$$\sigma_1 = \begin{pmatrix} 0 & 1 & 2 & 3 \\ 1 & 2 & 3 & 0 \end{pmatrix} \text{ and } \sigma_2 = \begin{pmatrix} 0 & 1 & 2 & 3 \\ 3 & 1 & 0 & 2 \end{pmatrix}$$

Then $\sigma_1 \Diamond \sigma_2 = \begin{pmatrix} 0 & 1 & 2 & 3 \\ 1 & 0 & 2 & 3 \end{pmatrix}$ and $\sigma_2 \Diamond \sigma_1 = \begin{pmatrix} 0 & 1 & 2 & 3 \\ 0 & 2 & 1 & 3 \end{pmatrix}$, and so both are permutations. However, $\sigma_1 \Diamond \sigma_2 \neq \sigma_2 \Diamond \sigma_1$. $\Diamond$

We denote the set of all permutations of the set Q by $\mathcal{S}_Q$. We use $\mathcal{S}_n$ as shorthand for $\mathcal{S}_{[n]}$. Composition clearly yields a binary operator on $\mathcal{S}_Q$:

$$\mathcal{S}_Q \times \mathcal{S}_Q \to \mathcal{S}_Q : (\sigma_1, \sigma_2) \to \sigma_1 \Diamond \sigma_2.$$

Our discussion of $F_R(Q)$ showed us that $\Diamond$ is associative, or $(\sigma_1 \Diamond \sigma_2) \Diamond \sigma_3 = \sigma_1 \Diamond (\sigma_2 \Diamond \sigma_3)$, and hence $(\mathcal{S}_Q, \Diamond)$ is a semigroup. However, Example 9 shows that it is *nonabelian*.

Now, the identity map $id_Q : Q \to Q : q \mapsto q$ $\left[\text{we write } 1_n \text{ for } id_{[n]} = \begin{pmatrix} 0 & 1 & 2 & \dots & n-1 \\ 0 & 1 & 2 & \dots & n-1 \end{pmatrix} \right]$ belongs to $\mathcal{S}_Q$, and since it is the identity for all of $F_R(Q)$, it is certainly the identity for $(\mathcal{S}_Q, \Diamond)$. Thus, $(\mathcal{S}_Q, \Diamond, id_Q)$ is a monoid.

Finally, for $\sigma \in \mathcal{S}_Q$ we define σ^{-1} to be the inverse map

$$\sigma^{-1} : Q \to Q : q \mapsto \text{ the unique } q' \text{ such that } (q')\sigma = q$$

The function σ^{-1} is well-defined because σ is bijective. Because σ is onto, there is at least one q' such that $(q')\sigma = q$; and because σ is one-to-one, that q' must be unique.

Example 10

$$\begin{pmatrix} 0 & 1 & 2 & 3 \\ 2 & 1 & 3 & 0 \end{pmatrix}^{-1} = \begin{pmatrix} 0 & 1 & 2 & 3 \\ 3 & 1 & 0 & 2 \end{pmatrix}$$

and

$$\begin{pmatrix} 0 & 1 & 2 & 3 \\ 1 & 2 & 0 & 3 \end{pmatrix}^{-1} = \begin{pmatrix} 0 & 1 & 2 & 3 \\ 2 & 0 & 1 & 3 \end{pmatrix}$$ $\Diamond$

From our definition of σ^{-1}, it follows that for all σ in $\mathcal{S}_Q$ and all q in Q

$$(q)[\sigma^{-1} \diamond \sigma] = ((q)\sigma^{-1})\sigma = q = (q)id_Q$$

and

$$(q)[\sigma \diamond \sigma^{-1}] = ((q)\sigma)\sigma^{-1} = q = (q)id_Q$$

Thus $\sigma^{-1} \diamond \sigma = id_Q = \sigma \diamond \sigma^{-1}$ for all σ in $\mathcal{S}_Q$, and so σ^{-1} is the inverse of σ. Hence:

THEOREM 8

$(\mathcal{S}_Q, \diamond, id_Q, ^{-1})$ is a (nonabelian†) group. We call $\mathcal{S}_Q$ the **symmetric group on** Q, and call $\mathcal{S}_n$ the **symmetric group on** n **letters.**   □

Example 11

If we denote the elements of $\mathcal{S}_3$ by

$$1_3 = \begin{pmatrix} 0 & 1 & 2 \\ 0 & 1 & 2 \end{pmatrix} \quad b = \begin{pmatrix} 0 & 1 & 2 \\ 1 & 2 & 0 \end{pmatrix} \quad c = \begin{pmatrix} 0 & 1 & 2 \\ 2 & 0 & 1 \end{pmatrix}$$

$$d = \begin{pmatrix} 0 & 1 & 2 \\ 0 & 2 & 1 \end{pmatrix} \quad e = \begin{pmatrix} 0 & 1 & 2 \\ 2 & 1 & 0 \end{pmatrix} \quad f = \begin{pmatrix} 0 & 1 & 2 \\ 1 & 0 & 2 \end{pmatrix}$$

then the multiplication table for $\mathcal{S}_3$ is Table 5–2.

Table 5–2

$\diamond$	1_3	b	c	d	e	f
1_3	1_3	b	c	d	e	f
b	b	c	1_3	e	f	d
c	c	1_3	b	f	d	e
d	d	f	e	1_3	c	b
e	e	d	f	b	1_3	c
f	f	e	d	c	b	1_3

By inspection of the table we have the following:

$$1_3^{-1} = 1_3; \ b^{-1} = c; \ c^{-1} = b; \ d^{-1} = d; \ e^{-1} = e; \ \text{and} \ f^{-1} = f. \qquad \diamond$$

---

†Exceptions are when $|Q| \leq 2$.

Let us now look at that part of $\mathcal{S}_3$ involving 1_3, b, and c in our last example, that is, the following:

$\diamond$	1_3	b	c
1_3	1_3	b	c
b	b	c	1_3
c	c	1_3	b

Substituting 0, 1, 2, and $+$ for 1_3, b, c, and $\diamond$, respectively, we obtain

$+$	0	1	2
0	0	1	2
1	1	2	0
2	2	0	1

i.e., the group of integers modulo 3. Thus, in a sense we can consider $\mathbf{Z}_3$ to be a "part" of $\mathcal{S}_3$.

The major importance of permutation groups is that any group with n elements is isomorphic to "a part" of $\mathcal{S}_n$. In Section 5–3 we shall make precise what we mean by "a part," and shall close by proving Theorem 5–3–19: Every group G is isomorphic to a subgroup of $\mathcal{S}_{|G|}$.

EXERCISES FOR SECTION 5–1

1.   Prove Theorem 3.
2.   Construct addition tables for $\mathbf{Z}_4$ and $\mathbf{Z}_5$.
3.   Write down the multiplication tables for $\mathbf{Z}_5\backslash\{0\}$, $\mathbf{Z}_6\backslash\{0\}$, $\mathbf{Z}_7\backslash\{0\}$, and $\mathbf{Z}_8\backslash\{0\}$. Note that $\mathbf{Z}_5\backslash\{0\}$ and $\mathbf{Z}_7\backslash\{0\}$ do yield groups, while $\mathbf{Z}_6\backslash\{0\}$ and $\mathbf{Z}_8\backslash\{0\}$ do not.
4.   Determine whether or not the map $(\mathbf{Z}_+, \cdot) \to (\mathbf{R}, +) : n \mapsto \log n$ is a semigroup homomorphism.
5.   Determine whether or not the map

$$(\mathbf{N}, +) \to (\mathbf{Z}, +) : n \mapsto \begin{cases} \dfrac{n}{2} & \text{if } n \text{ is even} \\ \dfrac{n+1}{2} & \text{if } n \text{ is odd} \end{cases}$$

is a semigroup homomorphism.
6.   Determine which of the following maps are group homomorphisms:
   (a) $(\mathbf{Z}, +, 0, -) \to (\mathbf{Q}\backslash\{0\}, \cdot, 1, {}^{-1}) : n \mapsto 2^{-n}$
   (b) $\mathbf{Z}_2 \to \mathbf{Z}_4 : n \mapsto n$
   (c) $\mathbf{Z}_2 \to \mathbf{Z}_4 : \begin{cases} 0 \mapsto 0 \\ 1 \mapsto 2 \end{cases}$

7. For the previous three exercises, determine which homomorphisms are:
  (a) epimorphisms
  (b) monomorphisms
  (c) isomorphisms.
8. Prove that $\cong$ is an equivalence relation.
9. **(i)** Is $\mathbf{Z}_3$ under addition isomorphic to $\mathbf{Z}_4\backslash\{0\}$ under multiplication?
  (ii) How many groups with three elements are there?
  (iii) Is $\mathbf{Z}_4$ under addition isomorphic to $\mathbf{Z}_5\backslash\{0\}$ under multiplication?
10. For the δ of Example 6, prove that δ^*_{w0} = reset to q_1, and δ^*_{w1} = reset to q_2 for every $w \in \{0,1\}^*$.
11. For the state-graph of Figure 5–3, tabulate $\delta^*_{1101101}$, δ^*_{1101}, δ^*_{101}, and verify by composition that

$$\delta^*_{1101101} = \delta^*_{1101} \diamond \delta^*_{101}.$$

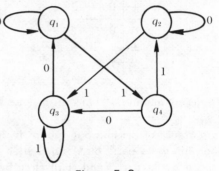

Figure 5–3

12. Given the 3-state machine of Figure 5–4, construct a table describing the elements of $F_R(\{q_1, q_2, q_3\})$ and then find S_δ.

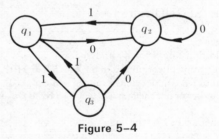

Figure 5–4

13. Write down all the permutations of $[4] = \{0, 1, 2, 3\}$.
14. Verify (whether Q is finite or infinite) that if σ_1 and σ_2 are both permutations of Q (i.e., bijections $Q \to Q$), then $\sigma_1 \diamond \sigma_2$ is also a permutation of Q.
15. Prove that $(S_\delta, \diamond, id_Q)$ is a monoid.
16. Prove that $S_\delta \cong X^*/\equiv$.

5–2   Direct Products and Machine Decomposition

We now continue our discussion of semigroups, monoids, and groups by seeing how to construct new algebraic systems (i.e., new semigroups, monoids, or groups) from old ones. We shall then study related concepts for constructing new automata from old ones.

Suppose S_1 and S_2 are semigroups under an operation · which we shall usually leave implicit, but refer to as multiplication. Then the Cartesian product of the underlying sets

$$S_1 \times S_2 = \{(a_1, a_2) \,|\, a_1 \in S_1, a_2 \in S_2\}$$

can also be made into a semigroup by defining the product of elements of $S_1 \times S_2$ by multiplying their corresponding components; i.e., by defining

$$(S_1 \times S_2) \times (S_1 \times S_2) \rightarrow (S_1 \times S_2) : [(a_1, a_2), (b_1, b_2)] \mapsto (a_1 \cdot b_1, a_2 \cdot b_2).$$

Quite often, the operator on $(S_1 \times S_2)$ is denoted by the same symbol as is the operator on S_1 and the operator on S_2. Therefore, we may often see

$$(a_1, a_2) \cdot (b_1, b_2) = (a_1 \cdot b_1, a_2 \cdot b_2)$$

In this circumstance, remember that multiplication on the left side of the equation is in the semigroup $S_1 \times S_2$, while on the right side multiplication is firstly in S_1, and then in S_2. Also, as we soon shall see, many times we have that $S_1 = S_2$. It is clear (Exercise 1) that with this operation we obtain a new semigroup $(S_1 \times S_2, \cdot)$ called the **direct product** of S_1 and S_2.

If S_1 and S_2 are monoids having identities 1_1 and 1_2, respectively, then for all $(a_1, a_2) \in S_1 \times S_2$ we have

$$\begin{aligned} (1_1, 1_2) \cdot (a_1, a_2) &= (1_1 \cdot a_1, 1_2 \cdot a_2) = (a_1, a_2) \\ &= (a_1 \cdot 1_1, a_2 \cdot 1_2) = (a_1, a_2) \cdot (1_1, 1_2) \end{aligned}$$

Thus, $(1_1, 1_2)$ is an identity, and hence, $(S_1 \times S_2, \cdot, (1_1, 1_2))$ is a monoid called the **direct product** of the monoids $(S_1, \cdot, 1_1)$ and $(S_2, \cdot, 1_2)$.

Finally, if S_1 and S_2 are both groups, then for all $(a_1, a_2) \in S_1 \times S_2$ there exists $(a_1^{-1}, a_2^{-1}) \in S_1 \times S_2$ such that

$$\begin{aligned} (a_1^{-1}, a_2^{-1}) \cdot (a_1, a_2) &= (a_1^{-1} \cdot a_1, a_2^{-1} \cdot a_2) = (1_1, 1_2) \\ &= (a_1 \cdot a_1^{-1}, a_2 \cdot a_2^{-1}) = (a_1, a_2) \cdot (a_1^{-1}, a_2^{-1}) \end{aligned}$$

Thus, (a_1^{-1}, a_2^{-1}) is an inverse of (a_1, a_2), and hence, $(S_1 \times S_2, \cdot, (1_1, 1_2), (^{-1}, ^{-1}))$ is a group, called the **direct product group.**

Example 1

Both **N** and **Z** are semigroups under multiplication. Thus, **N** $\times$ **Z** is a semigroup under multiplication. Obviously, **Z** $\times$ **N** is also a semigroup.

Since $\mathbf{N}$ and $\mathbf{Z}$ are both monoids under addition, then the monoid $\mathbf{N} \times \mathbf{Z}$ is the direct product of $\mathbf{N}$ and $\mathbf{Z}$. We can also form a monoid $\mathbf{Z} \times \mathbf{N}$ by taking the direct product of $\mathbf{Z}$ and $\mathbf{N}$.

By taking the direct product of $\mathbf{Z}$ with itself, we get $\mathbf{Z} \times \mathbf{Z}$, which is a group under addition, e.g.,

$$(3, -6) + (4, 2) = (3 + 4, -6 + 2) = (7, -4)$$

The direct product $\mathbf{Z}_2 \times \mathbf{Z}_2$ is a group under addition having the addition table

+	(0,0)	(0,1)	(1,0)	(1,1)
(0,0)	(0,0)	(0,1)	(1,0)	(1,1)
(0,1)	(0,1)	(0,0)	(1,1)	(1,0)
(1,0)	(1,0)	(1,1)	(0,0)	(0,1)
(1,1)	(1,1)	(1,0)	(0,1)	(0,0)

This group is often referred to as the **Klein* four-group.** Note that this group has a different structure from $\mathbf{Z}_4$. However, let us look only at the elements $(0,0)$ and $(0,1)$ of $\mathbf{Z}_2 \times \mathbf{Z}_2$. Addition for these elements is given by

+	(0,0)	(0,1)
(0,0)	(0,0)	(0,1)
(0,1)	(0,1)	(0,0)

Replacing $(0,0)$ by 0 and $(0,1)$ by 1, we obtain

+	0	1
0	0	1
1	1	0

i.e., the group of integers modulo 2. In this sense, therefore, we can think of $\mathbf{Z}_2$ as a subgroup of $\mathbf{Z}_2 \times \mathbf{Z}_2$. We leave the more formal result as an easy exercise for the reader. ◊

Having defined the direct product for $n = 2$ groups (or monoids, or semigroups), it becomes obvious how to extend this concept for any $n \geq 2$.

---

*Named for the German mathematician Felix Klein (1849–1925).

DEFINITION 1

Given n semigroups $S_1, S_2, \ldots, S_n$, we define a binary operator on $S_1 \times S_2 \times \cdots \times S_n$ by

$$(S_1 \times S_2 \times \cdots \times S_n) \times (S_1 \times S_2 \times \cdots \times S_n) \to (S_1 \times S_2 \times \cdots \times S_n):$$
$$[(a_1, a_2, \ldots, a_n), (b_1, b_2, \ldots, b_n)] \mapsto (a_1 \cdot b_1, a_2 \cdot b_2, \ldots, a_n \cdot b_n)$$

In case $S_1, S_2, \ldots, S_n$ are monoids having the identities $1_1, 1_2, \ldots, 1_n$, respectively, then the identity for the monoid $S_1 \times S_2 \times \cdots \times S_n$ is simply $(1_1, 1_2, \ldots, 1_n)$.

If in addition $S_1, S_2, \ldots, S_n$ are all groups, then the inverse for each $(a_1, a_2, \ldots, a_n) \in S_1 \times S_2 \times \cdots \times S_n$ is $(a_1^{-1}, a_2^{-1}, \ldots, a_n^{-1}) \in S_1 \times S_2 \times \cdots \times S_n$. The resultant structure is called the **direct product** of the S_j's.

○

Example 2

Addition for the group $\mathbf{Z}_2^3 = \mathbf{Z}_2 \times \mathbf{Z}_2 \times \mathbf{Z}_2$ is given by Table 5-3, in which, for the sake of convenience, instead of (a_1, a_2, a_3) we simply write $a_1 a_2 a_3$.

Table 5-3

+	000	100	010	110	001	101	011	111
000	000	100	010	110	001	101	011	111
100	100	000	110	010	101	001	111	011
010	010	110	000	100	011	111	001	101
110	110	010	100	000	111	011	101	001
001	001	101	011	111	000	100	010	110
101	101	001	111	011	100	000	110	010
011	011	111	001	101	010	110	000	100
111	111	011	101	001	110	010	100	000

◊

Turning now to automata, recall that we saw in Section 2-3 that any finite automaton may be simulated by a network of binary modules, provided that we allow loops. In other words, a very simple set of components can be used to build up arbitrary finite automata *if we allow loops*. Automata theorists have shown that we cannot build up arbitrary automata from a finite set of component types if we only allow loop-free synthesis, just as there is no finite set of integers from which all other integers can be built by multiplication (since there are infinitely many prime numbers) but all integers can be built from 1 and -1 by addition. The proof of this would take us too far afield in an introductory text such as this. Here we simply present a few examples of what *can* be achieved with loop-free composition of machines. In particular, we shall give concrete expression to our study of permutations and (in the next section) of normal subgroups.

Let us restate the definitions given in Section 2–4 of serial and parallel connection of machines (Figure 5–5) in a (slightly restricted) form suitable for the present theory.

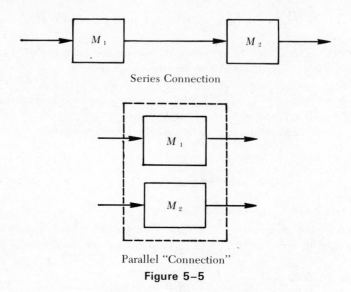

Series Connection

Parallel "Connection"
Figure 5–5

DEFINITION 2

The **series connection** of two machines $M_1 = (Q_1, X_1, Y_1, \delta_1, \beta_1)$ and $M_2 = (Q_2, X_2, Y_2, \delta_2, \beta_2)$ for which $Y_1 = X_2$ is the machine

$$M_s = (Q_1 \times Q_2, X_1, Y_2, \delta, \beta)$$

where

$$\delta((q, q'), x) = (\delta_1(q, x), \delta_2(q', \beta_1(q)))$$

and

$$\beta((q, q')) = \beta_2(q')$$ ○

DEFINITION 3

The **parallel "connection"** of two machines $M_1 = (Q_1, X_1, Y_1, \delta_1, \beta_1)$ and $M_2 = (Q_2, X_2, Y_2, \delta_2, \beta_2)$ is the machine

$$M_p = (Q_1 \times Q_2, X_1 \times X_2, Y_1 \times Y_2, \delta, \beta)$$

where

$$\delta((q, q'), (x, x')) = (\delta_1(q, x), \delta_2(q', x'))$$

and
$$\beta((q, q')) = (\beta_1(q), \beta_2(q'))$$ ○

Recall that, given a group G, we define the machine $M(G)$ of the group to be (Q, X, Y, δ, β), where

$$Q = X = Y = G$$

and
$$\delta(q, x) = q \cdot x \in G$$
$$\beta(q) = q \in G$$.

It will be seen in Section 5-3 that the monoid of the dynamics of $M(G)$ is a group isomorphic to G.

Example 3

To construct $M(\mathbf{Z}_3)$, we select

$$Q = X = Y = \mathbf{Z}_3 = \{0, 1, 2\}$$

and insist that

$$\delta(0, 0) = 0 \qquad \delta(1, 0) = 1 \qquad \delta(2, 0) = 2$$
$$\delta(0, 1) = 1 \qquad \delta(1, 1) = 2 \qquad \delta(2, 1) = 0$$
$$\delta(0, 2) = 2 \qquad \delta(1, 2) = 0 \qquad \delta(2, 2) = 1$$

The resulting state graph is shown in Figure 5-6.

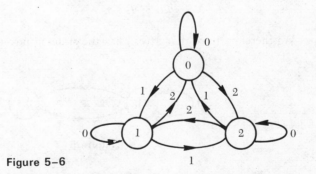

Figure 5-6

To double-check that the monoid (of the dynamics) of this machine is indeed isomorphic to $\mathbf{Z}_3$, we form Table 5-4.

Table 5-4

δ_w^* $\backslash$ q	0	1	2	
δ_Λ^*	0	1	2	
δ_0^*	0	1	2	
δ_1^*	1	2	0	
δ_2^*	2	0	1	
δ_{00}^*	0	1	$2 \Rightarrow \delta_{00}^* = \delta_0^*$	
δ_{01}^*	1	2	$0 \Rightarrow \delta_{01}^* = \delta_1^*$	
δ_{02}^*	2	0	$1 \Rightarrow \delta_{02}^* = \delta_2^*$	
δ_{10}^*	1	2	$0 \Rightarrow \delta_{10}^* = \delta_1^*$	
δ_{11}^*	2	0	$1 \Rightarrow \delta_{11}^* = \delta_2^*$	
δ_{12}^*	0	1	$2 \Rightarrow \delta_{12}^* = \delta_0^*$	
δ_{20}^*	2	0	$1 \Rightarrow \delta_{20}^* = \delta_2^*$	
δ_{21}^*	0	1	$2 \Rightarrow \delta_{21}^* = \delta_0^*$	
δ_{22}^*	1	2	$0 \Rightarrow \delta_{22}^* = \delta_1^*$	

It should now be quite apparent that the monoid of this machine is isomorphic to $\mathbf{Z}_3$. ◊

Example 4

Define the machine $M(\mathbf{Z}_2)$ by $M(\mathbf{Z}_2) = (Q, X, Y, \delta, \beta)$

where $\qquad\qquad Q = X = Y = \{0, 1\}$

and $\qquad\qquad \delta(q, x) = q \oplus w$ (addition modulo 2)

$$\beta(q) = q$$

We therefore have that $M(\mathbf{Z}_2)$ has the state-output graph of Figure 5-7.

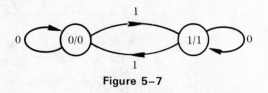

Figure 5-7

The parallel connection of two copies of $M(\mathbf{Z}_2)$ has the state-output graph of Figure 5-8. From this graph, let us construct Table 5-5, describing δ_w^*:

Table 5-5

δ_w^* \ q, q'	$0, 0$	$0, 1$	$1, 0$	$1, 1$
δ_Λ^*	$0, 0$	$0, 1$	$1, 0$	$1, 1$
$\delta_{0,0}^*$	$0, 0$	$0, 1$	$1, 0$	$1, 1 \Rightarrow \delta_{0,0}^* = \delta_\Lambda^*$
$\delta_{0,1}^*$	$0, 1$	$0, 0$	$1, 1$	$1, 0$
$\delta_{1,0}^*$	$1, 0$	$1, 1$	$0, 0$	$0, 1$
$\delta_{1,1}^*$	$1, 1$	$1, 0$	$0, 1$	$0, 0$
$\delta_{(0,0)(0,0)}^*$	$0, 0$	$0, 1$	$1, 0$	$1, 1 \Rightarrow \delta_{(0,0)(0,0)}^* = \delta_{0,0}^*$
$\delta_{(0,0)(0,1)}^*$	$0, 1$	$0, 0$	$1, 1$	$1, 0 \Rightarrow \delta_{(0,0)(0,1)}^* = \delta_{0,1}^*$
$\delta_{(0,0)(1,0)}^*$	$1, 0$	$1, 1$	$0, 0$	$0, 1 \Rightarrow \delta_{(0,0)(1,0)}^* = \delta_{1,0}^*$
$\delta_{(0,0)(1,1)}^*$	$1, 1$	$1, 0$	$0, 1$	$0, 0 \Rightarrow \delta_{(0,0)(1,1)}^* = \delta_{1,1}^*$
$\delta_{(0,1)(0,0)}^*$	$0, 1$	$0, 0$	$1, 1$	$1, 0 \Rightarrow \delta_{(0,1)(0,0)}^* = \delta_{0,1}^*$
$\delta_{(0,1)(0,1)}^*$	$0, 0$	$0, 1$	$1, 0$	$1, 1 \Rightarrow \delta_{(0,1)(0,1)}^* = \delta_{0,0}^*$
$\delta_{(0,1)(1,0)}^*$	$1, 1$	$1, 0$	$0, 1$	$0, 0 \Rightarrow \delta_{(0,1)(1,0)}^* = \delta_{1,1}^*$
$\delta_{(0,1)(1,1)}^*$	$1, 0$	$1, 1$	$0, 0$	$0, 1 \Rightarrow \delta_{(0,1)(1,1)}^* = \delta_{1,0}^*$
$\delta_{(1,0)(0,0)}^*$	$1, 0$	$1, 1$	$0, 0$	$0, 1 \Rightarrow \delta_{(1,0)(0,0)}^* = \delta_{1,0}^*$
$\delta_{(1,0)(0,1)}^*$	$1, 1$	$1, 0$	$0, 1$	$0, 0 \Rightarrow \delta_{(1.0)(0.1)}^* = \delta_{1,1}^*$
$\delta_{(1,0)(1,0)}^*$	$0, 0$	$0, 1$	$1, 0$	$1, 1 \Rightarrow \delta_{(1,0)(1,0)}^* = \delta_{0,0}^*$
$\delta_{(1,0)(1,1)}^*$	$0, 1$	$0, 0$	$1, 1$	$1, 0 \Rightarrow \delta_{(1,0)(1,1)}^* = \delta_{0,1}^*$
$\delta_{(1,1)(0,0)}^*$	$1, 1$	$1, 0$	$0, 1$	$0, 0 \Rightarrow \delta_{(1,1)(0,0)}^* = \delta_{1,1}^*$
$\delta_{(1,1)(0,1)}^*$	$1, 0$	$1, 1$	$0, 0$	$0, 1 \Rightarrow \delta_{(1,1)(0,1)}^* = \delta_{1,0}^*$
$\delta_{(1,1)(1,0)}^*$	$0, 1$	$0, 0$	$1, 1$	$1, 0 \Rightarrow \delta_{(1,1)(1,0)}^* = \delta_{0,1}^*$
$\delta_{(1,1)(1,1)}^*$	$0, 0$	$0, 1$	$1, 0$	$1, 1 \Rightarrow \delta_{(1,1)(1,1)}^* = \delta_{0,0}^*$

Thus, the monoid of the automaton is described by Table 5-6.

Table 5-6

$\diamond$	$\delta_{0,0}^*$	$\delta_{0,1}^*$	$\delta_{1,0}^*$	$\delta_{1,1}^*$
$\delta_{0,0}^*$	$\delta_{0,0}^*$	$\delta_{0,1}^*$	$\delta_{1,0}^*$	$\delta_{1,1}^*$
$\delta_{0,1}^*$	$\delta_{0,1}^*$	$\delta_{0,0}^*$	$\delta_{1,1}^*$	$\delta_{1,0}^*$
$\delta_{1,0}^*$	$\delta_{1,0}^*$	$\delta_{1,1}^*$	$\delta_{0,0}^*$	$\delta_{0,1}^*$
$\delta_{1,1}^*$	$\delta_{1,1}^*$	$\delta_{1,0}^*$	$\delta_{0,1}^*$	$\delta_{0,0}^*$

Note that this monoid is actually a group, and the group is isomorphic to $\mathbf{Z}_2 \times \mathbf{Z}_2$. In general, if $M(G_1)$ and $M(G_2)$ are the machines of groups G_1 and G_2, respectively, then the monoid of the parallel "connection" of them is isomorphic to the direct product group $G_1 \times G_2$. (See Exercise 5.) $\Diamond$

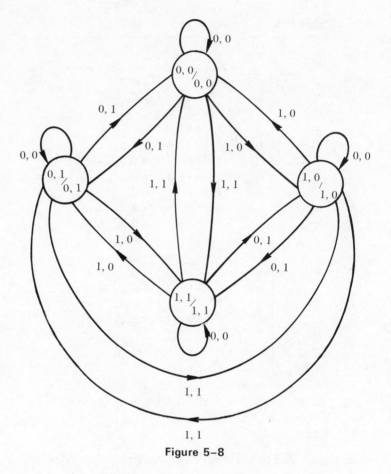

Figure 5-8

Example 5

The series connection of two copies of $M(\mathbf{Z}_2)$ has the state-output graph shown in Figure 5-9. In this case, δ_w^* is described by Table 5-7.

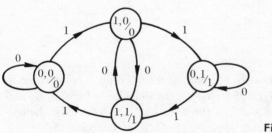

Figure 5-9

Table 5–7

δ_w^* \ q, q'	$0, 0$	$0, 1$	$1, 0$	$1, 1$
δ_Λ^*	$0, 0$	$0, 1$	$1, 0$	$1, 1$
δ_0^*	$0, 0$	$0, 1$	$1, 1$	$1, 0$
δ_1^*	$1, 0$	$1, 1$	$0, 1$	$0, 0$
δ_{00}^*	$0, 0$	$0, 1$	$1, 0$	$1, 1 \Rightarrow \delta_{00}^* = \delta_\Lambda^*$
δ_{01}^*	$1, 0$	$1, 1$	$0, 0$	$0, 1$
δ_{10}^*	$1, 1$	$1, 0$	$0, 1$	$0, 0$
δ_{11}^*	$0, 1$	$0, 0$	$1, 1$	$1, 0$
δ_{000}^*	$0, 0$	$0, 1$	$1, 1$	$1, 0 \Rightarrow \delta_{000}^* = \delta_0^*$
δ_{001}^*	$1, 0$	$1, 1$	$0, 1$	$0, 0 \Rightarrow \delta_{001}^* = \delta_1^*$
δ_{010}^*	$1, 1$	$1, 0$	$0, 0$	$0, 1$
δ_{011}^*	$0, 1$	$0, 0$	$1, 0$	$1, 1$
δ_{100}^*	$1, 0$	$1, 1$	$0, 1$	$0, 0 \Rightarrow \delta_{100}^* = \delta_1^*$
δ_{101}^*	$0, 0$	$0, 1$	$1, 1$	$1, 0 \Rightarrow \delta_{101}^* = \delta_0^*$
δ_{110}^*	$0, 1$	$0, 0$	$1, 0$	$1, 1 \Rightarrow \delta_{110}^* = \delta_{011}^*$
δ_{111}^*	$1, 1$	$1, 0$	$0, 0$	$0, 1 \Rightarrow \delta_{111}^* = \delta_{010}^*$

From the information contained in this table, we may form Table 5–8, describing the monoid of the series machine.

Table 5–8

$\diamond$	δ_Λ^*	δ_0^*	δ_1^*	δ_{01}^*	δ_{10}^*	δ_{11}^*	δ_{010}^*	δ_{011}^*
δ_Λ^*	δ_Λ^*	δ_0^*	δ_1^*	δ_{01}^*	δ_{10}^*	δ_{11}^*	δ_{010}^*	δ_{011}^*
δ_0^*	δ_0^*	δ_Λ^*	δ_{01}^*	δ_1^*	δ_{010}^*	δ_{011}^*	δ_{10}^*	δ_{11}^*
δ_1^*	δ_1^*	δ_{10}^*	δ_{11}^*	δ_0^*	δ_{011}^*	δ_{010}^*	δ_Λ^*	δ_{01}^*
δ_{01}^*	δ_{01}^*	δ_{010}^*	δ_{011}^*	δ_Λ^*	δ_{11}^*	δ_{10}^*	δ_0^*	δ_1^*
δ_{10}^*	δ_{10}^*	δ_1^*	δ_0^*	δ_{11}^*	δ_Λ^*	δ_{01}^*	δ_{011}^*	δ_{010}^*
δ_{11}^*	δ_{11}^*	δ_{011}^*	δ_{010}^*	δ_{10}^*	δ_{01}^*	δ_Λ^*	δ_1^*	δ_0^*
δ_{010}^*	δ_{010}^*	δ_{01}^*	δ_Λ^*	δ_{011}^*	δ_0^*	δ_1^*	δ_{11}^*	δ_{10}^*
δ_{011}^*	δ_{011}^*	δ_{11}^*	δ_{10}^*	δ_{010}^*	δ_1^*	δ_0^*	δ_{01}^*	δ_Λ^*

Thus, we see that the monoid of the series machine is again a group, but with *eight* distinct elements.   ◊

This example emphasizes that the series connection can have a larger monoid than the parallel connection. This is a consequence of the fact that the action of an input depends upon the state of the first machine.

The connection of machines in series and parallel may be subsumed in the following general way of combining machines, which explicitly includes encoding and decoding maps.

DEFINITION 4

Given any two (state-output) machines $M' = (Q', X', Y', \delta', \beta')$ and $M = (Q, X, Y, \delta, \beta)$, and a triple $K = (\eta, \mu, \gamma)$ comprising maps

$$\eta: \widetilde{X} \to X, \ \mu: \widetilde{X} \times Y \to X' \text{ and } \gamma: Y \times Y' \to \widetilde{Y},$$

we define the **cascade** of M' and M with **connection** K to be the machine

$$M' \ominus_K M = (Q' \times Q, \widetilde{X}, \widetilde{Y}, \delta_K, \beta_K)$$

where (Figure 5–10) δ_K and β_K are given by

$$\delta_K[(q', q), \widetilde{x}] = [\delta'(q', \mu(\widetilde{x}, \beta(q))), \delta(q, \eta(\widetilde{x}))]$$
$$\beta_K(q', q) = \gamma(\beta'(q'), \beta(q)) \qquad\qquad\qquad \bigcirc$$

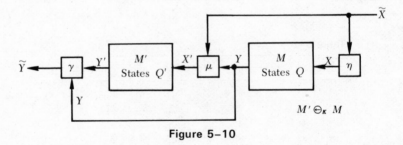

Figure 5–10

To get *series* connection (with encoders) (Figure 5–11), we make μ independent of $\widetilde{X}$ and γ independent of Y; to get *parallel* connection (with en-

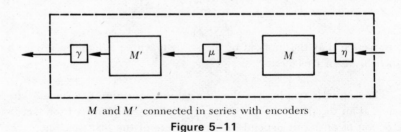

M and M' connected in series with encoders

Figure 5–11

coders) (Figure 5–12), we set $\alpha(\tilde{x}) = (\eta(\tilde{x}), \mu(\tilde{x}))$—i.e., μ is independent of Y. Clearly, there is *no* way of introducing *feedback* loops into a collection of

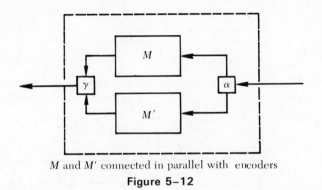

M and *M'* connected in parallel with encoders

Figure 5–12

automata by cascading them. The precise notion of loop-free composition that we shall employ, then, is that of repeated formation of cascades (which thus includes symbol-by-symbol encodings and decodings).

As an example of the use of cascades, let us briefly study a class of machines which have proved important in automata theory—machines for which an input resets the machine to a state determined by that input, or else the input leaves all states unchanged:

DEFINITION 5

M is an **identity-reset machine** if the output of the machine equals its state and if, for each $x \in X$, the map $\delta(\cdot, x): Q \to Q: q \mapsto \delta(q, x)$ is either the identity map on Q, or else is a constant ($=$ reset) map.   ○

Now let us consider the two-state identity-reset machine shown in Figure 5–13. This **"flip-flop"** F has states $\{q_0, q_1\}$, and inputs $\{e, x_0, x_1\}$ with the actions:

$$\delta(q, e) = q \text{ where } e \text{ is the identity input}$$

$$\delta(q, x_i) = q_i \text{ where } x_i \text{ is the "reset to } q_i\text{" input}$$

Figure 5–13   The state-output graph for the flip-flop.

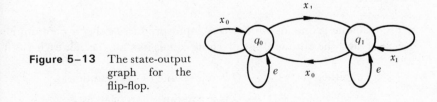

PROPOSITION 1

Any identity-reset machine may be simulated by a repeated cascade of m copies of the "flip-flop" F.

Construction

We only use encoding, decoding, and parallel connection (Figure 5–14). If M is an n-state identity-reset machine, choose m so that $n \leq 2^m$, and place

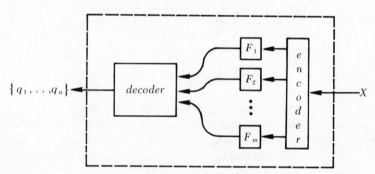

Figure 5–14   Identity-reset machine simulated by a parallel connection of flip-flops.

m copies of F in parallel to obtain F^m. We select n of the 2^m states of F^m at our whim and decode these as the outputs ($=$ states) $q_1, \ldots, q_n$ of M. If an input x to M acts as an identity, we encode it as the identity input to all m copies of F. If x acts as a reset to state q_i, we encode it as that configuration of resets which will cause F^m to go into the state which will be decoded as q_i. □

We shall next see how to decompose machines whose inputs either permute the states or reset them:

DEFINITION 6

A **PR machine** is one for which every input produces either a permutation or a reset, and the output of the machine equals its state; i.e., for each $x \in X$,

$$\text{either } \delta(\,\cdot\,, x): Q \to Q \text{ is one-to-one (a permutation)}$$
$$\text{or } \delta(\,\cdot\,, x): Q \to Q \text{ is a constant map (a reset)}$$

The permutations generate a group, called the **group** of the PR machine, which is not quite the monoid of the machine, but is obtained from it by deleting resets. ○

Example 6

Consider the machine of Figure 5-15.

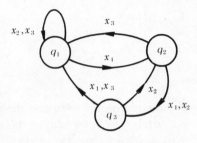

Figure 5-15

Since $\delta(q_1, x_1) = q_2$, $\delta(q_2, x_1) = q_3$, and $\delta(q_3, x_1) = q_1$, then $\delta(\cdot, x_1)$ is a permutation.

Since $\delta(q_1, x_2) = q_1$, $\delta(q_2, x_2) = q_3$, and $\delta(q_3, x_2) = q_2$, then $\delta(\cdot, x_2)$ is also a permutation.

Since $\delta(q_1, x_3) = q_1$, $\delta(q_2, x_3) = q_1$, and $\delta(q_3, x_3) = q_1$, then $\delta(\cdot, x_3)$ is a reset to q_1.

Thus, the given machine is a PR machine. To obtain the explicit description of the monoid of the machine, we construct Table 5-9.

Table 5-9

δ_w^* $\quad q$	q_1	q_2	q_3
δ_Λ^*	q_1	q_2	q_3
$\delta_{x_1}^*$	q_2	q_3	q_1
$\delta_{x_2}^*$	q_1	q_3	q_2
$\delta_{x_3}^*$	q_1	q_1	q_1
$\delta_{x_1 x_1}^*$	q_3	q_1	q_2
$\delta_{x_1 x_2}^*$	q_3	q_2	q_1
$\delta_{x_1 x_3}^*$	q_1	q_1	$q_1 \Rightarrow \delta_{x_1 x_3}^* = \delta_{x_3}^*$
$\delta_{x_2 x_1}^*$	q_2	q_1	q_3
$\delta_{x_2 x_2}^*$	q_1	q_2	$q_3 \Rightarrow \delta_{x_2 x_2}^* = \delta_\Lambda^*$
$\delta_{x_2 x_3}^*$	q_1	q_1	$q_1 \Rightarrow \delta_{x_2 x_3}^* = \delta_{x_3}^*$
$\delta_{x_3 x_1}^*$	q_2	q_2	q_2
$\delta_{x_3 x_2}^*$	q_1	q_1	$q_1 \Rightarrow \delta_{x_3 x_2}^* = \delta_{x_3}^*$
$\delta_{x_3 x_3}^*$	q_1	q_1	$q_1 \Rightarrow \delta_{x_3 x_3}^* = \delta_{x_3}^*$
$\delta_{x_3 x_1 x_1}^*$	q_3	q_3	q_3

Therefore, the monoid of the machine is described by Table 5–10, where, for the sake of convenience, we will denote δ_w^* simply by w.

Table 5–10

$\diamond$	Λ	x_1	x_2	x_3	x_1x_1	x_1x_2	x_2x_1	x_3x_1	$x_3x_1x_1$
Λ	Λ	x_1	x_2	x_3	x_1x_2	x_1x_2	x_2x_1	x_3x_1	$x_3x_1x_1$
x_1	x_1	x_1x_1	x_1x_2	x_3	Λ	x_2x_1	x_2	x_3x_1	$x_3x_1x_1$
x_2	x_2	x_2x_1	Λ	x_3	x_1x_2	x_1x_1	x_1	x_3x_1	$x_3x_1x_1$
x_3	x_3	x_3x_1	x_3	x_3	$x_3x_1x_1$	$x_3x_1x_1$	x_3x_1	x_3x_1	$x_3x_1x_1$
x_1x_1	x_1x_1	Λ	x_2x_1	x_3	x_1	x_2	x_1x_2	x_3x_1	$x_3x_1x_1$
x_1x_2	x_1x_2	x_2	x_1	x_3	x_2x_1	Λ	x_1x_2	x_3x_1	$x_3x_1x_1$
x_2x_1	x_2x_1	x_1x_2	x_1x_1	x_3	x_2	x_1	Λ	x_3x_1	$x_3x_1x_1$
x_3x_1	x_3x_1	$x_3x_1x_1$	$x_3x_1x_1$	x_3	x_3	x_2x_1	x_2	x_3x_1	$x_3x_1x_1$
$x_3x_1x_1$	$x_3x_1x_1$	x_3	x_2x_1	x_3	x_3x_1	x_2	x_1x_2	x_3x_1	$x_3x_1x_1$

By eliminating the rows and the columns that correspond to resets (i.e., x_3, x_3x_1, and $x_3x_1x_1$), we obtain the description of the group of the given *PR* machine. Note that this group is isomorphic to $\mathcal{S}_3$. $\qquad\diamond$

THEOREM 2

If M is a *PR* machine with permutation group G, then M can be simulated by a cascade of $M(G)$ and an identity-reset machine with the same state set as M.

Proof

In Figure 5–16, *IR* is an identity-reset machine with state set Q, the same as that of M. The input set of *IR* is $\{e\} \cup Q$. The identity input of *IR* is

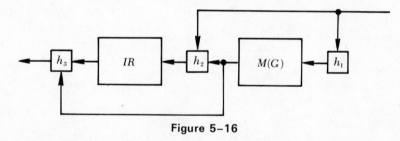

Figure 5–16

e, while input $q \neq e$ resets *IR* to state q. $M(G)$ is the machine of group G. Our task is to describe the codes h_1, h_2, and h_3 in such a way that the cascade simulates our *PR* machine M.

First we recall that G is the group part of the monoid of M. Thus, for each $g \in G$ and each $q \in Q$ the result $q \cdot g$ of acting upon q with g is well-defined. Hence, let us define h_3 in terms of this action by

$$h_3 : Q \times G \to Q : (q, g) \mapsto q \cdot g$$

Now, suppose $M(G)$ is in state g and IR is in state q, encoding the state $q \cdot g$ of M. Then we must specify h_1 and h_2 for two kinds of inputs:

(i) The action of input x upon M is the permutation g' from G. Clearly, if we set $h_1(x) = g'$ and $h_2(g, x) = e$, then $M(G)$ will change state from g to gg', IR will remain in state q, and the overall system output $h_3(q, gg') = q \cdot gg'$ will equal $(q \cdot g) \cdot g'$, the result of acting upon the previous state $q \cdot g$ with the permutation g', just as desired.

(ii) The action of input x upon M is to reset M to state $\widehat{q}$. Let us take $h_1(x)$ to be 1, the identity of the group G, so that $M(G)$ remains in state g. If $h_2(g, x) \neq e$, then IR will reset to state $h_2(g, x)$, and the overall system output will be $h_3(h_2(g, x), g) = h_2(g, x) \cdot g$. But we require that this output equal the desired state $\widehat{q}$ of M. However, $h_2(g, x) \cdot g = \widehat{q}$ is satisfied if we take $h_2(g, x) = \widehat{q} \cdot g^{-1}$, the result of acting upon the state $\widehat{q}$ with the permutation g^{-1} from G.

Hence, the cascade with h_1 and h_2 defined as below does indeed simulate M:

$$h_1(x) = \begin{cases} g' & \text{if } \delta_x^* = g' \in G \\ 1 & \text{if } \delta_x^* = \text{reset to } \widehat{q} \end{cases}$$

$$h_2(g, x) = \begin{cases} e & \text{if } \delta_x^* \in G \\ \widehat{q} \cdot g^{-1} & \text{if } \delta_x^* = \text{reset to } \widehat{q} \end{cases} \qquad \square$$

EXERCISES FOR SECTION 5-2

1. Given two semigroups, verify that the componentwise operation of their direct product is associative.

2. Construct the addition table for $\mathbf{Z}_2 \times \mathbf{Z}_3$. Does this group have the same structure as the symmetric group $\mathcal{S}_3$?

3. Prove that if G_1 and G_2 are abelian groups, then the direct product group $G_1 \times G_2$ is abelian.

4. Determine the state graph for $M(\mathbf{Z}_2 \times \mathbf{Z}_3)$.

5. Prove that if S_1 is the monoid of machine M_1, and S_2 is the monoid of M_2, then the parallel connection of M_1 and M_2 has as its monoid the direct product, $S_1 \times S_2$.

6. Using flip-flops, simulate the identity-reset machine of Figure 5-17.

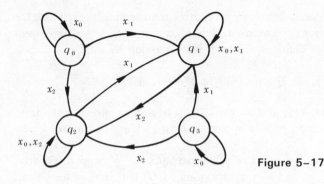

Figure 5–17

7. Determine the group of the *PR* machine shown in Figure 5–18.

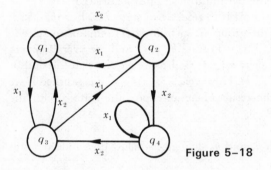

Figure 5–18

5–3   Subsemigroups, Submonoids and Subgroups

We now want to make precise the sense in which, at the end of Section 5–1, we noted that $\{1_3, b, c\}$ formed a part of the group $\mathcal{S}_3$. We note that in specifying $\mathcal{S}_3$ as a group, we specified three things: $\cdot$, 1_3, and $^{-1}$. The crucial property of $\{1_3, b, c\}$ was that it contained the composite of any two of its elements, it contained 1_3, and it contained the inverse of any of its elements. Thus, we could regard $(\{1_3, b, c\}, \cdot, 1_3, ^{-1})$ as a group simply by pretending that $\cdot$ and $^{-1}$ were operators on $\{1_3, b, c\}$ rather than on $\mathcal{S}_3$. This suggests the following definition:

DEFINITION 1

Let $m: S^n \to S$ be an *n*-ary operator on the set S, and let S' be a subset of S. Then we say that S' is **closed under** m if and only if $m[(S')^n] \subset S'$, that is, iff $m(s_1, s_2, \ldots, s_n) \in S'$ whenever each s_j is in S'. In this case we may define an *n*-ary operator on S' by

$$(S')^n \to S': (s_1, \ldots, s_n) \mapsto m(s_1, \ldots, s_n)$$

Usually, when no confusion can arise, we shall also label this operator by m. If $(m_1, \ldots, m_k)$ is a set of operators on S, we shall say that $S' \subset S$ is **closed under** $(m_1, \ldots, m_k)$ iff S' is closed under m_j for each $j = 1, 2, \ldots, k$.

If m is a 0-ary operator, then we may regard m as an element of S. To say that $S' \subset S$ is closed under m will then just be a fancy way of saying that $m \in S'$.   ○

With this mouthful of terminology, we may readily define the notion of a *subgroup* as our formalization of the sense in which $\{1_3, b, c\}$ is a part of $\mathcal{S}_3$.

DEFINITION 2

Let $(G, \cdot, 1, ^{-1})$ be a group, and let $H \subset G$ be closed under $(\cdot, 1, ^{-1})$. Then we call $(H, \cdot, 1, ^{-1})$ a **subgroup** of $(G, \cdot, 1, ^{-1})$. [Where the operators can be safely omitted without ambiguity, we may abbreviate the last sentence to read, "Then we call H a **subgroup** of G."] We denote this by $H < G$.   ○

Clearly, we may make corresponding definitions for monoids and semigroups:

DEFINITION 3

Let $(S, \cdot, 1)$ be a monoid, and let $H \subset S$ be closed under $(\cdot, 1)$. Then we call H a **submonoid** of S. We denote this by $H < S$.

Let $(S, \cdot)$ be a semigroup, and let $H \subset S$ be closed under $\cdot$. Then we call H a **subsemigroup** of S. We denote this by $H < S$.   ○

Example 1

(i) Since X^* is a semigroup under concatenation, as is X^+, and since $X^+ \subset X^*$, then X^+ is a subsemigroup of X^*.

(ii) Both $(\mathbf{Z}, +, 0)$ and $(\mathbf{N}, +, 0)$ are monoids. Since $\mathbf{N} \subset \mathbf{Z}$, then $\mathbf{N}$ is a submonoid of $\mathbf{Z}$. Similarly, $(\mathbf{N}, \cdot, 1)$ is a submonoid of $(\mathbf{Z}, \cdot, 1)$.

(iii) The group $(\mathbf{Z}, +, 0, -)$ is a subgroup of $(\mathbf{Q}, +, 0, -)$.

(iv) Consider the group $\mathbf{Z}_4$. Modulo 4 addition is given by

+	0	1	2	3
0	0	1	2	3
1	1	2	3	0
2	2	3	0	1
3	3	0	1	2

Since for the subset $\{0, 2\}$ we have

+	0	2
0	0	2
2	2	0

and

n	$-n$
0	0
2	2

$\{0, 2\}$ is a subgroup of $\mathbf{Z}_4$. However, for $\{0, 1\}$ we have

+	0	1
0	0	1
1	1	2

so $\{0, 1\}$ is not closed under modulo 4 addition, and hence is not a subgroup of $\mathbf{Z}_4$.

If S is a group (or monoid, or semigroup), then S is a **trivial** subgroup (or submonoid, or subsemigroup, respectively) of itself. On the other hand, if S is a group (or monoid) having identity 1, then $\{1\}$ is also a **trivial** subgroup (or submonoid) of S. ◊

Example 2

Consider the two semigroups $(\mathbf{N}, \max)$ and $(\mathbf{Z}_+, \max)$ of $\mathbf{N}$ and $\mathbf{Z}_+$ under the maximum operation. Clearly $(\mathbf{Z}_+, \max)$ is a subsemigroup of $(\mathbf{N}, \max)$. ◊

Example 3

Note that $(\mathbf{N}, \max)$ has identity 0, while $(\mathbf{Z}_+, \max)$ has identity 1. Thus, $\mathbf{Z}_+$ admits a monoid structure $(\mathbf{Z}_+, \max, 1)$ with respect to the same binary operation which makes $(\mathbf{Z}_+, \max)$ a subsemigroup of $(\mathbf{N}, \max)$. **But BE-WARE!** $(\mathbf{Z}_+, \max, 1)$ is *not a submonoid* of $(\mathbf{N}, \max, 0)$ because $\mathbf{Z}_+$ *is not closed under* 0 (i.e., does not contain 0). Ponder this example. ◊

Given a group G (don't get upset about now using G instead of S) and a subgroup H, in order to determine whether or not H is a subgroup of G, we must verify that H is closed under ·, 1, and $^{-1}$. In many cases, however, it is not necessary to do this directly. We may take a short cut in testing for a subgroup with the use of the following important lemma.

LEMMA 1

Suppose G is a group and H is a subset of G. Then H is a subgroup of G if and only if

$$h_1 \cdot h_2^{-1} \in H \quad \text{for all } h_1, h_2 \in H$$

Proof

In order to prove this theorem, we are required to show that if H is a subgroup, then $h_1 \cdot h_2^{-1} \in H$ for all $h_1, h_2 \in H$, and vice versa.

To prove the first part, assume that H is a subgroup of G, and let $h_1, h_2 \in H$. Since H is a subgroup, then $h_2^{-1} \in H$ and hence $h_1 \cdot h_2^{-1} \in H$.

To prove the converse, assume that $h_1 \cdot h_2^{-1} \in H$ for all $h_1, h_2 \in H$. We must now show that H is a subgroup of G. For any $h \in H$, let $h_1 = h_2 = h$. Thus, $h_1 \cdot h_2^{-1} = h \cdot h^{-1} = 1 \in H$ and H has an identity. Since $1 \in H$, for any $h \in H$ we have $1 \cdot h^{-1} = h^{-1} \in H$, and each element has an inverse. For all $h_1, h_2 \in H$, since $h_2^{-1} \in H$ we have $h_1 \cdot (h_2^{-1})^{-1} = h_1 \cdot h_2 \in H$, and $\cdot$ is a binary operator on H. $\qquad\square$

Example 4

If $f: G_1 \to G_2$ is a group homomorphism, then $f(G_1)$ is a subgroup of G_2, since $f(g_1) \cdot f(g_1')^{-1} = f(g_1) \cdot f(g_1'^{-1}) = f(g_1 \cdot g_1'^{-1}) \in f(G_1)$ for all g_1, g_1' in G_1. $\lozenge$

At this point, let us introduce one more important concept.

DEFINITION 4

Suppose that G is a group, and let K be a subset of G. Then we say that the set H defined by

$$H = \{k_1 \cdot k_2 \cdot k_3 \ldots k_n \,|\, n \in \mathbf{Z}_+ \text{ and either}$$

$$k_i \in K \text{ or } k_i^{-1} \in K \text{ for } i = 1, 2, 3, \ldots, n\}$$

is the set **generated** by K, and we write $H = \langle K \rangle$. $\qquad\bigcirc$

Example 5

Referring to the symmetric group $\mathcal{S}_3$ given in Example 5–1–11, suppose that $K = \{b\}$. Then the elements of $H = \langle K \rangle = \langle \{b\} \rangle$ are:

$$b$$
$$b^{-1} = c$$
$$b \cdot b = c$$
$$b \cdot b^{-1} = 1_3$$
$$b^{-1} \cdot b = 1_3$$
$$b \cdot b \cdot b = 1_3$$
$$b \cdot b \cdot b^{-1} = b$$
$$b \cdot b^{-1} \cdot b = b$$
$$b \cdot b^{-1} \cdot b^{-1} = c$$

etc.

Thus, $\langle \{b\} \rangle = \{1_3, b, c\}$.

For the case when $K = \{b, d\}$, we have all the elements in the list above (1_3, b, and c) as well as

$$d$$
$$d^{-1} = d$$
$$d \cdot d = 1_3$$
$$b \cdot d = e$$
$$d \cdot b = f$$

and since we have exhausted all the elements of $\mathcal{S}_3$, we have $\langle \{b, d\} \rangle = \mathcal{S}_3$.

◇

For the sake of notational convenience, from now on, if $K = \{a_1, a_2, \ldots, a_r\}$, instead of writing $\langle K \rangle = \langle \{a_1, a_2, \ldots, a_r\} \rangle$ we will simply write $\langle K \rangle = \langle a_1, a_2, \ldots, a_r \rangle$.

Example 6

Let $G = \mathbf{Z}_6$, the group of integers modulo 6 under addition. The elements of $\langle 1 \rangle$ are:

$$1$$
$$-1 = 5$$
$$1 + 1 = 2$$

$$1 + (-1) = 0$$
$$-1 + 1 = 0$$
$$-1 + (-1) = 5 + 5 = 4$$
$$1 + 1 + 1 = 3$$

and since this exhausts $\mathbf{Z}_6$, we have $\langle 1 \rangle = \mathbf{Z}_6$.
The elements of $\langle 2 \rangle$ are:

$$2$$
$$-2 = 4$$
$$2 + (-2) = 0$$
$$-2 + 2 = 0$$
$$2 + 2 = 4$$
$$2 + 2 + 2 = 0$$
$$2 + 2 + (-2) = 2$$

etc.

Thus, $\langle 2 \rangle = \{0, 2, 4\}$. $\qquad\qquad\qquad\qquad\qquad\qquad\qquad\qquad \Diamond$

Studying the previous examples, we note that in each case $\langle K \rangle$ is a subgroup of G. The reason is simple and is given as follows:

THEOREM 2

Suppose that G is a group and K is a subset of G. Then $\langle K \rangle$ is a subgroup of G.

Proof

Let $H = \langle K \rangle$ and let $h_1, h_2 \in H$. Thus, we can write h_1 and h_2 in the form

$$h_1 = k_{11} \cdot k_{12} \cdot k_{13} \cdot \ldots \cdot k_{1n}$$
$$h_2 = k_{21} \cdot k_{22} \cdot k_{23} \cdot \ldots \cdot k_{2m}$$

where either $k_{1i} \in K$ or $k_{1i}^{-1} \in K$ for $i = 1, 2, \ldots, n$ and either $k_{2j} \in K$ or $k_{2j}^{-1} \in K$ for $j = 1, 2, \ldots, m$. Therefore,

$$h_1 \cdot h_2^{-1} = (k_{11} \cdot k_{12} \cdot k_{13} \cdot \ldots \cdot k_{1n}) \cdot (k_{21} \cdot k_{22} \cdot k_{23} \cdot \ldots \cdot k_{2m})^{-1}$$
$$= k_{11} \cdot k_{12} \cdot k_{13} \cdot \ldots \cdot k_{1n} \cdot k_{2m}^{-1} k_{2(m-1)}^{-1} \cdot k_{2(m-2)}^{-1} \cdot \ldots \cdot k_{21}^{-1}$$

and thus, by the definition of $\langle K \rangle$, $h_1 \cdot h_2^{-1} \in \langle K \rangle$. Hence, $\langle K \rangle$ is a subgroup of G.   ☐

Exercise 12 gives an alternative definition for $\langle K \rangle$, the subgroup generated by K.

If G is a group and K is a subset of G, we have already seen that $\langle K \rangle$, the set generated by K, is a subgroup of G. Let us now consider the special case where K consists of a single element $g \in G$.

DEFINITION 5

Suppose that G is a group, and $g \in G$. Then we call $\langle g \rangle$ the **cyclic subgroup** generated by g.   ◯

Referring to the definition of the subgroup generated by K, we have that any element of $\langle g \rangle$ is of the form of either

$$g \cdot g^{-1} = 1$$

or

$$g \cdot g \cdot g \cdot \cdots \cdot g$$

or

$$g^{-1} \cdot g^{-1} \cdot g^{-1} \cdot \cdots \cdot g^{-1}$$

We denote the product of g with itself n times by g^n. Thus, the product of g^{-1} with itself n times is denoted by $(g^{-1})^n$. Consequently, by the associative law, we have that

$$(g^{-1})^n \cdot g^n = (g^{-1} \cdot g^{-1} \cdot g^{-1} \cdot \cdots \cdot g^{-1}) \cdot (g \cdot g \cdot g \cdot \cdots \cdot g) = 1$$

Hence, $(g^{-1})^n = (g^n)^{-1}$. We may therefore unambiguously denote both $(g^{-1})^n$ and $(g^n)^{-1}$ by g^{-n}.

Note: For the case that G is a group under addition, instead of writing g^n, $(g^{-1})^n$, $(g^n)^{-1}$, and g^{-n}, we write ng, $n(-g)$, $-(ng)$, and $-ng$, respectively.

Example 7

Suppose that $G = \mathbf{Z}_{12}$. Then the elements of $\langle 3 \rangle$, the cyclic subgroup generated by 3, are:

$$3$$
$$-3 = 9$$
$$3 + 3 = 6$$
$$-3 + (-3) = -6 = 6$$

$$-3 + 3 = 0$$
$$3 + 3 + 3 = 9$$
$$-3 + (-3) + (-3) = -9 = 3$$
$$3 + 3 + 3 + 3 = 0$$
$$-3 + (-3) + (-3) + (-3) = 0$$

Hence, $\langle 3 \rangle = \{0, 3, 6, 9\}$. ◊

DEFINITION 6

If G is a group, and if $g \in G$, then the smallest positive integer m (if it exists) such that $g^m = 1$ is called the **order** of g. ○

Clearly, such an integer exists if G is finite; to see this, suppose the contrary. Then for every integer i and j such that $i \neq j$, we have $g^i \neq g^j$, since $g^i = g^j \Rightarrow g^{i-j} = 1$, which contradicts our supposition. But, if $g^i \neq g^j$ for all distinct integers i and j, it must be true that G is infinite. This also contradicts our supposition. Thus, the integer m must exist, and clearly $m \leq |G|$ (Exercise 13).

Example 8

The permutation $\rho = \begin{pmatrix} 0 & 1 & 2 & 3 \\ 3 & 2 & 0 & 1 \end{pmatrix}$ has order 4, since $\rho^2 = \begin{pmatrix} 0 & 1 & 2 & 3 \\ 1 & 0 & 3 & 2 \end{pmatrix}$; $\rho^3 = \begin{pmatrix} 0 & 1 & 2 & 3 \\ 2 & 3 & 1 & 0 \end{pmatrix}$; and $\rho^4 = \begin{pmatrix} 0 & 1 & 2 & 3 \\ 0 & 1 & 2 & 3 \end{pmatrix}$, the identity. ◊

THEOREM 3

If the element g of the group G has order m, then

$$|\langle g \rangle| = m$$

Proof

Assume that $g^i = g^j$ for some i, j with $1 \leq i < j \leq m$. Then $g^{i-j} = 1$, contradicting the assumption that m is the order of g. Thus, the elements g^1, g^2, $g^3, \ldots, g^m = 1$ are distinct, and hence, $|\langle g \rangle| \geq m$. But it is clear that these elements form a group, for (given any i and j with $1 \leq j \leq m$) we have that $g^i \cdot (g^j)^{-1} = g^{i-j}$, and we then have either that $j > i$ so that $1 \leq i - j \leq m$;

or that $j \leq i$ so that

$$g^{i-j} = 1 \cdot g^{i-j} = g^m \cdot g^{i-j} = g^{m+i-j}$$

with $1 \leq m + i - j \leq m$.   □

By selecting any element g in a group G, we can form the cyclic subgroup $\langle g \rangle$. For the case $g = 1$, we have the trivial subgroup $\langle 1 \rangle = \{1\}$. Conversely, certain groups have the property that there is an element that generates the other trivial subgroup (the group itself).

DEFINITION 7

Suppose that G is a (possibly infinite) group. If there exists some $g \in G$ such that $\langle g \rangle = G$, we call G a **cyclic group**. We also say that g is a **generator** of G.   ○

Example 9

For the group $\mathbf{Z}_4$, we have that

$$\langle 1 \rangle = \{0, 1, 2, 3\}$$

Thus, $\mathbf{Z}_4$ is a cyclic group, and 1 is a generator of this group. Note, in addition, that $\langle 3 \rangle = \mathbf{Z}_4$. Hence, 3 is also a generator of the group.

In general, $\mathbf{Z}_m$ is a cyclic group and 1 is a generator of the group.

Whereas $\mathbf{Z}_m$ is a finite cyclic group, $\mathbf{Z}$ is an infinite cyclic group, and again 1 is a generator of $\mathbf{Z}$.

Let us consider the nonzero elements of $\mathbf{Z}_5$ under multiplication. This multiplication table is given by

·	1	2	3	4
1	1	2	3	4
2	2	4	1	3
3	3	1	4	2
4	4	3	2	1

Having verified that the result is a group under multiplication in Exercise 5-1-3, let us consider all the cyclic subgroups of this group. We have that

$$\langle 1 \rangle = \{1\}$$
$$\langle 2 \rangle = \{2, 4, 3, 1\}$$
$$\langle 3 \rangle = \{3, 4, 2, 1\}$$
$$\langle 4 \rangle = \{4, 1\}$$

Thus, this group is cyclic and both 2 and 3 are generators. Note, however, that if we rename the elements and the operation properly:

OLD NAME	NEW NAME
·	+
1	0
2	1
3	3
4	2

we obtain

+	0	1	2	3
0	0	1	2	3
1	1	2	3	0
2	2	3	0	1
3	3	0	1	2

which is $\mathbf{Z}_3$ under addition.   ◊

It can be shown (Exercise 14) that the elements and the operations of any cyclic group with m elements can be renamed to yield $\mathbf{Z}_m$. The elements and operation of any infinite cyclic group can be renamed such that the group $\mathbf{Z}$ under addition results.

The fact that a cyclic group has an element that generates the group enables us to prove the following property of cyclic groups.

THEOREM 4

Every cyclic group is abelian.

Proof

Suppose that G is a cyclic group, and let $g_1, g_2 \in G$. Since G is cyclic, there exists $g \in G$ such that $\langle g \rangle = G$. Thus, for some i and j, we have $g_1 = g^i$ and $g_2 = g^j$. Hence,

$$g_1 \cdot g_2 = g^i \cdot g^j = g^{i+j} = g^{j+i} = g^j \cdot g^i = g_2 \cdot g_1$$

and G is abelian.   □

Note: Do not under any circumstances assume that the converse of this theorem is true. An abelian group is not necessarily cyclic:

Example 10

The Klein four-group $\mathbf{Z}_2^2$, which (compare p. 376) is described by

·	00	01	10	11
00	00	01	10	11
01	01	00	11	10
10	10	11	00	01
11	11	10	01	00

is an abelian group. However, since

$$\langle 00 \rangle = \{00\}$$
$$\langle 01 \rangle = \{00, 01\}$$
$$\langle 10 \rangle = \{00, 10\}$$
$$\langle 11 \rangle = \{00, 11\}$$

the group is not cyclic.   ◊

Although the previous theorem may have been fairly obvious, the next theorem is somewhat less obvious.

THEOREM 5

Every subgroup of a cyclic group is a cyclic subgroup.

Proof

Suppose that G is a cyclic group, and $g \in G$ is the generator of the group. Let H be a nontrivial subgroup of G. Suppose that r is the smallest positive integer for which $g^r \in H$. (Why does such an r exist?) We will show that $\langle g^r \rangle = H$.

Since $g^r \in H$, clearly $\langle g^r \rangle \subset H$. To prove the converse, let $h \in H$. Since $h \in G$, there exists an integer s such that $g^s = h$. We have three cases:

(I) s is positive.

Assume that s is not a multiple of r. Then there exists a nonnegative integer n such that

$$(n + 1)r > s > nr$$

But $(n + 1)r > s > nr \Rightarrow r > -nr + s > 0$, and since

$$\begin{aligned} g^{-nr+s} &= g^{-nr} \cdot g^s \\ &= (g^r)^{-n} \cdot g^s \\ &\in H, \end{aligned}$$

this contradicts our assumption that r is the smallest integer such that $g^r \in H$. Hence, if s is positive, then s is a multiple of r.

(II) $s = 0$.

Under this circumstance, trivially, s is a multiple of r.

(III) s is negative.

Let $q = -s$. Then q is positive and $g^q = g^{-s} = (g^s)^{-1} = h^{-1} \in H$. We repeat the reasoning of case (I) to conclude that q, and hence s, is a multiple of r.

Thus, for each $h \in H$, there exists an integer m such that

$$h = g^s = g^{rm} = (g^r)^m$$

Thus

$$H \subset \langle g^r \rangle$$

Hence, $H = \langle g^r \rangle$, and H is a cyclic subgroup of G.   □

Let us next look at some basic properties of **cyclic semigroups,** i.e., *semigroups* of the form $\{a^m \mid m \geq 1\}$, and then apply them to the study of permutations.

First, we say that an element b of a semigroup is **idempotent** if $b = b^2$. [This implies $b^m = b^n$ for all positive integers—"idem" means "same" and "potens" is power, so that "idempotent" means "all powers are the same." In a *group*, the identity is the only idempotent.] We then have the following characterization:

THEOREM 6

Let a be an element of an arbitrary semigroup S. Let $\langle a \rangle$ be the cyclic subsemigroup of S generated by a, i.e., $\{a, a^2, a^3, \ldots\}$. If $\langle a \rangle$ is infinite, then all the powers of a are distinct. If $\langle a \rangle$ is finite, there exist two positive integers, the **index** r and the **period** m of a, such that $a^r = a^{r+m}$, and

$$\langle a \rangle = \{a, a^2, \ldots, a^{r+m-1}\}$$

the order of $\langle a \rangle$ being $r + m - 1$. The set

$$K_a = \{a^r, a^{r+1}, \ldots, a^{r+m-1}\}$$

is a cyclic group of order m. If n is the multiple of m satisfying $r \leq n \leq m + r - 1$, then a^n is idempotent and is the identity of K_a.

Proof

If $\langle a \rangle$ is not infinite, let s be the smallest integer for which there exists a yet smaller integer r for which $a^r = a^s$. The results then follow from Figure 5-19 with $m = s - r$. [Check the details!]   □

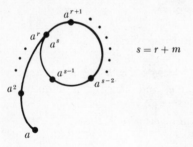

$$s = r + m$$

Figure 5-19

COROLLARY 7

Any finite semigroup S contains an idempotent—in fact, one of the form a^k for any a in S.   □

Let us now consider permutations of the finite set $\{0, 1, \ldots, n - 1\}$ in more detail.

A **transposition** is a permutation in which only two elements differ from their images. We denote by (ij) the permutation

$$i \mapsto j; \ j \mapsto i; \ x \mapsto x \text{ for } x \notin \{i, j\}$$

Thus,

$$(ij) = \begin{pmatrix} 0 & 1 \ldots i \ldots j \ldots n - 1 \\ 0 & 1 \ldots j \ldots i \ldots n - 1 \end{pmatrix} = (ji)$$

A **cycle** is a permutation specified by a sequence $a_1, a_2, \ldots, a_r$ such that

$$a_1 \mapsto a_2; \ a_2 \mapsto a_3; \ \ldots; \ a_{r-1} \mapsto a_r; \ a_r \mapsto a_1; \ x \mapsto x \text{ for } x \notin \{a_1, \ldots, a_r\}$$

We denote this cycle by $(a_1 a_2 \ldots a_r)$. Thus, any transposition is a cycle.

Example 11

$\begin{pmatrix} 0 & 1 & 2 & 3 \\ 2 & 1 & 0 & 3 \end{pmatrix} = (02) = (20)$ is a transposition, while

$\begin{pmatrix} 0 & 1 & 2 & 3 \\ 3 & 1 & 0 & 2 \end{pmatrix} = (032)$ and $\begin{pmatrix} 0 & 1 & 2 & 3 \\ 3 & 2 & 0 & 1 \end{pmatrix} = (0312)$ are cycles.   ◊

FACT 8

Any permutation can be expressed as a product of disjoint cycles, and this expression is unique, save for the order of writing.

Proof

The first cycle is $(0, (0)\rho, (0)\rho^2, \ldots)$. Then pick an element s not in the cycle and form $(s, (s)\rho, (s)\rho^2, \ldots)$, and so forth.   □

Example 12

$$\begin{pmatrix} 0 & 1 & 2 & 3 & 4 & 5 & 6 & 7 & 8 \\ 3 & 2 & 4 & 8 & 1 & 6 & 5 & 0 & 7 \end{pmatrix} = (0387)(124)(56).$$ ◊

COROLLARY 9

Any permutation can be expressed as a product of transpositions.

Proof

This follows from Fact 8 on noting that

$$(a_1 a_2 \ldots a_r) = (a_1 a_2)(a_1 a_3) \ldots (a_1 a_r)$$ □

Example 13

In $\mathcal{S}_4$, $(02)(03)(01) = (0231)$ since

$$\begin{pmatrix} 0 & 1 & 2 & 3 \\ 2 & 1 & 0 & 3 \end{pmatrix}\begin{pmatrix} 0 & 1 & 2 & 3 \\ 3 & 1 & 2 & 0 \end{pmatrix}\begin{pmatrix} 0 & 1 & 2 & 3 \\ 1 & 0 & 2 & 3 \end{pmatrix} = \begin{pmatrix} 0 & 1 & 2 & 3 \\ 2 & 1 & 3 & 0 \end{pmatrix}\begin{pmatrix} 0 & 1 & 2 & 3 \\ 1 & 0 & 2 & 3 \end{pmatrix}$$

$$= \begin{pmatrix} 0 & 1 & 2 & 3 \\ 2 & 0 & 3 & 1 \end{pmatrix}$$

$$= (0231) \qquad \Diamond$$

LEMMA 10

Any cycle $(a_1 a_2 \ldots a_r)$ with all a_j's distinct has period r.

Proof

Exercise 17. □

Given ρ in $\mathcal{S}_n$, an **inversion** is said to occur each time ρ changes the order of a pair of symbols; i.e., each time $i < j$ but $(i)\rho > (j)\rho$.

The permutation ρ is said to have **odd** or **even parity** according to whether the number of inversions is odd or even. We set $\varepsilon_\rho = +1$ if ρ is even, and $\varepsilon_\rho = -1$ if ρ is odd. Thus, $\varepsilon_\rho = (-1)^{\nu_\rho}$, where ν_ρ is the number of inversions in ρ. We then have (Exercise 19) that

$$\varepsilon_\rho = \prod_{i > j} \left(\frac{(i)\rho - (j)\rho}{i - j} \right)$$

Example 14

The number of inversions in $\rho = \begin{pmatrix} 0 & 1 & 2 & 3 & 4 \\ 4 & 2 & 0 & 3 & 1 \end{pmatrix}$ is

$$\nu_\rho = 3 \text{ (from 4)} + 1 \text{ (from 3)} + 2 \text{ (from 2)} + 1 \text{ (from 1)}$$
$$= 7$$

which is odd. We have

$$\varepsilon_\rho = \left(\underbrace{\frac{1-4}{4}}_{i=4} \cdot \underbrace{\frac{1-2}{3} \cdot \frac{1-0}{2} \cdot \frac{1-3}{1}}_{} \right) \cdot \left(\underbrace{\frac{3-4}{3} \cdot \frac{3-2}{2} \cdot \frac{3-0}{1}}_{i=3} \right)$$

$$\cdot \left(\underbrace{\frac{0-4}{2} \cdot \frac{0-2}{1}}_{i=2} \right) \cdot \left(\underbrace{\frac{2-4}{1}}_{i=1} \right) = -1 \qquad \Diamond$$

LEMMA 11

$$\varepsilon_{\rho\sigma} = \varepsilon_\rho \cdot \varepsilon_\sigma$$

Proof

$$\varepsilon_{\rho\sigma} = \prod_{i>j} \frac{(i)\rho\sigma - (j)\rho\sigma}{i - j}$$

$$= \prod_{i>j} \frac{(i)\rho\sigma - (j)\rho\sigma}{(i)\sigma - (j)\sigma} \cdot \frac{(i)\sigma - (j)\sigma}{i - j}$$

$$= \varepsilon_\rho \cdot \varepsilon_\sigma \qquad \qquad \square$$

COROLLARY 12

Every transposition has parity -1.

Proof

If $k < \ell$, then $(k\ell)$ has $(k - \ell)$ inversions from repositioning ℓ, and $(k - \ell - 1)$ from repositioning k, to yield an odd total of $2(k - \ell) - 1$. $\square$

COROLLARY 13

Inverse permutations have the same parity.

Proof

$\varepsilon_\rho^{-1} \cdot \varepsilon_\rho = \varepsilon_1 = +1$. But $\dfrac{+1}{-1} = -1$ and $\dfrac{+1}{+1} = +1$. $\square$

COROLLARY 14

The cycle $(a_1 \ldots a_r) = (a_r a_1) \ldots (a_3 a_1)(a_2 a_1)$, being a product of $r - 1$ transpositions, has parity $(-1)^{r-1}$.   □

FACT 15

(i) The set A_n of all even permutations of $\{0, 1, \ldots, n - 1\}$ forms a subgroup of $\mathcal{S}_n$ called the **alternating group of degree** n.

(ii) Further, the number of odd permutations of degree n equals the number of even permutations of degree n, so that both equal $\frac{1}{2}(n!)$.

Proof

(i) Since (even)(even)$^{-1}$ = even, A_n is a subgroup of $\mathcal{S}_n$.

(ii) ρ is even iff $(12)\rho$ is odd. Thus $2|A_n| = \mathcal{S}_n = n!$.   □

We closed Section 5–1 with the claim that any group with n elements is isomorphic to a "part" of $\mathcal{S}_n$. We shall now prove this in the formalized version that "any group with n elements is isomorphic to a subgroup of $\mathcal{S}_n$." In fact, we shall prove far more, and—in contrast to the usual approach of algebra textbooks—we shall do it in an intuitively appealing way, building on our knowledge of automata.

We saw in Section 2–2 that we could associate with any semigroup S the machine, $M(S)$, of S:

$$M(S) = (S, S, S, \delta_S, \beta_S)$$

Let us now compute the monoid S_{δ_S}—which we shall denote by $\widehat{S}$—of the machine $M(S)$, using the definition of Section 5–1.

Given any map $\delta : Q \times X \to Q$, the monoid S_δ is the submonoid of $F_R(Q)$ comprising all maps of the form

$$\delta_w^* : Q \to Q : q \mapsto \delta^*(q, w)$$

for some $w \in X^*$. In our particular case, then, in which our δ is

$$\delta_S : S \times S \to S : (s, s') \mapsto s \cdot s',$$

the monoid $\widehat{S} = S_{\delta_S}$ is the submonoid of $F_R(S)$ comprising all maps of the form

$$f_{(s_1, \ldots, s_n)} : S \to S : s \mapsto s \cdot (s_1 \cdot \cdots \cdot s_n)$$

for some $(s_1, \ldots, s_n) \in S^*$. Now, if $(s_1, \ldots, s_n) = \Lambda$, we get the map

$$f_\Lambda : S \to S : s \mapsto s, \text{ so that } f_\Lambda = id_S$$

Clearly, $s' \in S$ yields the same map, $f_{s'} = id_S$, iff $s = s \cdot s'$ for all $s \in S$, i.e., iff s' is a right identity for s.

If $(s_1, \ldots, s_n) \neq \Lambda$, it is clear that $f_{(s_1, \ldots, s_n)} = f_{s_1} \cdot \ldots \cdot s_n : S \to S : s \mapsto s \cdot (s_1 \cdot \ldots \cdot s_n)$.

Let us use the following notation: For any semigroup S, f_S is the subsemigroup $\{f_s \mid s \in S\}$ of $F_R(S)$. [Why is f_S a semigroup?] Recall that, for any semigroup T, we may form a monoid T^1 by the rule: If T contains an identity, then $T^1 = T$. If not, add a new element 1 to T, and then make it a monoid by setting $1 \cdot t = t \cdot 1 = t$ for all $t \in T \cup \{1\}$. Call the resulting monoid T^1. Then f_S^1 is a submonoid of $F_R(S)$. [Why?] With these notations we may summarize our progress as follows:

FACT 16

Let S be a semigroup with machine $M(S)$. Then the monoid of $M(S)$ is simply f_S^1. $\square$

We now show how simple f_S^1 turns out to be when S is itself a monoid (or, in particular, a group).

THEOREM 17

If S is a monoid, then $f_S^1 = f_S$ and $S \cong f_S$. In particular, then, S is isomorphic to a submonoid of $F_R(S)$.

Proof

Consider the map $f. : S \to f_S^1 : s \mapsto f_s$. It is clearly a homomorphism, since for all s, s_1, s_2 in S we have

$$(s)[f_{s_1} \diamond f_{s_2}] = (s \cdot s_1) f_{s_2} = (s \cdot s_1) \cdot s_2$$
$$= s \cdot (s_1 \cdot s_2) \text{ by associativity}$$
$$= (s) f_{s_1 \cdot s_2}.$$

Thus, $f_{s_1} \diamond f_{s_2} = f_{s_1 \cdot s_2}$ for all s_1, s_2 in S, and so the map $s_1 \overset{f.}{\mapsto} f_{s_1}$ is indeed a homomorphism. It only remains to check that $f.$ is a bijection.

That $f.$ is onto follows from our observation that f_S contains the identity, and thus equals f_S^1, as soon as S contains a right identity.

That f. is one-to-one also follows from the fact that S contains an identity 1, for if $f_{s_1} = f_{s_2}$ we must have that

$$s_1 = 1 \cdot s_1 = (1)f_{s_1} = (1)f_{s_2} = 1 \cdot s_2 = s_2$$

Thus f., being a homomorphism which is both one-to-one and onto, is indeed an isomorphism as claimed.   □

Before seeing what extra properties hold when S is a group, we had better give an example which destroys the tempting (but false!) conjecture that if S is a semigroup which is not a monoid, then we must have that $f_S^1 = S^1$.

Example 15

We take two copies of $\mathbf{Z}_2$

$$S_1 = \{0, 1\} \text{ and } S_2 = \{0', 1'\}$$

and turn $S = S_1 \cup S_2$ into a semigroup by decreeing that, in adding elements together, we ignore the primes:

$$0 + 0 = 0' + 0 = 0 + 0' = 0' + 0' = 0$$
$$= 1 + 1 = 1' + 1 = 1 + 1' = 1' + 1'$$
$$0 + 1 = 0' + 1 = 0 + 1' = 0' + 1' = 1$$
$$= 1 + 0 = 1' + 0 = 1 + 0' = 1' + 0'.$$

It is clear that no element is an identity since we can, for example, never have $0' + j = 0'$. Now let us tabulate f_S for each $s_j \in S$:

s	$(s)f_0$	$(s)f_{0'}$	$(s)f_1$	$(s)f_{1'}$
0	0	0	1	1
1	1	1	0	0
0'	0	0	1	1
1'	1	1	0	0

Thus $f_0 = f_{0'}, f_1 = f_{1'}$ and so f_S has only two elements $\{f_0, f_1\}$, while f_S^1 has *three* elements $\{f_0, f_1, id_S\}$, and so cannot be isomorphic to S^1, since it has five elements.   ◊

Note that our machine-theoretic approach makes Theorem 17 completely intuitive: Given a monoid (or group) S, we think of it dynamically as $M(S)$—and then we recapture S in isomorphism with $f_S < F_R(S)$ by identifying each s in our monoid S with the state-transition function f_s it induces as input to $M(S)$.

Now suppose that S is a group. Then from

$$s \cdot s^{-1} = 1 = s^{-1} \cdot s \quad \text{for each } s \in S,$$

and the fact that $f_\cdot$ is a monoid homomorphism, we deduce that

$$f_s \diamond f_{s^{-1}} = id_S = f_{s^{-1}} \diamond f_s$$

and hence that

$$f_{s^{-1}} = (f_s)^{-1}, \text{ the inverse of } f_s \text{ in } F_R(S)$$

In other words, if S is a group, then each f_s is invertible, hence a bijection, and hence an element of $\mathcal{S}_S$. We thus have our long-awaited theorem:

THEOREM 18

Every group G is isomorphic to the subgroup f_G of $\mathcal{S}_G$, where

$$f_G = \{f_{g'}\!:\! G \to G\!:\! g \mapsto g \cdot g' \,|\, g' \in G\} \qquad \square$$

The point of our approach to the above theorem is a dramatic one: Not only can we apply algebra to computer and information science, we can also apply computer and information science to algebra!

EXERCISES FOR SECTION 5–3

1.   Is $\{0, 2, 4\}$ a subgroup of Z_6? Is $\{0, 1, 2\}$? Is $\{0, 2\}$? Is $\{0, 3\}$?

2.   Find all the nontrivial subgroups of Z_3. Repeat for Z_4 and Z_5.

3.   For a fixed integer $m \in Z$, define

$$m Z = \{x \,|\, x \in Z \text{ and } x = m \cdot y \text{ for some } y \in Z\}$$

Prove that mZ is a subgroup of Z.

4.   Suppose that G is a group and H is a subset of G. Prove that H is a subgroup of G if and only if

$$h_1^{-1} \cdot h_2 \in H \quad \text{for all } h_1, h_2 \in H.$$

5.   Prove that $H_1 < G_1$ and $H_2 < G_2$ implies $H_1 \times H_2 < G_1 \times G_2$.

6.   Suppose that G is a group, and $H_1 < G$ and $H_2 < G$. Prove that $H_1 \cap H_2 < G$. Can you generalize this exercise?

7.   By means of constructing a counter-example, demonstrate that, in general, the union of two subgroups H_1 and H_2 of a group G is not a subgroup of G.

8.   Determine whether or not $H = \{0000, 0111, 1010, 1111\}$ is a subgroup of Z_2^4.

9.   Suppose that G_1 and G_2 are groups, and $G_1 \times G_2$ is the resulting direct product group. Let 1_1 and 1_2 be the identities of G_1 and G_2, respectively. Prove that

$$\{1_1\} \times G_2 = \{(1_1, a_2) \mid a_2 \in G_2\}$$

and

$$G_1 \times \{1_2\} = \{(a_1, 1_2) \mid a_1 \in G_1\}$$

are subgroups of $G_1 \times G_2$.

10.   For the symmetric group $\mathscr{S}_3$, find $\langle \{1_3\} \rangle$, $\langle \{b, c\} \rangle$, $\langle \{e\} \rangle$, and $\langle \{e, f\} \rangle$.

11.   For $\mathbf{Z}_6$, find $\langle 0 \rangle$, $\langle 3 \rangle$, $\langle 5 \rangle$, and $\langle 2, 4 \rangle$.

12.   Suppose that G is a group and K is a subset of G. Prove that the subgroup $\langle K \rangle$ is the smallest subgroup of G that contains K.

13.   Suppose that G is a finite group, and g in G has order m. Verify that $m \le |G|$.

14.   Let G be a cyclic group. Verify that $G \cong \mathbf{Z}$ if G is infinite; while $G \cong \mathbf{Z}_m$, if G is finite, with $|G| = m$.

15.   Determine whether or not

$$\left\{ \begin{pmatrix} 0 & 1 & 2 & 3 \\ 0 & 1 & 2 & 3 \end{pmatrix}, \begin{pmatrix} 0 & 1 & 2 & 3 \\ 0 & 1 & 3 & 2 \end{pmatrix}, \begin{pmatrix} 0 & 1 & 2 & 3 \\ 1 & 0 & 2 & 3 \end{pmatrix}, \begin{pmatrix} 0 & 1 & 2 & 3 \\ 1 & 0 & 3 & 2 \end{pmatrix} \right\}$$

is isomorphic to the Klein four-group.

16.   Verify that two cycles with no common element commute. For example,

for $n = 6$, if $\rho = (314)$ and $\sigma = (25)$ then $\rho\sigma = \sigma\rho = \begin{pmatrix} 0 & 1 & 2 & 3 & 4 & 5 \\ 0 & 4 & 5 & 1 & 3 & 2 \end{pmatrix}$

17.   Prove Lemma 10.

18.   Verify that if ρ is a product of disjoint cycles $\rho_1, \rho_2, \ldots, \rho_m$ with orders $r_1, r_2, \ldots, r_m$, then the order of ρ is the least common multiple of $\{r_1, r_2, \ldots, r_m\}$.

19.   Verify that $\varepsilon_\rho = \displaystyle\prod_{i > j} \left(\frac{(i)\rho - (j)\rho}{i - j} \right)$.

20.   In Example 15, we did not check that the multiplication on S was indeed associative. Remedy this once and for all by proving the following general result: Let S_1 be any semigroup, and let S_2 be a set disjoint from S_1, but in bijective correspondence $s \leftrightarrow s'$ with S_1. Define a binary operation on $S = S_1 \cup S_2$ by the rule

$$s_1 \cdot s_2 = s_1' \cdot s_2 = s_1 \cdot s_2' = s_1' \cdot s_2' \quad \text{for all } s_1, s_2 \in S$$

Then this operation is associative.

5–4   Normal Subgroups

Returning to the study of congruences initiated in Section 5–1, we shall now use our convenient shorthand of leaving the operators implicit, and speak of the group G when it is clear which $(G, \cdot, 1, {}^{-1})$ is to be understood.

Suppose now that G is a group and $g \in G$. Let us see what each equivalence class $[g]$ looks like for a congruence $\equiv$ on G.

We first see that $[1]$, the equivalence class of the identity, is a subgroup of G. Certainly 1 is in $[1]$; and if x and y belong to $[1]$, then

$$x \equiv 1 \text{ and } y \equiv 1 \Rightarrow x \cdot y \equiv 1 \cdot 1 = 1$$

so that $x \cdot y \in [1]$. Finally, if $x \equiv 1$, then $x^{-1} \equiv 1^{-1}$, but $1^{-1} = 1$ (Why?) and we are done.

Let us denote the subgroup $[1]$ of G by H. (Note that the equivalence class of 1 may well be different for different congruences, so that H was determined by our choice of $\equiv$.) We now show that for each g in G we have the two equalities

$$[g] = g \cdot H \text{ where } g \cdot H = \{g \cdot h \,|\, h \in H\}; \text{ and}$$
$$[g] = H \cdot g \text{ where } H \cdot g = \{h \cdot g \,|\, h \in H\}.$$

We first prove that $[g] \subset g \cdot H$:

Suppose that $g_1 \in [g]$. Then $g_1 \equiv g$ and so $g^{-1} \cdot g_1 \equiv g^{-1} \cdot g = 1$. Thus $g^{-1} \cdot g_1 \in H$, and so $g^{-1} \cdot g_1 = h$ for some $h \in H \Rightarrow g_1 = g \cdot h \Rightarrow g_1 \in g \cdot H$.
We next prove that $g \cdot H \subset [g]$:

If $g_1 = g \cdot h$, with $h \in H$, then $h \equiv 1$ and so $g_1 = g \cdot h \equiv g \cdot 1 = g$, and thus $g_1 \in [g]$.

Combining these, we deduce that $[g] = g \cdot H$. Similarly, $[g] = H \cdot g$ (Exercise 1) for $H = [1]$.

The above fact tells us that $H = [1]$ has the property that, for every $g \in G$, we have the equality

$$g \cdot H = H \cdot g$$

Let us show by an example that this property does *not* hold for every subgroup H of any group G:

Example 1

Again consider $\mathscr{S}_3$, the group of permutations on the set $\{0, 1, 2\}$. Suppose that H is the subgroup $H = \{1_3, e\}$, where

$$1_3 = \begin{pmatrix} 0 & 1 & 2 \\ 0 & 1 & 2 \end{pmatrix} \text{ and } e = \begin{pmatrix} 0 & 1 & 2 \\ 2 & 1 & 0 \end{pmatrix}$$

Let $f = \begin{pmatrix} 0 & 1 & 2 \\ 1 & 0 & 2 \end{pmatrix}$. Then

$$f \diamond H = f \diamond \{1_3, e\} = \{f, b\} \text{ where } b = \begin{pmatrix} 0 & 1 & 2 \\ 1 & 2 & 0 \end{pmatrix}$$

while

$$H \diamond f = \{1_3, e\} \diamond f = \{f, c\} \text{ where } c = \begin{pmatrix} 0 & 1 & 2 \\ 2 & 0 & 1 \end{pmatrix}$$

and we see that $f \diamond H$ is *not* equal to $H \diamond f$. Thus, a subgroup need not be the [1] of some congruence. ◊

In other words, to be the [1] of a group congruence, a subgroup H of G must have the special property expressed in the following definition:

DEFINITION 1

A subgroup H of G is called a **normal subgroup** if and only if

$$g \cdot H = H \cdot g \quad \text{for all } g \in G$$

We write $H \lhd G$ to denote that H is a normal subgroup of G. (Recall that $H < G$ denotes that H is a subgroup of G.) ○

Thus $\{1_3, e\}$ is *not* a normal subgroup of $\mathcal{S}_3$.

The sets $g \cdot H$ and $H \cdot g$, for $g \in G$, are of interest to us for *any* subgroup H of G, whether or not H is normal. We call each set $g \cdot H$ a **left coset** of H, and we call $H \cdot g$ a **right coset** of H.

Example 2

For the permutation group $\mathcal{S}_3$, let H be the subgroup $H = \{1_3, b, c\}$. Then the left cosets of H are:

$$1_3 \diamond H = 1_3 \diamond \{1_3, b, c\} = \{1_3 \diamond 1_3, 1_3 \diamond b, 1_3 \diamond c\} = \{1_3, b, c\} = H$$
$$b \diamond H = b \diamond \{1_3, b, c\} = \{b \diamond 1_3, b \diamond b, b \diamond c\} = \{b, c, 1_3\} = H$$
$$c \diamond H = c \diamond \{1_3, b, c\} = \{c \diamond 1_3, c \diamond b, c \diamond c\} = \{c, 1_3, b\} = H$$
$$d \diamond H = d \diamond \{1_3, b, c\} = \{d \diamond 1_3, d \diamond b, d \diamond c\} = \{d, f, e\}$$
$$e \diamond H = e \diamond \{1_3, b, c\} = \{e \diamond 1_3, e \diamond b, e \diamond c\} = \{e, d, f\} = d \diamond H$$
$$f \diamond H = f \diamond \{1_3, b, c\} = \{f \diamond 1_3, f \diamond b, f \diamond c\} = \{f, e, d\} = d \diamond H \quad ◊$$

Example 3

For $\mathbf{Z}_6$, the group of integers modulo 6, let $H = \{0, 2, 4\}$. Then the left cosets of H are:

$$0 + H = 0 + \{0, 2, 4\} = \{0 + 0, 0 + 2, 0 + 4\} = \{0, 2, 4\} = 0 + H$$
$$1 + H = 1 + \{0, 2, 4\} = \{1 + 0, 1 + 2, 1 + 4\} = \{1, 3, 5\}$$

$$2 + H = 2 + \{0, 2, 4\} = \{2 + 0, 2 + 2, 2 + 4\} = \{2, 4, 0\} = 0 + H$$
$$3 + H = 3 + \{0, 2, 4\} = \{3 + 0, 3 + 2, 3 + 4\} = \{3, 5, 1\} = 1 + H$$
$$4 + H = 4 + \{0, 2, 4\} = \{4 + 0, 4 + 2, 4 + 4\} = \{4, 0, 2\} = 0 + H$$
$$5 + H = 5 + \{0, 2, 4\} = \{5 + 0, 5 + 2, 5 + 4\} = \{5, 1, 3\} = 1 + H \quad \Diamond$$

Example 4

Given the group $\mathbf{Z}_2^3$ and the subgroup $H = \{000, 101, 011, 110\}$, two left cosets of H are

$$000 + H = \{000, 101, 011, 110\} \text{ and}$$
$$001 + H = \{001, 100, 010, 111\}$$

Since $000 + H$ and $001 + H$ already form a partition of $\mathbf{Z}_2^3$, the following lemma tells us that the coset of every other element must equal either $000 + H$ or $001 + H$. In fact, we can readily see that:

$$010 + H = 001 + H$$
$$011 + H = 000 + H$$
$$100 + H = 001 + H$$
$$101 + H = 000 + H$$
$$110 + H = 000 + H$$
$$111 + H = 001 + H \qquad \Diamond$$

Inspection of the above examples suggests the following:

LEMMA 1

If $H < G$ (i.e., whether or not the subgroup H is normal), then the left (respectively, right) cosets of H form a partition of G, called the **left** (respectively, **right**) **coset decomposition** of G by H. (These two decompositions coincide iff $H \lhd G$.)

Proof

It suffices to show that if two cosets have an element in common, they are the same coset; i.e., if $g_1 \cdot H \cap g_2 \cdot H \neq \varnothing$, then $g_1 \cdot H = g_2 \cdot H$.

Thus, suppose that

$$g_1 \cdot h_1 = g_2 \cdot h_2$$

Then

$$g_1 = g_2 \cdot h_2 \cdot h_1^{-1}$$

so

$$g_1 \cdot H = (g_2 \cdot h_2 \cdot h_1^{-1}) \cdot H$$
$$= g_2 \cdot (h_2 \cdot h_1^{-1} \cdot H)$$

which equals $g_2 \cdot H$ by Exercise 7.   □

To see the utility of cosets in the theory of error-correcting codes, consider the subgroup $\{000, 111\}$ of $\mathbf{Z}_2^3$. Now suppose that we want to transmit a sequence of 0's and 1's through a channel in which occasional errors of transmission occur, but such that the probability of more than one error occurring in three consecutive digits is negligible. Then if we send the sequence 000 we can be sure of receiving one of the sequences which differ from it in at most one place: namely 000, 100, 010, and 001. Similarly, if we send 111 we are sure to receive one of the sequences 111, 011, 101, or 110. Now note that the two sets $\{000, 100, 010, 001\}$ and $\{111, 011, 101, 110\}$ are disjoint, so that from the received message we can uniquely reconstruct the transmitted message. In other words, the encoding

$$f: \{0, 1\}^* \to \{0, 1\}^*$$

defined by the code words $f(0) = 000$ and $f(1) = 111$ has the property of correcting single errors if they do not occur more than once in every three consecutive transmitted symbols. Moreover, since the set of code words $\{000, 111\}$ forms a subgroup H of $\mathbf{Z}_2^3$, we can form the left cosets:

$$g_1 + H = 000 + H = \{000, 111\}$$
$$g_2 + H = 100 + H = \{100, 011\}$$
$$g_3 + H = 010 + H = \{010, 101\}$$
$$g_4 + H = 001 + H = \{001, 110\}$$

For each coset we have picked as "coset leader" the word g_j which represents the error of transmission, and we see that if the received word $\hat{w}$ is in coset $g_j + H$, then the transmitted word w is simply reconstructed by the rule $w = -g_j + \hat{w}$. For example, $010 \in g_3 + H$, and does indeed correspond to the transmitted word

$$w = -g_j + \hat{w} = 010 + 010 = 000$$

In view of the above discussion, we can see that for any integer n the group $\mathbf{Z}_2^n$, that is, the group of all binary n-tuples under componentwise modulo 2 addition, is of paramount importance in the study of error-correcting codes, with subgroups of $\mathbf{Z}_2^n$ being utilized for purposes of error-detection and correction. Consequently, we have the following:

DEFINITION 2

Subgroups of $\mathbf{Z}_2^n$ are called length n **binary group codes**. Subgroups of $\mathbf{Z}_m^n$ are referred to as m-**ary group codes** of length n.   ○

Example 5

The set $H = \{00000, 10111, 01101, 11010\}$ is a subgroup of $\mathbf{Z}_2^5$, and hence, a length 5 binary group code. The set $H = \{000000, 010101, 101010, 111111\}$ is a binary group code of length 6.   ◊

We shall exploit these ideas when we take up the algebraic study of error-correcting codes in Chapters 7 and 8.

Example 6

It can be shown (Exercise 11(c)) that for a subgroup H of a group G, we have $H \cdot H = H$. Let us here note that the same result does *not* hold for monoids or semigroups in general. For example, let A_k be the subsemigroup of X^* comprising all words of length $\geq k$. Then the reader may easily check that $A_k A_k = A_{2k} \neq A_k$.   ◊

An important property for determining whether or not two elements are in the same coset is given by the following necessary and sufficient condition.

LEMMA 2

Suppose that G is a group and H is a subgroup of G. Then the two elements $g_1, g_2 \in G$ are in the same left coset if and only if $g_1^{-1} \cdot g_2 \in H$; i.e.,

$$g_1 \cdot H = g_2 \cdot H \Leftrightarrow g_1^{-1} \cdot g_2 \in H$$

Proof

To prove necessity, suppose that $g_1 \cdot H = g_2 \cdot H$. Then there exists $h \in H$ such that

$$g_1 \cdot h = g_2 \cdot 1$$
$$\therefore g_1^{-1} \cdot g_2 = h \in H$$

To prove sufficiency, suppose that

$$g_1^{-1} \cdot g_2 = h \in H$$

Then,

$$g_2 = g_1 \cdot h$$

and

$$\begin{aligned} g_2 \cdot H &= (g_1 \cdot h) \cdot H \\ &= g_1 \cdot (h \cdot H) \\ &= g_1 \cdot H \end{aligned}$$ □

Example 6

Consider the subgroup $H = (1_3, e)$ of $\mathcal{S}_3$. Since

$$b^{-1} \cdot d = c \cdot d = f \notin H$$

then b and d are not in the same left coset of H. However, since

$$c^{-1} \cdot d = b \cdot d = e \in H$$

then c and d are in the same left coset of H.

Now consider the subgroup $H = \{0, 3, 6, 9, 12\}$ of the group $\mathbf{Z}_{15}$. Since

$$-5 + 7 = 10 + 7 = 2 \notin H$$

then 5 and 7 are not in the same left coset. However, since

$$-8 + 11 = 7 + 11 = 3 \in H$$

8 and 11 are in the same left coset.   ◊

Example 7

Consider the subgroup $H = \{00000, 10111, 01101, 11010\}$ of $\mathbf{Z}_2^5$. Since

$$-11001 + 010101 = 11001 + 01010 = 10011 \notin H$$

11001 and 01010 are not in the same left coset. However, since

$$-10001 + 11100 = 10001 + 11100 = 01101 \in H$$

10001 and 11100 are in the same left coset. ◊

Noting that $1 \in H$ for any $H < G$, we see that g lies in both $g \cdot H$ and $H \cdot g$. Thus the left coset decomposition and the right coset decomposition of G by H yield the same partition of G iff $g \cdot H = H \cdot g$ for each $g \in G$; i.e., iff $H \lhd G$. Let us now combine all our knowledge of group congruences and normal subgroups to prove the following theorem:

THEOREM 3

An equivalence relation $\equiv$ on a group G is a congruence on G iff its partition is the coset decomposition of G by a normal subgroup H of G.

Proof

We have already proved that if $\equiv$ is a congruence on G, then $H = [1]$ is a normal subgroup of G for which $[g] = g \cdot H = H \cdot g$ for every g in G.

Conversely, given $H \lhd G$, we must show that the equivalence relation

$$x \equiv_H y \Leftrightarrow x \cdot H = y \cdot H$$

is indeed a congruence on G. For this, we need only verify that it is compatible with multiplication; i.e., we must prove that

$$x \cdot H = x' \cdot H \text{ and } y \cdot H = y' \cdot H \Rightarrow (x \cdot y) \cdot H = (x' \cdot y') \cdot H$$

Now

$$
\begin{aligned}
(x \cdot y) \cdot H &= x \cdot y \cdot (H \cdot H) && \text{since } H \cdot H = H \\
&= x \cdot (y \cdot H) \cdot H && \text{by associativity} \\
&= x \cdot (H \cdot y) \cdot H && \text{since } H \lhd G \text{ so that } y \cdot H = H \cdot y \\
&= (x \cdot H) \cdot (y \cdot H) && \text{by associativity.}
\end{aligned}
$$

Similarly,

$$(x' \cdot y') \cdot H = (x' \cdot H) \cdot (y' \cdot H)$$

But $x \cdot H = x' \cdot H$ and $y \cdot H = y' \cdot H$, whence $(x \cdot y) \cdot H = (x' \cdot y') \cdot H$.

Thus $\equiv_H$ is indeed a congruence, and we are done. □

Since any congruence on G is thus completely determined by the normal subgroup H of G, which is the equivalence class of the identity, we write G/H as an unambiguous denotation of the **factor group** $G/\equiv_H$.

Given a group homomorphism $f: G \to G'$, we have seen how f determines a subgroup $f(G)$ of G'. We will now demonstrate how f also determines a normal subgroup of G. To do this, we introduce the following:

DEFINITION 3

Suppose that $f: S \to S'$ is a monoid homomorphism; then the **kernel** of f, denoted $\mathrm{Ker}\, f$, is the set

$$\mathrm{Ker}\, f = \{x \in S \mid f(x) = 1' \in S'\}$$

i.e., the kernel of f comprises all the elements in S that are mapped to the identity of S'.   ○

We already know from our study of congruences that a normal subgroup $H \lhd G$ determines a canonical epimorphism

$$\eta : G \to G/H : g \mapsto g \cdot H$$

whose kernel is H, since $1 \cdot H = H$ is the identity of G/H. In fact, the converse is also true:

THEOREM 4

If $f: G \to G'$ is a group homomorphism, then $\mathrm{Ker}\, f$ is a normal subgroup of G, and $f(g_1) = f(g_2) \Leftrightarrow g_1 \cdot \mathrm{Ker}\, f = g_2 \cdot \mathrm{Ker}\, f$. Thus

$$f(G) \cong G/\mathrm{Ker}\, f$$

Proof

We need only prove that the equivalence relation

$$g_1 \equiv_f g_2 \Leftrightarrow f(g_1) = f(g_2)$$

is a congruence, for then it immediately follows that $\mathrm{Ker}\, f = [1]_{\equiv_f}$ is a normal subgroup of G, and that $f(G) \cong G/\mathrm{Ker}\, f$.

But to check that $\equiv_f$ is a group congruence, we need only check that

$$g_1 \equiv_f g_2 \text{ and } g_3 \equiv_f g_4 \Rightarrow g_1 \cdot g_3 \equiv_f g_2 \cdot g_4$$

However, this follows immediately from the fact that f is a homomorphism, since $g_1 \equiv_f g_2$ and $g_3 \equiv_f g_4$ implies that

$$f(g_1 \cdot g_3) = f(g_1) \cdot f(g_3) = f(g_2) \cdot f(g_4)$$
$$= f(g_2 \cdot g_4)$$

so that $g_1 \cdot g_3 \equiv g_2 \cdot g_4$. □

The usual treatment of the factor group in algebra textbooks simply defines normal subgroups *ab initio,* and then verifies that the blocks of the coset decomposition of G by a normal subgroup H may indeed be treated as the elements of a group G/H with the following operations:

$$(x \cdot H) \cdot (y \cdot H) = (x \cdot y) \cdot H$$
$$1_{G/H} = H$$
$$(x \cdot H)^{-1} = (x^{-1}) \cdot H$$

The beauty of the present treatment is that it forced us to *discover* normal subgroups and coset decompositions as soon as we tried to find what partitions of a group were compatible with its operations; i.e., as soon as we looked at congruences.

Example 8

Since $H = \{1_3, b, c\}$ is a normal subgroup of S_3 (see Exercise 5), the cosets of H constitute the factor group S_3/H with the operation $\diamond$ given by

$\diamond$	$1_3 \diamond H$	$d \diamond H$
$1_3 \diamond H$	$1_3 \diamond H$	$d \diamond H$
$d \diamond H$	$d \diamond H$	$1_3 \diamond H$

Note that this group has the same structure as $\mathbf{Z}_2$.

Since $\mathbf{Z}_6$ is abelian, the subgroup $\langle 2 \rangle = \{0, 2, 4\}$ is normal. Thus, addition for the factor group $\mathbf{Z}_6/\langle 2 \rangle$ is given by

$+$	$0 + \langle 2 \rangle$	$1 + \langle 2 \rangle$
$0 + \langle 2 \rangle$	$0 + \langle 2 \rangle$	$1 + \langle 2 \rangle$
$1 + \langle 2 \rangle$	$1 + \langle 2 \rangle$	$0 + \langle 2 \rangle$

and this group also has the same structure as $\mathbf{Z}_2$.

On the other hand, since $\langle 3 \rangle = \{0, 3\}$ is also normal, addition for $\mathbf{Z}_6/\langle 3 \rangle$ is shown below:

$+$	$0 + \langle 3 \rangle$	$1 + \langle 3 \rangle$	$2 + \langle 3 \rangle$
$0 + \langle 3 \rangle$	$0 + \langle 3 \rangle$	$1 + \langle 3 \rangle$	$2 + \langle 3 \rangle$
$1 + \langle 3 \rangle$	$1 + \langle 3 \rangle$	$2 + \langle 3 \rangle$	$0 + \langle 3 \rangle$
$2 + \langle 3 \rangle$	$2 + \langle 3 \rangle$	$0 + \langle 3 \rangle$	$1 + \langle 3 \rangle$

Note that this group has the same structure as $\mathbf{Z}_3$.   ◊

Before relating this material to our study of machine decomposition in Section 5–2, it will be necessary to summarize some powerful results on group structure, which build upon the preceding discussion of normal subgroups.

DEFINITION 4

We say that a proper normal subgroup H of G is **maximal** if the only subgroup K such that

$$H < K \lhd G$$

is

$$K = H \text{ or } K = G. \qquad \bigcirc$$

In other words, H is maximal if it is contained in no larger proper normal subgroup of G. Note that this does *not* say that H has more elements than any other normal subgroup of G, for both $\langle 2 \rangle$ and $\langle 3 \rangle$ are maximal normal subgroups of $\mathbf{Z}_6$ even though $|\langle 3 \rangle| < |\langle 2 \rangle|$. This is illustrated in Figure 5–20.

Let us now prove the following important result.

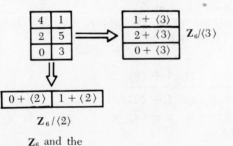

$\mathbf{Z}_6 / \langle 2 \rangle$

$\mathbf{Z}_6$ and the
cosets of $\langle 2 \rangle$ and $\langle 3 \rangle$

Figure 5–20

LEMMA 5

Suppose that G is a group and H is a normal subgroup of G. Then every subgroup of G/H is of the form K/H where $K < G$ and $H \lhd K$.

Proof

By definition, $G/H = \{g \cdot H \,|\, g \in G\}$. Let S be a subgroup of G/H. Then there exists some K which is the largest subset of G such that

$$S = \{k \cdot H \,|\, k \in K\}$$

Let $k_1, k_2 \in K$. Then $k_1 \cdot H$, $k_2 \cdot H \in S$, and S contains

$$(k_1 \cdot H) \cdot (k_2 \cdot H)^{-1}$$
$$= (k_1 \cdot H) \cdot (k_2^{-1} \cdot H)$$
$$= (k_1 \cdot k_2^{-1}) \cdot H$$

Thus, $k_1 \cdot k_2^{-1} \in K$, and so K is a subgroup of G.

Since H is the identity for G/H, it is the identity for S. Let $h \in H$. Then $h \cdot H = H \in S$. Thus, $h \in K$ and $H < K$. Since H is a normal subgroup of G, it must be a normal subgroup of K.   □

DEFINITION 5

We say that a group G is **simple** if its only normal subgroups are $\{1\}$ and G.   ○

We therefore have the following important result.

THEOREM 6

Suppose that G is a group and H is a normal subgroup of G. Then H is maximal if and only if G/H is simple.

Proof

First we assume that $H \lhd G$ is maximal. Let $K/H \lhd G/H$. Then $H \lhd K \lhd G$. Since H is maximal, then either $K = H$ or $K = G$. If $K = H$, we have $K/H = H/H = H$. If $K = G$, then $K/H = G/H$. Hence, G/H is simple.

Next we assume that $H \lhd G$ is not maximal, and we wish to show that G/H is not simple. This is equivalent to proving that G/H is simple $\Rightarrow H$ is maximal. If H is not maximal, then there exists a subgroup K such that $H < K \lhd G$, where $K \neq H$ and $K \neq G$. Since $H \lhd G$, it is clear that $H \lhd K$. Since K/H and G/H are groups, and since clearly $K/H \subset G/H$, we have $K/H < G/H$. Furthermore, since $K \lhd G$, we have that $K/H \lhd G/H$. But $K \neq H$ and $K \neq G$ means that G/H is not simple. $\qquad \square$

FACT 7

An abelian group G is simple iff $G \cong \mathbf{Z}_p$ for some prime p.

Proof

Let G be an abelian group, and g an element other than 1. Then $\langle g \rangle$ is a normal subgroup of G not equal to $\{1\}$. Thus, if G is simple, $G = \langle g \rangle$.

If $\langle g \rangle$ is infinite, then $\langle g^2 \rangle$ is a proper normal subgroup of G. Thus, if G is simple, $G = \langle g \rangle$ must be finite. But if

$$\langle g \rangle = \{ g^n = 1, g, g^2, \ldots, g^{n-1} \}$$

then $\langle g \rangle \cong \mathbf{Z}_n$ under the correspondence $g^j \leftrightarrow j$. However, if $n = mp$ where p is a prime, it is clear that $\langle g^m \rangle \cong \mathbf{Z}_p$ is a subgroup of $\langle g \rangle$; hence, an abelian G can be simple only if $|G|$ is prime. $\qquad \square$

Example 9

Returning now to $\mathbf{Z}_6$, let us take $\langle 2 \rangle$ as our maximal normal subgroup. The only maximal subgroup of $\langle 2 \rangle$ is $\{0\}$. We therefore have

$$\{0\} \lhd \langle 2 \rangle \lhd \mathbf{Z}_6$$

with the associated factor groups $\mathbf{Z}_6/\langle 2 \rangle \cong \mathbf{Z}_2$ and $\langle 2 \rangle/\{0\} \cong \mathbf{Z}_3$. If we take $\langle 3 \rangle$ as our maximal normal subgroup of $\mathbf{Z}_6$, its only maximal subgroup is also $\{0\}$, and we have

$$\{0\} \lhd \langle 3 \rangle \lhd \mathbf{Z}_6$$

with the associated factor groups $\mathbf{Z}_6/\langle 3 \rangle \cong \mathbf{Z}_3$ and $\langle 3 \rangle/\{0\} \cong \mathbf{Z}_2$. Similarly, as the reader may easily convince himself, we have for $\mathbf{Z}_{12}$ the series

$$\{0\} \lhd \langle 4 \rangle \lhd \langle 2 \rangle \lhd \mathbf{Z}_{12} \text{ with } \mathbf{Z}_{12}/\langle 2 \rangle \cong \mathbf{Z}_2, \langle 2 \rangle/\langle 4 \rangle \cong \mathbf{Z}_2, \langle 4 \rangle/\{0\} \cong \mathbf{Z}_3$$

$\{0\} \lhd \langle 6 \rangle \lhd \langle 3 \rangle \lhd \mathbf{Z}_{12}$ with $\mathbf{Z}_{12}/\langle 3 \rangle \cong \mathbf{Z}_3$, $\langle 3 \rangle/\langle 6 \rangle \cong \mathbf{Z}_2$, $\langle 6 \rangle/\{0\} \cong \mathbf{Z}_2$

$\{0\} \lhd \langle 6 \rangle \lhd \langle 2 \rangle \lhd \mathbf{Z}_{12}$ with $\mathbf{Z}_{12}/\langle 2 \rangle \cong \mathbf{Z}_2$, $\langle 2 \rangle/\langle 6 \rangle \cong \mathbf{Z}_3$, $\langle 6 \rangle/\{0\} \cong \mathbf{Z}_2$

$\Diamond$

DEFINITION 6

We call a series of **length** n

$$\{1\} = G_0 \lhd G_1 \lhd G_2 \lhd \cdots \lhd G_{n-1} \lhd G_n = G$$

a **principal series** if each G_j is a maximal normal subgroup of G_{j+1}, for $0 \le j < n$. We call the sequence $(G_n/G_{n-1}, G_{n-1}/G_{n-2}, \ldots, G_2/G_1, G_1/G_0)$ the **factor set** of the principal series. $\bigcirc$

In the examples of $\mathbf{Z}_{12}$ and $\mathbf{Z}_6$, we saw that the factor sets of different principal series of a given group differ only in the ordering of their factors. In fact, this holds true for all groups, and we have:

THEOREM 8 (SCHREIER'S THEOREM)

Any two principal series of a given group G are of the same length, and their factor sets differ only in the ordering of their factors. The simple groups, thus uniquely associated with the group G, are called the **composition factors** of G. $\square$

We shall not give the proof here, but instead refer the reader to any decent textbook on group theory. Instead, let us see what it implies for machine decomposition:

THEOREM 9

If G is a group, then $M(G)$ can be simulated by a cascade of the machines of the composition factors of G.

Proof

It will suffice to verify that, given a group G and a normal subgroup H, we can simulate $M(G)$ by a cascade of $M(G)$ and $M(G/H)$. This is because a repeated application of such a result will yield the theorem by induction:

Suppose that $\{1\} = G_0 \lhd G_1 \lhd G_2 \lhd \cdots \lhd G_{n-1} \lhd G_n = G$. Then construct $M(G_1)$ by cascading $M(G_1/G_0)$ with $M(G_0)$; $M(G_2)$ from $M(G_2/G_1)$ and $M(G_1)$, etc.; until finally we construct $M(G)$ as a cascade of the machines of its composition factors.

Let $H \lhd G$ and $K \cong G/H$. We have the cascade in Figure 5–21 (cf. Figure 5–10). For each coset $[g]$ of H in G, we choose a fixed element g' such that

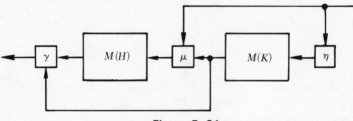

Figure 5–21

$[g] = [g'] = g' \cdot H$. (Such an element g' is called a **coset leader.**) Thus, for any $\widehat{g} \in G$, $[\widehat{g}] = [\widehat{g}'] = \widehat{g}' \cdot H = H \cdot \widehat{g}'$ so that there exists $h \in H$ for which $\widehat{g} = h \cdot \widehat{g}'$.

Suppose that $M(K)$ is in state $[a]$ and $M(H)$ is in state h. Then we shall interpret, via γ, the pair $([a], h)$ as encoding the element $\widehat{g} = h \cdot a' \in G$. Since $[\widehat{g}] = [\widehat{g}'] = [a'] = [a]$, we have that $\widehat{g} = h \cdot \widehat{g}'$. As seems natural, we use η to encode an input $g \in G$ to $M(G)$ as an input $[g]$ to $M(K)$. This will change the state of $M(K)$ to $[a] \cdot [g] = [a'] \cdot [g] = [\widehat{g}'] \cdot [g] = [\widehat{g}' \cdot g]$. The input $\mu(g, [a]) = \mu(g, [\widehat{g}'])$ to $M(H)$ will change its state to $h \cdot \mu(g, [\widehat{g}'])$. Thus, if the new state of $M(G)$ is to correspond to $\widehat{g} \cdot g$, we must have

$$\widehat{g} \cdot g = \text{encoding of } ([\widehat{g}' \cdot g], h \cdot \mu(g, [\widehat{g}']))$$

or
$$(h \cdot \widehat{g}') \cdot g = h \cdot \mu(g, [\widehat{g}']) \cdot (\widehat{g}' \cdot g)'$$

$$h \cdot \widehat{g}' \cdot g = h \cdot \mu(g, [\widehat{g}']) \cdot (\widehat{g}' \cdot g)'$$

from which
$$\mu(g, [\widehat{g}']) = (\widehat{g}' \cdot g) \cdot ((\widehat{g}' \cdot g)')^{-1}$$

$$\mu(g, [\widehat{g}]) = (\widehat{g}' \cdot g) \cdot ((\widehat{g}' \cdot g)')^{-1} \in H$$

since
$$[\widehat{g}' \cdot g] = [(\widehat{g}' \cdot g)']$$

We thus define η, μ, and γ as follows:

$$\eta : G \to K : g \mapsto [g]$$

$$\mu : G \times K \to H : (g, [\widehat{g}]) \mapsto (\widehat{g}' \cdot g) \cdot ((\widehat{g}' \cdot g)')^{-1}$$

$$\gamma : K \times H \to G : ([\widehat{g}], h) \mapsto h \cdot \widehat{g}'$$

Then the above cascade indeed simulates $M(G)$.   □

Example 10

Let us simulate $M(\mathbf{Z}_6)$ using the fact that

$$\{0\} \lhd \langle 2 \rangle \lhd \mathbf{Z}_6$$

We know that $\langle 2 \rangle = \{0, 2, 4\}$ and $\mathbf{Z}_6/\langle 2 \rangle \cong \mathbf{Z}_2$. We thus have Figure 5–22.

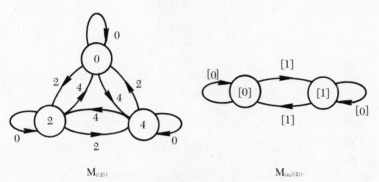

$M_{\langle\langle 2 \rangle\rangle}$ $M_{\langle \mathbf{Z}_6/\langle 2 \rangle\rangle}$

Figure 5–22

Since $\eta : \mathbf{Z}_6 \to \mathbf{Z}_6/\langle 2 \rangle : g \mapsto [g]$, then

$$\eta(0) = \eta(2) = \eta(4) = [0]$$
$$\eta(1) = \eta(3) = \eta(5) = [1]$$

Since $\mu : \mathbf{Z}_6 \times \mathbf{Z}_6/\langle 2 \rangle \to \langle 2 \rangle : (g, [\hat{g}]) \mapsto (\hat{g}' + g) + (-(\hat{g}' + g)')$, then

$$\mu(0, [0]) = (0 + 0) + (-(0 + 0)') = 0 + 0 = 0$$
$$\mu(0, [1]) = (1 + 0) + (-(1 + 0)') = 1 + 1 = 0$$
$$\mu(1, [0]) = (0 + 1) + (-(0 + 1)') = 1 + 1 = 0$$
$$\mu(1, [1]) = (1 + 1) + (-(1 + 1)') = 2 + 0 = 2$$
$$\mu(2, [0]) = (0 + 2) + (-(0 + 2)') = 2 + 0 = 2$$
$$\mu(2, [1]) = (1 + 2) + (-(1 + 2)') = 3 + 1 = 4$$
$$\mu(3, [0]) = (0 + 3) + (-(0 + 3)') = 3 + 1 = 4$$
$$\mu(3, [1]) = (1 + 3) + (-(1 + 3)') = 4 + 0 = 4$$
$$\mu(4, [0]) = (0 + 4) + (-(0 + 4)') = 4 + 0 = 4$$
$$\mu(4, [1]) = (1 + 4) + (-(1 + 4)') = 5 + 1 = 0$$
$$\mu(5, [0]) = (0 + 5) + (-(0 + 5)') = 5 + 1 = 0$$
$$\mu(5, [1]) = (1 + 5) + (-(1 + 5)') = 0 + 0 = 0$$

Finally, since $\gamma: \mathbf{Z}_6/\langle 2 \rangle \times \langle 2 \rangle \to \mathbf{Z}_6 : ([\widehat{g}], h) \mapsto h + \widehat{g}'$, then

$$\gamma([0], 0) = 0 + 0 = 0$$
$$\gamma([0], 2) = 2 + 0 = 2$$
$$\gamma([0], 4) = 4 + 0 = 4$$
$$\gamma([1], 0) = 0 + 1 = 1$$
$$\gamma([1], 2) = 2 + 1 = 3$$
$$\gamma([1], 4) = 4 + 1 = 5$$

$\Diamond$

EXERCISES FOR SECTION 5-4

1. Prove that $[g] = H \cdot g$, where $H = [1]$ for a congruence.

2. Prove the following:

(a) For any group G, both G and $\{1\}$—where 1 is the identity of G—are normal subgroups.

(b) Every subgroup of an abelian group is normal.

3. Suppose that G is a group, and H is a subgroup of G. Verify that H is a normal subgroup of G if and only if $g \cdot H \cdot g^{-1} \subset H$ for all $g \in G$.

4. Suppose that G is a group, and H_1 and H_2 are subgroups of G. Define $H_1 \cdot H_2$ by

$$H_1 \cdot H_2 = \{h_1 \cdot h_2 \mid h_1 \in H_1, h_2 \in H_2\}$$

(a) Prove that if *either* H_1 or H_2 is normal, then $H_1 \cdot H_2$ is a subgroup of G.

(b) Prove that if H_1 and H_2 are *both* normal, then $H_1 \cdot H_2$ is a normal subgroup of G.

5. Verify that $H = \{1_3, b, c\}$ is a normal subgroup of $\mathcal{S}_3$ by enumerating all the right cosets, and referring to Example 2.

6. For the subgroup $H = \{1_3, f\}$ of $\mathcal{S}_3$, enumerate all the left cosets. Is H normal?

7. Suppose that $H < G$. If $h \in H$, prove that $h \cdot H = H$.

8. Prove Lemma 1 for the right coset decomposition of G by H.

9. For $\mathbf{Z}_6$, find all the left cosets of $H = \{0, 3\}$.

10. Given the group $\mathbf{Z}_2^4$ and the subgroup

$$H = \{0000, 0011, 0101, 0110, 1001, 1010, 1100, 1111\},$$

find the left cosets of H.

11. Given a group G and a subgroup H,

(a) Prove that $g \cdot H = H$ if and only if $g \in H$.

(b) Prove that $|g \cdot H| = |H|$ for all $g \in G$.

(c) Prove that $H \cdot H = H$.

(d) Deduce from (b) that, if $|G|$ and $|H|$ are finite, the coset decomposition of G by H has $|G|/|H|$ blocks.

(e) Prove that if $|G|$ is a prime number, then either $H = \{1\}$ or $H = G$, and that G is a cyclic group.

12. (a) Use Exercise 11 to prove Lagrange's theorem: If G is a finite group and H is a subgroup of G, then $|H|$ divides $|G|$.

(b)   Verify that for *any* subgroup H of *any* group G for which there are exactly two cosets of H in G, we must have $H \lhd G$.

13.   For the subgroup $H = \{0, 5, 10, 15, 20\}$ of $\mathbf{Z}_{25}$, determine whether or not the following pairs of elements are in the same left coset.

(a)   2, 12
(b)   3, 22
(c)   6, 16
(d)   11, 14
(e)   7, 22
(f)   8, 13

14.   For $H < \mathbf{Z}_2^5$ given in Example 7, determine whether or not the following pairs of elements are in the same left coset.

(a)   11001, 00111
(b)   01101, 01000
(c)   01110, 11010
(d)   00011, 10100
(e)   10101, 01010
(f)   00111, 10000

15.   Verify that the kernel of a monoid homomorphism $f : S \to S'$ is a submonoid of S.

16.   Construct addition tables for the factor groups

$$\mathbf{Z}_{20}/\langle 4 \rangle \text{ and } \mathbf{Z}_{20}/\langle 5 \rangle$$

17.   Prove that G/H is a group if and only if H is a normal subgroup of G.
18.   Prove that $K/H \lhd G/H$ if and only if $K \lhd G$.
19.   Simulate $\mathbf{Z}_6$ using the fact that

$$\{0\} \lhd \langle 3 \rangle \lhd \mathbf{Z}_6$$

5–5   Complexity of Finite Networks

As an interesting application of the group theory just developed, we now present two complementary theories of complexity of finite networks:

(1) The Winograd-Spira theory considers the construction of combinational networks (recall Section 2–3) using modules of limited fan-in (i.e., there is a fixed bound r on the number of input lines to each module) and asks what is the smallest number of levels (see Figure 5–23) in any network which computes a given function. The main result of our presentation of their theory will be to show that it gives tight bounds on the complexity of multiplication in finite groups.

(2) The Minsky-Papert theory fixes the network to the two levels of Figure 5–24, with the first level consisting of preprocessors (i.e., the realizations of any Boolean function) feeding a single threshold logic unit (Section 2–3). [Such a network is called a **single-layer perceptron,** referring to the fact that there is only one layer of preprocessors.] We think of the output of the logic unit as dividing the set of input patterns on the "retina" which feeds the preprocessor units into two classes. The theory then asks, "How many

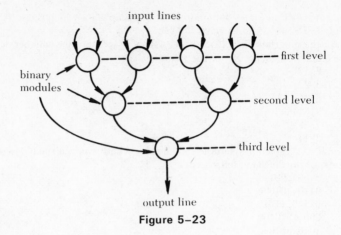

input lines

binary
modules

first level

second level

third level

output line

Figure 5–23

input lines must preprocessor units have if the network is to achieve some given classification?" A major result of our presentation of the Minsky-Papert theory will be that the classification of retinal patterns into those with an odd number of active input lines and those with an even number of active input lines requires at least one preprocessor unit to receive input lines from the whole retina.

Note the tradeoff between fixed fan-in, variable-level (the former theory), and fixed-level, variable fan-in (the latter).

We first turn to the Winograd-Spira theory. In what follows, an **(r)-circuit** is a network of binary modules in which each module is limited to have at most r input lines. We shall assume a unit delay in the operation

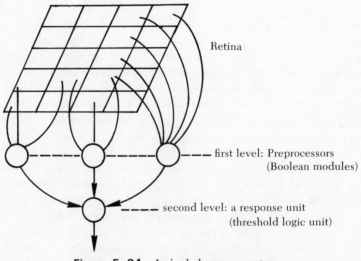

Retina

first level: Preprocessors
(Boolean modules)

second level: a response unit
(threshold logic unit)

Figure 5–24 A single-layer perceptron.

of all our modules. The theory is then based on the simple observation exemplified by Figure 5–23 where we see that if we consider (2)-circuits in which an output line depends on 2^3 input lines, then it takes at least three time units for an input configuration to yield its corresponding output. Lemma 1 below formalizes this observation, and is the basis for the lower bounds we obtain on computation time for various functions.

LEMMA 1

The output of a module of an (r)-circuit at time τ is determined by the state at time 0 of at most r^τ of the input lines.

Proof

Since each module has r inputs, and since there can be at most r levels, then clearly the maximum number of input lines affecting the output of a module is r^τ.   □

Rather than actually count levels in a network, we shall instead count how many unit delays intervene between the presentation of an input pattern and the stabilization of the corresponding output. To have a function

$$\phi : X_1 \times \cdots \times X_n \to Y$$

computed by a network, we must specify how elements of each of the $(n + 1)$ sets in the definition of ϕ are encoded as "patterns of activity" on the lines of the network. Consulting Figure 5–25, we are led to the following:

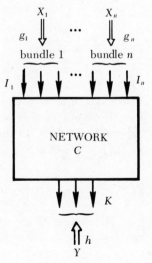

Figure 5–25 Encoding scheme for computing a function via a finite network.

DEFINITION 1

Suppose that a network C has its input lines partitioned into n bundles. We denote by I_j (for $j = 1, 2, \ldots, n$) the set of all possible input patterns which can be provided by the jth bundle. We denote by K the set of all possible output patterns of the network. Then we say that network C is **capable of computing a finite function** $\phi: X_1 \times X_2 \times \cdots \times X_n \to Y$ **in time** τ if there are maps $g_j: X_j \to I_j$ (for $j = 1, \ldots, n$) and an injection $h: Y \to K$ such that if C receives the same input $[g_1(x_1), \ldots, g_n(x_n)]$ from time 0 through time $\tau - 1$, the output at time τ will be $h(\phi(x_1, \ldots, x_n))$. $\qquad \qquad \Box$

We require h to be an injection so that distinct y's are encoded differently; otherwise, we could not read the results of all computations from the network. The reason that we have $h: Y \to K$ rather than $h: K \to Y$ is that the former convention ensures that the network C, rather than the map h, does the computing; otherwise, we can always compute ϕ in time 0 if we take

$$K = I_1 \times \cdots \times I_n$$

and allow h to compute ϕ via the formula

$$h(g_1(x_1), \ldots, g_n(x_n)) = \phi(x_1, \ldots, x_n)$$

provided that we choose each g_j to be an injection.

We now formalize the notion of a set of values from the set X_m which, in appropriate contexts, have distinct effects upon the jth output line of a given network C which computes ϕ.

DEFINITION 2

Let $\phi: X_1 \times X_2 \times \cdots \times X_n \to Y$ be a finite function; and for an (r)-circuit C which computes ϕ, let $h_j(y)$ be the value on the jth output line when the overall output of C is $h(y)$. Then the subset $S_m(j) \subset X_m$ is called an h_j-**separable set for C in the mth argument of** ϕ if for any distinct s_1 and s_2 in $S_m(j)$ there exist $x_1, x_2, \ldots, x_{m-1}, x_{m+1}, \ldots, x_n$ with $x_i \in X_i$ such that

$$h_j(\phi(x_1, \ldots, x_{m-1}, s_1, x_{m+1}, \ldots, x_n)) \neq h_j(\phi(x_1, \ldots, x_{m-1}, s_2, x_{m+1}, \ldots, x_n)) \quad \Box$$

This notion of an h_j-separable set allows us to use Lemma 1 to get a completely general lower bound on the time required by C to compute ϕ.

LEMMA 2 (THE BASIC LEMMA)

Let $\phi:X_1 \times X_2 \times \cdots \times X_n \to Y$. Let C be an (r)-circuit which computes ϕ in time τ. If $S_m(j)$ is an h_j-separable set for C in the mth argument of ϕ, then†

$$\tau \geq \max_{j} \{\lceil \log_r(\lceil \log_2|S_1(j)|\rceil + \cdots + \lceil \log_2|S_n(j)|\rceil)\rceil\}$$

Proof

First, we note that to encode the elements of $S_m(j)$ distinctly, we must have at least $\lceil \log_2|S_m(j)|\rceil$ input lines comprising the mth input bundle (which corresponds to I_m). The jth output at time τ must depend upon all of these input lines; otherwise, there would be two elements of $S_m(j)$ which were not h_j-separable. Thus, the jth output depends upon at least $\lceil \log_2|S_1(j)|\rceil + \cdots + \lceil \log_2|S_n(j)|\rceil$ input lines, from which $r^\tau \geq \lceil \log_2|S_1(j)|\rceil + \cdots + \lceil \log_2|S_n(j)|\rceil$ by Lemma 1. The result follows since τ is integral valued. □

It is worth stressing that this lemma only provides a *lower* bound on τ. Thus, to say that an (r)-circuit, which computes ϕ in time τ, must have $\tau \geq \tau_L$ in no way implies that there is any circuit which computes ϕ for which τ actually attains τ_L. It will only be in special cases (such as group multiplication; e.g., see Theorem 10) that τ_L is essentially achieved. To make this point, we first note that there are 2^{16} functions $\{0, 1\}^4 \to \{0, 1\}$. However, a module of the form shown in Figure 5–26 is capable of realizing at most

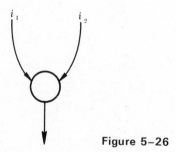

Figure 5–26

2^4 functions from $\{0, 1\}^2$ to $\{0, 1\}$. Specifically, these functions, say $f_1, f_2, \ldots, f_{16}$, are described by Table 5–11.

---

†We shall let $\lceil x \rceil$ be the smallest integer $\geq x$; let $\lfloor x \rfloor$ be the largest integer $\leq x$; and let $|S|$ be the number of elements in the set S. As usual, $Z_N = \{0, 1, \ldots, N - 1\}$.

Table 5–11

i_1	i_2	f_1	f_2	f_3	f_4	f_5	f_6	f_7	f_8	f_9	f_{10}	f_{11}	f_{12}	f_{13}	f_{14}	f_{15}	f_{16}
0	0	0	0	0	0	0	0	0	0	1	1	1	1	1	1	1	1
0	1	0	0	0	0	1	1	1	1	0	0	0	0	1	1	1	1
1	0	0	0	1	1	0	0	1	1	0	0	1	1	0	0	1	1
1	1	0	1	0	1	0	1	0	1	0	1	0	1	0	1	0	1

Thus, since it consists of three modules, a (2)-circuit of the form shown in Figure 5–27 can realize at most $(2^4)^3 = 2^{12}$ functions from $\{0,1\}^4$ to $\{0,1\}$,

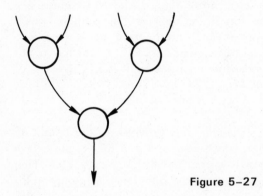

Figure 5–27

and no other (2)-circuit (try to find one) can realize more in time $\tau = 2$. Yet, Lemma 2 yields $\tau_L = 2$ for all 2^{16} functions $\{0,1\}^4 \to \{0,1\}$.

Example 1

Suppose that $\phi: \mathbf{Z}_N \times \mathbf{Z}_N \to \{0,1\}$ is defined by

$$\phi(x_1, x_2) = \begin{cases} 1 & \text{if } x_1 \le x_2 \\ 0 & \text{if } x_1 > x_2 \end{cases}$$

and suppose that the (r)-circuit C computes ϕ in time τ. Since the output encoding h is an injection, there exists some output line (say the jth) such that $h_j(0) \ne h_j(1)$. Thus, suppose that x and y are distinct elements of $\mathbf{Z}_N$, where $x > y$. Then

$$h_j(\phi(x,y)) \ne h_j(\phi(y,y))$$

so that x and y are h_j-separable to the first argument. In other words, $\mathbf{Z}_N$ is an h_j-separable set for C in the first argument of ϕ. Furthermore,

$$h_j(\phi(x, x)) \neq h_j(\phi(x, y))$$

so that $\mathbf{Z}_N$ is also an h_j-separable set for C in the second argument of ϕ. Hence, by Lemma 2, since $|\mathbf{Z}_N| = N$,

$$\tau \geq \lceil \log_r \lceil \log_2 N \rceil + \lceil \log_2 N \rceil \rceil = \lceil \log_r 2 \lceil \log_2 N \rceil \rceil \qquad \Diamond$$

Example 2

Suppose that $\phi: \mathbf{Z}_N \times \mathbf{Z}_N \to \mathbf{Z}_N$ is defined by

$$\phi(x_1, x_2) = \left\lfloor \frac{x_1 \cdot x_2}{N} \right\rfloor$$

and suppose that the (r)-circuit C computes ϕ in time τ. As in Example 1, pick j such that $h_j(0) \neq h_j(1)$. Let $m = \lfloor N^{1/2} \rfloor$, and consider the subset $\{1, 2, \dots, m\} \subset \mathbf{Z}_N$. Thus, suppose that x and y are distinct elements of $\{1, 2, \dots, m\}$, where $x > y$. Then we may choose $z \in \mathbf{Z}_N$ such that $x \cdot z < N \leq y \cdot z < 2N$ (Exercise 1). Hence,

$$h_j(\phi(x, z)) \neq h_j(\phi(y, z))$$

so that $\{1, 2, \dots, m\}$ is an h_j-separable set for C in the first argument of ϕ. By symmetry, we conclude the same for the second argument of ϕ.

Therefore, by Lemma 2,

$$\tau \geq \lceil \log_r 2 \lceil \log_2 m \rceil \rceil$$

where $m = \lfloor N^{1/2} \rfloor$. $\qquad \Diamond$

Note that in the above examples we have not made use of any explicit knowledge of the output encoding h. The next example will show that the size of separable sets can be strongly dependent upon the output encoding of a circuit which computes a given ϕ.

Example 3

Let $\phi: \mathbf{Z}_N \times \mathbf{Z}_N \to \mathbf{Z}_{N^2}$ be numerical multiplication with $N = 2^8$. Consider an output encoding in which, if the output value is M, then the ith output line ($0 \leq i < 16$) carries the ith bit in the binary expansion for M. Then, let us use 16 output lines. Pick any $x \neq y$ with $x, y \in \mathbf{Z}_N$. Then their binary expansions differ in at least one place, say the kth. Choose $z = 2^{8-k}$. Then

$$h_8(\phi(x, z)) \neq h_8(\phi(y, z))$$

and
$$h_8(\phi(z, x)) \neq h_8(\phi(z, y))$$

Hence there is an h_8-separable set of size 2^8 in both arguments of ϕ.

Now consider the same ϕ, but let the output encoding for M be the binary representation of the exponents in the prime decomposition of M. Let the first four output lines encode the exponent of 2 in the result. (Since $M < 2^{16}$, the exponent of 2 in the prime decomposition of M is less than 16. Hence, four lines suffice.) Pick $x, y \in \mathbf{Z}_N$ such that x and y do not have the same power of 2 in their prime decompositions; the powers of 2 differ in, say, the kth place of their binary expansions. Then, letting $z = 2^{4-k}$, we have that

$$h_4(\phi(x, z)) \neq h_4(\phi(y, z))$$
and
$$h_4(\phi(z, x)) \neq h_4(\phi(z, y))$$

Thus, since an element of $\mathbf{Z}_N$ can have eight different exponents of two in its prime decomposition, there is an h_4-separable set of size 8 in both arguments of ϕ. Since 2 is the smallest prime, one then sees that 8 is the maximal size of a separable set for any output line. Note, however, that this output code requires 45 output lines (Exercise 2).   ◊

We now show how Lemma 2 may be applied to give us information about group multiplication. Let G be a finite group, and let $\phi: G \times G \to G$ be group multiplication. Let C be an (r)-circuit which computes ϕ. Let $h_j(g)$ be the value on the jth output line of C when the output is $h(g)$.

DEFINITION 3

We define† two equivalence relations on G (Exercise 3) by:

$$xR_j y \quad \Leftrightarrow \quad h_j(xg) = h_j(yg) \text{ for all } g \in G$$
$$xL_j y \quad \Leftrightarrow \quad h_j(gx) = h_j(gy) \text{ for all } g \in G$$

Let us write R_j for $[1]_{R_j}$ and L_j for $[1]_{L_j}$, where 1 is the identity of G.   ◯

LEMMA 3

R_j and L_j are groups. Moreover,

$$[g]_{R_j} = R_j g \text{ and } [g]_{L_j} = gL_j$$

for all g in G.

---

†Let us simplify notation for the time being by writing the product $x \cdot y$ as xy for short.

Proof

To prove that R_j is a group, we will show that $ab^{-1} \in R_j$ for each a and b in R_j. For all g in G we have

$$
\begin{aligned}
h_j(ab^{-1}g) &= h_j(b^{-1}g) &&\text{since } aR_j1 \\
&= h_j(bb^{-1}g) &&\text{since } bR_j1 \\
&= h_j(g)
\end{aligned}
$$

so that $ab^{-1}R_j1$, as required. Moreover,

$$
\begin{aligned}
a \in [g]_{R_j} &\Leftrightarrow h_j(ay) = h_j(gy) &&\text{for all } y \text{ in } G \\
&\Leftrightarrow h_j(ag^{-1}z) = h_j(z) &&\text{for all } z = gy \text{ in } G \\
&\Leftrightarrow ag^{-1} \in R_j \\
&\Leftrightarrow a \in R_jg.
\end{aligned}
$$

Interchanging the order of multiplication yields the result for L_j.   □

With this lemma, we gain an elegant characterization of maximal h_j-separable sets when considering group multiplication (Exercise 4).

LEMMA 4

A maximal size $S \subset G$ which is h_j-separable in the first (respectively, second) argument consists of a representative from each left coset of R_j (respectively, right coset of L_j) in G. It thus has size $|G|/|R_j|$ (respectively, $|G|/|L_j|$).   □

Combining Lemma 2 and Lemma 4, we immediately deduce:

THEOREM 5

Let C be an (r)-circuit which computes the group multiplication $\phi: G \times G \to G$ in time τ. Then

$$
\tau \geq \max_j \left\{ \left\lceil \log_r \left(\left\lceil \log_2 \frac{|G|}{|R_j|} \right\rceil + \left\lceil \log_2 \frac{|G|}{|L_j|} \right\rceil \right) \right\rceil \right\}
$$

    □

These results could be important in the design of a circuit to compute ϕ, since they define which are the "good" and which are the "bad" output encodings; the desideratum is to make R_j and L_j as large as possible over all j. We now provide a lower bound on group multiplication time which does not depend on the choice of output encoding. First, we need some concepts which give us a firmer handle on the multiplicative structure of a group:

DEFINITION 4

Given a group H and an element $c \in H$, we say that $P(c, H)$ **holds** if every subgroup K of H (other than $\{1\}$) contains c. We then say that $P(H)$ **holds** if there is at least one $c \neq 1$ in H for which $P(c, H)$ holds; or if $H = \{1\}$.

For any $c \neq 1$ in a group G, let $\beta(c)$ be the maximum order of any subgroup of G not containing c. In addition, let

$$\beta(G) = \min\{\beta(c) \,|\, c \in G\backslash\{1\}\} \qquad\qquad \bigcirc$$

Note that $\beta(G) = 1$ iff $P(G)$ holds, since

$$\beta(c) = 1 \Leftrightarrow \{1\} \text{ is the largest subgroup of } G \text{ not containing } c$$
$$\Leftrightarrow P(c, G) \text{ holds}$$

so that

$$\beta(G) = 1 \Leftrightarrow P(c, G) \text{ holds for some } c \neq 1 \text{ in } G$$

Example 4

Consider $\mathbf{Z}_8 = \{0, 1, 2, 3, 4, 5, 6, 7\}$, the group of integers modulo 8. Then the proper subgroups of $\mathbf{Z}_8$ are:

$$\{0\}$$
$$\{0, 4\}$$
$$\{0, 2, 4, 6\}$$

Thus, $P(4, \mathbf{Z}_8)$ holds; and since $4 \neq 0$, $P(\mathbf{Z}_8)$ holds. Hence, $\beta(\mathbf{Z}_8) = 1$. For $\mathbf{Z}_8$, we also have:

$$\beta(1) = \beta(3) = \beta(5) = \beta(7) = 4$$
$$\beta(2) = \beta(6) = 2$$
$$\beta(4) = 1 \qquad\qquad \Diamond$$

Let us now prove the following:

LEMMA 6

For any finite group G we have that

$$|G| \geq \alpha(G)\beta(G)$$

where $\alpha(G)$ is the largest order of a subgroup H of G for which $P(H)$ holds.

Proof

Suppose that H is a subgroup of G of largest order for which $P(H)$ holds, so that $\alpha(G) = |H|$. In particular, suppose that $P(c, H)$ holds. Then let K be the largest subgroup of G not containing c, so that

$$|K| = \beta(c) \geq \beta(G)$$

Assume that there exist h_1, h_2 in H and k_1, k_2 in K such that

$$h_1 k_1 = h_2 k_2$$

Then, we may write

$$h_2^{-1} h_1 = k_2 k_1^{-1} = m$$

Since m is in K, the subgroup $\langle m \rangle$ that it generates lies in K and so cannot contain c. Since m is in H and $P(c, H)$ holds, $\langle m \rangle$ must contain c unless $m = 1$. We deduce that $m = 1$, and that $h_1 k_1$ cannot equal $h_2 k_2$ unless $h_1 = h_2$ and $k_1 = k_2$. Thus,

$$|G| \geq |H| \cdot |K| \geq \alpha(G)\beta(G) \qquad \square$$

THEOREM 7

Let G be a finite group. If C is an (r)-circuit to multiply in G in time τ, then

$$\tau \geq \left\lceil \log_r 2 \left\lceil \log_2 \frac{|G|}{\beta(G)} \right\rceil \right\rceil$$

which implies that

$$\tau \geq \lceil \log_r 2 \lceil \log_2 |\alpha(G)| \rceil \rceil$$

by Lemma 6.

Proof

Let $c \in G$ be such that $\beta(c) = \beta(G)$, and let j be such that $h_j(c) \neq h_j(1)$. Thus, $c \notin R_j$ and $c \notin L_j$. Hence, R_j and L_j must both have at most as many elements as the largest subgroup of G not containing c. Thus,

$$|R_j| \leq \beta(G) \text{ and } |L_j| \leq \beta(G)$$

Hence, the result follows from Theorem 5 and Lemma 6.   □

We shall now construct, for each finite group, a circuit which computes its multiplication within one time unit of the lower bound given in Theorem 7. Our first step in this direction is the following:

LEMMA 8

Let K be any subgroup of G. Define $\widehat{\phi}: G \times G \to \{0, 1\}$ by

$$\widehat{\phi}(a, b) = \begin{cases} 0 \text{ if } ab \in K \\ 1 \text{ if } ab \notin K \end{cases}$$

Then there exists an (r)-circuit to compute $\widehat{\phi}$ in time

$$\tau = 1 + \left\lceil \log_r \left\lceil \log_2 \frac{|G|}{|K|} \right\rceil \right\rceil$$

Proof

Let $M = \dfrac{|G|}{|K|}$. Pick a coset representative $v_i \in Kv_i$ for each distinct right coset of K in G. Then $\{v_i^{-1}\}$ will be a set of left coset representatives, for $v_i^{-1} K = v_j^{-1} K$ iff $v_i v_j^{-1} \in K$ iff $Kv_j = Kv_i$. We then define a map $z_1: G \to \{0, 1\}^n$, where $n = \lceil \log_2 M \rceil$, such that

$$z_1(g_1) = z_1(g_2) \text{ iff } Kg_1 = Kg_2$$

and define $z_2: G \to \{0, 1\}^n$ by requiring that

$$z_1(g) \oplus z_2(g^{-1}) = \overline{0}$$

where $\overline{0}$ is the all-zero n-tuple and $\oplus$ is componentwise addition modulo 2.

These are then the two input encodings for our circuit. Note that z_2 maps any two elements in the same left coset to the same n-tuple. We let the first level of the circuit consist of $\lceil \log_2 M \rceil$ modulo 2 adders. If ab is being computed, these adders sum $z_1(a)$ and $z_2(b)$ componentwise modulo 2. Thus, all outputs are 0 iff $a \in Kv_j$ and $b \in v_j^{-1}K$ for some common j; i.e., iff $ab \in K$. The rest of the circuit is a fan-in of r-input elements having output 0 iff all inputs are 0 and output 1 if at least one input is nonzero. This fan-in has depth $\lceil \log_r \lceil \log_2 M \rceil \rceil$. Thus, the circuit computes $\hat{\phi}$ in time

$$\tau = \lceil \log_r \lceil \log_2 M \rceil \rceil + 1 \qquad \square$$

COROLLARY 9

There is an (r)-circuit to compute whether $ab \in Ku$ for any $u \in G$ in time

$$\tau = 1 + \left\lceil \log_r \left\lceil \log_2 \frac{|G|}{|K|} \right\rceil \right\rceil$$

Proof

Exercise 5. $\qquad \square$

LEMMA 10

If G has subgroups $K_1, \ldots, K_n$ such that $\bigcap_{j=1}^{n} K_j = \{1\}$, then there exists an (r)-circuit to compute multiplication in G in time

$$\tau = 1 + \max_{1 \le j \le n} \left\lceil \log_r \left\lceil \log_2 \frac{|G|}{|K_j|} \right\rceil \right\rceil$$

Proof

First note that knowing the right cosets containing any $a \in G$ suffices to determine a, since $K_j a_1 = K_j a_2$ for all j; then

$$\bigcap_{j=1}^{n} K_j a_1 = \bigcap_{j=1}^{n} K_j a_2$$

and so $a_1 = a_2$. Now consider the circuit which is a parallel array, with one subcircuit constructed as in Corollary 9 for each right coset of each K_j, $1 \le j \le n$. Then this circuit computes multiplication in G by our above observation (there is an injection from G into the output of this parallel array) and clearly does so in time

$$\tau = 1 + \left\lceil \log_r \left\lceil \log_2 \frac{|G|}{|K_j|} \right\rceil \right\rceil \qquad \square$$

We finally obtain the following result:

THEOREM 11

For any $r \geq 2$ there is an (r)-circuit to multiply in a finite group G in time

$$\tau = 1 + \left\lceil \log_r \left\lceil \log_2 \frac{|G|}{\beta(G)} \right\rceil \right\rceil$$

Proof

For each $g \neq 1$ in G, let K_g be a largest subgroup of G not containing g. Let us then take $K_1, \ldots, K_n$ in Lemma 10 to be the set of distinct groups among the K_g. Then

$$\bigcap_{j=1}^{n} K_j = \{1\}$$

while

$$\min_{1 \leq j \leq n} |K_j| = \beta(G)$$

by the definition of $\beta(G)$. Thus, the circuit of Lemma 10 has in this case the computation time

$$\tau = 1 + \left\lceil \log_r \left\lceil \log_2 \frac{|G|}{|\beta(G)|} \right\rceil \right\rceil \qquad \square$$

To see how impressive this bound is, note that Theorem 7 told us that we must have

$$\tau \geq \left\lceil \log_r 2 \left\lceil \log_2 \frac{|G|}{|\beta(G)|} \right\rceil \right\rceil$$

where the right-hand side is the smallest integer greater than or equal to

$$\log_r 2 \left\lceil \log_2 \frac{|G|}{|\beta(G)|} \right\rceil = \log_r 2 + \log_r \left\lceil \log_2 \frac{|G|}{|\beta(G)|} \right\rceil$$

Hence, if $r = 2$, the bound is actually achieved.

The above circuit is almost optimum, in the sense that its multiplication time is within one time unit of the fastest obtainable. However, the input coding is highly redundant (compare Example 3). It is an exciting, but difficult, area of research to search for an equally good fit between upper and lower bounds for functions other than group multiplication, and to try to do so in a way which is far more economical in the number of modules required.

We now return to the scheme shown in Figure 5–23. There we consider a formalized "retina" as a set R of input lines arranged in a rectangular array on which "patterns" may be projected. We then identify a binary firing pattern (with a 0 for an inactive line and a 1 for an active line) on those lines, with the subset of R comprising the active lines.

We shall be interested in such pattern **predicates** ψ (i.e., $\psi(X)$ is true for some patterns $X \subset R$, and false for others) as: X is connected (Theorem 21), or, X is of odd parity (Theorem 19).

With each predicate ψ we shall associate the binary function

$$\ulcorner\psi(X)\urcorner = \begin{cases} 1 \text{ if } \psi(X) \text{ is true} \\ 0 \text{ if } \psi(X) \text{ is false} \end{cases}$$

We ask what predicates ψ can be computed by a network whose first layer consists of computing elements from a given set Φ of modules, and whose second layer consists of a single threshold module (a module whose output is 1 if and only if a certain weighted sum of its inputs exceeds its threshold). Thus, we are interested in $L(\Phi)$ defined by the following:

DEFINITION 5

Suppose that Φ is any collection of functions of the form $\phi: 2^R \to \{0, 1\}$. Then the **class of functions linear with respect to** Φ, denoted by $L(\Phi)$, consists of precisely those functions $\psi: 2^R \to \{0, 1\}$ for which $\psi(X) = 1$ iff it is true that

$$\sum_{\phi \in \Phi} \alpha_\phi \phi(X) \geq \theta$$

for some fixed choice of the real numbers α_ϕ (the "weights") and θ (the "threshold"). We denote this relationship by

$$\psi = \ulcorner \sum_\Phi \alpha_\phi \phi \geq \theta \urcorner$$

We shall say that a function ϕ from the set Φ is of **degree** k if we may associate it with a module having k input lines, each being a distinct line of R. We then say that the **order** of ψ is the smallest integer k such that $\psi \in L(\Phi)$ for some collection of functions in which every $\phi \in \Phi$ is of degree at most k. ○

Thus, a linear threshold function is of order 1, and every function in $L(\Phi)$ has order at most $|R|$. It is in this sense, then, that we say that Winograd and Spira ask how much time is required for a function if we bound the order, whereas Minsky and Papert ask how big an order is required for a function if we bound the time (by only allowing one level to be read out by a threshold element).

DEFINITION 6

The function $\phi : 2^R \to \{0, 1\}$ is called a **mask** on R if there is a set A such that $\phi(X) = \ulcorner A \subset X \urcorner$. We denote such a mask by ϕ_A. We write ϕ_x for $\phi_{\{x\}} = \ulcorner x \in X \urcorner$, and we denote the set of all masks on R by $\mathfrak{M}_R$. ○

Thus, ϕ_A is of degree $|A|$, and is simply an AND-gate with one input line for each element of A.

PROPOSITION 12

All masks are of order 1.

Proof

$$\phi_A = \ulcorner \sum_{x \in A} \phi_x \geq |A| \urcorner$$

□

PROPOSITION 13

If M is an integer $0 < M < |R|$, then the "counting function" $\psi^M(X) = \ulcorner |X| = M \urcorner$ is of order at most 2.

Proof

$$\psi^M(X) = \ulcorner (|X| - M)^2 \leq 0 \urcorner$$
$$= \ulcorner 0 \geq |X|^2 - 2|X|M + M^2 \urcorner$$
$$= \ulcorner (2M - 1)|X| - |X|(|X| - 1) \geq M^2 \urcorner$$
$$= \ulcorner (2M - 1) \sum_x \phi_x(X) + (-1) \sum_{x \neq x'} \phi_{\{x,x'\}}(X) \geq M^2 \urcorner$$

□

THEOREM 14

Every ψ is in $L(\mathfrak{M}_R)$; i.e., every ψ is a linear threshold function with respect to the set of all masks.

Proof

Take the disjunctive normal form (of Section 2–3) for ψ. Noting that at most one term is nonzero for any choice of the arguments, we may replace the $\vee$ by a numeral Σ and replace $\bar{x}$ by $1 - x$ to consider the form as an actual numerical expression

$$\psi(x_1, \ldots, x_n) = \sum \psi(\alpha_1, \ldots, \alpha_n)x_1^{\alpha_1} \ldots x_n^{\alpha_n}$$

Gathering terms, this becomes

$$\psi(X) = \sum \alpha_i \phi_i(X) \tag{1}$$

where each $\phi_i(X) = x_{j_1} \ldots x_{j_m}$ for some subset $(j_1, \ldots, j_m)$ of $(1, \ldots, n)$. But this just says that ϕ_i is a mask. Rewriting (1) in the form

$$\psi = \ulcorner \sum \alpha_i \phi_i \geq 1/2 \urcorner$$

we see that ψ does indeed belong to $L(\mathfrak{M}_R)$.   □

LEMMA 15

ψ is of order k iff $\psi \in (\Phi)$ where Φ is the set of masks of degree $\leq k$.

Proof

It is trivial that if $\psi \in L(\Phi)$, where Φ is the set of masks of degree $\leq k$, then ψ is of degree at most k.

To prove the converse, let

$$\psi(X) = \ulcorner \sum_\phi \alpha_\phi \phi(X) \geq \theta \urcorner$$

where each ϕ is of degree at most k. By the argument which led to (1), we see that each ϕ can be written as

$$\phi = \sum_i \alpha_i^\phi \phi_i$$

where the ϕ_i are now *masks* of degree at most k. But then

$$\psi(X) = \ulcorner \sum_i \left(\sum_\phi \alpha_\phi \alpha_i^\phi \right) \phi_i(X) \geq \theta \urcorner$$

$\square$

We shall now show that if a predicate is unchanged by various permutations, then we may use this fact to simplify its coefficients with respect to the set of masks; and that this simplified form will often enable us to place a lower bound on the order of the predicate (bearing in mind Lemma 15). Before giving the theory, we should make this clear by using the general method to prove the fact, which was obvious by visual inspection in Section 2–3, that a modulo 2 adder cannot be realized as a threshold logic unit.

Example 5

Let R have two elements and let $\psi(x_1, x_2) = x_1 \oplus x_2$, which is unchanged by transposing x_1 and x_2. We use this fact to show that ψ cannot be expressed as a linear threshold function. Suppose, to the contrary, that $\psi(x_1, x_2) = \ulcorner \alpha x_1 + \beta x_2 \geq \theta \urcorner$. Then by symmetry we must have $\psi(x_1, x_2) = \ulcorner \alpha x_2 + \beta x_1 \geq \theta \urcorner$, which yields $\psi(x_1, x_2) = \ulcorner \gamma x_1 + \gamma x_2 \geq \theta \urcorner$ where $\gamma = \dfrac{\alpha + \beta}{2}$; that is, $\psi(X) = \ulcorner \gamma |X| \geq \theta \urcorner$. But $\psi(0, 0) = 1$, $\psi(0, 1) = 0 = \psi(1, 0)$, and $\psi(1, 1) = 1$, which would imply

$$\gamma \cdot 0 \geq \theta; \ \gamma \cdot 1 < \theta; \ \gamma \cdot 2 \geq 0$$

However, this is impossible, since a linear function cannot change direction.

$\square$

We shall now see how the above analysis may be generalized. Let G be a group of permutations on R, with xg the image of $x \in R$ under $g \in G$. We then write

$$Xg = \{xg \,|\, x \in X\} \text{ for each } X \subset R \text{ and } g \in G$$

and use ϕg to denote the function with $\phi g(X) = \phi(Xg)$. We then say that ϕ is **equivalent** to ϕ' **with respect to** G, and write $\phi \underset{G}{\equiv} \phi'$, if and only if $\phi = \phi'g$ for *some* $g \in G$. We say that ψ is **invariant** under G if and only if $\psi = \psi g$ for *all* $g \in G$.

FACT 16

The set of all masks of degree at most k is closed under *any* group of permutations on R.

THEOREM 17 (THE GROUP INVARIANCE THEOREM)

Let G be a group of permutations of R and let Φ be a set of functions on R closed under G (i.e., $\phi \in \Phi$ and $g \in G$ implies $\phi g \in \Phi$). Then if ψ in $L(\Phi)$ is invariant under G, it has a linear representation

$$\psi = \ulcorner \sum_{\phi \in \Phi} \beta(\phi)\phi \geq \theta \urcorner$$

in which $\beta(\phi) = \beta(\phi')$ whenever $\phi \underset{G}{\equiv} \phi'$.

Proof

Given a representation

$$\psi = \ulcorner \sum \alpha(\phi)\phi \geq \theta \urcorner$$

form the quotient

$$\beta(\phi) = \frac{\sum_{g \in G} \alpha(\phi g)}{|G|}$$

which thus depends only on the equivalence class of ϕ. Then

$$\psi = \ulcorner \sum \beta(\phi)\phi \geq \theta \urcorner$$

as the reader may readily verify. $\qquad\square$

COROLLARY 18

Let $\Phi = \Phi_1 \cup \cdots \cup \Phi_m$, where each Φ_j is a block of $\underset{G}{\equiv}$. Let $N_j(X)$ be the *number* of ϕ's in Φ_j for which $\phi(X)$ is true. Then if ψ is in $L(\Phi)$, with Φ closed, and ψ invariant, under G, then ψ has a representation

$$\psi = \ulcorner \sum_{i=1}^{m} \alpha_i N_i \geq \theta \urcorner \qquad\square$$

We may now apply the group invariance theorem to show that some functions have order which increases markedly as $|R|$ increases.

THEOREM 19

The **parity function**

$$\psi_{PAR}(X) = \ulcorner |X| \text{ is an odd number} \urcorner$$

is of order $|R|$.

Proof

Since ψ_{PAR} is invariant under the group G of *all* permutations of R, Theorem 14 and Corollary 18 tell us that ψ_{PAR} has a representation

$$\psi_{PAR} = \ulcorner \sum_{\alpha} \alpha_j C_j \geq \theta \urcorner$$

where $C_j(X)$ is the number of masks ϕ of degree j with $\phi(X) = 1$, and thus equals the number of subsets of X with j elements:

$$C_j(X) = \binom{|X|}{j} = \frac{1}{j!}|X|(|X| - 1) \cdots (|X| - j + 1),$$

a polynomial of degree j in $|X|$.

If ψ_{PAR} is of order k, then $P(X) = \sum_{j=0}^{k} \alpha_j C_j(X) - \theta$ is a polynomial of degree $\leq k$ in $|X|$.

Now, let X_j have j points for each j among $0, 1, \ldots, |R|$. Then the sequence $P(|X_0|) < 0$, $P(|X_1|) \geq 0$, $P(|X_2|) < 0$, $\ldots$, $P(|X_R|)$ changes sign $|R| - 1$ times. Thus, P has degree $\geq |R|$, and so we conclude that ψ_{PAR} must have order $|R|$. ☐

Minsky and Papert [1969, Theorem 10.1] show that, in the threshold function for realizing ψ_{PAR}, the ratio of the largest to the smallest weights must be $2^{|R|-1}$, and they comment that this shows that a function which is theoretically realizable in a certain way need not be practically realizable.

THEOREM 20 (THE "ONE-IN-A-BOX" THEOREM)

Let $A_1, \ldots, A_m$ be disjoint subsets of R, and let

$$\psi(X) = \ulcorner (|X \cap A_i| > 0) \text{ for all } i \urcorner$$

i.e., $\psi(X)$ is true only if X contains a member of each A_i.

If $|A_i| = 4m^2$ for all i, then the order of ψ is $\geq m$.

Proof

Let G_i be the group of all permutations which leave $R \backslash A_i$ invariant $(i = 1, \ldots, m)$. Let G be the group generated by the G_i. Then ψ is invariant with respect to G. Let Φ^K be the set of masks of degree $\leq K$, with equivalence classes Φ_j under $\underset{G}{\equiv}$. We see that $\phi_1 \underset{G}{\equiv} \phi_2$ iff $|S(\phi_1) \cap A_i| = |S(\phi_2) \cap A_i|$ for each i, where $S(\phi)$ is the set of lines feeding the module of ϕ. Then clearly

$$N_j(X) = |\{\phi | \phi \in \Phi_j \text{ and } \phi(X)\}| = \binom{|X \cap A_1|}{|S(\phi) \cap A_1|} \cdots \binom{|X \cap A_m|}{|S(\phi) \cap A_m|}$$

(for any ϕ in ϕ_j). So $N_j(X)$ is a polynomial $P_j(y_1, \ldots, y_n)$ of degree $\leq K$ in the numbers $y_i = |X \cap A_i|$. Therefore, if ψ can be represented in terms of Φ^K, then there is a polynomial Q of degree $\leq K$ such that

$$\psi(X) = {}^\lceil Q(y_1, \ldots, y_m) \geq 0 \text{ with } y_i = |X \cap A_i| {}^\rceil$$

Thus, we require that for $0 \leq y_i \leq 4m^2$:

$$Q(y_1, \ldots, y_m) > 0 \Leftrightarrow (y_i > 0) \text{ for all } i$$

Set $y_i = (t - (2i - 1))^2$ so that Q becomes a polynomial of degree $\leq 2K$ in t. Now if t is odd, $y_i = 0$ for $i = \dfrac{t + 1}{2}$, but if t is even, $y_i > 0$. Thus, the degree of Q in t is $\geq 2m$. Hence $K \geq m$. $\qquad\square$

We close our discussion by applying the "One-in-a-Box" theorem to place a lower bound on the order of the connectedness predicate: Let us recall our interpretation of R as a set of squares in the plane, and say that two points of R are **adjacent** if they are squares with a common edge. We then say that X is **connected** if for each p and q in X we can find a sequence $p_1, p_2, \ldots, p_n$ of points, all of which are in X, with $p = p_1$, with p_j adjacent to p_{j+1} for $1 \leq j < n$, and with $p_n = q$.

THEOREM 21

The order of the predicate $\psi(X) = {}^\lceil X$ is connected${}^\rceil$ increases without bound as $|R| \to \infty$.

Proof

Consider a rectangle with $(2m + 1)$ rows, each of $4m^2$ squares. A figure containing all the odd-numbered rows will be connected iff it also contains at least one point from each of the m even-numbered rows. Thus, a solution to the connectedness problem for this array with $|R| = 4m^2(2m + 1)$ solves the one-in-a-box problem for the even rows, and so has order at least m. Thus, the order of ψ increases at least as fast as $\frac{1}{2}\sqrt[3]{|R|}$. $\square$

EXERCISES FOR SECTION 5-5

1.   Given $\{1, 2, \ldots, m\} \subset \mathbf{Z}_N$, where $m = \lfloor N^{1/2} \rfloor$, show that there exists some $z \in \mathbf{Z}_N$ such that $x \cdot z < N \leq y \cdot z < 2N$.

2.   Verify that 45 output lines are required in Example 3.

3.   Verify that R_j and L_j given in Definition 3 are indeed equivalence relations.

4.   Give a complete proof of Lemma 4.

5.   Prove Corollary 9.

6.   Prove the following refinement of Theorem 14: The coefficients α_i of the masks ϕ_i in (1) are unique.

7.   Apply Corollary 17 to masks of degree 1 to prove that if G is any **transitive** group of permutations on R (i.e., $xG = R$ for each $x \in R$), then the only order one predicates invariant under G are

$$\ulcorner |X| > m \urcorner, \quad \ulcorner |X| \geq m \urcorner, \quad \ulcorner |X| < m \urcorner \quad \text{and} \quad \ulcorner |X| \leq m \urcorner$$

for some m.

8.   Prove the following statements:

(a)   If $\psi_{PAR} \in L(\Phi)$ and Φ contains *only* masks, then Φ contains *every* mask. [Hint: Suppose that ϕ_A is not in Φ, and deduce that $\psi_{PAR}(X \cap A)$ is of order $< |A|$ to get a contradiction.]

(b)   If $\psi_{PAR} \in L(\Phi)$, then Φ must contain at least one ϕ of degree $|R|$.

(c)   If Φ is the set of all ψ_{PAR}^A for *proper* subsets A of R, then $\psi_{PAR} \notin L(\Phi)$.

5–6   Universal Algebras

We are now in a position to unify the concepts we have studied in Sections 5–1 through 5–4. We have seen that there are many different semigroups, but they all share the possession of a binary operator which we may, in general, label as m, though in particular cases we may rewrite $m(x, y)$ as $x \cdot y$, xy, or $x + y$, as proves convenient. In specifying a monoid, we must again specify a binary operator, which we may label m, as well as a nullary operator (i.e., a constant), which we may label 1. In talking of groups, we have employed three labels—m, 1, and i—for three operators which are binary, nullary, and unary. In short, in talking of a class of interesting algebraic structures we shall commonly specify a set of labels, which are to be interpreted as operators of given *arity* (we say that an n-ary operator has arity n) when we turn to any particular exemplar of that structure. Our task, then, is to specify a general language in which we may discuss algebraic structures of this kind. This is the language of *universal algebras*. We start by specifying when a set Ω may qualify as a set of operator labels, and then call any set A, which is equipped with a collection of operators appropriately labelled by elements of Ω, an Ω-algebra:

We say that a set Ω is a **label set** if it is equipped with a function $\nu:\Omega \to \mathbf{N}:\omega \mapsto \nu(\omega)$, and we call $\nu(\omega)$ the **arity** of ω.

The following definition makes clear the fact that we may use ω to label an n-ary operator if and only if $\nu(\omega) = n$:

DEFINITION 1

Given a label set Ω, an **Ω-algebra**† is a set A together with a collection of functions, one for each $\omega \in \Omega$, such that whenever $\nu(\omega) = n$ the corresponding function is of the form $A^n \to A$.

We usually label this function as ω_A. The set of operators on A so formed is then denoted by Ω_A and we denote the Ω-algebra by (A, Ω_A). We call A the **carrier** of (A, Ω_A), and often refer to the Ω-algebra simply by the name of its carrier when there is no doubt about which operators are to be applied.

$\bigcirc$

In other words, Ω is a set of labels, whereas Ω_A is an *interpretation* of these labels as operators on A—just as $+$ is a label which may be interpreted in many ways, as addition of real numbers, or of vectors, or of rationals, or of numbers modulo m, and in many other ways besides.

As we shall see, it will be important that a given ω must always be interpreted as a function of the same arity—for then we shall have a methodical way of comparing different interpretations of ω, and for building new interpretations from old ones.

Example 1

Suppose that Ω is the finite set $\{m, 1, i\}$ with the arity function $\nu:\Omega \to \mathbf{N}$ specified by the values $\nu(m) = 2$, $\nu(1) = 0$, $\nu(i) = 1$.

If we set $A = \mathbf{Z}$, $m_A = +$, $1_A = 0$, and $i_A = -$, then the Ω-algebra (A, Ω_A) is the usual group of the integers under addition.

However, if we take $B = \mathbf{N}$ with $m_B = +$, $1_B = 0$, and $i_B(x) = 2x$, then (B, Ω_B) is still an Ω-algebra for $\Omega = \{m, 1, i\}$, but is *not* a group. In building up to Definition 8 below, we shall specify the extra conditions that must be placed on an $\{m, 1, i\}$-algebra to ensure that it is indeed a group. $\Diamond$

Example 2

As in Section 5–2, by a *semiautomaton* we simply mean a function $\delta:Q \times X \to Q$ (which may be regarded as the *dynamics* of an automaton

---

†This is essentially the notion introduced in Section 4–3, though there we allowed labels with multiple arity. However, the present section does *not* depend on Chapter 4.

for which we are not interested in the outputs—hence, *semi*automaton). Now think of X as a label set with $\nu(x) = 1$ for each $x \in X$. Then the concepts of an X-algebra (Q, X_Q) and a *semiautomaton with input set X* are interchangeable:

Given a function $\delta: Q \times X \to Q$, we may define a unary operator $x: Q \to Q: q \mapsto q \cdot x$ for each $x \in X$ by the equations

$$q \cdot x \overset{\Delta}{=} \delta(q, x) \quad \text{for each } x \in X \text{ and each } q \in Q$$

Conversely, if we have an X-algebra with *carrier* Q, so that we have a unary operator $q \mapsto q \cdot x$ for each $x \in X$, we may define a semiautomaton δ with *state set* Q by the equation

$$\delta(q, x) \overset{\Delta}{=} q \cdot x \quad \text{for all } (q, x) \in Q \times X$$

In other words, we may regard each input x to a semiautomaton as labelling the state-transition function $\delta(\cdot, x): Q \to Q: q \mapsto \delta(q, x)$ [where we have turned the two-argument function δ into a one-argument function $\delta(\cdot, x)$ by filling in the value x, and indicating by a dot where the remaining argument may be inserted]. ◊

Example 3

Pursuing our interest in semiautomata, consider Figure 5–28, which depicts a $\{0, 1\}$-algebra with carrier $Q = \{q_0, q_1, q_2, q_3\}$ (i.e., a semiautomaton with

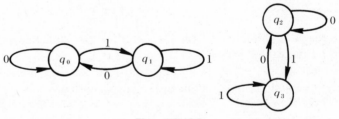

Figure 5–28

input set $\{0, 1\}$ and state set Q). This state graph may be converted into Table 5–12. ◊

Table 5–12

q	$q \cdot 0$	$q \cdot 1$
q_0	q_0	q_1
q_1	q_0	q_1
q_2	q_2	q_3
q_3	q_2	q_3

Given two states, q and q', of a (semi)automaton δ, we say (as in Section 2–5) that state q' is **reachable** from q if there exists some input sequence $w \in X^*$ which sends the machine from state q into q'; i.e., such that $\delta^*(q, w) = q'$. Given any subset $Q' = Q$, we call the set of states reachable from states of Q' the **closure** of Q'. We denote this by $\langle Q' \rangle$, and so we have

$$\langle Q' \rangle = \{\delta^*(q, w) | q \in Q' \text{ and } w \in X^*\}$$

We also say that Q' **generates** $\langle Q' \rangle$.

Thus, in the above example, $\langle \{q_0\} \rangle = \{q_0, q_1\} = \langle \{q_1\} \rangle$ and $\langle \{q_0, q_2\} \rangle = Q$, among other relationships.

Let us rephrase the above discussion in a way which will generalize to Ω-algebras. Recall that we defined $\delta^* : Q \times X^* \to Q$ inductively by the definition

$$\left. \begin{array}{l} \delta^*(q, e) = q \\ \delta^*(q, wx) = \delta(\delta^*(q, w), x) \text{ for all } w \in X^*, x \in X \end{array} \right\} \text{ for all } q \in Q$$

Transferring this to the view of a semiautomaton as an X-algebra, we see that we may *derive* from the given family of operators $x : Q \to Q : q \mapsto q \cdot x$ (where there is one for each $x \in X$) a new family of operators (of which there is one for each $w \in X^*$) by the formula

$$w : Q \to Q : q \mapsto q \cdot w \overset{\Delta}{=} \delta^*(q, w)$$

or, equivalently, by the induction scheme

$$\left. \begin{array}{l} q \cdot e = q \\ q \cdot (wx) = (q \cdot w) \cdot x \text{ for all } w \in X^*, x \in X \end{array} \right\} \text{ for all } q \in Q$$

Then, if we think of X^* as labelling the set of **derived operators** of X, we get the equation

$$\langle Q' \rangle = \{q \cdot w | q \in Q' \text{ and } w \in X^*\}$$

The above discussion suggests that, given *any* Ω-algebra (A, Ω_A), we may construct a set of operators Ω_A^* which can be built up, or *derived*, from the elements of the set Ω_A. We will denote the corresponding label set by Ω^*.

We shall now demonstrate this concept by means of another example.

Example 4

Consider the Ω-algebra (A, Ω_A) having the label set $\Omega = \{m, 1, i\}$ with the corresponding arity $\nu(m) = 2$, $\nu(1) = 0$, $\nu(i) = 1$.

Let us build up the operator f_1, having arity 3, as follows:

$$f_1(a_1, a_2, a_3) = m_A(a_1, m_A(a_2, a_3))$$

Similarly, we can derive an arity 3 operator f_2 given by

$$f_2(a_1, a_2, a_3) = m_A(m_A(a_1, a_2), a_3)$$

Some derived unary operators are:

$$f_3(a) = m_A(a, 1)$$
$$f_4(a) = a$$
$$f_5(a) = m_A(1, a)$$
$$f_6(a) = m_A(a, i(a))$$
$$f_7(a) = 1$$
$$f_8(a) = m_A(i(a), a)$$

In terms of these derived operators, the given Ω-algebra (A, Ω_A) is a group if and only if the following three conditions are satisfied:

I. $f_1(a_1, a_2, a_3) = f_2(a_1, a_2, a_3)$ for all $a_1, a_2, a_3 \in A$ (associativity)
II. $f_3(a) = f_4(a) = f_5(a)$ for all $a \in A$ (identity)
III. $f_6(a) = f_7(a) = f_8(a)$ for all $a \in A$ (inverse) $\Diamond$

The formal definition of derived operators that follows is somewhat formidable, and the reader may wish to pass directly to Definition 3.

DEFINITION 2

Let Ω be a label set with arity function $\nu: \Omega \to \mathbf{Z}_+$. For each $m \in \mathbf{Z}_+$ and each p with $0 \le p \le m$, let $S^{(m,p)}$ be a new label with arity m.

Let (A, Ω_A) be an Ω-algebra with $\omega_A: A^{\nu(\omega)} \to A$, for each $\omega \in \Omega$. For each $m \in \mathbf{Z}_+$ and each p with $1 \le p \le m$, let $S_A^{(m,p)}$ be the function
$$A^m \to A: (a_1, \ldots, a_p, \ldots, a_m) \mapsto a_p,$$
while $S^{(m,0)}$ is the function
$$A^m \to A^0: (a_1, \ldots, a_m) \mapsto \Lambda.$$

We then define the set Ω^* of de-rived labels with arity inductively as follows:

We then define the set Ω_A^* of de-rived operators inductively as follows:

Basis Step.
$$\Omega^{(0)} = \Omega \cup \{S^{(m,p)} \mid m \in \mathbf{Z}_+, \\ 0 \le p \le m\}$$

Basis Step.
$$\Omega_A^{(0)} = \Omega_A \cup \{S_A^{(m,p)} \mid m \in \mathbf{Z}_+, \\ 0 \le p \le m\}$$

Induction Step.

$$\Omega^{(n+1)} = \Omega^{(n)} \cup$$
$$\{\omega\omega_1 \ldots \omega_k \,|\, \omega_j \in \Omega^{(n)},$$
$$1 \leq j \leq k$$
$$\text{and } \omega \in \Omega$$
$$\text{with } \nu(\omega) = k\}$$

where $\nu(\omega\omega_1 \ldots \omega_k) \overset{\Delta}{=}$
$\max(\nu(\omega_1), \ldots, \nu(\omega_k))$

Induction Step.

$$\Omega_A^{(n+1)} = \Omega_A^{(n)} \cup$$
$$\{[\omega\omega_1 \ldots \omega_k]_A \,|\, \omega_j \in \Omega^{(n)},$$
$$1 \leq j \leq k$$
$$\text{and } \omega \in \Omega$$
$$\text{with } \nu(\omega) = k\}$$

where, if $\nu(\omega\omega_1 \ldots \omega_k) = m$,
we have
$$[\omega\omega_1 \ldots \omega_k]_A(a_1, \ldots, a_m) \overset{\Delta}{=}$$
$$\omega(\omega_1(a_1, \ldots, a_{\nu(\omega_1)}), \ldots,$$
$$\omega_k(a_1, \ldots, a_{\nu(\omega_k)})) \qquad \bigcirc$$

Example 5

In our study of semigroups, we are interested in the associative law

$$m(m(x,y), z) = m(x, m(y,z))$$

Let us see how the above definitions reveal the functions

$$f_1(x,y,z) = m(m(x,y), z)$$

and

$$f_2(x,y,z) = m(x, m(y,z))$$

as operators derived from m:

$$mmS^{(3,3)}(x,y,z)$$
$$= m(m(x,y), S^{(3,3)}(x,y,z))$$
$$= m(m(x,y), z)$$
$$= f_1(x,y,z)$$

Thus, $f_1 \in \{m\}^{(1)}$. Further,

$$mS^{(3,1)}(mS^{(3,2)}S^{(3,3)})(x,y,z)$$
$$= m(S^{(3,1)}(x,y,z), mS^{(3,2)}S^{(3,3)}(x,y,z))$$
$$= m(x, m(S^{(3,2)}(x,y,z), S^{(3,3)}(x,y,z)))$$
$$= m(x, m(y,z))$$
$$= f_2(x,y,z)$$

Thus, $f_2 \in \{m\}^{(2)}$. $\qquad\qquad\qquad\qquad\qquad \Diamond$

We see that the role of the functions $S^{(m,p)}$ is just "to put the arguments in the right places." Thus, Ω^* labels all operators that can be built up from operators labelled by Ω by repeatedly "shuffling" variables (with the $S^{(m,p)}$) and "hitting" the variables with Ω-operators.

We may now generalize our definition of closure:

DEFINITION 3

Let (A, Ω_A) be an Ω-algebra. Then the **closure** of a subset A' of A is the set

$$\langle A' \rangle = \{\widehat{\omega}_A(a_1, \ldots, a_n) \,|\, n \in \mathbf{N} \text{ with}$$
$$(a_1, \ldots, a_n) \in A^n, \, \widehat{\omega} \in \Omega^*, \text{ and } \nu(\widehat{\omega}) = n\}$$

If B is a subset of A which equals its own closure (i.e., if $B = \langle B \rangle$), then we say that B is **closed**. If B is closed, then each operator ω_A of Ω_A^* (and, *a fortiori*, each operator of Ω_A) of arity n maps B^n into B, and so its restriction to B^n is in fact an operator ω_B on B, where

$$\omega_B = \omega_A \,|\, B^n : B^n \to B : (b_1, \ldots, b_n) \mapsto \omega_A(b_1, \ldots, b_n) \in B$$

We call the Ω-algebra (B, Ω_B) so formed the **subalgebra** of A with carrier B. Thus, A has one subalgebra for each closed subset, and so, in particular, (A, Ω_A) always has itself as subalgebra. We call a subalgebra **proper** if it is not the whole algebra.   ○

The reader should recognize the above discussion as the appropriate generalization of our notions of subsemigroups, submonoids, and subgroups in Section 5-2.

Example 6

Returning to the 4-state semiautomaton of Figure 5–28, we see that there are three distinct closed sets, $\{q_0, q_1\}$, $\{q_2, q_3\}$, and Q, and thus there are two distinct proper subalgebras, one for each half of the state diagram.   ◊

Example 7

Consider the semigroup $\mathbf{N}$ under multiplication. Then the only label in Ω is the binary $\cdot$ (we denote $\cdot_{\mathbf{N}}(n_1, n_2)$ by $n_1 \cdot n_2$) and the induction scheme of Exercise 3 reduces to

$$\langle A' \rangle^{(0)} = A'$$
$$\langle A' \rangle^{(n+1)} = \langle A' \rangle^{(n)} \cup \{a_1 \cdot a_2 \,|\, a_1, a_2 \in \langle A' \rangle^{(n)}\}$$

Taking the simple case $A' = \{2\}$, we see that

$$\langle\{2\}\rangle^{(0)} = \{2\}$$
$$\langle\{2\}\rangle^{(1)} = \{2\} \cup \{2 \cdot 2\} = \{2, 2^2\}$$
$$\langle\{2\}\rangle^{(2)} = \{2, 2^2\} \cup \{2 \cdot 2, 2 \cdot 2^2, 2^2 \cdot 2, 2^2 \cdot 2^2\} = \{2, 2^2, 2^3, 2^4\}$$

and we may easily verify by induction that

$$\langle\{2\}\rangle^{(n)} = \{2^k \mid 1 \le k \le 2^n, k \in \mathbf{Z}_+\}$$

to deduce that

$$\langle\{2\}\rangle = \{2^k \mid k \in \mathbf{Z}_+\}$$

as our intuition would indeed lead us to expect.

Similarly, given any finite set $\{a_1, a_2, \ldots, a_n\}$ of integers, we may show that its closure in $(\mathbf{N}, \cdot)$ is precisely the set

$$\left\{ a_1^{k_1} a_2^{k_2} \ldots a_n^{k_n} \mid \text{each } k_i \in \mathbf{N} \text{ but } \sum_i k_i \ge 1 \right\}$$

which may be obtained from the initial set by repeated multiplication. ◊

Example 8

Since $\{2^n \mid n \in \mathbf{N}\}$ is closed under multiplication, $(\{2^n\}, \cdot)$ is a subsemigroup of $(\mathbf{N}, \cdot)$. ◊

Let us now see another way in which we may form new Ω-algebras from old ones by emulating the passage to congruence classes by which $\mathbf{Z}_m$ was formed from $\mathbf{Z}$, which we studied in Section 5–1. Consider, then, the $\mathbf{Z}$-algebra $(\mathbf{Z}, +, 0, -)$ [which is short for $(\mathbf{Z}, \{+, 0, -\}_{\mathbf{Z}})$] and the equivalence relation $\sim_m$ defined on $\mathbf{Z}$ by

$$k_1 \sim_m k_1' \Leftrightarrow k_1 - k_1' \text{ is a multiple of } m$$

We see that $\sim_m$ is compatible with $+$, 0, and $-$ in the sense that:

$$k_1 \sim_m k_1 \text{ and } k_2 \sim_m k_2' \Rightarrow k_1 + k_2 \sim_m k_1' + k_2'$$

0 is a constant, and so causes no trouble (since $\Lambda \sim_m \Lambda$, it is certainly true that for all x, x' in $\mathbf{Z}^0$, $x \sim_m x' \Rightarrow 0(x) \sim_m 0(x')$)

$$k_1 \sim_m k_1' \Rightarrow -k_1 \sim_m -k_1'$$

Because of this we were able to define three "barrel" functions, to obtain corresponding operators on $\mathbf{Z}_m = \mathbf{Z}/\!\sim_m$:

$$+ : \mathbf{Z}_m^2 \to \mathbf{Z}_m : ([k_1]_m, [k_2]_m) \mapsto [k_1 + k_2]_m$$
$$0 : \mathbf{Z}_m^0 \to \mathbf{Z}_m : \Lambda \mapsto [0]_m$$
$$- : \mathbf{Z}_m^1 \to \mathbf{Z}_m : [k_1]_m \mapsto [-k_1]_m$$

Clearly, the above situation immediately generalizes to that set forth in the following two definitions:

DEFINITION 4

Let $\equiv$ be an equivalence relation on the carrier A of an Ω-algebra (A, Ω_A). We say that $\equiv$ is a **congruence** on (A, Ω_A) if for any $\omega \in \Omega$, say $\nu(\omega) = n$, and any pair of samples $(a_1, \ldots, a_n)$ and $(a'_1, \ldots, a'_n)$ of A^n, we must always have that

$$a_1 \equiv a'_1, \ldots, a_n \equiv a'_n \Rightarrow \omega_A(a_1, \ldots, a_n) \equiv \omega_A(a'_1, \ldots, a'_n)$$

[Note that the above implication is trivially satisfied if $\nu(\omega) = 0$, since $\equiv$ is reflexive.]   ○

DEFINITION 5

Let $\equiv$ be a congruence on the Ω-algebra (A, Ω_A). Then for each $\omega \in \Omega$ we may define an operator $\omega_{A/\equiv} : (A/\equiv)^{\nu(\omega)} \to A/\equiv$ by the equation

$$\omega_{A/\equiv}([a_1]_\equiv, \ldots, [a_{\nu(\omega)}]_\equiv) \overset{\Delta}{=} \omega_A[a_1, \ldots, a_{\nu(\omega)}]_\equiv \text{ for all } (a_1, \ldots, a_{\nu(\omega)}) \in A^{\nu(\omega)} \quad \textbf{(1)}$$

The Ω-algebra $(A/\equiv, \Omega_{A/\equiv})$ so defined is called the **factor algebra** of (A, Ω_A) with respect to the congruence $\equiv$.   ○

Example 9

$(\mathbf{Z}_m, +, 0, -)$ is the factor algebra of $(\mathbf{Z}, +, 0, -)$ with respect to the congruence $\sim_m$.   ◊

Now let us consider the **canonical surjection** $A \to A/\equiv$ $a \mapsto [a]_\equiv$. If we write f for this map, and denote $A/\equiv$ by B, we see that, for $\nu(\omega) = n$, we may rewrite (1) as

$$\omega_B(f(a_1), \ldots, f(a_n)) = f(\omega_A(a_1, \ldots, a_n)) \quad \textbf{(2)}$$

This discussion suggests the following definition.

DEFINITION 6

Let (A, Ω_A) and (B, Ω_B) be two Ω-algebras. Then we say that a map $f : A \to B$ is an **(Ω-algebra) homomorphism** whenever

$$\omega_B(f(a_1), \dots, f(a_n)) = f(\omega_A(a_1, \dots, a_n))$$

for each $\omega \in \Omega$ with $\nu(\omega) = n$ and each $(a_1, \dots, a_n) \in A^n$.

If we define the map $f^n : A^n \to B^n$ by $f^n(a_1, \dots, a_n) = (f(a_1), \dots, f(a_n))$, then we may express the condition that f be a homomorphism by requiring that for each $\omega \in \Omega$ we have commutativity of the following diagram:

$$\begin{array}{ccc} A^n & \xrightarrow{\ f^n\ } & B^n \\ \omega_A \downarrow & & \downarrow \omega_B \\ A & \xrightarrow{\ f\ } & B \end{array} \qquad \text{where } n = \nu(\omega). \qquad \bigcirc$$

The following example reminds us that the definition of a homomorphism does *not* require that $f : A \to B$ be onto (i.e., surjective):

Example 10

If (A, Ω_A) is a proper subalgebra of (B, Ω_B), then the clearly nonsurjective inclusion map $f : A \to B : a \mapsto a$ is a homomorphism, since if $\nu(\omega) = n$

$$\begin{aligned} \omega_B(f(a_1), \dots, f(a_n)) &= \omega_B(a_1, \dots, a_n) && \text{since } f(a_j) = a_j \\ &= \omega_A(a_1, \dots, a_n) && \text{since } \omega_B | A^n = \omega_A \\ &= f(\omega_A(a_1, \dots, a_n)) && \text{since } A \text{ is closed and } f : a \mapsto a. \quad \Diamond \end{aligned}$$

DEFINITION 7

If $f : A \to B$ determines a homomorphism $(A, \Omega_A) \to (B, \Omega_B)$, we say that the homomorphism is

> an **epimorphism** iff f is surjective (onto);
> a **monomorphism** iff f is injective ($1 : 1$);
> an **isomorphism** iff f is bijective ($1 : 1$ and onto). $\qquad \bigcirc$

We have already seen that every congruence yields a homomorphism, and now we also find that every homomorphism determines a congruence, as is made clear in the following theorem:

THEOREM 1

Let $f: A \to B$ determine an Ω-algebra homomorphism from (A, Ω_A) to (B, Ω_B). Then the relation $\equiv_f$ defined on A by

$$a \equiv_f a' \Leftrightarrow f(a) = f(a')$$

is a congruence on A, and the Ω-algebra whose carrier is $f(A)$ is a subalgebra of B isomorphic to the factor algebra $(A/\equiv_f, \Omega_{A/\equiv_f})$.

Proof

We must check

(i) that $\equiv_f$ is a congruence;
(ii) that $f(A)$ is closed;
(iii) that there is a bijection $\varphi: f(A) \to A/\equiv_f$ which is a homomorphism.

To check (i), we must show that if $\nu(\omega) = n$, then for any $(a_1, \ldots, a_n)$ and $(a'_1, \ldots, a'_n)$ such that $a_j \equiv_f a'_j$ for $1 \le j \le n$, we must have that $\omega_A(a_1, \ldots, a_n) \equiv_f \omega_A(a'_1, \ldots, a'_n)$. But this follows immediately from the definition of $\equiv_f$ and the fact that f is a homomorphism, for

$$\omega_A(a_1, \ldots, a_n) \equiv_f \omega_A(a'_1, \ldots, a'_n) \Leftrightarrow$$
$$f\omega_A(a_1, \ldots, a_n) = f\omega_A(a'_1, \ldots, a'_n) \Leftrightarrow$$
$$\omega_A(f(a_1), \ldots, f(a_n)) = \omega_A(f(a'_1), \ldots, f(a'_n))$$

But the last equality is immediate, since to claim $a_j \equiv_f a'_j$ is just to say that $f(a_j) = f(a'_j)$.

The verification of (ii) simply uses the fact that f is a homomorphism. If $b_1, \ldots, b_n$ lie in $f(A)$, we can find $a_1, \ldots, a_n$ in A such that $b_j = f(a_j)$ for each j. But then

$$\omega_B(b_1, \ldots, b_n) = \omega_B(f(a_1), \ldots, f(a_n))$$
$$= f(\omega_A(a_1, \ldots, a_n)) \in f(A)$$

and so $f(A)$ is indeed closed.

To check (iii), we simply check that the obvious bijection $\varphi: f(A) \to A/\equiv_f : b \mapsto [f^{-1}(b)]_{\equiv_f}$ is indeed a homomorphism. The details are straightforward, and are left to the reader. $\square$

If η denotes the canonical epimorphism $\eta: A \to A/\equiv_f$, this theorem yields the following commutative diagram:

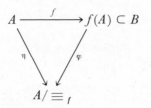

At this stage, let us recast our definitions of semigroup, monoid, and group in the language of Ω-algebras to see what must be added to our notion of Ω-algebra to do justice to such concepts:

We fix $\nu(m) = 2$, $\nu(1) = 0$, and $\nu(i) = 1$. Then:

A **semigroup** is an $\{m\}$-algebra which satisfies the equation

$$m(x, m(y, z)) = m(m(x,y), z) \text{ for all } x, y, z \text{ in its carrier}$$

A **monoid** is an $\{m, 1\}$-algebra which satisfies the equations

$$\left.\begin{array}{r} m(x, m(y, z)) = m(m(x,y), z) \\ m(x, 1) = x = m(1, x) \end{array}\right\} \text{ for all } x, y, z \text{ in its carrier.}$$

A **group** is an $\{m, 1, i\}$-algebra which satisfies the equations

$$\left.\begin{array}{r} m(x, m(y, z)) = m(m(x,y), z) \\ m(x, 1) = x = m(1, x) \\ m(x, i(x)) = 1 = m(i(x), x) \end{array}\right\} \text{ for all } x, y, z \text{ in its carrier.}$$

Recalling our discussion of derived operators, we have already seen that we can derive from m the operators f_1 and f_2 such that the first equation may be re-expressed by the equality of derived operators

$$f_1 = f_2 \tag{3}$$

since we have $f_1(x, y, z) = m(x, m(y, z))$ and $f_2(x, y, z) = m(m(x, y)z)$.

Let us perform the same service for the remaining equations.

From m and 1 we may derive three new operators:

$$f_3(x) = m(x, 1)$$
$$f_4(x) = x$$
$$f_5(x) = m(1, x)$$

to re-express the condition that 1 denotes an identity for m by the pair of equations

$$f_3 = f_4 \tag{4}$$
$$f_4 = f_5 \tag{5}$$

Again, from m, 1, and i we may derive three operators:

$$f_6(x) = m(x, i(x))$$
$$f_7(x) = 1$$
$$f_8(x) = m(i(x), x)$$

to re-express the condition that i denote an inverse for m by the pair of equations

$$f_6 = f_7 \qquad\qquad (6)$$
$$f_7 = f_8 \qquad\qquad (7)$$

Our definitions then become:

A **semigroup** is an $\{m\}$-algebra which satisfies equation (3).

A **monoid** is an $\{m, 1\}$-algebra which satisfies equations (3), (4), and (5).

A **group** is an $\{m, 1, i\}$-algebra which satisfies equations (3) through (7).

This clearly reveals each of the three concepts as an example of the general notion of an (Ω, E)-algebra, where we have the following definition:

DEFINITION 8

Let Ω be a label set, with Ω^* its set of derived labels. By an $\boldsymbol{\Omega}$-**equation** we shall mean a pair (f, f') of elements of Ω^* of the same arity. We say that an Ω-algebra (A, Ω_A) **satisfies** the Ω-equation (f, f') if we have $f_A = f'_A$ as operators $A^n \to A$, where $\nu(f) = \nu(f') = n$.

Let E be a set (finite or infinite) of Ω-equations. Then we say that the Ω-algebra (A, Ω_A) is an (Ω, E)-**algebra** if it satisfies every equation in E. ○

Fortunately, most of the hard work on (Ω, E)-algebras has been accomplished in our study of plain Ω-algebras, as the reader may see by providing the proof of the following theorem.

THEOREM 2

Let $f: A \to B$ be a homomorphism from the Ω-algebra (A, Ω_A) to the Ω-algebra (B, Ω_B). Then the following are true:

(i) f is compatible with every derived operator labelled by an element of Ω^*.

(ii) If (A, Ω_A) is an (Ω, E)-algebra, then $(f(A), \Omega_{f(A)})$ is also an (Ω, E)-algebra for the same set E of equations.

(iii) Let $\equiv$ be a congruence on the Ω-algebra (A, Ω_A). Then if (A, Ω_A) is an (Ω, E)-algebra, then $(A/\equiv, \Omega_{A/\equiv})$ is an (Ω, E)-algebra for the same E.

(iv) Every subalgebra of an (Ω, E)-algebra is also an (Ω, E)-algebra. $\square$

Thus, every sub-$\{m, 1, i\}$-algebra of a group is automatically a group, and every $\{m\}$-algebra which is a homomorphic image of a semigroup is also a semigroup, and so on. However, the following examples may serve to help the reader to avoid reading too much into the above assertions:

Example 11

$(\mathbf{N}, \max, 0)$ is a monoid, and the set $\mathbf{Z}_+$ is a closed subset of $\mathbf{N}$ under max. However, $0 \notin \mathbf{Z}_+$, and so $(\mathbf{Z}_+, \max, 0)$ is not a submonoid of $(\mathbf{N}, \max, 0)$. Neither is $(\mathbf{Z}_+, \max, 1)$, even though it *is* a monoid (why not?). $\Diamond$

Example 12

Let $\{0, 1\}$ be a group under $0 + 0 = 1 + 1 = 0$; $0 + 1 = 1 + 0 = 1$; with identity 0, and inverse $-0 = 0$ and $-1 = 1$. Let $\{2, 3\}$ be a group under $2 + 2 = 3 + 3 = 2$; $2 + 3 = 3 + 2 = 3$; with identity 2, and inverse $-2 = 2$ and $-3 = 3$. Then we may form a new $\{m, 1, i\}$-algebra with carrier $B = \{0, 1, 2, 3\}$ by defining

$+_B$	0	1	2	3		x	$i_B(x)$
0	0	1	0	2		0	1
1	1	0	1	3	$1_B = 0$	1	0
2	2	1	2	3		2	3
3	3	0	3	2		3	2

Then the injection $\{0, 1\} \to \{0, 1, 2, 3\}$ is clearly an $\{m, 1, i\}$-homomorphism whose image is a group, but this does not turn the whole set $\{0, 1, 2, 3\}$ into a group. $\Diamond$

To conclude, let us explicitly demonstrate that the study of direct products in Section 5-2 is also pertinent in the general setting of (Ω, E)-algebras.

Let (A, Ω_A) and (B, Ω_B) be two (Ω, E)-algebras. Then we may turn $A \times B$ into an Ω-algebra by taking

$$\omega_{A \times B} = \omega_A \times \omega_B : (A \times B)^{\nu(\omega)} \to A \times B:$$
$$((a_1, b_1), \dots, (a_{\nu(\omega)}, b_{\nu(\omega)})) \mapsto (\omega_A(a_1, \dots, a_{\nu(\omega)}), \omega_B(b_1, \dots, b_{\nu(\omega)}))$$

It only remains to check that $(A \times B, \Omega_{A \times B})$ satisfies the set E of equations satisfied by (A, Ω_A) and (B, Ω_B). Suppose, then, that $f = f'$ is an equation from E. It is straightforward to check that $f_{A \times B} = f_A \times f_B$ and $f'_{A \times B} = f'_A \times f'_B$. Let, then, $\nu(f) = \nu(f') = n$. Then for any $((a_1, b_1), \ldots, (a_n, b_n)) \in (A \times B)^n$ we have

$$
\begin{aligned}
f_{A \times B}((a_1, b_1), \ldots, (a_n, b_n)) &= (f_A(a_1, \ldots, a_n), f_B(b_1, \ldots, b_n)) \\
&= (f'_A(a_1, \ldots, a_n), f'_B(b_1, \ldots, b_n)) \\
&\quad \text{since } f = f' \text{ holds in both } (A, \Omega_A) \text{ and } (B, \Omega_B) \\
&= f'_{A \times B}((a_1, b_1), \ldots, (a_n, b_n)) \\
&\quad \text{so that } f = f' \text{ holds in } (A \times B, \Omega_{A \times B}).
\end{aligned}
$$

We then have the following result:

THEOREM 3

The direct product of (Ω, E)-algebras is again an (Ω, E)-algebra. □

We shall return to universal algebras in Section 7–2, when we see that rings, modules, and vector spaces are all (Ω, E)-algebras for appropriate label sets Ω and defining equations E. The virtue of this, of course, is that such concepts as submodule, module homorphism, and congruences are available in these new settings without extra effort on our part.

EXERCISES FOR SECTION 5–6

1. Specify the X-algebra corresponding to the semiautomata M_1 and M_2 of Figure 5–29.

For both M_1 and M_2, find $\langle \{q_1\} \rangle$, $\langle \{q_3, q_4\} \rangle$, and the smallest integer n for which an n-state subset of Q generates all of Q.

2. Draw the state graphs of all the proper subsemiautomata of the $\{0, 1\}$-algebra given by the state graph of Figure 5–30.

3. Prove that the closure of a subset A' of an Ω-algebra (A, Ω_A) may be equivalently defined by induction as follows:

Basis Step: $\langle A' \rangle^{(0)} = A'$

Induction Step: $\langle A' \rangle^{(n+1)} = \langle A' \rangle^{(n)} \cup \{\omega_A(a_1, \ldots, a_k) \mid \omega \in \Omega, \nu(\omega) = k,$ and

$$(a_1, \ldots, a_k) \in (\langle A' \rangle^{(n)})^k\}$$

Then $\langle A' \rangle = \displaystyle\bigcup_{n \geq 0} \langle A' \rangle^{(n)}$

M_1:

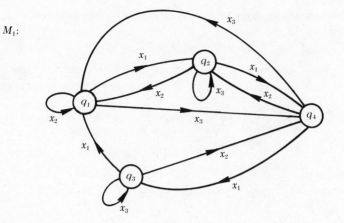

M_2:

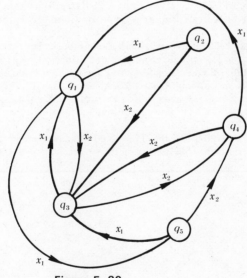

Figure 5-29

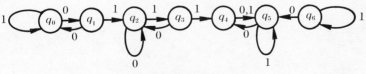

Figure 5-30

4.   Given the semigroup **Z** under addition, find the closure of
    (a) $\{3\}$
    (b) $\{m\}$
5.   Verify Theorem 2.
6.   Recall from Section 1–2 that if $\{A_\alpha \,|\, \alpha \in I\}$ is a family of sets indexed by the (finite or infinite) set I, then the direct product $\prod_{\alpha \in I} A_\alpha$ is the set of all functions

$f:I \to \bigcup_{\alpha \in A} A_\alpha$ such that $f(\alpha) \in A_\alpha$ for each $\alpha \in I$. Define the direct product of a family

$\{(A_\alpha, \Omega_{A_\alpha}) \,|\, \alpha \in I\}$ of (Ω, E)-algebras.

FURTHER READING FOR CHAPTER 5

    General background for the first few sections is provided by Hu [1965] and by MacLane and Birkhoff [1967]. The discussion of complexity in Section 5–4 is based on Minsky and Papert [1969], Spira [1969], and Winograd [1967]. Universal algebra (Section 5–6) is treated in great detail by Cohn [1965] and Grätzer [1968].

P. M. COHN [1965] Universal Algebra, New York: Harper and Row.
P. M. GRÄTZER [1968] Universal Algebra, Princeton, N.J.: Van Nostrand.
S. T. HU [1965] Elements of Modern Algebra, San Francisco: Holden-Day.
S. MACLANE and G. BIRKHOFF [1967] Algebra, New York: Macmillan.
M. L. MINSKY and S. PAPERT [1969] Perceptrons, Cambridge, Mass.: MIT Press.
P. M. SPIRA [1969] The Time Required for Group Multiplication, J. Assoc. Comp Mach., *16*, 235–243.
S. WINOGRAD [1967] On the Time Required to Perform Multiplication, J. Assoc. Comp. Mach., *14*, 793–802.

CHAPTER 6

Applied Probability Theory

This is the first of three chapters which, between them, provide an essentially self-contained introduction to information and coding theory. The basic results of information theory are presented in the present chapter, while Chapters 7 and 8 (which may be read independently of this chapter) provide an introduction to algebraic coding theory.

In Section 6–1, we provide the basic notions of discrete probability theory, serving two purposes: to provide one of the most important applications of the basic ideas of set theory developed in Section 1–2, and to provide the language in which we can couch our discussion of information theory. Then, in Section 6–2, we introduce the probabilistic measure of information which lies at the heart of the theory of reliable communication in the presence of noise. Shannon's noisy coding theorem, the key result of that theory, is developed in Section 6–4. But first, in Section 6–3, we develop Huffman's algorithm, which relates our measure of information to economical encoding schemes that seek to minimize the average number of symbols sent for the average message, given the probability with which different messages of an ensemble will be transmitted, and given that the channel has no noise for which we must compensate. Finally, in Section 6–5, we relate our study of probability theory to some of the notions of automata theory developed in Chapter 2.

6-1 Basic Notions of Discrete Probability Theory

One of the most important applications of the set-theoretic notions introduced in Section 1–2 has been in the axiomatic theory of probability. Thus, both to reinforce those notions and to prepare ourselves for the applications in the remainder of this chapter, we now turn to the basic notions of probability theory:

Suppose that the elements of a (finite or denumerable) set $S = \{s_1, s_2, s_3, \ldots\}$ correspond to all the outcomes of some experiment, in that, when the experiment is performed, we will identify the outcome with one and only one element s_i. We call the set S a **sample space** for the experiment, and any subset of S is said to be an **event**. Thus, the set of all events is the power set of S.

Example 1

Consider the experiment consisting of flipping a coin. For practical purposes we will assume that the coin eventually comes down, and ignore the case where the coin comes to rest on its edge. We may then take for our sample space $S = \{H, T\}$, where H and T denote the outcome of a flip being a head and a tail, respectively. Clearly, S is a valid sample space, since each time the coin is flipped the outcome will correspond to one and only one element of S. In this example there are four events: $\varnothing$, $\{H\}$, $\{T\}$, and S. (The null event $\varnothing$ signifies an outcome that is impossible.) $\lozenge$

Example 2

Now let us consider an experiment which consists of flipping a coin three times in succession in accordance with the assumptions stated for the previous example. (Equivalently, we can consider an experiment of flipping three distinct coins simultaneously.) A sample space is given by

$$S = \{HHH, HHT, HTH, HTT, THH, THT, TTH, TTT\}$$

where, for example, HTT indicates that the result of the first flip is a head, the second is a tail, and the third is also a tail.

We note that certain events may easily be characterized verbally, e.g., the subset $\{HHH, HHT, HTH, HTT\}$ is the event $\{\text{the first flip is a head}\}$, $\{HTT, THT, TTH\}$ is the event $\{\text{exactly two flips are tails}\}$, and $\{HHH, HHT, HTH, THH\}$ is the event $\{\text{at least two flips are heads}\}$. $\lozenge$

We will refer to a single performance of an experiment as a **trial.** Suppose that S is a sample space for an experiment and A is a subset of S. If the outcome $s \in S$ of a trial of the experiment is in A, then we say that event A has **occurred.** If $s \notin A$, then A has **not occurred.** At times it may be convenient to refer to certain special events. The event S is called the **certain event,** since the result of a trial must be some $s \in S$. Conversely, $\varnothing$ is the **impossible event** since the result of any trial is some $s \notin \varnothing$. Finally, a subset A of S consisting of the single element $s \in S$ (i.e., $A = \{s\}$) is an **elementary event.**

Since events are sets, we can talk about the union or intersection of two events A and B, and write $A \cup B$ or $A \cap B$, respectively. Two events A and B are said to be **mutually exclusive** if they are disjoint sets, that is, if $A \cap B = \varnothing$.

Let S then be a sample space. We associate with S a **probability measure** which assigns to *certain* events $A \subset S$ a number $P(A)$ called the **probability** of the event A. Later, we shall see the motivation for only defining P on a restricted family of subsets of S: the so-called "measurable" sets. For now, let us see what properties P should have to qualify as a probability:

Assume that we make successive trials in which no outcome is influenced in any way by the outcomes of previous trials. The intuitive idea of $P(A)$ is that if we make n trials, and obtain an occurrence of the event A (i.e., a point of A) some m times, then $\dfrac{m}{n}$ will be a good approximation to $P(A)$ for large n. Since $0 \le \dfrac{m}{n} \le 1$, this implies that $0 \le P(A) \le 1$ for each A. Our *frequency interpretation* then implies that a probability P must satisfy the following three axioms:

  I. $P(A) \ge 0$
 II. $P(S) = 1$
III. If $A \cap B = \varnothing$, then $P(A \cup B) = P(A) + P(B)$.

If $P(A)$ is a probability, we may say that $P(A)$ is the probability that A occurs.

Throughout this section, we shall only consider cases in which S is finite. However, in Section 6–5 we shall see applications in which we want to put a probability measure on the set of all infinite sequences of states of an automaton, and this set is infinite. In such applications we do not wish to have a probability estimate for all possible events, and so will designate a subset Ω of the power set 2^S of our sample space. The formal characterization of a probability space will then be:

DEFINITION 1

A **probability space** is a triple (S, Ω, P) where S is a set, and Ω is a nonempty subset of 2^S which is closed under (either finite or denumerable) union and under complementation. That is, if $\{A_i | i \in \mathbf{N}\}$ is any family of sets from Ω, then $\bigcup_{i \in \mathbf{N}} A_i$ belong to Ω. Further, if $A \in \Omega$, then $\bar{A} = S \backslash A \in \Omega$. Finally, $P : \Omega \to \{x | 0 \le x \le 1 \text{ and } x \text{ is a real number}\}$ satisfies the conditions:

(i) $P(S) = 1$

(ii) If $A = \bigcup_{i \in \mathbf{N}} A_i$ and $A_i \cap A_j = \varnothing$ for each $i \ne j$, then

$$P\left(\bigcup_{i \in \mathbf{N}} A_i\right) = \sum_{i \in \mathbf{N}} P(A_i). \qquad \bigcirc$$

Example 3

Let us check that the above conditions on Ω ensure that $S \in \Omega$, so that we can look at $P(S)$ as required in condition (i):

Since Ω is nonempty, there is some A in Ω. Then $\bar{A}$ is in Ω, and hence $S = A \cup \bar{A}$ must be in Ω as well. $\qquad \Diamond$

In the remainder of this section, we shall not worry about infinite unions, but shall simply make use of the fact that whenever $P(A)$ is defined so too is $P(\bar{A})$, and that if $P(A)$ and $P(B)$ are defined, so too is $P(A \cup B)$. Since $A \cap B = \bar{A} \cup \bar{B}$, we may deduce that $P(A \cap B)$ is then also defined.

Our frequency interpretation certainly suggests that $P(\varnothing) = 0$. We shall now show that this property follows from our axioms, which are certainly obeyed by any P satisfying Definition 1.

LEMMA 1

If P satisfies Axioms I to III, then $P(\varnothing) = 0$.

Proof

Since $A \cup \varnothing = A$, then

$$P(A \cup \varnothing) = P(A)$$

However, $A \cap \varnothing = \varnothing$. Thus, by Axiom III,

$$P(A \cup \varnothing) = P(A) + P(\varnothing)$$

Hence,

$$P(A) = P(A) + P(\varnothing)$$

whence $P(\varnothing) = 0$. $\qquad \square$

Example 4

Again consider the experiment of flipping a coin. If $0 < p < 1$ and we make the assignments:

$$P(\varnothing) = 0$$
$$P(\{H\}) = p$$
$$P(\{T\}) = 1 - p$$
$$P(S) = 1$$

then these numbers are indeed probabilities. We say that the coin is "fair" if $p = 1/2$; i.e., the occurrence of a head and a tail are equally likely.   ◊

Example 5

Consider the experiment of flipping the coin of the previous example three times. Let us make the following assignments for the *elementary* events:

$$P(\{HHH\}) = p^3$$
$$P(\{HHT\}) = p^2(1 - p)$$
$$P(\{HTH\}) = p^2(1 - p)$$
$$P(\{HTT\}) = p(1 - p)^2$$
$$P(\{THH\}) = p^2(1 - p)$$
$$P(\{THT\}) = p(1 - p)^2$$
$$P(\{TTH\}) = p(1 - p)^2$$
$$P(\{TTT\}) = (1 - p)^3$$

Note that if we then use Axiom III to define the probability of any other event, we do indeed obtain a probability P satisfying all axioms. For example,

$$
\begin{aligned}
P(\{\text{exactly two flips are tails}\}) &= P(\{HTT, THT, TTH\}) \\
&= P(\{HTT\}) + P(\{THT\}) + P(\{TTH\}) \\
&= 3p(1 - p)^2
\end{aligned}
$$

For the case when each experimental outcome is equally likely, we have that the probability of each elementary event is $1/8$; this corresponds to the condition $p = 1/2$.   ◊

We have stated above that a probability is a nonnegative number. We will now show that such a number cannot be greater than 1. We first prove a lemma.

LEMMA 2

$P(A) + P(\bar{A}) = 1.$

Proof

$P(A \cup \bar{A}) = P(S) = 1$ by Axiom II. Since $A \cap \bar{A} = \varnothing$, then by Axiom III,

$$P(A) + P(\bar{A}) = 1 \qquad \square$$

Since $P(A)$ and $P(\bar{A})$ are both probabilities, they are both nonnegative. Therefore, because they sum to 1, neither can be greater than 1. We have thus proved the following:

THEOREM 3

$0 \le P(A) \le 1.$ $\qquad \square$

Axiom III states that for mutually exclusive events A and B (i.e., $A \cap B = \varnothing$), we must have

$$P(A \cup B) = P(A) + P(B)$$

With the information at hand, we can now generalize this result.

THEOREM 4

$P(A \cup B) = P(A) + P(B) - P(A \cap B).$

Proof

From our study of set theory we know that

$$A \cup B = A \cup (\bar{A} \cap B)$$

and that A and $\bar{A} \cap B$ are mutually exclusive (check this). Thus,

$$P(A \cup B) = P(A) + P(\bar{A} \cap B) \qquad (1)$$

Similarly, from

$$B = (A \cap B) \cup (\bar{A} \cap B)$$

we deduce that

$$P(B) = P(A \cap B) + P(\bar{A} \cap B)$$

so that

$$P(\overline{A} \cap B) = P(B) - P(A \cap B) \tag{2}$$

Thus

$$P(A \cup B) = P(A) + P(\overline{A} \cap B) \qquad \text{from (1)}$$
$$= P(A) + P(B) - P(A \cap B) \text{ from (2)} \qquad \square$$

This theorem is indeed a generalization of Axiom III since, when A and B are mutually exclusive, we have

$$P(A \cup B) = P(A) + P(B) - P(A \cap B)$$
$$= P(A) + P(B) - P(\varnothing)$$
$$= P(A) + P(B)$$

Note: If $P(A) = 1$, this does *not* in general imply that $A = S$. For example, in our coin-tossing example, we might have taken S to be the three-element space $\{H, T, R\}$ where R corresponds to the coin falling on its rim, and then have set $P(\{H\}) = P(\{T\}) = 1/2$, while $P(\{R\}) = 0$.

Example 6

Given events A and B such that $P([A \cup B] \setminus [A \cap B]) = 0$, we will show that $P(A) = P(B) = P(A \cap B)$. We will first demonstrate that $P(A \setminus [A \cap B]) = 0$ and use the identity

$$A = [A \setminus (A \cap B)] \cup (A \cap B)$$

Since

$$A \setminus [A \cap B] \subset [A \cup B] \setminus [A \cap B]$$

then by Exercise 1,

$$0 = P([A \cup B] \setminus [A \cap B]) \geq P(A \setminus [A \cap B]) \geq 0$$

Thus, $P(A \setminus [A \cap B]) = 0$.
   Now,

$$A = [A \setminus (A \cap B)] \cup (A \cap B)$$

Also, $A \setminus (A \cap B)$ and $A \cap B$ are clearly mutually exclusive. Therefore,

$$P(A) = P([A \setminus (A \cap B)] \cup [A \cap B])$$
$$= P(A \setminus [A \cap B]) + P(A \cap B)$$
$$= 0 + P(A \cap B)$$
$$= P(A \cap B)$$

Similarly,

$$P(B) = P(A \cap B) \qquad \diamond$$

The above theorems and proofs have been based on an axiomatic approach to probability theory rather than that of a relative-frequency approach. Although a relative-frequency approach may be intuitively appealing, the axiomatic approach is preferred because of precision and rigor.

Its relation to the relative-frequency interpretation is known as the **law of large numbers** and may be stated as follows: Suppose that, for a given experiment, n trials are performed, each one of which is totally uninfluenced by any other. Further suppose that event A, having probability $P(A)$, occurs k times in these n trials. Then, for arbitrarily small positive numbers δ and ε, there exists a sufficiently large positive integer N such that for $n \geq N$ we have that the probability of the event

$$\left\{ \left| \frac{k}{n} - P(A) \right| > \delta \right\}$$

is at most ε. Note that this does not imply that

$$\lim_{n \to \infty} \frac{k}{n} = P(A)$$

but rather that for sufficiently large n there is a high probability that $\frac{k}{n}$ approximates $P(A)$. More will be said about this "law of large numbers" below.

Let us now turn to the idea of *conditional probabilities*, seeing how a relative-frequency interpretation may still suggest possible directions and definitions. Suppose that we make a series of trials in which the occurrences are always constrained to be in event B, and we want to estimate how often we obtain an occurrence of the event A. We may express this another way. Let us make a sequence of n unconstrained trials, and then discard those in which we do not get an occurrence of B. This means that approximately $P(B) \cdot n$ trials remain. In which of these remaining trials do we get an occurrence of A? Precisely when we have an occurrence of $A \cap B$, i.e., in approximately $P(A \cap B) \cdot n$ cases. Thus the frequency with which A occurs, when we know that B has occurred (assuming $P(B) \neq 0$), is approximated by

$$\frac{P(A \cap B) \cdot n}{P(B) \cdot n} = \frac{P(A \cap B)}{P(B)}$$

i.e., that fraction of the occurrences of B which are also occurrences of A. For this reason we make the following definition:

DEFINITION 2

The **conditional probability** of event A occurring, given that event B has occurred, is denoted by $P(A|B)$ and is defined as

$$P(A|B) = \frac{P(A \cap B)}{P(B)}$$

for $P(B) > 0$. If $P(B) = 0$, we define $P(A|B) = 0$. Note, then, that we always have $P(A \cap B) = P(A|B)P(B)$. ○

Suppose that A and B are mutually exclusive events and $P(B) > 0$. Then

$$P(A|B) = \frac{P(A \cap B)}{P(B)} = \frac{P(\emptyset)}{P(B)} = 0$$

This result clearly is to be expected. Since A and B are disjoint, knowing that B has occurred precludes the possibility of A occurring.

Example 7

Suppose that $A \subset B$. We will prove that $P(A|B) \geq P(A)$.

First suppose that $P(B) = 0$. Then $A \subset B$ implies $P(B) \geq P(A)$, by Exercise 1, and so $P(A) = 0$. Thus, by definition $P(A|B) = 0$ which is certainly greater than or equal to $P(A)$.

Now suppose that $P(B) > 0$. Then by definition,

$$P(A|B) = \frac{P(A \cap B)}{P(B)}$$

Since $A \subset B$, then $A \cap B = A$ and $P(A \cap B) = P(A)$. Thus,

$$P(A|B) = \frac{P(A)}{P(B)} \geq P(A)$$

since $0 < P(B) \leq 1$.   ◊

Example 8

Again let us consider the experiment of flipping a coin three times. We will assume that the coin is fair, and we will calculate the probability that the third flip is a head, given that exactly two of the flips are heads.

We first define the events:

$$A = \{\text{the third flip is a head}\}$$
$$B = \{\text{exactly two of the flips are heads}\}.$$

Obviously, then

$$A = \{HHH, HTH, THH, TTH\}$$
$$B = \{HHT, HTH, THH\}$$

Hence,

$$A \cap B = \{HTH, THH\}$$

and

$$P(A) = 4/8, \ P(B) = 3/8, \ P(A \cap B) = 2/8$$

Thus,

$$P(A|B) = \frac{P(A \cap B)}{P(B)} = \frac{2/8}{3/8} = 2/3$$ ◊

We have defined what we mean by conditional probability and have given an example of this concept. However, can we be sure that with this definition we will always obtain probabilities? In other words, will conditional probabilities indeed satisfy the axioms of probability measure? Our next task is to resolve these questions.

THEOREM 5

Suppose that S is a sample space, and suppose that G is any event such that $P(G) > 0$. To every event $A \subset S$ assign the number $P(A|G)$. Then these numbers satisfy the axioms of probability measure.

Proof

I. Since $A \cap G \subset S$, then $P(A \cap G) \geq 0$. Also, since $P(G) > 0$, then

$$P(A|G) = \frac{P(A \cap G)}{P(G)} \geq 0$$

II. Since $S \cap G = G$, we have

$$P(S|G) = \frac{P(S \cap G)}{P(G)} = \frac{P(G)}{P(G)} = 1$$

III. Suppose that $A \cap B = \emptyset$. Then

$$(A \cap G) \cap (B \cap G) = (A \cap B) \cap G = \emptyset \cap G = \emptyset$$

Consequently,

$$
\begin{aligned}
P(A \cup B|G) &= \frac{P([A \cup B] \cap G)}{P(G)} \\
&= \frac{P([A \cap G] \cup [B \cap G])}{P(G)} \\
&= \frac{P(A \cap G) + P(B \cap G)}{P(G)} \\
&= \frac{P(A \cap G)}{P(G)} + \frac{P(B \cap G)}{P(G)} \\
&= P(A|G) + P(B|G)
\end{aligned}
$$

for $A \cap B = \emptyset$. $\qquad\qquad\qquad\qquad\qquad\qquad\qquad\qquad\qquad\qquad$ □

By this theorem, we see that conditional probabilities are indeed probabilities. Thus, for the sake of convenience, instead of saying that $P(A|B)$ is the conditional probability of event A occurring given that event B has occurred, we will simply say that $P(A|B)$ is the **probability of A given B.**

Example 9

For the example of three tosses of an unbiased (fair) coin, we will calculate the conditional probabilities for all the elementary events given the event

$$B = \{HTT, THT, TTH\}$$

that exactly one flip is a head:

$$P(\{HHH\}|B) = \frac{P(\{HHH\} \cap B)}{P(B)} = \frac{P(\varnothing)}{P(B)} = \frac{0}{3/8} = 0$$

$$P(\{HHT\}|B) = \frac{P(\{HHT\} \cap B)}{P(B)} = \frac{P(\varnothing)}{P(B)} = \frac{0}{3/8} = 0$$

$$P(\{HTH\}|B) = \frac{P(\{HTH\} \cap B)}{P(B)} = \frac{P(\varnothing)}{P(B)} = \frac{0}{3/8} = 0$$

$$P(\{HTT\}|B) = \frac{P(\{HTT\} \cap B)}{P(B)} = \frac{P(\{HTT\})}{P(B)} = \frac{1/8}{3/8} = 1/3$$

$$P(\{THH\}|B) = \frac{P(\{THH\} \cap B)}{P(B)} = \frac{P(\varnothing)}{P(B)} = \frac{0}{3/8} = 0$$

$$P(\{THT\}|B) = \frac{P(\{THT\} \cap B)}{P(B)} = \frac{P(\{THT\})}{P(B)} = \frac{1/8}{3/8} = 1/3$$

$$P(\{TTH\}|B) = \frac{P(\{TTH\} \cap B)}{P(B)} = \frac{P(\{THT\})}{P(B)} = \frac{1/8}{3/8} = 1/3$$

$$P(\{TTT\}|B) = \frac{P(\{TTT\} \cap B)}{P(B)} = \frac{P(\varnothing)}{P(B)} = \frac{0}{3/8} = 0 \qquad \Diamond$$

PROBABILITY TREES

When an experiment is of a sequential nature, it is often convenient, especially for purposes of calculation, to represent the experiment graphically by a **probability tree.**

For our experiment of flipping a coin three times, let us now use more precise notation by denoting the result of the ith flip by H_i or T_i, for $i = 1$, 2, 3. We may construct a probability tree as shown in Figure 6–1.

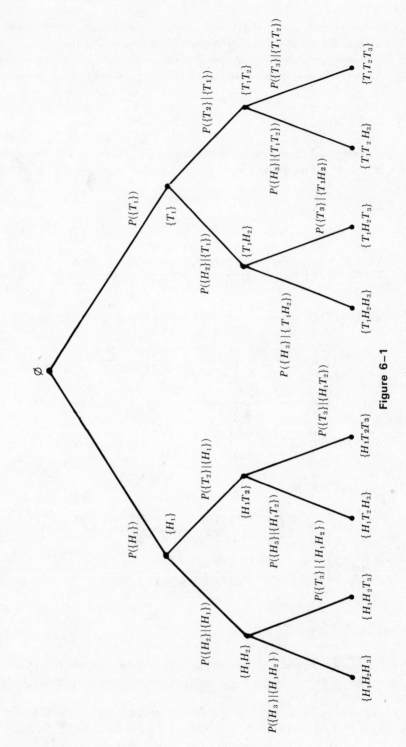

Figure 6–1

In this tree the vertices are labelled by the events of the experiment according to how much of the experiment has been completed. The edges, on the other hand, are labelled by the conditional probabilities required to descend from a vertex to an adjacent one. The probability associated with the event corresponding to a vertex is obtained by taking the product of the probabilities labelling the edges forming the unique path between the vertex under consideration and the root of the tree. This is simply a consequence of the definition of conditional probability. As an example, in the tree of Figure 6–1, we can write

$$P(\{H_1 T_2\}) = P(\{T_2\} \,|\, \{H_1\})P(\{H_1\})$$

since, actually, $\{H_1 T_2\} = \{H_1\} \cap \{T_2\}$. We may also write

$$P(\{H_1 T_2 H_3\}) = P(\{H_3\} \,|\, \{H_1 T_2\})P(\{H_1 T_2\})$$
$$= P(\{H_3\} \,|\, \{H_1 T_2\})P(\{T_2\} \,|\, \{H_1\})P(\{H_1\})$$

Note that in the probability tree, the events labelling the terminal vertices are those elementary events comprising the sample space of the completed experiment. Thus, to compute the probability of any given event, we need only sum the probabilities of the elementary events forming the given event.

Example 10

Our experiment consists of the following game played by flipping a fair coin. Players A and B alternate flipping the coin, player A starting first. The first player to flip a total of two heads wins and the other player loses, or the first player to flip a total of two tails loses and the other player wins. Let us calculate the probability that player A wins, to see if there is an advantage to the player that starts first. For the sake of convenience, we construct the probability tree of Figure 6–2.

For this tree, the subscripts indicate the sequence of heads and tails accrued by each player. The darkened vertices indicate those conditions under which player A wins. Since the probability corresponding to each edge is $1/2$, we have that

$$P(\{A \text{ wins}\}) = 2(1/8) + 2(1/16) + 4(1/32)$$
$$= 8/32 + 4/32 + 4/32 = 16/32$$
$$= 1/2$$

Hence, we conclude that there is no advantage for either player! (They might just as well flip the coin once and save themselves a lot of trouble.)   ◊

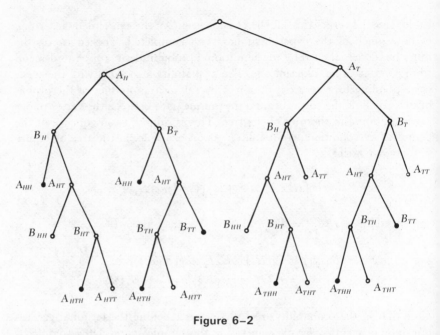

Figure 6–2

So far we have considered two examples for which the corresponding probability trees were of a finite structure. However, there are numerous situations in which an infinite structure is required. Let us illustrate:

Example 11

Player A flips a fair coin. If the outcome is a head, he wins; if it is a tail, player B flips. If B's flip is a head, he wins; if not, A flips the coin again. This process is repeated (ad infinitum, if necessary) until somebody wins. Let us calculate the probability that A wins.

We first construct the probability tree of Figure 6–3 to describe the experiment.

For this tree, the darkened vertices correspond to those elementary events for which A wins. Since the probability represented by each branch in the tree is $1/2$, we have

$$P(\{A \text{ wins}\}) = P(A_H) + P(A_{TH}) + P(A_{TTH}) + P(A_{TTTH}) + \cdots$$
$$= 1/2 + (1/2)^3 + (1/2)^5 + (1/2)^7 + \cdots$$

which is an infinite sum. However, in many problems such as this one, it is possible to obtain a closed form solution by using the series expansion

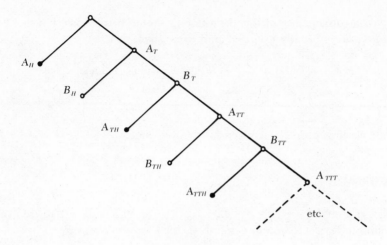

Figure 6–3

learned in freshman calculus:

$$\frac{1}{1-x} = 1 + x + x^2 + x^3 + \cdots = \sum_{i=0}^{\infty} x^i \text{ for } 0 \leq |x| < 1$$

Hence, by some juggling, we get

$$P(\{A \text{ wins}\}) = 1/2[1 + (1/2)^2 + (1/2)^4 + (1/2)^6 + \cdots$$
$$= 1/2[1 + 1/4 + (1/4)^2 + (1/4)^3 + \cdots$$
$$= 1/2\left[\frac{1}{1-1/4}\right] = 1/2\left[\frac{1}{3/4}\right] = (1/2)(4/3)$$
$$= 2/3$$

so there is definitely a big advantage for A to flip first, as we intuitively felt all along.   ◊

We begin our discussion of the theorem attributed to Bayes as follows:

DEFINITION 3

We say that the subsets $A_1, A_2, \ldots, A_n$ of S are **mutually exclusive** if $A_i \cap A_j = \emptyset$ for $i, j = 1, 2, \ldots, n$ and $i \neq j$. Furthermore, we say that the subsets are **exhaustive** if

$$\bigcup_{i=1}^{n} A_i = A_1 \cup A_2 \cup \cdots \cup A_n = S$$ ○

As a consequence of this definition, it should be obvious that if A_1, A_2, ..., A_n are mutually exclusive and exhaustive, then

$$P(A_1) + P(A_2) + \cdots + P(A_n) = P(A_1 \cup A_2 \cup \cdots \cup A_n)$$
$$= P(S)$$
$$= 1$$

A less obvious property is given by the following:

THEOREM 6

Suppose that the n events A_1, A_2, ..., A_n are subsets of S. If these events are mutually exclusive and exhaustive, then for any event B

$$P(B) = P(B|A_1)P(A_1) + P(B|A_2)P(A_2) + \cdots + P(B|A_n)P(A_n)$$

$$= \sum_{i=1}^{n} P(B|A_i)P(A_i)$$

Proof

Clearly, since $B = B \cap S = B \cap (A_1 \cup A_2 \cup \cdots \cup A_n)$, we have

$$B = (B \cap A_1) \cup (B \cap A_2) \cup \cdots \cup (B \cap A_n)$$

with each of the terms in the union being disjoint from all the others. Thus

$$P(B) = P([B \cap A_1] \cup [B \cap A_2] \cup \cdots \cup [B \cap A_n])$$
$$= P(B \cap A_1) + P(B \cap A_2) + \cdots + P(B \cap A_n)$$

However, by the definition of conditional probability,

$$P(B \cap A_i) = P(B|A_i)P(A_i)$$

so we have that

$$P(B) = P(B|A_1)P(A_1) + P(B|A_2)P(A_2) + \cdots + P(B|A_n)P(A_n) \qquad \square$$

Example 12

Of all the shoppers at a particular department store, 70% are women and 30% are men. Suppose that 20% and 25% of the female and male population, respectively, smoke cigarettes. We shall define a trial of an experiment to consist of arbitrarily selecting a shopper in the department store. Let us define the following events:

$$W = \{\text{woman shopper}\}$$
$$M = \{\text{man shopper}\}$$
$$C|W = \{\text{shopper smokes, given a woman shopper}\}$$
$$C|M = \{\text{shopper smokes, given a man shopper}\}$$

Clearly, from the information above we may assign the probabilities:

$$P(W) = 0.7$$
$$P(M) = 0.3$$
$$P(C|W) = 0.2$$
$$P(C|M) = 0.25$$

What is the probability that a shopper selected is: (1) a woman who smokes, (2) a man who smokes, (3) a smoker?

(1) We wish to find $P(W \cap C)$. Since

$$P(C|W) = \frac{P(C \cap W)}{P(W)}$$

then

$$
\begin{aligned}
P(W \cap C) = P(C \cap W) &= P(C|W)P(W) \\
&= (0.2)(0.7) \\
&= 0.14
\end{aligned}
$$

(2) To find $P(M \cap C)$, we note that

$$
\begin{aligned}
P(M \cap C) = P(C \cap M) &= P(C|M)P(M) \\
&= (0.25)(0.3) \\
&= 0.075
\end{aligned}
$$

(3) In order to determine $P(C)$, note that W and M are presumably mutually exclusive and exhaustive on the set of all shoppers. Thus, by the previous theorem,

$$
\begin{aligned}
P(C) &= P(C|W)P(W) + P(C|M)P(M) \\
&= 0.14 + 0.075 \\
&= 0.215 \qquad\qquad\qquad\qquad \Diamond
\end{aligned}
$$

As was stated, Theorem 6 is valid for any event B in case $A_1, A_2, \ldots,$ A_n are mutually exclusive and exhaustive. However, if $A_1, A_2, \ldots, A_n$ are mutually exclusive and not exhaustive, we can still apply the theorem to an event B, provided that $B \subset A_1 \cup A_2 \cup \cdots \cup A_n$.

In Example 12, we were actually reclassifying shoppers (men and women) as either smokers or non-smokers. We can represent this reclassification by the directed graph of Figure 6–4. The numbers labelling the edges of this

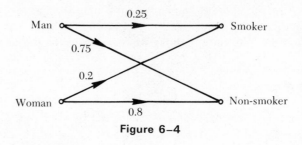

Figure 6–4

graph are the probabilities associated with the corresponding events; e.g., the probability that a man does not smoke is 0.75. Such a graph is called a **channel,** as it "channels" information from one form into (possibly) another. This particular channel is *binary,* as there are two categories of shoppers both before and after reclassification.

In the last theorem, we showed how to calculate $P(B)$ from $P(B|A_i)$ and $P(A_i)$ for $i = 1, 2, \ldots, n$. We now shall demonstrate that from $P(B|A_i)$ and $P(A_i)$ we can also determine $P(A_i|B)$ for $i = 1, 2, \ldots, n$. [Note that in general $P(B|A_i) \neq P(A_i|B)$.]

THEOREM 7 (BAYES' THEOREM)

Suppose that the n events $A_1, A_2, \ldots, A_n$ are subsets of S. If these events are mutually exclusive and exhaustive, then for any event B such that $P(B) > 0$ we have

$$P(A_i|B) = \frac{P(B|A_i)P(A_i)}{P(B)}$$

$$= \frac{P(B|A_i)P(A_i)}{P(B|A_1)P(A_1) + P(B|A_2)P(A_2) + \cdots + P(B|A_n)P(A_n)}$$

for $i = 1, 2, \ldots, n$.

Proof

$$P(A_i|B) = \frac{P(A_i \cap B)}{P(B)} \text{ by definition of conditional probability } P(A_i|B)$$

$$= \frac{P(B|A_i)P(A_i)}{P(B)} \text{ by definition of the conditional probability } P(B|A_i)$$

and we get the desired result by substituting $P(B|A_1)P(A_1) + \cdots + P(B|A_n)P(A_n)$ for $P(B)$. ☐

As mentioned above, if $A_1, A_2, \ldots, A_n$ are mutually exclusive and not exhaustive, we can still apply this theorem to an event B for which $P(B) > 0$ provided that $B \subset A_1 \cup A_2 \cup \cdots \cup A_n$.

Let us now reconsider Example 12. In order to find $P(M|C)$, we obviously may use Bayes' Theorem, that is,

$$P(M|C) = \frac{P(C|M)P(M)}{P(C|W)P(W) + P(C|M)P(M)}$$

However, since we know that conditional probabilities satisfy the axioms of probability measure, we may also use

$$P(M|C) = P(\bar{W}|C) = 1 - P(W|C)$$

The application of Bayes' Theorem sometimes yields results that are contrary to naive intuition. Such a case is demonstrated in the following example.

Example 13

Suppose that a laboratory test has been developed for detecting mononucleosis (mono, for short). The probability that a person selected at random has mono is 0.005. If a person has mono, 95% of the time the test will be positive. If a person doesn't have mono, the test will be positive only 4% of the time. These circumstances are described by the binary channel shown in Figure 6-5. We show that, given a positive test, the probability that a person has mono is, at first glance, surprisingly low.

Let $M = \{\text{person has mono}\}$
and $T = \{\text{positive mono test}\}$

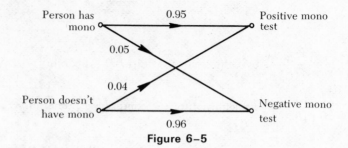

Figure 6–5

From the description above, we have:

$$P(M) = 0.005$$
$$P(\bar{M}) = 0.995$$
$$P(T|M) = 0.95$$
$$P(T|\bar{M}) = 0.04$$

Thus, by Bayes' Theorem,

$$P(M|T) = \frac{P(T|M)P(M)}{P(T|M)P(M) + P(T|\bar{M})P(\bar{M})}$$

$$= \frac{(.95)(.005)}{(.95)(.005) + (.04)(.995)}$$

$$= \frac{0.00475}{0.00475 + 0.0398} = \frac{0.00475}{0.04455}$$

$$= 0.107 \qquad \Diamond$$

This last example indicates why a discipline such as probability theory should be formal rather than intuitive.

Suppose that S is a sample space, and A and B are events. Consider the case for which $P(A|B) = P(A)$. In other words, knowing that event B has occurred does not affect the probability of event A occurring. Under this circumstance we feel that event A "does not depend" on the occurrence of event B. This gives rise to the following:

DEFINITION 4

If $P(A|B) = P(A)$, then we say that A is **independent** of B.   ○

As a consequence of this definition, if A is independent of B, $P(A) \neq 0$, and $P(B) \neq 0$, then

$$P(A) = P(A|B) = \frac{P(A \cap B)}{P(B)}$$

Thus

$$P(B) = \frac{P(B \cap A)}{P(A)} = P(B|A)$$

and B is independent of A. Thus, if $P(A|B) = P(A)$, we simply say that A and B are independent events. An equivalent definition of independence is given by the next theorem.

THEOREM 8

If $P(A) \neq 0$ and $P(B) \neq 0$, then A and B are independent events if and only if $P(A \cap B) = P(A)P(B)$.

Proof

Suppose that A and B are independent events. Then

$$P(A) = \frac{P(A \cap B)}{P(B)}$$

and so

$$P(A \cap B) = P(A)P(B)$$

By reversing the argument, the converse is proved.   □

Example 14

Let us return to our experiment of flipping an unbiased coin three times, and define the events:

$$C = \{\text{the first flip is a head}\}$$
$$= \{HHH, HHT, HTH, HTT\}$$

and

$$D = \{\text{the second flip is a head}\}$$
$$= \{HHH, HHT, THH, THT\}$$

Clearly, $P(C) = P(D) = 1/2$.
    We would like to know whether or not C and D are independent. Since

$$C \cap D = \{HHH, HHT\}$$

implies $\qquad\qquad P(C \cap D) = 1/4$, then

$$P(C \cap D) = P(C)P(D)$$

Hence, C and D are independent. $\qquad\qquad\qquad\qquad\qquad\qquad$ ◊

RANDOM VARIABLES

To prepare for later applications, we briefly discuss random variables and expected values. We consider a measurement space X, in which we can study observed properties $\mathbf{x}(s)$ of samples s from S:

DEFINITION 5

A **random variable** is a function $\mathbf{x}: S \to X$ together with a probability space (S, Ω, P) on S. $\qquad\qquad\qquad\qquad\qquad\qquad\qquad\qquad\qquad\qquad\qquad\qquad$ ○

The intuition is that, rather than conduct our trials on the original sample space S, we now observe the values $\mathbf{x}(s)$ in X. We may think of these samples as *varying randomly* in X. Then the probability measure P on S induces a probability measure $P_{\mathbf{x}}$ on X, with $P_{\mathbf{x}}(B)$, for $B \subset X$, being the probability that a trial in S should yield an s for which $\mathbf{x}(s) \in B$. Thus

$$P_{\mathbf{x}}(B) = P(\mathbf{x}^{-1}(B))$$

and so an event B on X is measurable iff $\mathbf{x}^{-1}(B) \in \Omega$. However, *in the ensuing discussion we shall only consider finite sets S and X,* so that all sets will be measurable, and we can ignore such technicalities. When S is finite or denumerable, we call the random variable x **discrete.** In distinction, *continuous* random variables have probability distributed over the real line, say, for S, and we must integrate probability measures rather than simply adding probabilities as we do here.

Example 15

Suppose that an experiment consists of rolling a pair of dice. Each die has six faces, and each face has a fixed number of dots on it. The number of dots on each face varies from one to six, and each distinct face has a distinct number of dots. In this case, then, our sample space S has 36 elements:

(1, 1)	(2, 1)	(3, 1)	(4, 1)	(5, 1)	(6, 1)
(1, 2)	(2, 2)	(3, 2)	(4, 2)	(5, 2)	(6, 2)
(1, 3)	(2, 3)	(3, 3)	(4, 3)	(5, 3)	(6, 3)
(1, 4)	(2, 4)	(3, 4)	(4, 4)	(5, 4)	(6, 4)
(1, 5)	(2, 5)	(3, 5)	(4, 5)	(5, 5)	(6, 5)
(1, 6)	(2, 6)	(3, 6)	(4, 6)	(5, 6)	(6, 6)

The most common random variable defined for this experiment is the total value of the toss. In this case X is the set $\{2, 3, \ldots, 12\}$ and $\mathbf{x}: S \to X: (i, j) \mapsto i + j$. For example, $\mathbf{x}(1, 3) = 4$ and $\mathbf{x}(4, 3) = 7$.

Let us define the event A to consist of all dice tosses which assign the number 5 to our random variable. We shall denote this event by

$$A = \{\mathbf{x} = 5\}$$

Clearly,

$$\{\mathbf{x} = 5\} = \mathbf{x}^{-1}(5) = \{(1, 4), (2, 3), (3, 2), (4, 1)\}$$

Similarly, the event

$$\{\mathbf{x} = 6\} = \{(1, 5), (2, 4), (3, 3), (4, 2), (5, 1)\}$$

Extending this notation, we have

$$\{\mathbf{x} \leq 3\} = \{(1, 1), (1, 2), (2, 1)\}$$
$$\{\mathbf{x} > 10\} = \{(5, 6), (6, 5), (6, 6)\}$$
$$\{8 \leq \mathbf{x} \leq 10\} = \{(2, 6), (3, 5), (4, 4), (5, 3), (6, 2), (3, 6),$$
$$(4, 5), (5, 4), (6, 3), (4, 6), (5, 5), (6, 4)\}$$

Now let us assume that our dice are "fair." That is, let us assume that each of the outcomes is equally likely. Consequently, we shall assign the probability 1/36 to each elementary event. We shall simplify our notation by writing $P\{\mathbf{x} = i\}$ to indicate $P(\{\mathbf{x} = i\})$. Since elementary events of an experiment are mutually exclusive, we can compute the probabilities of all the elementary events in X:

$$P\{\mathbf{x} = 1\} = P(\varnothing) = 0$$
$$P\{\mathbf{x} = 2\} = 1/36$$
$$P\{\mathbf{x} = 3\} = 2/36 = 1/18$$
$$P\{\mathbf{x} = 4\} = 3/36 = 1/12$$
$$P\{\mathbf{x} = 5\} = 4/36 = 1/9$$
$$P\{\mathbf{x} = 6\} = 5/36$$
$$P\{\mathbf{x} = 7\} = 6/36 = 1/6$$
$$P\{\mathbf{x} = 8\} = 5/36$$
$$P\{\mathbf{x} = 9\} = 4/36 = 1/9$$
$$P\{\mathbf{x} = 10\} = 3/36 = 1/12$$
$$P\{\mathbf{x} = 11\} = 2/36 = 1/18$$
$$P\{\mathbf{x} = 12\} = 1/36$$

It should be perfectly clear that if $\mathbf{x}:S \to \{x_1, \ldots, x_n\}$ is a random variable that assigns the numbers $x_1, x_2, \ldots, x_n$ to outcomes of an experiment, then in general

$$\sum_{i=1} P\{\mathbf{x} = x_i\} = 1$$

Because of mutual exclusivity, from the probabilities above it is convenient to calculate other probabilities. For example,

$$
\begin{aligned}
P\{\mathbf{x} < 6\} &= P\{\mathbf{x} = 2\} + P\{\mathbf{x} = 3\} + P\{\mathbf{x} = 4\} + P\{\mathbf{x} = 5\} \\
&= 1/36 + 2/36 + 3/36 + 4/36 \\
&= 10/36 \\
&= 5/18
\end{aligned}
$$

Now let us calculate some conditional probabilities. For the sake of simplicity instead of, for example, writing $P(\{\mathbf{x} = 3\} \,|\, \{\mathbf{x} < 6\})$, let us write $P\{\mathbf{x} = 3 \,|\, \mathbf{x} < 6\}$. Then

$$
\begin{aligned}
P\{\mathbf{x} = 3 \,|\, \mathbf{x} < 6\} &= \frac{P(\{\mathbf{x} = 3\} \cap \{\mathbf{x} < 6\})}{P\{\mathbf{x} < 6\}} \\[2mm]
&= \frac{P\{\mathbf{x} = 3\}}{P\{\mathbf{x} < 6\}} \\[2mm]
&= \frac{1/18}{5/18} \\[2mm]
&= 1/5
\end{aligned}
$$

and

$$
\begin{aligned}
P\{\mathbf{x} \geq 7 \,|\, 5 \leq \mathbf{x} \leq 8\} &= \frac{P(\{\mathbf{x} \geq 7\} \cap \{5 \leq \mathbf{x} \leq 8\})}{P\{5 \leq \mathbf{x} \leq 8\}} \\[2mm]
&= \frac{P\{7 \leq \mathbf{x} \leq 8\}}{P\{5 \leq \mathbf{x} \leq 8\}} \\[2mm]
&= \frac{P\{\mathbf{x} = 7\} + P\{\mathbf{x} = 8\}}{P\{5 \leq \mathbf{x} \leq 8\}} \\[2mm]
&= \frac{6/36 + 5/36}{20/36} \\[2mm]
&= 11/20
\end{aligned}
$$

Now suppose that we denote the event

$$\{\mathbf{x} = 3\} \cup \{\mathbf{x} = 5\} \cup \{\mathbf{x} = 7\} \cup \{\mathbf{x} = 9\} \cup \{\mathbf{x} = 11\}$$

by $\{\mathbf{x}$ is odd$\}$. Also, consider the event $\{5 \leq \mathbf{x} \leq 8\}$. Are these two events independent? Clearly, $P\{\mathbf{x}$ is odd$\} = 2/36 + 4/36 + 6/36 + 4/36 + 2/36 = 18/36 = 1/2$, and $P\{5 \leq x \leq 8\} = 4/36 + 5/36 + 6/36 + 5/36 = 5/9$. Furthermore,

$$\begin{aligned} P(\{\mathbf{x} \text{ is odd}\} \cap \{5 \leq \mathbf{x} \leq 8\}) &= P(\{\mathbf{x} = 5\} \cup \{\mathbf{x} = 7\}) \\ &= 4/36 + 6/36 \\ &= 10/36 \\ &= 5/18 \end{aligned}$$

Since $P\{\mathbf{x}$ is odd$\}P\{5 \leq \mathbf{x} \leq 8\} = (1/2)(5/9) = 5/18$, also, $\{\mathbf{x}$ is odd$\}$ and $\{5 \leq \mathbf{x} \leq 8\}$ are independent events. We might have alternatively verified this result by either

$$\begin{aligned} P\{\mathbf{x} \text{ is odd}|5 \leq \mathbf{x} \leq 8\} &= \frac{P(\{\mathbf{x} \text{ is odd}\} \cap \{5 \leq \mathbf{x} \leq 8\})}{P\{5 \leq \mathbf{x} \leq 8\}} \\ &= \frac{P(\{\mathbf{x} = 5\} \cup \{\mathbf{x} = 7\})}{P\{5 \leq \mathbf{x} \leq 8\}} \\ &= \frac{5/18}{5/9} \\ &= 1/2 = P\{\mathbf{x} \text{ is odd}\} \end{aligned}$$

or

$$\begin{aligned} P\{5 \leq \mathbf{x} \leq 8|\mathbf{x} \text{ is odd}\} &= \frac{P(\{\mathbf{x} = 5\} \cup \{\mathbf{x} = 7\})}{P\{\mathbf{x} \text{ is odd}\}} \\ &= \frac{5/18}{1/2} \\ &= 5/9 = P\{5 \leq \mathbf{x} \leq 8\} \qquad \Diamond \end{aligned}$$

Suppose that for a given experiment we would like a single number which is typical of the numbers assigned by a *numerical* (or *real*) random variable $\mathbf{x}$; in other words, we have $X \subset \mathbf{R}$. For an experiment in which any number is equally likely to appear, an intuitive choice may simply be the average of the numbers that can possibly appear. For example, if we roll a single fair die, and if we have a random variable $\mathbf{x}$ which assigns the integers 1 through 6 to the outcomes, we can say that a number that can be expected is the average

$$\frac{1 + 2 + 3 + 4 + 5 + 6}{6} = \frac{21}{6} = 3.5$$

Although $\mathbf{x}$ never assigns the number 3.5 to an outcome, this number is the average of the assigned numbers, and hence, is in a sense typical.

Now suppose that the numbers assigned by a random variable **x** are not equally likely. Instead of a simple average, a weighted average would seem appropriate. Consider the case when we roll a pair of fair dice 36 times. In the case of our previous example, in 36 rolls we would roughly expect the number 2 once, the number 3 twice, the number 4 thrice, and so forth. Thus, a typical number is in the vicinity of E, where

$$E = \frac{1(2) + 2(3) + 3(4) + 4(5) + 5(6) + 6(7) + 5(8) + 4(9) + 3(10) + 2(11) + 1(12)}{36}$$

$$= \frac{2 + 6 + 12 + 20 + 30 + 42 + 40 + 36 + 30 + 22 + 12}{36}$$

$$= \frac{252}{36}$$

$$= 7$$

In this case, the typical number is not only a number assigned by the random variable, but it is the most probable number assigned. This discussion is the basis of the following:

DEFINITION 6

Given a discrete random variable **x** which assigns the *numbers* $x_1, x_2, \ldots, x_n$ to the outcomes of an experiment, the **expected value** (or **expectation** or **mean**) of **x**, denoted by $E(\mathbf{x})$, is given by

$$E(\mathbf{x}) = \sum_{i=1}^{n} x_i P\{\mathbf{x} = x_i\}$$

○

Example 16

As demonstrated above, the mean of the random variable **x** which assigns a number equal to the sum of the dots on the faces of a pair of fair dice is $E(\mathbf{x}) = 7$. ◊

Suppose that $\mathbf{x}: S \to \mathbf{R}$ is a discrete random variable. If $f: \mathbf{R} \to \mathbf{R}: r \mapsto f(r)$ is a real function, then we denote by $f(\mathbf{x})$ the function

$$f(\mathbf{x}): S \to \mathbf{R}: s \mapsto f[\mathbf{x}(s)]$$

Thus, we see that $f(\mathbf{x})$ is also a discrete random variable on S, and we refer to $f(\mathbf{x})$ as a **function of the random variable x.** Then the **expected value** (or **expectation** or **mean**) of $f(\mathbf{x})$ is

$$E[f(\mathbf{x})] = \sum_{i=1}^{n} f(x_i)P\{\mathbf{x} = x_i\}$$

For the special case when $f(\mathbf{x}) = \mathbf{x}$ (i.e., when $f = id_{\mathbf{R}}$), this is, of course, just $E(\mathbf{x})$. For any real number c, if $f(\mathbf{x}) = c\mathbf{x}$ we have

$$E(c\mathbf{x}) = \sum_{i=1}^{n} cx_i P\{\mathbf{x} = x_i\}$$

$$= c \sum_{i=1}^{n} x_i P\{\mathbf{x} = x_i\}$$

$$= cE(\mathbf{x})$$

while if $f(\mathbf{x}) = c$, then

$$E(c) = \sum_{i=1}^{n} f(x_i)P\{\mathbf{x} = x_i\}$$

$$= \sum_{i=1}^{n} cP\{\mathbf{x} = x_i\}$$

$$= c \sum_{i=1}^{n} P\{\mathbf{x} = x_i\}$$

$$= c$$

Furthermore, if $f(\mathbf{x}) = f_1(\mathbf{x}) + f_2(\mathbf{x})$, then

$$E[f_1(\mathbf{x}) + f_2(\mathbf{x})] = \sum_{i=1}^{n} [f_1(x_i) + f_2(x_i)]P\{\mathbf{x} = x_i\}$$

$$= \sum_{i=1}^{n} [f_1(x_i)P\{\mathbf{x} = x_i\} + f_2(x_i)P\{\mathbf{x} = x_i\}]$$

$$= \sum_{i=1}^{n} f_1(x_i)P\{\mathbf{x} = x_i\} + \sum_{i=1}^{n} f_2(x_i)P\{\mathbf{x} = x_i\}$$

$$= E[f_1(\mathbf{x})] + E[f_2(\mathbf{x})]$$

and, obviously,

$$E[cf(\mathbf{x})] = cE[f(\mathbf{x})]$$

Of considerable importance is the case when $f(\mathbf{x}) = [\mathbf{x} - E(\mathbf{x})]^2$, i.e., when $f: \mathbf{R} \to \mathbf{R} : r \mapsto [r - E(\mathbf{x})]^2$. (Why not $r \mapsto [r - E(r)]^2$?) We thus define the following:

DEFINITION 7

Given a discrete random variable **x**, the **variance** of **x** is denoted by $\sigma_{\mathbf{x}}^2$ and is defined as

$$\sigma_{\mathbf{x}}^2 = E([\mathbf{x} - E(\mathbf{x})]^2)$$

$$= \sum_{i=1}^{n} [x_i - E(\mathbf{x})]^2 P\{\mathbf{x} = x_i\}$$

The non-negative square root $\sigma_{\mathbf{x}}$ of the variance is called the **standard deviation** of **x**. ○

THEOREM 8

$$\sigma_{\mathbf{x}}^2 = E(\mathbf{x}^2) - E(\mathbf{x})^2$$

where $E(\mathbf{x})^2 = E(\mathbf{x})E(\mathbf{x})$.

Proof

$$
\begin{aligned}
\sigma_{\mathbf{x}}^2 &= E([\mathbf{x} - E(\mathbf{x})]^2) \\
&= E(\mathbf{x}^2 - 2E(\mathbf{x})\mathbf{x} + E(\mathbf{x})^2) \\
&= E(\mathbf{x}^2) + E[-2E(\mathbf{x})\mathbf{x}] + E[E(\mathbf{x})^2] \\
&= E(\mathbf{x}^2) - 2E(\mathbf{x})E(\mathbf{x}) + E(\mathbf{x})^2 \qquad \text{since } E(\mathbf{x}) \text{ is a constant} \\
&= E(\mathbf{x}^2) - E(\mathbf{x})^2
\end{aligned}
$$

□

Example 17

Suppose that $0 < q < 1$. Then a random variable **x** which assigns the numbers 0 and 1 such that

$$P\{\mathbf{x} = 0\} = 1 - q$$
$$P\{\mathbf{x} = 1\} = q$$

is known as a **Bernoulli random variable.** We say that the event $\{\mathbf{x} = 0\}$ is a *failure* and the event $\{\mathbf{x} = 1\}$ is a *success*. For such a random variable we have

$$
\begin{aligned}
E(\mathbf{x}) &= 0 \cdot P\{\mathbf{x} = 0\} + 1 \cdot P\{\mathbf{x} = 1\} \\
&= 0 \cdot (1 - q) + 1 \cdot q \\
&= q
\end{aligned}
$$

and

$$
\begin{aligned}
E(\mathbf{x}^2) &= 0^2 \cdot P\{\mathbf{x} = 0\} + 1^2 \cdot P\{\mathbf{x} = 1\} \\
&= 0 \cdot (1 - q) + 1 \cdot q \\
&= q
\end{aligned}
$$

Thus,

$$
\begin{aligned}
\sigma_{\mathbf{x}}^2 &= E(\mathbf{x}^2) - E(\mathbf{x})^2 \\
&= q - q^2 \\
&= q(1 - q)
\end{aligned}
$$
       ◊

COROLLARY 9

Suppose that $\mathbf{x}$ is a discrete random variable and c is an arbitrary constant. Then for the random variable $\mathbf{y} = f(\mathbf{x}) = c\mathbf{x}$, we have that $\sigma_{\mathbf{y}}^2 = c^2\sigma_{\mathbf{x}}^2$.

Proof

$$
\begin{aligned}
\sigma_{\mathbf{y}}^2 &= E(\mathbf{y}^2) - E(\mathbf{y})^2 = E([c\mathbf{x}]^2) - E(c\mathbf{x})^2 \\
&= E(c^2\mathbf{x}^2) - E(c\mathbf{x})E(c\mathbf{x}) \\
&= c^2E(\mathbf{x}^2) - cE(\mathbf{x})cE(\mathbf{x}) \\
&= c^2[E(\mathbf{x}^2) - E(\mathbf{x})^2] \\
&= c^2\sigma_{\mathbf{x}}^2
\end{aligned}
$$
       □

We now begin our derivation of the *law of large numbers,* which will be of considerable import later. The first step in this direction is the *Chebyshev inequality,* which gives us an upper bound on the probability of the event $\{|\mathbf{x} - E(\mathbf{x})| > \delta > 0\}$; i.e., the probability that $\mathbf{x}$ assigns a number outside the closed interval $[E(\mathbf{x}) - \delta, E(\mathbf{x}) + \delta]$, as shown in Figure 6–6. Since

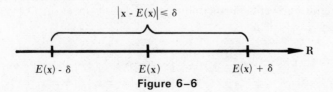

Figure 6–6

$$\sigma_{\mathbf{x}}^2 = \sum_{x_j} [x_j - E(\mathbf{x})]^2 P\{\mathbf{x} = x_j\}$$

$$= \sum_{x_j < E(\mathbf{x})-\delta} [x_j - E(\mathbf{x})]^2 P\{\mathbf{x} = x_j\} + \sum_{E(\mathbf{x})-\delta \leq x_j \leq E(\mathbf{x})+\delta} [x_j - E(\mathbf{x})]^2 P\{\mathbf{x} = x_j\}$$

$$+ \sum_{E(\mathbf{x})+\delta < x_j} [x_j - E(\mathbf{x})]^2 P\{\mathbf{x} = x_j\}$$

and since $[x_j - E(\mathbf{x})]^2 \geq 0$ and $P\{\mathbf{x} = x_j\} \geq 0$, we have that

$$\sigma_{\mathbf{x}}^2 \geq \sum_{x_j < E(\mathbf{x})-\delta} [x_j - E(\mathbf{x})]^2 P\{\mathbf{x} = x_j\} + \sum_{E(\mathbf{x})+\delta < x_j} [x_j - E(\mathbf{x})]^2 P\{\mathbf{x} = x_j\}$$

But for both $x_j < E(\mathbf{x}) - \delta$ and $E(\mathbf{x}) + \delta < x_j$ we have that $\delta^2 < [x_j - E(\mathbf{x})]^2$. Thus,

$$\sigma_{\mathbf{x}}^2 \geq \sum_{x_j < E(\mathbf{x})-\delta} \delta^2 P\{\mathbf{x} = x_j\} + \sum_{E(\mathbf{x})+\delta < x_j} \delta^2 P\{\mathbf{x} = x_j\}$$

so

$$\frac{\sigma_{\mathbf{x}}^2}{\delta^2} \geq \sum_{x_j < E(\mathbf{x})-\delta} P\{\mathbf{x} = x_j\} + \sum_{E(\mathbf{x})+\delta < x_j} P\{\mathbf{x} = x_j\}$$

which yields the **Chebyshev inequality**

$$P\{|\mathbf{x} - E(\mathbf{x})| > \delta\} \leq \frac{\sigma_{\mathbf{x}}^2}{\delta^2}$$

Let us now consider simultaneously the two random variables $\mathbf{x}:S \to X$ and $\mathbf{y}:S \to Y$, with X and Y both sets of real numbers, on the same sample space S. Since, for example, $\{\mathbf{x} = x_i\}$ and $\{\mathbf{y} = y_j\}$ are events, we can take their union or intersection, and we may wish to determine the probability of the resulting event. Furthermore, if we denote $\{\mathbf{x} = x_i\} \cap \{\mathbf{y} = y_j\}$ by $\{\mathbf{x} = x_i, \mathbf{y} = y_j\}$, then

$$P\{\mathbf{x} = x_i, \mathbf{y} = y_j\} = P\{\mathbf{x} = x_i | \mathbf{y} = y_j\} P\{\mathbf{y} = y_j\}$$
$$= P\{\mathbf{y} = y_j | \mathbf{x} = x_i\} P\{\mathbf{x} = x_i\}$$

Example 18

Suppose that $\mathbf{x}$ is defined for the experiment of rolling a pair of fair dice, as before. Define the random variable $\mathbf{y}$ as in Exercise 14.

First let us find $P\{\mathbf{x} = 6 \,|\, \mathbf{y} = 2\}$. We begin with

$$P\{\mathbf{x} = 6 \,|\, \mathbf{y} = 2\} = \frac{P\{\mathbf{x} = 6, \mathbf{y} = 2\}}{P\{\mathbf{y} = 2\}}$$

Now, $\{\mathbf{x} = 6\} = \{(1,5), (2,4), (3,3), (4,2), (5,1)\}$ and $\{\mathbf{y} = 2\} = \{(1,3), (3,1), (2,4), (4,2), (3,5), (5,3), (6,4), (4,6)\}$. Thus, $\{\mathbf{x} = 6, \mathbf{y} = 2\} = \{\mathbf{x} = 6\} \cap \{\mathbf{y} = 2\} = \{(2,4), (4,2)\}$, and $P\{\mathbf{x} = 6, \mathbf{y} = 2\} = 2/36$. Since $P\{\mathbf{y} = 2\} = 8/36$, then

$$P\{\mathbf{x} = 6 \,|\, \mathbf{y} = 2\} = \frac{2/36}{8/36}$$

$$= 1/4$$

Next let us find $P\{\mathbf{y} = 2 \,|\, \mathbf{x} = 6\}$. Now

$$P\{\mathbf{y} = 2 \,|\, \mathbf{x} = 6\} = \frac{P\{\mathbf{y} = 2, \mathbf{x} = 6\}}{P\{\mathbf{x} = 6\}}$$

Thus,

$$P\{\mathbf{y} = 2 \,|\, \mathbf{x} = 6\} = \frac{2/36}{5/36}$$

$$= 2/5 \qquad \qquad \Diamond$$

Suppose that $\mathbf{x}$ assigns the numbers $x_1, x_2, \ldots, x_n$ and $\mathbf{y}$ assigns the numbers $y_1, y_2, \ldots, y_m$ to the outcomes of an experiment. Clearly, if $i \neq j$, then

$$\{\mathbf{y} = y_i, \mathbf{y} = y_j\} = \{\mathbf{y} = y_i\} \cap \{\mathbf{y} = y_j\} = \varnothing$$

Furthermore,

$$\{\mathbf{y} = y_1\} \cup \{\mathbf{y} = y_2\} \cup \cdots \cup \{\mathbf{y} = y_m\} = S$$

Hence,

$$P\{\mathbf{x} = x_i\} = P(\{\mathbf{x} = x_i\} \cap S)$$

and

$$P\{\mathbf{x} = x_i\} = \sum_{j=1}^{m} P\{\mathbf{x} = x_i, \mathbf{y} = y_j\}$$

In a similar manner,

$$P\{\mathbf{y} = y_j\} = \sum_{i=1}^{n} P\{\mathbf{x} = x_i, \mathbf{y} = y_j\}$$

As a consequence of our discussion of two random variables $\mathbf{x}$ and $\mathbf{y}$ defined for the same experiment, it is natural to extend our definition of the expectation of $\mathbf{x}$.

DEFINITION 9

Suppose that $\mathbf{x}$ is a random variable which assigns the numbers $x_1, x_2, \ldots, x_n$ to the outcomes of an experiment. Then for any event A, the **conditional expected value** of $\mathbf{x}$ given A, denoted by $E(\mathbf{x}|A)$, is given by

$$E(\mathbf{x}|A) = \sum_{i=1}^{n} x_i P\{\mathbf{x} = x_i|A\}$$

Example 19

For our experiment of rolling a pair of fair dice, let us find the (conditional) expected value of $\mathbf{y}$ (specified in Exercise 14) given the event $\{\mathbf{x} = 6\}$. Since

$$P\{\mathbf{y} = 0|\mathbf{x} = 6\} = \frac{P\{\mathbf{y} = 0, \mathbf{x} = 6\}}{P\{\mathbf{x} = 6\}} = \frac{1/36}{5/36} = 1/5$$

$$P\{\mathbf{y} = 1|\mathbf{x} = 6\} = \frac{P\{\mathbf{y} = 1, \mathbf{x} = 6\}}{P\{\mathbf{x} = 6\}} = \frac{0}{5/36} = 0$$

$$P\{\mathbf{y} = 2|\mathbf{x} = 6\} = \frac{P\{\mathbf{y} = 2, \mathbf{x} = 6\}}{P\{\mathbf{x} = 6\}} = \frac{2/36}{5/36} = 2/5$$

$$P\{\mathbf{y} = 3|\mathbf{x} = 6\} = \frac{P\{\mathbf{y} = 3, \mathbf{x} = 6\}}{P\{\mathbf{x} = 6\}} = \frac{0}{5/36} = 0$$

$$P\{\mathbf{y} = 4|\mathbf{x} = 6\} = \frac{P\{\mathbf{y} = 4, \mathbf{x} = 6\}}{P\{\mathbf{x} = 6\}} = \frac{2/36}{5/36} = 2/5$$

$$P\{\mathbf{y} = 5|\mathbf{x} = 6\} = \frac{P\{\mathbf{y} = 5, \mathbf{x} = 6\}}{P\{\mathbf{x} = 6\}} = \frac{0}{5/36} = 0$$

then

$$E(\mathbf{y}\,|\,\mathbf{x} = 6) = \sum_{j=0}^{5} jP\{\mathbf{y} = j\,|\,\mathbf{x} = 6\}$$

$$= 0(1/5) + 1(0) + 2(2/5) + 3(0) + 4(2/5) + 5(0)$$
$$= 12/5 \qquad\qquad\qquad \Diamond$$

Let us now return to the concept of independence. Recall that two events A and B are independent if $P(A\,|\,B) = P(A)$. Suppose now that $\mathbf{x}$ and $\mathbf{y}$ are random variables which assign the numbers $x_1, x_2, \ldots, x_n$ and $y_1, y_2, \ldots, y_m$, respectively. If $A = \{\mathbf{x} = x_i\}$ and $B = \{\mathbf{y} = y_j\}$ for some i and j such that $1 \leq i \leq n$ and $1 \leq j \leq m$, clearly then $\{\mathbf{x} = x_i\}$ and $\{\mathbf{y} = y_j\}$ are independent if

$$P\{\mathbf{x} = x_i\,|\,\mathbf{y} = y_j\} = P\{\mathbf{x} = x_i\}$$

Naturally, this is to be expected by definition. However, if this relationship holds for all values of i and j, then the resulting relationship between $\mathbf{x}$ and $\mathbf{y}$ is given a special name:

DEFINITION 10

Suppose that $\mathbf{x}$ and $\mathbf{y}$ are random variables which assign the numbers $x_1, x_2, \ldots, x_n$ and $y_1, y_2, \ldots, y_m$, respectively. If

$$P\{\mathbf{x} = x_i\,|\,\mathbf{y} = y_j\} = P\{\mathbf{x} = x_i\}$$

for all $i = 1, 2, \ldots, n$ and $j = 1, 2, \ldots, m$, then we say that $\mathbf{x}$ and $\mathbf{y}$ are **statistically independent** random variables. $\qquad\qquad$ $\bigcirc$

Example 20

From previous examples it is clear that the random variables $\mathbf{x}$ and $\mathbf{y}$ defined for the experiment of rolling fair dice are not statistically independent. For instance, we have seen that

$$P\{\mathbf{x} = 6\,|\,\mathbf{y} = 2\} = 1/4$$

and

$$P\{\mathbf{x} = 6\} = 5/36$$

from which we conclude that

$$P\{\mathbf{x} = 6\,|\,\mathbf{y} = 2\} \neq P\{\mathbf{x} = 6\} \qquad\qquad\qquad \Diamond$$

Suppose that $\mathbf{x}:S \to \mathbf{R}$ and $\mathbf{y}:S \to \mathbf{R}$ are discrete random variables on S which assign the numbers $x_1, x_2, \ldots, x_n$ and $y_1, y_2, \ldots, y_m$, respectively. If $f:\mathbf{R} \times \mathbf{R} \to \mathbf{R}:(r, r') \mapsto f(r, r')$ is a real function, then we denote by $f(\mathbf{x}, \mathbf{y})$ the function

$$f(\mathbf{x}, \mathbf{y}):S \to \mathbf{R}:s \mapsto f[\mathbf{x}(s), \mathbf{y}(s)]$$

Then, clearly, $f(\mathbf{x}, \mathbf{y})$ is also a random variable on S, and we say that $f(\mathbf{x}, \mathbf{y})$ is a function of the random variables $\mathbf{x}$ and $\mathbf{y}$. Then the **joint** (or **compound**) **expected value** of $f(\mathbf{x}, \mathbf{y})$ is

$$E[f(\mathbf{x}, \mathbf{y})] = \sum_{i=1}^{n} \sum_{j=1}^{m} f(x_i, y_j) P\{\mathbf{x} = x_i, \mathbf{y} = y_j\}$$

For the special case when $f(\mathbf{x}, \mathbf{y}) = \mathbf{x} + \mathbf{y}$, we have

$$E(\mathbf{x} + \mathbf{y}) = \sum_{i=1}^{n} \sum_{j=1}^{m} (x_i + y_j) P\{\mathbf{x} = x_i, \mathbf{y} = y_j\}$$

$$= \sum_{i=1}^{n} \sum_{j=1}^{m} x_i P\{\mathbf{x} = x_i, \mathbf{y} = y_j\} + \sum_{i=1}^{n} \sum_{j=1}^{m} y_j P\{\mathbf{x} = x_i, \mathbf{y} = y_j\}$$

$$= \sum_{i=1}^{n} x_i \sum_{j=1}^{m} P\{\mathbf{x} = x_i, \mathbf{y} = y_j\} + \sum_{j=1}^{m} y_j \sum_{i=1}^{n} P\{\mathbf{x} = x_i, \mathbf{y} = y_j\}$$

$$= \sum_{i=1}^{n} x_i P\{\mathbf{x} = x_i\} + \sum_{j=1}^{m} y_j P\{\mathbf{y} = y_j\}$$

$$= E(\mathbf{x}) + E(\mathbf{y})$$

When $\mathbf{x}$ and $\mathbf{y}$ are statistically independent, we have

$$P\{\mathbf{x} = x_i, \mathbf{y} = y_j\} = P\{\mathbf{x} = x_i\} P\{\mathbf{y} = y_j\}$$

so that

$$E(\mathbf{xy}) = \sum_{i=1}^{n} \sum_{j=1}^{m} x_i y_j P\{\mathbf{x} = x_i\} P\{\mathbf{y} = y_j\}$$

$$= \sum_{i=1}^{n} x_i P\{\mathbf{x} = x_i\} \sum_{j=1}^{m} y_j P\{\mathbf{y} = y_j\}$$

$$= E(\mathbf{x})E(\mathbf{y})$$

LEMMA 10

Suppose that $\mathbf{x}$ and $\mathbf{y}$ are random variables on S. If $\mathbf{x}$ and $\mathbf{y}$ are statistically independent, then for the random variable $\mathbf{z} = f(\mathbf{x}, \mathbf{y}) = \mathbf{x} + \mathbf{y}$ we have that

$$\sigma_z^2 = \sigma_x^2 + \sigma_y^2$$

Proof

$$
\begin{aligned}
\sigma_z^2 &= E(z^2) - E(z)^2 \\
&= E([x + y]^2) - E(x + y)^2 \\
&= E(x^2 + 2xy + y^2) - [E(x) + E(y)]^2 \\
&= E(x^2) + 2E(xy) + E(y^2) - E(x)^2 - 2E(x)E(y) - E(y)^2 \\
&= E(x^2) + 2E(x)E(y) + E(y^2) - E(x)^2 - 2E(x)E(y) - E(y)^2 \\
&= E(x^2) - E(x)^2 + E(y)^2 - E(y)^2 \\
&= \sigma_x^2 + \sigma_y^2 \qquad\qquad\qquad\qquad\qquad\qquad\qquad\qquad \square
\end{aligned}
$$

Now suppose that we have r statistically independent random variables $x_1, x_2, \ldots, x_r$ (i.e., x_i and x_j are statistically independent if $i \neq j$), each of which is the same function as $x : S \to R$. Let us define the random variable y by

$$y = \frac{x_1 + x_2 + \cdots + x_r}{r} = \frac{1}{r} \sum_{i=1}^{r} x_i$$

Then

$$E(y) = E\left[\frac{1}{r} \sum_{i=1}^{r} x_i\right]$$

$$= \frac{1}{r} E\left(\sum_{i=1}^{r} x_i\right)$$

$$= \frac{1}{r} \sum_{i=1}^{r} E(x_i)$$

$$= E(x)$$

since $x_i = x$ for $i = 1, 2, \ldots, r$. Furthermore,

$$
\begin{aligned}
\sigma_y^2 &= \sigma_{(1/r)(x_1 + x_2 + \cdots + x_r)}^2 \\
&= \frac{1}{r^2} \sigma_{x_1 + x_2 + \cdots + x_r}^2 \qquad\qquad\text{by Corollary 9} \\
&= \frac{1}{r^2}(\sigma_{x_1}^2 + \sigma_{x_2}^2 + \cdots + \sigma_{x_r}^2) \text{ by Lemma 10 (and a little} \\
&\qquad\qquad\qquad\qquad\qquad\qquad\qquad\quad\text{further juggling)} \\
&= \frac{1}{r^2}(r\sigma_x^2) \\
&= \frac{\sigma_x^2}{r}
\end{aligned}
$$

But, from the Chebyshev inequality,

$$P\{|\mathbf{y} - E(\mathbf{y})| > \delta\} \le \frac{\sigma_{\mathbf{y}}^2}{\delta^2}$$

so that

$$P\left\{\left|\frac{1}{r}\sum_{i=1}^{r} \mathbf{x}_i - E(\mathbf{x})\right| > \delta\right\} \le \frac{\sigma_{\mathbf{x}}^2}{r\,\delta^2}$$

Thus,

$$\lim_{r\to\infty} P\left\{\left|\frac{1}{r}\sum_{i=1}^{r} \mathbf{x}_i - E(\mathbf{x})\right| > \delta\right\} = 0 \qquad \Box$$

Thus, using the terminology of Example 17, we have proved:

The Law of Large Numbers

If $\mathbf{x}$ is a Bernoulli random variable then for k successes in r trials and any $\delta > 0$ we have that

$$\lim_{r\to\infty} P\left\{\left|\frac{k}{r} - q\right| > \delta\right\} = 0 \qquad \Box$$

Decision Theory

An important application of some of the above ideas has been in decision theory; we illustrate this with a problem in pattern recognition diagrammed in Figure 6–7. We are given a sample space S of *objects,* each of which belongs

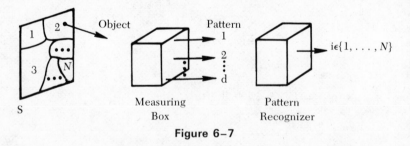

Figure 6–7

to one of N disjoint classes. Objects are picked at random, and measured by a box which encodes each object s from S into a *pattern* consisting of d measurements, each of which lies in a finite set $M \subset \mathbf{R}$ of real numbers (finite, since the measurements have limited precision). Thus, the measuring box provides us with a random variable

$$\mathbf{m}: S \to M^d$$

In general, the measurements will not provide enough information to determine exactly to which class an object s, whose pattern is $\mathbf{m}(s)$, belongs. The task of the pattern recognizer, then, is to classify patterns in such a way that the expected loss due to misclassification of objects is as small as possible, given some estimate $c(i|j)$ of the cost of classifying an object of class j as one of class i for $1 \leq i, j \leq N$. To do this, certain data are required. Let us assume, then, that as a result of constant comparison of the results of measurement with expert classification using more subtle cues, the following probabilities have been reliably (but see our comments on the frequency interpretation of probability) approximated:

(i) $P(a) = P\{\mathbf{m}(s) = a\}$, the probability of occurrence of pattern $a \in M^d$.
(ii) $P(a|i) = P\{\mathbf{m}(s) = a | s \in i\}$, the probability that an object in class i will yield pattern a when measured.
(iii) $P(i) = P\{s \in i\}$, the probability that an object will belong to class i.
(iv) $P(i|a) = P\{s \in i | \mathbf{m}(s) = a\}$, the probability that an object whose pattern is a will belong to class i.

The theory of adaptive networks or learning machines studies ways of building pattern recognition networks which can use performance feedback to update *estimates* of the above probabilities, and then use the estimates in a scheme of the type we shall present below. Important questions, which we shall not discuss here, are then those of *stability* (can the machine compensate for small changes in the initial estimates?) and *rate of convergence* (will the estimates improve quickly enough to yield tolerable classification in a reasonable time?).

In any case, given the data (i) to (iv) above, the expected loss in classifying an object with pattern a into class i is clearly the average over j of what the loss will be if the object actually belongs to class j. Thus, if we denote this expected loss by $\mathcal{L}(i|a)$, we have:

$$\mathcal{L}(i|a) = \sum_{j=1}^{N} c(i|j) P(j|a)$$

$$= \sum_{j=1}^{N} c(i|j) \frac{P(a|j)P(j)}{P(a)} \quad \text{by Bayes' rule (Theorem 7)}$$

$$= \frac{1}{P(a)} \left[\sum_{j=1}^{N} c(i|j) P(a|j) P(j) \right]$$

In particular, if we assume unit cost for each wrong decision and zero cost for the correct decision, we see that the best decision is that which minimizes

$$P(a)\mathcal{L}(i|a) = \sum_{j \neq i} P(a|j) P(j)$$

$$= P(a) - P(a|i) P(i)$$

since

$$P(a) = \sum_{j=1}^{N} P(a|j)P(j)$$

Thus, in this so-called symmetric-cost case of $c(i|j) = 1 - \delta_{ij}$, where

$$\delta_{ij} = \begin{cases} 1 & \text{if } i = j \\ 0 & \text{if } i \neq j \end{cases}$$

is the **Kronecker delta,** the best decision is that which maximizes

$$L(i|a) = P(a|i)P(i)$$

If all categories are equally likely, so that each $P(i) = \dfrac{1}{N}$, the decision reduces to picking the i which maximizes $P(a|i)$—the so-called **maximum-likelihood decision.**

Example 21

Let us put Example 13 into this framework. In this case, there are two classes, M (for mono) and $\bar{M}$, and the pattern set has two elements, T (for positive test) and $\bar{T}$.

Suppose that we use the following cost estimates:

$c(M|M) = 1000$ is the cost of relatively short hospitalization if disease is detected early

$c(M|\bar{M}) = 300$ is the cost of more extensive tests to rule out presence of the disease

$c(\bar{M}|\bar{M}) = 0$

$c(\bar{M}|M) = 5000$ is the cost of protracted hospitalization if the disease is not detected and is allowed to progress to a later stage

Then we have the following costs:

$$\begin{aligned} P(T)\mathcal{L}(M|T) &= c(M|M)P(T|M)P(M) + c(M|\bar{M})P(T|\bar{M})P(\bar{M}) \\ &= 1000(0.95)(0.005) + 300(0.04)(0.995) \\ &= 4.75 + 11.94 \\ &= 16.79 \end{aligned}$$

and

$$\begin{aligned} P(T)\mathcal{L}(\bar{M}|T) &= c(\bar{M}|M)P(T|M)P(M) + c(\bar{M}|\bar{M})P(T|\bar{M})P(\bar{M}) \\ &= 5000(0.95)(0.005) \\ &= 23.75 \end{aligned}$$

Thus, despite the very low probability (0.107) that someone with a positive test has mono, an assessment of costs tells us that a positive test should not be ignored. ◊

Returning to the symmetric-cost case, note that maximizing $\mathcal{L}(i|a)$ is equivalent to maximizing $\log \mathcal{L}(i|a)$, which equals

$$g_i(a) = \log P(a|i) + \log P(i)$$

If there are just two classes (let us now call them 0 and 1), then clearly the optimal classifier is described by the function

$$f(a) = \begin{cases} 1 & \text{if } g_1(a) \geq g_0(a) \\ 0 & \text{if not} \end{cases}$$

In fact, under quite reasonable assumptions we can replace this formula, which requires processors to compute $g_1(a)$ and $g_2(a)$, by a threshold element which computes $f(a)$ directly from the d components $(a_1, \ldots, a_d)$ of a. We proceed as follows:

Firstly,

$$g_1(a) - g_0(a) = [\log P(a|1) + \log P(1)] - [\log P(a|0) + \log P(0)]$$

$$= \log\left[\frac{P(a|1)}{P(a|0)}\right] + \log\left[\frac{P(1)}{1 - P(1)}\right] \tag{3}$$

since $P(0) + P(1) = 1$. Suppose, then, that our measuring device, and our objects, have the properties that in each class the components of a are statistically independent, so that

$$P(a|i) = P(a_1|i) \cdots P(a_d|i) \text{ for } i = 0, 1$$

Then (3) becomes

$$g_1(a) - g_0(a) = \sum_{k=1}^{d} \log\left[\frac{P(a_k|1)}{P(a_k|0)}\right] + \log\left[\frac{P(1)}{1 - P(1)}\right] \tag{4}$$

Let us further suppose that our measurements are all tests with just two outcomes, 0 or 1. Then, if we set

$$p_k = P(a_k = 1|1) \text{ so that } 1 - p_k = P(a_k = 0|1)$$

and

$$q_k = P(a_k = 1|0) \text{ so that } 1 - q_k = P(a_k = 0|0)$$

we can rewrite

$$\log\left[\frac{P(a_k\,|\,1)}{P(a_k\,|\,0)}\right]$$

as

$$\log\frac{p_k}{q_k}$$

if $a_k = 1$, and as

$$\log\left[\frac{1-p_k}{1-q_k}\right]$$

if $a_k = 0$. Then,

$$\log\left[\frac{P(a_k\,|\,1)}{P(a_k\,|\,0)}\right] = a_k\log\left[\frac{p_k}{q_k}\right] + (1-a_k)\log\left[\frac{1-p_k}{1-q_k}\right]$$

$$= a_k w_k + w'_k$$

where

$$w_k = \log\left[\frac{p_k}{q_k}\right] - \log\left[\frac{1-p_k}{1-q_k}\right] = \log\left[\frac{p_k(1-q_k)}{q_k(1-p_k)}\right]$$

and

$$w'_k = \log\left[\frac{1-p_k}{1-q_k}\right]$$

Thus, from (3) and (4) we obtain

$$g_1(a) - g_0(a) = \sum_{k=1}^{d} w_k a_k - \theta$$

where

$$\theta = -\sum_{k=1}^{d} w'_k - \log\left[\frac{P(1)}{1-P(1)}\right]$$

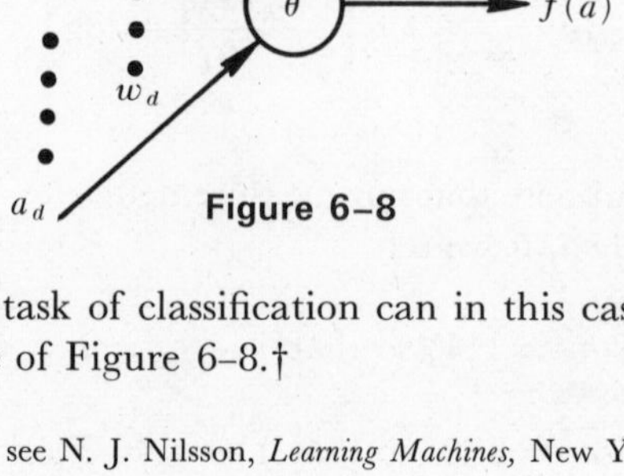

Figure 6–8

In other words, the task of classification can in this case be carried out by the threshold device of Figure 6–8.†

---

†For more on this topic, see N. J. Nilsson, *Learning Machines,* New York, McGraw-Hill, 1965.

EXERCISES FOR SECTION 6-1

1.   Suppose that $B \subset A$. Prove that $P(A) \geq P(B)$. [Hint: Use the fact that $A = B \cup A = B \cup (A \cap \bar{B})$.]

2.   Show that

$$P(A \cup B \cup C) = P(A) + P(B) + P(C) + P(A \cap B \cap C)$$
$$- P(A \cap B) - P(A \cap C) - P(B \cap C)$$

[Hint: First look at $P(A \cup [B \cup C])$, and recall that $A \cap (B \cup C) = (A \cap B) \cup (A \cap C)$.]

3.   Prove, by induction on n, that we always have

$$P(A_1 \cup A_2 \cup \cdots A_n) \leq P(A_1) + P(A_2) + \cdots + P(A_n)$$

4.   Use the equality $P(A \cup B) = P(A) + P(B) - P(A \cap B)$ to prove that if $P(A) = P(B) = 1$, then $P(A \cup B) = P(A \cap B) = 1$.

5.   Suppose that $B \subset A$ and $P(B) > 0$. Prove that $P(A|B) = 1$.

6.   For the experiment of flipping a fair coin three times, determine the probability that the third flip is a head, given that at least two of the flips are heads.

7.   Suppose that somebody has developed a fair three-sided coin. Our game consists of the following: Player A flips the coin first. If side 3 results, he wins; if not, player B flips the coin. If side 3 then results, player B wins. If not, player A then has the last flip whereupon side 3 makes him a winner, while side 1 or 2 makes him a loser. Determine the probability that player A wins the game (i.e., see if he who flips last, flips best).

8.   Three players alternate flipping a fair coin until one of them flips a head and wins. Find the probability that the first player to flip wins. Repeat your calculation for the second and third players.

9.   Rolling a pair of fair dice, a player obtains one of the integers between 2 and 12, inclusive. Now consider the following experiment: You roll a pair of fair dice. If you get 7 or 11, you win. Conversely, if you roll "craps" (2, 3, or 12), you lose. If you roll any other number (either 4, 5, 6, 8, 9, or 10), that number becomes your "point," and you keep rolling the dice until you get your point and you win, or you roll 7 and you lose. The name of this game is **craps.** Find the probability of winning at craps, given the following probabilities:

$$P(2) = P(12) = 1/36$$
$$P(3) = P(11) = 1/18$$
$$P(4) = P(10) = 1/12$$
$$P(5) = P(9) = 1/9$$
$$P(6) = P(8) = 5/36$$
$$P(7) = 1/6$$

10.   Compute $P(W|C)$ for the data of Example 12. Compute $P(M|C)$ in two distinct ways.

11.   For the conditions of Example 13, find $P(T)$; i.e., the probability that a person selected at random will have a positive mono test.

12.   A friend of yours with a thick foreign accent flips a fair coin and tells you the outcome. Because of his accent, when he says "head," the probability that you think he said "head" is 0.8; otherwise, you think he said "tail." In addition, when he says "tail," there is a 0.4 probability that you think he said "tail" and a 0.6 probability that you think he said "head." This situation, known as a *noisy* channel, is summarized in Figure 6–9. Given that you think your friend said "head," what is the probability that he actually flipped a head? What is the probability that he flipped a tail, given that you think he said "tail"?

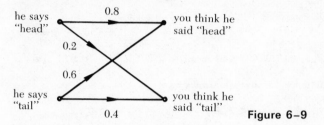

Figure 6–9

13. Suppose that A and B are independent. Prove that $\bar{A}$ and $\bar{B}$ are also independent. [Hint: Use DeMorgan's Law, $\bar{A} \cap \bar{B} = \overline{A \cup B}$.]

14. For the experiment of rolling a pair of fair dice, define a random variable $y:S \to Y = \{0, 1, 2, 3, 4, 5\}$ by $(i,j) \mapsto |i - j|$. Find the following:

(a) $P\{y = 0\}$
(b) $P\{y = 1\}$
(c) $P\{y = 2\}$
(d) $P\{y = 3\}$
(e) $P\{y = 4\}$
(f) $P\{y = 5\}$
(g) $P\{y = 0 | y \le 2\}$
(h) $P\{y \ge 3 | 2 \le y \le 4\}$

15. Given a pair of fair dice and the random variable y defined in the last exercise, find the expected value of y.

16. For Example 18, find

$$P\{x = 6 | y \le 3\}$$

17. For Example 18, verify that

$$P\{x = 6\} = \sum_{j=0}^{5} P\{x = 6, y = j\}.$$

18. Prove that

$$\sum_{i=1}^{n} \sum_{j=1}^{m} P\{x = x_i, y = y_j\} = 1$$

19. Show that the joint expected value of x and y for the experiment of rolling a pair of fair dice is $E(xy) = 245/18$.

20. Prove that, if x and y are statistically independent, then for $i = 1, 2, \ldots, n$ and $j = 1, 2, \ldots, m$ we have

$$P\{x = x_i, y = y_j\} = P\{x = x_i\}P\{y = y_j\}$$

21. Using the data of Examples 13 and 21, calculate the following expected losses:

   (a) $\mathcal{L}(M\,|\,T)$
   (b) $\mathcal{L}(\bar{M}\,|\,T)$
   (c) $\mathcal{L}(M\,|\,\bar{T})$
   (d) $\mathcal{L}(\bar{M}\,|\,\bar{T})$

22. Using the data of Examples 13 and 21, find the smallest value of $c(\bar{M}\,|\,M)$, leaving other costs fixed, which would render testing for mono a waste of time.

23. Using the data of Examples 13 and 21, compute the optimal action when the test is negative. Any comments?

6-2   A Measure of Information

One of the most important applications of probability theory has been to the design of systems for the reliable transmission of information. In this section, we discuss the general problems of information transmission and define a measure of information. In Section 6-3 we shall then discuss questions of efficiency of encoding, while in Section 6-4 we shall prove the existence of encoding schemes which reduce the sensitivity of messages to noise, or "static," during transmission.

The reliable transmission of information is a major concern in the field of electrical and computer engineering. Quite often there is a need to transfer data, in the form of electrical signals, from one point to another. In many cases (e.g., digital computer and pulse modulation systems) the information to be communicated is in digital form, that is, in the form of signals which at any instant of time assume only a finite number of discrete values. A general digital information transmission or communication system is shown in Figure 6-10.

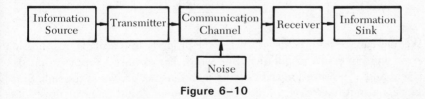

Figure 6-10

Initially, the digital data to be transmitted are produced by an information source. The information is then transferred through a communication channel by means of a transmitter. Typical of such channels are telephone and transmission lines, storage devices, and the atmosphere. Upon passing through a channel, a signal may be perturbed by undesirable disturbances such as lightning, sunspots, or other causes of electrical or electronic malfunction. This "noise" may result in the appearance at the receiver of a signal which is different from its corresponding transmitted signal. Regardless of any changes, whatever is received at the output of the channel goes to the destination or information sink. Thus, the resulting received information may contain errors.

As a specific example, suppose that at any instant of time a transmitter is capable of accepting only one of two possible inputs, say 0 or 1. Such a channel is called a *binary* channel. Suppose that an information source produces four distinct outputs. To serve as inputs to the channel, these four "messages" must be in terms of the binary digits 0 and 1. Assume, then, that the outputs of the source are the four binary sequences 00, 01, 10, and 11. For the case when the same sequence is received as transmitted, we say that no errors have occurred in transmission. However, suppose that the sequence 01 is transmitted and an error in transmission of the second digit occurs so that 00 is received. Clearly, there is no way for the sink to know whether 00 was sent and no errors occurred in transmission, or whether 01 was sent and one error occurred in transmission. Consequently, the set of sequences (or *code*) $S_1 = \{00, 01, 10, 11\}$ has no error-detecting capabilities.

To help alleviate this condition, let us increase the length of each sequence (or *code word*) by adding one digit in a manner such that the number of 1's in each new code word is even. The addition of this so-called "parity check" digit is summarized in Table 6–1. Hence, the new code is $S_2 = \{000, 011, 101, 110\}$.

Table 6–1

ORIGINAL CODE WORD	PARITY CHECK DIGIT
00	0
01	1
10	1
11	0

We now can see that the new code has the property that a single transmission error will not result in another code word. For example, suppose that 011 is sent and a transmission error occurs such that 111 arrives at the sink. Since 111 could not have been transmitted, it is obvious that an error must have occurred. Consequently, the new code has the ability to detect single errors and is called a *single-error-detecting* code. However, although this code enables the sink to detect errors, it does not lend itself to *error-correction*, since 100 may result from a single error in either 101 or 110.

This error-detecting capability has its price. The information, which was transmittable without any error-detecting capability by code words of length two, can be transmitted by using code words of length three so that all single errors are detectable. We can say that the new code has an *efficiency* or *rate* of $\frac{2}{3}$ of that of the original. Thus, the price paid is efficiency.

Consider next the possibility of making a transmission more reliable by the simple philosophy of repetition. As an example, assume that a new code

S_3 is formed from the code $S_1 = \{00, 01, 10, 11\}$ by repeating each code word three times, i.e., the new code is $S_3 = \{000000, 010101, 101010, 111111\}$. For this code we note that the change of a single digit in any code word will not result in another code word. Now suppose that a code word of S_3 is sent and a single error occurs in transmission. Can we determine the code word that was sent? The answer is yes. Because a code word in S_3 consists of a length-two binary sequence repeated three times, a single error will change only one of these length-two sequences. Thus if we agree to (a) take a received sequence, (b) partition it into thirds, and (c) change one of the length-two sequences such that it is the same as the remaining two sequences, we will be able to correct a single error occurring in any code word. Thus, we say that S_3 is a *single-error-correcting* code. The cost of this error-correcting capability becomes apparent when we note that S_3 is $\frac{2}{6} = \frac{1}{3}$ as efficient as S_1.

In the previous examples we were able to construct error-detecting and error-correcting codes from simple codes by adding *redundancy,* that is, by adding digits in some predetermined manner. This process is *error-correction encoding.* The inverse process of reconstructing the original code words from the received sequence is called *decoding.* We are thus led to the study of the system shown in Figure 6–11.

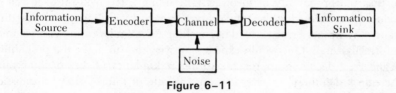

Figure 6–11

Here we will study only the "discrete" case, i.e., the case where messages and signals are regarded as sequences of symbols. The main result of our mathematical study of discrete information transmission will be Shannon's theorem, which provides very broad conditions under which there *exists* an encoding such that, despite noise, a message that is sent can be received as accurately as desired. In Sections 7–3 and 8–2 we shall turn to methods for actually *constructing* codes with error-correcting capabilities.

A rather general treatment of Shannon's theory entails the use of such concepts as measure theory, and is too sophisticated and much too lengthy for inclusion here. Instead, we shall follow Shannon's original approach [Shannon, 1948; Shannon and Weaver, 1949] by characterizing our information source by a random variable, by letting our channel be memoryless (defined below), and by omitting details of rigor in our mathematical proofs.

Here let us outline the strategy that leads up to Shannon's theorem: First, we must define a mathematical measure of information which depends only on the probability distribution describing a source. We can then set up our mathematical model of the source and channel, and associate with our source an *entropy H,* which is to be thought of as the average amount of information contained in each symbol produced by the source. The symbols emitted by the source will be encoded into channel symbols (*source encoding*) and transmitted through the channel one by one, the noise perturbing the channel symbols independently. (This independence is one of our simplifying assumptions.) We further assume that the present output depends on the present input and not on past inputs. Thus, we call the channel *memoryless.* The perturbation will clearly result in a loss of information in the channel. We then study the amount of information getting through the channel. Clearly we cannot receive more information than is sent. The information not getting through the channel is called the *equivocation,* and we regard it as the amount of uncertainty we have about the original message. For a given channel, different sources result in different amounts of information being transmitted. Consequently, we define the *capacity C* of the channel as the maximum information that we can transmit through the channel by suitable choice of source. Thus, C is the maximum amount of information that we can ever hope to transmit through our channel.

As we have indicated, by sending information in a redundant form we can obtain the ability to correct errors which occur in transmission. Because of this, the probability of incorrectly decoding a received message can be reduced, thus reducing the equivocation. Hence, by adding sufficient redundancy (by proper error-correction encoding), the equivocation can be made arbitrarily small. One would expect, however, that to make the probability of incorrect decoding approach zero, the redundancy of the encoding must increase indefinitely, thereby causing the rate of information transmission to approach zero. This is by no means true. Actually, by proper encoding, it is possible to send information through the channel at any rate less than C with as small an equivocation as desired. This statement is not true for any rate greater than C. These results are the main justification for the definition of C, and constitute Shannon's remarkable Fundamental Theorem for a Discrete Noisy Channel:

Let a discrete channel have capacity C and let a discrete source have entropy H. If $H < C$, there exists an encoding scheme such that the output of the source can be transmitted through the channel with an arbitrarily small equivocation. If $H > C$, there is no method of encoding which gives an equivocation less than $H - C$.

With this perspective, we now turn to the crucial measure, due to Hartley [1928], which associates with the probability of an event the amount of information the occurrence of that event may be said to convey. We begin with an example.

Suppose that you have a mild spirit of adventure, and therefore you have invested heavily in the stock market. When you return home every weekday at 5:30 P.M., you tune in the market report. Although the market can be quite unpredictable, you have been following it for a few years and, taking into consideration the economy, politics, and so forth, you have an idea of what to expect. You know that fluctuations of a few points up or down are quite common, and hence, not surprising. Consequently, when you return home one day and hear that the market closed up 1.21,† you are relatively unaffected. You could easily expect something like this—this event has a relatively high probability of occurrence, and you therefore received very little information from the market report.

Sometime later on another day, you listen to the market report and you hear that the average closed down 19.40. Such a big loss is not a frequent occurrence; i.e., the probability that this happens is fairly small. Because you were not really expecting this situation, the report supplied you with a substantial amount of information.

More than a month later, you receive the report that the market rose 47.35 in one day. This is almost unheard of. The probability that this can happen is extremely small. Yet, it happened. The information content of the report is so large that the market is the subject of conversation for days.

It is because of this example and others like it that we can imply a strong relation between probability and information. We naturally would feel that when an event having a high probability (close to 1) occurs, very little information is gained. On the other hand, when an event having a low probability (close to 0) occurs, a large amount of information is obtained. For this reason, we proceed as follows:

Suppose that an event A occurs with probability $P(A) = p$. We would like to have some function I which assigns a real number to the probability p, thereby indicating the amount of information gained when event A occurs. In other words, we would like to find a function $I:[0, 1] \rightarrow \mathbf{R}$ (that is, I maps the real numbers between 0 and 1 into the real numbers) which is decreasing. The reason for this is to have the information $I(p)$ get smaller as p gets larger. We also demand that I be continuous, since a miniscule change in probability of an event should have little effect on the information we gain from its occurrence.

Now suppose that B is an event having probability $P(B) = p'$. If A and B are independent events, then we know that $P(A \cap B) = P(A) \cdot P(B) = p \cdot p'$. Now the occurrence of A yields $I(p)$ units of information. Similarly, $I(p')$ units of information are gained when B occurs. Thus, if there is no dependence between A and B, when both occur simultaneously we should expect to have a total of $I(p) + I(p')$ units of information. Thus, let us constrain I to have the property

$$I(p \cdot p') = I(p) + I(p')$$

---

†That is, the Dow-Jones Industrials average (which at one time was around $1000) has increased by $1.21.

It can be proven mathematically that any continuous decreasing function I which satisfies this equation must be logarithmic:*

THEOREM 1

If $I:[0, 1] \to \mathbf{R}$ satisfies the conditions

 (i) $I(p)$ is a continuous decreasing function of p
(ii) $I(p_1 \cdot p_2) = I(p_1) + I(p_2)$ for all $p_1, p_2 \in [0, 1]$
then

$$I(p) = -\lambda \log_2 p$$

where λ is some positive constant.

Proof

We first note that, if $0 \leq p \leq 1$, then $\infty \geq -\log_2 p \geq 0$, and so we may find a positive rational number $\dfrac{m}{n}$ such that $(\frac{1}{2})^{m/n}$ approximates $p = (\frac{1}{2})^{-\log_2 p}$ with any desired accuracy.

But (ii) enables us to compute $I((\frac{1}{2})^{m/n})$ directly for any m/n: It is easy to deduce, by induction, that (ii) yields, for any $k \geq 2$,

$$I(p_1 \cdot p_2 \cdot \ldots \cdot p_k) = I(p_1) + I(p_2) + \cdots + I(p_k)$$

Thus

$$I((\tfrac{1}{2})^{m/n}) = I([(\tfrac{1}{2})^{1/n}]^m) = mI((\tfrac{1}{2})^{1/n})$$

But

$$I(\tfrac{1}{2}) = I([(\tfrac{1}{2})^{1/n}]^n) = nI((\tfrac{1}{2})^{1/n})$$

Thus

$$I((\tfrac{1}{2})^{m/n}) = \frac{m}{n}I(\tfrac{1}{2})$$

In other words, for any p of the form $(\frac{1}{2})^{m/n}$ for positive rational m/n, and which thus has $-\log_2 p = m/n$, we must have

$$I(p) = -\lambda \log_2 p \tag{1}$$

where $\lambda = I(\frac{1}{2})$. The requirement that I be a decreasing function of p forces λ to be positive. The requirement that I be a continuous function of p forces the formula (1) to hold for *all* p in $[0, 1]$ since, as we saw, any such p can be approximated to arbitrary accuracy by a p for which (1) has been shown to hold. $\square$

---

*In the remainder of this section we assume familiarity with a little "indiscrete" mathematics—namely the elementary properties of the logarithm.

Example 1

Let us toss a fair coin. Then $P\{\text{Head}\} = P\{\text{Tail}\} = \frac{1}{2}$, and the information content of either the event $\{\text{Head}\}$ or the event $\{\text{Tail}\}$ is

$$I(\tfrac{1}{2}) = -\lambda \log_2 (\tfrac{1}{2}) = \lambda$$

Clearly, then, the average amount of information in a coin toss is

$$H = P\{\text{Head}\} \cdot I(P\{\text{Head}\}) + P\{\text{Tail}\} \cdot I(P\{\text{Tail}\})$$
$$= \frac{1}{2} \cdot \lambda + \frac{1}{2} \cdot \lambda$$
$$= \lambda \qquad\qquad \lozenge$$

It has seemed reasonable to set $\lambda = 1$, so that a single toss of a fair coin yields exactly one unit of information. The resultant binary (since the base of the logarithm is 2) unit is contracted into the word **bit.** Henceforth, then, we shall take $\lambda = 1$, and write

$$I(p) = -\log_2 p$$

where the unit is the *bit*. Note, for simplicity of using tables, that $I(p) = \log_2 \left(\dfrac{1}{p} \right)$.

Example 2

Suppose that a coin is so biased that $P\{\text{Head}\} = \frac{1}{4}$ while $P\{\text{Tail}\} = \frac{3}{4}$. The information content of $\{\text{Head}\}$ is

$$I(\tfrac{1}{4}) = \log_2 4 = 2 \text{ bits}$$

while the information content of $\{\text{Tail}\}$ is

$$I(\tfrac{3}{4}) = \log_2 (\tfrac{4}{3}) = 0.4150 \text{ bits (from log tables)}$$

Thus, the average information per toss is

$$H = P\{\text{Head}\} \cdot I(P\{\text{Head}\}) + P\{\text{Tail}\} \cdot I(P\{\text{Tail}\})$$
$$= (1/4)(2) + (3/4)(0.4150)$$
$$= 0.5 + 0.31125$$
$$= 0.81125 \text{ bits of information} \qquad\qquad \lozenge$$

Hence, we see that when a coin is biased, we anticipate one side (the side with the higher probability) more than another, and thus, more than half of the time a smaller amount of information is gained. The result is less average information per toss. A plot of the average information H versus $P\{\text{Head}\} = p$ is shown in Figure 6–12. This average is defined by

$$H(p) = -p \log_2 p - (1 - p) \log_2 (1 - p)$$

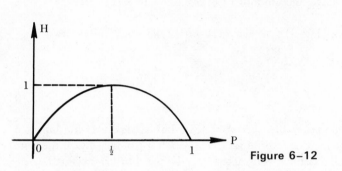

Figure 6–12

where, for the sake of consistency, we must define $0 \log_2 0 = 0$. Since we rule out the case of a zero-probability event ever occurring, it cannot make a nonzero contribution to our expected value.

Example 3

This example reminds us that we are using "information" in a limited technical sense. We do not give a sense of the word which carries the semantic connotations which render meaningful the question: "Which of these stories did you find to be most informative?":

Suppose that an author has a (rather limited!) vocabulary of 7000 words. Using these, he will write a 1000-word short story. Clearly, there are $(7000)^{1000}$ possible stories that can be written. Although many of these would be unbelievably bad, let us assume that every story is equally likely. (For some authors this is not an unwarranted assumption.) Thus, the probability of a specific story being written is $p = (7000)^{-1000}$. The information gained as a result of the story being furnished is [see Table 6–2 on page 472]

$$I(p) = \log_2 \left(\frac{1}{p}\right)$$

$$= \log_2 (7000)^{1000}$$

$$= 1000 \log_2 7000$$
$$= 1.2773 \times 10^4 \text{ bits}$$

Next suppose that an artist divides a canvas into 100 intervals horizontally and 90 intervals vertically. The result is a canvas that is partitioned into 9000 squares. Let us assume that each square is arbitrarily painted with one of seven colors. Hence, there are 7^{9000} possible paintings, each with a probability of $p = 7^{-9000}$. The amount of information in the final product is, therefore,

$$I(p) = \log_2 \left(\frac{1}{p}\right)$$

$$= \log_2 7^{9000}$$
$$= 9000 \log_2 7$$
$$= 2.5266 \times 10^4 \text{ bits}$$

Under the assumptions made in this example, we may now conclude that "one picture is worth (at least) a thousand words." [Abramson, 1963] ◊

Alas, this discussion sheds no light on the real meaning of the old saw, since for that purpose a highly sophisticated theory of *semantic* information is required which can handle meaningful relationships between pieces of information, rather than simply compute upon mere probabilities of occurrence. However, this criticism does not weaken the practicality of the theory of information transmission which Shannon has erected on Hartley's measure. In designing a telephone system, we want to ensure that the probability of a message being garbled is as low as possible. It seems an unreasonable demand that your telephone recognize when you are making an especially significant statement, and take special steps not to garble it!

Let us consider an information source

$$\mathbf{X} = \begin{pmatrix} x_1 & x_2 \ldots x_n \\ p_1 & p_2 \ldots p_n \end{pmatrix}$$

i.e., $\mathbf{X}$ produces source symbols $x_1, x_2, \ldots, x_n$ independently according to the following distribution:

$$P\{\mathbf{X} = x_1\} = p_1$$
$$P\{\mathbf{X} = x_2\} = p_2$$
$$\vdots$$
$$P\{\mathbf{X} = x_n\} = p_n$$

where we use the notation $\{\mathbf{X} = x_i\}$ to denote the event "the source produces symbol x_i." To be consistent, we must have

$$0 \leq p_i \leq 1 \text{ for } i = 1, 2, \ldots, n$$

and

$$\sum_{i=1}^{n} p_i = 1$$

If the source symbols are numbers, then the source $\mathbf{X}$ is a random variable in the limited sense of the term. As mentioned above, the information content of the event $\{\mathbf{X} = x_i\}$ is $-\log_2 p_i$ bits. Thus, we have the following:

DEFINITION 2

The average amount of information per symbol of the source $\mathbf{X} = \begin{pmatrix} x_1 \cdots x_n \\ p_1 \cdots p_n \end{pmatrix}$ is denoted by $H(\mathbf{X})$ and is called the **entropy** of $\mathbf{X}$; that is,

$$H(\mathbf{X}) = -\sum_{i=1}^{n} p_i \log_2 p_i$$

where the units of $H(\mathbf{X})$ are bits. ○

For a given collection of symbols, it is now reasonable to ask what probability distribution on their generation yields the maximum entropy. We can answer this question with one lemma and one theorem.

LEMMA 2

If $p_1, p_2, \ldots, p_n$ are positive numbers and $q_1, q_2, \ldots, q_n$ are non-negative numbers such that

$$\sum_{i=1}^{n} p_i = \sum_{i=1}^{n} q_i = 1$$

then

$$-\sum_{i=1}^{n} p_i \log_2 p_i \leq -\sum_{i=1}^{n} p_i \log_2 q_i$$

where equality holds if and only if $p_i = q_i$ for $i = 1, 2, \ldots, n$.

Proof

The key to this proof is the fact that $\log_2 x \leq x - 1$, with equality iff $x = 1$. This is "demonstrated" in Figure 6–13. (The reader may provide a "real" proof by calculus.)

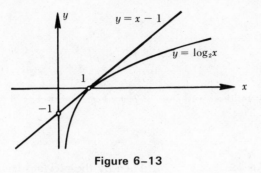

Figure 6-13

Thus, setting $x = q_i/p_i$, we get

$$\log_2 (q_i/p_i) \leq (q_i/p_i) - 1$$

with equality iff $q_i/p_i = 1$, or $q_i = p_i$. Hence,

$$p_i \log_2 (q_i/p_i) \leq p_i[(q_i/p_i) - 1]$$

and

$$\sum_{i=1}^{n} p_i \log_2 (q_i/p_i) \leq \sum_{i=1}^{n} p_i[(q_i/p_i) - 1] = \sum_{i=1}^{n} (q_i - p_i)$$

$$= \sum_{i=1}^{n} q_i - \sum_{i=1}^{n} p_i$$

$$= 1 - 1$$

Therefore,

$$\sum_{i=1}^{n} p_i(\log_2 q_i - \log_2 p_i) \leq 0$$

and so

$$-\sum_{i=1}^{n} p_i \log_2 p_i \leq -\sum_{i=1}^{n} p_i \log_2 q_i$$

with equality if and only if $p_i = q_i$ for $i = 1, 2, \ldots, n$. □

We now may prove the following important result.

THEOREM 3

$$H(\mathbf{X}) = -\sum_{i=1}^{n} p_i \log_2 p_i \leq \log_2 n$$

where equality holds if and only if $p_i = 1/n$ for $i = 1, 2, \ldots, n$.

Proof

Let $q_i = 1/n$ for $i = 1, 2, \ldots, n$. Then by the previous lemma,

$$H(\mathbf{X}) = -\sum_{i=1}^{n} p_i \log_2 p_i \leq -\sum_{i=1}^{n} p_i \log_2 (1/n) = -\log_2 (1/n)$$

so

$$H(\mathbf{X}) \leq \log_2 n$$

with equality if and only if $p_i = q_i = 1/n$ for $i = 1, 2, \ldots, n$. $\square$

We now conclude that the average information content of a source symbol is maximum when the symbols have an equal probability of being produced. Furthermore, this maximum is $\log_2 n$ bits.

It is commonly known that for a source which produces the symbols $x_1, x_2, \ldots, x_n$, we can represent each symbol with m binary digits provided that $2^m \geq n$, that is, $m \geq \log_2 n$. We now also realize that these m binary digits therefore contain an average of at most $\log_2 n$ bits of information. Hence, we can appreciate the relation between binary digits and binary units of information, and why they are sometimes confused.

EXERCISE FOR SECTION 6-2

1. Consider again the case in which a fair coin is flipped three times.
   (a) Find the information gained when an elementary event occurs.
   (b) Find the average information of an elementary event.
   (c) Find the average information of an elementary event for the following probability distribution (Note that $\log_2 3 = 1.585$):

$$P\{HHH\} = 3^3/4^3$$
$$P\{HHT\} = 3^2/4^3$$
$$P\{HTH\} = 3^2/4^3$$
$$P\{HTT\} = 3/4^3$$
$$P\{THH\} = 3^2/4^3$$
$$P\{THT\} = 3/4^3$$
$$P\{TTH\} = 3/4^3$$
$$P\{TTT\} = 1/4^3$$

6–3   Coding for Noiseless Channels

In this section, we see that our study of probability and entropy in the previous two sections enables us to solve the noiseless coding problem of transmitting information as economically as possible through a *noiseless* communication channel, i.e., a channel for which the received symbol is the same as the transmitted symbol.

To make our discussion self-contained, we briefly summarize the concepts of a semigroup and a semigroup homomorphism—the reader can find fuller treatments in Sections 2–2 and 5–1.

DEFINITION 1

A **semigroup** is a set S along with an operation $\cdot$, called **multiplication,** which is a mapping $\cdot: S \times S \to S: (s_1, s_2) \mapsto s_1 \cdot s_2$ such that for all $s_1, s_2, s_3 \in S$, the associative law

$$s_1 \cdot (s_2 \cdot s_3) = (s_1 \cdot s_2) \cdot s_3$$

is satisfied. ○

Example 1

The following is a list of just some of the many semigroups under ordinary multiplication:

(a) the positive integers
(b) the non-negative integers
(c) the integers
(d) the rational numbers
(e) the real numbers
(f) $\{2^i \mid i \in \mathbf{Z}\}$

By choosing ordinary addition as the operation, the sets (a) through (e) above yield five new semigroups. The set described in (f) is not a semigroup under addition. ◊

Of particular interest to us now is the case when the operation $\cdot$ signifies concatenation. For instance, we can concatenate the two binary sequences 1011 and 001 to obtain the single binary sequence 1011001, i.e.,

$$(1011) \cdot (001) = 1011001$$

We use the symbol X^+ to denote the set of all nonempty sequences of symbols from the alphabet X—it should now be obvious that X^+ is a semi-group under concatenation. (See Definition 2-1-3 on page 78.)

Suppose we have two semigroups, S_1 and S_2. (If there is no ambiguity as to the operation of a semigroup, its mention may be omitted.) We now give a special name to those functions $h: S_1 \to S_2$ for which it makes no difference as to whether elements in S_1 are operated upon before or after they are mapped. More formally, we have:

DEFINITION 2

Given semigroups S_1 and S_2, a map $h: S_1 \to S_2: s_1 \mapsto h(s_1)$ is said to be a **semigroup homomorphism** if for all $s_1, s_1' \in S_1$ we have that

$$h(s_1 \cdot s_1') = h(s_1) \cdot h(s_1')$$

Note that multiplication on the left side of this equation is the semigroup operation in S_1, while on the right side it is the operation in S_2.   ○

Example 2

Consider the semigroups $\mathbf{Z}$ under ordinary addition and $\{2^i \,|\, i \in \mathbf{Z}\}$ under ordinary multiplication. Then the map

$$h: \mathbf{Z} \to \{2^i \,|\, i \in \mathbf{Z}\} : n \mapsto h(n) = 2^n$$

is a semigroup homomorphism, since for any $j, k \in \mathbf{Z}$ we have

$$h(j + k) = 2^{j+k} = 2^j \cdot 2^k = h(j) \cdot h(k) \qquad \Diamond$$

At this point, let us simplify our notation by rewriting the semigroup product $s_1 \cdot s_2$, where s_1 and s_2 are elements of semigroup S, simply as $s_1 s_2$.

Suppose we wish to transmit messages from a source which generates sequences consisting of the four symbols A, B, C, and D via a noiseless channel which can only handle sequences of 0's and 1's. In order to transmit messages produced by the source, we must encode the source symbols, that is, represent these letters with binary digits. In this case we might represent each letter unambiguously with the use of two binary digits by the encoding h_1:

$$A \leftrightarrow 00$$
$$B \leftrightarrow 01$$
$$C \leftrightarrow 10$$
$$D \leftrightarrow 11$$

We say that each binary sequence which represents a source symbol is a *code word*. We call the collection of all code words a *code*. Furthermore, the number of digits in a code word is called the *length* of the word. In the example above, each code word has length two.

DEFINITION 3

An **encoding** from alphabet X to alphabet X' is a homomorphism $h : X^+ \rightarrow (X')^+$. We call each $h(x)$ for $x \in X$ a **code word;** we call $\{h(x) \mid x \in X\}$ the **code;** and we call $\ell(h) = \max \{\ell(h(x)) \mid x \in X\}$ the **length** of the code, where $\ell(w)$ denotes the length of sequence w.   ○

If the set X' has q elements, we call h a **q-ary encoding** and often find it convenient to standardize X' to be $\mathbf{Z}_q = \{0, 1, \ldots, q - 1\}$. For $q = 2$ we get **binary encodings,** and take $X' = \{0, 1\}$.

Note that each encoding is uniquely determined by the resulting code words, since each element w in X^+ can be written $x_1 x_2 \ldots x_n$ as some sequence of x_j's from X; and then the fact that h is a homomorphism implies that

$$h(w) = h(x_1 x_2 \ldots x_n) = h(x_1) h(x_2) \ldots h(x_n)$$

Suppose now that we are using the above code h_1 to encode symbols independently produced by some source according to the following probability distribution:

$$P(A) = 1/2$$
$$P(B) = 1/4$$
$$P(C) = 1/8$$
$$P(D) = 1/8$$

If ℓ_i is the length of the ith word of a code having n words, and if p_i is the probability that the ith word occurs, we define the **average length** L of a code word by

$$L = \sum_{i=1}^{n} p_i \ell_i$$

Clearly, the average length of a word in the above code is then 2.0. However, why should we represent both A and C by code words with the same length when an A is four times as probable as a C? Obviously, we shouldn't. (Morse had the right idea.) Perhaps it will be advantageous to assign A a shorter code word at the expense of representing C and D by longer code words. Let us therefore consider the encoding h_2 defined by the following correspondence:

$$A \leftrightarrow 1$$
$$B \leftrightarrow 01$$
$$C \leftrightarrow 001$$
$$D \leftrightarrow 000$$

For this code, the average length L of a code word is

$$L = \sum_{i=1}^{4} p_i \ell_i = (1/2)(1) + (1/4)(2) + (1/8)(3) + (1/8)(3)$$
$$= 1/2 + 1/2 + 3/8 + 3/8$$
$$= 1.75 \text{ binary digits}$$

Thus, on the average, a word for this code is shorter than a word for the previously given code.* Note that the entropy of the above source is

$$-\sum_{i=1}^{4} p_i \log_2 p_i = -(1/2) \log_2 (1/2) - (1/4) \log_2 (1/4)$$
$$- (1/8) \log_2 (1/8) - (1/8) \log_2 (1/8)$$
$$= 1/2 + 1/2 + 3/8 + 3/8$$
$$= 1.75 \text{ bits}$$

Do not, however, jump to the conclusion that we can always find a code having an average word length given by the entropy of the source. We shall see, though, that we can come close to doing so by an appropriate trick.

Suppose that our source produces the sequence

$$ABACBAAD$$

Encoding this with h_1, we have

$$0001001001000011$$

Since the channel is assumed to be noiseless, if this binary sequence is transmitted, the exact sequence will be received. (Note that both the transmitted and received sequences contain only 0's and 1's; there are no spaces! This is true for any binary channel, noiseless or noisy. Allowing a space would

---

*The noiseless coding problem deals with finding a code having the shortest possible average code word length.

be tantamount to adding a third symbol. We would then be dealing with a ternary, not binary, channel.) There is no problem in obtaining the original message, for we need only inspect the received sequence two digits at a time. However, suppose we decide to use h_2. Then the message

$$ABACBAAD$$

is encoded as

$$10110010111000$$

In order for h_2 to be useful, we should not be able to decode this sequence (or any other possible transmitted sequence) into any message except that which was originally transmitted. Try as you will, the only sequence from $\{A, B, C, D\}^+$ for which $h_2(w) = 10110010111000$ is $w = ABACBAAD$. We shall see why very shortly. First we will formalize our discussion:

DEFINITION 4

A code determined by the encoding $h : X^+ \to (X')^+$ is said to be **uniquely decodable** iff h is an injection.   ○

Example 3

Consider the encoding h_3 shown below:

Symbol	Code Word
A	0
B	10
C	11
D	101

For this code,

$$h_3(BCA) = 10110 = h_3(DB)$$

Thus the code is not uniquely decodable, since h_3 is obviously not injective. Next consider the previously given code h_2:

Symbol	Code Word
A	1
B	01
C	001
D	000

From the message

$$ABACBAAD$$

we obtained the sequence

$$10110010111000$$

The first bit in the sequence is a 1. By inspection of the code, no code word other than the one corresponding to A begins with a 1. Thus, the first code word is 1. The second bit is a 0. Thus, the second code word begins with a 0. This code word corresponds to either B, C, or D. Since the next bit is a 1, the only possibility is the word corresponding to B. Hence, the next code word is 01. We can proceed in this manner and decode this sequence. ◊

The reason for this simplicity of decoding lies in the fact that no code word is the beginning (or prefix) of another code word. Such a code is called a *prefix code*. Thus, as soon as a code word is formed, that code word can be removed from the sequence and the remainder of the sequence can then be decoded. This process is repeated until the sequence is completely decoded. Formally, we have the following:

DEFINITION 5

A code determined by the encoding $h: X^+ \to (X')^+$ is said to be a **prefix code** if whenever

$$h(x_1) = h(x)w' \text{ for some } x_1 \text{ and } x \text{ in } X, \text{ and } w' \text{ in } (X')^*$$

we must have that $x_1 = x$.   ○

THEOREM 1

Every prefix code is uniquely decodable.

Proof

We know that if $h(x_1) = h(x)w'$ for some x_1 and x in X and w' in $(X')^*$, then $x_1 = x$. We must prove that if $h(w_1) = h(w_2)$, then $w_1 = w_2$.

Suppose, then, that $h(w_1) = h(w_2)$, where $w_1 = x_1 \widehat{w}_1$ and $w_2 = x_2 \widehat{w}_2$.

Then

$$h(x_1)h(\widehat{w}_1) = h(x_2)h(\widehat{w}_2) \tag{1}$$

Without loss of generality, let us assume that $h(x_1)$ is no shorter than $h(x_2)$. Then (1) tells us that

$$h(x_1) = h(x_2)w' \text{ for some } w' \text{ in } (X')^*$$

and this implies that $x_1 = x_2$, so that $w' = \Lambda$. Hence we have $w_1 = x_1\widehat{w}_1$ and $w_2 = x_1\widehat{w}_2$; and it is clear from (1) that $h(\widehat{w}_1) = h(\widehat{w}_2)$. Continuing in this way, we can prove that later and later corresponding symbols of w_1 and w_2 are equal, and we thus deduce that $w_1 = w_2$, as desired.   □

In general, it is a simple matter of inspection to determine whether or not a given code is a prefix code. Conversely, it is generally quite tedious to apply known algorithms for testing unique decodability. Furthermore, we shall see that for every uniquely decodable code there is a prefix code that is just as "good." Consequently, we will only be concerned with prefix codes in this book. Note that a code in which each code word is a distinct word of the same length is certainly a prefix code.

We will now demonstrate how prefix codes can be represented by trees. We may then use this description in order to prove properties of prefix codes. As an example, consider the tree shown in Figure 6–14. For the binary case,

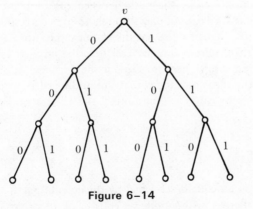

Figure 6–14

we label the branches 0 and 1 as indicated. The top vertex, labelled v, is called the *root* of the tree and may be addressed as Λ, the empty sequence from $\{0, 1\}^*$; while every other vertex in the tree may be addressed with the binary sequence obtained when the path between the root and that vertex is traversed. The result is shown in Figure 6–15.

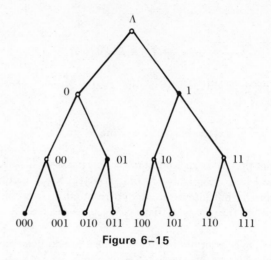

Figure 6–15

If a binary code consists of words with lengths no greater than three, we can associate the words with certain vertices of the tree. For the code

$$1$$
$$01$$
$$001$$
$$000$$

the darkened vertices in Figure 6–15 correspond to the code words. Since this code is a prefix code, the path between the root and a vertex corresponding to code word cannot pass through a vertex corresponding to another code word. Thus, we can represent the code by the subtree shown in Figure 6–16. It is in this manner that we can describe any prefix code by a tree. Note that we no longer need to darken the vertices, since in Figure 6–16 it is precisely the maximal nodes that are addressed by code words. In this manner, conversely, any tree (or subtree) describes a prefix code.

DEFINITION 6

Given a q-ary prefix code determined by the encoding $h:X^+ \to \mathbf{Z}_q^+$, the **tree of the code** is the tree whose node set consists of all strings of $\{0, 1, 2, \ldots, q-1\}^*$ which are prefixes of code words $h(x)$ for x in X. [Note that the code words thus address the maximal nodes of the tree.]   ○

Suppose we have a binary prefix code whose words have lengths ℓ_1, ℓ_2, $\ell_3, \ldots, \ell_n$. For the sake of convenience, we may assume that $\ell_1 \leq \ell_2 \leq \ell_3 \leq$

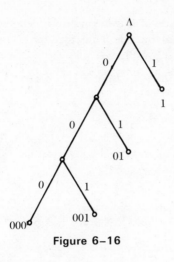

Figure 6–16

$\cdots \leq \ell_n$. We know that we can designate this code by certain vertices of a tree whose vertices are labelled with all the binary sequences of length ℓ_n and less. We also know that there are 2^{ℓ_n} vertices which are labelled with sequences of length ℓ_n. Now consider the subtree corresponding to the code. Because the code is a prefix code, it should be clear that a code word of length ℓ_i would prevent $2^{\ell_n - \ell_i}$ vertices labelled with sequences of length ℓ_n from representing code words. Thus, the total number of vertices labelled with sequences of length ℓ_n that cannot represent code words is

$$\sum_{i=1}^{n} 2^{\ell_n - \ell_i}$$

Since this number cannot be larger than 2^{ℓ_n}, we have

$$\sum_{i=1}^{n} 2^{\ell_n - \ell_i} \leq 2^{\ell_n}$$

so that

$$2^{\ell_n} \sum_{i=1}^{n} 2^{-\ell_i} \leq 2^{\ell_n}$$

from which

$$\sum_{i=1}^{n} 2^{-\ell_i} \leq 1$$

The term on the left side of this inequality is denoted by $\sigma(h)$ and is called the **characteristic sum** of the code. Thus, for a binary prefix code having words of length $\ell_1, \ell_2, \ldots, \ell_n$, we have

$$\sigma(h) = \sum_{i=1}^{n} 2^{-\ell_i} \leq 1$$

Using the exact reasoning described above, for the case of a q-ary prefix code we can write

$$\sigma(h) = \sum_{i=1}^{n} q^{-\ell_i} \leq 1$$

Now suppose that we are given positive integers $\ell_1, \ell_2, \ell_3, \ldots, \ell_n$ such that

$$\sum_{i=1}^{n} q^{-\ell_i} \leq 1$$

By essentially reversing the discussion above, we may conclude that there exists a q-ary prefix code having $\ell_1, \ell_2, \ell_3, \ldots, \ell_n$ as the word lengths. We thus have the following:

THEOREM 2

There exists a q-ary prefix code having word lengths $\ell_1, \ell_2, \ell_3, \ldots, \ell_n$ if and only if

$$\sum_{i=1}^{n} q^{-\ell_i} \leq 1 \qquad \qquad \square$$

(Note that even if a code has a characteristic sum no greater than one, it is not necessarily a prefix code.)

We know that a prefix code is uniquely decodable (though the converse is not necessarily so). Thus, if

$$\sum_{i=1}^{n} 2^{-\ell_i} \leq 1$$

then trivially there exists a uniquely decodable binary code having word lengths $\ell_1, \ell_2, \ell_3, \ldots, \ell_n$. Because our major concern is with prefix codes, we will only mention that the previous theorem is also valid for uniquely decodable codes; thus, if there exists a uniquely decodable code having the word lengths $\ell_1, \ell_2, \ell_3, \ldots, \ell_n$, then there also exists a prefix code having the same word lengths. Consequently, both codes have the same average length (with respect to a particular source).

As a result of our discussion of the characteristic sum of a code, we are now in a position to relate entropy to the average length of codes. First remember that we are dealing with noiseless channels. Thus, we need not be concerned with error-correction. However, it seems reasonable that for a given source we might wish to employ the most efficient code possible. We may simply define efficiency in terms of average length; the most efficient codes are those (there may be more than one) which have the smallest average length.

In addition to efficiency, we should be concerned with the ease of decoding messages. It should be clear that messages formed from the words of a prefix code are much more easily decoded than are messages formed by using non-prefix codes. Since for any uniquely decodable code there is a prefix code that is just as good (i.e., with the same average length), we have another reason for our emphasis on prefix codes.

We may now ask the following questions: For a given source, what is a lower bound for the average length of a code? When can this bound be attained? When this lower bound cannot be attained, what is the minimum average length? How are these optimum (minimum average length) codes constructed? We now proceed to answer these noiseless coding questions.

Previously, we saw a source for which there was a code having an average length L equal to the entropy of the source $H(\mathbf{X})$. We warned the reader not to conclude that we can always find a code with $L = H(\mathbf{X})$. However, we will now answer the first two of the above questions by demonstrating that $H(\mathbf{X})$ is the lower bound for L and by giving the conditions for which $L = H(\mathbf{X})$.

THEOREM 3

Suppose that $\mathbf{X} = \begin{pmatrix} x_1 \cdots x_n \\ p_1 \cdots p_n \end{pmatrix}$ is an information source, so that a binary prefix code (where ℓ_i is the length of the ith of its n words) has an average length of

$$L = \sum_{i=1}^{n} p_i \ell_i$$

Then

$$L \geq H(\mathbf{X})$$

with equality if and only if $p_i = 2^{-l_i}$ for $i = 1, 2, \ldots, n$.

Proof

By definition

$$H(\mathbf{X}) = -\sum_{i=1}^{n} p_i \log_2 p_i$$

By Lemma 6-2-2 we know that for any set of probabilities $\left\{ q_i \middle| \sum_{i=1}^{n} q_i = 1 \right\}$,

$$H(\mathbf{X}) \leq -\sum_{i=1}^{n} p_i \log_2 q_i$$

with equality if and only if $p_i = q_i$ for $i = 1, 2, \ldots, n$. Recalling that the characteristic sum is $\sigma = \sum_{j=1}^{n} 2^{-l_j}$, let us define

$$q_i = 2^{-l_i}/\sigma$$

for $i = 1, 2, \ldots, n$. (Verify that $0 < q_i \leq 1$ and that $\sum_{i=1}^{n} q_i = 1$.) Thus, we have

$$H(\mathbf{X}) \leq -\sum_{i=1}^{n} p_i \log_2 (2^{-l_i}/\sigma)$$

with equality if and only if $p_i = 2^{-l_i}/\sigma$ for $i = 1, 2, \ldots, n$. Continuing,

$$H(\mathbf{X}) \leq -\sum_{i=1}^{n} p_i (\log_2 2^{-l_i} - \log_2 \sigma)$$

$$\leq -\sum_{i=1}^{n} p_i \log_2 2^{-l_i} + \sum_{i=1}^{n} p_i \log_2 \sigma$$

$$\leq \sum_{i=1}^{n} p_i l_i + \log_2 \sigma$$

with equality if and only if $p_i = 2^{-\ell_i}/\sigma$ for $i = 1, 2, \ldots, n$. But $\log_2 \sigma \le 0$, since $\sigma \le 1$. Thus,

$$H(\mathbf{X}) \le \sum_{i=1}^{n} p_i \ell_i = L$$

Also,

$$H(\mathbf{X}) = L + \log_2 \sigma$$

if and only if $p_i = 2^{-\ell_i}/\sigma$ for $i = 1, 2, \ldots, n$. Furthermore, $\log_2 \sigma = 0$ if and only if $\sigma = 1$. Hence,

$$H(\mathbf{X}) = L$$

if and only if $p_i = 2^{-\ell_i}$ for $i = 1, 2, \ldots, n$ (which implies $\sigma = 1$). $\square$

Although the theorem considers binary prefix codes, it is also valid for binary uniquely decodable codes in general.

We have just seen that a lower bound for L is $H(\mathbf{X})$. We will now show that there always exists a prefix code for which L is less than $1 + H(\mathbf{X})$.

THEOREM 4

For any source $\mathbf{X}$ there exists a binary prefix code with average length L such that

$$H(\mathbf{X}) \le L < 1 + H(\mathbf{X})$$

Proof

Associated with the source are the probabilities $p_1, p_2, \ldots, p_n$. Clearly, for each $i = 1, 2, \ldots, n$ there exists a unique integer ℓ_i such that

$$-\log_2 p_i \le \ell_i < 1 - \log_2 p_i$$

In order to prove that a prefix code exists with these integers as the code word lengths, we must show that

$$\sum_{i=1}^{n} 2^{-\ell_i} \le 1$$

But $\log_2 p_i \geq -\ell_i$ implies that $p_i \geq 2^{-\ell_i}$ for $i = 1, 2, \ldots, n$. Hence,

$$\sum_{i=1}^{n} p_i \geq \sum_{i=1}^{n} 2^{-\ell_i}$$

that is

$$1 \geq \sum_{i=1}^{n} 2^{-\ell_i}$$

Thus, there exists a prefix code having word lengths $\ell_1, \ell_2, \ldots, \ell_n$. Furthermore, since

$$-\log_2 p_i \leq \ell_i < 1 - \log_2 p_i$$

for $i = 1, 2, \ldots, n$, multiplying by p_i we have

$$-p_i \log_2 p_i \leq p_i \ell_i < p_i - p_i \log_2 p_i$$

from which

$$-\sum_{i=1}^{n} p_i \log_2 p_i \leq \sum_{i=1}^{n} p_i \ell_i < \sum_{i=1}^{n} p_i - \sum_{i=1}^{n} p_i \log_2 p_i$$

or

$$H(\mathbf{X}) \leq L < 1 + H(\mathbf{X}) \qquad \qquad \square$$

At this point, let us work a few examples. In the process, we will wish to take some logarithms. We thus present in Table 6–2 a partial list of logarithms to the base 2.

Table 6–2

i	$\log_2 i$
1	0.00000
2	1.00000
3	1.58496
4	2.00000
5	2.32193
6	2.58496
7	2.80735
8	3.00000
9	3.16993
10	3.32193

Example 4

Let us find a prefix code for the probability distribution:

$$p_1 = p_2 = 1/4, p_3 = p_4 = p_5 = 1/8, p_6 = 1/16, p_7 = p_8 = 1/32$$

From the last theorem, we know that there exists a prefix code with average length L such that $H(\mathbf{X}) \leq L < 1 + H(\mathbf{X})$, and we can obtain such a code by letting ℓ_i be the integer for which $-\log_2 p_i \leq \ell_i < 1 - \log_2 p_i$.

In this example we have

$$H(\mathbf{X}) = -\sum_{i=1}^{8} p_i \log_2 p_i$$

$$
\begin{aligned}
&= -(1/4)\log_2(1/4) - (1/4)\log_2(1/4) - (1/8)\log_2(1/8) \\
&\quad - (1/8)\log_2(1/8) - (1/8)\log_2(1/8) - (1/16)\log_2(1/16) \\
&\quad - (1/32)\log_2(1/32) - (1/32)\log_2(1/32) \\
&= 2/4 + 2/4 + 3/8 + 3/8 + 3/8 + 4/16 + 5/32 + 5/32 \\
&= 2.6875 \text{ bits}
\end{aligned}
$$

To determine the ℓ_i, we begin with

$$-\log_2 p_1 \leq \ell_1 < 1 - \log_2 p_1$$

Thus,

$$-\log_2(1/4) \leq \ell_1 < 1 - \log_2(1/4)$$
$$2 \leq \ell_1 < 3$$

and $\ell_1 = 2$. In a similar manner we have $\ell_2 = 2$, $\ell_3 = \ell_4 = \ell_5 = 3$, $\ell_6 = 4$, $\ell_7 = \ell_8 = 5$. One possible choice of a prefix code with these word lengths is shown in Figure 6–17. The average length of a word in this code is

$$L = \sum_{i=1}^{8} p_i \ell_i$$

$$
\begin{aligned}
&= (1/4)(2) + (1/4)(2) + (1/8)(3) + (1/8)(3) \\
&\quad + (1/8)(3) + (1/16)(4) + (1/32)(5) + (1/32)(5) \\
&= 2.6875 \text{ binary digits}
\end{aligned}
$$

Thus, in this example $L = H(\mathbf{X})$. However, this should be no surprise since, by Theorem 3, this occurs if and only if $p_i = 2^{-\ell_i}$ for $i = 1, 2, \ldots, 8$. ◊

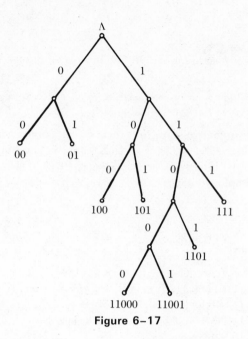

Figure 6–17

Example 5

Now let us consider the probabilities

$$p_1 = 0.3, p_2 = p_3 = 0.2, p_4 = p_5 = 0.1,$$
$$p_6 = 0.05, p_7 = 0.03, p_8 = 0.02$$

The entropy is given by

$$H(\mathbf{X}) = -\sum_{i=1}^{8} p_i \log_2 p_i$$

$$= -(0.3)\log_2(0.3) - (0.2)\log_2(0.2) - (0.2)\log_2(0.2)$$
$$\quad - (0.1)\log_2(0.1) - (0.1)\log_2(0.1) - (0.05)\log_2(0.05)$$
$$\quad - (0.03)\log_2(0.03) - (0.02)\log_2(0.02)$$
$$= (0.3)(1.73697) + (0.2)(2.32193) + (0.2)(2.32193)$$
$$\quad + (0.1)(3.32193) + (0.1)(3.32193) + (0.05)(4.32193)$$
$$\quad + (0.03)(5.05890) + (0.02)(5.64386)$$

$$= 0.52109 + 0.46439 + 0.46439$$
$$+ 0.33219 + 0.33219 + 0.21610$$
$$+ 0.15176 + 0.11288$$
$$= 2.59499 \text{ bits}$$

In order to determine the lengths of the words of a prefix code for which $H(\mathbf{X}) \leq L < 1 + H(\mathbf{X})$, we note that

$$-\log_2 p_1 = 1.73697 \Rightarrow \ell_1 = 2$$
$$-\log_2 p_2 = 2.32193 \Rightarrow \ell_2 = 3$$
$$\ell_3 = 3$$
$$-\log_2 p_4 = 3.32193 \Rightarrow \ell_4 = 4$$
$$\ell_5 = 4$$
$$-\log_2 p_6 = 4.32193 \Rightarrow \ell_6 = 5$$
$$-\log_2 p_7 = 5.05890 \Rightarrow \ell_7 = 6$$
$$-\log_2 p_8 = 5.64386 \Rightarrow \ell_8 = 6$$

One possible code is shown in Figure 6–18. The average length of a word

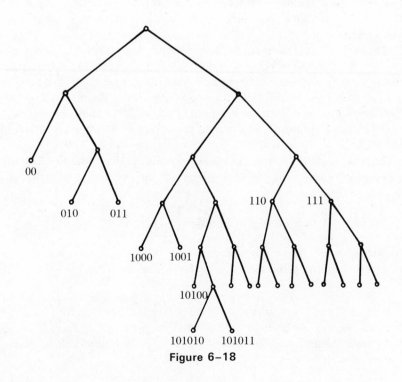

Figure 6–18

in this code is

$$L = \sum_{i=1}^{8} p_i \ell_i$$

$$= (.3)(2) + (.2)(3) + (.2)(3) + (.1)(4) + (.1)(4)$$
$$+ (.05)(5) + (.03)(6) + (.02)(6)$$
$$= 3.15 \text{ binary digits}$$

and indeed, $H(\mathbf{X}) \leq L < 1 + H(\mathbf{X})$. In this case we may have noticed before calculating the average length that, since $p_i \neq 2^{-\ell_i}$ for $i = 1, 2, \ldots, 8$, we must have $L > H(\mathbf{X})$. ◊

In the previous two examples we have considered a case where the average length of a code attains the lower bound, and a case where it does not. In the latter, investigation of Figure 6–18 indicates that we can easily select another prefix code having a smaller value for L than the one given. We can make this statement since, for example, we may select the vertices corresponding to 110 and 111 rather than use the vertices corresponding to 101010 and 101011. Thus, the lengths of two code words can be reduced from 6 to 3. The result is a reduction in L. (This new code is still not optimum; i.e., it does not have minimum average length.) Let us, then, study how to determine the smallest possible value for L and a method of constructing the corresponding code.

In 1952, D. A. Huffman devised a simple, yet elegant, combinatorial technique for the construction of optimum (minimum average length) prefix codes. We will first apply Huffman's algorithm, and then compute the minimum average length from the code obtained. (Recall that for any uniquely decodable code there is a prefix code with the same average word length. Thus, an optimum prefix code is also an optimum uniquely decodable code.)

In general there is more than one optimum prefix code. For example, given one optimum code, a second can be obtained simply by interchanging the 1's and 0's.

We begin with a set of probabilities $\{p_1, p_2, \ldots, p_n\}$, where $\sum_{i=1}^{n} p_i = 1$, that corresponds to some information source. Without loss of generality, we can make the simplifying assumption that

$$p_1 \geq p_2 \geq p_3 \geq \cdots \geq p_{n-1} \geq p_n$$

Huffman reasoned as follows: Suppose that $\ell_1, \ell_2, \ell_3, \ldots, \ell_{n-1}, \ell_n$ are the word lengths of an optimum binary prefix code. We can conclude that

$$\ell_1 \leq \ell_2 \leq \ell_3 \leq \cdots \leq \ell_{n-1} \leq \ell_n$$

If this were not the case, then $\ell_i > \ell_j$ for some $i < j$. Under the circumstance that $p_i > p_j$, we can form a new code in which the ith word has length $\ell_i' = \ell_j$ and the jth word has length $\ell_j' = \ell_i$. Clearly, the new code has a smaller average length than the original—a contradiction to our assumption that the original is optimum. Hence, our conclusion above about the lengths of the code words.

We now make the claim that $\ell_{n-1} = \ell_n$. We already know that $\ell_{n-1} \leq \ell_n$. So assume that $\ell_{n-1} < \ell_n$. Since no prefix of the code word of length ℓ_n is a code word, eliminate all but the first ℓ_{n-1} binary digits of the word. The resulting code is still a prefix code, since this new word cannot be a prefix of any other code word. (No other code word has length greater than ℓ_{n-1}. No other code word of length ℓ_{n-1} can be the same as this code word, since the original code was a prefix code.) Clearly, the new code has a smaller average length than the original code, which is a contradiction. Thus, $\ell_{n-1} = \ell_n$.

Now, suppose that $h(x_{n-1}) = wx$, with $x = 0$ or 1, is a code word. Setting $\bar{x} = 1 - x$, it follows that $w\bar{x}$ must also be a code word, for if it were not, we could recode $h(x_{n-1})$ as w without violating the prefix code condition. But our code is optimum, and so no shorter encoding of x_{n-1} is possible. Thus, by interchanging the code word $w\bar{x}$ with the one associated with x_n, the new code is still an optimum code. Hence, there is an optimum code in which the code words associated with p_{n-1} and p_n both have length $\ell_{n-1} = \ell_n$, and they differ only in the last binary digit. It is such a code that is obtained with Huffman's algorithm.

Now consider an optimum code for which we have $h(x_{n-1}) = wx$ and $h(x_n) = w\bar{x}$, with $x = 0$ or 1. Suppose that for the original set of probabilities we replace the two probabilities p_{n-1} and p_n by their sum $p_{n-1} + p_n$, thereby decreasing the number of probabilities from n to $n - 1$. We claim that eliminating wx and $w\bar{x}$ from the code and replacing them by the single word w yields a code that is optimum for the new set of probabilities. To prove this, assume to the contrary that the code so obtained has average length L and is not optimum, so that there exists some optimum code with average length $L' < L$. So take the code word w_1 corresponding to $p_{n-1} + p_n$ and form two code words $w_1 0$ and $w_1 1$. This new code has an average length of $L' + p_{n-1} + p_n$ for the original set of probabilities (Verify this!), while the old code has an average length of $L + p_{n-1} + p_n$ for the original probabilities. However, $L + p_{n-1} + p_n > L' + p_{n-1} + p_n$, which contradicts the fact that the original code was an optimum prefix code. Hence, our claim is substantiated.

From our discussion above, we see that if we sum the two smallest probabilities and if we can find an optimum code for the new set of probabilities, we can then obtain an optimum code for the original set of probabilities. However, we can apply the same reasoning to the new set of probabilities; i.e., we can consider the new set of probabilities as some other original set. We can repeat this until we obtain a set consisting of two probabilities. At this point we trivially know the optimum prefix code: a 0 and a 1. We reverse the manner in which the probabilities were merged, and thereby obtain an optimum prefix code for the original set of probabilities.

THEOREM 5

We have justified the following nested algorithm due to Huffman: Given a source $\mathbf{X} = \begin{pmatrix} x_1 \cdots x_n \\ p_1 \cdots p_n \end{pmatrix}$, $n \geq 2$, we form a tree as follows:

1. Create n nodes labelled $p_1, \ldots, p_n$.
2. Set $k = n$, and set $q_1 = p_1, q_2 = p_2, \ldots, q_k = p_k$.
3. Does $k = 2$?
   If so, create one new node labelled $q_1 + q_2$ with successors labelled q_1 and q_2, and *halt*.
   If not, go to 4.
4. Let q_i and q_j be the smallest pair of q's. (Make an arbitrary choice if there are several candidates.)
5. Create one new node labelled $q_i + q_j$ having as its successors the nodes labelled q_i and q_j.
6. Replace k by $k - 1$, and form the new list $q_1, \ldots, q_{k-1}$ in terms of the old values $q_1, q_2, \ldots, q_{i-1}, q_{i+1}, \ldots, q_{j-1}, q_{j+1}, \ldots, q_k, q_i + q_j$.
7. Go to 3.

    The tree that results from this algorithm represents an optimum binary prefix code. $\square$

Example 6

Suppose that we are given the set of probabilities

$$\{0.3, 0.2, 0.2, 0.1, 0.1, 0.05, 0.03, 0.02\}$$

Then the scheme of Theorem 5 yields the tree shown in Figure 6–19, where we have marked with a (k) the node formed when k had the indicated value, and

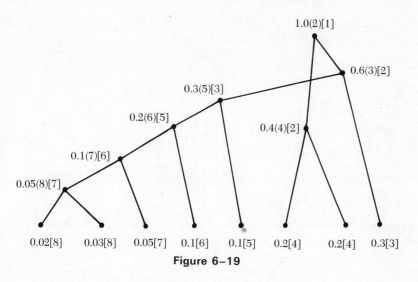

0.3(5)[3]

0.2(6)[5]

0.4(4)[2]

0.1(7)[6]

0.05(8)[7]

0.02[8]   0.03[8]   0.05[7]   0.1[6]   0.1[5]   0.2[4]   0.2[4]   0.3[3]

1.0(2)[1]

0.6(3)[2]

Figure 6–19

with a [k] the nodes removed from consideration when that node was created. Note that we made arbitrary choices at stages 6 and 5. Note also that we were unfortunate in that our choice of probabilities did not allow us to form the tree directly without having to cross any branches. However, we may redraw this tree so that the resulting structure does not have branches that cross. This is exemplified by the tree shown in Figure 6–20.

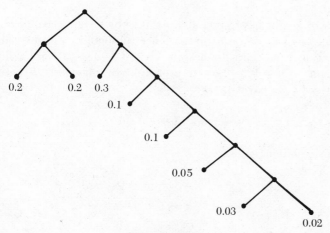

0.2   0.2   0.3

0.1

0.1

0.05

0.03

0.02

Figure 6–20

Choosing one of the possible labellings of the branches of the tree with 0's and 1's, we obtain the following code words:

$$
\begin{array}{l}
10 \\
00 \\
01 \\
110 \\
1110 \\
11110 \\
111110 \\
111111
\end{array}
$$

Thus, these words constitute an optimum prefix code, and the average length of a code word is

$$
\begin{aligned}
L = \sum_{i=1}^{8} p_i \ell_i &= (.3)(2) + (.2)(2) + (.2)(2) + (.1)(3) \\
&\quad + (.1)(4) + (.05)(5) + (.03)(6) + (.02)(6) \\
&= 2.65 \text{ binary digits}
\end{aligned}
$$

The entropy in this case is $H(\mathbf{X}) = 2.59499$ bits.   ◊

Huffman's algorithm can be generalized to the q-ary case quite readily. Instead of merging the smallest two probabilities in each list, we merge the smallest q probabilities in each list, except possibly the first. For the original list, we merge the smallest m probabilities, where $2 \leq m \leq q$, so that by merging the q smallest probabilities in each succeeding list we obtain the single probability 1.0.

If we originally have n probabilities, then by merging m of these, our second list has $n - (m - 1)$ probabilities. Since q probabilities are merged for each succeeding list, the third list has $n - (m - 1) - (q - 1)$ probabilities; the fourth has $n - (m - 1) - 2(q - 1)$ probabilities; and so forth. Eventually, for some integer i, we have

$$
n - (m - 1) - i(q - 1) = 1
$$

From this equation, we have

$$
\begin{aligned}
-i(q - 1) &= 1 - [n - (m - 1)] \\
i(q - 1) &= -1 + n - (m - 1) \\
&= n - m
\end{aligned}
$$

Thus,

$$
i = (n - m)/(q - 1)
$$

We therefore select m, where $2 \leq m \leq q$, such that $(n - m)/(q - 1)$ is an integer.

Again consider a source which produces the symbols $A, B, C, \ldots$ independently. We have seen that we can encode each of these symbols with a distinct word of a binary prefix code which has an average length L, where

$$H(\mathbf{X}) \leq L < 1 + H(\mathbf{X})$$

and $H(\mathbf{X})$ is the entropy of the source. Thus, the average number of binary digits needed to represent a source symbol is at least $H(\mathbf{X})$. (For some sources, the average number is exactly $H(\mathbf{X})$. This, however, is a very special case.) We shall now present a coding scheme for which the average number of binary digits needed to represent a source symbol can be made arbitrarily close to $H(\mathbf{X})$, regardless of the source, so long as we encode sufficiently long sequences.

Suppose that we wait for a source to produce two symbols, and we encode pairs of symbols; i.e., instead of encoding the symbols $A, B, C, \ldots$ separately, we encode the pairs $AA, AB, AC, BA, BB, BC, \ldots$. For the sake of calculation, we may think of each of these pairs as one output of a source which is formed by connecting together two independent sources, each of which is identical to the original source. (The first letter of each pair is produced by one of the identical sources, and the second letter is produced by the other.) One of our conditions in the development of a measure of information was to have the information from two independent sources equal to the sum of the information from each separate source. For this reason, the average information per pair is

$$H(\mathbf{X}) + H(\mathbf{X}) = 2H(\mathbf{X})$$

Furthermore, we know that we can encode these pairs with a binary prefix code having an average word length of L_2, where

$$2H(\mathbf{X}) \leq L_2 < 1 + 2H(\mathbf{X})$$

Continuing to reason in this manner, we can encode the symbols produced by a source, r symbols at a time, with a binary prefix code having an average length of L_r, where

$$rH(\mathbf{X}) \leq L_r < 1 + rH(\mathbf{X})$$

Dividing this inequality by r, we obtain

$$H(\mathbf{X}) \leq L_r/r < (1/r) + H(\mathbf{X})$$

Since a code word in such a code represents r symbols, and since L_r is the average length of a code word, then L_r/r is the average number of binary digits representing one symbol. From the last inequality, therefore, we now conclude that *if we encode blocks of symbols, rather than encode symbols independently, then the average number of binary digits needed to represent a source symbol may, by appropriate encoding, be made to approach* $H(\mathbf{X})$. *The cost of encoding longer and longer blocks is the necessity of employing larger and larger codes.*

We have now completed our discussion of the problem of coding for the case in which no errors can occur during transmission and in which our concern is solely with the efficiency of codes and their decodability. In the next section, we shall further be concerned with the occurrence of errors; i.e., we must try to reconstruct a transmitted sequence from a received sequence that contains errors. To do this, we will encode large blocks of information efficiently so that, at the decoder, the probability of reconstructing the transmitted information can be made arbitrarily close to 1. In Chapters 7 and 8 we shall increase our algebraic knowledge while learning how to *construct* codes explicitly for communicating through *noisy* channels.

EXERCISES FOR SECTION 6-3

1. Is the set of negative integers a semigroup under ordinary addition? Under ordinary multiplication?

2. Given the semigroup $\mathbf{Z}_+$ under multiplication and the semigroup $\mathbf{R}$ of real numbers under addition, show that the map

$$h:\mathbf{Z}_+ \to \mathbf{R}:i \to h(i) = \log_{10} i$$

is a semigroup homomorphism.

3. Recast the proof of Theorem 1 as a formal proof by induction.

4. Let $n_1, n_2, \ldots, n_k$ be any k distinct integers from $\mathbf{N}$. Let 1^n be the string of n consecutive 1's. Show that the encoding $\{x_1, \ldots, x_k\}^+ \to \{0, 1\}^+$ given by $x_j \mapsto 1^{n_j}$ results in a code that is not uniquely decodable, while the encoding given by $x_j \mapsto 01^{n_j}$ results in one that is uniquely decodable.

5. Show the trees of the following binary prefix codes:

(a)	(b)	(c)
0	00	00
11	11	10
100	0100	010
101	0101	011
		110
		111

6. Provide a full proof of Theorem 2 for the binary case.

7. Calculate the characteristic sum for the three binary prefix codes given in Exercise 5. [For example, in case (a), we have

$$\sigma = \sum_{i=1}^{4} 2^{-l_i} = 2^{-1} + 2^{-2} + 2^{-3} + 2^{-3}$$

$$= 1/2 + 1/4 + 1/8 + 1/8 = 1.]$$

8.   Prove the extension of Theorem 3 to the case of q-ary prefix codes. The theorem then states that

$$L \geq H(\mathbf{X})/\log_2 q$$

with equality if and only if $p_i = q^{-l_i}$ for $i = 1, 2, \ldots, n$.

9.   Prove Theorem 4 as generalized to the q-ary case with the result that

$$H(\mathbf{X})/\log_2 q \leq L < 1 + H(\mathbf{X})/\log_2 q$$

10.   In Example 6, find a sequence of choices in Huffman's algorithm which will yield the code:

> 00
> 10
> 010
> 110
> 111
> 0110
> 01110
> 01111

Although the set of code word lengths for this code is different from the code of Example 6, they are both optimum. Hence, they must have the same average length. Calculate L to confirm this.

11.   Apply Huffman's algorithm to find an optimum binary prefix code for the following set of probabilities: $\{1/4, 1/4, 1/8, 1/8, 1/8, 1/16, 1/32, 1/32\}$. Calculate the average length of a word for the resulting code.

12.   Apply Huffman's algorithm to find an optimum quaternary $(q = 4)$ prefix code for the set of probabilities: $\{0.22, 0.20, 0.18, 0.15, 0.10, 0.08, 0.05, 0.02\}$. [Since $n = 8$, we must select m such that $2 \leq m \leq 4$ and $(8 - m)/3$ is an integer. Consequently, $m = 2$.]

13.   By reversing a code word $x_1 x_2 \ldots x_r$, we mean the sequence $x_r x_{r-1} \ldots x_1$. Show that the code obtained by reversing the words of a prefix code is uniquely decodable.

14.   Give an example of a uniquely decodable code which is neither a prefix code nor a code obtained by reversing the words of a prefix code.

15.   Given the following probabilities:

$$p_1 = 0.4 \qquad p_2 = 0.2 \qquad p_3 = p_4 = p_5 = p_6 = 0.1$$

(a)   Find three optimum binary prefix codes such that no two have the same word-length structure.

(b)   What is the average length of a code word?

16.   Given an information source that produces the symbols A, B, C, and D independently according to the probabilities:

$$P(A) = 0.4 \qquad P(B) = 0.3 \qquad P(C) = 0.2 \qquad P(D) = 0.1$$

(a)   Find an optimum binary prefix code for this source if the symbols are encoded one at a time.

(b)   What is the average number of binary digits needed to encode a source symbol?

(c)   What is the entropy of the source?

17. For the source given in problem 16:

(a) Find an optimum binary prefix code if the symbols are encoded two at a time.

(b) What is the average number of binary digits needed to encode a source symbol?

6–4   The Noisy Coding Theorem

The next step in the development of Shannon's theory is the introduction of the concept of channel capacity. In order to define this term, we will first discuss what is meant by conditional entropy. We begin with an example.

Suppose we have the binary channel shown in Figure 6–21. For this

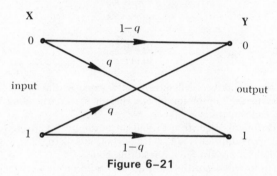

Figure 6–21

channel, the probability that the output is 0, given that the input is 0, is $1 - q$. The probability that the output is 1, given that the input is 0, is q. Similar statements can be made about the output when the input is 1. Because of the symmetry of this channel, it is referred to as the **Binary Symmetric Channel (BSC)**. If the input to the channel is produced by some source **X**, we may describe the input to the channel by the random variable **X**. The channel, in conjunction with a source, can be thought of as another source **Y**. Thus, we may describe the output of the channel by the random variable **Y**. In summary, the BSC is characterized by the following conditional probabilities:

$$P\{\mathbf{Y} = 0 \,|\, \mathbf{X} = 0\} = 1 - q$$
$$P\{\mathbf{Y} = 0 \,|\, \mathbf{X} = 1\} = q$$
$$P\{\mathbf{Y} = 1 \,|\, \mathbf{X} = 0\} = q$$
$$P\{\mathbf{Y} = 1 \,|\, \mathbf{X} = 1\} = 1 - q$$

For each distinct value of q, for $0 \leq q \leq 1$, we have a distinct BSC. Thus, there are an infinite number of binary symmetric channels.

We know that the entropy of the source $H(\mathbf{X})$ is a measure of the average amount of information contained in a source symbol. For a source which produces two symbols, we also know that $H(\mathbf{X}) \leq 1$ bit of information. In particular, the information contents of $\{X = 0\}$ and $\{X = 1\}$ are $-\log_2 P\{X = 0\}$ and $-\log_2 P\{X = 1\}$, respectively.

Let us now determine the information content of the input of a BSC, given that the output is known. We should feel that the information content of the input will, on the average, be decreased when the output is revealed. This would occur because the revelation of the output supplies us with some of the information originally contained in the input. In particular, suppose that we know that the output is 0. Then the information content of the event $\{X = 0 | Y = 0\}$ is

$$-\log_2 P\{X = 0 | Y = 0\}$$

and the information content of $\{X = 1 | Y = 0\}$ is

$$-\log_2 P\{X = 1 | Y = 0\}$$

Thus, the average information content of an input symbol given that the output is 0 is

$$
\begin{aligned}
H(X|Y = 0) = &-P\{X = 0 | Y = 0\} \log_2 P\{X = 0 | Y = 0\} \\
&- P\{X = 1 | Y = 0\} \log_2 P\{X = 1 | Y = 0\}
\end{aligned}
$$

Similarly, the average information content of an input symbol, given that the output is 1, is

$$
\begin{aligned}
H(X|Y = 1) = &-P\{X = 0 | Y = 1\} \log_2 P\{X = 0 | Y = 1\} \\
&- P\{X = 1 | Y = 1\} \log_2 P\{X = 1 | Y = 1\}
\end{aligned}
$$

Once we are given the probability distribution of the source, say $P\{X = 0\} = p$ and $P\{X = 1\} = 1 - p$, it is a simple matter to determine the conditional probabilities above. By Bayes' Theorem,

$$
P\{X = 0 | Y = 0\} = \frac{P\{Y = 0 | X = 0\}P\{X = 0\}}{P\{Y = 0 | X = 0\}P\{X = 0\} + P\{Y = 0 | X = 1\}P\{X = 1\}}
$$

$$
P\{X = 1 | Y = 0\} = \frac{P\{Y = 0 | X = 1\}P\{X = 1\}}{P\{Y = 0 | X = 0\}P\{X = 0\} + P\{Y = 0 | X = 1\}P\{X = 1\}}
$$

$$
P\{X = 0 | Y = 1\} = \frac{P\{Y = 1 | X = 0\}P\{X = 0\}}{P\{Y = 1 | X = 0\}P\{X = 0\} + P\{Y = 1 | X = 1\}P\{X = 1\}}
$$

$$
P\{X = 1 | Y = 1\} = \frac{P\{Y = 1 | X = 1\}P\{X = 1\}}{P(Y = 1 | X = 0\}P\{X = 0\} + P\{Y = 1 | X = 1\}P\{X = 1\}}
$$

From these equations, we have

$$P\{X = 0 \,|\, Y = 0\} = \frac{(1-q)p}{(1-q)p + q(1-p)}$$

$$P\{X = 1 \,|\, Y = 0\} = \frac{q(1-p)}{(1-q)p + q(1-p)}$$

$$P\{X = 0 \,|\, Y = 1\} = \frac{qp}{qp + (1-q)(1-p)}$$

$$P\{X = 1 \,|\, Y = 1\} = \frac{(1-q)(1-p)}{qp + (1-q)(1-p)}$$

Example 1

For a BSC with $q = 7/8$, let us find the average information content of an input (source) symbol, given each possible output symbol. We shall do this for the binary source in which $p = 1/2$. We have

$$P\{X = 0 \,|\, Y = 0\} = \frac{(7/8)(1/2)}{(7/8)(1/2) + (1/8)(1/2)} = 7/8$$

and

$$P\{X = 1 \,|\, Y = 0\} = \frac{(1/8)(1/2)}{(7/8)(1/2) + (1/8)(1/2)} = 1/8$$

Thus,

$$
\begin{aligned}
H(X \,|\, Y = 0) &= -(7/8)\log_2(7/8) - (1/8)\log_2(1/8) \\
&= (0.875)(0.19265) + (0.125)(3.0) \\
&= 0.16857 + 0.375 \\
&= 0.54357 \text{ bits}
\end{aligned}
$$

Also,

$$P\{X = 0 \,|\, Y = 1\} = \frac{(1/8)(1/2)}{(1/8)(1/2) + (7/8)(1/2)} = 1/8$$

$$P\{X = 1 \,|\, Y = 1\} = 1 - P\{X = 0 \,|\, Y = 1\} = 7/8$$

and

$$
\begin{aligned}
H(X \,|\, Y = 1) &= -(1/8)\log_2(1/8) - (7/8)\log_2(7/8) \\
&= 0.54357 \text{ bits} \qquad \Diamond
\end{aligned}
$$

Knowing the average information per source symbol, and given a particular output symbol, we can calculate the average information per source symbol given an average output symbol. We denote this by $H(X \,|\, Y)$ and define

$$H(X \,|\, Y) = P\{Y = 0\}H(X \,|\, Y = 0) + P\{Y = 1\}H(X \,|\, Y = 1)$$

We say that $H(X \,|\, Y)$ is the **conditional entropy** of **X** given **Y**.

Example 2

For the BSC given in the last example ($q = 7/8$), let us calculate the conditional entropy of $\mathbf{X}$ given $\mathbf{Y}$ when $p = 1/2$.

We must first calculate $P\{\mathbf{Y} = 0\}$ and $P\{\mathbf{Y} = 1\}$. We have

$$P\{\mathbf{Y} = 0\} = P\{\mathbf{Y} = 0 \,|\, \mathbf{X} = 0\}P\{\mathbf{X} = 0\} + P\{\mathbf{Y} = 0 \,|\, \mathbf{X} = 1\}P\{\mathbf{X} = 1\}$$
$$= (1 - q)p + q(1 - p) = (7/8)(1/2) + (1/8)(1/2) = 1/2 = 0.5$$

and

$$P\{\mathbf{Y} = 1\} = P\{\mathbf{Y} = 1 \,|\, \mathbf{X} = 0\}P\{\mathbf{X} = 0\} + P\{\mathbf{Y} = 1 \,|\, \mathbf{X} = 1\}P\{\mathbf{X} = 1\}$$
$$= qp + (1 - q)(1 - p) = 1 - P\{\mathbf{Y} = 0\} = 1/2 = 0.5$$

Thus,

$$H(\mathbf{X}\,|\,\mathbf{Y}) = (0.5)(0.54357) + (0.5)(0.54357) = 0.54357 \text{ bits} \qquad \Diamond$$

The average information content of an input symbol is $H(\mathbf{X})$. On the average, upon revealing the output, the average information content of an input symbol is $H(\mathbf{X}\,|\,\mathbf{Y})$. Thus, in the process of revealing the output, the average information per input symbol changes from $H(\mathbf{X})$ to $H(\mathbf{X}\,|\,\mathbf{Y})$. Hence, we can say that $\mathbf{Y}$ conveys or transmits $H(\mathbf{X}) - H(\mathbf{X}\,|\,\mathbf{Y})$ bits of information (on the average) about $\mathbf{X}$. Therefore, it is this quantity, $H(\mathbf{X}) - H(\mathbf{X}\,|\,\mathbf{Y})$, that gives us a measure of the information transmitted through a channel. Conversely, the quantity $H(\mathbf{X}\,|\,\mathbf{Y})$ is that part of the original $H(\mathbf{X})$ bits of information that is not revealed by $\mathbf{Y}$; i.e., $H(\mathbf{X}\,|\,\mathbf{Y})$ bits do not get transmitted through the channel. Thus, we say that this information gets lost during transmission. (Remember, the channel is noisy and some errors occur during transmission. The result is a loss of information.) For this reason, we say that $H(\mathbf{X}\,|\,\mathbf{Y})$ is a measure of uncertainty, and hence, we refer to $H(\mathbf{X}\,|\,\mathbf{Y})$ as **equivocation.**

Recapitulating, the average information content of a source symbol is $H(\mathbf{X})$ bits. Placing such a source at the input of a channel and revealing the output reduces the average information content of a source symbol to $H(\mathbf{X}\,|\,\mathbf{Y})$ bits. The average information transmitted through the channel is, therefore, $H(\mathbf{X}) - H(\mathbf{X}\,|\,\mathbf{Y})$ bits. The information which does not get through the channel is $H(\mathbf{X}\,|\,\mathbf{Y})$ bits.

Example 3

Given the BSC having $q = 7/8$, we will find the information transmitted through the channel when the input is connected to a binary source with $p = 1/2$.

We know that for this source that $H(\mathbf{X}) = 1.0$ bit. Thus,

$$H(\mathbf{X}) - H(\mathbf{X}\,|\,\mathbf{Y}) = 1.0 - 0.54357 = 0.45643 \text{ bits} \qquad \Diamond$$

The purpose of Example 3 and Exercises 3 and 4 is to demonstrate that different sources may result in different amounts of information being transmitted through the same channel. Suppose we try all possible sources for a particular channel. Let C denote the maximum amount of average information which is transmitted through the channel; i.e.,

$$C = \max \{H(\mathbf{X}) - H(\mathbf{X}|\mathbf{Y})\}$$

where the maximum is taken over all sources $\mathbf{X}$ which can feed the channel. We therefore say that the *capacity* of the channel is C, or more simply, that C is the *channel capacity*. Hence, the channel capacity is the largest average amount of information per symbol that we can ever hope to transmit through a channel.

For the three sources in Example 3 and Exercises 3 and 4, the one for which $p = 1/2$ resulted in the most information being transmitted. It can be shown that no other source can yield a greater information transmission. Thus, the capacity of the BSC in which $q = 7/8$ is $C = 0.45643$ bits.

In general, it can be shown (Exercise 5) that for a BSC, the channel capacity is attained when we use a binary source having $p = 1/2$. Furthermore, the capacity is given by

$$
\begin{aligned}
C &= 1 + q \log_2 q + (1 - q) \log_2 (1 - q) \\
&= 1 + \log_2 q[(1 - q)/q]^{1-q}
\end{aligned}
\tag{1}
$$

We may now summarize, as well as generalize, our previous discussion:

Given a source $\mathbf{X}$ which produces symbols $x_1, x_2, \ldots, x_n$ independently, the average information content of a symbol is given by the *entropy* of the source

$$H(\mathbf{X}) = - \sum_{i=1}^{n} p_i \log_2 p_i$$

where $p_i = P\{\mathbf{X} = x_i\}$.

Suppose that the source is connected to a channel through which the source symbols are transmitted. At the output of the channel we receive the symbols $y_1, y_2, \ldots, y_m$. This is shown in Figure 6–22.

DEFINITION 1

The average information content of an input symbol given a specific output symbol y_j is

$$H(\mathbf{X}|\mathbf{Y} = y_j) = - \sum_{i=1}^{n} P\{\mathbf{X} = x_i | \mathbf{Y} = y_j\} \log_2 P\{\mathbf{X} = x_i | \mathbf{Y} = y_j\}$$

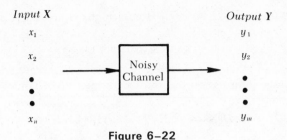

Input X   *Output Y*

x_1 y_1

x_2 y_2

•   •
•   •
•   •

x_n y_m

Figure 6–22

while the average information of an input symbol given an average output symbol is

$$H(\mathbf{X}|\mathbf{Y}) = \sum_{j=1}^{m} P\{\mathbf{Y} = y_j\} H(\mathbf{X}|\mathbf{Y} = y_j)$$

We refer to the conditional entropy $H(\mathbf{X}|\mathbf{Y})$ as **equivocation.** The average information transmitted through the channel for the given source is

$$H(\mathbf{X}) - H(\mathbf{X}|\mathbf{Y})$$

The maximum amount of average information that can be transmitted through a channel is

$$C = \max_{\text{all sources}} \{H(\mathbf{X}) - H(\mathbf{X}|\mathbf{Y})\}$$

and C is called the **channel capacity.** The units of $H(\mathbf{X})$, $H(\mathbf{X}|\mathbf{Y})$, and C are all given in bits.   ○

Shannon's theorem essentially says the following: Suppose that a noisy channel has capacity C and that an information source $\mathbf{X}$ has entropy $H(\mathbf{X})$. If $H(\mathbf{X}) < C$, then it is possible to transmit, after suitable encoding, the information produced by $\mathbf{X}$ through the channel in such a way that the equivocation (i.e., the information lost) is arbitrarily small.

In our example of the BSC having $q = 7/8$, we stated that the capacity of the channel is $C = 0.45643$ bits. In order to achieve this capacity, we have to "stuff" the channel by using a source in which $H(\mathbf{X}) = 1.0$ bit. Consequently, $H(\mathbf{X}|\mathbf{Y}) = 1.0 - 0.45643 = 0.54357$ bits of information which is produced by the source does not get through the channel.

Suppose now that we do not try to force so much information through this channel. Thus, let us consider the binary source in which $p = 1/16$. By Exercise 4 we know that

$$H(\mathbf{X}) = 0.33729 \text{ bits}$$

In this case, therefore, $H(\mathbf{X}) < C$. However, the equivocation is

$$H(\mathbf{X}|\mathbf{Y}) = 0.21885 \text{ bits}$$

and the average information transmitted through the channel is

$$H(\mathbf{X}) - H(\mathbf{X}|\mathbf{Y}) = 0.11844 \text{ bits}$$

Thus, all the information produced by the source does not get transmitted through the channel. Is this a counter-example to Shannon's theory? The answer is no. Let us explain:

In our discussion above, we have a source for which $H(\mathbf{X}) < C$. Connecting this source to the channel results in the transmission of an average amount of information which is less than $H(\mathbf{X})$. In this case, though, we are transmitting the source symbols one-by-one directly through the channel. The keys to Shannon's theory, however, are first to wait for the source to produce a block of N source symbols, and then to encode this block of symbols before transmission. We shall see that, in order to make the equivocation arbitrarily small, we will have to make N increasingly large.

THEOREM 1 (SHANNON'S FUNDAMENTAL THEOREM)

Given an information source $\mathbf{X}$ and a noisy channel with capacity C. If $H(\mathbf{X}) < C$, it is possible to encode the source information in such a way that this information can be transmitted through the channel with an arbitrarily small equivocation. Conversely, if $H(\mathbf{X}) > C$, no encoding scheme will result in an equivocation which is less than $H(\mathbf{X}) - C$.

Proof

The proof of the converse, by way of contradiction, is a relatively simple matter. Therefore, let us first assume that there exists an encoding scheme which results in an equivocation $H(\mathbf{X}|\mathbf{Y})$ such that

$$H(\mathbf{X}|\mathbf{Y}) < H(\mathbf{X}) - C$$

From this equation, we have

$$C < H(\mathbf{X}) - H(\mathbf{X}|\mathbf{Y})$$

However, this is a contradiction of our definition of channel capacity. Hence, the equivocation cannot be less than $H(\mathbf{X}) - C$, and we have proved the converse.

In the process of proving the remainder of the theorem, we will require some results from probability theory. We first recall the law of large numbers. When applied to an information source, we state it as follows:

Suppose that an information source $\mathbf{X}$ produces the symbols $x_1, x_2, \ldots,$ x_n independently. For $i = 1, 2, \ldots, n$, let $P\{\mathbf{X} = x_i\} = p_i$, and let k_i denote the number of times x_i occurs in a sequence of N consecutive symbols produced by the source. Then for arbitrarily small positive numbers δ and ε, there exists a sufficiently large positive integer N_0 such that for $N \geq N_0$ we have

$$P\left\{\left|\frac{k_i}{N} - p_i\right| > \delta\right\} \leq \varepsilon$$

for $i = 1, 2, \ldots, n$.

If we choose very small numbers for δ and ε, the law of large numbers states that for a very long sequence produced by the source, there is a very high probability that the relative frequency of occurrence of symbol x_i will approximately be equal to p_i.

Now let us consider a very long typical sequence which is produced by the source. If this sequence is N symbols long, then by the law of large numbers we are practically assured that the ith symbol appears approximately $p_i N$ times in the sequence, for $i = 1, 2, \ldots, n$. Because the symbols are produced independently, the probability p that a specific very long typical sequence is produced is, thus, well approximated by

$$p = p_1^{p_1 N} p_2^{p_2 N} \cdots p_n^{p_n N}$$

Taking the logarithm of both sides of this equation, we obtain

$$\log_2 p = \sum_{i=1}^{n} p_i N \log_2 p_i$$

$$= N \sum_{i=1}^{n} p_i \log_2 p_i$$

$$= -NH(\mathbf{X})$$

so that

$$p = 2^{-NH(\mathbf{X})}$$

On the other hand, by the law of large numbers, the probability that a source produces a very long non-typical sequence (i.e., a sequence in which

x_i does not appear approximately $p_i N$ times for $i = 1, 2, \ldots, n$) is very small. Thus, we conclude that the probabilities of the typical sequences approximately sum to one. Since the probability that a specific typical sequence is produced is approximately $2^{-NH(\mathbf{X})}$, the implication is that there are approximately $2^{NH(\mathbf{X})}$ typical sequences.

Now let N be very large. Since $H(\mathbf{X}) < C$, there exists some source $\mathbf{X}'$ such that $H(\mathbf{X}) < H(\mathbf{X}') - H(\mathbf{X}'|\mathbf{Y}) \le C$. We shall use the typical sequences produced by $\mathbf{X}'$ for the purpose of encoding the information (in the form of typical sequences) produced by $\mathbf{X}$. Therefore, let us first consider the consequences of using $\mathbf{X}'$ as the input to the channel. We now state the following facts:

(1) There are about $2^{NH(\mathbf{X}')}$ typical input sequences which are produced by $\mathbf{X}'$. The probability that the sequence produced by $\mathbf{X}'$ is one of these is very high (close to one). The probability that any other sequence is produced is very small (close to zero).

Since we may describe the output of the channel by the random variable $\mathbf{Y}$, we have:

(2) There are about $2^{NH(\mathbf{Y})}$ typical output sequences. The probability that one of these typical sequences appears at the output is very high. The probability that any other sequence appears at the output is very small.

The average information content of an input symbol is $H(\mathbf{X}')$, and that of an output symbol is $H(\mathbf{Y})$. From these entropies we can obtain the approximate number of typical input and output sequences, $2^{NH(\mathbf{X}')}$ and $2^{NH(\mathbf{Y})}$, respectively. Since the average information content of an input symbol, given an average output symbol, is $H(\mathbf{X}'|\mathbf{Y})$, we conclude:

(3) Given a typical output sequence y, there are about $2^{NH(\mathbf{X}'|\mathbf{Y})}$ typical input sequences which are likely to produce the output sequence y. The probability that one of these typical input sequences produces y is very high. The probability that any other sequence produces y is very small.

Finally, the average information content of an output symbol, given an average input symbol, is $H(\mathbf{Y}|\mathbf{X}')$; hence:

(4) Given a typical input sequence x', there are about $2^{NH(\mathbf{Y}|\mathbf{X}')}$ typical output sequences which are likely to be produced by this input sequence x'. The probability that one of these typical output sequences is produced by x' is very high. The probability that any other sequence is produced by x' is very small.

The four statements given above are summarized in Figure 6–23.

We shall now encode the information produced by the original source $\mathbf{X}$. Since we assume N to be very large, the probability that a non-typical sequence is produced by $\mathbf{X}$ is very small. Thus, we will neglect such sequences.

Let S be the set of all typical sequences produced by $\mathbf{X}$. Similarly, let S' be the set of all typical sequences produced by $\mathbf{X}'$. We select the following "random" encoding scheme:

For each typical sequence $s \in S$, we arbitrarily select a typical sequence $s' \in S'$ as the encoding for $s \in S$. (Note that under this circumstance, it is

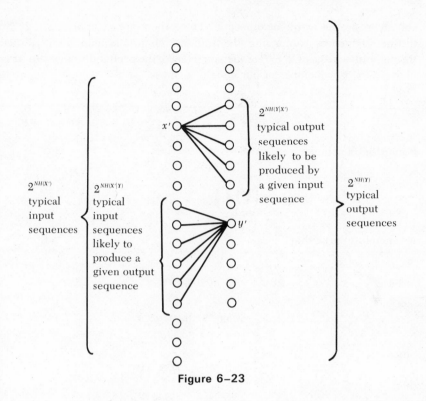

Figure 6-23

quite possible for both $s_1 \in S$ and $s_2 \in S$ to be encoded as the same sequence, say $s_1' \in S'$. Intuitively, this possibility appears distasteful; however, it is actually, in the end, of no consequence.) Hence, our code is some subset of S'.

Each time the source **X** produces $s \in S$, we transmit $s' \in S'$ through the channel. So suppose that y is received. We would like to determine the probability that y will be decoded correctly. First, however, we must decide upon a decoding scheme. Let us choose the following:

Suppose that y is received. From our previous discussion we know that there are approximately $2^{NH(\mathbf{X}'|\mathbf{Y})}$ elements in S' which are most likely to produce y. (One is the sequence that was transmitted.) Of these elements, consider only those which are in our code. Now arbitrarily select one of these code words. We will assume that this sequence was transmitted.

For any decoding scheme, we will decode y correctly only if the sequence we select was the one actually transmitted. Thus, for the above decoding scheme, an error in decoding is possible only if, in addition to the sequence transmitted, one or more of the approximately $2^{NH(\mathbf{X}'|\mathbf{Y})}$ sequences most likely to produce y is a code word. Hence, the probability p_e that y is decoded incorrectly can be bounded from above as follows:

There are $2^{NH(\mathbf{X}')}$ typical sequences from which $2^{NH(\mathbf{X})}$ are arbitrarily chosen to be the words of our code. Thus, there are no more than $2^{NH(X)}$ distinct sequences comprising the code which are randomly distributed throughout a space of $2^{NH(X')}$ sequences. Hence, the probability that a particular $s' \in S'$ is a member of our code is at most

$$\frac{2^{NH(X)}}{2^{NH(X')}} = 2^{N[H(X)-H(X')]}$$

Using the fact that

$$P\left(\bigcup_{i=1}^{n} A_i\right) \leq \sum_{i=1}^{n} P(A_i)$$

we therefore have that

$$p_e \leq \sum_{i=1}^{2^{NH(X'|Y)}} 2^{N[H(X)-H(X')]}$$

$$\leq 2^{NH(X'|Y)} 2^{N[H(X)-H(X')]}$$
$$\leq 2^{N[H(X'|Y)-H(X')+H(X)]}$$

Since

$$H(X) < H(X') - H(X'|Y)$$

then

$$H(X'|Y) - H(X') + H(X) < 0$$

Now, let

$$\Delta = -[H(X'|Y) - H(X') + H(X)]$$

Since Δ is positive, and since

$$p_e \leq 2^{-N\Delta} = \frac{1}{2^{N\Delta}}$$

we have that

$$\lim_{N \to \infty} p_e = \lim_{N \to \infty} \frac{1}{2^{N\Delta}} = 0$$

Therefore, as N becomes increasingly large, the probability that y is incorrectly decoded approaches zero. This means that we can make the equivocation arbitrarily small by choosing N sufficiently large.

This completes our recounting of Shannon's original informal "proof" of his theorem. □

We have now seen that we can reliably transmit information through a noisy channel. In order to accomplish this feat, we must first encode the information before transmitting it. Shannon's theory states that there exists a code which can be used for reliable transmission. The theorem is proved by using an arbitrarily selected code (this is known as *random coding*), since there is a high probability that such a code will do the job. However, for large values of N, actually selecting a code in this manner is not only computationally horrendous, but it is impossible to implement practically.

In Chapters 7 and 8, we shall consider the problem of finding the (error-correcting) codes promised by Shannon's theorem.

For the purpose of proving Shannon's theorem, we were able to utilize a somewhat arbitrary decoding scheme. However, for the actual transmission of information, the problem of decoding must be given more serious thought. Thus, let us now consider the problem of determining the best possible decoding scheme. We will call a best possible decoder an *ideal observer*.

Given a channel in which elements of the set $\{t_1, t_2, \ldots, t_n\}$ are transmitted and elements of the set $\{r_1, r_2, \ldots, r_m\}$ are received (these elements may be either symbols or sequences of symbols), the event $\{t_i$ is transmitted$\}$ will be denoted by $\{\mathbf{T} = t_i\}$, and the event $\{r_j$ is received$\}$ will be denoted by $\{\mathbf{R} = r_j\}$. Any map $f: \{r_1, r_2, \ldots, r_m\} \to \{t_1, t_2, \ldots, t_n\}$ is said to be a **decoding scheme,** and that which performs a decoding scheme is called a **decoder.**

Suppose that t_i is transmitted and r_j is received. Also suppose that the decoder decodes r_j as t_j. If $t_j = t_i$, then the decoding is *correct;* otherwise (if $t_j \neq t_i$), the decoding is *incorrect.* Consequently, the probability that r_j is decoded correctly is equal to the probability that, given r_j is received, t_j was actually transmitted; i.e.,

$$P\{\mathbf{T} = t_j \mid \mathbf{R} = r_j\}$$

It then follows that the average probability of correct decoding p_c is

$$p_c = \sum_{j=1}^{m} P\{\mathbf{R} = r_j\} P\{\mathbf{T} = t_j \mid \mathbf{R} = r_j\}$$

A decoding scheme that maximizes p_c is called an **ideal observer.**

Regardless of what decoding scheme may be used, $P\{\mathbf{R} = r_j\}$ remains the same. This is because $P\{\mathbf{R} = r_j\}$ depends only on the characteristics of the channel and the probabilities associated with what is transmitted. Thus, we can maximize p_c by maximizing

$$P\{\mathbf{T} = t_j \mid \mathbf{R} = r_j\}$$

for $j = 1, 2, \ldots, m$. In summary, therefore, a decoder which, given a received r_j, selects t_j such that p_c is maximized is an ideal observer.

For the special case when all inputs are equally likely, i.e., when

$$P\{\mathbf{T} = t_1\} = P\{\mathbf{T} = t_2\} = \cdots = P\{\mathbf{T} = t_n\} = 1/n$$

we can be more specific about the ideal observer. From our discussion of probability theory, we know that

$$P(\{T = t_j\} \cap \{R = r_j\}) = P\{T = t_j | R = r_j\}P\{R = r_j\}$$
$$= P\{R = r_j | T = t_j\}P\{T = t_j\}$$

Thus,

$$p_c = \sum_{j=1}^{m} P\{R = r_j | T = t_j\}P\{T = t_j\}$$

$$= 1/n \sum_{j=1}^{m} P\{R = r_j | T = t_j\}$$

and by maximizing

$$P\{R = r_j | T = t_j\}$$

for $j = 1, 2, \ldots, m$, we can maximize p_c. Hence, in order to obtain an ideal observer when all inputs are equally likely, for each r_j we simply have the decoder select the element t_j for which $P\{R = r_j | T = t_j\}$ is a maximum. The reader should compare this with the discussion of pattern recognition which closed Section 6–1.

EXERCISES FOR SECTION 6–4

1. Carry out the calculations corresponding to Example 1 for the BSC with $p = 1/4$.

2. Determine the calculation corresponding to Example 2 for $p = 1/4$.

3. Verify that for $p = 1/4$ the result corresponding to Example 3 is

$$H(X) - H(X|Y) = 0.35248 \text{ bits}$$

while for $p = 1/8$ we have that

$$H(X) - H(X|Y) = 0.21431 \text{ bits}$$

4. Calculate the information transmitted through the BSC having $q = 7/8$ for a binary source with $p = 1/16$.

5. Derive equation (1) by proving that the capacity of a BSC is attained when $p = 1/2$. [Hint: Let $r = p + q - 2pq$ and choose r such that $-r \log_2 r - (1 - r) \log_2 (1 - r)$ is maximum.]

6. Consider the channel of Figure 6–24. Suppose that a binary source with $P\{X = 0\} = P\{X = 1\} = 1/2$ is connected to the input of this channel. Determine the following entropies:
  - **(a)** $H(X)$
  - **(b)** $H(Y)$
  - **(c)** $H(X|Y)$

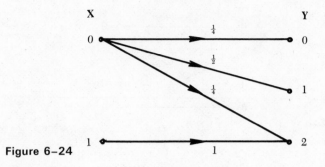

Figure 6-24

(d) $H(\mathbf{Y}|\mathbf{X})$
(e) $H(\mathbf{X}) - H(\mathbf{X}|\mathbf{Y})$
(f) $H(\mathbf{Y}) - H(\mathbf{Y}|\mathbf{X})$

7.   Suppose that the random variables $\mathbf{X}$ and $\mathbf{Y}$ take on values $x_1, x_2, \ldots, x_n$ and $y_1, y_2, \ldots, y_m$, respectively. Define the **joint** (or **compound**) entropy of $\mathbf{X}$ and $\mathbf{Y}$, denoted $H(\mathbf{X}, \mathbf{Y})$, to be

$$H(\mathbf{X}, \mathbf{Y}) = - \sum_{i=1}^{n} \sum_{j=1}^{m} P(\{\mathbf{X} = x_i\} \cap \{\mathbf{Y} = y_j\}) \log_2 P(\{\mathbf{X} = x_i\} \cap \{\mathbf{Y} = y_j\})$$

Show that $H(\mathbf{X}) + H(\mathbf{Y}|\mathbf{X}) = H(\mathbf{X}, \mathbf{Y})$.

8.   Use Exercise 7 to prove that

$$H(\mathbf{X}) - H(\mathbf{X}|\mathbf{Y}) = H(\mathbf{Y}) - H(\mathbf{Y}|\mathbf{X})$$

9.   With $H(\mathbf{X}, \mathbf{Y})$ defined as in Exercise 7, prove that

$$H(\mathbf{X}, \mathbf{Y}) \le H(\mathbf{X}) + H(\mathbf{Y})$$

where equality holds if and only if $\mathbf{X}$ and $\mathbf{Y}$ are statistically independent.

10.   Use Exercise 9 to prove that

$$H(\mathbf{X}|\mathbf{Y}) \le H(\mathbf{X})$$

where equality holds if and only if $\mathbf{X}$ and $\mathbf{Y}$ are statistically independent.

11.   Given a discrete noisy channel with input $\mathbf{X}$ and output $\mathbf{Y}$, we can define the following terms:

The channel is
   I.   **lossless** if $H(\mathbf{X}|\mathbf{Y}) = 0$ for all input distributions.
  II.   **deterministic** if $H(\mathbf{Y}|\mathbf{X}) = 0$ for all input distributions.
 III.   **noiseless** if it is both lossless and deterministic.
 IV.   **useless** if its capacity is $C = 0$.

Identify each of the following channels with the appropriate descriptors of the above four terms:

(a)

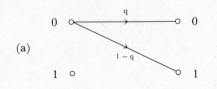

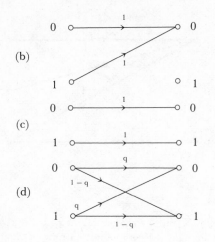

6–5   Markov Chains and Stochastic Automata

In most of our discussion in this chapter we have stressed finite sample spaces, with a sample being taken at a given time. In proving Shannon's noisy coding theorem, we relaxed this somewhat and considered the encoding of long sequences. Yet, our study was still based on a model in which symbols were independently generated at the source, and independently perturbed in the channel. However, we often come upon situations (such as the sequence of daily weather readings at some particular place) which are described by a sequence of highly correlated phenomena. In such a case, it is the whole *time series* that constitutes the sample, and even if there are only finitely many different readings that can be made at any one time, it may be mathematically appropriate to consider any finite sequence of such readings as constituting an event on the sample space of infinite sequences of readings. In this section, we shall give a general language for such processes, and then consider the special cases known as Markov chains. Furthermore, we shall see how the language of Markov chains can be used to describe automata in which the current state and input do not determine the next state completely, but only determine a probability for each possible next state.

Consider, then, a device M which has a (possibly infinite) set of states $Q = \{q_0, q_1, q_2, \ldots\}$ and which operates at discrete times (for simplicity, say at times $t = 0, 1, 2, \ldots$). To each map $q:\mathbf{N} \to Q$ let us associate the infinite sequence $q(0), q(1), q(2), \ldots$. We then let $q:\mathbf{N} \to Q$ correspond to the device being in state $q(t)$ at time t. Furthermore, let us associate with this device the sample space $Q^{\mathbf{N}}$, where

$$Q^{\mathbf{N}} = \{q(0), q(1), q(2), \ldots | q:\mathbf{N} \to Q\}$$

Since we associate the map $q:\mathbf{N} \to Q$ with the sequence $q(0), q(1), q(2), \ldots$, we may for purposes of brevity denote $Q^{\mathbf{N}}$ by

$$Q^{\mathbf{N}} = \{q | q:\mathbf{N} \to Q\}$$

Clearly then, Q^N is an infinite sample space. As discussed in Definition 6-1-1, we can single out a special class Ω of events for which we shall assign probabilities. In this case we let each event in Ω be comprised of all the sample space elements that begin with some finite specified sequence. For example, given the elements $q_{i_0}, q_{i_1}, \ldots, q_{i_m} \in Q$, we define the event $(q_{i_0}, q_{i_1}, \ldots, q_{i_m})$ by

$$(q_{i_0}, q_{i_1}, \ldots, q_{i_m}) = \{q \in Q^N \,|\, q(t) = q_{i_t} \text{ for } t = 0, 1, 2, \ldots, m\}$$

Having done this, we may identify the set of all events with Q^*, where Λ is the certain event and $(q_{i_0}, q_{i_1}, \ldots, q_{i_m}) \in Q^*$ corresponds to the device M being in state q_{i_j} at time j (for $j = 0, 1, 2, \ldots, m$). We then let P be a probability measure defined only on certain subsets of the sample space Q^N, where we assume that all the subsets corresponding to the elements of Q^* are included. "Real world" considerations demand that if M is in some state at time t, then it must be some state (possible the same) at time $t + 1$. This, and other considerations, suggest the following concept.

DEFINITION 1

A probability measure (map) $P: Q^* \to [0, 1]$ is a **stochastic process** if the following two conditions are satisfied:

(i) $\sum\limits_{q_j \in Q} P(q_j) = 1$

(ii) $\sum\limits_{q_j \in Q} P(q_{i_0}, q_{i_1}, \ldots, q_{i_m}, q_j) = P(q_{i_0}, q_{i_1}, \ldots, q_{i_m})$ ○

Suppose we denote the event $\{q \in Q^N \,|\, q(t) = q_k\}$ that M is in state q_k at time t by $q_k(t)$. Then the probability that M is in state q_j at time $t + 1$, given that M is in state q_k at time t, is

$$P(q_j(t + 1) \,|\, q_k(t)) = \frac{P(q_j(t + 1) \cap q_k(t))}{P(q_k(t))}$$

$$= \frac{\sum\limits_{\substack{q_{i_r} \in Q \\ 0 \leq r < t}} P(q_{i_0}, q_{i_1}, \ldots, q_{i_{t-1}}, q_k, q_j)}{\sum\limits_{\substack{q_{i_r} \in Q \\ 0 \leq r < t}} P(q_{i_0}, q_{i_1}, \ldots, q_{i_{t-1}}, q_k)}$$

where we take $P(q_j(t + 1) \,|\, q_k(t)) = 0$ if $P(q_k(t)) = 0$. We call such a probability a **transition probability.**

Example 1

A stochastic process $P: \{q_0, q_1\} \to [0, 1]$ is defined for sequences of length at most three by the probability tree shown in Figure 6-25. Clearly, this definition can be continued indefinitely by choosing $P(wq_0)$ to be any value between 0 and $P(w)$ and then taking $P(wq_1) = P(w) - P(wq_0)$.

500

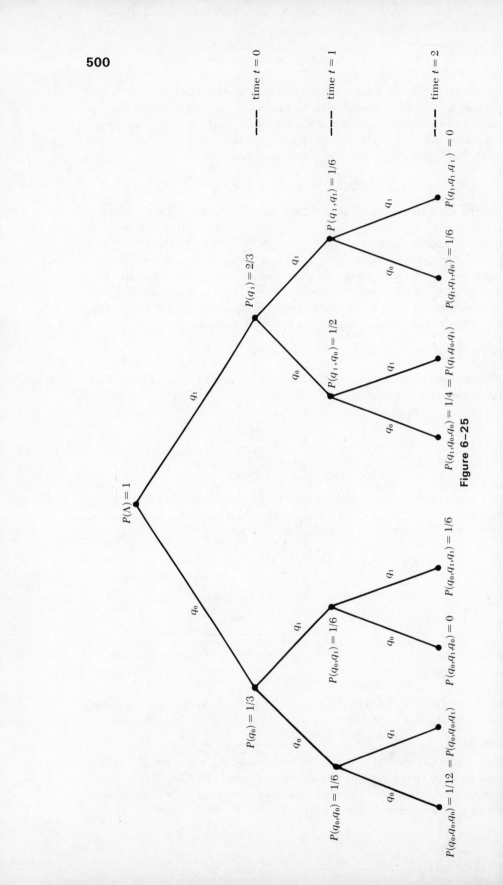

Figure 6-25

Let us now determine some transition probabilities. We have

$$P(q_0(2)|q_0(1)) = \frac{P(q_0, q_0, q_0) + P(q_1, q_0, q_0)}{P(q_0, q_0) + P(q_1, q_0)}$$

$$= \frac{1/12 + 1/4}{1/6 + 1/2} = \frac{4/12}{4/6} = 1/2$$

and

$$P(q_0(1)|q_0(0)) = \frac{P(q_0, q_0)}{P(q_0)} = \frac{1/6}{1/3} = 1/2$$

so that the probability of transition from state q_0 to state q_0 is the same at time $t = 0$ as at time $t = 1$. However, since

$$P(q_0(2)|q_1(1)) = \frac{P(q_0, q_1, q_0) + P(q_1, q_1, q_0)}{P(q_0, q_1) + P(q_1, q_1)}$$

$$= \frac{0 + 1/6}{1/6 + 1/6} = 1/2$$

and

$$P(q_0(1)|q_1(0)) = \frac{P(q_1, q_0)}{P(q_1)} = \frac{1/2}{2/3} = 3/4$$

the probability of transition from state q_1 to state q_0 is not the same at time $t = 0$ as at time $t = 1$.

Furthermore,

$$q_1(1) \cap q_0(0) = (q_0, q_1)$$

$$q_1(1) \cap q_1(0) = (q_1, q_1)$$

so that

$$P(q_0(2)|q_1(1) \cap q_0(0)) = \frac{P(q_0, q_1, q_0)}{P(q_0, q_1)} = \frac{0}{1/6} = 0$$

and

$$P(q_0(2)|q_1(1) \cap q_1(0)) = \frac{P(q_1, q_1, q_0)}{P(q_1, q_1)} = \frac{1/6}{1/6} = 1$$

Thus, the probability of changing from state q_1 to state q_0 can be influenced by past history. Thus, we see that the probability of a transition from state q_i to state q_j at time t for a general stochastic process may or may not depend on the time t, and may or may not depend on the states of the process prior to time t.   ◊

We say that P is a Markov† chain if it is a stochastic process in which, when the present state is q_k, the probability that q_j is the next state is independent of any additional information about the past. More formally we have the following:

---

†Named for the Russian mathematician A. A. Markov (1856–1922).

DEFINITION 2

A stochastic process P is a **Markov chain** if for all t and $q_j, q_k \in Q$ we have that

$$P(q_j(t + 1) \,|\, q_k(t))$$
$$= P(q_j(t + 1) \,|\, q_a(0) \cap q_b(1) \cap \cdots \cap q_r(t - 1) \cap q_k(t)) \quad \textbf{(1)}$$

for every $q_a, q_b, \ldots, q_r \in Q$. ○

We call equation (1) the **Markov property.** It has the pleasant paraphrase, "A stochastic process is a Markov chain if, given the present, the past and future are independent." In other words, "All relevant information about the past is contained in the present state," which means that a state of a Markov chain shares a common property with a state of a deterministic automaton.

DEFINITION 3

We say that the Markov chain P is **stationary** if, for all j and k, we have that $P(q_j(t + 1) \,|\, q_k(t))$ is independent of t. For a stationary P, we denote this constant value by p_{kj}. ○

LEMMA 1

Let P be a stationary Markov chain. Then P is completely determined by the transition probabilities

$$p_{kj} = P(q_j(t + 1) \,|\, q_k(t)) \quad \textbf{(2)}$$

for any t, and the initial values

$$p_j = P(q_j(0)) \quad \textbf{(3)}$$

for $q_j \in Q$.

Proof

We must prove that the data (2) and (3) determine

$$P(q_{i_0}, q_{i_1}, \ldots, q_{i_n})$$

for all $(q_{i_0}, q_{i_1}, \ldots, q_{i_n})$ in Q^*. We do this by induction. For length 1, the value is given directly by equation (3). Suppose, then, that we already know the probability $P(q_{i_0}, q_{i_1}, \ldots, q_{i_{n-1}})$ in terms of (2) and (3), and wish to compute $P(q_{i_0}, q_{i_1}, \ldots, q_{i_n})$. Then

$$P(q_{i_0}, q_{i_1}, \ldots, q_{i_n}) = P(q_{i_0}, q_{i_1}, \ldots, q_{i_{n-1}})P(q_{i_n}(n) \mid q_{i_0}(0), q_{i_1}(1), \ldots, q_{i_{n-1}}(n-1))$$
$$\text{by the definition of}$$
$$\text{conditional probability}$$

$$= P(q_{i_0}, q_{i_1}, \ldots, q_{i_{n-1}})P(q_{i_n}(n) \mid q_{i_{n-1}}(n-1))$$
$$\text{by the Markov property}$$

$$= P(q_{i_0}, q_{i_1}, \ldots, q_{i_{n-1}})p_{i_{n-1}, i_n} \text{ by (2)}$$

In fact, it is immediately clear from the last equation that we have the general formula:

$$P(q_{i_0}, q_{i_1}, \ldots, q_{i_n}) = p_{i_0}p_{i_0,i_1} \cdots p_{i_{n-1},i_n} \qquad \textbf{(4)} \quad \square$$

Henceforth, we shall assume that P is stationary and that Q has n elements. Then we may immediately deduce that

$$0 \le p_{ij} \le 1 \qquad \textbf{(5a)}$$

and

$$\sum_{j=1}^{n} p_{ij} = 1$$
$$\textbf{(5b)}$$

In other words, if M is in state q_i at time t, then M *must* (with probability one) be in some state at time $t+1$.

A matrix $\mathcal{P}$ whose elements p_{ij} satisfy (5) is called a **Markov matrix** or **stochastic matrix;**† i.e., a matrix is **Markov** if all of its elements are non-negative, and each *row* sums to 1.

Example 2

The following are three stochastic matrices for $n = 2, 3,$ and 4, respectively:

$$\begin{bmatrix} 1 & 0 \\ 0 & 1 \end{bmatrix} \qquad \begin{bmatrix} 1/2 & 1/2 & 0 \\ 1/3 & 1/3 & 1/3 \\ 1/4 & 1/8 & 5/8 \end{bmatrix} \qquad \begin{bmatrix} 1.0 & 0.0 & 0.0 & 0.0 \\ 0.3 & 0.2 & 0.1 & 0.4 \\ 0.1 & 0.1 & 0.6 & 0.2 \\ 0.1 & 0.6 & 0.0 & 0.3 \end{bmatrix} \qquad \Diamond$$

Example 3

Given a stationary Markov chain with n states $\{q_1, q_2, \ldots, q_n\}$ and a stochastic matrix $\mathcal{P}$, let us denote the probability $P(q_j(t+r) \mid q_i(t))$ by p_{ij}^r. We will now compute the probability $p_{ij}^2 = P(q_j(t+2) \mid q_i(t))$ that if q_i is the state at time t, then q_j will be the state at time $t+2$. Clearly, the event $q_j(t+2) \cap q_k(t+1)$ can be written as the union of the n mutually exclusive events $A_1, A_2, \ldots,$

---

†Until Lemma 5, we use no matrix theory in this section beyond the definitions of a matrix and of matrix multiplication. Most readers will know these, but others may find it helpful first to study Section 7–1. Warning: Other concepts discussed in Chapter 7 will also be utilized in later parts of this section.

A_n, where A_k is the event $q_j(t + 2) \cap q_k(t + 1) \cap q_i(t)$. Reasoning as we did in developing equation (4), we have that

$$P(A_k) = P(q_i(t))p_{ik}p_{kj}$$

Thus,

$$\begin{aligned} p_{ij}^2 &= P(q_j(t + 2)\,|\,q_i(t)) \\ &= \frac{P(q_j(t + 2) \cap q_i(t))}{P(q_i(t))} \\ &= \frac{\displaystyle\sum_{k=1}^{n} p(A_k)}{P(q_i(t))} \\ &= \sum_{k=1}^{n} p_{ik}p_{kj} \end{aligned}$$

Thus, p_{ij}^2 is the generic element of the square of the matrix $\mathcal{P}$, and we may thus write

$$\mathcal{P}^2 = (p_{ij}^2)$$

without ambiguity. ◊

It is now immediate by an easy induction that the following holds.

THEOREM 2

For a stationary Markov chain with stochastic matrix $\mathcal{P}$, the rth power of $\mathcal{P}$ is $\mathcal{P}^r = (p_{ij}^r)$, where p_{ij}^r is the probability that if the chain is in state q_i at time t, it will be in state q_j at time $t + r$. □

Thus, we may think of a Markov chain as being a stochastic process, taking place on a discrete time scale, characterized by n states $q_1, \ldots, q_n$ and a Markov matrix $\mathcal{P}$. We call $\mathcal{P}$ the **transition matrix** of the chain, and say that the process has the Markov property.

Let us briefly see a role in which Markov chains have appeared in automata theory. In Chapter 2, we considered deterministic automata in which the present state q and input x uniquely determine the next state and present output. We now turn to probabilistic automata (called *stochastic sequential machines*), in which q and x determine only the *probability* that the present output will be y and the next state will be q'. Such an automaton arises, for example, from a network in which we have a certain amount of random malfunctioning of components.

It is worthwhile to note that stochastic sequential machines may be

considered as models for communication channels, while deterministic automata are models for encoders and decoders. However, here we emphasize
results obtained for probabilistic automata in relation to facts about deterministic automata.

DEFINITION 4

A **stochastic sequential machine (SSM)** is a quadruple $M = (X, Y, Q, P)$,
where:

> X is a finite set called the set of **inputs,**
>
> Y is a finite set called the set of **outputs,**
>
> Q is a finite set called the set of **states,** and
>
> P is a conditional probability measure $P(q', y | q, x)$; that is,

$$P(q', y | q, x) \geq 0 \text{ and } \sum_{y \in Y} \sum_{q' \in Q} P(q', y | q, x) = 1$$

○

We interpret $P(q', y | q, x)$ as the probability that the present output will
be $y \in Y$ and the next state will be $q' \in Q$, given that the machine is in state
$q \in Q$ when the input $x \in X$ is applied.

Rather than concentrate on the finite set Q, it is more natural to consider
Π, the set of probability distributions on Q, as an extended state set. If
$Q = \{q_1, q_2, \ldots, q_n\}$, a typical element of Π will be $\pi = (\pi_1, \pi_2, \ldots, \pi_n)$, with
each $\pi_i \geq 0$ being the probability that M is in state q_i, and with $\Sigma \pi_i = 1$.
We may embed Q in Π by identifying q_j with the probability vector having
a 1 in the jth position and a 0 elsewhere, and call such a state **pure.**

The **input-output function** of a distribution-state π is then defined to
be the function $P_\pi^M : (Y \times X)^* \to [0, 1]$ given by

$$P_\pi^M(y_1, \ldots, y_n | x_1, \ldots, x_n) = \sum_{\substack{q_k \in Q \\ 1 \leq k \leq n}} \pi_{q_1} \prod_{k=1}^{n-1} P(q_{k+1}, y_k | q_k, x_k),$$

and is the probability, given an initial distribution-state π and input sequence
$x_1, \ldots, x_n$, that the output sequence is $y_1, \ldots, y_n$.

We say that distribution-states π and π' are *equivalent* if they have the
same input-output functions, i.e., if $P_\pi^M(\cdot | \cdot) = P_{\pi'}^M(\cdot | \cdot)$.

DEFINITION 5

Two SSM's are **equivalent** if they have the same set of input-output functions.

○

Recall that in Section 2–1 we saw how every deterministic automaton with output map of the form $\lambda: Q \times X \to Y$ could be replaced by one whose output map was of the form $\beta: Q \to Y$. We now give the corresponding result for stochastic machines.

DEFINITION 6

A **state-output SSM** is one in which the output y is a function f of the state q'; i.e., $P(q', y \mid q, x) = 0$ unless $y = f(q')$. ○

THEOREM 3

Every SSM is equivalent to a state-output SSM.

Proof

Just take the new finite-state set $Q \times Y$, and use the transition function

$$P((q,y'),y'' \mid (q,y), x) = \begin{cases} 0 & \text{if } y' \neq y'' \\ P(q,y' \mid q, x) & \text{if } y' = y'' \end{cases}$$ □

Let us now re-examine the definition of a stochastic sequential machine. Its behavior is determined by the conditional probability measure P, where $P(q', y \mid q, x)$ is the probability that the next state is q' and the present output is y, given that the present state is q and the present input is x. Thus, a stochastic sequential machine is not only a generalization of an automaton, but also a generalization of a Markov chain. In fact, a stochastic machine may be thought of as a controlled Markov chain, in that the transition matrix depends upon a parameter which may be chosen by the experimenter at each step. The fact that we have outputs as well as states need cause no difficulty, since we may regard the state-output pairs as elements of an enlarged state set.

The techniques of Markov matrices are immediately applicable to this more general situation, and we obtain the following results:

Let the stochastic sequential machine M have n states, and let $M(y \mid x)$ be the $n \times n$ matrix with ij element $m_{ij}(y \mid x) = P(q_j, y \mid q_i, x)$. Then $M(x) = \sum_{y \in Y} M(y \mid x)$ is a Markov matrix (Exercise 4), called the **state-transition matrix**. The element $m_{ij}(x)$ is the probability that M will go into state q_j if it receives input x when in state q_i. If $u = x_1 \ldots x_n \in X^*$ and $v = y_1 \ldots y_n \in Y^*$, then

$$M(v \mid u) = M(y_1 \mid x_1)M(y_2 \mid x_2) \ldots M(y_n \mid x_n) \tag{6}$$

has for ij element the probability that if we start M in state q_i and apply input sequence u, we shall receive output sequences v and end up in state q_j. Similarly,

$$M(u) = M(x_1) \ldots M(x_n) \tag{7}$$

has for ij element the probability that if we start M in state q_i and apply input sequence u, we shall end up in state q_j.

As in the deterministic case, we may draw state graphs to describe a machine. However, an arrow leading from one state to another must now be labelled not only with the output accompanying the transition, but also with the probability of that transition.

Example 4

Consider the stochastic automaton with $X = Y = Q = \{0, 1\}$ having the following matrices:

$$M(0|0) = \begin{bmatrix} 0 & \dfrac{1}{2} \\ \dfrac{3}{4} & 0 \end{bmatrix} \text{ and } M(1|0) = \begin{bmatrix} \dfrac{1}{4} & \dfrac{1}{4} \\ 0 & \dfrac{1}{4} \end{bmatrix} \Rightarrow M(0) = \begin{bmatrix} \dfrac{1}{4} & \dfrac{3}{4} \\ \dfrac{3}{4} & \dfrac{1}{4} \end{bmatrix}$$

$$M(0|1) = \begin{bmatrix} \dfrac{1}{3} & 0 \\ 0 & 0 \end{bmatrix} \text{ and } M(1|1) = \begin{bmatrix} \dfrac{2}{3} & 0 \\ 0 & 1 \end{bmatrix} \Rightarrow M(1) = \begin{bmatrix} 1 & 0 \\ 0 & 1 \end{bmatrix}$$

We *omit* arrows for 0-probability transitions, and obtain the state graph shown in Figure 6-26. ◊

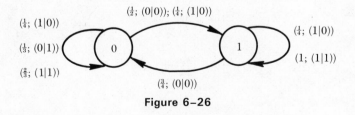

$(\frac{1}{2}; (0|0)); (\frac{1}{4}; (1|0))$

$(\frac{1}{4}; (1|0))$

$(\frac{1}{3}; (0|1))$

$(\frac{2}{3}; (1|1))$

$(\frac{1}{4}; (1|0))$

$(1; (1|1))$

$(\frac{3}{4}; (0|0))$

Figure 6-26

DEFINITION 7

We say that q_i is **reachable** from q_j if there is some sequence in X^* for which the probability of going from q_i to q_j is positive; i.e., whenever there is a directed path from q_i to q_j in the state graph. We say that q_j is **accessible** from a distribution-state π if there is a sequence w such that $\pi \cdot M(w)_j > 0$, that is, if the jth entry of $\pi \cdot M(w)$ is nonzero. This occurs whenever there is a state q_k from which q_i is reachable and $\pi_k > 0$. ○

LEMMA 4

If q_j is accessible from π, then there is a string w of length less than n such that $\pi \cdot M(w)_j > 0$.

Proof

This is just a replay of the reachability arguments in Section 2–5. Simply let

$$S_0^\pi = \text{the set of states } q_k \text{ with } \pi_k > 0$$

and let

$$S_{m+1}^\pi = S_m^\pi \cup \{q_\ell \,|\, \text{there exists } q_k \in S_m^\pi \text{ and } x \in X \text{ with } M(x)_{k\ell} > 0\}$$

Then S_m^π is clearly the set of states reachable from the states of S_0^π by applying input sequences of length at most m. It is clear that if $S_m^\pi = S_{m+1}^\pi$, then $S_m^\pi = S_{m'}^\pi$ for all $m' \geq m$. Hence (why?), S_{n-1}^π must contain all states accessible from π. □

Let $h(v|u)$ be the n-component column vector whose ith component is $\sum_{j=1}^{n} P(q_j, v | q_i, u)$, which we now label as $P_i(v|u)$. This is simply the probability that if M is in state q_i and receives input sequence u, it will emit output sequence v. Let all components of the n-component vector e have the value 1. Then clearly

$$h(v|u) = M(v|u)e$$

since

$$P_i(v|u) = \sum_{j=1}^{n} m_{ij}(v|u) \cdot 1$$
$$= \{M(v|u)e\}_i$$

We then have that

$$h(vv'|uu') = M(vv'|uu')e$$
$$= M(v|u)M(v'|u')e$$
$$= M(v|u)h(v'|u')$$

Let $\pi = (\pi_1, \ldots, \pi_n)$ be any initial distribution for M; i.e., π_i is the probability that M is in state q_i at the initial moment. Then

$$P_\pi(v \mid u) = \pi \cdot h(v \mid u) \qquad \text{(8)}$$

is the probability $\Sigma \pi_i P_i(v \mid u)$ that v is the response of M when u is applied starting with the initial distribution π.

We now give an analysis of equivalence of distribution-states for the stochastic case.

DEFINITION 8

Let k be a non-negative integer. We say that the initial distribution π for the stochastic machine M is **k-equivalent** to the initial distribution λ for the stochastic machine N (or that (M, π) and (N, λ) are **k-equivalent machines**) if

$$P_\pi^M(v \mid u) = P_\lambda^N(v \mid u)$$

for all u and v of length at most k. If k-equivalence holds for all k, then (M, π) and (N, λ) are **equivalent**; otherwise, they are **distinguishable**.   ○

Just as Section 2–5 had both reachability and observability results, so do we have the following companion to Lemma 4.

LEMMA 5

If M is a stochastic sequential machine with n states, and if π and λ are any two initial distributions for M, then the $(n - 1)$-equivalence of π and λ is a necessary and sufficient condition for their equivalence.

Proof

Recalling (8), we see that π and λ are k-equivalent if

$$(\pi - \lambda)h(v \mid u)$$

vanishes for all v and u of length at most k, i.e., if and only if the linear map $\phi(z) = (\pi - \lambda)z$ vanishes on the linear subspace of the n-dimensional space spanned by the vectors $h(v \mid u)$ for all v and u of length at most k; call it $L_k(M)$. Corresponding to the argument in Lemma 4, we have

(i) $$L_k \subset L_{k+1}$$

and

(ii) $$L_k = L_{k+1} \Rightarrow L_g = L_k \text{ for all } g \geq k$$

Thus, L_k must eventually become constant. So let J be the first k such that $L_g^k = L_k$ for all $g \geq k$. Since our space only has n dimensions and since L_0 is spanned by e and thus has dimension 1, we conclude that $J \leq n - 1$. This $L_j(M)$ is the union of all $L_k(M)$'s.

Hence π and λ are equivalent if and only if they are $(n - 1)$-equivalent. $\square$

THEOREM 6

If M has n states, N has m states, and π and λ are initial distributions for M and N, respectively, then the $(n + m - 1)$-equivalence of (M, π) and (N, λ) is a necessary and sufficient condition for their equivalence.

Proof

Let $M + N$ be the *sum machine*, whose state set is the union of those of M and N, defined by

$$(M + N)(y|x) = \begin{bmatrix} M(y|x) & 0 \\ 0 & N(y|x) \end{bmatrix}$$

Then (M, π) and (N, λ) are equivalent if $(\pi, 0)$ and $(0, \lambda)$ are equivalent with regard to $M + N$. The result then follows. $\square$

DEFINITION 9

Two stochastic sequential machines M and N are said to be **state-equivalent** if to each pure state of M there corresponds an equivalent pure state of N, and vice versa. A **reduced form** of M is a machine that is state-equivalent to M and has the minimum number of pure states for such equivalents. A machine is in **reduced form** if any two pure states are distinguishable. $\bigcirc$

The next two theorems tell us that N is a reduced form of M if and only if N is in reduced form (and hence justifies our terminology); but that, unlike deterministic machines, reduced forms for stochastic machines may *not* be unique.

THEOREM 7

Let M be an n-state machine with at least one pair of equivalent states. Then there exist $(n - 1)$-state machines which are state-equivalent to M. In particular, if s and r are equivalent states of M, let $N(y|x)$ be the matrix obtained from $M(y|x)$ by deleting row r and column r and replacing column s with the sum of columns s and r; then $N = N(y|x)$ is an $(n-1)$-state machine which is equivalent to M.

Proof

Exercise 6.   □

THEOREM 8

Let M be a machine having n states, and let $L = L_J(M)$ be the associated linear space (introduced in the proof of Lemma 5). Also, let H be an $n \times (\dim L)$ matrix whose columns form a basis for L, and let $N(y|x)$ be any set of $n \times n$ matrices with non-negative elements satisfying

$$N(y|x)H = M(y|x)H \tag{8}$$

Then $N = N(y|x)$ is an n-state machine which is state-equivalent to M; in fact, (N, q_i) is equivalent to (M, q_i) for $i = 1, 2, \ldots, n$. The converse is also true.

Proof

Recall that L is the space spanned by all vectors of the form $h^M(v|u)$, including e; and that the column space of H is L. Thus, for each u and v there exists a column vector $\eta(v|u)$ such that

$$h^M(v|u) = H\eta(v|u) \tag{9}$$

In particular, using $e = H\eta$, we have

$$N(y|x)e = N(y|x)H\eta = M(y|x)H\eta = M(y|x)e$$

Summing over y for fixed x,

$$N(x)e = \sum_{y \in Y} N(y|x)e = \sum_{y \in Y} M(y|x)e = M(x)e$$

and so $N(x)$ is Markov and thus $N(y|x)$ specifies a machine.

We may now prove that N behaves as desired by simple induction: Letting $h = H\eta$, we have for any x in X and y in Y that

$$\begin{aligned} h^N(y|x) = N(y|x)e &= N(y|x)H\eta \\ &= M(y|x)H\eta \quad \text{by (8)} \\ &= h^M(y|x) \end{aligned}$$

The general result then follows because, if we already know that

$h^N(v|u) = h^M(v|u)$, we may deduce that

$$
\begin{aligned}
h^N(yv|xu) &= N(y|x)h^N(v|u) \\
&= N(y|x)h^M(v|u) \quad \text{by induction hypothesis} \\
&= N(y|x)H\eta(v|u) \quad \text{by (9)} \\
&= M(y|x)H\eta(v|u) \quad \text{by (8)} \\
&= M(y|x)h^M(v|u) \quad \text{by (9)} \\
&= h^M(yv|xu) \qquad\quad \text{as desired}
\end{aligned}
$$

Conversely, if (N, q_i) is equivalent to (M, q_i), we have that

$$
h^M(yv|xu) = h^N(yv|xu)
$$

for all y, v, x, and u, so that

$$
N(y|x)L^M(v|u) = M(y|x)L^N(v|u)
$$

and

$$
N(y|x)h = M(y|x)h
$$

for any $h \in L$. Thus, it is certainly true that

$$
N(y|x)H = M(y|x)H
$$

for any H whose column space is (contained in) L. $\qquad\square$

With this, we conclude our formal study of probability theory. However, we shall see much more of automata and of error-correcting codes in the remainder of this book; and the reader may find it interesting to pursue, in the literature, the stochastic generalization of many of the problems and solutions that we discuss.

EXERCISES FOR SECTION 6-5

1. For the probability tree of Figure 6–25, calculate $P(q_1(2)|q_1(1))$, $P(q_1(2)|q_1(0))$, $P(q_1(2)|q_1(1) \cap q_1(0))$, and $P(q_1(1)|q_1(0))$.

2. Prove that the identity matrix

$$
I = [\delta_{ij}]_{n \times n}
$$

is stochastic for each n, where δ_{ij} is the Kronecker delta defined by

$$
\delta_{ij} = \begin{cases} 1 \text{ if } i = j \\ 0 \text{ otherwise} \end{cases}
$$

3. Is there a Markov matrix which could generate the probability trees of Figure 6–27(a), (b), (c), and (d)? If so, give p_i and p_{ij}.

4. Verify that $M(x)$ with elements $m_{ij}(x) = \sum_{y \in Y} P(q_j, y | q_i, x)$ is a Markov matrix.

5. Show that deterministic automata may be identified with stochastic automata, every entry of whose $M(x|y)$ and $M(x)$ matrices is either 0 or 1.

6. Prove Theorem 7.

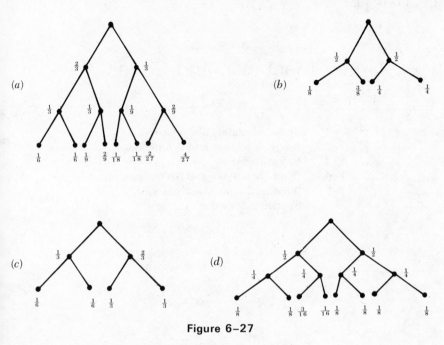

Figure 6-27

Further Reading for Chapter 6

There are a number of books that deal in part or entirely with information theory. For an introductory treatment see Raisbeck [1963] or Shannon and Weaver [1949], the latter containing Shannon's [1948] original papers. Beckmann [1967] has two chapters on information theory, while some of the more recent books on the subject are Abramson [1963], Ash [1965], Gallager [1968], Ingels [1971], Jelinek [1968], and Young [1971]. Further reading for Section 6-5 is provided by Paz [1971].

NORMAN ABRAMSON [1963], *Information Theory and Coding*, New York, McGraw-Hill.

ROBERT ASH [1965], *Information Theory*, New York, John Wiley and Sons.

PETR BECKMANN [1967], *Probability in Communication Engineering*, New York, Harcourt, Brace and World.

ROBERT G. GALLAGER [1968], *Information Theory and Reliable Communication*, New York, John Wiley and Sons.

R. V. L. HARTLEY [1928], "Transmission of Information," *Bell System Tech. J.*, Vol. 7, pp. 535-563, July.

FRANKLIN M. INGELS [1971], *Information and Coding Theory*, Scranton, Pa., Intext.

FREDERICK JELINEK [1968], *Probabilistic Information Theory*, New York, McGraw-Hill.

A. PAZ [1971], *Introduction to Probabilistic Automata*, New York, Academic Press.

GORDON RAISBECK [1963], *Information Theory*, Cambridge, Mass., MIT Press.

C. E. SHANNON [1948], "A Mathematical Theory of Communication," *Bell System Tech. J.*, Vol. 27, pp. 379-423 (Pt. I), July; pp. 623-656 (Pt. II), October.

C. E. SHANNON and WARREN WEAVER [1949], *The Mathematical Theory of Communication*, Urbana, Ill., Univ. Illinois Press.

JOHN F. YOUNG [1971], *Information Theory*, New York, John Wiley and Sons.

CHAPTER 7

Linear Machines and Codes

In this chapter, we introduce a number of key concepts of linear algebra and show their applications in coding theory and in linear machine theory, which latter subject is of interest in its own right to control theorists and is also important in its applications to coding theory. In Section 7–1, we introduce the key notions of rings, modules, fields, and matrices in such a way that the only prerequisite for the reader is a knowledge of the basic concepts of Sections 2–2 and 2–4. Then, in Section 7–2, which may be omitted without any damage by the reader more interested in applications, we show how the concepts of Section 7–1 may be placed in interesting theoretical perspective by using the notion of universal algebra introduced in Section 5–6. Following this preamble, we develop our remaining theory in the context of applications. In Section 7–3 we show how the ideas of field, module, and matrix may be brought together in introducing the class of codes which are called *group codes* (on the basis of their group properties in case the codes are binary). We shall return to related questions in coding theory in Chapter 8, but in Section 7–4 we bring together our current concepts with the automata theory ideas of Chapter 2 by introducing linear machines (together with a special case, shift registers, which will prove important in Chapter 8), and then devote Section 7–5 to adapting the theory of Section 2–5 on building automata with specified behavior to the case in which the automata are linear machines.

514

7–1 Rings, Modules and Matrices

In this section, we summarize the basic concepts of rings, modules, and matrices which are required in the study of coding theory and linear machine theory. The reader who is familiar with linear algebra will find it sufficient to skim this section quickly, to see how concepts he has seen for fields and vector spaces generalize easily to rings and modules. In the next section, we give a more sophisticated algebraic perspective on much of the material in this section; but Section 7–2 may be omitted by any reader more interested in applications.

Before proceeding further, readers should make sure that they are familiar with the concepts of *associativity* and *commutativity*, of *semigroup, monoid,* and *group,* and of *inverse* and *identity* from Section 2–2; and the properties of *equivalence relations* developed in Section 2–4 through Definition 3 and Example 6. All the concepts we now study may be considered as the result of imposing additional structure on abelian groups.

We may recall from Chapter 1 that **Z, Q,** and **R** shared (among others) the following properties:

(1) The binary operation $+$ is associative and commutative, and admits an identity and inverse.
(2) The binary operation $\cdot$ is associative.
(3) The operation $+$ distributes over $\cdot$ in that we have the distributive laws

$$r_1 \cdot (r_2 + r_3) = (r_1 \cdot r_2) + (r_1 \cdot r_3)$$

and

$$(r_2 + r_3) \cdot r_1 = (r_2 \cdot r_1) + (r_3 \cdot r_1)$$

Further, they share the property: (4) that $\cdot$ is commutative and admits an identity, while for **Q** and **R** we further have: (5) that $\cdot$ admits inverses. However, let us first concentrate on structures which share the properties (1), (2), (3) listed above:

DEFINITION 1

A **ring** is a triple $(R, +, \cdot)$ where R is the underlying set, and $+$ and $\cdot$ are binary operations on R, such that:

(i) $(R, +)$ is an abelian group (with identity 0, and inverse $r \mapsto -r$);
(ii) $(R, \cdot)$ is a semigroup;
(iii) $r_1 \cdot (r_2 + r_3) = (r_1 \cdot r_2) + (r_1 \cdot r_3)$
$(r_2 + r_3) \cdot r_1 = (r_2 \cdot r_1) + (r_3 \cdot r_1)$ for all $r_1, r_2, r_3 \in R$ ○

Note. From now on, we will assume that multiplication is performed before addition. Thus, in (iii) above, we can write $(r_i \cdot r_j) + (r_i \cdot r_k)$ as $r_i \cdot r_j + r_i \cdot r_k$.

We say that a ring is **unitary** if $\cdot$ admits an identity; we say it is **commutative** if $\cdot$ is abelian. Thus **Z, Q,** and **R** are all commutative, unitary rings, and for them condition (ii) in the definition of a ring can be strengthened to read "$(R, \cdot)$ is an abelian monoid." The same is true for $\mathbf{Z}_m$ (Exercise 1).

DEFINITION 2

We say that the ring $(R, +, \cdot)$ is a **field** if $(R \backslash \{0\}, \cdot)$ is an abelian group (with identity 1 and inverse $r \mapsto r^{-1}$, say). $\qquad\qquad\qquad\qquad\bigcirc$

Some authors do not demand that $(R \backslash \{0\}, \cdot)$ be abelian. However, we would (though the need will not arise in this book) refer to a ring for which $(R \backslash \{0\}, \cdot)$ was a (not necessarily abelian) group as a **skew field.**

It is clear, then, that **Q, R,** and **C** are fields, but that **Z** is not a field. In any case, it is obvious from the definition of a field that every ring property is a field property, but that there exist field properties which are not possessed by those rings which are not fields.

To make sure that the definition of a ring is clearly understood, let us check a few simple consequences of the definition, and then give some more exotic examples.

FACT 1

Let $(R, +, \cdot)$ be a ring. Then for all r_1, r_2 in R we have:

(a) $r_1 \cdot 0 = 0 = 0 \cdot r_1$

and

(b) $r_1 \cdot (-r_2) = -(r_1 \cdot r_2) = (-r_1) \cdot r_2$

Proof

(a)
$$
\begin{aligned}
0 &= -(r_1 \cdot 0) + (r_1 \cdot 0) \\
&= -(r_1 \cdot 0) + (r_1 \cdot (0 + 0)) \\
&= -(r_1 \cdot 0) + (r_1 \cdot 0 + r_1 \cdot 0) \\
&= (-(r_1 \cdot 0) + r_1 \cdot 0) + r_1 \cdot 0 \\
&= 0 + r_1 \cdot 0 \\
&= r_1 \cdot 0
\end{aligned}
$$

Similarly we can prove that $0 = 0 \cdot r_1$.

(b) $r_1 \cdot (-r_2) + r_1 \cdot r_2 = r_1 \cdot (-r_2 + r_2)$ by distributivity
$$= r_1 \cdot 0$$
$$= 0 \qquad \text{by (a)}$$

By the uniqueness of the inverse in the group $(R, +)$ we deduce that $r_1 \cdot (-r_2) = -(r_1 \cdot r_2)$. Similarly, $(-r_1) \cdot r_2 = -(r_1 \cdot r_2)$.   □

We now see that polynomials form a ring:

DEFINITION 3

By a formal **polynomial** in the single **indeterminate** x with **coefficients** in the ring R we shall mean an expression of the form

$$a_0 + a_1 x + \cdots + a_{n-1} x^{n-1} + a_n x^n \text{ (for some } n \geq 0) \tag{1}$$

(for $n = 0$ this reduces to the form a_0) where each coefficient $a_j \in R, 0 \leq j \leq n$. We denote by $R[x]$ the collection of all polynomials in x with coefficients in R.   ○

With each $f = a_0 + a_1 x + \cdots + a_n x^n$ in $R[x]$ we may associate a function $\widehat{f} : R \to R : r \mapsto f(r)$ by the obvious rule:

$$\widehat{f}(r) = \sum_{j=0}^{n} a_j \cdot r^j$$

Note that, whereas in expression (1) x was a symbol, here r is a ring element; so we can indeed, given r, compute r^j, multiply it by a_j, and then add up the $(n + 1)$ terms $a_j \cdot r^j$ so obtained. We shall not distinguish the polynomial

$$a_0 + \cdots + a_n x^n + 0x^{n+1} + \cdots + 0x^{n+k-1} + 0x^{n+k}$$

from the polynomial $a_0 + \cdots + a_n x^n$. This is indeed consistent with the assignment of a function $\widehat{f} : R \to R$ to each f.

Given two polynomials

$$f = a_0 + a_1 x + \cdots + a_{n-1} x^{n-1} + a_n x^n = \sum_{i=0}^{n} a_i x^i$$

and

$$g = b_0 + b_1 x + \cdots + b_{m-1} x^{m-1} + b_m x^m = \sum_{j=0}^{m} b_j x^j$$

we may define their sum by the rule

$$f + g = (a_0 + b_0) + (a_1 + b_1)x + \cdots + (a_{k-1} + b_{k-1})x^{k-1} + (a_k + b_k)x^k$$

where $k = \max(m, n)$ and, for example, if $m < n$ (so that $k = n$) we set $b_n = b_{n-1} = \cdots = b_{m+1} = 0$.

For example, in $\mathbf{Z}[x]$ we have

$$(1 + 15x + 2x^2 + 3x^3) + (7 + 2x)$$
$$= (1 + 7) + (15 + 2)x + (2 + 0)x^2 + (3 + 0)x^3$$
$$= 8 + 17x + 2x^2 + 3x^3$$

The above definition is motivated by the fact (verify!) that for ring elements r we do indeed have $\hat{f}(r) + \hat{g}(r) = (\widehat{f + g})(r)$.

Similarly, if we define multiplication by the rule

$$f \cdot g = \sum_{k=0}^{m+n} \left(\sum_{i+j=k} a_i \cdot b_j \right) x^k$$

we have that $\hat{f}(r) \cdot \hat{g}(r) = (\widehat{f \cdot g})(r)$ for all r in R. For example, $(1 + 15x + 2x^2 + 3x^3) \cdot (7 + 2x) = 7 + 107x + 44x^2 + 25x^3 + 6x^4$.

THEOREM 2

Given any ring R, then $(R[x], +, \cdot)$ is a ring.

Proof

(i) $(R[x], +)$ is an abelian group.
   (a) The reader may readily see that $+$ is associative and commutative using the fact that $(R, +)$ is itself an abelian group.
   (b) Using the fact that 0 is the identity for $(R, +)$, we see that the polynomial with one term, 0, is in fact the identity for $(R[x], +)$, since $\Sigma a_j x^j + 0 = \Sigma(a_j + 0)x^j = \Sigma a_j x^j$.
   (c) Since each a_j has inverse $-a_j$ in $(R, +)$, we see that the inverse of $\Sigma a_j x^j$ in $(R[x], +)$ is $\Sigma(-a_j)x_j$ because

$$\sum a_j x^j + \sum (-a_j)x^j = \sum [a_j + (-a_j)]x^j = \sum 0x^j = 0$$

Note that in the last equality we use our convention that we identify with each other two polynomials that only differ by the adjunction of terms with coefficient 0.

(ii) The operation $\cdot$ is associative, since

$$\left[\left(\sum a_i x^i\right) \cdot \left(\sum b_j x^j\right)\right] \cdot \left(\sum c_\ell x^\ell\right) = \left[\sum_{i+j=k}\left(\sum a_i \cdot b_j\right) x^k\right] \cdot \left(\sum c_\ell x^\ell\right)$$

$$= \sum\left[\sum_{k+\ell=p}\left(\sum_{i+j=k} a_i \cdot b_j\right) \cdot c_\ell\right] x^p$$

$$= \sum\left(\sum_{i+j+\ell=p} a_i \cdot b_j \cdot c_\ell\right) x^p$$

and, by symmetry, this clearly equals $(\Sigma a_i x^i) \cdot [(\Sigma b_j x^j) \cdot (\Sigma c_\ell x^\ell)]$.

(iii) The operation $\cdot$ is distributive over $+$. We prove the left case:

$$\left(\sum a_i x^i\right) \cdot \left[\sum b_j x^j + \sum c_\ell x^\ell\right]$$

$$= \left(\sum a_i x^i\right) \cdot \left[\sum (b_j + c_j) x^j\right]$$

$$= \sum\left(\sum_{i+j=k} a_i \cdot (b_j + c_j)\right) x^k$$

$$= \sum\left(\sum_{i+j=k} (a_i \cdot b_j + a_i \cdot c_j)\right) x^k \quad \text{by distributivity in } R$$

$$= \left(\sum a_i x^i\right) \cdot \left(\sum b_j x^j\right) + \left(\sum a_i x^i\right) \cdot \left(\sum c_\ell x^\ell\right) \qquad \square$$

Example 1

From Exercise 1 we have that $\mathbf{Z}_2 = \{0, 1\}$ is a ring for addition and multiplication given by the following tables:

+	0	1
0	0	1
1	1	0

$\cdot$	0	1
0	0	0
1	0	1

We may therefore refer to $\mathbf{Z}_2$ as the ring of integers modulo 2.

Suppose that in $\mathbf{Z}_2[x]$ we choose

$$f = 1 + x + x^4 + x^5$$

and

$$g = 1 + x^3 + x^4$$

Then we have that

$$f + g = x + x^3 + x^5$$

and

$$f \cdot g = 1 + x + x^3 + x^4 + x^7 + x^9 \qquad \diamond$$

Note that in $\mathbf{Z}_2[x]$ every polynomial is "monic", in the sense that we shall now define:

DEFINITION 4

Let f be the polynomial $a_0 + a_1 x + \cdots + a_n x^n$. Then the largest integer t, $0 \leq t \leq n$, such that $a_t \neq 0$ is called the **degree** of f and is written $\deg f$. We call $a_{\deg f}$ the **leading coefficient** of f, and say that f is **monic** if $a_{\deg f} = 1$. If $f = 0$, we define $\deg(0) = -\infty$. $\qquad \bigcirc$

Note that if R is not only a ring but also a field, then $R[x]$ is a unitary, commutative ring (having as the identity the polynomial with one term, 1), as the reader may easily check. However, if $1 \neq 0$, then $R[x]$ is not a field, for suppose that $a_n \neq 0$ and $b_m \neq 0$. Then the coefficient of x^{m+n} in

$$\left(\sum_{i=0}^{n} a_i x^i \right) \cdot \left(\sum_{j=0}^{m} b_j x^j \right) \text{ is } a_n \cdot b_m, \text{ and this cannot be 0 since}$$

$$a_n \cdot b_m = 0 \text{ and } b_m \neq 0 \Rightarrow (a_n \cdot b_m) \cdot b_m^{-1} = 0 \cdot b_m^{-1} = 0$$
$$\Rightarrow a_n \cdot (b_m \cdot b_m^{-1}) = a_n = 0$$

contrary to our assumption that $a_n \neq 0$ (i.e., fields do *not* have **nonzero divisors** of 0). Thus, if the degree of f is $n > 1$ and $g \neq 0$, we have that

$$\deg(f \cdot g) = \deg f + \deg g \geq \deg f$$

Hence, we can only have $f \cdot g = 1$ if $\deg f = 1$, in which case $f = a_0$ for some $a_0 \in R$, and f has the inverse $g = a_0^{-1}$.

We now introduce the crucial notions of subring, homomorphism, congruence, and quotient (or factor) ring.

DEFINITION 5

We say that a ring $(R_1, +_1, \cdot_1)$ is a **subring** of the ring $(R, +, \cdot)$ if R_1 is a subset of R, and if $+_1$ and $\cdot_1$ are simply the restrictions of $+$ and $\cdot$, respectively, to R_1. Further, if $(R_1, +_1, \cdot_1)$ is a field, we say that it is a **subfield** of $(R, +, \cdot)$.   ○

   Thus (leaving the usual $+$ and $\cdot$ implicit), we have that **R** and **Q** are subfields of **C,** but that **Z** is only a subring. Thus, a subring of a field need *not* be a subfield.

DEFINITION 6

Given any family $\{(R_\alpha, +_\alpha, \cdot_\alpha) | \alpha \in I\}$ of rings, we define their **product** to have underlying set

$$\prod_{\alpha \in I} R_\alpha = \left\{ f : I \to \bigcup_{\alpha \in I} R_\alpha \,\middle|\, f(\alpha) \in R_\alpha \right\}$$

with addition and multiplication given by

$$(f + f')(\alpha) = f(\alpha) +_\alpha f'(\alpha) \text{ for all } \alpha \text{ in } I$$
$$(f \cdot f')(\alpha) = f(\alpha) \cdot_\alpha f'(\alpha) \text{ for all } \alpha \text{ in } I$$

Their **coproduct** is the subring with underlying set

$$\bigoplus_{\alpha \in I} R_\alpha = \{ f \,|\, \{\alpha \,|\, f(\alpha) \neq 0\} \text{ is finite} \}$$ ○

   Thus, if I is finite, $\displaystyle\prod_{\alpha \in I} R_\alpha = \bigoplus_{\alpha \in I} R_\alpha$, but this is never true for infinite I.

The reader should verify (Exercise 4) that the product and coproduct are indeed rings.

Example 2

Let K_1 and K_2 be fields with $0 \neq 1$. Then $K_1 \times K_2$ is a unitary, commutative ring with zero (additive identity) element $(0, 0)$, unit (multiplicative identity) $(1, 1)$, and multiplication given by $(r_1, r_2) \cdot (r_3, r_4) = (r_1 \cdot r_3, r_2 \cdot r_4)$. [Note that, for example, in the element $(0, 0)$, the left 0 is the $0 \in K_1$, while the 0 on the right is the $0 \in K_2$.] But $K_1 \times K_2$ is *not* a field, because for any $s \neq 0$, the nonzero element $(s, 0)$ does not have an inverse; i.e., there is no solution to the equation $(s, 0) \cdot (r_1, r_2) = (1, 1)$ unless $0 = 1$ in K_2. $\Diamond$

DEFINITION 7

Let R_1 and R_2 be rings (which may or may not be fields). Then a map $h: R_1 \to R_2$ is a **ring homomorphism** if and only if

$$h(r_1 + r_2) = h(r_1) + h(r_2)$$
$$h(r_1 \cdot r_2) = h(r_1) \cdot h(r_2)$$

for all r_1 and r_2 in R_1. We say that h is an **isomorphism** (or, respectively, a **monomorphism** or **epimorphism**) iff it is a bijection (or, respectively, an injection or surjection). We say that R_1 and R_2 are **isomorphic** if there exists an isomorphism from R_1 to R_2. $\bigcirc$

Noting that

$$h(0) = h(0 + 0) = h(0) + h(0)$$

we deduce that in R_2

$$0 = [h(0) + h(0)] - h(0) = h(0)$$

so that h preserves 0. Then

$$h(r) + h(-r) = h(r + (-r)) = h(0) = 0$$

yields

$$h(-r) = -h(r)$$

since the additive inverse of $h(r)$ is unique.

Example 3

The map $\mathbf{Z} \to \mathbf{Z}_m : k \mapsto [k]_m$, which sends k into its remainder after dividing k by m, is a ring homomorphism. $\Diamond$

DEFINITION 8

An equivalence relation $\equiv$ on the ring R (which may or may not be a field) is a **congruence** iff $\equiv$ is compatible with both $+$ and $\cdot$, that is,

$$r_1 \equiv r_1' \text{ and } r_2 \equiv r_2' \Rightarrow r_1 + r_2 \equiv r_1' + r_2'$$
$$\text{and}$$
$$r_1 \cdot r_2 \equiv r_1' \cdot r_2' \qquad\qquad \bigcirc$$

Suppose that $\equiv$ is a congruence on the ring R, and consider the factor set $R/\equiv$. We already know that $R/\equiv$ is a group under the additive operation

$$[r_1] + [r_2] = [r_1 + r_2]$$

Since R is abelian, so is $R/\equiv$. Furthermore, if we define multiplication on $R/\equiv$ by

$$[r_1] \cdot [r_2] = [r_1 \cdot r_2],$$

it is easily verified that this operation is well-defined and that it follows that $R/\equiv$ is a ring. Such a ring is called a **factor ring** or a **quotient ring.**

Example 4

Let $(\mathbf{Z}, +, \cdot)$ be the ring of the integers under ordinary addition and multiplication. Then the equivalence relation

$$n_1 \sim_m n_2 \Leftrightarrow n_1 = n_2 + k \cdot m \text{ for some } k \in \mathbf{Z}$$

is compatible with both $\cdot$ and $+$, and we may thus define multiplication and addition on the factor set $\mathbf{Z}_m = \mathbf{Z}/\sim_m$ by:

$$[n_1]_m + [n_2]_m = [n_1 + n_2]_m$$
$$[n_1]_m \cdot [n_2]_m = [n_1 \cdot n_2]_m$$

Then $(\mathbf{Z}_m, +, \cdot)$ is the factor ring of $(\mathbf{Z}, +, \cdot)$ with respect to the ring congruence $\sim_m$. We call $\mathbf{Z}_m$ the **ring of integers modulo** m. $\Diamond$

A comparison between Examples 3 and 4 then suggests the intimate connection between homomorphisms and congruences, which is in fact confirmed in the next theorem.

THEOREM 3

Let R_1 and R_2 be rings, and let $h: R_1 \to R_2$ be any map. Let $\equiv_h$ be the equivalence relation on R_1 defined by

$$r_1 \equiv_h r_2 \Leftrightarrow h(r_1) = h(r_2)$$

Then h is a homomorphism iff $\equiv_h$ is a congruence; and in this case $h(R_1)$ is isomorphic to the quotient ring with underlying set $R_1/\equiv_h$, where addition and multiplication are defined by

$$[r_1]_h + [r_2]_h = [r_1 + r_2]_h$$
and
$$[r_1]_h \cdot [r_2]_h = [r_1 \cdot r_2]_h$$

The reader may either prove this as an exercise (Exercise 6) or note that it follows from general principles (see the proof of Theorem 7-2-2). In any case, the isomorphism is given by

$$h(R_1) \to R_1/\equiv_h : h(r) \mapsto [r]_h \qquad\qquad \square$$

Given a ring R, let $[0]$ be the equivalence class of 0 with respect to some congruence $\equiv$. Then for all a and b in $[0]$ we have (see Exercise 7)

$$[a + (-b)] = [a] + [-b] = [0] + [0] = [0]$$

so that $[0]$ is a *subgroup* of R. In other words, $[0]$ contains 0, and for every a and b in $[0]$, it also contains $a + b$ and $-a$.

Because $\equiv$ is a congruence not only with respect to $+$, but also with respect to $\cdot$, if $r_1 \equiv 0$, then for any r in R we must have that

$$r \cdot r_1 \equiv r \cdot 0 = 0$$
and
$$r_1 \cdot r \equiv 0 \cdot r = 0$$

Let H be any subset of R. We use the notation $r + H$ for the set

$$r + H = \{r + h \mid h \in H\}$$

and call $r + H$ a **coset** or a **residue class** of H. Then it is clear that

$$
\begin{aligned}
r' \in [r] &\Leftrightarrow r \equiv r' \Leftrightarrow r - r \equiv r' - r \\
&\Leftrightarrow r' - r \equiv 0 \\
&\Leftrightarrow r' - r \in [0] \\
&\Leftrightarrow r' \in r + [0]
\end{aligned}
$$

Thus, the congruence classes of $\equiv$ are precisely the cosets of $[0]$. We thus call the partitioning of R into these congruence classes the **coset decomposition** of R by $[0]$. Hence, we have proved that if $\equiv$ is a congruence on R, then $R/\equiv$ is given by the coset decomposition of R by H, where H is an *ideal* of $(R, +, \cdot)$ in the following sense:

DEFINITION 9

We say that a subset H of the underlying set R of a ring $(R, +, \cdot)$ is an **ideal** if

(a) H is a subgroup of $(R, +)$; and
(b) for any $h \in H$ and $r \in R$, both $h \cdot r$ and $r \cdot h$ belong to H; i.e., $(H \cdot R) \cup (R \cdot H) \subset H$, where we define the product of A and B by $A \cdot B = \{a \cdot b \mid a \in A \text{ and } b \in B\}$. $\bigcirc$

Example 5

Let $H = [0]_m$ be the equivalence class of 0 for the congruence $\sim_m$ on $(\mathbf{Z}, +, \cdot)$. Then H contains precisely those integers which are multiples of m.

Thus, $h_1, h_2 \in H$ implies $h_1 = k_1 \cdot m$ and $h_2 = k_2 \cdot m$ for some $k_1, k_2 \in \mathbf{Z}$; and then $-h_1 + h_2 = (-k_1 + k_2) \cdot m \in H$ (see Exercise 7), while for any $n \in \mathbf{Z}, h_1 \cdot n = n \cdot h_1 = (n \cdot k_1) \cdot m \in H$. Thus, H is indeed an ideal of $(\mathbf{Z}, +, \cdot)$. $\Diamond$

Example 6

Given a commutative ring $(R, +, \cdot)$, consider the polynomial ring $(R[x], +, \cdot)$ consisting of all polynomials having coefficients in R. Choose a fixed $f \in R[x]$. Define the set $\langle f \rangle$ to be

$$\langle f \rangle = \{g \in R[x] \mid g = f_1 \cdot f \text{ for } f_1 \in R[x]\}$$

i.e., $\langle f \rangle$ is the set of all polynomial multiples of f. Then $\langle f \rangle$ is an ideal of $(R[x], +, \cdot)$ (Exercise 8). $\Diamond$

The characterization of $[0]_m$ in Example 5 as all multiples of m shows it to be an example of a "principal" ideal, defined as follows:

DEFINITION 10

An ideal H of a ring R is said to be a **principal ideal** if there exists an element h such that

$$H = R^1 \cdot h \cdot R^1 \tag{2}$$

[Recall from Section 2–2 that $R^1 = R$ if R is a unitary ring; while $R^1 = R \cup \{1\}$ where $1 \notin R$ obeys $1 \cdot r = r = r \cdot 1$, if not. We then see that (2) is a convenient shorthand for $H = \{h\} \cup R \cdot h \cup h \cdot R \cup R \cdot h \cdot R$.] A ring in which every ideal is a principal ideal is called a **principal ideal ring**.

Clearly, if the ring R is unitary, then the polynomial 1 belongs to $R[x]$; and the ideal $\langle f \rangle$ of the commutative ring $(R[x], +, \cdot)$ is a principal ideal, called the principal ideal **generated** by f.   ○

We have seen that any congruence on a ring $(R, +, \cdot)$ corresponds to the coset decomposition of $(R, +)$ by a subgroup H of $(R, +)$ which is also an ideal. Let us see that the converse also holds.

THEOREM 4

Let $(R, +, \cdot)$ be a ring and let H be a subgroup of $(R, +)$. Then the equivalence relation $\equiv_H$ defined by

$$g_1 \equiv_H g_2 \Leftrightarrow g_1 + H = g_2 + H$$

is a ring congruence iff H is an ideal of R. In particular, if $h : R_1 \to R_2$ is a homomorphism with the kernel $\text{Ker } h = \{r \in R_1 \mid h(r) = 0\}$, we have that

$$h(R_1) \cong R_1 / \text{Ker } h$$

Proof

We have already verified the "only if" part, i.e., that $\equiv$ is a congruence only if it is $\equiv_H$ for some ideal H of R.

Conversely, suppose that H is an ideal of $(R, +)$. This ensures that $\equiv_H$ is a congruence for $+$, and so it only remains to show that $\equiv_H$ is a congruence for $\cdot$. But

$$g_1 \equiv_H g_1' \text{ and } g_2 \equiv_H g_2' \Rightarrow \text{there exist } h_1, h_2 \text{ in } H \text{ such that}$$
$$g_1 = g_1' + h_1 \text{ and } g_2 = g_2' + h_2$$
$$\Rightarrow g_1 \cdot g_2 = g_1' \cdot g_2' + (h_1 \cdot g_2' + h_1 \cdot h_2 + g_1' \cdot h_2)$$

Since H is an ideal, each term $h_1 \cdot g_2'$, $h_1 \cdot h_2$, and $g_1' \cdot h_2$ must be in H. Then, since H is a subgroup, their sum must be in H, and so $g_1 \cdot g_2 = g_1' \cdot g_2' + h$ for some $h \in H$. Thus $g_1 \cdot g_2 \equiv_H g_1' \cdot g_2'$ and so $\equiv_H$ is indeed a ring congruence.

The fact that $h(R) \cong R_1/\mathrm{Ker}\; h$ is then immediate from Theorem 7–1–3. $\square$

Example 7

Consider the ring $(\mathbf{Z}_2[x], +, \cdot)$ and the ideal $\langle f \rangle$, where $f = 1 + x^3$. Then, we have that

$$\langle f \rangle = \{0 \cdot f, 1 \cdot f, x \cdot f, (1 + x) \cdot f, x^2 \cdot f, (1 + x^2) \cdot f, \ldots\}$$
$$= \{0, 1 + x^3, x + x^4, 1 + x + x^3 + x^4, x^2 + x^5, 1 + x^2 + x^3 + x^5, \ldots\}$$

The residue class (coset) decomposition of $\mathbf{Z}_2[x]$ by $\langle f \rangle$ is thus:

$$\langle f \rangle = [0] = \{0, 1 + x^3, x + x^4, 1 + x + x^3 + x^4,$$
$$x^2 + x^5, 1 + x^2 + x^3 + x^5, \ldots\}$$

$$[1] = \{1, x^3, 1 + x + x^4, x + x^3 + x^4,$$
$$1 + x^2 + x^5, x^2 + x^3 + x^5, \ldots\}$$

$$[x] = \{x, 1 + x + x^3, x^4, 1 + x^3 + x^4,$$
$$x + x^2 + x^5, 1 + x + x^2 + x^3 + x^5, \ldots\}$$

$$[1 + x] = \{1 + x, x + x^3, 1 + x^4, x^3 + x^4,$$
$$1 + x + x^2 + x^5, x + x^2 + x^3 + x^5, \ldots\}$$

$$[x^2] = \{x^2, 1 + x^2 + x^3, x + x^2 + x^4,$$
$$1 + x + x^2 + x^3 + x^4, x^5, 1 + x^3 + x^5, \ldots\}$$

$$[1 + x^2] = \{1 + x^2, x^2 + x^3, 1 + x + x^2 + x^4,$$
$$x + x^2 + x^3 + x^4, 1 + x^5, x^3 + x^5, \ldots\}$$

$$[x + x^2] = \{x + x^2, 1 + x + x^2 + x^3, x^2 + x^4,$$
$$1 + x^2 + x^3 + x^4, x + x^5, 1 + x + x^3 + x^5, \ldots\}$$

$$[1 + x + x^2] = \{1 + x + x^2, x + x^2 + x^3, 1 + x^2 + x^4,$$
$$x^2 + x^3 + x^4, 1 + x + x^5, x + x^3 + x^5, \ldots\}$$

It can be verified (either by careful inspection of the above display, or by the general theory of Section 8–1) that the above residue classes comprise the factor ring $\mathbf{Z}_2[x]/\langle 1 + x^3 \rangle$, called the *ring of polynomials modulo* $1 + x^3$. In this ring we have, for example,

$$[1 + x] + [1 + x^2]$$
$$= [(1 + x) + (1 + x^2)] = [x + x^2]$$

and

$$[1 + x] \cdot [1 + x^2]$$
$$= [(1 + x) \cdot (1 + x^2)] = [1 + x^2 + x + x^3]$$
$$= [(1 + x^3) + (x + x^2)] = [1 + x^3] + [x + x^2] = [0] + [x + x^2]$$
$$= [x + x^2]$$

while

$$[1 + x^2] \cdot [x + x^2] = [(1 + x^2) \cdot (x + x^2)] = [x + x^2 + x^3 + x^4]$$
$$= [x + x^2 + x^3 + x \cdot x^3] = [(x + x \cdot x^3) + (x^2 + x^3)]$$
$$= [x \cdot (1 + x^3) + (x^2 + 1 + 1 + x^3)]$$
$$= [x \cdot (1 + x^3)] + [(1 + x^2) + (1 + x^3)]$$
$$= [x] \cdot [1 + x^3] + [1 + x^2] + [1 + x^3]$$
$$= [x] \cdot [0] + [1 + x^2] + [0]$$
$$= [1 + x^2]$$

Note that the cosets $[0]$, $[1 + x]$, $[x + x^2]$, and $[1 + x^2]$ comprise an ideal of $\mathbf{Z}_2[x]/\langle 1 + x^3 \rangle$. More will be said about this in Chapter 8.   ◊

We shall now see that congruences do not destroy "fieldness."

THEOREM 5

Let $\equiv$ be a ring congruence on the field $(K, +, \cdot)$. Then the quotient ring $(K/\equiv, +, \cdot)$ is also a field.

Proof

We need only show that $[1]$ is a multiplicative identity for $K/\equiv$ and that each $[r] \neq [0]$ has a multiplicative inverse.

We first note that $[1] \neq [0]$, or else the problem is trivial, since otherwise we would have $r = r \cdot 1 \equiv r \cdot 0 = 0$ for each $r \in K$.

But then $[1] \cdot [r] = [1 \cdot r] = [r] = [r \cdot 1] = [r] \cdot [1]$ for all $r \in K$; and if $[r] \neq [0]$, then $r \neq 0$ so that r^{-1} exists. Thus, we have $[r] \cdot [r^{-1}] = [r \cdot r^{-1}] = [1] = [r^{-1} \cdot r] = [r^{-1}] \cdot [r]$, so that $[r^{-1}]$ is an inverse for $[r]$; i.e., $[r^{-1}] = [r]^{-1}$.   □

In fact, ring congruences have the delightful property that they can sometimes (but not always) turn rings into fields, as the next example shows.

Example 8

We have already seen that for each integer $m \geq 2$, the equivalence relation $\sim_m$ turns the infinite ring $(\mathbf{Z}, +, \cdot)$ into a finite ring $(\mathbf{Z}_m, +, \cdot)$. Readers of Section 5–1 will have further seen that $(\mathbf{Z}_m\backslash\{0\}, \cdot\,\}$ was an abelian group for $m = 2, 3, 5, 7$ but not for $m = 4, 6, 8,$ or 9. For example, we have the two finite fields:

$(\mathbf{Z}_2, +, \cdot)$:

+	0	1
0	0	1
1	1	0

$\cdot$	1
1	1

$(\mathbf{Z}_3, +, \cdot)$:

+	0	1	2
0	0	1	2
1	1	2	0
2	2	0	1

$\cdot$	1	2
1	1	2
2	2	1

while $(\mathbf{Z}_4, +, \cdot)$ is not a field, since $2 \cdot 2 = 0$, so it has nonzero divisors of 0.

$\Diamond$

The above observation on $\mathbf{Z}_4$ quickly yields the following fact.

FACT 6

If $m \geq 2$ is not prime, then $(\mathbf{Z}_m, +, \cdot)$ is *not* a field.

Proof

Since m is not a prime, there exist integers $n_1, n_2 \in \mathbf{Z}$ such that $m > n_1, n_2 > 1$ and $n_1 \cdot n_2 = m$. But then

$$[n_1]_m \cdot [n_2]_m = [m]_m = [0]_m$$

while neither $[n_1]_m$ nor $[n_2]_m$ equals $[0]_m$. Hence, $(\mathbf{Z}_m, +, 0)$ has nonzero divisors of 0, and so cannot be a field. $\Box$

To obtain the complementary result we need the following property of the integers.

THEOREM 7 (EUCLIDEAN DIVISION ALGORITHM)

Let r_1 and r_2 be any two integers. Then there exist integers t_1 and t_2 such that

$$\text{g.c.d.}(r_1, r_2) = t_1 \cdot r_1 + t_2 \cdot r_2$$

where g.c.d.(r_1, r_2) is the **greatest common divisor** of r_1 and r_2, i.e., the largest integer which divides both r_1 and r_2.

Proof

We prove the theorem by actually presenting an algorithm known as the **Euclidean Division Algorithm** for finding t_1 and t_2. We proceed as follows:

Suppose, without loss of generality (why?), that $0 < r_2 \le r_1$. Divide r_2 into r_1 to get

$$r_1 = p_2 \cdot r_2 + r_3, \text{ where } 0 \le r_3 < r_2$$

If $r_3 = 0$, then $r_2 = $ g.c.d.(r_1, r_2); and we may take $t_1 = 0$, $t_2 = 1$ and stop. If $r_3 \ne 0$, then we may note that

$$\text{g.c.d.}(r_2, r_3) = \text{g.c.d.}(r_1, r_2)$$

since k divides $r_3 = r_1 - p_2 \cdot r_2$ and r_2 iff k divides r_1 and r_2. (Verify!)

Thus we have replaced the problem of finding g.c.d.(r_1, r_2) by the problem of finding g.c.d.(r_2, r_3). Repeating the process several times, we will find numbers $r_4, \ldots, r_k$ and $p_3, \ldots, p_{k-1}$ such that for each j (where $4 \le j \le k$) we have

$$r_j = r_{j-2} - (p_{j-1} \cdot r_{j-1}) \tag{3}$$

and

$$\text{g.c.d.}(r_{j-1}, r_j) = \text{g.c.d.}(r_1, r_2)$$

where $r_1 > r_2 > r_3 > r_4 > \cdots > r_k$; and we finally have (why?)

$$r_{k-1} = p_k \cdot r_k$$

so that $r_k = $ g.c.d.$(r_{k-1}, r_k) = $ g.c.d.(r_1, r_2). But then we may obtain t_1 and t_2 by reconstructing r_k from r_1 and r_2 by repeated use of the equations (3) for $j = k, k-1, \ldots, 3$. $\square$

Example 9

Let $r_1 = 11$, $r_2 = 7$.

$$\text{Then } r_1 = 1 \cdot r_2 + 4 \text{ so that } r_3 = 4 = r_1 - 1 \cdot r_2$$
$$\text{Then } r_2 = 1 \cdot r_3 + 3 \text{ so that } r_4 = 3 = r_2 - 1 \cdot r_3$$
$$\text{Then } r_3 = 1 \cdot r_4 + 1 \text{ so that } r_5 = 1 = r_3 - 1 \cdot r_4$$
$$\text{Then } r_4 = 3 \cdot r_5$$

Hence g.c.d.(11, 7) = r_5 = 1. We then obtain t_1 and t_2 by reconstruction as follows:

$$r_5 = r_3 - 1 \cdot r_4$$
$$= r_3 - (r_2 - 1 \cdot r_3)$$
$$= 2 \cdot r_3 - r_2$$
$$= 2 \cdot (r_1 - r_2) - r_2$$
$$= 2 \cdot r_1 - 3 \cdot r_2$$

Checking this, we find that $2 \cdot 11 - 3 \cdot 7 = 22 - 21 = 1$, as claimed.   ◊

With this lemma in hand, we can now give the desired characterization of $(\mathbf{Z}_m, +, \cdot)$. We can in fact strengthen our previous observations by the following:

THEOREM 8

If $m \geq 2$, then $(\mathbf{Z}_m, +, \cdot)$ is a field iff m is a prime number.

Proof

Given Fact 6, it only remains to show that a m being prime implies that $(\mathbf{Z}_m \backslash \{[0]\}, \cdot)$ is an abelian group. Now $(\mathbf{Z}_m \backslash \{[0]\}, \cdot)$ is clearly an abelian monoid, since $[1] \cdot [n] = [1 \cdot n] = [n]$ and $[n_1] \cdot [n_2] = [n_1 \cdot n_2] = [n_2 \cdot n_1] = [n_2] \cdot [n_1]$. Thus, we must show that to each $[r] \neq [0]$, where $0 \leq r < m$, there corresponds an $[s]$ such that $[r] \cdot [s] = [1]$, i.e., such that $r \cdot s = k \cdot m + 1$ for some k in $\mathbf{Z}$. But by Theorem 7, there exist integers t_1 and t_2 such that $t_1 \cdot r + t_2 \cdot m = $ g.c.d.$(r, m) = 1$. Hence,

$$r \cdot t_1 = -t_2 \cdot m + 1$$

and so
$$[r] \cdot [t_1] = [-t_2 \cdot m + 1] = [1]$$

so that $[t_1]$ is the desired multiplicative inverse of $[r]$.   □

DEFINITION 11

The field $(\mathbf{Z}_p, +, \cdot)$ for a prime p is called a **prime field** and is referred to as the **Galois field** with p elements, denoted $GF(p)$.   ○

We now turn to the study of modules over rings (these reduce to the more familiar notion of *vector spaces* when the rings are fields), with *matrices* representing "linear maps" from one module to another.

Let R be a ring, let n be a positive integer, and let R^n be the set of all n-tuples (vectors) having components from R. We shall use x to denote the vector $\begin{bmatrix} x_1 \\ x_2 \\ \vdots \\ x_n \end{bmatrix}$ in R^n. We may then define addition for R^n by the rule that the jth component of $x + x'$ is the sum of the jth components of x and x', i.e.,

$$(x + x')_j = x_j + x'_j$$

and we then see that R^n is an abelian group under $+$, with identity 0 where $0_j = 0 \in R$, and with x having inverse $-x$, where $(-x)_j = -x_j$ so that for each j

$$(x + (-x))_j = x_j + (-x_j) = 0 \in R$$

Further, we can define a function $R \times R^n \to R^n : (r, x) \mapsto rx$ by the rule:

$$(rx)_j = r \cdot x_j$$

We call R^n, when endowed with addition and this function $R \times R^n \to R^n$ of multiplication of a vector (an element of R^n) on the left by a scalar (an element of R), an *R-module*. If R is a *field*, then we call R^n so structured a *vector space over R*.

The reader should convince himself that this is consistent with the following general notion. [Henceforth, x_1 and x_2 will usually denote vectors, rather than components of vectors, save in the motivating example of R^n.]

DEFINITION 12

Let R be a unitary ring. Then a (left) **R-module** A is an abelian group $(A, +)$ together with a function

$$R \times A \to A : (r, x) \mapsto rx$$

called **multiplication by a scalar**, which satisfies the following axioms for all r_1, r_2 in R and all x_1, x_2 in A:

   I. $r_1(x_1 + x_2) = r_1 x_1 + r_1 x_2$
  II. $(r_1 + r_2)x_1 = r_1 x_1 + r_2 x_1$
 III. $(r_1 r_2)x_1 = r_1(r_2 x_1)$
 IV. $1x_1 = x_1$ (where 1 is the multiplicative identity of R)

If K is a field, then a (left) K-module is called a **vector space** over K.   ◯

As an exercise in working from the general definition, we offer the following:

FACT 9

Let A be an R-module with zero 0. Then

$$r0 = 0$$

for all r in R.

Proof

This proof should look familiar:

$$
\begin{aligned}
r0 &= r(0 + 0) && \text{since } 0 + 0 = 0 \\
&= r0 + r0 && \text{by Axiom I} \\
\therefore 0 &= r0 && \text{on adding } -(r0) \text{ to both sides.}
\end{aligned}
$$

□

DEFINITION 13

Let A_1 and A_2 be two R-modules. We say that a map $f:A_1 \to A_2$ is **linear** if, for every x_1, x_2 in A_1, and every r_1, r_2 in R, we have that

$$f(r_1 x_1 + r_2 x_2) = r_1 f(x_1) + r_2 f(x_2)$$

○

[The introduction of modules and linear maps here is very easy, but also very ad hoc. The justification of these definitions, and the observation that there exist modules of forms other than R^n for finite n, may be found in Section 7–2.]

Our task in the rest of this section is to see how matrices arise as the natural way to characterize linear maps of the form $R^n \to R^m$.

Let us use $e_i^{(n)}$ to denote the vector x in R^n for which x_j is 1 if $j = i$, but is otherwise 0. It is then clear that for all x in R^n we have that

$$x = x_1 e_1^{(n)} + x_2 e_2^{(n)} + \cdots + x_n e_n^{(n)}$$

Example 10

In $\mathbf{Z}^3$, $e_1^{(3)} = \begin{bmatrix} 1 \\ 0 \\ 0 \end{bmatrix}$, $e_2^{(3)} = \begin{bmatrix} 0 \\ 1 \\ 0 \end{bmatrix}$, and $e_3^{(3)} = \begin{bmatrix} 0 \\ 0 \\ 1 \end{bmatrix}$.   Then

$$\begin{bmatrix} 3 \\ 17 \\ -4 \end{bmatrix} = \begin{bmatrix} 3 \\ 0 \\ 0 \end{bmatrix} + \begin{bmatrix} 0 \\ 17 \\ 0 \end{bmatrix} + \begin{bmatrix} 0 \\ 0 \\ -4 \end{bmatrix} = 3e_1^{(3)} + 17e_2^{(3)} + (-4)e_3^{(3)}. \qquad \lozenge$$

Thus, if $f: R^n \to R^m$ is linear, we have that

$$f(x) = x_1 f(e_1^{(n)}) + x_2 f(e_2^{(n)}) + \cdots + x_n f(e_n^{(n)})$$

and so f is completely characterized by the n vectors in the array

$$[f(e_1^{(n)}) \quad f(e_2^{(n)}) \cdots f(e_n^{(n)})]$$

Since each vector $f(e_i^{(n)})$ has m elements, this array has m rows and n columns. We refer to any such array with entries from R as an $m \times n$ *matrix* (over R).

To avoid the introduction of a lot of linear algebra, we offer the following definition as a convenient summary.

DEFINITION 14

We say that an R-module A is **finite dimensional** iff there is a positive integer n (the **dimension** of A) and a linear map $h: R^n \to A$ which is a *bijection*.

For any linear bijection $h: R^n \to A$, we call the n vectors $e_1 = h\left(\begin{bmatrix} 1 \\ 0 \\ \vdots \\ 0 \end{bmatrix}\right)$,

$e_2 = h\left(\begin{bmatrix} 0 \\ 1 \\ \vdots \\ 0 \end{bmatrix}\right), \ldots, e_n = h\left(\begin{bmatrix} 0 \\ 0 \\ \vdots \\ 1 \end{bmatrix}\right)$ a **basis** for A. Since every vector $x \in A$ is

the image of a unique $\begin{bmatrix} x_1 \\ x_2 \\ \vdots \\ x_n \end{bmatrix}$ in R^n, and since linearity then tells us that

$$x = h\left(\begin{bmatrix} x_1 \\ x_2 \\ \vdots \\ x_n \end{bmatrix}\right) = x_1 e_1 + x_2 e_2 + \cdots + x_n e_n$$

we call $\begin{bmatrix} x_1 \\ x_2 \\ \vdots \\ x_n \end{bmatrix}$ the **vector of x with respect to the basis** $\{e_1, e_2, \ldots, e_n\}$.

If $f: A \to A'$ is any linear map, we then have

$$f(x) = f(x_1 e_1 + \cdots + x_n e_n) = x_1 f(e_1) + \cdots + x_n f(e_n).$$

Thus, A is completely determined by the display of n vectors

$$[f(e_1) \quad f(e_2) \cdots f(e_n)]$$

and we refer to this as the **matrix** of f with respect to the basis $\{e_1, e_2, \ldots, e_n\}$. (It is usual to represent the vectors $f(e_j)$ with respect to some basis for A'.)

○

The reader should convince himself that if $A = R^n$, $A' = R^m$, and we

take the "standard basis" $\begin{bmatrix} 1 \\ \vdots \\ 0 \end{bmatrix}, \ldots, \begin{bmatrix} 0 \\ \vdots \\ 1 \end{bmatrix}$ in each case, then the above defini-

tions of "vector" and "matrix" are consistent with those that preceded them.

Suppose that A is an $m \times n$ matrix. If $m = n$ we say that A is a **square matrix.** If $m = 1$, then A is called a **row matrix,** while if $n = 1$, then A is called a **column matrix.**

Example 11

Let $f: \mathbf{Z}^3 \to \mathbf{Z}^2$ be the linear map (verify the linearity) defined by

$$f\left(\begin{bmatrix} x_1 \\ x_2 \\ x_3 \end{bmatrix}\right) = \begin{bmatrix} 3x_1 + x_3 \\ 2x_2 - x_3 \end{bmatrix}$$

Then we have that $f(e_1^{(3)}) = \begin{bmatrix} 3 \\ 0 \end{bmatrix}$, $f(e_2^{(3)}) = \begin{bmatrix} 0 \\ 2 \end{bmatrix}$, and $f(e_3^{(3)}) = \begin{bmatrix} 1 \\ -1 \end{bmatrix}$;

so f yields the 2×3 matrix over $\mathbf{Z}$:

$$\begin{bmatrix} 3 & 0 & 1 \\ 0 & 2 & -1 \end{bmatrix} \qquad \qquad \Diamond$$

Conversely, let A be any $m \times n$ matrix with columns $a_1, a_2, \ldots a_n$ in R^m. Then the correspondence

$$x \mapsto x_1 a_1 + x_2 a_2 + \cdots + x_n a_n$$

defines a linear (check this) map from R^n to R^m. Thus, we shall henceforth identify a linear map $f: R^n \to R^m$ with the $m \times n$ matrix $[f(e_1^{(n)}) \ldots f(e_n^{(n)})]$.

Let, then, $A = [a_1 \ldots a_n]$ be the matrix representing the linear map f. Then we write Ax rather than $f(x)$, and from the rule

$$Ax = \sum_{j=1}^{n} x_j a_j$$

we deduce the component-by-component rule for multiplying a vector by a matrix, when we use a_{ij} to denote the ith entry in column j (the jth column is denoted by a_j):

$$\begin{bmatrix} a_{11} & a_{12} & \cdots & a_{1n} \\ a_{21} & a_{22} & \cdots & a_{2n} \\ \vdots & \vdots & & \vdots \\ a_{m1} & a_{m2} & \cdots & a_{mn} \end{bmatrix} \begin{bmatrix} x_1 \\ x_2 \\ \vdots \\ x_m \end{bmatrix} = \begin{bmatrix} \sum_j a_{1j} x_j \\ \sum_j a_{2j} x_j \\ \vdots \\ \sum_j a_{mj} x_j \end{bmatrix} \tag{4}$$

"To get the ith entry of the column Ax, multiply corresponding terms of the ith row of A and of x, and then sum the resulting terms."

Example 12

For the matrix $\begin{bmatrix} 3 & 0 & 1 \\ 0 & 2 & -1 \end{bmatrix}$ of the previous example, equation (4) yields

$$\begin{bmatrix} 3 & 0 & 1 \\ 0 & 2 & -1 \end{bmatrix} \begin{bmatrix} x_1 \\ x_2 \\ x_3 \end{bmatrix} = \begin{bmatrix} 3x_1 + 0x_2 + 1x_3 \\ 0x_1 + 2x_2 + (-1)x_3 \end{bmatrix} = \begin{bmatrix} 3x_1 + x_3 \\ 2x_2 - x_3 \end{bmatrix}$$

as indeed it should. ◊

Given two linear maps $B: M_1 \to M_2$ and $A: M_2 \to M_3$, we may compose them in the usual way to form $A \circ B: M_1 \to M_3 : x \mapsto A(B(x))$. Note that $A \circ B$ is also linear, since

$$\begin{aligned} (A \circ B)(r_1 x_1 + r_2 x_2) &= A(B(r_1 x_1 + r_2 x_2)) && \text{by definition} \\ &= A(r_1 B(x_1) + r_2 B(x_2)) && \text{by the linearity of } B \\ &= r_1 A \circ B(x_1) = r_2 A \circ B(x_2) && \text{by the linearity of } A \end{aligned}$$

Now suppose that we compose two matrices. We want to define the product $B \cdot A$ of two matrices A and B so that $B \cdot A$ is the matrix of the composite of their functions.

If $A:R^n \to R^m$ and $B:R^m \to R^p$, then $B \circ A:R^n \to R^p$ has for the jth column of its matrix

$$B(Ae_j^{(n)}) = Ba_j = B \begin{bmatrix} a_{1j} \\ a_{2j} \\ \vdots \\ a_{mj} \end{bmatrix} = \begin{bmatrix} \sum_{k=1}^{m} b_{1k}a_{kj} \\ \vdots \\ \sum_{k=1}^{m} b_{pk}a_{kj} \end{bmatrix}$$

so that $B \cdot A = [Ba_1 \, Ba_2 \ldots Ba_n]$.

In other words, we recapture the well-known formula for matrix multiplication. If A is $m \times n$ and B is $p \times m$, then the product $B \cdot A$ is the $p \times n$ matrix with ij-element

$$\sum_{k=1}^{m} b_{ik}a_{kj}$$

Example 13

If

$$A = \begin{bmatrix} 1 & 0 & 2 \\ -3 & 1 & -1 \\ \frac{1}{2} & -1 & 0 \\ 2 & 2 & 4 \end{bmatrix} \quad \text{and} \quad B = \begin{bmatrix} 1 & -1 \\ 0 & 2 \\ 3 & 2 \end{bmatrix}$$

then

$$A \cdot B = \begin{bmatrix} 1 \cdot 1 + 0 \cdot 0 + 2 \cdot 3 & 1 \cdot (-1) + 0 \cdot 2 + 2 \cdot 2 \\ (-3) \cdot 1 + 1 \cdot 0 + (-1) \cdot 3 & (-3) \cdot (-1) + 1 \cdot 2 + (-1) \cdot 2 \\ (\frac{1}{2}) \cdot 1 + (-1) \cdot 0 + 0 \cdot 3 & (\frac{1}{2}) \cdot (-1) + (-1) \cdot (2) + 0 \cdot 2 \\ 2 \cdot 1 + 2 \cdot 0 + 4 \cdot 3 & 2 \cdot (-1) + 2 \cdot 2 + 4 \cdot 2 \end{bmatrix}$$

$$= \begin{bmatrix} 7 & 3 \\ -6 & 3 \\ \frac{1}{2} & -\frac{5}{2} \\ 14 & 10 \end{bmatrix}$$

Note that A is 4×3, B is 3×2, and thus, $A \cdot B$ is 4×2.

If

$$A = \begin{bmatrix} 2 & 1 \\ 1 & 0 \end{bmatrix} \quad \text{and} \quad B = \begin{bmatrix} 1 & 2 \\ -1 & 3 \end{bmatrix}$$

then

$$A \cdot B = \begin{bmatrix} 2 \cdot 1 + 1 \cdot (-1) & 2 \cdot 2 + 1 \cdot 3 \\ 1 \cdot 1 + 0 \cdot (-1) & 1 \cdot 2 + 0 \cdot 3 \end{bmatrix} = \begin{bmatrix} 1 & 7 \\ 1 & 2 \end{bmatrix}$$

while

$$B \cdot A = \begin{bmatrix} 1 \cdot 2 + 2 \cdot 1 & 1 \cdot 1 + 2 \cdot 0 \\ (-1) \cdot 2 + 3 \cdot 1 & (-1) \cdot 1 + 3 \cdot 0 \end{bmatrix} = \begin{bmatrix} 4 & 1 \\ 1 & -1 \end{bmatrix}$$

Thus, we see that $A \cdot B \neq B \cdot A$ in general. As a matter of fact, in the first part of this example, $B \cdot A$ does not even exist. ◊

Given two linear maps $A : M_1 \to M_2$ and $B : M_1 \to M_2$, we define their sum by the formula $(A + B) : M_1 \to M_2 : x \mapsto A(x) + B(x)$. Then $A + B$ is again linear. (Check this!) If A and B are both $m \times n$ matrices, we define their sum $A + B$ to be the matrix whose ij-entry is $a_{ij} + b_{ij}$. Then we have that

$$(A + B)x = Ax + Bx$$

for all x in R^n, since

$$[(A + B)x]_i = \sum_{k=1}^{n} (a_{ik} + b_{ik})x_k$$

$$= \sum_{k=1}^{n} (a_{ik}x_k + b_{ik}x_k) \qquad \text{by distributivity in } R$$

$$= \sum_{k=1}^{n} a_{ik}x_k + \sum_{k=1}^{n} b_{ik}x_k \qquad \begin{array}{l} \text{by associativity and} \\ \text{commutativity of addition in } R \end{array}$$

$$= [Ax]_i + [Bx]_i \qquad \text{as was to be shown}$$

FACT 10

Let M_1 and M_2 be R-modules, and let A, B, and C all be linear maps from M_1 to M_2. Then

$$(A + B) + C = A + (B + C)$$

Proof

Let x be any element of M_1. Then

$$
\begin{aligned}
((A + B) + C)(x) &= (A + B)(x) + C(x) \\
&= (A(x) + B(x)) + C(x) \\
&= A(x) + (B(x) + C(x)) \quad \text{by associativity of } + \text{ in } M_2 \\
&= (A + (B + C))(x) \qquad\qquad\qquad\qquad\qquad\qquad \Box
\end{aligned}
$$

In particular, because of the associative law of addition of a ring R, we see that addition of matrices of the same size is also associative. Hence, we can write $A + B + C$ without fear of ambiguity. Similarly, we may conclude that matrix addition is commutative.

Now suppose that A, B, and C are $m \times n$, $n \times r$, and $r \times p$ matrices, respectively, over the ring R. We would like to know whether or not matrix multiplication is associative. The following more general considerations show that it is.

FACT 11

Let M_1, M_2, M_3 and M_4 be R-modules, and let $C : M_1 \to M_2$, $B : M_2 \to M_3$, and $A : M_3 \to M_4$ be linear maps. Then

$$A(BC) = (AB)C : M_1 \to M_4$$

[*Note:* We now simplify notation by leaving out the composition symbol.]

Proof

Trivially, $A(BC)(x) = A(B(C(x))) = (AB)C(x)$, since composition of functions is associative, whether or not they are linear. $\qquad \Box$

Example 13

Suppose that

$$
A = \begin{bmatrix} 1 & 0 & 3 \\ -2 & -1 & 1 \end{bmatrix}, \quad
B = \begin{bmatrix} 1 & 0 \\ 4 & 0 \\ -1 & 2 \end{bmatrix} \quad \text{and} \quad
C = \begin{bmatrix} 1 & 1 & -2 & 2 \\ 3 & -1 & 0 & 0 \end{bmatrix}
$$

Then

$$A \cdot (B \cdot C) = \begin{bmatrix} 1 & 0 & 3 \\ -2 & -1 & 1 \end{bmatrix} \cdot \left(\begin{bmatrix} 1 & 0 \\ 4 & 0 \\ -1 & 2 \end{bmatrix} \cdot \begin{bmatrix} 1 & 1 & -2 & 2 \\ 3 & -1 & 0 & 0 \end{bmatrix} \right)$$

$$= \begin{bmatrix} 1 & 0 & 3 \\ -2 & -1 & 1 \end{bmatrix} \cdot \begin{bmatrix} 1 & 1 & -2 & 2 \\ 4 & 4 & -8 & 8 \\ 5 & -3 & 2 & -2 \end{bmatrix} = \begin{bmatrix} 16 & -8 & 4 & -4 \\ -1 & -9 & 14 & -14 \end{bmatrix}$$

and

$$(A \cdot B) \cdot C = \left(\begin{bmatrix} 1 & 0 & 3 \\ -2 & -1 & 1 \end{bmatrix} \cdot \begin{bmatrix} 1 & 0 \\ 4 & 0 \\ -1 & 2 \end{bmatrix} \right) \cdot \begin{bmatrix} 1 & 1 & -2 & 2 \\ 3 & -1 & 0 & 0 \end{bmatrix}$$

$$= \begin{bmatrix} -2 & 6 \\ -7 & 2 \end{bmatrix} \cdot \begin{bmatrix} 1 & 1 & -2 & 2 \\ 3 & -1 & 0 & 0 \end{bmatrix} = \begin{bmatrix} 16 & -8 & 4 & -4 \\ -1 & -9 & 14 & -14 \end{bmatrix}$$

$$\Diamond$$

Since matrix multiplication is associative, it is not ambiguous to write $A \cdot B \cdot C$.

We have already mentioned that matrix multiplication is not necessarily commutative, that is, $A \cdot B \neq B \cdot A$ in general. Furthermore, $B \cdot A$ might not actually be defined. Even for the special case when A and B are square matrices, that is, $n \times n$ matrices, multiplication will not necessarily be commutative.

Finally, let us consider the distributive law. If $A = (a_{ij})$ is an $m \times n$ matrix, and $B = (b_{ij})$ and $C = (c_{ij})$ are $n \times r$ matrices, then we can form $A \cdot (B + C)$ as well as $A \cdot B + A \cdot C$. Now we would like to know whether or not the two quantities are equal. We have that

$$[A \cdot (B + C)]_{ij}$$

$$= \sum_{k=1}^{n} a_{ik}(b_{kj} + c_{kj}) \text{ for } i = 1, 2, \ldots, m \text{ and } j = 1, 2, \ldots, r$$

$$= \sum_{k=1}^{n} (a_{ik}b_{kj} + a_{ik}c_{kj}) \text{ by the distributive law for our ring}$$

$$= \sum_{k=1}^{n} a_{ik}b_{kj} + \sum_{k=1}^{n} a_{ik}c_{kj}$$

$$= [A \cdot B + A \cdot C]_{ij}$$

This is, as the reader should have realized, a special case of the following (Exercise 13):

FACT 12

Let $A:M_2 \to M_3$, $B:M_1 \to M_2$ and $C:M_1 \to M_2$ be linear maps. Then

$$(AB + AC) = A(B + C):M_1 \to M_3$$

Thus, the left distributive law holds for matrices of appropriate size. □

In summary, provided that the sizes of the matrices are such that the operations are defined, we have the following properties for matrices over a fixed ring R:

I. $(A + B) + C = A + (B + C)$ associative law of addition
II. $A + B = B + A$ commutative law of addition
III. $(A \cdot B) \cdot C = A \cdot (B \cdot C)$ associative law of multiplication
IV. $A \cdot (B + C) = A \cdot B + A \cdot C$ left distributive law
V. $(A + B) \cdot C = A \cdot C + B \cdot C$ right distributive law

The $n \times n$ **unit** or **identity matrix**, denoted by I_n, is the matrix $I_n = (\delta_{ij})$ given by the **Kronecker delta**

$$\delta_{ij} = \begin{cases} 1 & \text{if } i = j \\ 0 & \text{otherwise} \end{cases}$$

The entries on the **main diagonal** of the unit matrix are 1, while all of the off-diagonal elements are 0. The $m \times n$ **zero matrix**, denoted by $0_{m \times n}$, has *every* entry 0. We write 0_n for $0_{n \times n}$. We then have the following, which we leave to the reader to verify.

THEOREM 14

Let $R^{n \times n}$ be the set of all $n \times n$ matrices over a unitary ring R. Then $R^{n \times n}$ is a unitary ring with the addition and multiplication defined above, and with the matrix 0_n as zero and the matrix I_n as identity. □

Example 14

The 3×3 unit matrix for the real numbers is

$$I_3 = \begin{bmatrix} 1 & 0 & 0 \\ 0 & 1 & 0 \\ 0 & 0 & 1 \end{bmatrix}$$

From our discussion above, I_3 corresponds to a function $f: \mathbf{R}^3 \to \mathbf{R}^3$. It should be obvious that this function is $f = 1_{\mathbf{R}^3}$, the identity function on $\mathbf{R}^3$. ◊

The reader may also verify the following:

THEOREM 15

$R^{n \times n}$ is not only a unitary ring in its own right, but is also an R-module with $R \times R^{n \times n} \to R^{n \times n}: (r, A) \mapsto rA$ defined by $(rA)_{ij} = ra_{ij}$ [i.e., we may just think of $R^{n \times n}$ as R^{n^2} and think of a matrix as a vector of length n^2 rather than as a rectangular array]. □

Again, the reader should have suspected this to be a special case of a general result:

THEOREM 16

Let M be a fixed R-module. Then the set $L(M)$ of all linear maps $M \to M$ is an R-module with addition and multiplication defined above; with zero the map $x \mapsto 0$ and identity the map $x \mapsto x$; and with multiplication by a scalar defined by

$$rA : M \to M : x \mapsto r \cdot A(x) \qquad \qquad □$$

The **transpose** of a matrix A, denoted by A^t, is the matrix obtained from A by interchanging its rows and columns; i.e., if A is the $m \times n$ matrix

$$A = \begin{bmatrix} a_{11} & a_{12} & a_{13} & \cdots & a_{1n} \\ a_{21} & a_{22} & a_{23} & \cdots & a_{2n} \\ a_{31} & a_{32} & a_{33} & \cdots & a_{3n} \\ \vdots & \vdots & \vdots & & \vdots \\ a_{m1} & a_{m2} & a_{m3} & \cdots & a_{mn} \end{bmatrix}$$

then A^t is the $n \times m$ matrix

$$A^t = \begin{bmatrix} a_{11} & a_{21} & a_{31} & \cdots & a_{m1} \\ a_{12} & a_{22} & a_{32} & \cdots & a_{m2} \\ a_{13} & a_{23} & a_{33} & \cdots & a_{m3} \\ \vdots & \vdots & \vdots & & \vdots \\ a_{1n} & a_{2n} & a_{3n} & \cdots & a_{mn} \end{bmatrix}$$

EXAMPLE 15

For the matrix

$$P = \begin{bmatrix} 2 & 3 & 0 \\ 1 & 0 & -2 \\ -1 & 1 & 4 \\ 0 & 1 & 3 \end{bmatrix}$$

we have that

$$P^t = \begin{bmatrix} 2 & 1 & -1 & 0 \\ 3 & 0 & 1 & 1 \\ 0 & -2 & 4 & 3 \end{bmatrix} \qquad \Diamond$$

It is often convenient to **partition** a matrix into submatrices contained in the matrix. For example, the first four columns of the matrix

$$A = \begin{bmatrix} 1 & 0 & 0 & 0 & 2 & 4 \\ 0 & 1 & 0 & 0 & -1 & 3 \\ 0 & 0 & 1 & 0 & 1 & 0 \\ 0 & 0 & 0 & 1 & 0 & 1 \end{bmatrix}$$

form I_4. Thus, in this case we may write

$$A = [I_4 \mathrel{\vdots} B]$$

or more simply

$$A = [I_4 B]$$

where B is the 4×2 matrix

$$B = \begin{bmatrix} 2 & 4 \\ -1 & 3 \\ 1 & 0 \\ 0 & 1 \end{bmatrix}$$

Furthermore, we can express B as

$$B = \begin{bmatrix} C \\ I_2 \end{bmatrix}$$

where

$$C = \begin{bmatrix} 2 & 4 \\ -1 & 3 \end{bmatrix}$$

Thus, an alternative form of A is

$$A = \left[I_4 \ \begin{array}{c} C \\ \hline I_2 \end{array} \right]$$

From the definition of the transpose of a matrix, if

$$P = \left[\begin{array}{c|c} A & B \\ \hline C & D \end{array} \right]$$

then it should be perfectly clear that

$$P^t = \left[\begin{array}{c|c} A^t & C^t \\ \hline B^t & D^t \end{array} \right]$$

With these tools, we may proceed immediately to the study of group codes in Section 7–3, or to the study of linear machines in Section 7–4. However, the reader interested in a broader algebraic perspective on the material in this section may wish first to read Section 7–2.

EXERCISES FOR SECTION 7–1

1.   For any m, we define addition and multiplication on $\mathbf{Z}_m = \{0, 1, \ldots, m-1\}$ by the rule "Form $a + b$ (or $a \cdot b$) as for ordinary numbers, and then take the remainder after division by m." (See pp. 122–123.) Verify that $(\mathbf{Z}_m, +, \cdot)$ is a ring.

2.   **(a)**   Verify that $\mathbf{Z}_2$ (see Exercise 1) is a field if we define modulo 2 multiplication in the natural way: $[a_1] \cdot [a_2] = [a_1 \cdot a_2]$, where $a_1 \cdot a_2$ is the product of a_1 and a_2 using ordinary multiplication.

(b)   Verify that $\mathbf{Z}_3$ is a field if we define modulo 3 multiplication in the natural way.

(c)   Verify that $\mathbf{Z}_4$ is *not* a field if we define modulo 4 multiplication in the natural way.

3.   Prove that $\deg(f + g) \leq \max [\deg f, \deg g]$ while $\deg(f \cdot g) \leq \deg f + \deg g$, with equality holding except in the rare case that the leading coefficients have product 0.

4.   Verify that the product and coproduct defined in Definition 6 are indeed rings.

5.   **(a)**   Verify that addition and multiplication for the direct product ring $\mathbf{Z}_2 \times \mathbf{Z}_2$ are given by the following tables:

+	$(0,0)$	$(0,1)$	$(1,0)$	$(1,1)$
$(0,0)$	$(0,0)$	$(0,1)$	$(1,0)$	$(1,1)$
$(0,1)$	$(0,1)$	$(0,0)$	$(1,1)$	$(1,0)$
$(1,0)$	$(1,0)$	$(1,1)$	$(0,0)$	$(0,1)$
$(1,1)$	$(1,1)$	$(1,0)$	$(0,1)$	$(0,0)$

·	$(0,0)$	$(0,1)$	$(1,0)$	$(1,1)$
$(0,0)$	$(0,0)$	$(0,0)$	$(0,0)$	$(0,0)$
$(0,1)$	$(0,0)$	$(0,1)$	$(0,0)$	$(0,1)$
$(1,0)$	$(0,0)$	$(0,0)$	$(1,0)$	$(1,0)$
$(1,1)$	$(0,0)$	$(0,1)$	$(1,0)$	$(1,1)$

and, hence, that $\mathbf{Z}_2 \times \mathbf{Z}_2$ is not a field.

(b)   Verify that if multiplication is instead given by the table

·	$(0,0)$	$(0,1)$	$(1,0)$	$(1,1)$
$(0,0)$	$(0,0)$	$(0,0)$	$(0,0)$	$(0,0)$
$(0,1)$	$(0,0)$	$(1,1)$	$(0,1)$	$(1,0)$
$(1,0)$	$(0,0)$	$(0,1)$	$(1,0)$	$(1,1)$
$(1,1)$	$(0,0)$	$(1,0)$	$(1,1)$	$(0,1)$

then the result is a field.

6.   Prove Theorem 3.

7.   Let G be any group (abelian or nonabelian) with operation $\cdot$. We say that $H \subset G$ is a **subgroup** of G if 1 is in H, h^{-1} is in H for each h in H, and $h_1 \cdot h_2$ is in H for all h_1, h_2 in H. Prove that H is a subgroup of G iff $h_1 \cdot h_2^{-1}$ is in H for all h_1, h_2 in H.

8.   Prove that the $\langle f \rangle$ of Example 6 is an ideal.

9.   Prove that $R^1 \cdot h \cdot R^1$ is always an ideal, for any element h of any ring R.

10.   Determine the addition and multiplication tables for $\mathbf{Z}_2[x]/\langle 1 + x + x^2 \rangle$, that is, the ring of polynomials modulo $1 + x + x^2$. Is this ring a field? Represent the residue class $[a + bx]$ by the pair (a, b) and compare this ring with the four-element field given in Exercise 5.

11.   Find the greatest common divisor of $r_1 = 1651$ and $r_2 = 390$. Find t_1 and t_2 such that

$$\text{g.c.d.}(r_1, r_2) = t_1 \cdot r_1 + t_2 \cdot r_2$$

12.   Given that A_1 and A_2 are two R-modules, prove that $f : A_1 \to A_2$ is linear iff $f(rx_1 + x_2) = rf(x_1) + f(x_2)$ for all x_1, x_2 in A_1.

13.   Verify Fact 12.

14.   Suppose that A and B are $m \times n$ matrices, and C is an $n \times r$ matrix. Show that the right distributive law is obeyed; i.e., show that

$$(A + B) \cdot C = A \cdot C + B \cdot C$$

7-2   Rings, Modules and Ω-algebras

This section places the concepts of rings and modules in the broad context of Ω-algebras provided by Section 5-6. Though mathematically enlightening, this new perspective will not be used in the remainder of the book. Thus the applications-oriented reader, or the reader who has not yet studied Section 5–6, should omit this section and proceed directly to the applications in Sections 7–3 and 7–4.

We start by noting that our definition (7–1–1) of a ring may be rewritten in the language of Ω-algebras as follows:

DEFINITION 1

Let Ω_R be the label set $(+, \cdot, -, 0)$ with arities $\nu(+) = 2 = \nu(\cdot)$, $\nu(-) = 1$ and $\nu(0) = 0$. Let E_R be the set of equations of derived operators which yield:

(a) $(r_1 + r_2) + r_3 = r_1 + (r_2 + r_3)$
(b) $r_1 + r_2 = r_2 + r_1$
(c) $r_1 + 0 = r_1 = 0 + r_1$
(d) $r_1 + (-r_1) = 0 = (-r_1) + r_1$
(e) $(r_1 \cdot r_2) \cdot r_3 = r_1 \cdot (r_2 \cdot r_3)$
(f) $r_1 \cdot (r_2 + r_3) = r_1 \cdot r_2 + r_1 \cdot r_3$
(g) $(r_2 + r_3) \cdot r_1 = r_2 \cdot r_1 + r_3 \cdot r_1$

Then a **ring** is an (Ω_R, E_R)-algebra.   ○

The old definition is easier to read, but the new one allows us to use the terms *subring, ring homomorphism, ring congruence,* and *quotient ring* without further definition.

We also have immediately the notion of the direct product of rings: Given any family $\{R_\alpha | \alpha \in I\}$ of rings, we have to define $+$ and $\cdot$ on

$$\prod_{\alpha \in I} R_\alpha = \{f : I \to \bigcup_{\alpha \in I} R_\alpha | f(\alpha) \in R_\alpha\}$$

Note that to define a function $f_1 \circ f_2 : I \to \bigcup_{\alpha \in I} R_\alpha$ in $\prod_{\alpha \in I} R_\alpha$ we must specify an $(f_1 \circ f_2)(\alpha)$ in R_α for each $\alpha \in I$. We thus define $+$ and $\cdot$ by the rules:

$$(f_1 + f_2)(\alpha) = f_1(\alpha) + f_2(\alpha)$$
$$(f_1 \cdot f_2)(\alpha) = f_1(\alpha) \cdot f_2(\alpha)$$

where the operators on the left side are on $\prod_{\alpha \in I} R_\alpha$, while those on the right side are on R_α. The general theory of (Ω, E)-algebras then assures us that the $\left(\prod_{\alpha \in I} R_\alpha, +, \cdot\right)$ so defined is indeed a ring.

At this stage, we can quickly see that fields are *not* (Ω, E)-algebras for any set E of equations; for whereas the direct product of two (Ω, E)-algebras is again an (Ω, E)-algebra for the given (Ω, E), the direct product of fields is not a field (Example 7–1–2).

The point we are making is that an (Ω, E)-algebra (A, Ω_A) is required to satisfy an equation $f = f'$ for *all* $\nu(\omega)$-tuples from A. However, if i is the multiplicative inverse in a field K, the field is *not* required to satisfy the equations

$$r \cdot i(r) = 1 \qquad \text{and} \qquad i(r) \cdot r = 1$$

for *all* r in K, but only for *nonzero* r. One might hope that this simply showed that the obvious defining equation was inappropriate, and that the multiplicative inverse of nonzero elements could be characterized by some other, more subtle, set of equations; but the fact that the direct product of fields is *not* a field shows that such a hope is unfounded. Thus, in what follows we *cannot* use (Ω, E)-algebra concepts for fields without checking the range of their validity. Therefore, we shall, for example, call a map $L : K_1 \to K_2$ a (field) homomorphism from the field K_1 to the field K_2 if and only if it is a ring homomorphism. But first, let us clarify the nature of such a concept as ring homomorphism. As an exercise in the techniques used in Section 5–1 to simplify the criteria for homomorphisms and congruences of groups, the reader should verify the following:

FACT 1

Let R_1 and R_2 be rings. Then:
   (a) A map $h : R_1 \to R_2$ is a ring homomorphism (in the sense of a homorophism with respect to $(+, \cdot, -, 0)$) iff

$$h(r_1 + r_2) = h(r_1) + h(r_2)$$

and

$$h(r_1 \cdot r_2) = h(r_1) \cdot h(r_2)$$

for all r_1, r_2 in R_1 (where the operations on the left-hand sides of the equations are in R_1, and those on the right-hand sides are in R_2); i.e., iff h is a semigroup homomorphism both for $(R_1, +) \to (R_2, +)$ and for $(R_1, \cdot) \to (R_2, \cdot)$.
   (b) An equivalence relation $\equiv$ on R_1 is a ring congruence (in the sense of a congruence with respect to $(+, \cdot, -, 0)$) iff $[r_1 \equiv r_1'$ and $r_2 \equiv r_2'] \Rightarrow [r_1 + r_2 \equiv r_1' + r_2'$ and $r_1 \cdot r_2 \equiv r_1' \cdot r_2']$; i.e., iff $\equiv$ is a semigroup congruence both for $(R_1, +)$ and $(R_1, \cdot)$.   □

Our general theory then gives us the following result.

THEOREM 2

Let R_1 and R_2 be rings, and let $h: R_1 \to R_2$ be any map. Let $\equiv_h$ be the equivalence relation defined by

$$r_1 \equiv_h r_2 \Leftrightarrow h(r_1) = h(r_2)$$

Then h is a homomorphism iff $\equiv_h$ is a congruence on R_1; and in this case $h(R_1) \cong R_1/\equiv_h$; i.e., the image $h(R_1)$ is isomorphic to the quotient ring $R_1/\equiv_h$.   □

Let K_1 and K_2 be fields. On general Ω-algebra grounds, we might feel that, to deserve the title of field homomorphism, a ring homomorphism $h: K_1 \to K_2$ must satisfy two further properties:

(a) $h(1) = 1$
(b) $h(r^{-1}) = h(r)^{-1}$

Now, property (a) will always be satisfied unless $h(1) = 0$, because

$$h(1) = h(1 \cdot 1) = h(1) \cdot h(1)$$

since h is a ring homomorphism. But then if $h(1) \neq 0$, it has a multiplicative inverse, and so

$$1 = h(1) \cdot h(1)^{-1} = [h(1) \cdot h(1)] \cdot h(1)^{-1} = h(1)$$

by associativity. Note that if $h(1) = 0$, then for any $r \in K$ we have that $h(r) = h(1 \cdot r) = h(1) \cdot h(r) = 0 \cdot h(r) = 0$. Hence, condition (a) only rules out the trivial homomorphism which maps all of K_1 to $0 \in K_2$.

However, insistence on property (b) makes us pay too heavy a price, for it only makes sense if, whenever r^{-1} is defined, so too is $h(r)^{-1}$, i.e., if $r \neq 0$ implies $h(r) \neq 0$. But this means that h is an injection, for if $h(r_1) = h(r_2)$, then

$$\begin{aligned} h[r_1 + (-r_2)] &= h(r_1) + [-h(r_2)] \\ &= h(r_1) + [-h(r_1)] = 0 \end{aligned}$$

Thus, if $r \neq 0$ implies $h(r) \neq 0$, it follows that $r_1 + (-r_2) = 0$ and thus that $r_1 = r_2$.

But if the only homomorphisms we can consider are those which are injective, this means that the only congruence we may consider is that for which each element is the only member in its equivalence class, and that makes life very dull indeed. So, we resign ourselves to a bad situation and make the definition below, consistent with our usage in Section 7–1, conceding that our homomorphisms need not preserve multiplicative inverses.

DEFINITION 2

Let K_1 and K_2 be fields. Then $h: K_1 \to K_2$ is called a **(field) homomorphism** iff h is a ring homomorphism.   ○

By the same token, we define congruences on fields as follows:

DEFINITION 3

Let K be a field. Then an equivalence relation $\equiv$ on K is called a **(field) congruence** iff $\equiv$ is a ring congruence.   ○

However, our fears that such congruences could destroy "fieldness" turn out to be essentially unfounded, as the reader may see by consulting Theorem 7–1–5.

We hinted, in Section 5–4, that groups of the form $\mathbf{Z}_m^n$ (the direct product of n copies of the *group* $\mathbf{Z}_m$) were important in coding theory. The reader will recall† from his study of Euclidean geometry or linear algebra that vector spaces of the form $\mathbf{R}^n$ (the direct product of n copies of the *field* $\mathbf{R}$ of real numbers) played an important role there. This suggests the need for a careful study of (Ω, E)-algebras of the form A^n, where A is a given (Ω, E)-algebra; in view of the comments we have just made, we will treat K^n, where K is a field, as a ring whose extra properties are to be investigated.

It turns out to be no extra work to consider direct products of an arbitrary number (finite or infinite) of copies of A, and in fact it will simplify our notation to use the functional form

$$A^I = \{f \mid f: I \to A\}$$

and if we take $I = \{1, 2, \ldots, n\}$ we recapture A^n in the form

$$A^{\{1,2,\ldots,n\}} = \{f \mid f: \{1, 2, \ldots, n\} \to A\}$$

by identifying the function f with the n-vector (which it will now be convenient to write in column form)

$$\begin{bmatrix} f(1) \\ f(2) \\ \vdots \\ f(n) \end{bmatrix}$$

---

† If the reader does not so recall, he will still find the mathematical development depending only on material in this book, though somewhat less motivated.

Now each element $a \in A$ gives rise to the constant function

$$c_a : I \to A : \alpha \mapsto a$$

and it is clear that the map

$$c. : A \to A^I : a \mapsto c_a$$

is an injection of A into A^I.

This enables us to turn $A \cup A^I$ into an Ω-algebra, by defining Ω_B, for $B = A \cup A^I$, by the rule

$$(f_1, \ldots, f_n)\omega_B = (\widehat{f_1}, \ldots, \widehat{f_n})\omega_{A^I}$$

where for each $f \in B$, we set $\widehat{f} = f$ if $f \in A^I$, and set $\widehat{f} = c_f$ if $f \in A$.

That (A^I, Ω_{A^I}) is an (Ω, E)-algebra was established by our general theory of Section 5-6. But this immediately implies that (B, Ω_B) is an (Ω, E)-algebra, since if $\omega = \omega'$ is an equation in E, and $\nu(\omega) = \nu(\omega') = n$, then we have for all $(f_1, \ldots, f_n) \in B^n$ that

$$\begin{aligned}
(f_1, \ldots, f_n)\omega_B &= (\widehat{f_1}, \ldots, \widehat{f_n})\omega_{A^I} \quad \text{by definition of } \omega_B \\
&= (\widehat{f_1}, \ldots, \widehat{f_n})\omega'_{A^I} \quad \text{since } (A^I, \Omega_{A^I}) \text{ obeys } \omega = \omega' \\
&= (f_1, \ldots, f_n)\omega'_B
\end{aligned}$$

so that each equation in E is satisfied by (B, Ω_B) for $B = A \cup A^I$.

Example 1

Let $(G, \cdot)$ be a group, and let I be a set. Then G^I is a group with

$$\left.\begin{aligned}
\text{multiplication } (f_1 \cdot f_2)(\alpha) &= f_1(\alpha) \cdot f_2(\alpha) \\
\text{identity } c_1(\alpha) &= 1 \\
\text{inverse } f^{-1}(\alpha) &= f(\alpha)^{-1}
\end{aligned}\right\} \text{ for each } \alpha \in I$$

and multiplication is defined for combinations of elements from G and G^I:

$$\left.\begin{aligned}
(g \cdot f)(\alpha) &= g \cdot f(\alpha) \\
(f \cdot g)(\alpha) &= f(\alpha) \cdot g
\end{aligned}\right\} \text{ for each } g \in G, f \in G^I, \alpha \in I$$

and, in addition to the satisfaction of the group equations in G and G^I alone, we also have

$$(f_1 \cdot f_2) \cdot f_3 = f_1 \cdot (f_2 \cdot f_3) \quad \text{for all } f_1, f_2, \text{ and } f_3 \text{ in } G \cup G^I \qquad \Diamond$$

Example 2

If $(G, +)$ is an abelian group, we change multiplication to addition in the previous example, and add the laws for commutativity of addition.

For example, if $G = \mathbf{Z}_2$ and $I = \{1, 2, 3\}$, we represent elements of $G^I = \mathbf{Z}_2^3$ as triples of 0's and 1's, and have

$$000 + 1 = 111, \ 010 + 0 = 010, \text{ etc.}$$

and find that associativity and commutativity does indeed hold for "mixed samples" as in the cases

$$1 + 001 = 111 + 001 = 110 = 001 + 111 = 001 + 1$$

and

$$(1 + 010) + 0 = 101 + 000 = 101 = 111 + 010$$
$$= 1 + (010 + 000) = 1 + (010 + 0) \qquad \Diamond$$

Example 3

Let $(R, +, \cdot)$ be a ring, and let I be a set. Then R^I is a ring with

$$\left.\begin{array}{rl} \text{addition} & (f_1 + f_2)(\alpha) = f_1(\alpha) + f_2(\alpha) \\ \text{zero} & c_0(\alpha) = 0 \\ \text{negative} & (-f)(\alpha) = -f(\alpha) \\ \text{multiplication} & (f_1 \cdot f_2)(\alpha) = f_1(\alpha) \cdot f_2(\alpha) \end{array}\right\} \text{ for each } \alpha \in I$$

Addition and multiplication are defined for combinations of elements from R and R^I:

$$\left.\begin{array}{l} (r + f)(\alpha) = r + f(\alpha) \\ (f + r)(\alpha) = f(\alpha) + r \\ (r \cdot f)(\alpha) = r \cdot f(\alpha) \\ (f \cdot r)(\alpha) = f(\alpha) \cdot r \end{array}\right\} \text{ for all } f \in R^I, r \in R, \text{ and } \alpha \in I$$

and, in addition to the satisfaction of the ring equations in R and R^I alone, we also have

$$\left.\begin{array}{l} (f_1 + f_2) + f_3 = f_1 + (f_2 + f_3) \\ (f_1 \cdot f_2) \cdot f_3 = f_1 \cdot (f_2 \cdot f_3) \\ f_1 \cdot (f_2 + f_3) = f_1 \cdot f_2 + f_1 \cdot f_3 \\ (f_2 + f_3) \cdot f_1 = f_2 \cdot f_1 + f_3 \cdot f_1 \end{array}\right\} \text{ for all } f_1, f_2, f_3 \text{ in } R \cup R^I \qquad \Diamond$$

Example 4

If $(K, +, \cdot)$ is a field, then $(K, +, \cdot)$ is, in particular, a unitary commutative ring. Since the unitary commutative rings do form a class of (Ω, E)-algebras

(Why?), we conclude that, for each set I, K^I is a unitary commutative ring and satisfies all the properties of the last example, while further having an identity c_1 and satisfying the commutative laws for multiplication.

For example, consider

$$\mathbf{R}^3 = \left\{ \begin{bmatrix} x_1 \\ x_2 \\ x_3 \end{bmatrix} \middle| x_j \in \mathbf{R} \right\}$$

Then we have

$$\begin{bmatrix} x_1 \\ x_2 \\ x_3 \end{bmatrix} + \begin{bmatrix} x_1' \\ x_2' \\ x_3' \end{bmatrix} = \begin{bmatrix} x_1 + x_1' \\ x_2 + x_2' \\ x_3 + x_3' \end{bmatrix} = \begin{bmatrix} x_1' + x_1 \\ x_2' + x_2 \\ x_3' + x_3 \end{bmatrix} = \begin{bmatrix} x_1' \\ x_2' \\ x_3' \end{bmatrix} + \begin{bmatrix} x_1 \\ x_2 \\ x_3 \end{bmatrix}$$

and

$$1 \cdot \begin{bmatrix} x_1 \\ x_2 \\ x_3 \end{bmatrix} = \begin{bmatrix} 1 \cdot x_1 \\ 1 \cdot x_2 \\ 1 \cdot x_3 \end{bmatrix} = \begin{bmatrix} x_1 \\ x_2 \\ x_3 \end{bmatrix} \qquad \Diamond$$

It turns out that there exist interesting structured sets called Banach spaces and Hilbert spaces (see Padulo and Arbib [1973]) which share many properties with the R^I and K^I of the above examples, but do not share the property that we can add scalars and vectors. [For example, one Hilbert space comprises all functions $f: \mathbf{N} \to \mathbf{R}$ for which $\sum_{n=0}^{\infty} f(n)^2 < \infty$, and it is clear that c_r does not belong to this space for any nonzero r.] We thus present next the two definitions, which capture the properties of R^I and K^I that have proved most useful in applications. First, we repeat Definition 7–1–12 (p. 532):

DEFINITION 4

Let R be a unitary ring. Then a (left) **R-module** A is an additive abelian group together with a function

$$R \times A \to A : (r, a) \mapsto ra$$

which satisfies the following axioms for r_1, r_2, $1 \in R$ and a_1, $a_2 \in A$:

$$r_1(a_1 + a_2) = r_1 a_1 + r_1 a_2 \tag{1}$$

$$(r_1 + r_2)a_1 = r_1 a_1 + r_2 a_1 \tag{2}$$

$$(r_1 r_2)a_1 = r_1(r_2 a_1) \tag{3}$$

$$1a_1 = a_1 \tag{4}$$

$\bigcirc$

Clearly, for any unitary ring R and any set I, R^I is a left R-module: Since $(R^I, +, \cdot)$ is a ring, $(R^I, +)$ is certainly an additive abelian group; $R \times R^I \to R^I$ is given by our multiplication of scalars (elements of R) by vectors (elements of R^I), and then we recognize equations (1) and (2) as the two forms the distributive law takes when the scalar appears on the left of the product; (3) is the associative law for multiplication when the first two terms are scalars; while (4) expresses the fact that 1 is a (left) multiplicative identity. In particular, each R^n, for R a ring, is an R-module.

Intriguingly enough, for each ring R the class of R-modules (and thus, for each field K the class of vector spaces over K) may be represented as a class of (Ω, E)-algebras:

Given R, let $\Omega_R = \{+, 0, -\} \cup R$.

For a given left R-module A, $\{+_A, 0_A, -_A\}$ is then the set of operators which make A an abelian group, and these satisfy the equations E_1 which define abelian groups. For each $r \in R$, r_A is then the operator $a \mapsto ra$ on A. For each r_1, r_2 in R, we then have an equation in r and $+$ corresponding to (1), an equation in r_1, r_2, and $+$ corresponding to (2), an equation in r_1 and r_2 corresponding to (3) [the last is simply $(r_1 r_2) = r_1 \circ r_2$], plus the single equation $1 =$ identity for (4).

Thus, a ring (or vector space) homomorphism $f: A_1 \to A_2$ is simply a group homomorphism which respects all the operators in R:

$$f(ra) = rf(a) \text{ for all } r \text{ in } R, a \text{ in } A_1$$

We call such a map *linear*. We thus recapture Definition 7-1-13 in our general setting:

DEFINITION 5

Let A_1 and A_2 be R-modules. Then a map $f: A_1 \to A_2$ is **linear** iff

$$\left.\begin{matrix} f(a_1 + a_2) = f(a_1) + f(a_2) \\ f(ra_1) = rf(a_1) \end{matrix}\right\} \text{ for all } a_1, a_2 \text{ in } A \text{ and all } r \text{ in } R \qquad \bigcirc$$

FACT 3

The map $f: A_1 \to A_2$ is linear iff $f(r_1 a_1 + r_2 a_2) = r_1 f(a_1) + r_2 f(a_2)$ for all r_1, r_2 in R and all a_1, a_2 in A_1.

Proof

We first prove that the condition ensures that f is linear:

$$f(a_1 + a_2) = f(1a_1 + 1a_2) = 1f(a_1) + 1f(a_2) = f(a_1) + f(a_2)$$

and

$$f(ra_1) = f(ra_1 + 0) = f(ra_1 + r0) = rf(a_1) + rf(0)$$

But

$$f(0) = f(0 + 0) = f(0) + f(0)$$

and so $f(0)$ is 0 and thus $rf(0)$ is 0. Hence

$$f(ra_1) = rf(a_1)$$

Conversely, if f is linear then

$$f(r_1a_1 + r_2a_2) = f(r_1a_1) + f(r_2a_2) = r_1f(a_1) + r_2f(a_2) \qquad \Box$$

This completes our presentation of the Ω-algebra perspective on rings and modules.

7-3   GROUP CODES

Let R be any ring. We have seen in Section 7–1 that a map $f: R^n \to R^m$ is linear iff there exists an $m \times n$ matrix A such that $f(x) = Ax$ for all x in R^n. Since a ring R is an abelian group under addition, so are R^m and R^n. Further, a linear map $R^n \to R^m$ is then certainly a group homomorphism. In this section, we shall study block codes which may be specified by such group homomorphisms. In most of our applications, then, we shall take R to be the finite ring $\mathbf{Z}_m$ for some integer $m \geq 2$, and we will be particularly interested in binary codes, i.e., the case in which $R = \mathbf{Z}_2 = \{0, 1\}$.

In Section 5–4, we motivated the consideration of a subgroup of the group $\mathbf{Z}_m^n$ as a code (called a **group code of length** n) by an example[†] which we now rephrase in a form suitable for our current purposes.

Example 1

We wish to transmit binary digits through a system in which occasional errors occur, but in which the occurrence of more than one error in three successive digits is negligible. Let us encode 0 as 000 and 1 as 111, so that 000 and 111 are the code words of the code $\{000, 111\}$ defined by the map $h(0) = 000$ and $h(1) = 111$.

Given our assumption on error distribution, we note that 000 will be received as 000, 001, 010 or 100, while 111 will be received as 111, 110, 101

[†]We shall frequently denote $(a_1, a_2, \ldots, a_n)$ simply by $a_1 a_2 \ldots a_n$. Thus, we may write $(0, 1, 0) \in \mathbf{Z}_2^3$ simply as 010.

or 011. Since these elements comprise sets that are disjoint, we may define a **decoding map** $g:\mathbf{Z}_2^3 \rightarrow \mathbf{Z}_2$ by the rule:

$$g(000) = g(001) = g(010) = g(100) = 0$$
$$g(111) = g(110) = g(101) = g(011) = 1$$

Now our code $H = \{000, 111\}$ is a subgroup of $\mathbf{Z}_2^3$, and is thus the kernel of a map from $\mathbf{Z}_2^3$. In fact, we may explicitly take it to be the kernel of the linear map $f:\mathbf{Z}_2^3 \rightarrow \mathbf{Z}_2^2$ defined by

$$f(x_1 x_2 x_3) = \begin{bmatrix} 1 & 1 & 0 \\ 0 & 1 & 1 \end{bmatrix} \cdot \begin{bmatrix} x_1 \\ x_2 \\ x_3 \end{bmatrix}$$

for which

$$f^{-1}(00) = \{000, 111\} = 000 + H$$
$$f^{-1}(01) = \{001, 110\} = 001 + H$$
$$f^{-1}(10) = \{100, 011\} = 100 + H$$
$$f^{-1}(11) = \{010, 101\} = 010 + H$$

Notice that in each coset, the *error vector* is the word with the fewest 1's, namely 000 in $f^{-1}(00)$, 001 in $f^{-1}(01)$, 100 in $f^{-1}(10)$, and 010 in $f^{-1}(11)$; and that to retrieve the original code word we simply add the received vector to the error vector in its coset—so that $001 + 001 = 000$, $011 + 100 = 111$, etc.
$\Diamond$

This has suggested to coding theorists that we may turn the above process round: We *start* with a linear map $f:\mathbf{Z}_m^n \rightarrow \mathbf{Z}_m^p$, take its kernel, Ker f, to be our code, define the error vectors by choosing as leader of each coset a word with the fewest nonzero components, and then retrieve code words by subtracting from a received element of $\mathbf{Z}_m^n$ the *leader* (error vector) of its coset.

Rephrasing this in the language of matrices, if P is a $p \times n$ matrix having entries in $\mathbf{Z}_m$, then the kernel of the function $f:\mathbf{Z}_m^n \rightarrow \mathbf{Z}_m^p$ corresponding to P is an m-ary group code. We call P a **parity check matrix** for the code, and may refer to Ker f as a **parity check code**.

Example 2

We have already seen that $\{000, 111\}$ is the binary group code defined by the matrix $P = \begin{bmatrix} 1 & 1 & 0 \\ 0 & 1 & 1 \end{bmatrix}$.
$\Diamond$

Suppose that H is an m-ary group code of length n, i.e., $H \lhd \mathbf{Z}_m^n$. If we simplify our notation by representing the set $S = \{s_1, s_2, s_3, \ldots\}$ as $S = s_1 s_2 s_3 \ldots$, then enumerating all the cosets of H we obtain:

$$
\begin{array}{llll}
H = h_1 & h_2 & h_3 & \cdots \\
g_1 + H = g_1 + h_1 & g_1 + h_2 & g_1 + h_3 \cdots \\
g_2 + H = g_2 + h_1 & g_2 + h_2 & g_2 + h_3 \cdots \\
\quad \vdots \\
g_r + H = g_r + h_1 & g_r + h_2 & g_r + h_3 \cdots
\end{array}
$$

It is often convenient to select h_1 to be the identity element. Under this circumstance, the left-most elements in the cosets ($h_1 = 0^n$, $g_1 + h_1 = g_1$, $g_2 + h_1 = g_2, \ldots, g_r + h_1 = g_r$) are called **coset leaders** and the resulting table is referred to as a **standard array**.

Example 3

For $H = \{0000, 1001, 0110, 1111\} \lhd \mathbf{Z}_2^4$, we may form the following standard array:

$$
\begin{array}{llll}
H = 0000 & 1001 & 0110 & 1111 \\
0001 + H = 0001 & 1000 & 0111 & 1110 \\
0010 + H = 0010 & 1011 & 0100 & 1101 \\
1100 + H = 1100 & 0101 & 1010 & 0011
\end{array}
$$

which we may use as a decoding table. $\lozenge$

As we have already suggested, if a standard array is to be used for decoding purposes, it should be so formed that each coset leader is an element containing the maximum number of zeros with respect to all the elements in the coset. If two or more elements in the same coset contain the maximum number of zeros, we arbitrarily select one as the coset leader. A standard array formed in this manner and used as a decoding table is an example of what is usually referred to as a *maximum-likelihood decoder*.[†] In the last example, when a binary symmetric channel is assumed, using the standard array as a decoding table yields maximum-likelihood decoding.

Suppose that some m-ary n-tuple x is received and we are going to use a standard array as a decoding table. If x appears in the $(i + 1)$st row and jth column of the array, then we assume that the code word h_j has been transmitted. More importantly, however, from the definition of a standard array, we can write

$$x = g_i + h_j$$

[†] It is assumed that the code words are equally likely to be selected.

where g_i is the coset leader of the coset comprising the ith row. From this equation we have

$$h_j = -g_i + x$$

Thus, given x, we need only determine the leader of the coset that contains x in order to calculate h_j, the assumed transmitted code word. Hence, we have eliminated the need for an entire decoding table, as we can use only the coset leaders. However, for a given x, we must somehow determine the leader of $x + H$. We now proceed to describe such a technique.

Let our parity check matrix P be $p \times n$. Then two elements x_1 and x_2 are in the same coset of the code H determined by P iff $Px_1 = Px_2$. [Why?] Thus, for each element x in $\mathbf{Z}_m^n$, let us refer to Px (the image of x under P) as the **syndrome** of x. We thus have that two m-ary n-tuples are in the same coset if and only if they have the same syndrome.

To decode, we list each coset leader along with its syndrome. Upon the reception of an m-ary n-tuple x, we form its syndrome Px, and search for the coset leader, say g_i, with the same syndrome. We then decode x as $h = -g_i + x$.

Decoding in this manner, we are required to consider only the coset leaders and their syndromes rather than an entire standard array. However, even under this circumstance, it is not unreasonable to have on the order of $2^{50} \approx 1{,}126{,}000{,}000{,}000{,}000$ coset leaders and an equal number of syndromes. (Can you imagine the size of the entire standard array?) A list of this magnitude is unworkable. Thus, let us not think about it any more. Instead, let's consider the following strategy:

For each received n-tuple x, we calculate its syndrome. To (maximum-likelihood) decode x, we try to determine an n-tuple g_i having the same syndrome as x and such that no other n-tuple with the same syndrome contains more zeros than g_i. We choose g_i as the coset leader and decode x as $h = -g_i + x$.

Unfortunately, in general, there is no simple way of finding such coset leaders. Thus, in practical terms, the problem of maximum-likelihood decoding an arbitrary group code remains unsolved.

Let us now turn our attention to determining the parity check matrix for certain group codes. We will demonstrate that such a matrix exists by showing how to construct it.

First we begin by restating our definition of a subgroup that is generated by a set, in terms of group codes.

DEFINITION 1

Suppose that J is a subset of $\mathbf{Z}_m^n$. Then the subgroup $\langle J \rangle$ given by

$$\langle J \rangle = \{ h_1 + h_2 + \cdots + h_r | r \in \mathbf{Z}_+ \text{ and either} \\ h_i \in J \text{ or } -h_i \in J \text{ for } i = 1, 2, 3, \ldots, r \}$$

is called the subgroup **generated** by J, and we say that J is a **set of generators** for $\langle J \rangle$. ○

Clearly, any group code $H \lhd \mathbf{Z}_m^n$ is a set of generators for itself, since $\langle H \rangle = H$. However, we will be interested in a smallest set of generators. Thus, let us define the following:

DEFINITION 2

Suppose that H is a group code and that the smallest set of generators of H contains k elements. Then we say that the code has **dimension** k. ○

Example 4

The binary group codes

$$H_1 = \{000, 011, 101, 110\}$$

and
$$H_2 = \{00000, 10111, 01101, 11010\}$$

each have dimension $k = 2$, since in each case any two nonzero code words will generate the code. ◊

Now let us consider a *binary* group code H having dimension k, so that there exists a set of generators, say $J = \{g_1, g_2, \ldots, g_k\}$, and no subset of this generates H. In a binary group code, each element is its own inverse. Thus, any $g \in H$ can be written as a sum of elements in J. With sufficient applications of the associative and commutative laws, if an element $g_i (i = 1, 2, \ldots, k)$ appears in a sum an odd number of times, the net result is that g_i appears only once. Similarly, if g_i appears an even number of times, the net effect is the complete elimination of g_i from the sum. We now ask how many distinct sums can be formed from elements of J. Since g_1 may or may not be in a sum, and g_2 may or may not be, etc., there are 2^k possible sums. We would like to know whether or not these sums yield distinct code words. For this, assume that two distinct sums result in the same code word, i.e., suppose that

$$g_{i_1} + g_{i_2} + \cdots + g_{i_r} = g_{j_1} + g_{j_2} + \cdots + g_{j_s}$$

where $g_{i_1}, g_{i_2}, \ldots, g_{i_r}, g_{j_1}, g_{j_2}, \ldots, g_{j_s} \in J$, and at least one term, say g_{j_s}, occurs on only one side of the equation. But then

$$(g_{j_{s-1}} + \cdots + g_{j_2} + g_{j_1}) + (g_{i_1} + g_{i_2} + \cdots + g_{i_r}) = g_{j_s}$$

so that g_{j_s} can be expressed as a sum of elements of J, contradicting our assumption that J is a minimum set of generators of H. This contradiction indicates that two distinct sums of elements of J result in different code words. Therefore, we have just proved the following theorem.

THEOREM 1

If H is a binary group code of dimension k, then $|H| = 2^k$.   □

As a result of the previous discussion, we can establish the number of cosets, and hence syndromes, for an m-ary group code when m is prime:

If m is prime and H is an m-ary code of dimension k and length n, then $|H| = m^k$ (Exercise 5). Thus, there are m^k columns in a standard array. Clearly, the number of rows in the array is $|\mathbf{Z}_m^n/H|$. Since the number of entries in a standard array must be $|\mathbf{Z}_m^n| = m^n$, we have that

$$|\mathbf{Z}_m^n/H| \cdot m^k = m^n$$

or

$$|\mathbf{Z}_m^n/H| = m^{n-k}$$

Hence, there are m^{n-k} cosets for an m-ary group code of length n and dimension k.

At this point, let us assume that a parity check matrix P has a specific form. Under such an assumption we will see that it is a simple matter to obtain a set of generators for the corresponding group code. We will shortly see that for all binary and many m-ary group codes the restriction placed upon P is of no particular consequence. Thus, let us suppose that $n > p$, and P is an m-ary $p \times n$ parity check matrix of the form $P = [BI_p]$, where I_p is the $p \times p$ unit matrix. Then, corresponding to P is a function $f: \mathbf{Z}_m^n \to \mathbf{Z}_m^p$. Note that under this circumstance, f is a surjection, since any syndrome $(a_1, a_2, \ldots, a_p)$ is the image of the n-tuple $(0, 0, \ldots, 0, a_1, a_2, \ldots, a_p)$ under f.

Suppose that m is still prime, and that the m-ary parity check code corresponding to P has dimension k, that is, $|\mathrm{Ker}\ f| = m^k$. Since $|\mathbf{Z}_m^n| = m^n$, $|\mathbf{Z}_m^p| = m^p$, and $\mathbf{Z}_m^n/\mathrm{Ker}\ f \cong \mathbf{Z}_m^p$, we have that

$$|\mathbf{Z}_m^n/\mathrm{Ker}\ f| = |\mathbf{Z}_m^p|$$

or

$$m^{n-k} = m^p$$

from which we get

$$n - k = p$$

Thus, the dimension of the group code $H = \mathrm{Ker}\ f$ is $k = n - p$.

We will now show how to easily obtain a set of generators for such a code. We first define the following:

DEFINITION 3

Suppose that the k code words which form a smallest generating set for an m-ary group code of dimension k are the rows of a matrix G. Then G is said to be a **generator matrix** for the code. ◯

Suppose that the $p \times n$ parity check matrix P is of the form $P = [BI_p]$. Consider the $k \times n$ matrix G of the form $G = [I_k A]$, where I_k is the $k \times k$ unit matrix and $k = n - p$. We will now demonstrate that if m is prime we can choose A such that G is a generator matrix for the parity check code corresponding to P.

We begin by taking the matrix product

$$P \cdot G^T = [BI_p] \cdot \begin{bmatrix} I_k \\ A^T \end{bmatrix}$$

$$= B + A^T$$

where we have used the fact that A is $k \times p$ and B is $p \times k$ to block multiply the partitioned matrices. Thus, for the case $A = -B^T$, we have that

$$P \cdot G^T = 0_{p \times k}$$

Under this circumstance, we note that each row of G (which is a column of G^T) is in Ker f. Consequently, the rows of G generate a subgroup $H' < \text{Ker} f$. We also note that the rows of G are a minimum set of generators for H'. This result is due to the fact that the ith row of G has a 1 in the ith position, and no other row of G has this property. Thus, the ith row of G is not in the closure of the other rows of G. Therefore, the subgroup H' has dimension k. Since $|H'| = |\text{Ker} f| = m^k$ and $H' < \text{Ker} f$, this implies $H' = \text{Ker} f$. Hence, the matrix $G = [I_k, -B^T]$ is a generator matrix for the parity check code Ker f. Note that the general equation $A = -B^T$ reduces to $A = B^T$ for the binary case.

We mentioned above that the assumption that a parity check matrix be in the form $P = [BI_p]$ was not a significant restriction. The following example presents one reason for making such a statement.

Example 5

Let us consider the parity check matrix

$$P = \begin{array}{c} \begin{array}{ccccccc} 1 & 2 & 3 & 4 & 5 & 6 & 7 \end{array} \\ \begin{bmatrix} 0 & 0 & 0 & 1 & 1 & 1 & 1 \\ 0 & 1 & 1 & 0 & 0 & 1 & 1 \\ 1 & 0 & 1 & 0 & 1 & 0 & 1 \end{bmatrix} \end{array}$$

Let us now determine the kernel $f^{-1}(000)$ of this f. To do this, we can apply the map to each of the $2^7 = 128$ elements of $\mathbf{Z}_2^7$ and note which ones are mapped into 000. Clearly, $0000000 \in \text{Ker} f$. It can be verified exhaustively that the remainder of the kernel of f consists of the following 15 binary septuples:

$$
\begin{array}{lll}
1110000 & 1011010 & 0010110 \\
1001100 & 0011001 & 1010101 \\
0101010 & 1100110 & 0001111 \\
1101001 & 0100101 & 0110011 \\
0111100 & 1000011 & 1111111
\end{array}
$$

Thus, the corresponding length 7 parity check code has $2^k = 16$ code words, and hence, has dimension $k = 4$. Although this matrix does not have the form $P = [BI_3]$, by permuting the columns of P we may form the matrix P_π given by:

$$
P_\pi = \begin{array}{c}
\begin{array}{ccccccc} 3 & 5 & 6 & 7 & 4 & 2 & 1 \end{array} \\
\left[\begin{array}{ccccccc}
0 & 1 & 1 & 1 & 1 & 0 & 0 \\
1 & 0 & 1 & 1 & 0 & 1 & 0 \\
1 & 1 & 0 & 1 & 0 & 0 & 1
\end{array}\right]
\end{array}
$$

The kernel of f_π is equivalent to the kernel of f, in the sense that each code word in $\text{Ker} f_\pi$ can be obtained from a code word in $\text{Ker} f$ by permuting the positions as was done for the parity check matrix. For example, since

$$
\begin{array}{ccccccc}
1 & 2 & 3 & 4 & 5 & 6 & 7 \\
1 & 0 & 0 & 1 & 1 & 0 & 0
\end{array}
$$

is in $\text{Ker} f$, then

$$
\begin{array}{ccccccc}
3 & 5 & 6 & 7 & 4 & 2 & 1 \\
0 & 1 & 0 & 0 & 1 & 0 & 1
\end{array}
$$

is in $\text{Ker} f_\pi$. Since P and P_π are $p \times n = 3 \times 7$ matrices, and since their corresponding parity check codes are isomorphic, the dimension of each code is $k = n - p = 4$, as mentioned above.

Since P_π is in the form $P_\pi = [BI_3]$, where

$$
B = \begin{bmatrix}
0 & 1 & 1 & 1 \\
1 & 0 & 1 & 1 \\
1 & 1 & 0 & 1
\end{bmatrix}
$$

we can easily find a generator matrix G_π for Ker f_π. The matrix is:

$$
G_\pi = [I_4 B^T] =
\begin{array}{c}
\begin{array}{ccccccc} 3 & 5 & 6 & 7 & 4 & 2 & 1 \end{array} \\
\left[\begin{array}{ccccccc}
1 & 0 & 0 & 0 & 0 & 1 & 1 \\
0 & 1 & 0 & 0 & 1 & 0 & 1 \\
0 & 0 & 1 & 0 & 1 & 1 & 0 \\
0 & 0 & 0 & 1 & 1 & 1 & 1
\end{array}\right]
\end{array}
$$

From this matrix it is a trivial matter to form a generator matrix G for Ker f. By permuting the columns of G_π, we obtain:

$$
G =
\begin{array}{c}
\begin{array}{ccccccc} 1 & 2 & 3 & 4 & 5 & 6 & 7 \end{array} \\
\left[\begin{array}{ccccccc}
1 & 1 & 1 & 0 & 0 & 0 & 0 \\
1 & 0 & 0 & 1 & 1 & 0 & 0 \\
0 & 1 & 0 & 1 & 0 & 1 & 0 \\
1 & 1 & 0 & 1 & 0 & 0 & 1
\end{array}\right]
\end{array}
\qquad \Diamond
$$

When a generator matrix has the form $G = [I_k A]$, we say that the matrix is in **reduced echelon form.** The codes generated by these matrices are given special names.

DEFINITION 4

If a group code has a generator matrix of the form $G = [I_k A]$, then the code is called a **systematic code.** $\bigcirc$

We note in Example 5 that the binary group code Ker f_π is a systematic code. We will now see that such codes can be "encoded" rather easily.

Suppose that a discrete source produces information in binary form. Let's assume that the output of the source at any time is any one of the 2^k possible binary k-tuples. Since information in this form does not possess error-correcting capability, we may want to transmit this information with the use of an (error-correcting) group code. In order to do this, we must associate a code word with each one of the k-tuples. For the case when an error-correcting code is a systematic group code, this encoding process can be realized relatively easily. Let $a = (a_1, a_2, \ldots, a_k)$ be an arbitrary binary k-tuple. Then if the generator matrix of a code is in reduced echelon form, i.e., $G = [I_k B^T]$, the matrix product $a \cdot G = g$ is given by

$$
\begin{aligned}
g = a \cdot G &= (a_1, a_2, \ldots, a_k) \cdot [I_k B^T] \\
&= (a_1, a_2, \ldots, a_k, b_1, b_2, \ldots, b_p)
\end{aligned}
$$

where the value of $b_i(i = 1, 2, \ldots, p)$ depends on the matrix B^T. Since g is a sum of elements in a generating set of a binary group code, g is a code word. Note also that the first k bits of g form the binary representation of the information which is to be transmitted. Consequently, the first k bits of a systematic code word are called the **information bits**. The remaining bits, which are a function of the matrix B^T that is established by the parity check matrix $P = [BI_p]$, are known as **parity check bits**. Thus, for each binary k-tuple we can determine a unique code word. Hence, the encoding process for a systematic group code can be accomplished by matrix multiplication. Clearly, we can extend this discussion to include the case of m-ary systematic group codes.

We mentioned earlier that the job of decoding is, in general, rather distasteful. However, for certain codes, decoding can be a fairly simple chore. One such class of codes is composed of the binary *Hamming*† *codes*. An example of a Hamming code is the previously considered simple code corresponding to the parity check matrix

$$P = \begin{bmatrix} 0 & 1 & 1 \\ 1 & 0 & 1 \end{bmatrix}$$

The key property of this matrix is that the binary pair constituting the ith column is the binary representation of the number i. Clearly, if no errors occur in a code word, a syndrome of 00 will result. However, if a single error occurs, say in the jth position, since the function $f: \mathbf{Z}_2^3 \to \mathbf{Z}_2^2$ corresponding to P is a homomorphism, the resulting syndrome will be the binary representation of the number j. For example, suppose that the code word $111 \in$ Ker f is altered by an error in the second position so that the triple 101 results. Since we can write

$$101 = 111 + 010$$

we have that

$$\begin{aligned} f(101) &= f(111 + 010) \\ &= f(111) + f(010) \\ &= 00 + f(010) \\ &= f(010) \\ &= 10 \end{aligned}$$

which is the binary representation of the number 2, and this indicates that the second digit of the triple is incorrect.

More generally, if the jth digit of a code word g is in error, we can write

---

†Named for the American engineer Richard W. Hamming.

the resulting triple g_r as

$$g_r = g + e_j^{(3)}$$

where $e_j^{(3)}$ is the triple whose jth digit is 1 and whose remaining digits are 0. We then have that

$$
\begin{aligned}
f(g_r) &= f(g + e_j^{(3)}) \\
&= f(g) + f(e_j^{(3)}) \\
&= 00 + f(e_j^{(3)}) \\
&= f(e_j^{(3)})
\end{aligned}
$$

and because of matrix multiplication, $f(e_j^{(3)})$ is the binary representation of the number j.

As a consequence of this property, we can use, as a decoding rule, the following: If a binary triple has a syndrome of 00, we assume that triple is the correct code word. If the syndrome of a triple g_r is the binary representation of the number j, then we assume that the jth digit of g_r is in error and we choose g as our code word, where $g = g_r + e_j^{(3)}$. Clearly, if no more than one error occurs in any code word, the syndrome will indicate which digit was in error, and correct decoding will ensue. This, however, will not be the case if more than one error occurs. We, therefore, say that such a code is a single-error-correcting code.

In general, we define a **binary Hamming code** to be the parity check code established by a $p \times n$ parity check matrix whose ith column is the binary representation of the number i. In the above example, we have a case in which $n = 2^p - 1$. For the case that $n < 2^p - 1$, the codes are referred to as "shortened" Hamming codes.

From our previous discussion, it should be clear that every binary Hamming code is a single-error-correcting code. To further convince the reader that this is so, let us reconsider the Hamming code corresponding to the parity check matrix

$$
P = \begin{bmatrix}
0 & 0 & 0 & 1 & 1 & 1 & 1 \\
0 & 1 & 1 & 0 & 0 & 1 & 1 \\
1 & 0 & 1 & 0 & 1 & 0 & 1
\end{bmatrix}
$$

In Example 5 we enumerated all of the 16 words in this code. Inspection of these code words reveals that any two words differ in at least three positions. For example, the words

$$1\ 1\ 1\ 0\ 0\ 0\ 0$$

and

$$1 \quad 0 \quad 0 \quad 1 \quad 1 \quad 0 \quad 0$$

differ in four positions, the second, third, fourth, and fifth; while

$$1 \quad 1 \quad 1 \quad 0 \quad 0 \quad 0 \quad 0$$

and

$$1 \quad 1 \quad 0 \quad 1 \quad 0 \quad 0 \quad 1$$

differ in three positions, the third, fourth, and seventh. Consequently, if a single error occurs in any code word, the resulting septuple will differ in only one position from the original code word, while it will differ in at least two positions from any other code word.

We therefore see that the words of the code are sufficiently "far apart" that a single error to a code word will produce a septuple that is "closer" to that code word than any other. More formally, we have the following:

DEFINITION 5

The number of positions in which two n-tuples differ is called the **Hamming distance** between them. The number of nonzero components of an n-tuple is called its **Hamming weight.** ○

In the Hamming code given above, the distance between any two code words is three or greater. Thus, we say that this code has **minimum distance** $d = 3$.

If we decode a septuple as the code word to which it is closest, then clearly, the Hamming code given above is capable of correcting all possible single error patterns. (*Note:* The reader should convince himself that for a binary symmetric channel with $0 < q < \frac{1}{2}$ decoding an n-tuple as its closest code word is actually maximum-likelihood decoding.)

In general, if we decode an n-tuple as the code word to which it is closest, then a group code having minimum distance $d = 2t + 1$ is capable of correcting all error patterns of weight t or less. We call such a code a t-**error-correcting code.**

Suppose that $x = x_1 x_2 x_3 \ldots x_n$ and $y = y_1 y_2 y_3 \ldots y_n$ are words of an m-ary group code. Clearly then, $-y = (-y_1)(-y_2)(-y_3) \ldots (-y_n)$ is a code word, as is $x + (-y) = x - y = (x_1 - y_1)(x_2 - y_2)(x_3 - y_3) \ldots (x_n - y_n)$. Thus, the ith component of $x - y$ is 0 if and only if $x_i = y_i$. We can therefore conclude that the distance between two code words, x and y, is the weight of the code word $x - y$. For this reason, the minimum distance of a code (the distance between the two closest distinct code words) is equal to the minimum weight of the nonzero code words of the code. Consequently, the terms "minimum distance" and "minimum weight" of a code are often used interchangeably.

In Example 5, we considered a length $n = 7$ binary group code of dimension $k = 4$ and minimum distance $d = 3$. This was an example of an $(n, k, d) = (7, 4, 3)$ binary group code. In general, a (non-shortened) binary Hamming code is a $(2^p - 1, 2^p - 1 - p, 3)$ binary group code. The fact that $n = 2^p - 1$ is a consequence of the fact that the parity check matrix P is a $p \times n$ matrix, and there are $2^p - 1$ nonzero p-tuples which constitute the columns of P. Furthermore, we have already seen that if P is such a $p \times n$ matrix, then $k = n - p = 2^p - 1 - p$. Finally, all of the columns of P are distinct. Thus, no nonzero code word can have weight two or less. This implies that $d \geq 3$. However, since the first three columns of P sum to zero, there exists a code word having weight 3 (namely $11100\ldots0$), and the code therefore has a minimum weight of $d = 3$.

EXERCISES FOR SECTION 7-3

1. **(a)** Find the binary group code defined by the parity check matrix

$$P = \begin{bmatrix} 0 & 1 & 1 & 0 \\ 1 & 0 & 1 & 1 \end{bmatrix}$$

(b) Repeat part (a) for the matrix

$$P = \begin{bmatrix} 1 & 0 & 1 & 0 \\ 1 & 1 & 0 & 0 \end{bmatrix}$$

2. Construct a standard array for the following binary group code:

$$H = \{00000, 10111, 01101, 11010\} \lhd \mathbf{Z}_2^5.$$

3. Construct a maximum-likelihood decoding table for the binary group code given in Exercise 2.

4. Determine the dimension of the length 6 binary group code $H = \{000000, 111000, 100110, 010101, 011110, 110011, 101101, 001011\}$ by finding a smallest generating set.

5. Show that if m is a prime number Theorem 1 can be generalized to the m-ary case; i.e., if, for prime m, H is an m-ary group code of dimension k, then $|H| = m^k$.

6. The parity check matrix for a binary group code is given by

$$P = \begin{bmatrix} 1 & 1 & 1 & 0 & 0 \\ 1 & 0 & 0 & 1 & 0 \\ 1 & 1 & 0 & 0 & 1 \end{bmatrix}$$

Find a generator matrix for this code.

7. A binary parity check code has the following generator matrix:

$$G = \begin{bmatrix} 0 & 0 & 1 & 1 & 1 & 1 & 0 & 0 & 0 \\ 0 & 1 & 0 & 1 & 1 & 0 & 1 & 0 & 0 \\ 1 & 1 & 0 & 1 & 0 & 0 & 0 & 1 & 0 \\ 1 & 1 & 1 & 0 & 0 & 0 & 0 & 0 & 1 \end{bmatrix}$$

Find a parity check matrix for this group code.

8.   **(a)**   Find a generator matrix for an $(n, k, d) = (15, 11, 3)$ binary systematic group code.

   (b)   Find a generator matrix for a length 15 binary Hamming code.

   (c)   Find a generator matrix for a length 12 binary "shortened" Hamming code.

7-4   Linear Machines and Shift Registers.

Although this section will appear better motivated to a reader who has carefully studied Chapter 2, it is so written as to be fully accessible to the reader who has not, and who wishes to use the present section purely as background for the further coding theory presented in Chapter 8.

DEFINITION 1

A **linear machine** (over the unitary ring R) is a sextuple

$$M = (Q, X, Y, F, G, H)$$

where Q, X, and Y are R-modules, called the spaces of **states, inputs,** and **outputs,** respectively; and where $F:Q \to Q$, $G:X \to Q$ and $H:Q \to Y$ are all linear maps.   ○

For the sake of notational convenience in what follows, we will write, for example, $Hq = y$ rather than $H(q) = y$. We shall think of M as operating on a discrete-time scale ($t = 0, 1, 2, 3, \ldots$) in such a way that if at time t its state is $q(t)$ in Q and its input is $x(t)$ in X, then its output at time t is

$$y(t) = Hq(t) \tag{1}$$

while at time $t + 1$, its state will have changed to

$$q(t + 1) = Fq(t) + Gx(t) \tag{2}$$

We may readily extend these formulas to obtain the effect of arbitrary input sequences:

LEMMA 1

Let the linear machine M be in state $q(t)$ at time t, and receive the sequence of inputs $x(t), x(t + 1), \ldots, x(t + n - 1)$ at times $t, t + 1, \ldots, t + n - 1$, respectively. Then at time $t + n$, its state will be

$$q(t + n) = F^n q(t) + \sum_{k=0}^{n-1} F^{n-1-k} Gx(t + k) \tag{3}$$

(where F^0 is the identity map, by definition) while its output will be

$$y(t + n) = HF^n q(t) + \sum_{k=0}^{n-1} HF^{n-1-k} Gx(t + k) \tag{4}$$

Proof

Since (3) reduces to (2) in case $n = 1$, it is certainly true for $n = 1$. We now prove it for all n by induction. Supposing that (3) holds for n, we verify it for $n + 1$:

$q(t + n + 1)$

$$= Fq(t + n) + Gx(t + n) \qquad \text{by equation (2)}$$

$$= F[F^n q(t) + \sum_{k=0}^{n-1} F^{n-1-k} Gx(t + k)] + Gx(t + n) \qquad \text{by the induction hypothesis}$$

$$= F^{n+1} q(t) + \sum_{k=0}^{n-1} F^{n-k} Gx(t + k) + Gx(t + n) \qquad \text{since } F \text{ is linear}$$

$$= F^{n+1} q(t) + \sum_{k=0}^{n} F^{n-1-k} Gx(t + k) \qquad \text{since } F^0 \text{ is the identity map}$$

which is just the form of equation (3) for $n + 1$. Of course, (4) follows immediately from (3), since

$$y(t + n) = Hq(t + n)$$

and H is linear.   □

Let us now see how to build M from a simple set of components in case Q, X, and Y are all finite-dimensional and equal R^n, R^m, and R^p, respectively. (The reader familiar with Chapter 2 may find it of interest to compare the constructions of Section 2–3. Prudence dictates that what we called "modules" in Section 2–3 be called devices here!)

We introduce the three devices shown in Figure 7–1. Each input line and each output line carries a signal from the ring R. Each **adder** and each **scaler** are delayless: if the inputs to an n-input adder are $r_1, \ldots, r_n$ at time

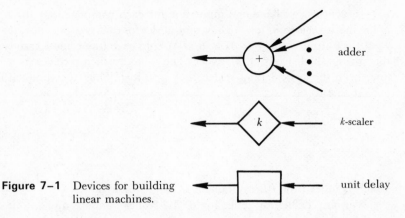

adder

k-scaler

Figure 7–1 Devices for building
linear machines.

unit delay

t, then $r_1 + \cdots + r_n$ will be its output at time t; if the input to the k-scaler
($k \in R$) is r at time t, then its output will be kr at time t. The **unit delay**
is just that: if its input is r at time t, then its output will be r at time $t + 1$.

We can build a **matrix multiplier** for any $m \times n$ matrix

$$A = \begin{bmatrix} a_{11} & \cdots & a_{1n} \\ \vdots & & \vdots \\ a_{m1} & \cdots & a_{mn} \end{bmatrix}$$

as a network of adders and k-scalers. As an example, the matrix multiplier
for

$$A = \begin{bmatrix} 0 & 2 & 1 \\ 3 & -1 & 2 \end{bmatrix}$$

is shown in Figure 7–2.

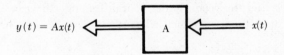

$$y(t) = Ax(t) \quad \Longleftarrow \quad \boxed{A} \quad \Longleftarrow \quad x(t)$$

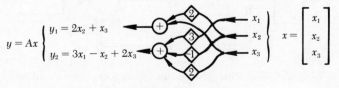

$$y = Ax \begin{cases} y_1 = 2x_2 + x_3 \\ y_2 = 3x_1 - x_2 + 2x_3 \end{cases} \qquad x = \begin{bmatrix} x_1 \\ x_2 \\ x_3 \end{bmatrix}$$

Figure 7–2

In general, we have one input line for each component x_1 through x_n of the input vector x in R^n. We have one adder for each component y_1 through y_m of the output vector $y = Ax$ in R^m. We split each input line x_j into m lines, the ith of which feeds an a_{ij}-scaler. The y_i adder then receives its n input lines from the a_{i1}-scaler, a_{i2}-scaler, $\ldots$, a_{in}-scaler. Thus, the value on the y_i output line is

$$\sum_{j=1}^{n} a_{ij}x_j$$

which is indeed the ith component of Ax, as desired.

We may define an adder for R^n by using n adders, and a unit delay for R^n by using n delay elements, as shown in Figure 7–3.

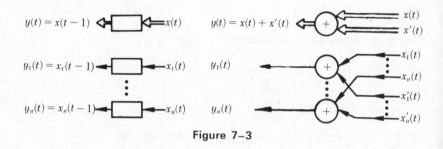

Figure 7–3

Using the notational conventions of Figures 7–2 and 7–3, we now see that the linear machine of Definition 1 may (given that $Q = R^n$, $X = R^m$, and $Y = R^p$) be expressed in the form of Figure 7–4, where the box F contains n^2 scalers and n adders; the box G contains nm scalers and n adders; the box H contains pn scalers and p adders; while the vector unit delay contains n delay devices, and the vector adder contains n adder devices.

Note that in the case (which will prove to be the most important one

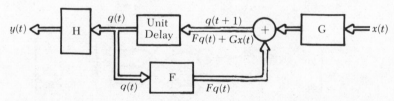

Figure 7–4 Building a linear machine from scalers, adders and unit delays.

in our applications to coding theory) that $R = Z_2$, we may dispense with scalers: the only elements of Z_2 are 0 and 1, and scaling by 0 means "remove the line" while scaling by 1 means "leave the line alone," so no special devices are required. Conversely, any system built from binary unit delays and modulo 2 adders (and such that each loop contains at least one delay) gives rise to a binary linear machine, whose state set is the vector of output values of the delay devices. (The proof is left as an exercise for the more conscientious reader; here we just give examples.)

Example 1

As an example of a binary linear machine, let us consider the machine shown in Figure 7–5. We regard the present output of a delay as the bit (0 or 1) it is presently storing, and its present input as the next quantity to be stored. For the machine shown in Figure 7–5, the current outputs of the delays are

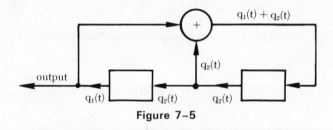

Figure 7–5

$q_1(t)$ and $q_2(t)$ so that the inputs to the delays must be $q_2(t)$ and $q_1(t) + q_2(t)$, respectively; the initial output of the machine is $q_1(t)$. Thus, the next quantities to be stored are $q_2(t)$ and $q_1(t) + q_2(t)$ and the next output of the machine will be $q_2(t)$.

This machine has $Q = Z_2^2$, $X = Z_2^0$, and $Y = Z_2$. Since $X = Z_2^0$, we need not mention the input in our equations—any such machine, which has $|X| = 1$, is called **autonomous**. The machine of Figure 7–5 is described by the equations:

$$\begin{bmatrix} q_1(t+1) \\ q_2(t+1) \end{bmatrix} = \begin{bmatrix} 0 & 1 \\ 1 & 1 \end{bmatrix} \begin{bmatrix} q_1(t) \\ q_2(t) \end{bmatrix}$$

$$y(t) = [1 \quad 0] \begin{bmatrix} q_1(t) \\ q_2(t) \end{bmatrix}$$

Thus, in this example, we have $F = \begin{bmatrix} 0 & 1 \\ 1 & 1 \end{bmatrix}$ and $H = [1 \quad 0]$.

In the absence of any input, formula (4) reduces to

$$y(t + n) = HF^n q(t)$$

Computing F^n for $n \geq 1$, we have

$$F = \begin{bmatrix} 0 & 1 \\ 1 & 1 \end{bmatrix} \qquad \text{and } HF = [0 \quad 1]$$

$$F^2 = \begin{bmatrix} 0 & 1 \\ 1 & 1 \end{bmatrix}\begin{bmatrix} 0 & 1 \\ 1 & 1 \end{bmatrix} = \begin{bmatrix} 1 & 1 \\ 1 & 0 \end{bmatrix} \qquad \text{and } HF^2 = [1 \quad 1]$$

$$F^3 = \begin{bmatrix} 0 & 1 \\ 1 & 1 \end{bmatrix}\begin{bmatrix} 1 & 1 \\ 1 & 0 \end{bmatrix} = \begin{bmatrix} 1 & 0 \\ 0 & 1 \end{bmatrix} \qquad \text{and } HF^3 = [1 \quad 0]$$

Since $F^3 = I$, the sequence of outputs repeats every three steps, so that if $q(t) = q$, the subsequent outputs are:

$$Hq, HFq, HF^2q, Hq, HFq, HF^2q, Hq, \ldots$$

We say that the output sequence is **periodic** with period 3.

Specifically, suppose that the initial state $q(0)$ of the machine is $\begin{bmatrix} 0 \\ 1 \end{bmatrix}$. Then the binary sequence produced by this linear machine is

$$0, 1, 1, 0, 1, 1, 0, 1, 1, 0, 1, 1, \ldots$$

If we had chosen $q(0) = \begin{bmatrix} 1 \\ 0 \end{bmatrix}$ the result would be the output sequence

$$1, 0, 1, 1, 0, 1, 1, 0, 1, 1, 0, \ldots$$

It should be clear that the machine has the state-transition graph shown in Figure 7–6.   ◊

The machine shown in Figure 7–5 is an example of what is known as

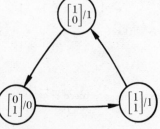
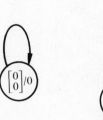

Figure 7–6

a **linear feedback shift register,** and it is a special case of the more general switching circuit shown in Figure 7–7. This circuit is also called a **shift register**

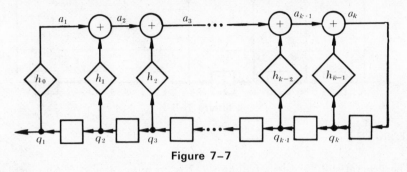

Figure 7–7

generator. In the schematic for the shift register generator, the outputs of the adders are labeled $a_2, a_3, \ldots, a_{k-1}, a_k$. Between the unit delays and the adders are scalar multipliers $h_0, h_1, h_2, \ldots, h_{k-2}, h_{k-1}$. In the binary case, these will simply mean that if $h_i = 0$ there is no connection, and if $h_i = 1$ there is a connection. The initial contents of the register are $q_1, q_2, \ldots, q_{k-1}, q_k$. If we set $g_0 = q_1, g_1 = q_2, \ldots, g_{k-1} = q_k$, we can then define g_{k+i} for $i \geq 0$ recursively by using the **recurrence relation** or **difference equation**

$$g_{k+i} = \sum_{j=0}^{k-1} h_j g_{j+i} \qquad \text{for } i = 0, 1, 2, \ldots \tag{5}$$

We then note that the output of the shift register generator is exactly the sequence $g_0, g_1, g_2, \ldots$. Thus, given a recurrence relation like (5), we now see how we can generate a solution by constructing a shift register generator which has its multipliers determined by the values of $h_j(j = 0, 1, 2, \ldots, k - 1)$ and selecting arbitrary initial conditions (i.e. values for $g_0, g_1, \ldots, g_{k-1}$):

Example 2

Suppose that we are given the binary difference equation

$$y_{6+i} = y_i + y_{1+i} + y_{2+i} + y_{3+i} \qquad \text{for } i = 0, 1, 2, \ldots$$

By inspection, we have that

$$h_0 = h_1 = h_2 = h_3 = 1$$

and

$$h_4 = h_5 = 0$$

A linear shift register which generates solutions of this equation is then given in Figure 7–8. ◊

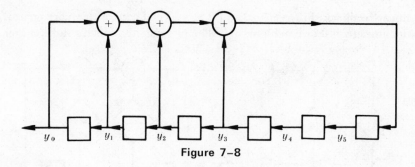

Figure 7–8

LEMMA 1

The general shift register of Figure 7–7 is an autonomous linear machine and is described by the equations

$$q(t + 1) = Fq(t)$$
$$y(t) = Hq(t)$$

where F is described by the **transition matrix**

$$F = \begin{bmatrix} 0 & 1 & 0 & \ldots & 0 \\ 0 & 0 & 1 & \ldots & 0 \\ \vdots & \vdots & \vdots & & \vdots \\ 0 & 0 & 0 & \ldots & 1 \\ h_0 & h_1 & h_2 & \ldots & h_{k-1} \end{bmatrix}$$

while

$$H = \begin{bmatrix} 1 & 0 & 0 & \ldots & 0 \end{bmatrix} \qquad\qquad \square$$

Using y_t to denote the output at time t, we note that the state at time t must be

$$q(t) = \begin{bmatrix} y_t \\ y_{t+1} \\ y_{t+2} \\ \vdots \\ y_{t+k-1} \end{bmatrix}$$

while we have $y_{t+k} = \sum_{j=0}^{k-1} h_j y_{t+j}$ for all $t \geq 0$.

Given any no-input linear equations

$$q(t + 1) = Fq(t)$$
$$y(t) = Hq(t)$$

we have seen that $y(t) = HF^t q(0)$, so that if $q(0)$ and $q'(0)$ are two different initial states with corresponding output sequences $y(t)$, $t \geq 0$, and $y'(t)$, $t \geq 0$, then it is clear that $rq(0) + r'q'(0)$ will have output sequence $ry(t) + r'y'(t)$ for $t \geq 0$. In particular, the initial state 0 yields an output sequence that is constantly 0. If F and H come from a shift register, we then have the following:

FACT 2

For a binary shift register generator with k unit delays there are 2^k initial states, and each yields a distinct output sequence (since the first k outputs are the k components of the initial states). Thus, there are exactly 2^k distinct solutions to the recurrence relation which defines the machine. □

This result will prove important when we return to coding theory in Chapter 8.

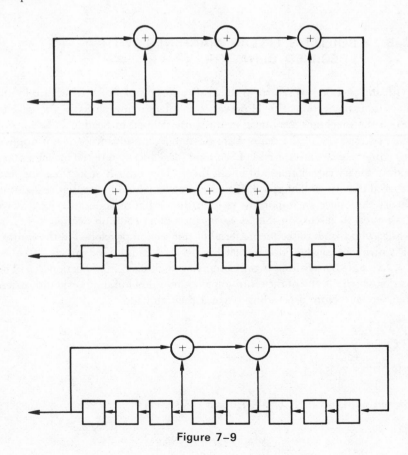

Figure 7–9

EXERCISES FOR SECTION 7–4

1.   For each recurrence relation below, construct the corresponding shift register generator and draw the state-transition graph:

(a) $y_i + y_{i+1} + y_{i+2} = y_{i+3}$ for $i = 0, 1, 2, \ldots$
(b) $y_i + y_{i+1} = y_{i+3}$ for $i = 0, 1, 2, \ldots$

2.   For each of the shift register generators in Figure 7–9, determine the corresponding recurrence relations. (Each line carries 0 or 1.)

7–5   BUILDING LINEAR MACHINES WITH SPECIFIED BEHAVIOR

With this section, we return to the realization problem for which we found a solution in Section 2–5. However, our interest now shifts to the case in which the machines are linear in the sense defined in Section 7–4. Since it makes strong use of the material in Section 2–5, and since it is not applied to coding theory until the end of Section 8–4, readers interested in elementary coding theory rather than automata theory may omit it at first reading and proceed directly to Chapter 8. However, readers should note that realization theory does play an important part in the design of coding devices, as we shall stress in discussing the *key equation* for BCH codes in Section 8–4. The reader who wishes to see the material of this section developed in the context of control theory should consult Chapter 8 of Padulo and Arbib [1974].

We start by recalling two theorems we shall need from Section 2–5. The reader who finds any of the terminology or notation unfamiliar should review that section before proceeding beyond their statements.

THEOREM 2–5–11

Given any behavior $f: X^* \to Y$, form the system

$$M_f = (Q_f, X, Y, \delta_f, \beta_f)$$

where:

$$Q_f = X^*/E_f (\text{where } w_1 E_f w_2 \Leftrightarrow f \circ L_{w_1} = f \circ L_{w_2})$$
$$\delta_f : Q_f \times X \to Q_f : ([w], x) \mapsto [wx]$$
$$\beta_f : Q_f \to Y : [w] \mapsto f(w)$$

Then the initialized machine $(M_f, [\Lambda])$ is a **minimal realization** of f, in that it is reachable and observable, and differs from the minimized form of any other realization of f only by the relabelling of states.   □

THEOREM 2–5–15

Let $f : X^* \to Y$ be any behavior. Let us define the k-indistinguishability relation of f on X^* by

$$w_1 E_f^k w_2 \Leftrightarrow f(w_1 w) = f(w_2 w) \text{ for all } w \text{ in } X^* \text{ such that } \ell(w) \leq k$$

and the k-reachable set of M_f by

$$S_k^f = \{[w] \mid \ell(w) \leq k\} \subset Q_f$$

Then if $S_p^f = S_{p+1}^f$ we have $S_p^f = Q_f$; and if $E_f^u = E_f^{u+1}$ we have $E_f^u = E_f$. Hence, if p and u are such that

$$S_p^f = S_{p+1}^f \text{ and } E_f^u = E_f^{u+1}$$

we deduce that

$$Q_f = \{w \in X^* \mid \ell(w) \leq p\}/E_f^u \qquad \square$$

In particular, we deduced that if $|Q_f| \leq N$, then

$$Q_f = \{w \in X^* \mid \ell(w) \leq N - 1\}/E_f^{N-2}$$

Although our main aim in this section will be to see what happens when we replace "arbitrary machines with finite state sets" by "linear machines with finite-dimensional state-spaces," we shall gain additional insight into arbitrary linear machines as well. We start, then, by recasting Definition 7–4–1 in a form closer to the automata-theoretic language of Chapter 2:

DEFINITION 1

A **linear machine** is a state-output automaton

$$M = (Q, X, Y, \delta, \beta)$$

where Q, X and Y are R-modules (for some fixed unitary ring R) and there exist linear maps $F:Q \to Q$, $G:X \to Q$, and $H:Q \to Y$ such that

$$\delta(q, x) = Fq + Gx$$

and

$$\beta(q) = Hq$$

for all q in Q and x in X.   ○

The **zero-state response** of M to a given input sequence w is simply the response of the machine in the zero-state 0 to w, that is, $M_0(w)$. Thus, the zero-state response of a linear machine to a sequence $w = x_k \ldots x_1 x_0$ is, by equation 7–4–(4),

$$M_0(w) = \sum_{l=0}^{k} HF^l Gx_l \tag{1}$$

so that it may be computed once we know the linear transformations HF^lG for each $l \in \mathbf{N}$.

Conversely, given M_0 we can determine the linear transformations HF^lG for $l \geq 0$. In fact, if the input space X is m-dimensional (recall Definition 7–1–14) with basis

$$e_1 = \begin{bmatrix} 1 \\ 0 \\ 0 \\ \vdots \\ 0 \end{bmatrix} \quad e_2 = \begin{bmatrix} 0 \\ 1 \\ 0 \\ \vdots \\ 0 \end{bmatrix} \quad \ldots \quad e_m = \begin{bmatrix} 0 \\ 0 \\ 0 \\ \vdots \\ 1 \end{bmatrix}$$

(where we now denote $e_i^{(m)}$ simply by e_i) and G has matrix

$$G = [g_1, g_2, \ldots, g_m] = [Ge_1, Ge_2, \ldots, Ge_m]$$

with respect to this basis, then we may determine the matrix

$$A_l = HF^lG = [HF^lGe_1, HF^lGe_2, \ldots, HF^lGe_m] \tag{2}$$

as follows:

We denote by 0^k, the length k sequence of zero m-vectors, i.e.,

$$0^k = \left(\begin{bmatrix} 0 \\ 0 \\ 0 \\ \vdots \\ 0 \end{bmatrix}, \begin{bmatrix} 0 \\ 0 \\ 0 \\ \vdots \\ 0 \end{bmatrix}, \ldots, \begin{bmatrix} 0 \\ 0 \\ 0 \\ \vdots \\ 0 \end{bmatrix} \right) \quad m \text{ zeros}$$

$$\underbrace{\phantom{\begin{bmatrix} 0 \\ 0 \\ 0 \\ 0 \\ 0 \end{bmatrix} \begin{bmatrix} 0 \\ 0 \\ 0 \\ 0 \\ 0 \end{bmatrix} \begin{bmatrix} 0 \\ 0 \\ 0 \\ 0 \\ 0 \end{bmatrix}}}_{k \text{ vectors}}$$

But by (1), we have for $j = 1, 2, \ldots m$ that

$$M_0(e_j 0^\ell) = HF^0 G0 + HF^1 G0 + \cdots + HF^{\ell-1} G0 + HF^\ell G e_j$$
$$= HF^\ell G e_j$$

Hence, we can determine the matrix $A_\ell = HF^\ell G$ by applying inputs:

$$A_\ell = [M_0(e_1 0^\ell), M_0(e_2 0^\ell), \ldots, M_0(e_m 0^\ell)] \tag{3}$$

Thus, the realization problem breaks down into two parts, one empirical and one mathematical. The empirical problem is to measure "sufficiently many" A_k, guided by formula (3). The mathematical problem, for which we shall use Theorem 2–5–11 as our key, is to go from the A_ℓ to a set of minimal F, G, and H such that $A_\ell = HF^\ell G$ for each ℓ; and, along the way, to specify what we mean by "sufficiently many."

Before proceeding further, we shall make an observation that will allow us to treat a map like M_0 in (1) as a linear function, rather than as just a map.

Given two R-modules X and Y, and a sequence of linear transformations $(A_0, A_1, \ldots, A_\ell \ldots)$ from X to Y, we may, as in the case $A_\ell = HF^\ell G$ of (1), form an associated function

$$f : X^* \to Y : x_k \ldots x_0 \mapsto \sum_{\ell=0}^{k} A_\ell x_\ell \tag{4}$$

Let us now see that X^* can be changed slightly to yield an R-module $X^\S$ such that f becomes a *linear* map from $X^\S$ to Y:

Observe from expression (4) that $f(w) = f(0^m w)$ for any $m \in \mathbf{N}$; i.e., $f(w)$ does not change if we preload w with (adjoin to the left of w) any sequence of 0's. Thus, for each $x_k \ldots x_1 x_0 \in X^*$, let us form the left-infinite sequence $\ldots 0 \ldots 0 x_k \ldots x_1 x_0$. We shall denote the set of all such left-infinite sequences by $X^\S$.

It will now be convenient for us to think of the sequence $w = x_n \ldots x_1 x_0$ as a function $w : \mathbf{N} \to X$ defined by

$$w(\ell) = \begin{cases} x_\ell & \text{if } 0 \leq \ell \leq k \\ 0 & \text{if } \ell > k \end{cases}$$

We thus see that the sequences $x_k \ldots x_1 x_0$ and $0 \ldots 00 x_k \ldots x_1 x_0$ are identified with the same function. This notion allows us to recast X^* into the form:

$$X^\S = \{ w : \mathbf{N} \to X \mid w(\ell) \neq 0 \text{ for only finitely many } \ell \}$$

We shall say that the **support** of w, abbreviated supp(w), is the set defined as

$$\text{supp}(w) = \{ \ell \in \mathbf{N} \mid w(\ell) \neq 0 \}$$

Consequently, let us recast expression (4) into the form

$$f:X^{\S} \to Y:w \mapsto \sum_{\text{supp}(w)} A_{\ell}w(\ell) \tag{5}$$

where the definition of $X^{\S}$ assures us that the sum in (5) has finitely many terms, and is thus well-defined. We think of $X^{\S}$ as the input space by regarding $w(\ell)$ as the input ℓ times ago, under "input regime" w. We turn $X^{\S}$ into an R-module simply by defining operations componentwise; i.e., by taking

$$(w + w')(\ell) = w(\ell) + w'(\ell) \tag{6a}$$

$$(rw)(\ell) = r(w(\ell)) \tag{6b}$$

where we define the left-hand side operations in $X^{\S}$ by the already available right-hand side operations in X (Exercise 1). [In fact, the reader who recalls Definition 7–1–6 will see that $X^{\S}$ is just the coproduct $\bigoplus_{\ell \in \mathbf{N}} R_{\ell}$ where for each ℓ, R_{ℓ} is simply a copy of X.]

To verify that the f of (5) is a linear map, let us denote $\text{supp}(rw + r'w')$ by S, $\text{supp}(w)$ by S_1, and $\text{supp}(w')$ by S_2.
Then

$$S = \{\ell \in \mathbf{N} \mid (rw + r'w')(\ell) \neq 0\}$$
$$= \{\ell \in \mathbf{N} \mid (rw)(\ell) + (r'w')(\ell) \neq 0\}$$
$$= \{\ell \in \mathbf{N} \mid rw(\ell) + r'w'(\ell) \neq 0\} \quad \subset S_1 \cup S_2$$

Thus,

$$f(rw + r'w') = \sum_{S} A_{\ell}(rw + r'w')(\ell)$$

$$= \sum_{S_1 \cup S_2} A_{\ell}(rw + r'w')(\ell)$$

$$= \sum_{S_1 \cup S_2} A_{\ell}[rw(\ell) + r'w'(\ell)] \qquad \text{by (6a)}$$

$$= \sum_{S_1 \cup S_2} A_{\ell}(r[w(\ell)] + r'[w'(\ell)]) \quad \text{by (6b)}$$

$$= \sum_{S_1 \cup S_2} [rA_{\ell}w(\ell) + r'A_{\ell}w'(\ell)] \quad \text{since } A_{\ell} \text{ is linear}$$

$$= r\sum_{S_1} A_{\ell}w(\ell) + r'\sum_{S_2} A_{\ell}w'(\ell) \quad \text{by Exercise 6}$$

$$= rf(w) + r'f(w') \qquad\qquad\qquad \text{as desired}$$

Thus, giving a sequence $(A_0, A_1, \ldots, A_k, \ldots)$ of linear transformations is equivalent to giving a linear transformation f from $X^\S$ to Y. Note that a given f need not have *any* finite-dimensional realization.

Let us be given a **linear response function**

$$f: X^\S \to Y: w \mapsto \sum_{\text{supp}(w)} A_\ell w(\ell)$$

and apply, to the corresponding behavior $X^* \to Y: x_k \cdots x_1 x_0 \mapsto \sum_{\ell=0}^{k} A_\ell x_\ell$,

the method summarized in Theorem 2-5-11. If for each $w \in X^*$ we denote the length of w by $|w|$, then we have that

$$
\begin{aligned}
w_1 E_f w_2 &\Leftrightarrow f(w_1 w) = f(w_2 w) &&\text{for all } w \text{ in } X^* \\
&\Leftrightarrow f(w_1 0^{|w|}) = f(w_2 0^{|w|}) &&\text{for all } w \text{ in } X^* \text{ by Exercise 2} \\
&\Leftrightarrow f(w_1 0^n) = f(w_2 0^n) &&\text{for all } n \in \mathbf{N}
\end{aligned}
$$

Therefore, if we define the map

$$\tilde{f}: X^\S \to Y^{\mathbf{N}}$$

which assigns to each $w \in X^\S$ the infinite sequence $\tilde{f}(w) = (f(w), f(w0), \ldots, f(w0^n), \ldots)$ identified with the function $\mathbf{N} \to Y: n \to f(w0^n)$ in $Y^{\mathbf{N}}$, we have the important result that

$$w_1 E_f w_2 \Leftrightarrow \tilde{f}(w_1) = \tilde{f}(w_2) \tag{7}$$

Now, it is obvious that the linearity of f implies the linearity of $\tilde{f}$, and so (Exercise 3) we can take

$$Q_f = X^\S / \text{Ker } \tilde{f}$$

which is itself an R-module. Note that Λ in X^* corresponds to $0 = (\ldots, 0, \ldots, 0, 0)$ in $X^\S$, so that M_f will have f as the response function of its zero-state $0 = [(\ldots, 0, \ldots, 0, 0)]$.

It remains to analyze the form of δ_f and β_f. But for any linear machine with $\delta(q, x) = Fq + Gx$ and $\beta(q) = Hq$, we have

$$
\begin{aligned}
\delta(q, x) &= (Fq + G0) + (F0 + Gx) \\
&= \delta(q, 0) + \delta(0, x)
\end{aligned}
$$

since any linear map sends 0 to 0. (Note that the 0 in $\delta(q, 0)$ is the $0 \in X$, while the 0 in $\delta(0, X)$ is the $0 \in Q$.) Hence, in the case of our M_f with state-module $Q_f = X^\S / \text{Ker } \tilde{f}$ and linear maps F_f, G_f, and H_f, we have

$$
\begin{aligned}
\delta_f([w], x) &= \delta_f([w], 0) + \delta_f([\Lambda], x) \\
&= [w0] + [x]
\end{aligned}
$$

where x in X becomes $(\ldots, 0, \ldots, 0, x)$ in $X^\S$, while, for w in $X^\S$, $w0$ is just $(\ldots, w(2), w(1), w(0), 0)$. As always (even for nonlinear f) we have $\beta_f([w]) = f(w)$. Hence, we have the general result (irrespective of whether or not f has a finite-dimensional realization):

THEOREM 1 (REALIZATION THEOREM FOR LINEAR MACHINES)

Let $f: X^\S \to Y$ be a linear map which induces

$$\tilde{f}: X^\S \to Y^\mathbf{N}: w \mapsto (f(w), f(w0), \ldots, f(w0^n), \ldots)$$

Then the initialized linear machine $(M_f, 0)$ with

$$M_f = (Q_f, X, Y, \delta_f, \beta_f)$$

where $Q_f = X^\S/\mathrm{Ker}\,\tilde{f}$ with equivalence classes $[w]$ and the linear maps F_f, G_f, H_f defined by

$$F_f([w]) = [w0]$$
$$G_f(x) = [x]$$
$$H_f([w]) = f(w)$$

respectively, is a minimal realization of M_f.   □

Note the beautiful fact that our *general* method of Section 2–5 yields a *linear* minimal (reachable and observable) realization of a *linear f*. We shall analyze this "coincidence" more carefully in Chapter 9.

Unfortunately, Theorem 1 does not yield an *algorithm* for constructing M_f. To make use of Theorem 2–5–15, we shall now impose the assumption that we have some bound N on the dimension of Q_f. After we have used this to obtain an algorithm (Corollary 2), we shall study a partial realization algorithm (Corollary 3) which enables us to make successive approximations to M_f if no such bound N is known.

It is clear by the definition of S_k^f in Theorem 2–5–15 that each S_k^f is a *submodule* of S_{k+1}^f:

$$S_k^f = \{[x_{k-1} \ldots x_0]\} = \{[0x_{k-1} \ldots x_0]\} \subset \{[x_k x_{k-1} \ldots x_0]\} = S_{k+1}^f$$

Clearly S_0^f has dimension 0, and S_{k+1}^f either equals S_k^f, or exceeds it in dimension by at least 1. Thus, in going from S_0^f to Q_f (via $S_1^f, S_2^f, \ldots$) there can be at most N increases in dimension. Hence, by the time we reach S_N^f, the maximal dimension must have been reached. Thus,

$$X_f = S_N^f \tag{7}$$

Similarly, we must have

$$E_f = E_f^{N-1} \tag{8}$$

since E_f^0 must yield observations along at least one dimension, or we always have zero output (in which case $E_f = E_f^0$, and (7) is valid *a fortiori*).

Thus, given a guarantee that M_f has dimension at most N, we have that

$$w_1 E_f w_2 \Leftrightarrow f(w_1 w) = f(w_2 w) \quad \text{for all } w \text{ with } |w| \leq N - 1$$
$$\Leftrightarrow f(w_1 0^n) = f(w_2 0^n) \quad \text{for all } n \leq N - 1$$

Hence, if for any w in X^* we define the **full-state vector** $\langle w \rangle$ to be

$$\langle w \rangle = \begin{bmatrix} f(w) \\ f(w0) \\ \vdots \\ f(w0^{N-1}) \end{bmatrix}$$

then two input sequences are equivalent under E_f iff $\langle w_1 \rangle = \langle w_2 \rangle$. Now it is clear (on noting Exercise 4 and recalling equation (7) above) that we can reach every state of M_f with a w which is a linear combination of the $e_\ell 0^k$ (where $[e_1, \ldots, e_m]$ is a basis for X, and $0 \leq k < N$), and hence it follows that every $\langle w \rangle$ is a linear combination of such $\langle e_\ell 0^k \rangle$ (Exercise 5). Let us fix k. We then see [recalling equations (2) and (3)] that

$$[\langle e_1 0^k \rangle, \ldots, \langle e_m 0^k \rangle] = \begin{bmatrix} f(e_1 0^k) & \cdots & f(e_m 0^k) \\ f(e_1 0^{k+1}) & \cdots & f(e_m 0^{k+1}) \\ \vdots & & \vdots \\ f(e_1 0^{k+N}) & \cdots & f(e_m 0^{k+N}) \end{bmatrix}$$

$$= \begin{bmatrix} A_k \\ A_{k+1} \\ \vdots \\ A_{k+N} \end{bmatrix} \tag{9}$$

when we partition our matrix by rows instead of columns.

Combining equations (7), (8) and (9), we conclude that, if M_f has dimension at most N, we need only use A_{k+j} for $0 \leq k < N$ and $0 \leq j < N$ in finding a basis for the columns of the block-partitioned matrix

$$\mathcal{K}_N = \begin{bmatrix} A_0 & A_1 & \cdots & A_{N-1} \\ A_1 & A_2 & \cdots & A_N \\ \vdots & \vdots & & \vdots \\ A_{N-1} & A_N & \cdots & A_{2N-2} \end{bmatrix}$$

which is called the (size N) **Hankel matrix** of the given response function f.

Thus, the problem of finding Q_f is reduced to the algorithmic level, and Theorem 1 reduces to the following useful form:

COROLLARY 2 (REALIZATION ALGORITHM FOR LINEAR MACHINES)

Let $f : X^\S \to Y$ be an R-linear map $w \mapsto \sum_{\text{supp}(f)} A_l w(l)$, for which X has basis $e_1, \ldots, e_m$, and for which it is guaranteed that there exists a realization of dimension at most N. Then a minimal realization M_f may be constructed as follows:

Select a basis for the space spanned by the array of vectors

$$\mathcal{K}_N = [\langle e_1 \rangle, \ldots, \langle e_m \rangle, \langle e_1 0 \rangle, \ldots, \langle e_m 0 \rangle, \ldots, \langle e_1 0^{N-1} \rangle, \ldots, \langle e_m 0^{N-1} \rangle]$$

Say that this basis consists of the vectors $\langle w_1 \rangle, \ldots, \langle w_{n'} \rangle$ with $n' \le N$, and let $[w]$ be the column vector whose entries are the coefficients of $\langle w \rangle$ with respect to this basis. Then, with respect to this basis, M_f is defined by the matrices

$$F_N = [[w_1 0], \ldots, [w_{n'} 0]]$$
$$G_N = [[e_1], \ldots, [e_m]]$$
$$H_N = [f(w_1), \ldots, f(w_{n'})]$$

Proof

Recall from Theorem 1 that

$$F_f([w]) = [w0]$$
$$G_f(x) = [x]$$
$$H_f([w]) = f(w)$$

Our task is now simply to specify the matrices F_N, G_N, and H_N which represent the linear transformations F_f, G_f, and H_f, respectively. Recall that the matrix of a linear transformation $h:A \to B$ is $[h(a_1), \ldots, h(a_k)]$, whose jth column is the image $h(a_j)$ of the jth vector of the basis $(a_1, \ldots, a_k)$ for A with respect to which the matrix is being computed. We thus immediately deduce that

$$F_N = [F_f([w_1]), \ldots, F_f([w_{n'}])] = [[w_1 0], \ldots, [w_{n'} 0]]$$
$$G_N = [G_f(e_1), \ldots, G_f(e_m)] = [[e_1], \ldots, [e_m]]$$
$$H_N = [H_f([w_1]), \ldots, H_f([w_{n'}])] = [f(w_1), \ldots, f(w_{n'})]$$

Note that we use the assumption that f has a realization of dimension at most N to guarantee that the full-state vectors $\langle w_1 0 \rangle, \ldots, \langle w_{n'} 0 \rangle$ are linearly dependent on $\langle w_1 \rangle, \ldots, \langle w_{n'} \rangle$, so that the expressions $[w_1 0], \ldots, [w_{n'} 0]$ are well-defined with repect to the basis. Clearly, to ensure that they are well-defined, it suffices to know that rank $\mathcal{3C}_N$ = rank $\mathcal{3C}_{N+1}$. □

Example 1

Suppose that we wish to compute the canonical realization of an input-output function

$$f : \mathbf{R}^\S \to \mathbf{R}$$

(i.e., both input and output are real scalars) when we are guaranteed that a three-dimensional realization exists. Our crucial matrix is then 3×3 and, identifying $[1]$ and e_1, takes the form:

$$\mathcal{3C}_3 = \begin{bmatrix} f(1) & f(10) & f(100) \\ f(10) & f(100) & f(1000) \\ f(100) & f(1000) & f(10000) \end{bmatrix} = [\langle 1 \rangle \langle 10 \rangle \langle 100 \rangle]$$

Let us see how our approach works with the specific values:

$$\mathcal{3C}_3 = \begin{bmatrix} 1 & -1 & -7 \\ -1 & -7 & -9 \\ -7 & -9 & 17 \end{bmatrix}$$

We seek a basis for the column space of $\mathcal{3C}_3$—in fact, it is $\langle 1 \rangle$ and $\langle 10 \rangle$, since the third column is linearly dependent with $\langle 100 \rangle = -5\langle 1 \rangle + 2\langle 10 \rangle$. (Thus, we get by with a two-dimensional realization, and do not need the full three-dimensional state-module for which we were prepared.) Recalling that

$[w]$ is the vector $\begin{bmatrix} q_1 \\ q_2 \end{bmatrix}$ such that $w = q_1\langle 1 \rangle + q_2\langle 10 \rangle$, we immediately read from our general formulas that

$$G_3 = [[e_1]] = \begin{bmatrix} 1 \\ 0 \end{bmatrix}$$

$$F_3 = [[10], [100]] = \begin{bmatrix} 0 & -5 \\ 1 & 2 \end{bmatrix}$$

$$H_3 = [f(1), f(10)] = [1 \quad -1]$$

and the reader can easily verify that these do yield the specified values of f.

$\Diamond$

Example 2

We find a minimal realization for the sequence $\{f(1), f(10), f(100), \ldots\}$ equal to the set of Fibonacci numbers given by

$$\{h_i\} = \{1, 1, 2, 3, 5, 8, 13, \ldots\}$$

We know that the Fibonacci sequence is defined by

$$h_t = h_{t-1} + h_{t-2}$$

This suggests that we take as our state the vector in $\mathbf{Z}^2$ comprising the two most recent values of the sequence, and start at time 0 by plugging a 1 into the present-output component of the state:

$$q(t+1) = \begin{bmatrix} 0 & 1 \\ 1 & 1 \end{bmatrix} q(t) + \begin{bmatrix} 0 \\ 1 \end{bmatrix} x(t)$$

$$y(t) = [0 \quad 1]q(t)$$

and this is indeed reachable and observable: [*Moral:* Don't plug in general algorithms when special knowledge allows a short cut.] $\Diamond$

We close with an important generalization of Corollary 2, in which we remove the condition that "it is guaranteed that there exists a realization of dimension at most N." (The reader for whom the concept of the *rank* of a matrix is unfamiliar should skip this corollary.)

COROLLARY 3 (PARTIAL REALIZATION ALGORITHM FOR LINEAR MACHINES)

Let $A_0, A_1, \ldots, A_{2N-3}, A_{2N-2}$ be a sequence of linear transformations from X to Y, where X has basis $(e_1, \ldots, e_m)$. For $j = 1, 2, \ldots, N + 1$, we define the Hankel matrix

$$
\mathfrak{IC}_j = \begin{bmatrix} A_0 & A_1 & \cdots & A_{j-1} \\ A_1 & A_2 & \cdots & A_j \\ \vdots & \vdots & & \vdots \\ A_{j-1} & A_j & \cdots & A_{2j-2} \end{bmatrix} = [\langle e_1 \rangle_j, \ldots, \langle e_m 0^{j-1} \rangle_j]
$$

If $\mathfrak{IC}_N$ and $\mathfrak{IC}_{N+1}$ have the same rank, select a basis $\langle w_1 \rangle, \ldots, \langle w_{n'} \rangle$ for the column space of $\mathfrak{IC}_{N'}$ and let $[w]$ be the column vector whose entries are the coefficients of $\langle w \rangle$ with respect to this basis. Then if we define

$$
\begin{aligned}
G_N &= [[e_1], \ldots, [e_m]] \\
F_N &= [[w_1 0], \ldots, [w_n 0]] \\
H_N &= [f(w_1), \ldots, f(w_{n'})]
\end{aligned}
$$

we have that (F_N, G_N, H_N) are matrices of minimal dimension such that

$$
A_\ell = H_N F_N^\ell G_N \text{ for } \ell = 0, 1, 2, \ldots, 2N - 2
$$

Proof

The condition that $\mathfrak{IC}_N$ and $\mathfrak{IC}_{N+1}$ have the same rank simply ensures that F_N is well-defined (compare the proof of Corollary 2), i.e., that each $\langle w_j 0 \rangle$ depends linearly upon the basis $\langle w_1 \rangle, \ldots, \langle w_{n'} \rangle$. Now, if we define the sequence $\bar{A}_\ell$ by

$$
\bar{A}_\ell = H_N F_N^\ell G_N \text{ for } all \ \ell
$$

it follows from Corollary 1 that we obtain a minimal realization of this sequence; and it is clear that $\bar{A}_\ell = A_\ell$ for $\ell = 0, 1, 2, \ldots, 2N - 2$. $\square$

This completes our study of the realization problem for linear machines. In Chapter 9 we shall see how it may be subsumed in an elegant general theory of "Machines in a Category."

EXERCISES FOR SECTION 7–5

1.   Let X be any R-module. Prove that, as a result of equation (6), $(X^{\S}, +, x \xmapsto{\lambda} rx)$ is also an R-module.

2.   Let $f(x_n \ldots x_0) = \sum_{k=0}^{n} A_k x_k$ for all $x_n \ldots x_0$ in X^*. Pick any m with $0 \leq m \leq k$ and observe that

$$\sum_{k=0}^{n} A_k x_k = \sum_{k=m+1}^{n} A_k x_k + \sum_{k=0}^{m} A_k x_k$$

$$= \sum_{k=0}^{n} A_k x_k' + \sum_{k=0}^{m} A_k x_k$$

where $x_k' = x_k$ if $m < k \leq n$, while $x_k' = 0$ if $0 \leq k \leq m$. Deduce that:

   (a) $f(w_1 w) = f(w_1 0^{|w|}) + f(w)$ for all w_1 and w in X^*, where $w_1 0^{|w|}$ is the sequence w_1 followed by an all-zero sequence of the same length as w.

   (b) $f(w_1 w) = f(w_2 w) \Leftrightarrow f(w_1 0^{|w|}) = f(w_2 0^{|w|})$.

3.   Prove the following generalization of Theorem 7–1–3: Let A_1 and A_2 be R-modules, and $g : A_1 \to A_2$ a linear map. Then we define the equivalence relation $\equiv_g$ by

$$a \equiv_g a' \Leftrightarrow g(a) = g(a')$$

Clearly $[a + a']_g = [a]_g + [a']_g$ and $[ra]_g = r[a]_g$. Thus, the factor set $A_1/\equiv_g$ may be turned into an R-module. Then $A_1/\equiv_g$ is isomorphic to $g(A_1)$, since the map $A_1/\equiv_g \to g(A_1) : [a]_g \mapsto g(a)$ is both linear and a bijection. Note (cf. Theorem 7–1–4) that $A_1/\equiv_g \cong A_1/\mathrm{Ker}\ g$.

4.   Prove that a q is of the form $\sum_{k=0}^{n} F^k G x_k$ for some $n \leq N$ iff q is of the form

$$\sum_{k=0}^{N} F^k G x_k'$$

[Hint: Take $x_k' = x_k$ for $0 \leq k \leq n$; $x_k' = 0$ for $n < k \leq N$.]

5.   Let $w = x_{N-1} \ldots x_0$ be any X-sequence of length N. Let

$$x_k = \sum_{l=1}^{m} a_{kl} e_l$$

be the representation of x_k with respect to the basis $\{e_l\}$ for X. Then use the full-state vector

$$\langle w \rangle = \begin{bmatrix} f(w) \\ f(w0) \\ \vdots \\ f(w0^{N-1}) \end{bmatrix}$$

to deduce that

$$\langle w \rangle = \sum_{k=0}^{N-1} \sum_{l=1}^{m} a_{kl} \langle e_l 0^k \rangle$$

6. Let A be an R-module, let r and r' be scalars, and let $a_1, \ldots, a_n, a'_1, \ldots, a'_n$ be elements of A. Use the module axioms to verify, by induction on n, that

$$\sum_{k=1}^{n} (ra_k + r'a'_k) = r \sum_{k=1}^{n} a_k + r' \sum_{k=1}^{n} a'_k$$

7. Find a two-dimensional realization for the linear map

$$f : \mathbf{Z}^{\S} \to \mathbf{Z} : x \mapsto \sum_{\text{supp}(w)} (-k)x(k)$$

(Hint: Let H be of the form $[1 \quad 0]$.)

8. Show that the validity of Corollaries 2 and 3 is not affected if we replace $\mathfrak{K}_N$ by any matrix $\hat{\mathfrak{K}}$ whose rows (respectively columns) are linear combinations of rows (columns) of $\mathfrak{K}_N$ and which span the row space (column space) of $\mathfrak{K}_N$.

Further Reading for Chapter 7

A number of books discuss error-correcting codes and their relationship to linear machines. Some of the more recent books are Ash [1965], Beckmann [1967], Berlekamp [1968], Gallager [1968], Ingels [1971], Lin [1970], and Peterson and Weldon [1972].

ROBERT ASH [1965], *Information Theory*, John Wiley and Sons, New York, New York.

PETER BECKMANN [1967], *Probability in Communication Engineering*, Harcourt, Brace, and World, New York, New York.

ELWYN R. BERLEKAMP [1968], *Algebraic Coding Theory*, McGraw-Hill, New York, New York.

ROBERT C. GALLAGER [1968], *Information Theory and Reliable Communication*, John Wiley and Sons, New York, New York.

FRANKLIN M. INGELS [1971], *Information and Coding Theory*, Intext, Scranton, Pennsylvania.

SHU LIN [1970], *An Introduction to Error-Correcting Codes*, Prentice-Hall, Englewood Cliffs, New Jersey.

LOUIS PADULO and MICHAEL A. ARBIB [1974], *System Theory*, W. B. Saunders Co., Philadelphia, Pennsylvania.

W. WESLEY PETERSON and E. J. WELDON, JR. [1972], *Error-Correcting Codes*, MIT Press, Cambridge, Massachusetts.

CHAPTER 8

Algebraic Coding Theory

In this chapter, we build upon our study of linear machines and codes in Chapter 7 to study a class of codes known as cyclic codes, while at the same time developing our understanding of ring theory. One of the most important ways of constructing a ring from a given field is to consider the collection of all polynomials in one variable which take coefficients in the field. We develop the basic properties of such polynomial rings over a field in Section 8–1. Then, in Section 8–2 we apply both this theory of polynomial rings, and our study of shift registers in Section 7–4, to provide an introduction to cyclic codes, namely those codes in which each code word is transformed into another code word under a cyclic shift of its constituent letters. The last two sections then present special cases of cyclic codes. In Section 8–3 we introduce the study of minimum polynomials, and see how they can be used to design maximum-length codes. Then, we close in Section 8–4 by developing properties of extension fields, and relating them to the Bose-Chaudhuri-Hocquenghem codes.

8–1   Polynomial Rings over a Field

In this section, we develop a number of properties of the polynomial ring $K[x]$, comprising formal polynomials in the indeterminate x with coefficients in a *field* K. In the next three sections, we shall then apply these results to coding theory, making the assumption that K is a *finite* field. Most usefully, we shall take $K = GF(2)$, the two-element field $\{0, 1\}$, in order to obtain binary codes.

The essential ingredient in our theory of polynomial rings is that the Euclidean Division Algorithm is available not only for $\mathbf{Z}$ but also for $K[x]$, where K is any field. The crucial point about the proof for the ring $\mathbf{Z}$ was that given r_2 and r_1, we could meaningfully say that $0 < r_2 \leq r_1$, we could then find r_3 and p_2 in $\mathbf{Z}$ such that

$$r_1 = p_2 r_2 + r_3 \text{ with } 0 \leq r_3 < r_2, \tag{1}$$

and that for each r_1 any series of the form $r_1 \geq r_2 > \cdots > r_k > \cdots \geq 0$ must be finite.

In turning to polynomials, we compare not the "size" of the polynomials but rather their degrees, and so write $0 < \deg f_2 \leq \deg f_1$ rather than $0 < r_2 \leq r_1$. Clearly, for any given f_1, any series of the form $\deg f_1 \geq \deg f_2 > \cdots > \deg f_k > \cdots \geq 0$ must have a finite number of terms. Let us finally check that the analog of (1) holds in $K[x]$.

LEMMA 1

Let f_1 and f_2 be any two polynomials from $K[x]$, where K is a field. If $\deg f_2 \leq \deg f_1$, then there exist polynomials p_2 and f_3 such that

$$f_1 = p_2 f_2 + f_3 \text{ where } -\infty \leq \deg f_3 < \deg f_2$$

Proof

Let f_1 have leading coefficient $a \neq 0$ and let f_2 have leading coefficient $b \neq 0$. Let

$$g_1 = f_1 - (ab^{-1} x^{\deg f_1 - \deg f_2}) \cdot f_2$$

Then $\deg g_1 \leq \deg f_1 - 1$. If $\deg g_1 < \deg f_2$, we are done, and may take $p_2 = ab^{-1} x^{\deg f_1 - \deg f_2}$ and $f_3 = g_1$. In any case, we have found g_1 and h_1 such that

$$f_1 = h_1 f_2 + g_1 \quad \text{and} \quad \deg g_1 \leq \deg f_1 - 1$$

Clearly, then, proceeding in this way we must find a sequence

$$g_1 = h_2 f_2 + g_2$$
$$\vdots$$
$$g_{k-1} = h_k f_2 + g_k$$

where $\deg g_j \leq \deg g_{j-1} - 1$, and we finally have $\deg g_k < \deg f_2$. But then

$$f_1 = \left(\sum_{j=1}^{k} h_j\right)f_2 + g_k$$

and we are done, with $p_2 = \sum_{j=1}^{k} h_j$ and $f_3 = g_k$.   □

This lemma gives us polynomial division, as outlined below:

Given polynomials p and s, we know that there exist polynomials q and r such that

$$s = p \cdot q + r$$

where $\deg r < \deg p$. We shall leave it as an exercise for the reader to prove that these polynomials are unique (up to multiplication by constants). We refer to q as the **quotient** and r as the **remainder.** For the case that there is zero remainder (that is, for $r = 0$) we have that

$$s = p \cdot q$$

and we say that s is **divisible** by p, or p **divides** s, or p is a **factor** of s.

Thus armed, we may immediately deduce (Exercise 3) the following:

LEMMA 2

Let f_1 and f_2 be any two polynomials from $K[x]$, for K a field. Then there exist g_1 and g_2 from $K[x]$ such that

$$\text{g.c.d. } (f_1, f_2) = g_1 f_1 + g_2 f_2$$

where g.c.d. (f_1, f_2) is 0 if either f_1 or f_2 is 0, but is otherwise the monic polynomial of highest degree which divides both f_1 and f_2.   □

From this moment on, we will also use the alternative notation $p(x)$ to emphasize that p is a polynomial.

Example 1

Recall Example 7-1-7. There, we let $R = GF(2)$, and considered $GF(2)[x]$, the ring of polynomials with coefficients in the field of integers modulo 2. Also, we let $H = \langle p(x) \rangle$ be the principal ideal comprising all the polynomials which are multiples of the polynomial $p(x) = 1 + x^3$. We denoted this ideal by $\langle 1 + x^3 \rangle$. Then we called the quotient ring $GF(2)[x]/\langle 1 + x^3 \rangle$ the *ring of polynomials modulo* $1 + x^3$ (with coefficients in $GF(2)$).

The ideal $H = [0]$ consists of all polynomials which differ from 0 by a multiple of $p(x)$, i.e., all the multiples of $p(x)$. To form a second residue class $[s(x)]$, we chose a polynomial $s(x) \notin H$ and formed the set $s(x) + H$. A third residue class was obtained by selecting a polynomial $t(x)$ such that $t(x) \notin H$ and $t(x) \notin s(x) + H$, etc. In this manner, we obtained the set $\{[0], [1], [x], [1 + x], [x^2], [1 + x^2], [x + x^2], [1 + x + x^2]\}$ of residue classes which comprise $GF(2)[x]/\langle 1 + x^3 \rangle$. Here we represent each residue class by a polynomial of smallest degree in the class. (We soon shall see that such a polynomial is unique.) In fact, since any polynomial with coefficients in the field of integers modulo 2 is in one of the residue classes given above, no new residue class can be formed. However, this is by no means obvious. Hence, we will shortly apply our division theory to replace blind search. But first, let us continue with the present example.

We know that the set of residue classes given above is a ring under addition and multiplication defined by:

$$[r_1] + [r_2] = [r_1 + r_2]$$
$$[r_1] \cdot [r_2] = [r_1 \cdot r_2]$$

Addition in this factor ring is no more difficult than addition in the original ring, e.g.,

$$
\begin{aligned}
[1 + x] + [1 + x^2] &= [(1 + x) + (1 + x^2)] \\
&= [1 + 1 + x + x^2] \\
&= [x + x^2] \quad \text{(since } 1 + 1 = 0 \text{ in } GF(2))
\end{aligned}
$$

A similar statement can be made about multiplication, e.g.,

$$
\begin{aligned}
[1 + x] \cdot [1 + x^2] &= [(1 + x) \cdot (1 + x^2)] \\
&= [1 + x + x^2 + x^3] \\
&= [(1 + x^3) + (x + x^2)] \\
&= [1 + x^3] + [x + x^2] \\
&= [0] + [x + x^2] \\
&= [x + x^2]
\end{aligned}
$$

We will shortly establish a short-cut for carrying out multiplication manipulations.

Since $GF(2)[x]/\langle 1 + x^3 \rangle$ is also a ring, we can form principal ideals here, too. We denote by $\langle [x] \rangle$ the ideal in $GF(2)[x]/\langle 1 + x^3 \rangle$ which consists of all multiples of the residue class $[x]$. The elements of this ideal are:

$$[0] \cdot [x] = [0 \cdot x] = [0]$$
$$[1] \cdot [x] = [1 \cdot x] = [x]$$
$$[x] \cdot [x] = [x \cdot x] = [x^2]$$
$$[1 + x] \cdot [x] = [(1 + x) \cdot x] = [x + x^2]$$
$$[x^2] \cdot [x] = [x^2 \cdot x] = [x^3] = [1 + (1 + x^3)]$$
$$= [1] + [1 + x^3] = [1] + [0] = [1]$$
$$[1 + x^2] \cdot [x] = [(1 + x^2) \cdot x] = [x + x^3] = [(1 + x) + (1 + x^3)]$$
$$= [1 + x] + [1 + x^3] = [1 + x]$$
$$[x + x^2] \cdot [x] = [(x + x^2) \cdot x] = [x^2 + x^3]$$
$$= [(1 + x^2) + (1 + x^3)] = [1 + x^2]$$
$$[1 + x + x^2] \cdot [x] = [(1 + x + x^2) \cdot x] = [x + x^2 + x^3]$$
$$= [(1 + x + x^2) + (1 + x^3)] = [1 + x + x^2]$$

Thus, we see that the ideal generated by $[x]$ is the entire ring, that is, $\langle [x] \rangle = GF(2)[x]/\langle 1 + x^3 \rangle$. Hence, $\langle [x] \rangle$ is trivial. To try to determine a nontrivial ideal, suppose we select $[1 + x]$ as the generator for a principal ideal. All the multiples of $[1 + x]$ are:

$$[0] \cdot [1 + x] = [0 \cdot (1 + x)] = [0]$$
$$[1] \cdot [1 + x] = [1 \cdot (1 + x)] = [1 + x]$$
$$[x] \cdot [1 + x] = [x \cdot (1 + x)] = [x + x^2]$$
$$[1 + x] \cdot [1 + x] = [(1 + x) \cdot (1 + x)] = [1 + x + x + x^2] = [1 + x^2]$$
$$[x^2] \cdot [1 + x] = [x^2 \cdot (1 + x)] = [x^2 + x^3]$$
$$= [(1 + x^2) + (1 + x^3)] = [1 + x^2]$$
$$[1 + x^2] \cdot [1 + x] = [(1 + x^2) \cdot (1 + x)] = [1 + x + x^2 + x^3]$$
$$= [(x + x^2) + (1 + x^3)] = [x + x^2]$$
$$[x + x^2] \cdot [1 + x] = [(x + x^2) \cdot (1 + x)] = [x + x^2 + x^2 + x^3]$$
$$= [(1 + x) + (1 + x^3)] = [1 + x]$$
$$[1 + x + x^2] \cdot [1 + x] = [(1 + x + x^2) \cdot (1 + x)]$$
$$= [1 + x + x + x^2 + x^2 + x^3] = [1 + x^3] = [0]$$

Since there are no more new residue clases that are multiples of $[1 + x]$ (why?), the ideal $\langle [1 + x] \rangle$ consists of the four residue classes:

$$[0]$$
$$[1 + x]$$
$$[x + x^2]$$
$$[1 + x^2]$$

$\diamond$

Let us now systematize this as follows:

LEMMA 3

If deg $p = n$, then in each residue class of $K[x]/\langle p(x)\rangle$ there is one and only one polynomial of degree less than n.

Proof

Consider the quotient ring $K[x]/\langle p(x)\rangle$ of polynomials modulo $p(x)$ with coefficients in the field K. Let deg $p(x) = n$. We know that any polynomial $s(x)$ is in some residue class, specifically, $s(x) \in [s(x)]$. Furthermore, no two polynomials of degree less than n can be in the same class; for suppose that $s_1(x) \in [s(x)]$ and $s_2(x) \in [s(x)]$, where deg $s_1 < n$ and deg $s_2 < n$. Since $s_1(x)$ and $s_2(x)$ are in the same residue class (coset), $-s_1(x) + s_2(x) \in [0] = \langle p(x)\rangle$. Thus, $[-s_1(x) + s_2(x)] = [0]$ and the degree of $-s_1(x) + s_2(x)$ is less than n. However, $[0]$ consists only of multiples of $p(x)$. Thus, $-s_1(x) + s_2(x) = 0$, which implies that $s_1(x) = s_2(x)$. $\square$

Given an arbitrary polynomial $s(x)$, it is now a simple task to determine the unique polynomial of smallest degree which is in the same residue class as $s(x)$. We simply divide $s(x)$ by $p(x)$ to obtain

$$s(x) = p(x) \cdot q(x) + r(x)$$

where deg $r <$ deg $p = n$. We then may write

$$-r(x) + s(x) = p(x) \cdot q(x)$$

so that

$$\begin{aligned}[-r(x) + s(x)] &= [p(x) \cdot q(x)]\\ &= [p(x)] \cdot [q(x)]\\ &= [0] \cdot [q(x)]\\ &= [0]\end{aligned}$$

Hence, $r(x)$ and $s(x)$ are in the same residue class; and since deg $r < n$, $r(x)$ is the unique polynomial of smallest degree in this residue class.

Example 2

In the ring $GF(2)[x]/\langle 1 + x^3\rangle$, let us find the polynomial of degree 2 or less that is in the same residue class as $x^2 + x^3 + x^7$. By polynomial division (remember, this is modulo 2 arithmetic), we obtain:

$$
\begin{array}{r}
x^4 + x + 1 = q(x) \\
p(x) = x^3 + 1 \overline{)\, x^7 + x^3 + x^2 } = s(x) \\
\underline{x^7 + x^4 } \\
x^4 + x^3 + x^2 \\
\underline{x^4 + x } \\
x^3 + x^2 + x \\
\underline{x^3 + 1} \\
x^2 + x + 1 = r(x)
\end{array}
$$

Thus, we see that

$$ s(x) = p(x) \cdot q(x) + r(x) $$

or

$$ x^2 + x^3 + x^7 = (1 + x^3) \cdot (1 + x + x^4) + (1 + x + x^2) $$

from which

$$ (1 + x + x^2) + (x^2 + x^3 + x^7) = (1 + x^3) \cdot (1 + x + x^4) \in [0] $$

Hence

$$ [1 + x + x^2] = [x^2 + x^3 + x^7] \qquad\qquad \lozenge $$

We now develop a general property of ideals in the ring of polynomials modulo $p(x)$.

THEOREM 4

Suppose that H is an ideal in the ring $K[x]/\langle p(x)\rangle$. Let $g(x)$ be a nonzero polynomial of minimum degree such that $[g(x)] \in H$. Then $[s(x)] \in H$ if and only if $g(x)$ divides $s(x)$.

Proof

First assume that $[s(x)] \in H$. Then by polynomial division we can write $s(x) = g(x) \cdot q(x) + r(x)$, where the degree of $r(x)$ is less than the degree of $g(x)$. Thus, $[s(x)] = [g(x) \cdot q(x) + r(x)] = [g(x)] \cdot [q(x)] + [r(x)]$, from which $-[g(x)] \cdot [q(x)] + [s(x)] = [r(x)]$. Since $[g(x)] \in H$, we have $[g(x)] \cdot [q(x)] \in H$, and $-[g(x)] \cdot [q(x)] + [s(x)] = [r(x)] \in H$. But the degree of $r(x)$ is less than the degree of $g(x)$. Thus, $r(x) = 0$, and so $g(x)$ divides $s(x)$.

Conversely, assume that $g(x)$ divides $s(x)$. Then there exists some $q(x)$ such that $s(x) = g(x) \cdot q(x)$. Thus, $[s(x)] = [g(x) \cdot q(x)] = [g(x)] \cdot [q(x)]$. Since $[g(x)] \in H$, we have $[g(x)] \cdot [q(x)] = [s(x)] \in H$. $\qquad\square$

As a result of the previous theorem, we see that if H is an ideal in the ring of polynomials modulo $p(x)$, there is a polynomial $g(x)$ such that for any $[s(x)] \in H$, $g(x)$ divides $s(x)$. Hence, there exists a polynomial $q(x)$ such that $s(x) = g(x) \cdot q(x)$ and $[s(x)] = [g(x)] \cdot [q(x)]$. Since each $[s(x)] \in H$ is a multiple of $[g(x)]$, and since any multiple of $[g(x)]$ is in H, then H is the principal ideal generated by $[g(x)]$. Hence, (recall Definition 7–1–10) we have proven the following result:

FACT 5

The ring of polynomials modulo $p(x)$ is a principal ideal ring.   □

We will now show that the polynomial $g(x)$ described in Theorem 4 is essentially unique.

COROLLARY 6

Suppose that H is an ideal in the ring of polynomials modulo $p(x)$. Let $g(x)$ be a nonzero polynomial of minimum degree such that $[g(x)] \in H$. Then $g(x)$ is unique up to multiplication by a scalar.

Proof

Assume that there are two nonzero polynomials $g(x)$ and $g'(x)$ of minimum degree such that $[g(x)] \in H$ and $[g'(x)] \in H$. By Theorem 4, $g(x)$ divides $g'(x)$ and $g'(x)$ divides $g(x)$. But $g(x)$ and $g'(x)$ have the same degree, and thus, differ by at most a scalar.   □

Another property of the polynomial $g(x)$ is given by the following:

THEOREM 7

Suppose that H is an ideal in the ring of polynomials modulo $p(x)$, and let $g(x)$ be a nonzero polynomial of minimum degree such that $[g(x)] \in H$. Then $g(x)$ divides $p(x)$.

Proof

By polynomial division we can write $p(x) = g(x) \cdot q(x) + r(x)$, where the degree of $r(x)$ is less than the degree of $g(x)$. Since $[p(x)] = [0]$, we have $[0] = [g(x)] \cdot [q(x)] + [r(x)]$. Thus, $[r(x)] = -[g(x)] \cdot [q(x)] \in H$. But $g(x)$ is a nonzero polynomial of smallest degree such that $[g(x)] \in H$. Hence, $r(x) = 0$ and $p(x) = g(x) \cdot q(x)$. $\qquad \Box$

We are now in a position to present a major result.

THEOREM 8

Let us be given the ring $K[x]/\langle p(x) \rangle$ of polynomials modulo $p(x)$ and a monic polynomial $g(x)$ which divides $p(x)$. Then in $H = \langle [g(x)] \rangle$, the principal ideal generated by $[g(x)]$, the polynomial $g(x)$ is the nonzero monic polynomial of minimum degree such that $[g(x)] \in H$.

Proof

Suppose that the monic polynomial $g(x)$ divides $p(x)$ and H is the ideal generated by $[g(x)]$ in the ring of polynomials modulo $p(x)$. If $[s(x)] \in H$, then there exists a polynomial $q(x)$ such that $[s(x)] = [g(x)] \cdot [q(x)] = [g(x) \cdot q(x)]$. Since $s(x)$ and $g(x) \cdot q(x)$ are in the same residue class, there exists a polynomial $t(x)$ such that $s(x) = g(x) \cdot q(x) + p(x) \cdot t(x)$. But $g(x)$ divides $p(x)$. Thus, for some $u(x)$, $p(x) = g(x) \cdot u(x)$. Therefore, $s(x) = g(x) \cdot q(x) + g(x) \cdot u(x) \cdot t(x) = g(x) \cdot (q(x) + u(x) \cdot t(x))$, and $g(x)$ divides $s(x)$. Hence, if $s(x) \neq 0$, the degree of $s(x)$ is no less than the degree of $g(x)$. $\qquad \Box$

Since $g(x)$ is the monic polynomial of minimum degree such that $[g(x)] \in H$, and H can be formed by taking all multiples of $[g(x)]$, we will refer to the polynomial $g(x)$ as the **generator polynomial** (or, more simply, the **generator**) of the ideal H, and we say that H is **generated** by $g(x)$.

Henceforth, we focus on the case in which K is a finite field, and, in particular, the case $K = GF(2)$. Our first task will then be to determine the order of an ideal H in the ring of polynomials modulo $p(x)$ without having to enumerate the elements of H.

First we recall from Lemma 3 that if $\deg p = n$, then each distinct polynomial

$$a_0 + a_1 x + a_1 x^2 + \cdots + a_{n-1} x^{n-1}$$

where $a_i \in K$ for $i = 0, 1, 2, \ldots, n - 1$, is in one and only one residue class; and these residue classes form $K[x]/\langle p(x) \rangle$. Obviously, there are exactly $|K|^n$ such polynomials, where $|K|$ is the number of elements of the finite field K. For example, then,

$$|GF(2)[x]/\langle p(x) \rangle| = 2^n$$

Now suppose that $g(x)$ is the generator polynomial of H. Then $g(x)$ divides $p(x)$, and there exists a polynomial $h(x)$ such that $p(x) = g(x) \cdot h(x)$. If $h(x)$ has degree k, then the degree of $g(x)$ is $n - k$. Thus, the polynomials $g(x)$, $x \cdot g(x), x^2 \cdot g(x), \ldots, x^{k-1} \cdot g(x)$ have degree $n - k, n - k + 1, n - k + 2, \ldots,$ $n - 1$, respectively. In addition, the residue classes $[g(x)], [x \cdot g(x)], [x^2 \cdot g(x)],$ $\ldots, [x^{k-1} \cdot g(x)]$ are in the ideal. To see that these k residue classes are a set of generators for the subgroup H when $K = GF(2)$, suppose that $[s(x)] \in H$, where $s(x)$ has degree less than n. We know that $g(x)$ divides $s(x)$. Thus, there exists a polynomial $q(x)$ such that $s(x) = g(x) \cdot q(x)$, where $q(x)$ has degree less than k. Therefore, we can write $q(x) = q_0 + q_1 x + q_2 x^2 + \cdots + q_{k-1} x^{k-1}$, where $q_i \in \{0, 1\}$ for $i = 0, 1, 2, \ldots, k - 1$. Consequently,

$$
\begin{aligned}
[s(x)] &= [g(x) \cdot q(x)] \\
&= [g(x) \cdot (q_0 + q_1 x + q_2 x^2 + \cdots + q_{k-1} x^{k-1})] \\
&= [q_0 \cdot g(x)] + [q_1 x \cdot g(x)] + [q_2 x^2 \cdot g(x)] + \cdots + (q_{k-1} x^{k-1} \cdot g(x)]
\end{aligned}
$$

Thus, the k residue classes $[g(x)], [x \cdot g(x)], [x^2 \cdot g(x)], \ldots, [x^{k-1} \cdot g(x)]$ generate the subgroup H. If these residue classes are a minimum set of generators, then the order of H is 2^k. Now, for the sake of contradiction, assume that such a set is not minimum; that is, assume that there are distinct integers $i_1, i_2, \ldots, i_r$ between 0 and $k - 1$ such that $[x^{i_1} \cdot g(x)] + [x^{i_2} \cdot g(x)] + \cdots + [x^{i_{r-1}} \cdot g(x)] = [x^{i_r} \cdot g(x)]$. Thus, $[0] = [x^{i_1} \cdot g(x)] + [x^{i_2} \cdot g(x)] + \cdots + [x^{i_r} \cdot g(x)] = [(x^{i_1} + x^{i_2} + \cdots + x^{i_r}) \cdot g(x)]$. But, since $i_1, i_2, \ldots, i_r$ are distinct, $x^{i_1} + x^{i_2} + \cdots + x^{i_r} \neq 0$. Furthermore, the degree of $(x^{i_1} + x^{i_2} + \cdots + x^{i_r}) \cdot g(x)$ is less than n. Thus, $[x^{i_1} \cdot g(x) + x^{i_2} \cdot g(x) + \cdots + x^{i_r} \cdot g(x)]$ $\neq [0]$, which is a contradiction. Hence, the set of generators of the subgroup H is minimum. We have now proved the following theorem for the case $K = GF(2)$.

THEOREM 9

Suppose that $g(x)$ is the generator polynomial for the ideal $H \subset K[x]/\langle p(x) \rangle$. Then $p(x) = g(x) \cdot h(x)$ and $|H| = |K|^k$, where k is the degree of $h(x)$. $\square$

The thorough reader may find it convenient to use vector space arguments in proving the theorem in general.

EXERCISES FOR SECTION 8-1

1.   Construct addition and multiplication tables for $GF(2)[x]/\langle x + x^2 \rangle$. Determine whether or not this ring is a field.

2.   Find the residue classes comprising the ideal $\langle [1 + x] \rangle \subset GF(2)[x]/\langle 1 + x^4 \rangle$.

3. Use Lemma 1 to rewrite the proof of the Euclidean Division Algorithm for **Z**, and use the result to prove Lemma 2 for $K[x]$ for any field K.

4. Let H be an ideal in the ring $K[x]/\langle p(x)\rangle$ of polynomials modulo $p(x)$. Define the set $S = \{g(x) \mid g(x) \neq 0, \ [g(x)] \in H, \ g(x) \text{ has minimum degree}\}$. Prove that S contains a monic polynomial.

5. Consider the factor ring $GF(2)[x]/\langle p(x)\rangle$. Give an example of a nontrivial ideal $\langle [s(x)]\rangle$, showing that if $s(x)$ does not divide $p(x)$, then $s(x)$ is not the polynomial of minimum degree for which $[s(x)] \in \langle [s(x)]\rangle$.

6. Give an example of a nontrivial ideal $H \subset GF(2)[x]/\langle p(x)\rangle$ for which $H = \langle [s_1(x)]\rangle = \langle [s_2(x)]\rangle$, where $\deg s_1 \leq \deg s_2 < \deg p$.

8-2 An Introduction to Cyclic Codes

Because of Lemma 8-1-3, for a polynomial $p(x)$ of degree n we may represent any element of $K[x]/\langle p(x)\rangle$ as an n-tuple of elements of K, i.e., the element of K^n comprising, low order digit first, the coefficients of the unique polynomial of degree less than n in the residue class. Since $K[x]/\langle p(x)\rangle$ is a (factor) ring, K^n inherits a ring structure in which addition is simply component-wise field K addition of two n-tuples, but in which the multiplication of two n-tuples must correspond to the product of the two corresponding residue classes in $K[x]/\langle p(x)\rangle$.

Example 1

Let us return to the ring $GF(2)[x]/\langle 1 + x^3\rangle$. The elements of this ring and the corresponding binary triples are (abbreviating (a_0, a_1, a_2) to $a_0a_1a_2$):

$$[0] \leftrightarrow 000$$
$$[1] \leftrightarrow 100$$
$$[x] \leftrightarrow 010$$
$$[1 + x] \leftrightarrow 110$$
$$[x^2] \leftrightarrow 001$$
$$[1 + x^2] \leftrightarrow 101$$
$$[x + x^2] \leftrightarrow 011$$
$$[1 + x + x^2] \leftrightarrow 111$$

Since in this ring

$$[1 + x] \cdot [1 + x^2] = [1 + x + x^2 + x^3] = [x + x^2]$$

we then have that

$$(110) \cdot (101) = (011) \qquad \Diamond$$

Again consider the ideal H generated by $g(x) = 1 + x$ in this factor ring. The elements forming this ideal, along with the corresponding binary representations, are:

$$[0] \leftrightarrow 000$$
$$[1 + x] \leftrightarrow 110$$
$$[x + x^2] \leftrightarrow 011$$
$$[1 + x^2] \leftrightarrow 101$$

Since H is an ideal, these four binary triples are a subgroup of $\mathbf{Z}_2^3$, and hence constitute a binary group code (recall Section 7–3). Inspection of this group code reveals that taking the last bit of any code word and placing it in front of the other two bits yields another code word. Codes with this property are quite important and are given a special name:

DEFINITION 1

Given an n-tuple $a = (a_0, a_1, a_2, \ldots, a_{n-1})$, we say that the n-tuple $(a_{n-1}, a_0, a_1, \ldots, a_{n-2})$ is obtained from a by a single **cyclic shift** to the right. A code in which a single cyclic shift to the right of any code word results in another code word is called a **cyclic code.** $\bigcirc$

Note that a cyclic code is not necessarily a cyclic group. The term "cyclic" when used to modify codes and groups has different meanings.

We see that the binary code given in Example 1 is cyclic. We now demonstrate that cyclic codes of length n correspond to ideals in the ring of polynomials modulo $1 - x^n$.

THEOREM 1

A group code of length n that is a vector space over the field K is cyclic if and only if it corresponds to an ideal in $K[x]/\langle 1 - x^n \rangle$, the ring of polynomials modulo $1 - x^n$.

Proof

Given a cyclic, group code of length n that is a vector space over K, consider the subgroup

$$H = \{[a_0 + a_1 x + \cdots + a_{n-1} x^{n-1}] \,|\, (a_0, a_1, \ldots, a_{n-1}) \text{ is a code word}\}$$
$$\subset K[x]/\langle 1 - x^n \rangle.$$

If $(a_0, a_1, \ldots, a_{n-1})$ is a code word, then so is $(a_{n-1}, a_0, \ldots, a_{n-2})$. Since $[1 - x^n] = [0]$ (i.e., $[1] = [x^n]$), we have that

$$[x] \cdot [a_0 + a_1 x + \cdots + a_{n-1} x^{n-1}]$$
$$= [a_0 x + a_1 x^2 + \cdots + a_{n-2} x^{n-1} + a_{n-1} x^n]$$
$$= [a_0 x + a_1 x^2 + \cdots + a_{n-2} x^{n-1}] + [a_{n-1}] \cdot [x^n]$$
$$= [a_{n-1}] + [a_0 x + a_1 x^2 + \cdots + a_{n-2} x^{n-1}]$$
$$= [a_{n-1} + a_0 x + a_1 x^2 + \cdots + a_{n-2} x^{n-1}] \in H$$

This implies that

$$[x^i] \cdot [a_0 + a_1 x + \cdots + a_{n-1} x^{n-1}] \in H$$

for any i. Also, since the code is a vector space over K, for any $r \in K$ and any code word $(a_0, a_1, \ldots, a_{n-1})$, we have that

$$r(a_0, a_1, \ldots, a_{n-1}) = (r \cdot a_0, r \cdot a_1, \ldots, r \cdot a_{n-1})$$

is a code word. Therefore,

$$[r \cdot a_0 + r \cdot a_1 x + \cdots + r \cdot a_{n-1} x^{n-1}] = [r] \cdot [a_0 + a_1 x + \cdots a_{n-1} x^{n-1}] \in H$$

Thus, for any $[a_0 + a_1 x + \cdots + a_{n-1} x^{n-1}] \in H$ and any $[r_0 + r_1 x + \cdots + r_{n-1} x^{n-1}] \in K[x]/\langle 1 - x^n \rangle$, it follows that

$$[r_0 + r_1 x + \cdots + r_{n-1} x^{n-1}] \cdot [a_0 + a_1 x + \cdots + a_{n-1} x^{n-1}]$$
$$= [r_0] \cdot [a_0 + a_1 x + \cdots + a_{n-1} x^{n-1}]$$
$$+ [r_1] \cdot [x] \cdot [a_0 + a_1 x + \cdots a_{n-1} x^{n-1}]$$
$$+ \cdots + [r_{n-1}] \cdot [x^{n-1}] \cdot [a_0 + a_1 x + \cdots + a_{n-1} x^{n-1}] \in H$$

Hence, H is an ideal.

Conversely, suppose that H is an ideal of $K[x]/\langle 1 - x^n \rangle$, the ring of polynomials modulo $1 - x^n$. If $(a_0, a_1, \ldots, a_{n-1})$ is a code word in the corresponding code, then $[a_0 + a_1 x + \cdots + a_{n-1} x^{n-1}] \in H$. Since H is an ideal,

$$[x] \cdot [a_0 + a_1 x + \cdots + a_{n-1} x^{n-1}] \in H$$

But, as above,

$$[x] \cdot [a_0 + a_1 x + \cdots + a_{n-1} x^{n-1}] = [a_{n-1} + a_0 x + \cdots + a_{n-2} x^{n-1}]$$

Thus, $(a_{n-1}, a_0, \ldots, a_{n-2})$ is a code word. Hence, the code is cyclic. $\square$

Note that a binary group code is a vector space over $GF(2)$. Thus, a binary group code of length n is cyclic if and only if it corresponds to an ideal in $GF(2)[x]/\langle 1 + x^n \rangle$.

By Theorem 8–1–7, if $g(x)$ is a generator polynomial of an ideal $H \subset K[x]/\langle p(x)\rangle$, then there exists some polynomial $h(x)$ such that

$$p(x) = g(x) \cdot h(x)$$

If $\deg p = n$ and $\deg g = n - k$, then $\deg h = k$ and $|H| = |K|^k$, with a minimum set of generators for the subgroup H consisting of the residue classes:

$$[g(x)], \; [x \cdot g(x)], \; [x^2 \cdot g(x)], \; \ldots, \; [x^{k-1} \cdot g(x)]$$

Thus, from the discussion above, if $p(x) = 1 - x^n$, then H corresponds to a cyclic code of length n and dimension k.

Example 2

Consider the ring of polynomials in $GF(2)[x]$ modulo $p(x) = 1 + x^7$. Since $1 + x^7 = (1 + x + x^3) \cdot (1 + x + x^2 + x^4)$ modulo 2, we may select $g(x) = 1 + x + x^3$ and $h(x) = 1 + x + x^2 + x^4$. Then the ideal generated by $g(x)$ has order $2^4 = 16$, and the corresponding binary cyclic code has length 7 and dimension $k = 4$. However, the residue classes $[g(x)], [x \cdot g(x)], [x^2 \cdot g(x)], \ldots, [x^{k-1} \cdot g(x)]$ are a minimum set of generators for the subgroup. In this case they are

$$[g(x)] = [1 + x + x^3]$$
$$[x \cdot g(x)] = [x + x^2 + x^4]$$
$$[x^2 \cdot g(x)] = [x^2 + x^3 + x^5]$$
$$[x^3 \cdot g(x)] = [x^3 + x^4 + x^6]$$

The binary septuple representations of these residue classes, when written as the rows of G, yield the following generator matrix for the code:

$$G = \begin{bmatrix} 1 & 1 & 0 & 1 & 0 & 0 & 0 \\ 0 & 1 & 1 & 0 & 1 & 0 & 0 \\ 0 & 0 & 1 & 1 & 0 & 1 & 0 \\ 0 & 0 & 0 & 1 & 1 & 0 & 1 \end{bmatrix}$$

Thus, we see that the n-tuple representation of $g(x)$ along with $k - 1$ successive cyclic shifts form a generator matrix for a binary (n, k) cyclic code.

According to the above described manner in which a generator matrix G is formed, G will not in general be in reduced echelon form. However, a slightly modified form is easily obtainable. First, we note that if we divide x^i (for $n - k \leq i \leq n - 1$) by $g(x)$, we can write $x^i = g(x) \cdot q_i(x) + r_i(x)$, where the degree of $r_i(x)$ is less than $n - k$. Thus, $-r_i(x) + x^i = g(x) \cdot q_i(x)$ is a polynomial representing the residue class $[-r_i(x) + x^i]$, which corresponds to a code word with only one nonzero digit among the last k digits. The formation of a matrix having rows corresponding to such residue classes produces a generator matrix of the form $G = [AI_k]$. Hence, it is a simple matter to form the corresponding parity check matrix $P = [I_{n-k}(-A)^T]$.

Also note that because $P = [I_{n-k}(-A)^T]$, then $P^T = \begin{bmatrix} I_{n-k} \\ -A \end{bmatrix}$. However, the rows of $-A$ are the binary representations of the remainders $r_i(x)$. Thus, the jth row of P^T is the binary representation of the polynomial which is the remainder obtained when x^j is divided by $g(x)$, for $j = 0, 1, 2, \ldots, n - 1$.

$\lozenge$

Example 3

Referring to the cyclic code given in the previous example, we note that

$$x^3 = (1 + x + x^3) \cdot 1 + (1 + x)$$
$$\Rightarrow 1 + x + x^3 = (1 + x + x^3) \cdot 1$$
$$x^4 = (1 + x + x^3) \cdot x + (x + x^2)$$
$$\Rightarrow x + x^2 + x^4 = (1 + x + x^3) \cdot x$$
$$x^5 = (1 + x + x^3) \cdot (1 + x^2) + (1 + x + x^2)$$
$$\Rightarrow 1 + x + x^2 + x^5 = (1 + x + x^3) \cdot (1 + x + x^2)$$
$$x^6 = (1 + x + x^3) \cdot (1 + x + x^3) + (1 + x^2)$$
$$\Rightarrow 1 + x^2 + x^6 = (1 + x + x^3) \cdot (1 + x + x^3)$$

Thus, writing the septuple representations of the residue classes $[1 + x + x^3]$, $[x + x^2 + x^4]$, $[1 + x + x^2 + x^5]$ and $[1 + x^2 + x^6]$ as the rows of a matrix G yields

$$G = \begin{bmatrix} 1 & 1 & 0 & 1 & 0 & 0 & 0 \\ 0 & 1 & 1 & 0 & 1 & 0 & 0 \\ 1 & 1 & 1 & 0 & 0 & 1 & 0 \\ 1 & 0 & 1 & 0 & 0 & 0 & 1 \end{bmatrix}$$

Hence,

$$P = \begin{bmatrix} 1 & 0 & 0 & 1 & 0 & 1 & 1 \\ 0 & 1 & 0 & 1 & 1 & 1 & 0 \\ 0 & 0 & 1 & 0 & 1 & 1 & 1 \end{bmatrix}$$

$\lozenge$

Let us compare our current situation with that on which we closed Section 7–4.

LEMMA 2

An (n, k) code is cyclic if and only if there exist polynomials $g(x)$ and $h(x)$ such that

$$1 - x^n = g(x) \cdot h(x)$$

where $\deg g = n - k$ and $\deg h = k$, for which the $|K|^k$ elements of the code are precisely the n low order coefficients of polynomials divisible by $g(x)$.   □

Let us now relate all this to the shift registers of Section 7–4. Generalizing Fact 2 of that section from $GF(2)$ to an arbitrary finite field K, we see that, given any sequence $h_0, h_1, \ldots, h_{k-1}$ of elements of K, there are $|K|^k$ different sequences $y_0, y_1, \ldots, y_l, \ldots$ which satisfy the recurrence relation

$$y_{k+i} = \sum_{j=0}^{k-1} h_j y_{j+i} \quad \text{for } i = 0, 1, 2, \ldots \tag{1}$$

namely, one for each vector $(y_0, y_1, \ldots, y_{k-1})$ of initial conditions.

Let us now associate with the shift register coefficients $h_0, h_1, \ldots, h_{k-1}$ the polynomial

$$h(x) = h_0 + h_1 x + \cdots + h_{k-1} x^{k-1} + h_k x^k$$

with $h_k = -1$ and represent the solution $y_0, y_1, \ldots$ by the formal series

$$y(x) = \sum_{l=0}^{\infty} y_l x^{-l}$$

Then

$$h(x) \cdot y(x) = \sum_{j=0}^{k} h_j x^j \cdot \sum_{l=0}^{\infty} y_l x^{-l}$$

$$= \sum_{i=-k}^{\infty} \left(\sum_{\substack{l-j=i \\ 0 \leq j \leq k \\ l \geq 0}} h_j y_l \right) x^{-i}$$

$$= \alpha(x) + \sum_{i \geq 0} \left(\sum_{j=0}^{k} h y_{j+i} \right) x^{-i}$$

where $\alpha(x)$ is a polynomial with 0 constant term.

On noting that $h_k = -1$ allows us to rework equation (1) in the form $\sum_{j=0}^{k} h_j y_{j+i} = 0$, we immediately deduce that

$$h(x) \cdot y(x) = \text{a polynomial with 0 constant term} \tag{2}$$

for any solution of (1). Could the $|K|^k$ code words associated with $g(x) = (1 - x^n)/h(x)$ in Lemma 2 have any connection with the $|K|^k$ different solutions of (1)? The answer is a pleasantly complete "yes." But before giving it, we must show that every $h(x)$ in an interestingly broad range does in fact divide $1 - x^n$ for some n.

In Section 7–4, we saw that the transition matrix of the shift register associated with $h(x)$ was

$$F = \begin{bmatrix} 0 & 1 & 0 & \cdots & 0 \\ 0 & 0 & 1 & \cdots & 0 \\ \vdots & \vdots & \vdots & & \vdots \\ 0 & 0 & 0 & \cdots & 1 \\ h_0 & h_1 & h_2 & \cdots & h_{k-1} \end{bmatrix}$$

Moving down the first column to the end, we see that*

$$\det(F) = (-1)^{k-1} h_0 \det(I_{k-1}) = (-1)^{k-1} h_0$$

Sticking with our assumption that F has coefficients in a finite field K, we see that F is invertible iff $h_0 \neq 0$. But, referring to Figure 7–7, we see that the case $h_0 = 0$ corresponds, essentially, to a shift register with only $(k - 1)$ delay devices, since q_1 has no effect upon the behavior of any of the devices, and so simply reports, with unit delay, the output sequence emitted by the shift register obtained from that of Figure 7–7 by deleting the leftmost delay device. For this reason, we may restrict our study to the case where $h_0 \neq 0$, and thus to the case in which F is invertible.

Let, now, K be a finite field with θ elements. There are then only θ^{k^2-1} nonzero $k \times k$ matrices with entries in K, and so at least two of the nonzero matrices $I, F, F^2, \ldots, F^{\theta^{k^2-1}}$ must be equal, say $F^i = F^j$ with $0 \leq i < j \leq \theta^{k^2-1}$. But if F is invertible, we then have

$$F^n = I \text{ where } 0 < n \leq \theta^{k^2-1} \tag{4}$$

on taking $n = j - i$. We call the smallest n for which (4) holds the **period** of F.

Consider now the sequence put out by the shift register of $h(x)$ for initial condition $1, 0, \ldots, 0$ (1 followed by $k - 1$ zeros). Let it be

$$y_0, y_1, \ldots, y_k, y_{k+1}, y_{k+2}, \ldots, y_{k+j+1}, \ldots = 1, 0, \ldots, 0, g_0, g_1, \ldots, g_j, \ldots \tag{5}$$

Since $F^n = I$, the state $(y_n, \ldots, y_{n+k-1})$ at time n must equal the state

---

*The reader unfamiliar with determinants should accept the fact that $\det(F) \neq 0$ iff F is invertible; where we say that $k \times k$ matrix F is *invertible* if there exists a $k \times k$ matrix F^{-1} such that $FF^{-1} = F^{-1}F = I_k$.

$(y_0, \ldots, y_k)$ at time 0. Thus we infer from (5) that

$$g_{n-k} = 1 \text{ while } g_{n-k+j} = 0 \text{ for } 1 \leq j < k$$

Since $\begin{bmatrix} 0 \\ 0 \\ \vdots \\ g_0 \end{bmatrix}$ is the state $F \begin{bmatrix} 1 \\ 0 \\ \vdots \\ 0 \end{bmatrix}$ of the shift register obtained in a single transition,

we also deduce that

$$g_0 = h_0 \tag{6}$$

For the y-sequence of (5), we now compute:

$$
\begin{aligned}
h(x) \cdot y(x) &= h(x) \cdot [1 + g_0 x^{-k} + \cdots + g_{n-k-1} x^{-n+1} + x^{-n} + g_0 x^{-n-k} \\
&\qquad\qquad + \text{lower order terms}] \\
&= (h(x) - h_0) + h_0 + h(x) \cdot (g_0 x^{-k} + \cdots + g_{n-k-1} x^{-n+1} + x^{-n}) \\
&\qquad\qquad + h_k x^k \cdot g_0 x^{-n-k} + \text{higher order terms} \tag{7}
\end{aligned}
$$

But by (2), the coefficients of x^{-l}, for $l \geq 0$, are all zero. Thus, on recalling that $h_0 = g_0$ by (6), and that $h_k = -1$, we may equate the coefficients of x^{-l} in (7), for $0 \leq l \leq n + k$, to zero to obtain

$$h(x) \cdot (g_0 x^{-k} + \cdots + g_{n-k-1} x^{-n+1} + x^{-n}) + g_0(1 - x^{-n}) = 0$$

so that

$$h(x) \cdot g(x) = 1 - x^n$$

where

$$g(x) = -g_0^{-1}(g_0 x^{n-k} + \cdots + g_{n-k-1} x + 1) \tag{8}$$

so that in the field $\{0, 1\}$ we have

$$
\begin{aligned}
g(x) &= g_0 x^{n-k} + \cdots + g_{n-k-1} x + 1 \\
&= y_k x^{n-k} + \cdots + y_{n-1} x + y_n \tag{9}
\end{aligned}
$$

We now make the following definitions:

DEFINITION 2

A sequence

$$s_0, s_1, s_2, \ldots$$

is said to be **periodic with period** n if n is a positive integer such that

$$s_{n+i} = s_i \quad \text{for } i = 0, 1, 2, \ldots \qquad \bigcirc$$

DEFINITION 3

Suppose that $f(x)$ is a polynomial with coefficients in some field K. Then the smallest positive integer n such that $f(x)$ divides $1 - x^n$ is called the **period** of $f(x)$. $\bigcirc$

(Note: For $K = GF(2)$, we have that $1 - x^n = 1 + x^n$.)

We thus have the elegant result:

THEOREM 3

Given a polynomial

$$h(x) = h_0 + h_1 x + h_2 x^2 + \cdots + h_{k-1} x^{k-1} - x^k$$

of period n, the solutions of the recurrence relation

$$g_{k+i} = \sum_{j=0}^{k-1} h_j g_{j+i} \quad \text{for } i \in \mathbf{N}$$

are periodic with period n. Moreover, by associating the first period $s_0, s_1, s_2, \ldots s_{n-1}$ of a solution with the residue class

$$[s_{n-1} + s_{n-2}x + \cdots + s_1 x^{n-2} + s_0 x^{n-1}] \in K[x]/\langle 1 - x^n \rangle$$

the set of all solutions corresponds to the ideal generated by $g(x) = (1 - x^n)/h(x)$ in the ring $K[x]/\langle 1 - x^n \rangle$. $\square$

Example 4

The polynomial $g(x) = 1 + x + x^3$ divides $1 + x^7$ (returning to the case $K = GF(2)$) and thus generates an ideal in the ring of polynomials modulo $1 + x^7$. We can form $h(x) = (1 + x^7)/(1 + x + x^3) = 1 + x + x^2 + x^4$, and use a shift register generator as an encoder for the corresponding cyclic code. Since the first seven bits of an output sequence form a code word in reverse order, by redrawing the shift register upside down, the first seven bits of an output sequence (when read from left to right) form a code word. This fact is demonstrated in Figure 8–1 for the initial conditions $s_0 = 1, s_1 = 0, s_2 = 1,$ $s_3 = 1$.   ◊

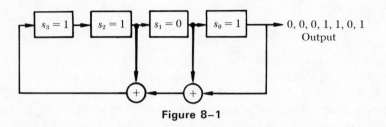

| $s_3 = 1$ | $s_2 = 1$ | $s_1 = 0$ | $s_0 = 1$ |

0, 0, 0, 1, 1, 0, 1
Output

Figure 8–1

We have seen that cyclic codes of length n correspond to ideals in $K[x]/\langle p(x)\rangle$, where $p(x) = 1 - x^n$. However, for the case that $p(x) \neq 1 - x^n$, the code corresponding to such an ideal is not necessarily cyclic. Thus, we will refer to such a code as a **pseudo-cyclic code.**

Let us close this section by investigating the relationship between cyclic codes and pseudo-cyclic codes. We begin with an example:

Example 5

Again consider the cyclic code dealt with in the previous two examples. Suppose that we form a new generator matrix G' from the original one by eliminating the last two rows and columns. The result is

$$G' = \begin{bmatrix} 1 & 1 & 0 & 1 & 0 \\ 0 & 1 & 1 & 0 & 1 \end{bmatrix}$$

Any such code obtained by deleting the last i rows and i columns, subject to the restriction $1 \leq i \leq k - 1$, from the generator matrix of a cyclic (n, k) code is called a **shortened cyclic code.**

The words of the code generated by G' are:

$$
\begin{array}{ccccc}
0 & 0 & 0 & 0 & 0 \\
1 & 1 & 0 & 1 & 0 \\
0 & 1 & 1 & 0 & 1 \\
1 & 0 & 1 & 1 & 1
\end{array}
$$

Thus, both the length and the dimension of the original code have been shortened by two. (However, the minimum distance remains the same.) Clearly, this code is not cyclic. Yet we may think of these code words as the binary representations of residue classes in the ring of polynomials modulo some polynomial $p(x)$ of degree 5. The residue classes, therefore, would be:

$$
\begin{array}{ccccc}
0 & 0 & 0 & 0 & 0 \leftrightarrow [0] \\
1 & 1 & 0 & 1 & 0 \leftrightarrow [1 + x + x^3] \\
0 & 1 & 1 & 0 & 1 \leftrightarrow [x + x^2 + x^4] \\
1 & 0 & 1 & 1 & 1 \leftrightarrow [1 + x^2 + x^3 + x^4]
\end{array}
$$

Since $1 + x + x^2 + x^5 = (1 + x + x^3) \cdot (1 + x^2)$, let's select $p(x) = 1 + x + x^2 + x^5$. However, $1 + x + x^3$ is the generator of an ideal of order 2^2. Since $1 + x + x^3$ divides both $x + x^2 + x^4$ and $1 + x^2 + x^3 + x^4$ but no other nonzero polynomial of degree less than 5, the set of the four residue classes given above constitutes the ideal. Thus, we see that this shortened cyclic code is a pseudo-cyclic code. This demonstrates a special case of the following general result. ◊

THEOREM 4

Every shortened binary cyclic code is a pseudo-cyclic code.

Proof

A binary cyclic code corresponds to an ideal H in the ring $GF(2)[x]/\langle 1 - x^n \rangle$. Suppose that $g(x)$ has degree $n - k$ and is the generator of H. Then the binary n-tuples corresponding to $[g(x)], [x \cdot g(x)], [x^2 \cdot g(x)], \ldots, [x^{k-1} \cdot g(x)]$ are a set of generators for the subgroup H. A shortened cyclic code of length $n' = n - i$ (for $1 \leq i \leq k - 1$) is the subgroup generated by the n'-tuples corresponding to the n' low order coefficients of $g(x)$, $x \cdot g(x)$, $x^2 \cdot g(x)$, $\ldots$, $x^{k-1-i} \cdot g(x)$. We would like to show that this subgroup of order 2^{k-i} corresponds to the ideal generated by $g(x)$ in the ring of polynomials modulo some polynomial $p(x)$ having degree n'.

Dividing $g(x)$ into $x^{n'}$, we get

$$
x^{n'} = g(x) \cdot h(x) + r(x)
$$

where the degree of $r(x)$ is less than the degree of $g(x)$. Consequently, we let

$$
p(x) = -r(x) + x^{n'} = g(x) \cdot h(x)
$$

Since $1 \leq i \leq k - 1$, we have $x^{n'} \neq r(x)$, and thus $p(x)$ is nonzero, has degree n', and is divisible by $g(x)$. Thus $g(x)$ generates an ideal in the ring of polynomials modulo $p(x)$, and since $\deg g = n - k$, the ideal has order $2^{n'-(n-k)} = 2^{k-i}$. In addition, $[g(x)], [x \cdot g(x)], [x^2 \cdot g(x)], \ldots, [x^{k-1-i} \cdot g(x)]$ are residue classes in this ideal. Since these residue classes are a minimum set, they generate a subgroup or order 2^{k-i}. Thus, this subgroup is exactly the ideal. Hence, the binary shortened cyclic code of dimension $k - i$ corresponds to this ideal, and is thus a pseudo-cyclic code.   □

Again, we leave the generalization of this theorem to the case of $K[x]/\langle 1 - x^n \rangle$ for those readers who are familiar with linear algebra and are so inclined.

Example 6

Let us consider the ring $GF(2)[x]/\langle p(x) \rangle$ of polynomials modulo $p(x) = 1 + x^2 + x^4 + x^5 + x^6 + x^7$. This polynomial can be written as $p(x) = g(x) \cdot h(x)$, where $g(x) = 1 + x^2 + x^3 + x^4$ and $h(x) = 1 + x + x^3$. We know that the pseudo-cyclic code corresponding to the ideal having the generator polynomial $g(x)$ has a generator matrix of

$$
G = \begin{bmatrix} 1 & 0 & 1 & 1 & 1 & 0 & 0 \\ 0 & 1 & 0 & 1 & 1 & 1 & 0 \\ 0 & 0 & 1 & 0 & 1 & 1 & 1 \end{bmatrix}
$$

Forming all possible sums of the rows of G yields the following additional words, which complete the code:

$$
\begin{array}{ccccccc}
0 & 0 & 0 & 0 & 0 & 0 & 0 \\
1 & 1 & 1 & 0 & 0 & 1 & 0 \\
0 & 1 & 1 & 1 & 0 & 0 & 1 \\
1 & 0 & 0 & 1 & 0 & 1 & 1 \\
1 & 1 & 0 & 0 & 1 & 0 & 1
\end{array}
$$

Inspection reveals that this code is a cyclic code. This is because $g(x)$ divides $1 + x^7$ as well as $1 + x^2 + x^4 + x^5 + x^6 + x^7$. Hence, $g(x)$ also generates an ideal in the ring of polynomials modulo $1 + x^7$. In fact, we have an almost complete converse to Theorem 4. Again our proof is for the binary case $K = GF(2)$.   ◊

THEOREM 5

A binary pseudo-cyclic code of length n and minimum distance 3 or greater that is generated by a polynomial of period n' is either a cyclic code or a shortened cyclic code.

Proof

By definition a binary pseudo-cyclic code of length n corresponds to an ideal H in some ring $GF(2)[x]/\langle p(x) \rangle$, where the degree of $p(x)$ is n. Suppose that $g(x)$ has degree m, period n', and is the generator polynomial of H. If $n' = n$, then H corresponds to a cyclic code. If $n' < n$, then $[1 - x^{n'}] \in H$, and this residue class corresponds to a code word of weight 2. Therefore, $n' > n$. Now $g(x)$ generates an ideal H' in the ring of polynomials modulo $1 - x^{n'}$. This ideal H' is a subgroup which has generators $[g(x)]$, $[x \cdot g(x)]$, $[x^2 \cdot g(x)]$, $\ldots$, $[x^{n'-m-1} \cdot g(x)]$ that constitute a minimum set. By shortening the dimension and length of the corresponding cyclic code by $n' - n$, the resulting code corresponds to the subgroup of residue classes generated by $[g(x)]$, $[x \cdot g(x)]$, $[x^2 \cdot g(x)]$, $\ldots$, $[x^{n-m-1} \cdot g(x)]$ in the ring $GF(2)[x]/\langle p(x) \rangle$. But this subgroup is exactly the ideal H. Hence, the theorem follows. □

EXERCISES FOR SECTION 8–2

1.   What is the length of the shortest binary cyclic code which corresponds to an ideal having a generator polynomial of $1 + x^5 + x^{10}$? Find a generator matrix in the form $G = [AI_k]$ for this code.

2.   Consider the binary cyclic code which corresponds to the ideal generated by $g(x)$ in the ring of polynomials modulo $1 + x^n$, where n is the period of $g(x)$. Prove that the code has minimum distance 3 or greater. [Hint: Consult Definition 8–3–2.]

3.   The following is a generator matrix for a binary group code.

$$G = \begin{bmatrix} 1 & 1 & 0 & 1 & 1 & 1 & 0 & 0 & 0 & 0 \\ 0 & 1 & 1 & 0 & 1 & 1 & 1 & 0 & 0 & 0 \\ 0 & 0 & 1 & 1 & 0 & 1 & 1 & 1 & 0 & 0 \\ 0 & 0 & 0 & 1 & 1 & 0 & 1 & 1 & 1 & 0 \\ 0 & 0 & 0 & 0 & 1 & 1 & 0 & 1 & 1 & 1 \end{bmatrix}$$

Is this code a cyclic code? If your answer is yes, what is the generator polynomial of the corresponding ideal? If your answer is no, why not?

4.   The matrix P given below is a parity check matrix for a binary cyclic code.

$$P = \begin{bmatrix} 1 & 0 & 0 & 0 & 0 & 1 & 1 & 1 \\ 0 & 1 & 0 & 0 & 0 & 1 & 0 & 0 \\ 0 & 0 & 1 & 0 & 0 & 0 & 1 & 0 \\ 0 & 0 & 0 & 1 & 0 & 0 & 0 & 1 \\ 0 & 0 & 0 & 0 & 1 & 1 & 1 & 1 \end{bmatrix}$$

Find the generator polynomial for the ideal corresponding to the cyclic code.

5.   Generalize Fact 7–4–2 from $GF(2)$ to any finite field K.

6.   The solutions of the difference equation

$$g_i + g_{i+1} + g_{i+4} = 0 \quad \text{for } i = 0, 1, 2, \ldots$$

are periodic with period 15. Find a set of generators for the group of solutions.

7.   Give an example of a difference equation which has a nontrivial solution of period n and a nontrivial solution of period less than n.

8.   Verify equation (7).

9.   Determine a shift register encoder for the length n binary cyclic code corresponding to the ideal generated by $g(x)$, where:

$$\text{(a) } n = 6, g(x) = 1 + x + x^2$$
$$\text{(b) } n = 8, g(x) = 1 + x + x^4 + x^5$$

8-3   Minimum Polynomials and Maximum-Length Codes

In this section we develop some further properties of finite groups and fields, especially extension fields, and minimum polynomials. We then apply these ideas to the study of maximum-length codes.

Recall that if p is a prime number, then $\mathbf{Z}_p$, the ring of integers modulo p, is a finite field called the **Galois*** field with p elements. This field, denoted $GF(p)$, is an example of a prime field. However, there are finite fields that are not prime. We now give an example of one such nonprime field.

Example 1

In Exercise 10 of Section 7-1, we asked the reader to determine the addition and multiplication tables for $GF(2)[x]/\langle 1 + x + x^2 \rangle$, the ring of polynomials modulo $1 + x + x^2$. These tables are shown below:

+	[0]	[1]	[x]	[1 + x]
[0]	[0]	[1]	[x]	[1 + x]
[1]	[1]	[0]	[1 + x]	[x]
[x]	[x]	[1 + x]	[0]	[1]
[1 + x]	[1 + x]	[x]	[1]	[0]

·	[0]	[1]	[x]	[1 + x]
[0]	[0]	[0]	[0]	[0]
[1]	[0]	[1]	[x]	[1 + x]
[x]	[0]	[x]	[1 + x]	[1]
[1 + x]	[0]	[1 + x]	[1]	[x]

We already know that this ring is commutative and has a multiplicative identity, that being the element [1]. By inspection, we see that each nonzero

---

*Named for the French mathematician Evariste Galois (1811–1832).

element has a multiplicative inverse. Hence, this ring is a finite field, specifically the Galois field $GF(4)$. From Exercise 1 of Section 8–1, we know that $GF(2)[x]/\langle x + x^2 \rangle$ is not a field. Is $GF(2)[x]/\langle 1 + x^2 \rangle$ a field (Exercise 1)?

◊

We shall now describe how fields like the one in Example 1 can be constructed. In order to do this, we must first define the following:

DEFINITION 1

Suppose that $f(x)$ is a polynomial of degree n with coefficients in any field K. Then $f(x)$ is said to be **irreducible** over K if there is no polynomial of degree r, $0 < r < n$, with coefficients in K that divides $f(x)$; otherwise, $f(x)$ is **reducible** over K.

○

Example 2

The polynomial $p_1(x) = 1 + x + x^2$ is irreducible over $GF(2)$, as is $p_2(x) = 1 + x^3 + x^4$. However, the polynomial $p_3(x) = 1 + x + x^2 + x^5 = (1 + x + x^3) \cdot (1 + x^2)$, and is thus reducible.

◊

In Example 1, we saw that the ring of polynomials modulo $1 + x + x^2$ is a field. We shall now see that this is a consequence of the fact that $1 + x + x^2$ is irreducible over $GF(2)$. More generally, we have the following:

THEOREM 1

The ring $K[x]/\langle p(x) \rangle$ is a field if and only if $p(x)$ is irreducible over K.

Proof

It suffices to demonstrate the existence of multiplicative inverses for all the nonzero ring elements.

First consider the ring of polynomials modulo $p(x)$, where $p(x)$ has degree n and is a reducible polynomial. Then there exist polynomials $q(x)$ and $r(x)$, where $0 < \deg q < n$ and $0 < \deg r < n$, such that $p(x) = q(x) \cdot r(x)$. Thus, $[0] = [p(x)] = [q(x) \cdot r(x)] = [q(x)] \cdot [r(x)]$. If $[q(x)]$ has a multiplicative inverse $[q(x)]^{-1}$, then $[0] = [q(x)]^{-1} \cdot [0] = [q(x)]^{-1} \cdot [q(x)] \cdot [r(x)] = [r(x)]$; this is a contradiction, since $r(x)$ is not a multiple of $p(x)$. Therefore, $[q(x)]$ has no inverse. This implies that the ring of polynomials modulo $p(x)$ is not a field. Hence, if the ring of polynomials modulo $p(x)$ is a field, then $p(x)$ is irreducible.

Conversely, assume that $p(x)$ is an irreducible polynomial. We claim that for every residue class $[s(x)] \neq [0]$ there exists a multiplicative inverse $[s(x)]^{-1}$. Thus, consider the residue class $[s(x)]$, where the degree of $s(x)$ is $m < n$. If $m = 0$, then $s(x) = s_0 \in K$ and $[s(x)]^{-1} = [s_0^{-1}]$. So suppose that $0 < m < n$. Since $p(x)$ is irreducible, the greatest common divisor of $s(x)$ and $p(x)$ is 1. Thus, there exist polynomials $u(x)$ and $v(x)$ such that $1 = u(x) \cdot s(x) + v(x) \cdot p(x)$. Hence, $[1] = [u(x) \cdot s(x) + v(x) \cdot p(x)] = [u(x) \cdot s(x)] + [v(x) \cdot p(x)] = [u(x) \cdot s(x)] + [0] = [u(x)] \cdot [s(x)]$, and $[u(x)] = [s(x)]^{-1}$. Therefore, the ring of polynomials modulo $p(x)$ is a field.   ☐

The field K given in Theorem 1 is said to be a **ground field,** and the ring of polynomials modulo a polynomial which is irreducible over K is called an **extension field.** We have already given an example in which the ground field is $GF(2)$ and the extension field is the ring of polynomials modulo $1 + x + x^2$. Note also that if k and k' are distinct elements in the ground field, then $[k] \neq [k']$ is in the extension field (unless p is itself a scalar). In the sense which identifies k and $[k]$, then, the ground field is a subfield of the extension field.

Consider the Galois field $GF(2)$. We know that the order of the ring of polynomials modulo $p(x)$, where $p(x)$ has degree m, is 2^m. Thus, if $GF(2)$ is the ground field and $p(x)$ is irreducible and of degree m, the resulting extension field is denoted $GF(2^m)$.

Now consider $GF(p)$, the ring of integers modulo a prime number p. In general, if $p(x)$† has degree m and is irreducible over $GF(p)$, the resulting extension field has order p^m and is therefore called $GF(p^m)$. However, there is no reason why such an extension field cannot be used as a ground field for yet another extension field. Thus, if $q(x)$ is a polynomial of degree n which is irreducible over $GF(p^m)$, we can form the extension field $GF(p^{m \cdot n})$.

THEOREM 2

If K is a finite field, then $|K| = p^m$, where p is a prime number and m is a positive number.

Proof

Let 1 denote the *multiplicative* identity of K. Form the following sums: $1 + 1$, $1 + 1 + 1$, $1 + 1 + 1 + 1$, etc. Denote these respectively by the integers 2, 3, 4, etc. Let p be the order of the *additive* subgroup S_1 of K so generated by 1. If p is not prime, then there exist positive integers q and r such that

---

†A different p!

$1 < q < p$, $1 < r < p$, and $q \cdot r = p$. Thus, $q \cdot r = 0$—a contradiction since a field cannot have nonzero divisors of 0. Hence, p is a prime number.

If $S_1 = K$, then $m = 1$ and we are done. If not, pick $\alpha \in K$ such that $\alpha \notin S_1$. Form the set

$$S_2 = \{a_0 + a_1 \cdot \alpha \, | \, a_0, a_1 \in S_1\} \subset K$$

Then all of the elements in S_2 are distinct; for suppose that

$$a_0 + a_1 \cdot \alpha = b_0 + b_1 \cdot \alpha$$

where a_0, a_1, b_0, $b_1 \in S_1$ and $(a_0, a_1) \neq (b_0, b_1)$. Then

$$\begin{aligned} a_0 - b_0 &= b_1 \cdot \alpha - a_1 \cdot \alpha \\ &= (b_1 - a_1) \cdot \alpha \end{aligned}$$

If $a_1 \neq b_1$, then

$$\alpha = (b_1 - a_1)^{-1} \cdot (a_0 - b_0) \in S_1$$

which is a contradiction to the fact that $\alpha \notin S_1$. If $a_1 = b_1$, then

$$a_0 - b_0 = 0$$

so

$$a_0 = b_0$$

which is a contradiction to the fact that $(a_0, a_1) \neq (b_0, b_1)$.

Since $|S_1| = p$, we have that $|S_2| = p^2$. If $S_2 = K$, then $m = 2$ and we are done. If not, pick $\beta \in K$ such that $\beta \notin S_2$. Form the set

$$S_3 = \{a_0 + a_1 \cdot \alpha + a_2 \cdot \beta \, | \, a_0, a_1, a_2 \in S_1\} \subset K$$

As in the above discussion, we conclude that the elements in S_3 are distinct and $|S_3| = p^3$.

Continuing in this manner, we conclude that for some positive number m, we have that $|K| = p^m$, where p is a prime number.   □

It is known that over any finite field there exists an irreducible polynomial of degree m, where m is any positive integer. Thus, for any prime number p and any positive integer m, there exists a finite field $GF(p^m)$. Furthermore, by Theorem 2, if a finite field contains q elements, then $q = p^m$ for some prime number p and some positive integer m. It follows from the proof of Theorem 2 that such a field is isomorphic to $GF(p^m)$. Thus, there is only one finite field with $q = p^m$ elements, and that is the Galois field $GF(q)$. No finite field with q elements exists if q is not a power of a prime.

We shall now establish some of the important properties of Galois fields. We begin by discussing the relationships between the field elements and the roots of the polynomial $x - x^q$.

DEFINITION 2

Suppose that $p(x)$ is a polynomial with coefficients in a field K, and suppose that $x - k$ divides $p(x)$, where $k \in K$. Then there exists a polynomial $q(x)$ such that $p(x) = (x - k) \cdot q(x)$. Thus, $p(k) = 0$, and k is called a **root** of $p(x)$.   ○

According to our definition, for each root k we can factor the term $x - k$ from the polynomial $p(x)$. Therefore, if $p(x)$ has r roots, the degree of $p(x)$ is at least r. Conversely, if $p(x)$ has degree n, it cannot have more than n roots.

Example 3

In the Galois field $GF(2)$, the roots of a polynomial are either 0 or 1. The polynomial $p_1(x) = x + x^2$ can be factored into the form $p_1(x) = x \cdot (1 + x)$. Thus, $p_1(x)$ has 0 and 1 as its two roots. The polynomial $p_2(x) = 1 + x^3 = (1 + x) \cdot (1 + x + x^2)$, however, has only a single root, that being 1. On the other hand, $p_3(x) = 1 + x + x^2 + x^3 + x^4 + x^5 + x^6 = (1 + x + x^3) \cdot (1 + x^2 + x^3)$ has no roots in $GF(2)$, while $p_4(x) = 1 + x^4 = (1 + x) \cdot (1 + x) \cdot (1 + x) \cdot (1 + x)$ has four roots, all of which are 1.   ◊

Suppose that we are given a polynomial $p(x) = p_0 + p_1 x + p_2 x^2 + \cdots + p_n x^n$, where $p_i \in GF(p)$ for $i = 0, 1, 2, \ldots, n$. Since $GF(p)$ is a subfield of $GF(p^m)$, let us consider the same polynomial with the coefficients considered as the elements of the extension field $GF(p^m)$; that is, consider $p(x) = [p_0] + [p_1]x + [p_2]x^2 + \cdots + [p_n]x^n$, where $[p_i] \in GF(p^m)$ for $i = 0, 1, 2, \ldots, n$. Clearly, if $a \in GF(p)$ is a root of the polynomial $p(x)$ with coefficients in $GF(p)$, then $[a] \in GF(p^m)$ is a root of $p(x)$ having coefficients in $GF(p^m)$. In the latter case, however, there may be roots in $GF(p^m)$ that are not in $GF(p)$.

In the discussion that follows, we can avoid confusion by representing the residue classes comprising the ring of polynomials modulo a polynomial of degree n as n-tuples. Specifically, we will represent any residue class

$$[a_0 + a_1 x + a_2 x^2 + \cdots + a_{n-1} x^{n-1}]$$

as

$$(a_0, a_1, a_2, \ldots, a_{n-1})$$

or, more simply, as

$$a_0 a_1 a_2 \cdots a_{n-1}$$

Example 4

For the factor ring $GF(2)[x]/\langle 1 + x + x^2 \rangle$, that is, for $GF(2^2) = GF(4)$, we have the following associations:

$$[0] \leftrightarrow 00$$
$$[1] \leftrightarrow 10$$
$$[x] \leftrightarrow 01$$
$$[1 + x] \leftrightarrow 11$$

Hence, rewriting the addition and multiplication tables for this field results in:

+	00	10	01	11
00	00	10	01	11
10	10	00	11	01
01	01	11	00	10
11	11	01	10	00

·	00	10	01	11
00	00	00	00	00
10	00	10	01	11
01	00	01	11	10
11	00	11	10	01

(Note that the elements of $GF(4)$ under addition actually comprise the Klein four-group of Section 5-2.)

Let us consider the polynomial $p(x) = x + x^4 = x \cdot (1 + x) \cdot (1 + x + x^2)$ having coefficients in $GF(2)$. Clearly, $p(x)$ has a single root 0 and a single root 1. Suppose, then, that the coefficients of $p(x)$ are elements of $GF(4)$. Then $p(x) = (10)x + (10)x^4$. Since $p(00) = (10)(00) + (10)(00)^4 = 00$ and $p(10) = (10)(10) + (10)(10)^4 = 10 + 10 = 00$, the elements 00 and 10 in $GF(4)$ are roots, as we expect. However, we now see that since $p(01) = (10)(01) + (10)(01)^4 = 01 + (10)(01) = 01 + 01 = 00$ and $p(11) = (10)(11) + (10)(11)^4 = 11 + (10)(11) = 11 + 11 = 00$, the elements 01 and 11 are also roots of $p(x)$. Thus, we see that the elements of $GF(4)$ are the four roots of $p(x) = (10)x + (10)x^4$. Hence, we can write $p(x) = (x + 00)(x + 01)(x + 10)(x + 11)$. $\Diamond$

This last example has been a demonstration of the following theorem for the case $q = 4$.

THEOREM 3

The elements of $GF(q)$ are all the roots of the polynomial $x - x^q$. (*Note:* Recall that $x - x^q = x + x^q$ in the binary case.)

Proof

Clearly, $0 \in GF(q)$ is a root of $x - x^q$. We now claim that each nonzero element of $GF(q)$ is also a root of $x - x^q = x \cdot (1 - x^{q-1})$.

Since there are $q - 1$ nonzero elements in $GF(q)$, and since they form a group under multiplication, the order of each nonzero element divides $q - 1$. Thus, if $\alpha \in GF(q)$, then $\alpha^{q-1} = 1$. Hence, $1 - \alpha^{q-1} = 0$, and α is a root of $1 - x^{q-1}$ and, thus, of $x - x^q$. Since $x - x^q$ has no more than q roots, and since each element in $GF(q)$ is a root, these are all the roots of $x - x^q$.   □

Example 5

Over $GF(2)$, the polynomial $p(x) = 1 + x + x^3 + x^4$ is reducible and can be factored as $p(x) = (1 + x) \cdot (1 + x) \cdot (1 + x + x^2)$. In this case, $p(x)$ has two roots, both of which are 1. Now, the polynomial $1 + x + x^2$ can be factored completely over $GF(2^2)$. As was seen in Example 4, each element of $GF(2^2)$ is a root of $x - x^4$. Since $1 + x + x^2$ divides $x - x^4$, the polynomial $1 + x + x^2$ can also be completely factored in $GF(4)$. Now, if $s(x) = 1 + x + x^2$, then

$$s(01) = 10 + 01 + (01)^2 = 10 + 01 + 11 = 00$$

and

$$s(11) = 10 + 11 + (11)^2 = 10 + 11 + 01 = 00$$

Thus, 01 and 11 are the roots of $s(x)$. Since $1 \in GF(2)$ is a double root of $p(x)$, then $10 \in GF(4)$ is a double root of $p(x)$. Hence, we finally have $p(x) = (x + 01) \cdot (x + 11) \cdot (x + 10)^2$.   ◊

Let us now consider the element $010 \in GF(8)$. By Theorem 3, 010 is a root of $x - x^8$ and, hence, of $1 - x^7$. We may now ask, "What are all the polynomials of degree less than 7 with coefficients in $GF(2)$ such that 010 is a root of all the corresponding polynomials with coefficients in $GF(8)$?" By exhaustion, using Exercise 4, we can determine the polynomials to be:

$$0$$

$$1 + x + x^3$$

$$x + x^2 + x^4 = x \cdot (1 + x + x^3)$$

$$1 + x^2 + x^3 + x^4 = (1 + x) \cdot (1 + x + x^3)$$

$$x^2 + x^3 + x^5 = x^2 \cdot (1 + x + x^3)$$

$$x + x^3 + x^4 + x^5 = (x + x^2) \cdot (1 + x + x^3)$$

$$1 + x + x^2 + x^5 = (1 + x^2) \cdot (1 + x + x^3)$$

$$1 + x^4 + x^5 = (1 + x + x^2) \cdot (1 + x + x^3)$$

$$x^3 + x^4 + x^6 = x^3 \cdot (1 + x + x^3)$$

$$1 + x + x^4 + x^6 = (1 + x^3) \cdot (1 + x + x^3)$$

$$1 + x^2 + x^6 = (1 + x + x^3) \cdot (1 + x + x^3)$$

$$1 + x + x^2 + x^3 + x^4 + x^5 + x^6 = (1 + x^2 + x^3) \cdot (1 + x + x^3)$$

$$1 + x^3 + x^5 + x^6 = (1 + x + x^2 + x^3) \cdot (1 + x + x^3)$$

$$x + x^2 + x^3 + x^6 = (x + x^3) \cdot (1 + x + x^3)$$

$$x^2 + x^4 + x^5 + x^6 = (x^2 + x^3) \cdot (1 + x + x^3)$$

$$x + x^5 + x^6 = (x + x^2 + x^3) \cdot (1 + x + x^3)$$

We now note that all these polynomials have one property in common; they are all divisible by $m(x) = 1 + x + x^3$. In addition, it should be obvious that any polynomial that is divisible by $m(x)$ has 010 as a root. Since $m(x)$ divides $1 - x^7$, it is a generator polynomial for an ideal H in the ring of polynomials modulo $1 - x^7$. Furthermore, $[s(x)] \in H$ if and only if $s(x)$ is divisible by $m(x)$. Thus, the above list consists of those polynomials which are the representations of the residue classes which constitute H. Thus, we see that by specifying an element in an extension field to be a root of a polynomial, a unique ideal can be defined.

Now note that the polynomial $m(x) = 1 + x + x^3$ is irreducible over $GF(2)$ and is the polynomial of smallest degree which has 010 as a root. Such a polynomial is given a special name.

DEFINITION 3

Suppose that α is an element in an extension field of a ground field K. Let $m(x)$ be a minimum degree monic polynomial with coefficients in K such that $m(\alpha) = 0$. Then $m(x)$ is said to be a **minimum polynomial** of α. (Here 0 denotes the additive identity of the extension field.)   ○

Clearly, if $m(x)$ is a minimum polynomial of α, then $m(x)$ is irreducible over K. If this were not so, then we could write $m(x) = p(x) \cdot q(x)$. Since $0 = m(\alpha) = p(\alpha) \cdot q(\alpha)$, this implies either $p(\alpha) = 0$ or $q(\alpha) = 0$—a contradiction to the definition of a minimum polynomial.

THEOREM 4

Let α be an element in an extension field of K, and suppose that $m(x)$ is a minimum polynomial of α. Then α is a root of $p(x)$, where $p(x)$ has coefficients in K, if and only if $m(x)$ divides $p(x)$.

Proof

Clearly, if $m(x)$ divides $p(x)$, then $p(x) = m(x) \cdot q(x)$ and $p(\alpha) = m(\alpha) \cdot q(\alpha) = 0$. Thus, α is a root of $p(x)$.

Now suppose that α is a root of $p(x)$. By polynomial division we can write

$$p(x) = m(x) \cdot q(x) + r(x)$$

where the degree of $r(x)$ is less than the degree of $m(x)$. But

$$p(\alpha) = m(\alpha) \cdot q(\alpha) + r(\alpha)$$
$$0 = 0 \cdot q(\alpha) + r(\alpha)$$
$$0 = r(\alpha).$$

If $r(x) \neq 0$, this contradicts the fact that $m(x)$ is a minimum polynomial of α. Hence, $r(x) = 0$ and $m(x)$ divides $p(x)$. □

COROLLARY 5

Let $m_1(x)$ and $m_2(x)$ both be minimum polynomials of α. Then, since $m_1(x)$ divides $m_2(x)$ and vice versa, $m_1(x) = m_2(x)$ and the minimum polynomial is unique. □

Recall (Theorem 8-2-1) that cyclic codes correspond to ideals in $K[x]/\langle 1 - x^n \rangle$. One way of generating such ideals can be summarized as follows:

THEOREM 6

Given a nonzero element α in $GF(2^m)$, form a code whose words correspond precisely to those $[s(x)]$ for which α is a root of $s(x)$. Then the code is a binary cyclic code whose length is the order of α; and the generator polynomial $g(x)$ of the corresponding ideal is $m(x)$, the minimum polynomial of α.

Proof

Suppose that α is a nonzero element of $GF(2^m)$, and suppose that $m(x)$ is the minimum polynomial of α. We know by Theorem 3 that α is a root of $x - x^{2^m}$ and, hence, of $1 - x^{2^m-1}$. However, if the order* of α is $n < 2^m - 1$, then α is also a root of $1 - x^n$. Thus, $m(x)$ divides $1 - x^n$, and n is the smallest integer such that $1 - x^n$ is divisible by $m(x)$, i.e. n is the period of $m(x)$. If this were not the case, then since α is a root of $m(x)$, the

---

*Recall that the nonzero elements of a field are a group under multiplication.

order of α would be less than n. Hence, letting $g(x) = m(x)$, we see that $g(x)$ generates an ideal in the ring of polynomials modulo $1 - x^n$, and this ideal corresponds to a binary cyclic code.   □

Example 6

Let $\alpha = 010 \in GF(2^3)$, where this field is defined by the ring of polynomials modulo $1 + x + x^3$. We will find a generator matrix for a cyclic code corresponding to the ideal H for which $[s(x)] \in H$ if and only if α is a root of $s(x)$. Since the order of α divides $2^3 - 1 = 7$, and since $\alpha \neq 100$, then the order of α is $n = 7$. The minimum polynomial of α is $m(x) = 1 + x + x^3$. Thus, $g(x) = 1 + x + x^3$ is a generator polynomial for an ideal in the ring of polynomials modulo $1 + x^7$. This ideal corresponds to a cyclic code having a generator matrix given by

$$G = \begin{bmatrix} 1 & 1 & 0 & 1 & 0 & 0 & 0 \\ 0 & 1 & 1 & 0 & 1 & 0 & 0 \\ 0 & 0 & 1 & 1 & 0 & 1 & 0 \\ 0 & 0 & 0 & 1 & 1 & 0 & 1 \end{bmatrix}$$

In Example 8-2-3, we saw that a parity check matrix for this code is

$$P = \begin{bmatrix} 1 & 0 & 0 & 1 & 0 & 1 & 1 \\ 0 & 1 & 0 & 1 & 1 & 1 & 0 \\ 0 & 0 & 1 & 0 & 1 & 1 & 1 \end{bmatrix}$$

Note that the columns of P consist of all the possible nonzero binary triples. Hence, P is a parity check matrix for a cyclic code that is equivalent to a Hamming code. (The codes are equivalent in the sense that the digits of the code words are simply reordered.) We eventually shall see that this result is a consequence of the choice of α.   ◊

To develop our understanding of $GF(q)$, we must first prove a property of finite abelian groups. We begin with the following.

DEFINITION 4

Let G be a finite abelian group under multiplication. Suppose that e is the order of $g \in G$, and no other element in G has order greater than e. Then e is called the **exponent** of G.   ○

This definition gives rise to an important property.

LEMMA 7

Suppose that G is a finite abelian group having exponent e. Then the order of every element of G divides e.

Proof

Since the exponent of G is e, there exists $g \in G$ such that the order of g is e. Assume that there exists $g' \in G$, where the order of g' is e', such that e' does not divide e. Then, there exists a prime p with associated powers r and s such that

$$e = p^r \cdot n$$
$$e' = p^s \cdot m$$

where $s > r \geq 0$, and p does not divide n or m (why?).

Consider the element $g_1 = g^{p^r}$. Since $g_1^n = (g^{p^r})^n = g^e = 1$, the order of g_1 divides n. If the order of g_1 is less than n, then the order of g is less than e—a contradiction. Thus, the order of g_1 is n. Now consider the element $g_2 = (g')^m$. As argued above, the order of g_2 is p^s.

Next form the element $g_1 \cdot g_2$. Since $(g_1 \cdot g_2)^{p^s \cdot n} = (g_1^n)^{p^s} \cdot (g_2^{p^s})^n = 1$, then the order of $g_1 \cdot g_2$ divides $p^s \cdot n$. Let d be the order of $g_1 \cdot g_2$. Thus, $1 = (g_1 \cdot g_2)^d = g_1^d \cdot g_2^d$ from which $g_1^d = g_2^{-d}$. Let the cyclic subgroups generated by g_1 and g_2 be denoted by G_1 and G_2, respectively. But $g_2^{-d} = g_1^d \in G_1$ and $g_1^d = g_2^{-d} \in G_2$. Since the order of G_1 is n and the order of G_2 is p^s, the order of the cyclic subgroup generated by g_1^d divides both n and p^s. However, n and p^s are relatively prime. Thus, $g_1^d = 1$. Hence, $g_2^d = 1$. Therefore, n divides d, as does p^s. But n and p^s are relatively prime. Thus, $p^s \cdot n$ divides d. From above, d divides $p^s \cdot n$. Hence, $d = p^s \cdot n > p^r \cdot n$—a contradiction since $p^r \cdot n$ is the exponent of G. Therefore, e' divides e, and the order of every element in G divides e. □

Having proved this lemma, it is now a simple matter for us to prove the next theorem.

THEOREM 8

The nonzero elements of $GF(q)$ are a *cyclic* group under multiplication.

Proof

We know that the nonzero elements of $GF(q)$ are a finite abelian group under multiplication, and this group has order $q - 1$. Let e be the exponent of this group. Since the order of any element g in this group divides e, then $g^e = 1$. Thus, g is a root of $1 - x^e$, for every element g in the group. However, there are at most e roots of $1 - x^e$. Therefore, $e \geq q - 1$. Conversely, the exponent of a group is at most the order of the group. Thus, $e \leq q - 1$. Hence, $e = q - 1$, which implies that the group is cyclic. □

As we shall see, the role of a generator of the cyclic group described in the previous theorem is of considerable importance to us. Consequently, we have the following:

DEFINITION 5

Suppose that $\alpha \in GF(q)$ is a generator for the cyclic group consisting of all the nonzero elements in $GF(q)$. Then α is said to be a **primitive element** of $GF(q)$. ○

Example 7

We can form $GF(16)$ by constructing the ring of polynomials modulo the irreducible polynomial $1 + x + x^2 + x^3 + x^4$. We know that the identity element $[1]$ cannot be a generator for the 15 nonzero elements. Thus, let us test the element $\alpha = [x]$. Since

$$\alpha = [x]^1 = [x] = 0100$$
$$\alpha^2 = [x] \cdot [x] = [x^2] = 0010$$
$$\alpha^3 = [x] \cdot [x^2] = [x^3] = 0001$$
$$\alpha^4 = [x] \cdot [x^3] = [1 + x + x^2 + x^3] = 1111$$
$$\alpha^5 = [x] \cdot [1 + x + x^2 + x^3] = [1] = 1000$$

then the order of $\alpha = 0100$ is 5, and α is therefore not a primitive element of $GF(16)$. However, for the element $\beta = [1 + x]$ we have:

$$\beta = [1 + x]^1 = [1 + x] = 1100$$
$$\beta^2 = [1 + x] \cdot [1 + x] = [1 + x^2] = 1010$$
$$\beta^3 = [1 + x] \cdot [1 + x^2] = [1 + x + x^2 + x^3] = 1111$$
$$\beta^4 = [1 + x] \cdot [1 + x + x^2 + x^3] = [x + x^2 + x^3] = 0111$$
$$\beta^5 = [1 + x] \cdot [x + x^2 + x^3] = [1 + x^2 + x^3] = 1011$$
$$\beta^6 = [1 + x] \cdot [1 + x^2 + x^3] = [x^3] = 0001$$
$$\beta^7 = [1 + x] \cdot [x^3] = [1 + x + x^2] = 1110$$
$$\beta^8 = [1 + x] \cdot [1 + x + x^2] = [1 + x^3] = 1001$$

$$\beta^9 = [1 + x] \cdot [1 + x^3] = [x^2] = 0010$$

$$\beta^{10} = [1 + x] \cdot [x^2] = [x^2 + x^3] = 0011$$

$$\beta^{11} = [1 + x] \cdot [x^2 + x^3] = [1 + x + x^3] = 1101$$

$$\beta^{12} = [1 + x] \cdot [1 + x + x^3] = [x] = 0100$$

$$\beta^{13} = [1 + x] \cdot [x] = [x + x^2] = 0110$$

$$\beta^{14} = [1 + x] \cdot [x + x^2] = [x + x^3] = 0101$$

$$\beta^{15} = [1 + x] \cdot [x + x^3] = [1] = 1000$$

Thus, we see that the order of β is 15, and hence $\beta = 1100$ is a primitive element of $GF(16)$. Since the order of any element divides the order of the group, any nonzero element other than 1000 has order 3, 5, or 15. Hence, in the above list, once it was determined that $\beta^5 \neq 1000$, we were assured that β is a primitive element. However, we continued the list so as to enumerate the nonzero elements of $GF(16)$ explicitly as powers of β.   ◊

DEFINITION 6

If an irreducible polynomial of degree m from $GF(2)[x]$ has a root which is a primitive element in $GF(2^m)$, then it is said to be a **primitive polynomial.**

○

Of course, a similar definition holds for $GF(p)$, but for simplicity we shall leave the generalization to the reader in the remainder of this chapter.

We have left it to the reader (Exercise 7) to show that a polynomial $p(x)$, which has degree m and which is irreducible over $GF(2)$, divides $1 - x^{2^m - 1}$. Thus, since all the nonzero elements of $GF(2^m)$ are the roots of $1 - x^{2^m - 1}$, the roots of $p(x)$ are nonzero elements of $GF(2^m)$. If one of these roots is a primitive element of $GF(2^m)$, then $p(x)$ is a primitive polynomial.

We will now prove a very important theorem about primitive polynomials.

THEOREM 9

Suppose that $p(x)$ has degree m and is irreducible over $GF(2)$. Then $p(x)$ is a primitive polynomial if and only if its period is $2^m - 1$.

Proof

Let $p(x)$ be a primitive polynomial of degree m, where the primitive element $\alpha \in GF(2^m)$ is a root of $p(x)$. Assume that the period of $p(x)$ is $n < 2^m - 1$. Then $p(x)$ divides $1 - x^n$. Since α is a root of $p(x)$, α must be a root of $1 - x^n$.

Thus, $\alpha^n = 1$, which is a contradiction since α is primitive. But we know that $p(x)$ divides $1 - x^{2^m-1}$. Hence, the period of $p(x)$ is $2^m - 1$.

Now suppose that the period of $p(x)$ is $2^m - 1$. Let $\alpha \in GF(2^m)$ be a root of $p(x)$. Assume that α is not primitive. Then the order of α is $n < 2^m - 1$, and α is a root of $1 - x^n$. Since $p(x)$ is the minimum polynomial of α, then $p(x)$ divides $1 - x^n$, which is a contradiction since the period of $p(x)$ is $2^m - 1$. Hence, α is a primitive element, and $p(x)$ is a primitive polynomial. $\qquad\square$

Let us now recall our discussion of difference equations and their solutions. For the difference equation

$$\sum_{j=0}^{k} h_j g_{j+i} = 0 \quad \text{for } i = 0, 1, 2, \ldots$$

in which $h_0 = -h_k = 1$, we saw that a solution $s_0, s_1, s_2, \ldots$ was periodic with period n, where n is the smallest positive integer such that $h(x) = 1 + h_1 x + h_2 x^2 + \cdots + h_{k-1} x^{k-1} - x^k$ divides $1 - x^n$. We also saw that we could construct a shift register generator that could calculate such solutions. (The feedback connections of this register were determined by the values of h_i for $i = 0, 1, 2, \ldots, k - 1$.)

Suppose now that $h(x)$ is a primitive polynomial. Then the smallest positive integer n for which $h(x)$ divides $1 - x^n$ is $n = 2^k - 1$. Hence, the solutions to the equation are periodic with period $2^k - 1$. Are there any of these solutions with period less than $2^k - 1$? We soon shall see.

Example 8

The difference equation

$$g_i + g_{1+i} + g_{3+i} = 0 \quad \text{for } i = 0, 1, 2, \ldots$$

corresponds to the irreducible polynomial $h(x) = 1 + x + x^3$. Since the roots of $h(x)$ are nonzero elements in $GF(2^3)$, the order of a root divides $2^3 - 1 = 7$. Since a root of $h(x)$ is clearly not the multiplicative identity of $GF(8)$, the root must have order 7. Hence, $h(x)$ is a primitive polynomial, and the period of $h(x)$ is $2^3 - 1 = 7$. Consequently, the solutions of the difference equation are periodic with period 7.

Suppose now that we form the solution $s_0, s_1, s_2, s_3, \ldots$ by selecting $s_0 = 0$, $s_1 = 1$, $s_2 = 1$ and calculating $s_3, s_4, s_5, s_6, \ldots$ with the use of the given recurrence relation. The resulting solution is

$$0, 0, 1, 0, 1, 1, 1, 0, 0, 1, 0, 1, 1, 1, \ldots$$

and is periodic with period 7. Such a solution is produced by the shift register generator shown in Figure 8–2. $\diamond$

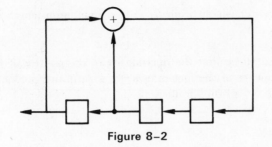

Figure 8–2

We may ask, "What is the maximum period of a sequence which can be produced by a 3-delay register?" We know that the initial content of the register fixes the output sequence. Consequently, knowledge of the content at any time implies knowledge of the output at any time in the future. So let us consider the output sequence

$$y_0, y_1, y_2, y_3, \cdots$$

where y_0, y_1, y_2 is the initial content. If y_1, y_2, y_3 is the same triple as y_0, y_1, y_2, then the output has period one. If, on the other hand, y_2, y_3, y_4 is the same triple as y_0, y_1, y_2, then the output has period two. In general, if i is the smallest integer such that y_i, y_{i+1}, y_{i+2} is the same as y_0, y_1, y_2, then the output is periodic with period i. Clearly, under this circumstance, it cannot happen that there exist integers q and r, where $0 < r < q \leq i$, such that y_r, y_{r+1}, y_{r+2} is the same as y_q, y_{q+1}, y_{q+2}. If this were the case, it would imply that $y_{q-r}, y_{q-r+1}, y_{q-r+2}$ is the same as y_0, y_1, y_2—a contradiction of the minimality of i.

The question is, then, "What is the largest possible value of i?" Since there are exactly $2^3 - 1 = 7$ distinct nonzero triples, and each successive triple in the sequence $y_0, y_1, y_2, y_3, \ldots$ must be different, the maximum value of i is 7. More generally:

FACT 10

A shift register generator with k delay elements cannot produce output sequences with periods greater than $2^k - 1$.   □

Since any nonzero sequence produced by the register shown in Figure 8–2 must have a period which divides 7, and since $1, 1, 1, \ldots$ is not a solution, the period of every nonzero solution is exactly 7.

DEFINITION 7

If the largest possible period, $2^k - 1$, is attained by the output sequence of a k-delay register, we say that it is a **maximum-length sequence,** and we refer to the register which produces it as a **maximum-length shift register generator.**

    ○

We shall now see that the maximality of the register of Figure 8–2 is more a consequence of the fact that $h(x)$ is a primitive polynomial than of the fact that 7 is a prime number.

THEOREM 11

A shift register generator which corresponds to a primitive polynomial $h(x)$ of degree k is a maximum-length shift register generator. Moreover, every sequence produced by such a register has period $2^k - 1$.

Proof

Because the period of $h(x)$ is $2^k - 1$, the generator is capable of producing a sequence of period $2^k - 1$. We are guaranteed that the sequence $\widehat{y}_0 = y_0,$ $y_1, y_2, \ldots, y_{n-1}, y_0, y_1, y_2, \ldots$ with $(y_0, y_1, \ldots, y_{k-1}) = (1, 0, \ldots, 0)$ which corresponds to the polynomial (recall (8) of Section 7–4)

$$g(x) = (1 - x^n)/h(x) = y_n + y_{n-1}x + \cdots + y_k x^{n-k}$$

where $n = 2^k - 1$, is such a sequence. But, the sequence $\widehat{y}_1 = y_1, y_2, y_3, \ldots,$ $y_{n-1}, y_0, y_1, y_2, \ldots$ is also a solution of the difference equation, and hence is another possible output of the shift register generator. The period of $\widehat{y}_1$ must also be $2^k - 1$, for otherwise there would be a contradiction to the periodicity of $\widehat{y}_0$. Similarly, the periods of the solutions

$$\widehat{y}_2 = y_2, y_3, y_4, \ldots, y_{n-1}, y_0, y_1, y_2, \ldots$$
$$\widehat{y}_3 = y_3, y_4, y_5, \ldots, y_{n-1}, y_0, y_1, y_2, \ldots$$
$$\vdots$$
$$\widehat{y}_{n-1} = y_{n-1}, y_0, y_1, \ldots, y_{n-1}, y_0, y_1, y_2, \ldots$$

all must be $2^k - 1$. However, there are exactly $2^k - 1$ nonzero solutions. Hence, $\widehat{y}_0, \widehat{y}_1, \widehat{y}_2, \ldots, \widehat{y}_{n-1}$ are all the solutions. Therefore, each solution has a period of exactly $2^k - 1$, so we see that every nonzero sequence produced by a maximum-length shift register generator is a maximum-length sequence.

    □

Example 9

Consider the primitive polynomial $h(x) = 1 + x + x^3$ and the corresponding recurrence relation of Example 8. Let us first look at the ideal H corresponding to the first period of the solutions of the difference equation. We know that the generator polynomial for H is

$$g(x) = (1 - x^7)/h(x) = 1 + x + x^2 + x^4$$

Because the shift register in Figure 8-2 generates maximum-length sequences, the cyclic code corresponding to this ideal is called a **maximum-length code.** This particular code has a generator matrix given by

$$G = \begin{bmatrix} 1 & 1 & 1 & 0 & 1 & 0 & 0 \\ 0 & 1 & 1 & 1 & 0 & 1 & 0 \\ 0 & 0 & 1 & 1 & 1 & 0 & 1 \end{bmatrix}$$

For reasons that will be apparent immediately, we shall list the remaining nonzero words of the code. They are:

$$\begin{array}{ccccccc} 1 & 0 & 0 & 1 & 1 & 1 & 0 \\ 0 & 1 & 0 & 0 & 1 & 1 & 1 \\ 1 & 1 & 0 & 1 & 0 & 0 & 1 \\ 1 & 0 & 1 & 0 & 0 & 1 & 1 \end{array}$$

We may note that, in addition to the fact that this is a minimum distance $(d = 4)$ code, each nonzero code word has weight 4. Thus, every pair of code words differ in exactly 4 positions. This is a demonstration of a special property of maximum-length codes.   ◊

THEOREM 12

If a maximum-length code has dimension k, then the minimum distance of the code is $d = 2^{k-1}$ and each nonzero code word has weight 2^{k-1}.

Proof

We know that each code word corresponds to a solution of the associated difference equations. In the last example, we had the solution:

$$0, 0, 1, 0, 1, 1, 1, 0, 0, 1, 0, 1, 1, 1, \ldots.$$

Since this is a maximum-length sequence of period 7, the first 7 consecutive triples are distinct, and hence, comprise all of the nonzero triples. We can easily verify this by reference to Figure 8-3.

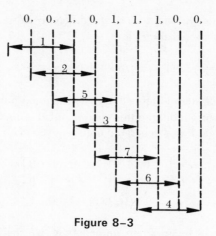

0, 0, 1, 0, 1, 1, 1, 0, 0,

Figure 8–3

Here, each binary triple is denoted by its corresponding decimal representation. We know that there are exactly $2^3 = 8$ binary triples, and hence a total of $3 \cdot 8 = 24$ bits. By symmetry, half of these must be 0 and half must be 1. Thus, there are $3 \cdot \frac{8}{2} = 12$ bits which are 1. By ignoring the triples consisting entirely of 0's, we see that of the 7 nonzero triples, there are still 12 bits which are 1. In the solution given in Figure 8–3, we have formed all the 7 nonzero triples. Since the first two bits in the second period are actually the first two bits in the first period, we have counted each bit three times. Therefore, the first period has $\frac{12}{3} = 4$ bits which are 1. Consequently, the weight of the corresponding code word is 4. Since every sequence has maximum length, the weight of every nonzero code word and, hence, the minimum distance d of the code are exactly 4.

In general, there are 2^k binary k-tuples having a total of $k \cdot 2^k$ bits, of which $k \cdot 2^k/2 = k \cdot 2^{k-1}$ are 1. Thus, $k \cdot 2^{k-1}$ bits of the $2^k - 1$ nonzero k-tuples are 1. Since the first period of a maximum-length sequence having period $2^k - 1$ contains all the nonzero k-tuples if each bit is counted k times, the first period has $k \cdot 2^{k-1}/k = 2^{k-1}$ bits which are 1. Thus, the weight of every nonzero code word of a maximum-length code is 2^{k-1}. Hence, such a code is an $(n, k, d) = (2^k - 1, k, 2^{k-1})$ binary group code. $\square$

In our discussion of the development of maximum-length codes, we concentrated on the binary case, that is, $GF(2)$ and its extension field $GF(2^m)$. However, it is possible (Exercise 11) to generalize these results to the nonbinary case with the employment of $GF(p)$ and $GF(p^m)$.

EXERCISES FOR SECTION 8–3

1. Determine whether or not $GF(2)[x]/\langle 1 + x^2 \rangle$ is a field.

2. Determine which of the following polynomials are irreducible over $GF(2)$:

(a) $1 + x + x^3$

(b) $1 + x + x^2 + x^3$

(c) $1 + x^3$
(d) $1 + x^2 + x^3$
(e) $1 + x + x^4$

3.   Give an example of a polynomial having distinct roots in $GF(2)$ and repeated roots in $GF(2^m)$.

4.   Use the irreducible polynomial $1 + x + x^3$ to construct addition and multiplication tables for $GF(2^3) = GF(8)$. Are the nonzero elements of this field a cyclic group under multiplication? If your answer is yes, find a generator for this group.

5.   The polynomial $1 + x^2 + x^3$ has period 7 and has as its roots three elements in an extension field of $GF(2)$. Find these roots.

6.   Prove that if α is a root of a monic irreducible polynomial $m(x)$, then $m(x)$ is the minimum polynomial of α.

7.   Suppose that $p(x)$ is a polynomial of degree m which is irreducible over $GF(2)$. Prove that $p(x)$ divides $1 - x^{2^m-1}$. [Hint: Use the fact that $GF(2)[x]/\langle p(x) \rangle = GF(2^m)$, and show that $p(x)$ is the minimum polynomial of the element $[x] \in GF(2^m)$.]

8.   Determine the elements of $GF(2^5)$ (in terms of a primitive element, as in Example 7) by utilizing the irreducible polynomial $1 + x^2 + x^5$.

9.   Prove that every root of a degree m primitive polynomial with coefficients in $GF(2)$ is a primitive element of $GF(2^m)$.

10.   Determine the generator polynomial $g(x)$ of an ideal which corresponds to an $n = 31$, $k = 5$, $d = 16$ maximum-length binary cyclic code. What are the roots of $g(x)$?

11.   State and prove the variant of Theorem 11 appropriate for $GF(p)$.

12.   Prove that a polynomial of degree n with coefficients in $GF(2)$ has exactly n roots (with possible repetitions) in some extension field of $GF(2)$.

8-4   BCH Codes

Our main interest in this section will be an important class of codes called *Bose-Chaudhuri-Hocquenghem* (*BCH*) codes. To build toward them, we start by generalizing the concept (Theorem 8-3-6) of defining a cyclic code by specifying one root of the generator polynomial $g(x)$. Suppose that $\alpha_1, \alpha_2, \ldots, \alpha_r \in GF(2^m)$ are distinct. We now define the generator polynomial $g(x)$ of an ideal H by specifying that $\alpha_1, \alpha_2, \ldots, \alpha_r$ be roots of $g(x)$. (This polynomial may have other roots as well.) In particular, our specification of H in $GF(2)[x]/\langle 1 - x^n \rangle$ is that $[s(x)] \in H$ if and only if $\alpha_1, \alpha_2, \ldots, \alpha_r$ are roots of $s(x)$.

Suppose that $m_i(x)$ is the minimum polynomial for α_i, for $i = 1, 2, \ldots, r$. Since $m_i(x)$ divides every polynomial for which α_i is a root, $g(x)$ is divisible by $m_i(x)$, for $i = 1, 2, \ldots, r$. Does this imply that $g(x) = m_1(x) \cdot m_2(x) \cdots m_r(x)$? The answer is yes only if $m_i(x) \neq m_j(x)$ for $i \neq j$. To see this, suppose that $m_i(x) = m_j(x)$ for some $j \neq i$. Then, since $\prod_{\substack{i=1 \\ i \neq j}}^{r} m_i(x)$ has $\alpha_1, \alpha_2, \ldots, \alpha_r$ as roots

and since it divides $\prod_{i=1}^{r} m_i(x)$, the latter polynomial cannot be the generator polynomial of the ideal. Consequently, $g(x)$ is a product in which each minimum polynomial appears once and only once. More formally, the generator polynomial $g(x)$ is the **least common multiple** of $m_1(x)$, $m_2(x)$, ..., $m_r(x)$, that is, a polynomial of smallest degree such that $m_i(x)$ divides $g(x)$ for each $i = 1, 2, \ldots, r$.

The ideal H is in the ring of polynomials modulo $1 - x^n$, where n is the period of $g(x)$. Since α_1, α_2, ..., α_r are roots of $g(x)$, they are roots of $1 - x^n$. Hence, the order of each α_i divides n. However, if e_1, e_2, ..., e_r are the orders of α_1, α_2, ..., α_r, respectively, then n is in general not equal to the product $e_1 \cdot e_2 \cdot \cdots \cdot e_r$. To see this, consider the case in which e_j divides e_i for some $j \neq i$. Thus, $n' = \prod_{\substack{i=1 \\ i \neq j}}^{r} e_i$, and the order of each α_i divides n'.

Therefore, α_i is a root of $1 - x^{n'}$ for $i = 1, 2, \ldots, r$, which implies that $g(x)$ divides $1 - x^{n'}$. But n' cannot be less than n. Hence, n is the least common multiple of e_1, e_2, ..., e_r, that is, the smallest integer such that e_i divides n for each $i = 1, 2, \ldots, r$.

Let us now give an example of a cyclic code defined by some distinct elements α_1, α_2, ..., α_r of an extension field $GF(2^m)$.

Example 1

Suppose that $\beta = 1100 \in GF(16)$ as given in Example 8-3-7. We will determine the ideal H in which $[s(x)] \in H$ if and only if β, β^2, β^3, and β^4 are roots of $s(x)$. We have seen that the multiplicative group consisting of the nonzero elements of $GF(q)$ is actually a cyclic group. Since the order of each element divides 15, and the order of β is exactly 15, then $n = 15$. We will soon be concerned with procedures for finding minimum polynomials. For the moment, we will simply state that the irreducible polynomial $m_1(x) = 1 + x^3 + x^4$ is the minimum polynomial of β. With the help of Example 8-3-7 this can be confirmed, since

$$m_1(\beta) = 1000 + \beta^3 + \beta^4$$
$$= 1000 + 1111 + 0111 = 0000$$

Additionally, $m_1(x)$ is also the minimum polynomial of β^2 and β^4, since

$$m_1(\beta^2) = 1000 + (\beta^2)^3 + (\beta^2)^4 = 1000 + \beta^6 + \beta^8$$
$$= 1000 + 0001 + 1001 = 0000$$

and

$$m_1(\beta^4) = 1000 + (\beta^4)^3 + (\beta^4)^4 = 1000 + \beta^{12} + \beta$$
$$= 1000 + 0100 + 1100 = 0000$$

Furthermore, the irreducible polynomial $m_3(x) = 1 + x + x^2 + x^3 + x^4$ is the minimum polynomial of β^3, since

$$m_3(\beta^3) = 1000 + \beta^3 + (\beta^3)^2 + (\beta^3)^3 + (\beta^3)^4$$
$$= 1000 + \beta^3 + \beta^6 + \beta^9 + \beta^{12}$$
$$= 1000 + 1111 + 0001 + 0010 + 0100 = 0000$$

Hence, the generator polynomial for the ideal H is

$$g(x) = m_1(x) \cdot m_3(x)$$
$$= (1 + x^3 + x^4) \cdot (1 + x + x^2 + x^3 + x^4)$$
$$= 1 + x + x^2 + x^4 + x^8$$

and the corresponding binary cyclic code has length 15 and dimension $15 - 8 = 7$.

It should be noticed that if $m_1(x)$ is the minimum polynomial of β, then $m_1(x)$ is also the minimum polynomial of β^2 and β^4 as well. Is $m_1(x)$ also the minimum polynomial of β^6? Since

$$m_1(\beta^6) = 1000 + (\beta^6)^3 + (\beta^6)^4 = 1000 + \beta^3 + \beta^9$$
$$= 1000 + 1111 + 0010 = 0101$$

the answer is no. But

$$m_1(\beta^8) = 1000 + (\beta^8)^3 + (\beta^8)^4 = 1000 + \beta^9 + \beta^2$$
$$= 1000 + 0101 + 1010 = 0000$$

Thus, $m_1(x)$ is also the minimum polynomial of β^8. Since the degree of $m_1(x)$ is 4, then β, β^2, β^4, and β^8 are all roots of $m_1(x)$. $\Diamond$

We shall now see that if one root of an irreducible polynomial is known, then all the roots are known.

To begin with, consider α, $\beta \in GF(2^m)$. Clearly,

$$(\alpha + \beta)^2 = (\alpha + \beta)(\alpha + \beta) = \alpha^2 + \alpha\beta + \alpha\beta + \beta^2$$

However, for any $\gamma \in GF(2^m)$, we have $\gamma + \gamma = 0$. Thus,

$$(\alpha + \beta)^2 = \alpha^2 + \beta^2$$

With this fact, we can prove the following theorem.

THEOREM 1

Suppose that $\alpha \in GF(2^m)$ is a root of the polynomial $p(x)$ having coefficients in $GF(2)$. Then α^2 is also a root of $p(x)$.

Proof

Suppose that $p(x) = p_0 + p_1 x + p_2 x^2 + p_3 x^3 + \cdots p_n x^n$. Then

$$p(\alpha^2) = p_0 + p_1(\alpha^2) + p_2(\alpha^2)^2 + p_3(\alpha^2)^3 + \cdots + p_n(\alpha^2)^n$$
$$= p_0 + p_1(\alpha^2) + p_2(\alpha^2)^2 + p_3(\alpha^3)^2 + \cdots + p_n(\alpha^n)^2$$

But, if $p_i \in GF(2)$, then $p_i^2 = p_i$. Thus,

$$p(\alpha^2) = p_0^2 + p_1^2(\alpha^2) + p_2^2(\alpha^2)^2 + p_3^2(\alpha^3)^2 + \cdots + p_n^2(\alpha^n)^2$$
$$= p_0 + (p_1\alpha)^2 + (p_2\alpha^2)^2 + (p_3\alpha^3)^2 + \cdots + (p_n\alpha^n)^2$$

However, since $(\alpha + \beta)^2 = \alpha^2 + \beta^2$, we have

$$p(\alpha^2) = (p_0 + p_1\alpha + p_2\alpha^2 + p_3\alpha^3 + \cdots + p_n\alpha^n)^2$$
$$= [p(\alpha)]^2$$
$$= 0 \qquad\qquad \square$$

Thus, if α is a root of a degree r polynomial $p(x)$ with coefficients in $GF(2)$ then $\alpha, \alpha^2, \alpha^{2^2}, \alpha^{2^3}, \ldots, \alpha^{2^{r-1}}$ are all roots (possibly nondistinct) of $p(x)$. However, if $p(x)$ should be irreducible, then these roots will be distinct (Exercise 1). We thus have the following result:

THEOREM 2

Suppose that $\alpha \in GF(2^m)$, and suppose that $m(x)$ is the minimum polynomial of α. If r is the degree of $m(x)$, then

$$\alpha, \alpha^2, \alpha^{2^2}, \alpha^{2^3}, \ldots, \alpha^{2^{r-1}}$$

are all the roots of $m(x)$. $\qquad\qquad \square$

Although we have been mainly concerned with $GF(2)$ and its extension fields, the above results can be generalized to $GF(p)$ and its extension fields. For example, if $\alpha, \beta \in GF(p^m)$, then $(\alpha + \beta)^p = \alpha^p + \beta^p$. From this result, it can easily be shown that if α is a root of $p(x)$, then α^p is also a root of $p(x)$. Finally, if $m(x)$ is the minimum polynomial of $\alpha \in GF(p^m)$ and the degree of $m(x)$ is n, then

$$\alpha, \alpha^p, \alpha^{p^2}, \alpha^{p^3}, \ldots, \alpha^{p^{n-1}}$$

are all the roots of $m(x)$.

We shall now demonstrate that if $\alpha_1, \alpha_2, \ldots, \alpha_r \in GF(2^m)$ are used to define a cyclic code, it is not necessary to employ $GF(2^m)$ explicitly, or actually to find the minimum polynomials of $\alpha_1, \alpha_2, \ldots, \alpha_r$, in order to determine the length and dimension of the code.

Example 2

Suppose that $\alpha \in GF(2^6)$ is a primitive element. Let us find the length and dimension for the cyclic code corresponding to the ideal H defined by: $[s(x)] \in H$ if and only if $\alpha, \alpha^2, \alpha^3, \ldots, \alpha^{10}$ are roots of $s(x)$. Since α is primitive, its order is $2^6 - 1 = 63$. Thus, the least common multiple of the orders of $\alpha, \alpha^2, \alpha^3, \ldots, \alpha^{10}$ is 63, and the resulting cyclic code has length $n = 63$. Now let $m_i(x)$ denote the minimum polynomial of α^i. Since $m_1(x)$ is the minimum polynomial of α, then by the previous theorem, all the roots of $m_1(x)$ are:

$$\alpha, \alpha^2, \alpha^4, \alpha^8, \alpha^{16}, \alpha^{32}$$

There are no additional roots, since $\alpha^{64} = \alpha$. Thus, the degree of $m_1(x)$ is 6. Also note that $m_1(x) = m_2(x) = m_4(x) = m_8(x)$. Now consider $m_3(x)$. Since α^3 is a root of $m_3(x)$, then all the roots of $m_3(x)$ are:

$$\alpha^3, \alpha^6, \alpha^{12}, \alpha^{24}, \alpha^{48}, \alpha^{96} = \alpha^{33}$$

Again, since $\alpha^{66} = \alpha^3$, these must be all the roots. We see that $m_3(x) = m_6(x)$ and also has degree 6. Next, the roots of $m_5(x) = m_{10}(x)$ are:

$$\alpha^5, \alpha^{10}, \alpha^{20}, \alpha^{40}, \alpha^{80} = \alpha^{17}, \alpha^{34}$$

and its degree is 6. The minimum polynomial $m_7(x)$ has the roots:

$$\alpha^7, \alpha^{14}, \alpha^{28}, \alpha^{56}, \alpha^{112} = \alpha^{49}, \alpha^{93} = \alpha^{35}$$

Thus, the degree of $m_7(x)$ is also 6. Finally, the roots of $m_9(x)$ are:

$$\alpha^9, \alpha^{18}, \alpha^{36}$$

In this case, therefore, $m_9(x)$ has degree 3. Since the generator polynomial of the ideal is the least common multiple of the minimum polynomials of $\alpha, \alpha^2, \alpha^3, \ldots, \alpha^{10}$, we have

$$g(x) = m_1(x) \cdot m_3(x) \cdot m_5(x) \cdot m_7(x) \cdot m_9(x)$$

This means that the degree of $g(x)$ is 27, and hence, the dimension of the corresponding cyclic code is $k = 63 - 27 = 36$.   ◊

Example 3

Suppose that $\alpha \in GF(2^6)$ is a primitive element. Let $\beta = \alpha^3$ and consider the ideal H defined as follows: $[s(x)] \in H$ if and only if β, β^2, β^3, β^4 are roots of $s(x)$. Since $2^6 - 1 = 63 = 3 \cdot 21$, then $\beta^{21} = (\alpha^3)^{21} = \alpha^{63} = 1$ and the order of β divides 21. If the order of β is less than 21, then the order of α is less than 63—a contradiction, since α is primitive. Thus, the order of β is 21. Now, $(\beta^2)^{21} = (\beta^{21})^2 = (\alpha^{63})^2 = 1$ and the order of β^2 divides 21. The same statement can be made about β^3 and β^4. Thus, the least common multiple of the orders is $n = 21$. If $m_i(x)$ denotes the minimum polynomial of β^i, then the roots of $m_1(x)$ are:

$$\beta, \; \beta^2, \; \beta^4, \; \beta^8, \; \beta^{16}, \; \beta^{32} = \beta^{11}$$

and the roots of $m_3(x)$ are:

$$\beta^3, \; \beta^6, \; \beta^{12}$$

Thus, $m_1(x) = m_2(x) = m_4(x)$ has degree 6, while $m_3(x)$ has degree 3. Since $g(x) = m_1(x) \cdot m_3(x)$, the generator polynomial of the ideal H has degree 9. Hence, the corresponding binary cyclic code has length $n = 21$ and dimension $k = 21 - 9 = 12$. ◊

We now turn our attention to the problem of finding the minimum polynomial of some element $\alpha \in GF(2^m)$. Let's consider $GF(16)$ as given in Example 1. Suppose that we wish to find the minimum polynomial $m_1(x)$ of $\beta = 1100$. We know that the roots of $m_1(x)$ must be β, β^2, β^4, and β^8. Since

$$m_1(x) = (x + \beta) \cdot (x + \beta^2) \cdot (x + \beta^4) \cdot (x + \beta^8)$$

we have

$$
\begin{aligned}
m_1(x) &= (\beta^3 + (\beta + \beta^2)x + x^2) \cdot (\beta^{12} + (\beta^4 + \beta^8)x + x^2) \\
&= \beta^3\beta^{12} + (\beta^3(\beta^4 + \beta^8) + (\beta + \beta^2)\beta^{12})x \\
&\quad + (\beta^3 + (\beta + \beta^2)(\beta^4 + \beta^8) + \beta^{12})x^2 \\
&\quad + (\beta + \beta^2 + \beta^4 + \beta^8)x^3 + x^4 \\
&= \beta^{15} + (\beta^7 + \beta^{11} + \beta^{13} + \beta^{14})x + (\beta^3 + \beta^5 + \beta^6 + \beta^9 \\
&\quad + \beta^{10} + \beta^{12})x^2 + (\beta + \beta^2 + \beta^4 + \beta^8)x^3 + x^4 \\
&= 1000 + (1110 + 1101 + 0110 + 0101)x \\
&\quad + (1111 + 1011 + 0001 + 0010 + 0011 + 0100)x^2 \\
&\quad + (1100 + 1010 + 0111 + 1001)x^3 + x^4 \\
&= 1 + x^3 + x^4
\end{aligned}
$$

Now we will find the minimum polynomial $m_3(x)$ of $\alpha = \beta^3$, for β given in Example 1, by a second technique. We know that the roots of $m_3(x)$ are

$\beta^3, \beta^6, \beta^{12}$, and $\beta^{24} = \beta^9$. Thus, the degree of $m_3(x)$ is 4, and in general, $m_3(x)$ is of the form:

$$m_3(x) = p_0 + p_1 x + p_2 x^2 + p_3 x^3 + x^4$$

Since $m_3(\alpha) = 0$, we have

$$0 = p_0 + p_1 \alpha + p_2 \alpha^2 + p_3 \alpha^3 + \alpha^4$$
$$= p_0 + p_1 \beta^3 + p_2 \beta^6 + p_3 \beta^9 + \beta^{12}$$

Thus,

$$0000 = p_0(1000) + p_1(1111) + p_2(0001) + p_3(0010) + (0100)$$

Therefore, we must choose $p_0, p_1, p_2,$ and p_3 such that this last equation is satisfied. Let us rewrite this equation in the form:

$$0000 = p_0 000 + p_1 p_1 p_1 p_1 + 000 p_2 + 00 p_3 0 + 0100$$

From this we get the four simultaneous equations:

$$0 = p_0 + p_1$$
$$0 = p_1 + 1$$
$$0 = p_1 + p_3$$
$$0 = p_1 + p_2$$

From the second equation, we obtain $p_1 = 1$. With this, the remaining three equations yield $p_0 = p_2 = p_3 = 1$. Hence, $m_3(x) = 1 + x + x^2 + x^3 + x^4$.

We are now in a position to define the promised special class of cyclic codes.

DEFINITION 1

Suppose that $\alpha \in GF(2^m)$ and let ℓ and d be integers such that $0 < \ell < 2^m$ and $1 < d < 2^m$. We specify an ideal as follows: $[s(x)] \in H$ if and only if α^ℓ, $\alpha^{\ell+1}, \alpha^{\ell+2}, \ldots, \alpha^{\ell+(d-2)}$ are roots of $s(x)$. The corresponding binary cyclic code is known as a **BCH (Bose-Chaudhuri-Hocquenghem) code.**[*]   ○

We will shortly see that such a code has a minimum distance of at least d. (This assertion is known as the *BCH bound*.) In many cases, the minimum distance is exactly d.

We now realize that the codes described in Examples 1, 2, and 3 are BCH codes. The values of d are 5, 11, and 5, respectively. In each case $\ell = 1$.

---

[*]Needless to say, the concept of BCH codes can be extended to the q-ary case simply by letting $\alpha \in GF(q^m)$ and proceeding in a similar manner.

In Example 1, $\beta \in GF(2^4)$ is a primitive element, as is $\alpha \in GF(2^6)$ in Example 2. We may then say that such codes are BCH codes that are generated by primitive elements. The binary cyclic code given in Example 3 is an example of a BCH code that is generated by a non-primitive element.

In Examples 2 and 3, the lengths of the cyclic codes were given by the orders of β, α, and β, respectively. To see that this is a general property of BCH codes, let us consider the elements $\alpha^l, \alpha^{l+1}, \alpha^{l+2}, \ldots, \alpha^{l+(d-2)}$. Of course, if $d = 2$, we have the special case of only one element α^l, and the length of the resulting cyclic code is the order of α^l. Thus, suppose that $d > 2$. Let n be the least common multiple of the orders of $\alpha^l, \alpha^{l+1}, \alpha^{l+2}, \ldots, \alpha^{l+(d-2)}$, and let e be the order of α. Since the order of α^l divides n, then $(\alpha^l)^n = \alpha^{l \cdot n} = 1$. But the order of α^{l+1} also divides n. Thus, $(\alpha^{l+1})^n = \alpha^{(l+1)n} = \alpha^{l \cdot n + n} = \alpha^{l \cdot n} \alpha^n = 1$. Hence, $\alpha^n = 1$, and e divides n. Now $\alpha^e = 1$. Thus, $(\alpha^e)^i = 1$ for all i, and $(\alpha^i)^e = 1$ for all i. Since the order of each α^i divides e, then n divides e. Hence, $n = e$.

As a result of this discussion, we see:

FACT 3

A BCH code generated by a primitive element of $GF(2^m)$ has length $n = 2^m - 1$. In addition, a non-primitive element will generate a BCH code having a length n which divides $2^m - 1$. Conversely, for every n which divides $2^m - 1$, there is a BCH code having length n. $\qquad\square$

Let us now give a proof of the BCH bound.

THEOREM 4 (BCH Bound)

Given the length n binary BCH code corresponding to the ideal H defined by:

$$[s(x)] \in H \Leftrightarrow \alpha^l, \alpha^{l+1}, \alpha^{l+2}, \ldots, \alpha^{l+d-2} \text{ are roots of } s(x),$$

where $\alpha \in GF(2^m)$. Then the minimum distance of the code is at least d.

Proof

Suppose that $[s(x)]$ corresponds to a code word of weight $b < d$. We may then write $s(x)$ of the form

$$s(x) = x^{k_1} + x^{k_2} + \cdots + x^{k_b}$$

where $0 \leq k_1 < k_2 < \cdots < k_b$. For all j, we may write:

$$s(\alpha^j) = (\alpha^j)^{k_1} + (\alpha^j)^{k_2} + \cdots + (\alpha^j)^{k_b}$$
$$= (\alpha^{k_1})^j + (\alpha^{k_2})^j + \cdots + (\alpha^{k_b})^j$$

Now, let us define the polynomial

$$p(x) = (x - \alpha^{k_1}) \cdot (x - \alpha^{k_2}) \cdot \cdots \cdot (x - \alpha^{k_b})$$
$$= x^b + p_1 x^{b-1} + p_2 x^{b-2} + \cdots + p_b$$

By the definition of $p(x)$, we have that

$$p(\alpha^{k_1}) = p(\alpha^{k_2}) = \cdots = p(\alpha^{k_b}) = 0$$

Hence, for all j,

$$(\alpha^{k_1})^{j-b} p(\alpha^{k_1}) + (\alpha^{k_2})^{j-b} p(\alpha^{k_2}) + \cdots + (\alpha^{k_b})^{j-b} p(\alpha^{k_b})$$
$$= (\alpha^{k_1})^{j-b} 0 + (\alpha^{k_2})^{j-b} 0 + \cdots + (\alpha^{k_b})^{j-b} 0 = 0 \quad \textbf{(1)}$$

We leave it as an exercise in arithmetic to show that equation (1) can be written in the form

$$0 = s(\alpha^j) + p_1 s(\alpha^{j-1}) + p_2 s(\alpha^{j-2}) + \cdots + p_b s(\alpha^{j-b}) \quad \textbf{(2)}$$

for all integers j. Since $[s(x)]$ corresponds to a code word, we know:

$$s(\alpha^l) = s(\alpha^{l+1}) = s(\alpha^{l+2}) = \cdots = s(\alpha^{l+d-2}) = 0$$

Thus, by choosing $j = b + l - 1$, equation (2) yields:

$$s(\alpha^{l-1}) = 0$$

We next select $j = b + l - 2$, and again use equation (2) to obtain:

$$s(\alpha^{l-2}) = 0$$

We continue this reasoning to obtain:

$$s(\alpha^0) = s(\alpha^1) = s(\alpha^2) = \cdots = s(\alpha^{l+d-2}) = 0$$

Traversing in the opposite direction, we eventually conclude that

$$s(\alpha^0) = s(\alpha^1) = s(\alpha^2) = \cdots = s(\alpha^{n-1}) = 0$$

where n is the order of α, and hence, the length of the BCH code. Since the order of α is n, the elements α^0, α^1, α^2, $\ldots$, α^{n-1} are distinct, and they are all the roots of $1 - x^n$.

Since α^0, α^1, α^2, $\ldots$, α^{n-1} are roots of $s(x)$, $1 - x^n$ divides $s(x)$. Hence,

$$[s(x)] = [0]$$

and there can be no nonzero code word of weight less than d. $\qquad\square$

We have seen that we can specify an ideal H, and hence a cyclic code, as follows: $[s(x)] \in H$ if and only if α_1, α_2, $\ldots$, α_r are roots of $s(x)$. From this, we are able to determine the generator polynomial of the ideal, and hence a generator matrix for the cyclic code. We shall now demonstrate how directly to obtain a parity check matrix for the code.

Suppose that $[s(x)] \in H$, where $s(x) = s_0 x^0 + s_1 x^1 + s_2 x^2 + \cdots + s_{n-1} x^{n-1}$. Since α_i is a root of $s(x)$ for $i = 1, 2, \ldots, r$, we have:

$$s(\alpha_i) = s_0 \alpha_i^0 + s_1 \alpha_i^1 + s_2 \alpha_i^2 + \cdots + s_{n-1} \alpha_i^{n-i} = 0$$

We may rewrite this equation as the matrix product:

$$[s_0, s_1, s_2, \ldots, s_{n-1}] \cdot \begin{bmatrix} \alpha_i^0 \\ \alpha_i^1 \\ \alpha_i^2 \\ \vdots \\ \alpha_i^{n-1} \end{bmatrix} = 0$$

Since this equation is satisfied for $i = 1, 2, \ldots, r$, we have the matrix equation

$$s \cdot P^t = 0$$

where $s = [s_0, s_1, s_2, \ldots, s_{n-1}]$ and

$$P^t = \begin{bmatrix} \alpha_1^0 & \alpha_2^0 & \alpha_3^0 & \cdots & \alpha_r^0 \\ \alpha_1^1 & \alpha_2^1 & \alpha_3^1 & \cdots & \alpha_r^1 \\ \alpha_1^2 & \alpha_2^2 & \alpha_3^2 & \cdots & \alpha_r^2 \\ \vdots & \vdots & \vdots & & \vdots \\ \alpha_1^{n-1} & \alpha_2^{n-1} & \alpha_3^{n-1} & \cdots & \alpha_r^{n-1} \end{bmatrix}$$

We now see that if $[s(x)] \in H$, then $s \cdot P^t = 0$. Furthermore, if $s \cdot P^t = 0$, then $s(x)$ has α_1, α_2, $\ldots$, α_r as roots, and $[s(x)] \in H$. Thus, $s = (s_0, s_1, s_2, \ldots, s_{n-1})$ is a code word if and only if $s \cdot P^t = 0$. Hence, the matrix P is actually a parity check matrix for the cyclic code corresponding to H.

Suppose now that α_i and α_j have the same minimum polynomial $m(x)$. If $[s(x)] \in H$, then $s(x)$ is divisible by $m(x)$. Thus, $s(\alpha_i) = 0$ if and only if

$s(\alpha_j) = 0$. Hence, if P^t contains powers of α_i, it need not contain powers of α_j. Consequently, the number of columns in P^t depends on the elements α_1, $\alpha_2, \ldots, \alpha_r$.

Example 4

Consider the BCH code described in Example 1 in which $[s(x)] \in H$ if and only if $\beta, \beta^2, \beta^3, \beta^4$ are roots of $s(x)$. In this case $\alpha_1 = \beta$, $\alpha_2 = \beta^2$, $\alpha_3 = \beta^3$, and $\alpha_4 = \beta^4$. However, $m_1(x) = m_2(x) = m_4(x)$. Thus, we need only consider $\alpha_1 = \beta$ and $\alpha_3 = \beta^3$. Therefore, we have:

$$P^t = \begin{bmatrix} \alpha_1^0 & \alpha_3^0 \\ \alpha_1^1 & \alpha_3^1 \\ \alpha_1^2 & \alpha_3^2 \\ \vdots & \vdots \\ \alpha_1^{14} & \alpha_3^{14} \end{bmatrix} = \begin{bmatrix} \beta^0 & (\beta^3)^0 \\ \beta^1 & (\beta^3)^1 \\ \beta^2 & (\beta^3)^2 \\ \vdots & \vdots \\ \beta^{14} & (\beta^3)^3 \end{bmatrix}$$

Hence,

$$P^t = \begin{bmatrix} 1 & 1 \\ \beta & \beta^3 \\ \beta^2 & \beta^6 \\ \beta^3 & \beta^9 \\ \beta^4 & \beta^{12} \\ \beta^5 & 1 \\ \beta^6 & \beta^3 \\ \beta^7 & \beta^6 \\ \beta^8 & \beta^9 \\ \beta^9 & \beta^{12} \\ \beta^{10} & 1 \\ \beta^{11} & \beta^3 \\ \beta^{12} & \beta^6 \\ \beta^{13} & \beta^9 \\ \beta^{14} & \beta^{12} \end{bmatrix} = \begin{bmatrix} 1 & 0 & 0 & 0 & 1 & 0 & 0 & 0 \\ 1 & 1 & 0 & 0 & 1 & 1 & 1 & 1 \\ 1 & 0 & 1 & 0 & 0 & 0 & 0 & 1 \\ 1 & 1 & 1 & 1 & 0 & 0 & 1 & 0 \\ 0 & 1 & 1 & 1 & 0 & 1 & 0 & 0 \\ 1 & 0 & 1 & 1 & 1 & 0 & 0 & 0 \\ 0 & 0 & 0 & 1 & 1 & 1 & 1 & 1 \\ 1 & 1 & 1 & 0 & 0 & 0 & 0 & 1 \\ 1 & 0 & 0 & 1 & 0 & 0 & 1 & 0 \\ 0 & 0 & 1 & 0 & 0 & 1 & 0 & 0 \\ 0 & 0 & 1 & 1 & 1 & 0 & 0 & 0 \\ 1 & 1 & 0 & 1 & 1 & 1 & 1 & 1 \\ 0 & 1 & 0 & 0 & 0 & 0 & 0 & 1 \\ 0 & 1 & 1 & 0 & 0 & 0 & 1 & 0 \\ 0 & 1 & 0 & 1 & 0 & 1 & 0 & 0 \end{bmatrix}$$

In general, the rows of P (the columns of P^t) may not be a minimal set; i.e., there may be one row which is a sum of other rows of P. This, however, is not the case in this example. ◊

Suppose that $\alpha \in GF(2^m)$, add H is an ideal such that $[s(x)] \in H$ if and only if α is a root of $s(x)$. We know that the generator polynomial for H

is $m(x)$, the minimum polynomial of α. In addition, the length n of the corresponding cyclic code is given by the order of α. We have just seen, however, that if

$$P^t = \begin{bmatrix} \alpha^0 \\ \alpha^1 \\ \alpha^2 \\ \vdots \\ \alpha^{n-1} \end{bmatrix}$$

then P is a parity check matrix for the binary group code. If α is a primitive element, therefore, then $n = 2^m - 1$ and the rows of P^t are distinct. Thus, the columns of P are all the $2^m - 1$ nonzero binary m-tuples. Hence, when α is primitive, the resulting cyclic code is (equivalent to) a Hamming code.

As a consequence of the definition of a primitive polynomial, we see that if $\alpha \in GF(2^m)$ is a primitive element, then its minimum polynomial $m(x)$ is a primitive polynomial. Hence, the Hamming code described above corresponds to an ideal generated by a primitive polynomial.

Now consider an ideal H generated by a primitive polynomial $m(x)$. Since $m(x)$ is primitive, there exists a primitive element $\alpha \in GF(2^m)$ which is a root of $m(x)$. But $[s(x)] \in H$ if and only if $m(x)$ divides $s(x)$. Thus, $[s(x)] \in H$ if and only if α is a root of $s(x)$. Hence, the cyclic code corresponding to an ideal generated by a primitive polynomial is a Hamming code.

We close by stressing the fact that each cyclic code has an associated shift register, which is a linear machine. Thus, the problem of code construction may be viewed as a case of the linear realization theory of Section 7-5. The interested reader should see the discussion of the "key equation" in Berlekamp [1968].

EXERCISES FOR SECTION 8–4

1.   Suppose that $\alpha \in GF(2^m)$. Let $m(x)$ be the minimum polynomial of α, where the degree of $m(x)$ is r. Prove that the roots of $m(x)$,

$$\alpha, \alpha^2, \alpha^{2^2}, \alpha^{2^3}, \ldots, \alpha^{2^{r-1}}$$

are distinct. (Note: This exercise is more involved than usual, and takes a bit of doing. For help, see Peterson and Weldon [1972]).

2.   Suppose that $\alpha \in GF(2^4)$ is a primitive element. Find the length and dimension of the binary cyclic code corresponding to the ideal defined as follows: $[s(x)] \in H$ if and only if α, α^2, α^3, α^4, α^5, α^6 are roots of $s(x)$.

3.   Describe a binary BCH code of length $n = 31$ that is generated by a primitive element and has $d = 5$. What is the dimension of this code? Find the generator polynomial of the ideal which corresponds to this code.

4.   Suppose that $\alpha \in GF(2^{11})$ is a primitive element. Let $\beta = \alpha^{89}$. Define an ideal as follows: $[s(x)] \in H$ if and only if β is a root of $s(x)$. Find the length, dimension, and a lower bound for the minimum distance of the corresponding cyclic code.

5.   Show that equation (1) can be written in the form of equation (2).

Further Reading for Chapter 8

The following books are devoted entirely to the subject of algebraic coding theory:

ELWYN R. BERLEKAMP [1968], *Algebraic Coding Theory,* McGraw-Hill, New York, New York.

SHU LIN [1970], *An Introduction to Error-Correcting Codes,* Prentice-Hall, Englewood Cliffs, New Jersey.

W. WESLEY PETERSON and E. J. WELDON, JR. [1972], *Error-Correcting Codes,* MIT Press, Cambridge, Massachusetts.

JACOBUS H. VAN LINT [1971], *Coding Theory,* Springer-Verlag, New York, New York.

CHAPTER 9

Machines in a Category

In the preceding eight chapters of this volume, we have encountered many different algebraic structures and many different applications. We start this chapter by introducing, in Section 9–1, the powerful general language of *category theory,* which allows us to set forth a number of key notions common to many different branches of mathematics. With this new vocabulary we may study the Arbib-Manes theory of machines in a category. First we establish, in Section 9–2, a general definition of *machine* which is as simple (once we can talk category-ese!) as the original definition of Section 2–1, and yet which encompasses the tree automata of Chapter 4 and the linear machines of Chapter 7. Then, in Section 9–3, we see that our study of how to build machines with specified behavior (Sections 2–5 and 7–5) may be simply transposed into our general setting—and prove the validity of this new approach by seeing how easily it yields a realization theory for tree automata.

9–1   An Introduction to Category Theory

In this section we introduce the general vocabulary of category theory. This will enable us to abstract the crucial properties required of a collection of structured sets and mappings so that in the next two sections we may develop the general realization theory due to Arbib and Ernest G. Manes. [For alternative approaches to a general realization theory see Bainbridge [1973] and Goguen [1972]. For more on category theory, see MacLane [1972].]

644

DEFINITION 1

A **category** $\mathcal{K}$ consists of the following three things:

I. A class of objects.

II. For each ordered pair (A, B) of objects, there is a (possibly empty) set $\mathcal{K}(A, B)$, an element of which is referred to as a $\mathcal{K}$-**morphism** from A to B. [Although a $\mathcal{K}$-morphism is not necessarily a map, it is an abstraction of the concept of a map; so we write $f\colon A \to B$ or $A \overset{f}{\to} B$ to indicate that $f \in \mathcal{K}(A, B)$, i.e., that f is a $\mathcal{K}$-morphism.]

III. For each ordered triple (A, B, C) of objects, there is a map (in the ordinary set-theoretic sense)

comp: $\mathcal{K}(A, B) \times \mathcal{K}(B, C) \to \mathcal{K}(A, C)\colon\ (A \overset{f}{\to} B,\ B \overset{g}{\to} C) \mapsto A \overset{gf}{\to} C$

called **composition of $\mathcal{K}$-morphisms,** where:

(a) for all $\mathcal{K}$-morphisms $A \overset{f}{\to} B$, $B \overset{g}{\to} C$, and $C \overset{h}{\to} D$, we have the associative law $h(gf) = (hg)f$.

(b) for each object A, there is a $\mathcal{K}$-morphism $id_A \in \mathcal{K}(A, A)$ such that for all $A \overset{f}{\to} B$, we have

$$A \xrightarrow{id_A} A \overset{f}{\to} B = A \overset{f}{\to} B = A \overset{f}{\to} B \xrightarrow{id_B} B \quad \text{i.e.,}$$

comp $(A \xrightarrow{id_A} A,\ A \overset{f}{\to} B) = A \overset{f}{\to} B =$ comp $(A \overset{f}{\to} B,\ B \xrightarrow{id_B} B)$
or $f(id_A) = f = (id_B)f$.   ○

[In this chapter we shall no longer use $\cdot$ for composition, save when it is needed as punctuation to avoid ambiguity.]

Example 1

The class of all sets is a category and is denoted by $\mathcal{S}$. The objects of the class are sets, and the $\mathcal{S}$-morphisms constituting $\mathcal{S}(A, B)$ are all the maps from A to B. Composition of $\mathcal{S}$-morphisms is given by the composition operation for maps, while for id_A we select the identity map $A \to A\colon a \mapsto a$. It is precisely for this reason (that the morphism id_A is an abstraction of the identity map) that we use the symbol id_A in the definition of a category as we do.   ◊

Example 2

The class of all monoids is **Mon,** the category of monoids, when **Mon** (A, B) is the collection of all monoid homomorphisms (Exercise 2) from A to B. Since composition of monoid homomorphisms yields a monoid homomorphism and the identity map on a monoid is certainly a monoid homomorphism, we do indeed have another category.   ◊

Example 3

R-**Mod** is the category whose objects are R-modules, and whose R-**Mod**-morphisms are linear maps. This conclusion is based on the fact that when f and g are linear maps, then gf is; and the identity map is certainly linear.
◊

    Examples 1, 2, and 3 all conform to the intuition that a category is a collection of structured sets together with maps which preserve that structure. However, we shall now give an example which shows that the concept of a category is much broader than this intuition.

Example 4

Let $\mathcal{K}$ have for objects all of the integers; i.e., all the elements of the set **Z**. For each m and n in **Z**, we define the set $\mathcal{K}(m, n)$ by

$$\mathcal{K}(m, n) = \begin{cases} \{1_{mn}\} & \text{if } m \leq n \\ \varnothing & \text{if } m > n \end{cases}$$

Thus, there is at most one $\mathcal{K}$-morphism for each ordered pair (m, n) of objects, and it is by no means a map. If $m \leq n$, let us denote the $\mathcal{K}$-morphism by 1_{mn}; while if $m > n$, there is no $\mathcal{K}$-morphism for the pair (m, n).
    In defining composition for $\mathcal{K}$-morphisms

$$\mathcal{K}(m, n) \times \mathcal{K}(n, p) \to \mathcal{K}(m, p)$$

we need only spell out what happens when both $\mathcal{K}(m, n)$ and $\mathcal{K}(n, p)$ are nonempty. Thus, there is only one possible way to define composition, that being

$$1_{np} \cdot 1_{mn} = 1_{mp}$$

whenever $n \leq p$ and $m \leq n$, so that $m \leq p$ as required for 1_{mp} to exist. It is then clear that

$$(1_{pr}) \cdot (1_{np} \cdot 1_{mn}) = 1_{pr} \cdot 1_{mp} = 1_{mr}$$

and

$$(1_{pr} \cdot 1_{np}) \cdot (1_{mn}) = 1_{nr} \cdot 1_{mn} = 1_{mr}$$

so that associativity holds. Finally, by taking id_m to be 1_{mm}, we have that

$$1_{mn} \cdot 1_{mm} = 1_{mn} = 1_{nn} \cdot 1_{mn}$$

or

$$m \xrightarrow{1_{mm}} m \xrightarrow{1_{mn}} n = m \xrightarrow{1_{mn}} n = m \xrightarrow{1_{mn}} n \xrightarrow{1_{nn}} n$$

Hence, $\mathcal{K}$ is a category.
◊

In much of automata theory, we are concerned with machines that are unique up to "relabelling." To make such a concept available in our general study of machines in a category, we must first abstract the notion of an isomorphism in any category.

We know (Exercise 5) that for two sets X and Y, the following two conditions are equivalent:

(i) There exists a map $f:X \to Y$ which is bijective.
(ii) There exist two maps $f:X \to Y$ and $g:Y \to X$ such that $gf = id_X$ and $fg = id_Y$; i.e., gf and fg are the identity maps on X and Y, respectively.

Furthermore, a necessary condition for two sets to be isomorphic is that there exists a bijection between them. Unfortunately, however, condition (i) above does not extend to an arbitrary category, since $\mathcal{K}$-morphisms are not necessarily maps. Thus, we take an approach suggested instead by condition (ii).

DEFINITION 2

In a category $\mathcal{K}$, we say that the $\mathcal{K}$-morphism $f:A \to B$ is an **isomorphism** if and only if there exists a $\mathcal{K}$-morphism $g:B \to A$ such that the diagram

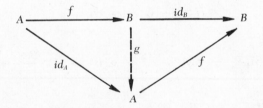

commutes. If there exists an isomorphism $f:A \to B$, then we say that A and B are **isomorphic** and write $A \cong B$.   ○

Reiterating, to say that a diagram commutes is to say that we get the same overall composition regardless of which route we take from a given place to a given destination. Thus, for the diagram of Definition 2, commutivity simply says that

$$gf = id_A \quad \text{and} \quad fg = id_B$$

(as well as $f(id_A) = (id_B)f$; however, for a category this is trivially true by definition).

Since $id_A:A \to A$ is an isomorphism (Exercise 7), it is now easy to check (Exercise 8) that $\cong$ is an equivalence relation on the objects of a category. We may think, heuristically, that $A \cong B$ if "A and B have the same 'abstract structure'."

We now introduce a functor as a structure-preserving map from one *category* into another:

DEFINITION 3

A **functor** (of categories) is a function H defined for objects by

$$H: \mathcal{C}_1 \to \mathcal{C}_2 : A \mapsto AH$$

and for morphisms by

$$H: \mathcal{C}_1(A, B) \to \mathcal{C}_2(AH, BH) : (A \xrightarrow{f} B) \mapsto (AH \xrightarrow{fH} BH)$$

such that

$$(fg)H = (fH)(gH) \text{ for all composable } f \text{ and } g \text{ in } \mathcal{C}_1$$

and

$$id_A H = id_{AH} \text{ for all } A \text{ in } \mathcal{C}_1$$

We denote a functor simply by either $H: \mathcal{C}_1 \to \mathcal{C}_2$ or $\mathcal{C}_1 \xrightarrow{H} \mathcal{C}_2$. ○

Example 5

Suppose that $\mathcal{C}_1 = \mathcal{C}_2 = \mathcal{C}$ and that the function H is given by

$$H: \mathcal{C} \to \mathcal{C} : A \mapsto AH = A$$

and

$$H: \mathcal{C}(A, B) \to \mathcal{C}(A, B) : (A \xrightarrow{f} B) \mapsto (A \xrightarrow{fH = f} B)$$

Since

$$(fg)H = fg = (fH)(gH) \text{ for all composable } f \text{ and } g \text{ in } \mathcal{C}$$

and

$$id_A H = id_A = id_{AH} \quad \text{for all } A \text{ in } \mathcal{C}$$

then $H: \mathcal{C} \to \mathcal{C}$ is a functor, called the **identity functor,** and is denoted by $id_\mathcal{C}$. ◊

Example 6

From Chapter 7, we know that for a unitary ring R, an R-module is an abelian group $(A, +)$ together with a function $\lambda: R \times A \to A : (r, x) \mapsto rx$ subject to the four axioms of Definition 7–1–12. Thus, let us denote an R-module by the triple $(A, +, \lambda)$.

Consider the function H defined by:

$$H: R\text{-}\mathbf{Mod} \to \mathbf{Mon} : (A, +, \lambda) \mapsto (A, +, \lambda)H = (A, +)$$

and

$$H:R\text{-}\mathbf{Mod}\ [(A_1, +, \lambda_1), (A_2, +, \lambda_2)] \rightarrow \mathbf{Mon}\ [(A_1, +), (A_2, +)]:$$

$$[(A_1, +, \lambda_1) \xrightarrow{f} (A_2, +, \lambda_2)] \mapsto [(A_1, +) \xrightarrow{fH = f} (A_2, +)]$$

Since

$$(fg)H = fg = (fH)(gH) \text{ for all composable } f \text{ and } g \text{ in } R\text{-}\mathbf{Mod}$$

and

$$id_{(A,+,\lambda)}H = id_{(A,+)} = id_{(A,+,\lambda)H} \text{ for all } (A, +, \lambda) \text{ in } R\text{-}\mathbf{Mod}$$

then $H:R\text{-}\mathbf{Mod} \rightarrow \mathbf{Mon}$ is a functor.   ◊

Example 7

Consider $H:\mathbf{Mon} \rightarrow \mathcal{S}$ defined by:

$$H:(S, \cdot) \mapsto (S, \cdot)H = S$$

and

$$H:[(S_1, \cdot) \xrightarrow{f} (S_2, \cdot)] \mapsto (S_1 \xrightarrow{fH = f} S_2)$$

Then, similarly to Example 6, we have that H is a functor. We call such a functor a **forgetful functor,** since it "forgets" the monoid operation and only remembers that a monoid homomorphism is a mapping of sets.   ◊

Example 8

Consider $\mathcal{S}$, the category of sets, and let us arbitrarily select some object in this category, say the set X_0. Let us define a function which crosses a set with X_0, denoted by $-\times X_0$, as follows:

$$-\times X_0:\mathcal{S} \rightarrow \mathcal{S}:Q \mapsto Q \times X_0$$

and

$$-\times X_0:\mathcal{S}(Q, Q') \rightarrow \mathcal{S}(Q \times X_0, Q' \times X_0):(Q \xrightarrow{f} Q') \mapsto$$

$$(Q \times X_0 \xrightarrow{f \times id_{X_0}} Q' \times X_0)$$

i.e.,

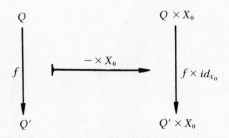

where
$$f \times id_{X_0} : (q, x) \mapsto (f(q), x)$$
Since
$$fg \times id_{X_0} : (q, x) \mapsto (fg(q), x)$$
and
$$(f \times id_{X_0})(g \times id_{X_0}) : (q, x) \mapsto (f[g(q)], x) = (fg(q), x)$$
then
$$fg \times id_{X_0} = (f \times id_{X_0})(g \times id_{X_0}) \text{ for all } f \text{ and } g \text{ composable in } \mathcal{S}$$
Also,
$$id_Q \times id_{X_0} : (q, x) \mapsto (q, x)$$
and
$$id_{Q \times X_0} : (q, x) \mapsto (q, x)$$
so
$$id_Q \times id_{X_0} = id_{Q \times X_0}$$

Hence, $\mathcal{S} \xrightarrow{\ - \times X_0\ } \mathcal{S}$ is indeed a functor.   ◊

We have already defined what we mean when we say that two objects of a category are isomorphic. We now define what it means to say that two categories are isomorphic.

DEFINITION 4

We say that a functor $H : \mathcal{K}_1 \to \mathcal{K}_2$ is an **isomorphism** if either of the following two equivalent conditions holds:

(i) $H : A \mapsto AH$ is a bijection on objects and
$H : f \mapsto fH$ is a bijection on morphisms.
(ii) There exists a functor $H^{-1} : \mathcal{K}_2 \to \mathcal{K}_1$ such that the diagram

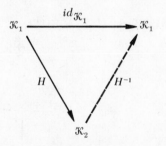

commutes. If there exists an isomorphism $H : \mathcal{K}_1 \to \mathcal{K}_2$, then we say that $\mathcal{K}_1$ and $\mathcal{K}_2$ are **isomorphic.**   ○

The final ingredient we need for our general theory of automata is the concept of "freeness." We start with monoids and then generalize.

DEFINITION 5

Given a set X, then the monoid X^* is called the **free monoid** on the basis X of generators.   ○

We may characterize the notion of a free monoid as follows:

THEOREM 1

A monoid S is isomorphic to X^* if and only if there exists a map $\eta: X \to S$ such that for any monoid S' and any map $f: X \to S'$ there exists a unique monoid homomorphism $\psi: S \to S'$ such that

(1)

commutes; i.e., $\psi \, \eta(x_j) = f(x_j)$ for all $x_j \in X$.

Proof

(i) Suppose that $S \cong X^*$, with $\alpha: X^* \to S$ an isomorphism. Define η to be the restriction of α to X, so that $\eta(x) = \alpha(x)$ for each x in X. Suppose that we are given $f: X \to S'$. Then by (1) we must have:

$$\psi \alpha(x) = f(x) \qquad (2)$$

Let now, $\alpha(x_1 \ldots x_n)$ be any element of S. Then if we define

$$\psi(\alpha(x_1 \ldots x_n)) \text{ to be } f(x_1) \ldots f(x_n)$$

it is clear that ψ is a homomorphism, since

$$\psi(\alpha(x_1 \ldots x_n) \cdot \alpha(x_1' \ldots x_m'))$$
$$= \psi(\alpha(x_1 \ldots x_n x_1' \ldots x_n')) \text{ since } \alpha \text{ is a homomorphism}$$
$$= f(x_1) \ldots f(x_n) f(x_1') \ldots f(x_m') \text{ by definition}$$
$$= \psi(\alpha(x_1 \ldots x_n)) \, \psi(\alpha(x_1' \ldots x_m'))$$

Moreover, this ψ is clearly the only homomorphism $S \to S'$ which satisfies (2).

(ii) Conversely, suppose that S is such that every $X \overset{f}{\to} S'$ has a unique homomorphic extension as defined by (1). In particular, taking $f = i_X : X \to X^* : x \mapsto x$, we have a unique homomorphism ψ such that

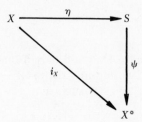

(3)

commutes. But, by part (i), X^* also has the property (interchanging the roles of S and X^* in (3)) which assures us that there exists a unique homomorphism ψ' such that the following diagram commutes:

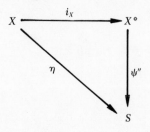

(4)

Splicing (3) and (4) together in two ways, we obtain the two commutative diagrams

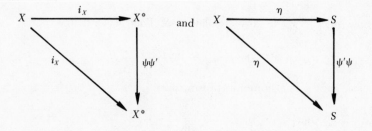

But we clearly also have the commutative diagrams

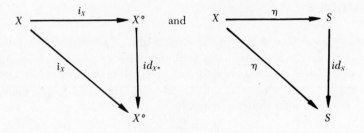

By the uniqueness property of the homomorphic extensions, we see that

$$\psi\psi' = id_{X^*}$$

since both are homomorphic extensions of i_X, while

$$\psi'\psi = id_S$$

since both are homomorphic extensions of η. We thus deduce that $\psi : S \to X^*$ is an isomorphism, so $S \cong X^*$ as was to be proved. $\qquad\square$

This theorem suggests the following formulation for the concept of freeness: Suppose we denote the forgetful functor by $\mathfrak{U} : \mathbf{Mon} \to \mathbf{S}$, i.e.,

$$\mathfrak{U} : (S, \cdot, 1) \mapsto (S, \cdot, 1)\mathfrak{U} = S$$

$$\mathfrak{U} : [(S_1, \cdot, 1) \xrightarrow{\ f\ } (S_2, \cdot, 1)] \mapsto (S_1 \xrightarrow{\ f\mathfrak{U} = f\ } S_2)$$

Then a monoid $M = (S, \cdot, 1)$, with $X \subset S$ and equipped with any "inclusion of the generators" map $\eta : X \to M\mathfrak{U}$, is *free* over X if for each $M' = (S', \cdot, 1')$ in **Mon** and each map $f : X \to M'\mathfrak{U}$, there exists a unique homomorphism $\psi : M \to M'$ in **Mon** such that $(\psi\mathfrak{U})\eta = f$; i.e., such that the diagram

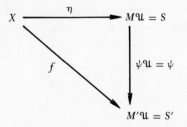

commutes.

This suggests the following as the appropriate general definition (we provide heuristics afterwards):

DEFINITION 6

Given categories $\mathcal{C}$ and $\mathcal{B}$ with A an object of $\mathcal{C}$, B an object of $\mathcal{B}$, a functor $H:\mathcal{C} \to \mathcal{B}$, and $\eta:B \to AH$ a $\mathcal{B}$-morphism, then we say that the pair (A, η) is **free** over B with respect to H if for any object A' in $\mathcal{C}$ and any $\mathcal{B}$-morphism $f:B \to A'H$, there exists a unique $\mathcal{C}$-morphism $\psi:A \to A'$ such that $(\psi H)\eta = f$; i.e., such that the diagram

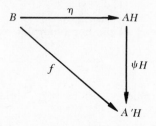

commutes. We refer to ψ as the **unique $\mathcal{C}$-morphic extension** of f.

Given a functor $H:\mathcal{C} \to \mathcal{B}$, if for all B in $\mathcal{B}$ there exists a pair (A, η) [with A in $\mathcal{C}$ and $\eta:B \to AH$ in $\mathcal{B}$] which is free over B with respect to H, then we say that H has a **left adjoint**.   ○

Heuristic meanings: Think of $\mathcal{C}$ as a category of $\mathcal{B}$-objects with additional structure and of H as the forgetful functor that throws away this structure. If B is a "basis" object and A is in $\mathcal{C}$, we generalize "B is a subset of A," which really says "B is a subset of AH," by specifying a map $\eta: B \to AH$. We then generalize our notion of the generators of a monoid to think of A as a "free object with η as inclusion of generators", although η need not be "one-to-one" in the general setting. The definition then asserts that every map f on B extends uniquely to an $\mathcal{C}$-morphism ψ.

We close the section by showing that B determines the A which is free over B up to isomorphism (Theorem 2), and then by showing that if $\mathcal{U}$ has a left adjoint, there exists a functor which provides the free objects (Theorem 3). However, we shall not need to use these facts, and some readers may wish to move straight on to the next section.

THEOREM 2

If (A, η) and (A', η') are both free over B with respect to H, then $A \cong A'$ in the strong sense that there exists an isomorphism $\phi:A \to A'$ such that $(\phi H)\eta = \eta'$.

Proof

We state the proof concisely, leaving it to the reader to fill in the details, using part (ii) of the proof of Theorem 1 as a model:

By freeness, there exist unique morphisms $A \xrightarrow{\phi} A'$ and $A' \xrightarrow{\psi} A$ such that we have the commutative diagram:

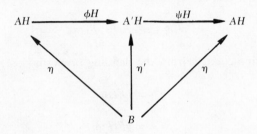

Thus $\eta = (\psi H)(\phi H)\eta = (\psi\phi)H \cdot \eta$. But it is clear that $\eta = (id_A)H \cdot \eta$. We may thus deduce, using the uniqueness assertion of Definition 6, that $\psi\phi = id_A$. Similarly, $\phi\psi = id_{A'}$. Thus, ϕ is an isomorphism, and we do indeed have that $(\phi H)\eta = \eta'$. □

THEOREM 3

Let $\mathcal{C} \xrightarrow{H} \mathcal{B}$ have a left adjoint. Define an object mapping $\mathcal{B} \xrightarrow{F} \mathcal{C}: B \mapsto BF$ by letting (BF, η) be our choice (unique up to isomorphism) of a free pair over B with respect to H. Given a $\mathcal{B}$-morphism $B \xrightarrow{f} B'$, we define fF to be the unique morphism which renders commutative the diagram:

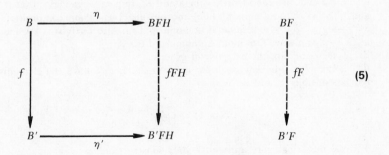

(5)

Then the pair $(B \mapsto BF, f \mapsto fF)$ defines a functor.

Proof

If $f = id_B : B \to B$, then we may take $\eta = \eta'$ and $fF = id_{BF}$ to render (5) commutative, for since H is a functor $(id_{BF})H = id_{BFH}$, so the left-hand diagram reduces to the truism $\eta \cdot id_B = id_{BFH} \cdot \eta$, which just says that $\eta = \eta$.

If $f = B \xrightarrow{g} B'' \xrightarrow{h} B'$, we may take $fF = BF \xrightarrow{gF} B''F \xrightarrow{hF} B'F$ to render (5) commutative, for H is a functor $(hF \cdot gF)H = hFH \cdot gFH$, so that the left-hand diagram reduces to

$$\eta'(hg) = hFH \cdot gFH\eta$$

which follows immediately from the defining properties

$$\eta'h = hFH\eta''$$

and

$$\eta''g = gFH \cdot \eta$$

for hF and gF, respectively. Thus, $(id_B)F = id_{BF}$, and $(hg)F = hF \cdot gF$, so that F is indeed a functor. $\qquad\qquad\qquad\qquad\qquad\qquad\qquad\qquad\qquad\square$

EXERCISES FOR SECTION 9–1

1. Given a category $\mathcal{K}$ and any object A, show that id_A is unique.

2. Recall that a map $f : S \to S'$ from one monoid to another is a **monoid homomorphism** if

$$f(s_1 \cdot s_2) = f(s_1) \cdot f(s_2) \text{ for all } s_1, s_2 \in S$$

and

$$f(1) = 1'$$

where 1 and $1'$ are the identities for S and S', respectively. Verify that if $f : S \to S'$ and $g : S' \to S''$ are monoid homomorphisms, then their composition $gf : S \to S'' : s \mapsto g(f(s))$ is also a monoid homomorphism. Also verify that the identity map $id_S : S \to S$ is always a monoid homomorphism.

3. Describe **Gp**, the category of groups.

4. Let $(P, \leq)$ be any partially ordered set. Let $\mathcal{K}$ have the elements of P for its class of objects, and define

$$\mathcal{K}(a, b) = \begin{cases} \{1_{ab}\} & \text{if } a \leq b \\ \varnothing & \text{if not} \end{cases}$$

Turn $\mathcal{K}$ into a category and verify your construction.

5. Given the sets X and Y, suppose that the map $f : X \to Y$ is a bijection. Prove that $f^{-1} : Y \to X$ is such that $ff^{-1} = id_Y$ and $f^{-1}f = id_X$. Conversely, prove that if

$f: X \to Y$ and $g: Y \to X$ are maps for which $fg = id_Y$ and $gf = id_X$, then f and g are bijections and $f^{-1} = g$.

6.   Using Definition 2, prove that a group homomorphism is an isomorphism if and only if the homomorphism is one-to-one and onto. State and verify the corresponding result for R-**Mod,** and for the category of Exercise 4.

7.   In a category $\mathcal{K}$, show that $id_A: A \to A$ is an isomorphism, and hence, $A \cong A$.

8.   Show that $\cong$ is an equivalence relation (i.e., A is related to B iff A is isomorphic to B) on the objects of a category $\mathcal{K}$.

9.   Describe a functor $H: R\text{-}\mathbf{Mod} \to \mathbf{Gp}$. (See Exercise 3.)

10.   Write out a more detailed proof of Theorem 2, using part (ii) of the proof of Theorem 1 as a model.

11.   Let the set X be a subset of a monoid S which is isomorphic to X^*. Define a homomorphism $\alpha: X^* \to S$ by the rule

$$\alpha(x_{i_1} x_{i_2} \ldots x_{i_n}) = x_{i_1} \cdot x_{i_2} \cdot \cdots \cdot x_{i_n}$$

where multiplication on the left is concatenation in X^*, while multiplication on the right is multiplication in S. Prove that α is an isomorphism.

9-2   The General Definition

Let us recapitulate the notion of a dynamorphism given in Section 2–5:

Suppose that we are given two machines $M = (Q, X_0, Y, \delta, \beta)$ and $M' = (Q', X_0, Y', \delta', \beta')$ having the same input set X_0. We refer to the maps $\delta: Q \times X_0 \to Q$ and $\delta': Q' \times X_0 \to Q'$ as the **dynamics** of their respective machines. We say that a map $h: Q \to Q'$ is a **dynamorphism** ("dynamic homomorphism") if the following diagram commutes:

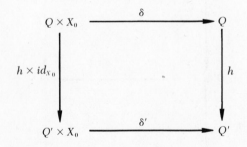

i.e., if $h[\delta(q, x)] = \delta'(h(q), x)$ for all $q \in Q$ and $x \in X_0$.

Now recall (Example 9–1–8) that by the definition of the functor $- \times X_0: \mathcal{S} \to \mathcal{S}$, the map $h: Q \to Q'$ is sent by this functor to the map $h \times X_0: Q \times X_0 \to Q' \times X_0$, where $h \times X_0$ is defined to be $h \times id_{X_0}$; i.e., $h \times X_0: (q, x) \mapsto (h(q), x)$ for all $q \in Q$ and $x \in X_0$. Thus, we may express the commutative diagram above in the equivalent form:

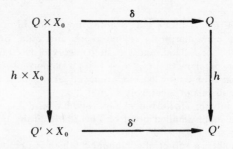

i.e., $\delta'(h \times X_0) = h\delta$.

Consider all the machines that have X_0 as their input set. We form the class whose objects are the dynamics of these machines. To each pair of dynamics $(\delta: Q \times X_0 \to Q, \ \delta': Q' \times X_0 \to Q')$ we associate the set of all dynamorphisms from Q to Q'. We claim that this results in a category, which will be denoted by $\mathbf{Dyn}(X_0)$. To verify this contention, we proceed as follows: If $h: Q \to Q'$ and $h': Q' \to Q''$ are dynamorphisms, let us define (morphism) composition by using the usual definition of composition of maps. We must, then, first check that $h'h: Q \to Q''$ is indeed a dynamorphism.

Let us take the commutative diagrams corresponding to the dynamorphisms $h: Q \to Q'$ and $h': Q' \to Q''$ and combine them to form the following commutative diagram:

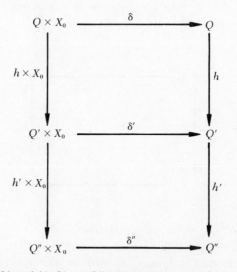

Since $h: Q \to Q'$ and $h': Q' \to Q''$ are maps, we can form the composite map $h'h: Q \to Q''$ and then the map $h'h \times X_0: Q \times X_0 \to Q'' \times X_0$. Representing these maps in the previous diagram, we have:

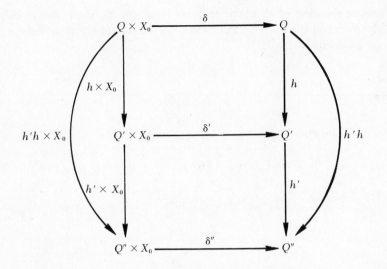

We must demonstrate that this diagram commutes [i.e., $\delta''(h'h \times X_0) = h'h\delta$] in order to show that $h'h$ is a dynamorphism. Since $- \times X_0 : \mathcal{S} \to \mathcal{S}$ is a functor (see Example 9-1-8), we have that

$$h'h \times X_0 = (h' \times X_0)(h \times X_0) \tag{1}$$

Since h and h' are dynamorphisms, we have

$$\delta'(h \times X_0) = h\delta \tag{2}$$

and

$$\delta''(h' \times X_0) = h'\delta' \tag{3}$$

respectively. Hence, we have that

$$
\begin{aligned}
\delta''(h'h \times X_0) &= \delta''(h' \times X_0)(h \times X_0) &&\text{by (1)}\\
&= h'\delta'(h \times X_0) &&\text{by (3)}\\
&= h'h\delta &&\text{by (2)}
\end{aligned}
$$

where we have used the associative property of map composition without explicit mention. Hence, we have that $h'h$ is a dynamorphism.

Clearly, now, the associativity of maps implies the associativity of dynamorphisms. Furthermore, $id_Q : Q \to Q$ is obviously a dynamorphism with the property that $h(id_Q) = h = (id_{Q'})h$ for any dynamorphism $h : Q \to Q'$. Hence, $\mathbf{Dyn}(X_0)$ is indeed a category. The objects of this category are dynamics $[\delta : Q \times X_0 \to Q$ is an object of $\mathbf{Dyn}(X_0)]$ and the $\mathbf{Dyn}(X_0)$-morphisms are dynamorphisms $[h : Q \to Q' \in \mathbf{Dyn}(X_0)(\delta : Q \times X_0 \to Q, \delta' : Q' \times X_0 \to Q')]$.

The crucial result for our general theory of machines in a category is that, among the class of all machines with input set X_0, there always exist "free' dynamics in the sense of Definition 9–1–6. We state this in technical language as follows:

THEOREM 1

The forgetful functor

$$\mathfrak{U}: \mathbf{Dyn}(X_0) \to \mathfrak{S}: [\delta: Q \times X_0 \to Q] \mapsto Q$$

has a left adjoint.

Proof

In accordance with Definition 9–1–6, we must demonstrate that for any set Q in $\mathfrak{S}$, there exist a dynamics (call it δ_Q) in $\mathbf{Dyn}(X_0)$ and a map ($\mathfrak{S}$-morphism) $\eta_Q: Q \to \delta_Q \mathfrak{U}$ such that (δ_Q, η_Q) is free over Q with respect to $\mathfrak{U}$. We shall show that this can be done by defining the dynamics δ_Q on the state set $\delta_Q \mathfrak{U} = Q \times X_0^*$ as follows:

$$\delta_Q: (Q \times X_0^*) \times X_0 \to Q \times X_0^*: ((q, w), x) \mapsto (q, wx)$$

Thus, the corresponding machine "remembers" (via registers, say) an element of Q and a string from X_0^*, and reacts to each input symbol from X_0 simply by adjoining it to the end of the X_0^*-register. We select the inclusion of generators map $\eta_Q: Q \to \delta_Q \mathfrak{U} = Q \times X_0^*$ to be $\eta_Q: q \mapsto (q, \Lambda)$. This simply inserts q into the Q-register and does not place anything in the X_0^*-register.

To verify that (δ_Q, η_Q) is free over Q with respect to $\mathfrak{U}$, we must check (see Definition 9–1–6) that for any dynamics $\delta': Q' \times X_0 \to Q'$ in $\mathbf{Dyn}(X_0)$ and any map $f: Q \to Q'$, there exists a unique dynamorphism $\psi: Q \times X_0^* \to Q'$ such that the diagram

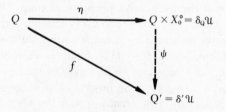

commutes. However, since ψ is a dynamorphism, it must also be true (by the definition of dynamorphism) that the diagram

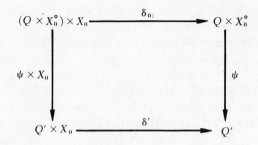

commutes. Thus, by the former diagram we require

$$\psi(\eta_Q(q)) = f(q)$$

or

$$\psi(q, \Lambda) = f(q) \tag{4}$$

for all $q \in Q$, while by the latter diagram we want

$$\psi \delta_Q((q, w), x) = \delta'(\psi \times X_0)((q, w), x)$$

or

$$\psi(q, wx) = \delta'(\psi(q, w), x) \tag{5}$$

for all $q \in Q$ and $w \in X_0^*$, and $x \in X_0$. Setting $w = \Lambda$ in equation (5), we get

$$\psi(q, \Lambda x) = \delta'(\psi(q, \Lambda), x)$$

and by (4),

$$\psi(q, x) = \delta'(f(q), x) \tag{6}$$

Next, setting $w = x_1$ in (5) yields

$$\begin{aligned}\psi(q, x_1 x) &= \delta'(\psi(q, x_1), x)\\&= \delta'(\delta'(f(q), x_1), x) \quad \text{by (6)}\\&= (\delta')^*(f(q), x_1 x)\end{aligned}$$

where $(\delta')^*: Q' \times X_0^* \to Q'$ is the inductive extension of $\delta': Q' \times X_0 \to Q'$. One may then verify (Exercise 1) by induction on the length of w that we must have

$$\psi(q, w) = (\delta')^*(f(q), w)$$

for all $q \in Q$ and $w \in X_0^*$. Thus, ψ is uniquely specified. Since this ψ results in the commutivity of the previous two diagrams, the pair (δ_Q, η_Q) is indeed free over Q with respect to $\mathfrak{U}$. $\qquad\square$

Let us now generalize the notions given above by replacing the functor $- \times X_0 : \mathcal{S} \to \mathcal{S}$ by a functor $X : \mathcal{K} \to \mathcal{K}$. Firstly, if Q is an object of the category $\mathcal{K}$, we define an X-**dynamics** to be any $\mathcal{K}$-morphism $\delta : QX \to Q$. (For the case $\mathcal{K} = \mathcal{S}$, by setting $X = - \times X_0 : \mathcal{S} \to \mathcal{S}$, the X-dynamics $\delta : QX \to Q$ recaptures the dynamics $\delta : Q \times X_0 \to Q$.) Because of this more general definition, we will be able to consider dynamics for machines which "live" in other categories $\mathcal{K}$ in addition to $\mathcal{S}$. (The astute reader may well suspect that linear machines "live" in R-**Mod,** the category of R-modules.) Secondly, given X-dynamics $\delta : QX \to Q$ and $\delta' : Q'X \to Q'$, we say that the $\mathcal{K}$-morphism $h : Q \to Q'$ is an X-**dynamorphism** if the diagram

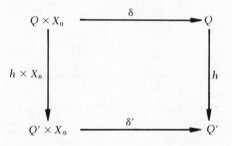

commutes. Note that if we specifically let $\mathcal{K} = \mathcal{S}$ and $X = - \times X_0$, then this definition of X-dynamorphism reverts to the original definition of dynamorphism.

Now, the class of all X-dynamics along with the associated X-dynamorphisms forms a category and is denoted by $\mathbf{Dyn}(X)$. The reader may formally establish this fact by using the procedure given for verifying that $\mathbf{Dyn}(X_0)$ is a category as a guide (Exercise 2).

For an arbitrary functor $X : \mathcal{K} \to \mathcal{K}$, we cannot in general expect the forgetful functor

$$\mathfrak{U} : \mathbf{Dyn}(X) \to \mathcal{K} : [\delta : QX \to Q] \mapsto Q$$

to have a left adjoint. However, the central idea of our theory of machines in a category is that we can extend many results of automata theory to any functor X which has the property that was established for the functor $- \times X_0$ in Theorem 1; namely, that X has a left adjoint. We call any such X an *input process.*

In summary, we will make the validity of Theorem 1 the axiom for our general definition, after making the crucial change in viewpoint of thinking of the input for a dynamics in $\mathbf{Dyn}(X_0)$ not as the set X_0 but as the functor $- \times X_0 : \mathcal{S} \to \mathcal{S}$. We shall reserve the symbol X for the entire "process" $Q \mapsto Q \times X_0$, explaining why we switch from X to X_0 to denote the set of inputs in the "classical" case. More formally we have:

DEFINITION 1

A **process** in an arbitrary category $\mathcal{K}$ is a functor $X: \mathcal{K} \to \mathcal{K}$. The **category of X-dynamics,** denoted **Dyn**(X), has as objects X-**dynamics** and has as morphisms X-**dynamorphisms.** The X-dynamics are the $\mathcal{K}$-morphisms $\delta: QX \to Q$, where Q is in $\mathcal{K}$. The X-dynamorphisms from X-dynamics $\delta: QX \to Q$ to $\delta': Q'X \to Q'$ are the $\mathcal{K}$-morphisms $h: Q \to Q'$ for which the diagram

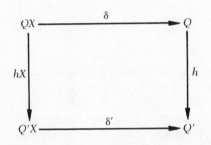

commutes. Composition and identities are defined as in $\mathcal{K}$ so that **Dyn**(X) is a category equipped with the obvious forgetful functor

$$\mathcal{U}: \mathbf{Dyn}(X) \to \mathcal{K}: [\delta: QX \to Q] \mapsto Q$$

which extracts the "state-object" of an X-dynamics. We say that X is an **input process** if and only if $\mathcal{U}$ has a left adjoint. In this case, the free dynamics over Q will be denoted $\delta_Q: (QX^@)X \to QX^@$ and the "inclusion of generators" will be denoted $\eta_Q: Q \to QX^@$. ○

In other words, $QX^@$ is an object in $\mathcal{K}$ (which corresponds to the set $Q \times X_0^*$ when $X = -\times X_0$), while $\delta_Q: (QX^@)X \to QX^@$ is a $\mathcal{K}$-morphism (which corresponds to $\delta_Q: (Q \times X_0^*) \times X_0 \to Q \times X_0^*: ((q, w), x) \mapsto (q, wx)$ when $X = -\times X_0$), and inclusion of generators $\eta_Q: Q \to QX^@$ is a $\mathcal{K}$-morphism (which corresponds to $\eta_Q: Q \to Q \times X_0^*$ when $X = -\times X_0$). Thus, the condition that δ_Q, η_Q) is free over Q is simply that for any X-dynamics $\delta': Q'X \to Q'$ in **Dyn**(X) and any $\mathcal{K}$-morphism $f: Q \to Q'$, there exists a unique X-dynamorphism $\psi: QX^@ \to Q'$ such that the diagram

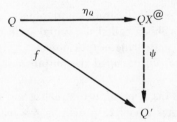

commutes, where the condition that ψ is an X-dynamorphism is simply that the diagram

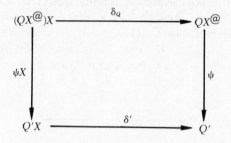

commutes. We refer to ψ as the **unique dynamorphic extension** of f.

Now let us remind ourselves of what enters the definition of a machine with input *set* X_0 so that we may formally define what we mean by a machine with input *process* X. We start with the dynamics $\delta: Q \times X_0 \to Q$, which generalizes to an X-dynamics $\delta: QX \to Q$. We specify an output *map* $\beta: Q \to Y$, and we generalize this to a $\mathcal{K}$-*morphism* $\beta: Q \to Y$, so that the output *set* Y in S is generalized to an output *object* Y in $\mathcal{K}$. We specify an *initial state* q_0 in Q in much of ordinary automata theory. However, for tree automata we often specify a whole *set* of initial states, and this specification may be given by a map $\tau: I \to Q$ which assigns a state $\tau(i)$ to each i in some set of labels for initial states. We generalize this to call for a $\mathcal{K}$-morphism $\tau: I \to Q$. Then, in ordinary automata theory, we can take $I = \{0\}$ and refer to $\tau(0) = q_0$ as *the* initial state. Putting all this together, we obtain our official definition:

DEFINITION 2

A **machine** in the category $\mathcal{K}$ is a septuple

$$M = (X, Q, \delta, I, \tau, Y, \beta)$$

where:

    X is an input process

    $\delta: QX \to Q$ is an X-dynamics in $\mathbf{Dyn}(X)$ and the object Q of $\mathcal{K}$ is called the **state object**

    I is an object of $\mathcal{K}$ called the **initial state object**

    $\tau: I \to Q$ is a $\mathcal{K}$-morphism called the **initial state morphism**

    Y is an object of $\mathcal{K}$ called the **output object**

    $\beta: Q \to Y$ is a $\mathcal{K}$-morphism called the **output morphism.**   ○

Why free machines? This is because the realization theory of Section 2–5 noted that it was always trivial to provide a *free* realization of a response function $f: X_0^* \to Y$, namely the machine

$$F_f = (X_0^*, X_0, Y, \text{conc}, f)$$

and we see that the dynamics

$$\text{conc}: X_0^* \times X_0 \to X_0^*:(w, x) \mapsto wx$$

is just the free dynamics on a one-input set Q, for if $Q = \{q_0\}$ then

$$Q \times X_0^* \to X_0^*:(q_0, w) \mapsto w$$

is not only a bijection of states for F_f and δ_Q, but is in fact a dynamorphism; i.e., the dynamics of F_f "is" the free dynamics on a one-element Q. Since the existence of F_f proved to be the starting point for our classical realization theory, it will come as no surprise to the reader that the ability to construct free machines will be a crucial property for any functor X which is to act as input process for machines with an interesting realization theory.

We shall now demonstrate how linear machines (discussed in Section 7–5) fit into this framework:

We begin by selecting as $\mathcal{K}$ the category R-**Mod** of R-modules and linear maps. Given R-modules X_0 and Q, we can form the R-module $Q \oplus X_0$ as the **direct sum** defined by the set

$$Q \oplus X_0 = \{(q, x) \mid q \in Q, x \in X_0\}$$

together with the operators

$$(q, x) + (q', x') = (q + q', x + x')$$

and

$$r(q, x) = (rq, rx)$$

We define the function $-\oplus X_0$ for objects (R-modules) of R-**Mod** by

$$-\oplus X_0: R\text{-}\mathbf{Mod} \to R\text{-}\mathbf{Mod}: Q \mapsto Q \oplus X_0$$

and for R-**Mod**-morphisms (linear maps) by

$$- \oplus X_0:(Q \xrightarrow{f} Q') \mapsto (Q \oplus X_0 \xrightarrow{f \oplus id_{X_0}} Q' \oplus X_0)$$

where $f \oplus id_{X_0}: Q \oplus X_0 \to Q' \oplus X_0:(q, x) \mapsto (f(q), x)$.

It can readily be checked that $-\oplus X_0: R\text{-}\mathbf{Mod} \to R\text{-}\mathbf{Mod}$, thus defined, is a functor (Exercise 3), so that $X = -\oplus X_0$ is a process. Thus, we may specify the X-dynamics when $X = -\oplus X_0$. By definition, the X-dynamics are the R-**Mod**-morphisms (linear maps) of the form:

$$\delta : QX \to Q$$

For any linear map

$$\delta : Q \oplus X_0 \to Q : (q, x) \mapsto \delta(q, x)$$

we have that

$$\delta(q, x) = \delta(q, 0) + \delta(0, x)$$

where the 0 in $\delta(q, 0)$ is the 0 in the R-module X_0, while the 0 in $\delta(0, x)$ is the 0 in the R-module Q.

Now the map

$$F : Q \to Q : q \mapsto Fq = \delta(q, 0)$$

is (by Exercise 4) clearly a linear map, as is

$$G : X_0 \to Q : x \mapsto Gx = \delta(0, x)$$

Thus, any linear map $Q \oplus X_0 \to Q$ can be cast into the form

$$\delta : Q \oplus X_0 \to Q : (q, x) \mapsto \delta(q, x) = Fq + Gx$$

Conversely, given *any* linear maps

$$F : Q \to Q : q \mapsto Fq$$

and

$$G : X_0 \to Q : x \mapsto Gx$$

the map δ defined by

$$\delta : Q \oplus X_0 \to Q : (q, x) \mapsto \delta(q, x) = Fq + Gx \tag{7}$$

is then a linear map (Exercise 5). Thus, the X-dynamics are exactly the maps of the form of expression (7).

To specify the X-dynamorphisms when $X = - \oplus X_0$, suppose that $h : Q \to Q'$ is an X-dynamorphism. Then by definition we must have that the diagram

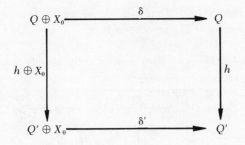

commutes. Under this condition, we have that

$$h\delta(q, x) = \delta'(h \oplus X_0)(q, x)$$
$$= \delta'(h(q), x)$$

or (representing δ' in terms of F' and G')

$$h(Fq + Gx) = F'h(q) + G'x$$

for all q in Q and x in X_0. Specifically, when $q = 0$, we have

$$hGx = G'x$$

for all $x \in X_0$; while by setting $x = 0$, we obtain

$$hFq = F'h(q)$$

for all $q \in Q$. Thus, if h is an X-dynamorphism we must have that

$$hG = G' \qquad \text{and} \qquad hF = F'h \tag{8}$$

Conversely, by working backwards, we see that any linear map $h: Q \to Q'$ satisfying (8) is an X-dynamorphism. Thus, (8) is a necessary and sufficient condition for h to be an X-dynamorphism.

We shall now demonstrate that X is an input process by exhibiting the free dynamics

$$\delta_Q : (QX^@)X \to QX^@$$

and the inclusion of generators morphism

$$\eta_Q : Q \to QX^@$$

for each Q.

We first recall from Section 7-5 that for any R-module Q, we can form the R-module, denoted $Q^\S$, that consists of all finite-support, left-infinite sequences of elements of Q. In other words,

$$Q^\S = \{w : \mathbf{N} \to Q \mid w(n) \neq 0 \text{ for only finitely many } n\}$$

where we may write w in the form $(\ldots, w_n, \ldots, w_2, w_1, w_0)$ for $w_n = w(n)$, and the operations for $Q^\S$ are defined componentwise by

$$(w + w')(n) = w(n) + w'(n)$$
$$(rw)(n) = rw(n)$$

where the left-hand-side operations in $Q^\S$ are defined in terms of the known right-hand-side operations in the R-module Q. In a similar manner, we can form the R-module $X_0^\S$. Additionally, let us define the maps

$$z : X_0^\S \to X_0^\S : (\ldots, x_n, \ldots, x_1, x_0) \mapsto (\ldots, x_{n-1}, \ldots, x_0, 0)$$
$$\bar{z} : Q^\S \to Q^\S : (\ldots, q_n, \ldots, q_1, q_0) \mapsto (\ldots, q_{n-1}, \ldots, q_0, 0)$$

which shift sequences to the left and adjoin a 0; and the maps

$$in_0 : X_0 \to X_0^\S : x \mapsto (\ldots, 0, \ldots, 0, x)$$
$$\overline{in_0} : Q \to Q^\S : q \mapsto (\ldots, 0, \ldots, 0, q)$$

which insert an element into the zero position of a left-infinite sequence. Thus, z is the shift (or successor) and in_0 is for zero insertion.

To show that X is an input process, we now claim that $QX^@ = Q^\S \oplus X_0^\S$ is the state-module for a free dynamics $\delta_Q(QX^@)X \to QX^@$ given by the linear map

$$\delta_Q : (Q^\S \oplus X_0^\S) \oplus X_0 \to Q^\S \oplus X_0^\S : [(w_1, w_2), x] \mapsto (\bar{z}w_1, zw_2 + in_0 x)$$

and inclusion of generators $\eta_Q : Q \to QX^@$ is given by the linear map

$$\eta_Q : Q \to Q^\S \oplus X_0^\S : q \mapsto (\overline{in_0}q, 0)$$

where the 0 of $(\overline{in_0}q, 0)$ is the all-zero sequence of $X_0^\S$. Note that $zw_2 + in_0 x$ has the same effect as has, in ordinary automata theory, the concatenation operation $X_0^* \times X_0 \to X_0^* : (w_2, x) \mapsto w_2 x$ which places a new input x at the end of a string w_2 of previously encountered inputs. Also note that the all-zero sequence of $X_0^\S$ corresponds to Λ in the classical case.

To substantiate our claim above, we must check that (δ_Q, η_Q) is indeed free over Q with respect to the forgetful functor:

$$\mathfrak{U} : \mathbf{Dyn}(- \oplus X_0) \to R\text{-}\mathbf{Mod} : (Q^\S \oplus X_0^\S) \oplus X_0 \mapsto Q^\S \oplus X_0^\S$$

According to Definition 9-1-6 and the definition of an X-dynamorphism, we have to show that for each linear map $f:Q \to Q'$ (i.e., $\mathcal{K}$-morphism for $\mathcal{K} = R\text{-}\mathbf{Mod}$) and each X-dynamics $\delta(q, x) = Fq + Gx$, there exists a unique X-dynamorphism

$$\psi:Q^\S \oplus X_0^\S \to Q'$$

such that each of the two diagrams

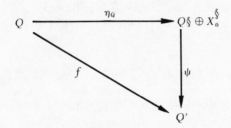

and

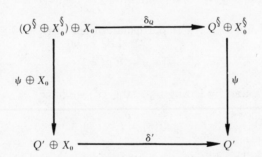

commutes. By the very argument that led us to the representation (7) of any $\delta(q, x)$ as $Fq + Gx$ for suitable F and G, it should be clear that ψ must take the form $\psi(w_1, w_2) = \alpha(w_1) + \gamma(w_2)$ for suitable linear maps $\alpha:Q^\S \to Q'$ and $\gamma:X_0^\S \to Q'$. We will now establish these maps.

To say that the former diagram commutes is to say that

$$\begin{aligned}
f(q) &= \psi\eta_Q(q) \\
&= \psi(\overline{in}_0 q, 0) \\
&= \alpha(\overline{in}_0 q) + \gamma(0) \\
&= \alpha(\overline{in}_0 q)
\end{aligned} \tag{9}$$

for all $q \in Q$. By another appeal to the argument yielding (7), we may express δ_Q as

$$\delta_Q[(w_1, w_2), x] = F_Q(w_1, w_2) + G_Q x$$

and δ' as

$$\delta'(w', x) = F'w' + G'x$$

for all $w_1 \in Q^\S$, $w_2 \in X_0^\S$, $w' \in Q'$, and $x \in X_0$. But, by definition of δ_Q, we have

$$
\begin{aligned}
\delta_Q[(w_1, w_2), x] &= (\bar{z}w_1, zw_2 + in_0 x) \\
&= (\bar{z}w_1, zw_2) + (0, in_0 x)
\end{aligned}
$$

Thus, $F_Q(w_1, w_2) = (\bar{z}w_1, zw_2)$, while $G_Q x = (0, in_0 x)$.

By (8), the condition that ψ is an X-dynamorphism is equivalent to saying that

$$\psi F_Q = F'\psi \qquad \text{and} \qquad \psi G_Q = G'$$

We have

$$\psi F_Q(w_1, w_2) = \psi(\bar{z}w_1, zw_2) = \alpha(\bar{z}w_1) + \gamma(zw_2) = \alpha\bar{z}(w_1) + \gamma z(w_2)$$

and

$$F'\psi(w_1, w_2) = F'[\alpha(w_1) + \gamma(w_2)] = F'\alpha(w_1) + F'\gamma(w_2)$$

for all $w_1 \in Q^\S$ and $w_2 \in X_0^\S$. In particular, by letting $w_2 = 0 \in X_0^\S$, we obtain

$$\alpha\bar{z}(w_1) = F'\alpha(w_1) \tag{10}$$

for all $w_1 \in Q^\S$, and by letting $w_1 = 0 \in Q^\S$, we have

$$\gamma z(w_2) = F'\gamma(w_2) \tag{11}$$

for all $w_2 \in X_0^\S$. In addition, we have that

$$G'x = \psi G_Q x = \psi(0, in_0 x) = \alpha(0) + \gamma(in_0 x) = \gamma(in_0 x) \tag{12}$$

for all $x \in X_0$.

We may now describe the unique linear map $\alpha : Q^\S \to Q'$. We have

$$\alpha(\ldots, q_n, \ldots, q_1, q_0) = \alpha \sum_{j \geq 0} z^j in_0(q_j) \qquad \text{by definition of } z \text{ and } in_0$$

$$= \sum_{j \geq 0} \alpha[z^j in_0(q_j)] \qquad \text{by the linearity of } \alpha$$

$$= \sum_{j \geq 0} (F')^j \alpha[in_0(q_j)] \qquad \text{by repeated application of } (10)$$

Thus, by (9) we have

$$\alpha(\ldots, q_n, \ldots, q_1, q_0) = \sum_{j \geq 0} (F')^j f(q_j) \tag{13}$$

which describes the linear map $\alpha: Q^\S \to Q'$ uniquely. Similarly,

$$\gamma(\ldots, x_n, \ldots, x_1, x_0) = \gamma \sum_{j \geq 0} z^j in_0(x_j) \qquad \text{by definition of } z \text{ and } in_0$$

$$= \sum_{j \geq 0} \gamma[z^j in_0(x_j)] \qquad \text{by the linearity of } \gamma$$

$$= \sum_{j \geq 0} (F')^j \gamma[in_0(x_j)] \quad \text{by repeated application of (11)}$$

Thus, by (12) we have

$$\gamma(\ldots, x_n, \ldots, x_1, x_0) = \sum_{j \geq 0} (F')^j G' x_j \tag{14}$$

which describes the linear map $\gamma: X_0^\S \to Q'$ uniquely. Hence, the existence of the unique linear map ψ indeed establishes that $-\oplus X_0$ is an input process, and so is encompassed by our general theory.

The reader, while relieved that the constructs of linear machine theory have all proved to live in the category R-**Mod,** may nonetheless feel that since linear machines are so clearly a special case of ordinary machines, it is hardly necessary to go to so much trouble to unify the two theories. To offset this feeling, we shall soon offer a result that may come as a considerable surprise, namely, that our general definition of machines in a category includes tree automata, despite the fact that the definition so far has only been seen to apply to ordinary machines. But first, we might comment that the general realization theorem of the next section has the following important property: If we define a **group machine** $M = (Q, X_0, Y, \delta, \beta)$ to be one for which Q, X_0, and Y are groups, and for which there exist homomorphisms $F: Q \to Q$, $G: X_0 \to Q$, and $H: X \to Y$ such that

$$\delta(q, x) = F(q) \cdot G(x) \text{ and } \beta(q) = H(q) \text{ for all } q \text{ in } Q \text{ and } x \text{ in } X$$

then the ordinary theory of Section 2-5 applied to the response M_e of the identity state in the state-group G does *not* in general yield a group machine as the minimal machine, whereas the categorical theory of the next section does always yield a group machine (see Padulo and Arbib [1974], Section

8–6 for details). This is in striking contrast to the situation found in Section 7–5, in which we saw that the ordinary theory when applied to a linear response function $f: X_0^§ \to Y$ did always yield a linear machine as the minimal machine.

Let us now recall the notions of a multigraded set, an Ω-tree, and an Ω-algebra from Section 4–3:

A **multigraded set** is a set Ω together with a function $\nu: \Omega \to 2^{\mathbf{N}}$ which assigns to each $\omega \in \Omega$ a finite set of **arities** $\nu(\omega) \subset \mathbf{N}$. Then an Ω-**tree** is a tree $T \subset \mathbf{N}^*$ together with a function $g: T \to \Omega$ such that if $w \in T$ has n successors, then $n \in \nu(g(w))$. An Ω-**algebra** (Q, δ) is a set Q (called the **carrier**) together with a map δ which assigns to each $\omega \in \Omega$ and $n \in \nu(\omega)$ a function

$$\delta_\omega^n : Q^n \to Q$$

Let us also recall the concept of an Ω-algebra homomorphism: Given two Ω-algebras (Q, δ) and (Q', δ') and a map $h: Q \to Q'$, let us define the map $h^n: Q^n \to (Q')^n$ by:

$$h^n(q_1, q_2, \ldots, q_n) = (h(q_1), h(q_2), \ldots, h(q_n))$$

We then say that h is an Ω-**algebra homomorphism** if

$$h(\delta_\omega^n(q_1, q_2, \ldots, q_n)) = (\delta')_\omega^n(h(q_1), h(q_2), \ldots, h(q_n))$$

for all $q_1, q_2, \ldots, q_n \in Q$; i.e., if the diagram

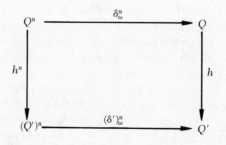

commutes.

We will now show that tree automata live in $\mathbb{S}$ and that they are incorporated in our general theory. We begin by defining a functor $X: \mathbb{S} \to \mathbb{S}$ such that the X-dynamics are precisely the Ω-algebras and the X-dynamorphisms are precisely the Ω-algebra homomorphisms.

For each Q in $\mathbb{S}$, let us define QX by

$$QX = \coprod_{n \in \mathbf{N}} Q^n \times \{\omega \mid n \in \nu(\omega)\}$$

$$= \{(q_1, q_2, \ldots q_n, \omega) \mid q_1, q_2, \ldots, q_n \in Q \text{ and } n \in \nu(\omega)\} \quad \textbf{(15)}$$

where $\amalg$ denotes a disjoint union of sets, emphasizing that no two of the sets can have any elements in common.

Example 1

Suppose that $Q = \{q_1, q_2\}$ and $\Omega = \{\omega_1, \omega_2, \omega_3\}$, where $\nu(\omega_1) = \{1\}$, $\nu(\omega_2) = \{2\}$, and $\nu(\omega_3) = \{1, 2\}$. Then we have that:

$$QX = \{(q_1, \omega_1), (q_2, \omega_1), (q_1, \omega_3), (q_2, \omega_3), (q_1, q_1, \omega_2),$$
$$(q_1, q_2, \omega_2), (q_2, q_1, \omega_2), (q_2, q_2, \omega_2), (q_1, q_1, \omega_3), (q_1, q_2, \omega_3),$$
$$(q_2, q_1, \omega_3), (q_2, q_2, \omega_3)\}$$

For the sake of notational convenience, let us rewrite (15) as:

$$QX = \coprod_{n \in \nu(\omega)} Q^n \times \{\omega\}$$

Now, an X-dynamics is just a map $\delta: QX \to Q$. However, to specify a map

$$\delta: \coprod_{n \in \nu(\omega)} Q^n \times \{\omega\} \to Q$$

is just to specify, for each $n \in \mathbf{N}$ and each $\omega \in \Omega$ such that $n \in \nu(\omega)$, a map

$$\delta_\omega^n : Q^n \to Q$$

Thus, an X-dynamics is an Ω-algebra. Since the converse is rather apparent, we see that the X-dynamics are precisely the Ω-algebras.

Next let us establish the X-dynamorphisms: Given any map $h: Q \to Q'$, let us define $hX: QX \to Q'X$ by:

$$hX: \coprod_{n \in \nu(\omega)} Q^n \times \{\omega\} \to \coprod_{n \in \nu(\omega)} (Q')^n \times \{\omega\} : (q_1, q_2, \dots, q_n, \omega) \mapsto$$

$$(h(q_1), h(q_2), \dots, h(q_n), \omega) \quad \textbf{(16)}$$

Then $h: Q \to Q'$ is an X-dynamorphism if and only if the diagram

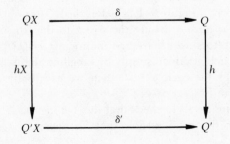

commutes; i.e., $h\delta = \delta'(hX)$. This, in turn, means that $h: Q \to Q'$ is an X-dynamorphism if and only if

$$h\delta(q_1, q_2, \ldots, q_n, \omega) = \delta'(hX)(q_1, q_2, \ldots, q_n, \omega) \tag{17}$$

for all $q_1, q_2, \ldots, q_n \in Q$ and $\omega \in \Omega$ such that $n \in \nu(\omega)$. However, since each X-dynamics is an Ω-algebra, equation (17) is equivalent to

$$
\begin{aligned}
h\delta_\omega^n(q_1, q_2, \ldots, q_n) &= \delta'(hX)(q_1, q_2, \ldots, q_n, \omega) \\
&= \delta'(h(q_1), h(q_2), \ldots, h(q_n), \omega) \\
&= (\delta')_\omega^n(h(q_1), h(q_2), \ldots, h(q_n))
\end{aligned}
$$

for all $q_1, q_2, \ldots, q_n \in Q$. Hence, $h: Q \to Q'$ is an X-dynamorphism if and only if it is an Ω-algebra homomorphism; and we have established our contention about the X-dynamorphisms. [*Note:* The thorough reader should formally establish (Exercise 6) that $X: \mathcal{S} \to \mathcal{S}$ defined by (15) and (16) is indeed a functor.]

Now that we have constructed the process X, let us verify that X is an input process; specifically, that we can construct a free dynamics

$$\delta_Q: (QX^@)X \to QX^@ \text{ for each } Q \text{ in } \mathcal{S}$$

Let Ω_Q be the multigraded set $\Omega_Q = \Omega \cup Q$ having the arity function $\nu_Q: \Omega_Q \to 2^{\mathbf{N}}$ defined by

$$
\nu_Q(\omega_Q) = \begin{cases} \nu(\omega_Q) & \text{if } \omega_Q \in \Omega \\ \{0\} & \text{if } \omega_Q \in Q \end{cases}
$$

and let $QX^@$ be the set of all the Ω_Q-trees. It is clear from their definition that an Ω_Q-tree is just like an Ω-tree save that some of the terminal nodes (i.e., nodes with no successors) of an Ω_Q-tree may be labelled with elements of Q.

By (15), we have that

$$(QX^@)X = \{(t_1, t_2, \ldots, t_n, \omega) \,|\, t_1, t_2, \ldots, t_n \text{ are } \Omega_Q\text{-trees and } n \in \nu(\omega)\}$$

We define the free dynamics $\delta_Q: (QX^@)X \to QX^@$ by taking $\delta_Q(t_1, \ldots, t_n, \omega)$ to be the tree shown in Figure 9–1, which is the Ω_Q-tree obtained by labelling the Λ-node with ω and attaching the tree t_j to the jth successor of Λ. For inclusion of generators, we choose the map $\eta_Q: Q \to QX^@$ which sends q to the one-node Ω_Q-tree obtained simply by labelling the Λ-node with q. [Note that if $\nu(\omega) = \{1\}$ for each $\omega \in \Omega$, then we essentially have the case of ordinary automata (Exercise 7).]

It only remains for us to check that the X-dynamics $\delta: (QX^@)X \to QX^@$ is indeed free. To do this, we show that for any map $f: Q \to Q'$ and any

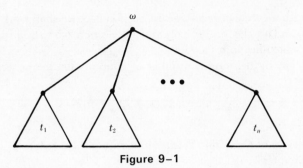

Figure 9–1

X-dynamics $\delta':Q'X \to Q'$, there exists a unique X-dynamorphism (i.e., an Ω-algebra homomorphism) $\psi:QX^@ \to Q'$ such that the following two diagrams commute:

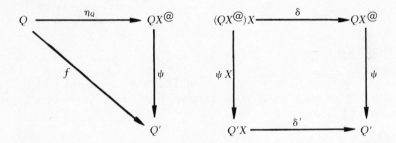

We proceed as follows:

We use $f:Q \to Q'$ to relabel terminal nodes to form, from an Ω_Q-tree, a corresponding $\Omega_{Q'}$-tree. Recalling the notion of a "run" from Section 4–3, we then run the δ'-dynamics on this tree and read out the result from the Λ-node. Formally, we define $\psi(t)$ inductively as follows:

Basis Step: If t is a one-node tree, then there are two cases:

a) If $t(\Lambda) = q \in Q$, take $\psi(t):\{\Lambda\} \to Q':\Lambda \mapsto f(q)$.
b) If $t(\Lambda) = \omega \in \Omega$ with $0 \in \nu(\omega)$, take $\psi(t):\{\Lambda\} \to Q':\Lambda \mapsto (\delta')^0_\omega$.

Induction Step: If $t = \delta_Q(t_1, t_2, \ldots, t_n, \omega)$ with $n \in \nu(\omega)$, define $\psi(t)$ in terms of $\psi(t_1), \psi(t_2), \ldots, \psi(t_n)$ by the rule

$$\psi(t) = (\delta')^n_\omega(\psi(t_1), \psi(t_2), \ldots, \psi(t_n)) \qquad \textbf{(18)}$$

Hence, this clearly defines a unique map $\psi:QX^@ \to Q'$ such that the previous two diagrams commute. Thus, the theory of tree automata is sustained in our general theory of machines in a category.

We now define the response, or the behavior, of any machine in a category, and then define the realization problem to be that of finding a machine with a specified behavior. In Section 9–3, we shall work within this framework and use the intuition obtained in Section 2–5 to build a realization theory for machines in a category.

We begin by defining a number of concepts for the general machine

$$M = (X, Q, \delta, I, \tau, Y, \beta)$$

in a category $\mathcal{K}$ of Definition 2, after motivating them by the usual concepts given in Chapter 2.

First, we note that the construction of a free dynamics $\delta_Q : (QX^@)X \to QX^@$, with the corresponding inclusion of generators $\eta_Q : Q \to QX^@$, is available for any object Q in $\mathcal{K}$. In particular, then, it is available for the initial state object I. Let us start by examining $IX^@$ for $X = - \times X_0$.

Example 2

If $X = - \times X_0$ in $\mathcal{S}$, from the proof of Theorem 1 we know that $QX^@ = Q \times X_0^*$. If we want the classical case, we take I to be a one-element set; say $I = \{0\}$. Then we have that

$$IX^@ = \{0\} \times X_0^* \cong X_0^*$$

where the obvious bijection is $(0, w) \leftrightarrow w$. Then $IX^@$ is just the set of all input sequences and is referred to as the "object of inputs."

Given the machine $M = (- \times X_0, Q, \delta, I, \tau, Y, \beta)$, where $I = \{0\}$ and $\tau(0) = q_0 \in Q$, let us study r, the unique dynamorphic extension of τ, i.e., the unique r for which each of the two diagrams

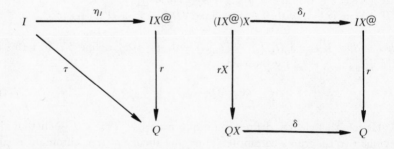

commutes. In the present case, by referring to the proof of Theorem 1, we see that these two diagrams take the form

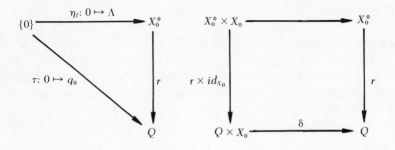

Thus, we have that

$$r\eta_I(0) = \tau(0)$$
$$r(\Lambda) = q_0$$

and

$$r(\text{conc})(w, x) = \delta(r \times id_{X_0})(w, x)$$
$$r(wx) = \delta(r(w), x)$$

for all $w \in X_0^*$ and $x \in X_0$. Hence, just as in the proof of Theorem 1, we conclude that

$$r : X_0^* \to Q : w \mapsto \delta^*(q_0, w)$$

We thus call r the *reachability map,* since it sends the input string w to the state which w causes M to reach from the initial state q_0.

Since $r : X_0^* \to Q$ and $\beta : Q \to Y$, we can define $f : X_0^* \to Y$ by $f = \beta r$; and

$$f(w) = \beta r(w) = \beta[\delta^*(q_0, w)] = M_{q_0}$$

which is the response to w of M when started in state q_0. We call $f = M_{q_0}$ the *response,* or *behavior,* of M. Note that in Section 2–1 we spoke of M_q as the response of M *when started in state q.* If we do not specify q, it is to be understood that q_0 is intended, since the specification of M that we now use actually includes the initial state. Further, in Section 2–1 we called any function f of the form $f : X_0^* \to Y$ a behavior and said that an automaton M with initial state q_0 *realizes* a behavior $f : X_0^* \to Y$ iff $f = Mq_0$.   ◊

We saw in Section 2–5 that any behavior $X_0^* \to Y$ has a (not necessarily finite-state) realization; just as we saw in Section 7–5 (and see Example 3 below) that any linear behavior $X_0^\S \to Y$ has a (not necessarily finite-dimensional) realization as the behavior of a linear machine. In the next section, we shall prove a general realization theorem for which these two results are special cases. Moreover, the general theorem will yield a realization theory for tree automata as well.

We now formalize the notions observed in Example 2.

DEFINITION 3

Suppose that $M = (X, Q, \delta, I, \tau, Y, \beta)$ is a machine in a category $\mathcal{K}$ with $\delta_I : (IX^@)X \to IX^@$ as the free dynamics over I and with inclusion of generators $\eta_I : I \to IX^@$. We then call $IX^@$ the **object of inputs** for M. The **reachability morphism** $r : IX^@ \to Q$ of M is the unique dynamorphic extension of the initial state morphism $\tau : I \to Q$, i.e., the unique $\mathcal{K}$-morphism r for which both of the diagrams

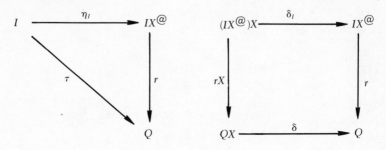

commute. The **response,** or **behavior,** of M is the composition $\beta r : IX^@ \to Y$; i.e.,

$$IX^@ \xrightarrow{r} Q \xrightarrow{\beta} Y$$

For fixed I, X, and Y, a **response morphism** is any $\mathcal{K}$-morphism $f : IX^@ \to Y$. Finally, we say that a machine M **realizes** f, or is a **realization** of f, if and only if $f = \beta r$ for M.   ○

Next let us consider the case of linear machines.

Example 3

Recalling Definition 7–5–1, let us consider the linear machine $M = (Q, X_0, Y, \delta, \beta)$ defined by the linear maps $F : Q \to Q$, $G : X_0 \to Q$, and $H : Q \to Y$. We take the input object to be the trivial R-module $\{0\}$, so that since $\tau : \{0\} \to Q$ is linear, we must have that $\tau(0) = 0 \in Q$.

Clearly, $\{0\}^{\S}$ has only one element; namely, the all-zero, left-infinite sequence. Obviously then $\{0\}^{\S}$ is isomorphic to $\{0\}$ as an R-module. It is also clear that $\{0\} \oplus A \cong A$ for any R-module A. Thus, by our general formula, $QX^@ = Q^{\S} \oplus X_0^{\S}$ for $X = -\oplus X_0$, the object of inputs for our linear machine is

$$IX^@ = I^{\S} \oplus X_0^{\S}$$
$$= \{0\}^{\S} \oplus X_0^{\S}$$
$$\cong X_0^{\S}$$

Reassuringly, then, the general theory tells us that $X_0^\S$ is the appropriate object of inputs for linear machines, just as we had concluded by *ad hoc* methods in Section 7–5. The reachability map $r : X_0^\S \to Y$ then yields the commutative diagrams:

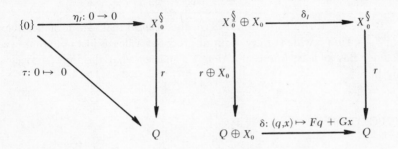

Thus, by equation (14), we have that

$$r(\ldots, x_n, \ldots, x_1, x_0) = \sum_{j \geq 0} F^j G x_j$$

which is indeed the familiar formula from Section 7–4.

Finally, using the fact that $\beta = H : Q \to Y$ is linear, we have

$$f(\ldots, x_n, \ldots, x_1, x_0) = \beta r(\ldots, x_n, \ldots, x_1, x_0)$$

$$= \beta \sum_{j \geq 0} F^j G x_j$$

$$= H \sum_{j \geq 0} F^j G x_j$$

$$= \sum_{j \geq 0} H F^j G x_j$$

recapturing equation (1) of Section 7–5, the zero-state response of a linear machine.   ◊

Example 4

Let $X : \S \to \S : Q \mapsto QX$ be the Ω-algebra functor (15) such that for any set Q, $QX^@$ is the set of Ω_Q-trees. Then the object of inputs, $IX^@$, is simply the set of Ω_I-trees, which are just like Ω-trees, save that some terminal nodes may bear initial state labels from I. Then $r : (IX^@)X \to Q$ for a tree automaton $M = (X, Q, \delta, I, \tau, Y, \beta)$, being the unique dynamorphic extension of

$\tau : I \to Q$, acts on an Ω_Q-tree t simply by relabelling [compare (18)] any terminal node labelled $i \in I$ with the state $\tau(i) \in Q$, and then running on the resultant Ω_Q-tree with δ to obtain the Q-tree $\bar{t}$, to yield $r(t) = \bar{t}(\Lambda)$. We then have the response function $\beta r : IX^@ \to Y$ yielding $\beta[\bar{t}(\Lambda)]$, the output associated with the state on the Λ-node of the tree $\bar{t}$. $\Diamond$

Before we turn, in Section 9–3, to the *minimal* realization of behaviors $f : IX^@ \to Y$ for a wide variety of input processes X, let us just note that every behavior has at least one realization, no matter what the input process X may be.

PROPOSITION 2

Let X be an input process and let $f : IX^@ \to Y$ be a behavior. Let $\delta_I : (IX^@)X \to IX^@$ be the free dynamics over I, with inclusion of the generators $\eta_I : I \to IX^@$. Then the machine

$$F_f = (X, IX^@, \delta_I, I, \eta_I, Y, f)$$

is a realization of f, called the **free realization** of f.

Proof

Since we have the diagram

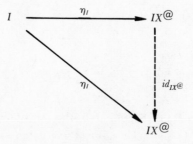

and since $id_{IX^@}$ is certainly a dynamorphism of δ_I into itself, we conclude that id_{IX} is the unique dynamorphic extension of the initial state morphism η_I of F_f, and is thus the reachability morphism of F_f. Thus, the behavior of F_f is

$$IX^@ \xrightarrow{id_{IX^@}} IX^@ \xrightarrow{f} Y$$

which equals f, as was to be shown. $\square$

This, of course, reduces for $X = - \times X_0$ in $\mathcal{S}$ to the familiar machine $F_f = (X_0, X_0^*, \text{conc}, Y, f)$, with initial state Λ, of Section 2–5.

EXERCISES FOR SECTION 9–2

1.   As described in the proof of Theorem 1, prove by induction on the length of w that

$$\psi(q, w) = (\delta')^*(f(q), w)$$

for all q in Q and w in X_0^*.

2.   Verify that $\mathbf{Dyn}(X)$ is a category by using as a guide the procedure which established that $\mathbf{Dyn}(X_0)$ is a category.

3.   Show that $- \oplus X_0 : R\text{-}\mathbf{Mod} \to R\text{-}\mathbf{Mod}$ defined by

$$- \oplus X_0 : Q \mapsto Q \oplus X_0$$

and

$$- \oplus X_0 : f \mapsto f \oplus id_{X_0}$$

is a functor.

4.   Given the linear map

$$\delta : Q \oplus X_0 \to Q : (q, x) \mapsto \delta(q, x)$$

in the category $R\text{-}\mathbf{Mod}$, prove that the maps F and G defined by

$$F : Q \to Q : q \mapsto Fq = \delta(q, 0)$$

and

$$G : X_0 \to Q : x \mapsto Gx = \delta(0, x)$$

are linear.

5.   Given any linear maps

$$F : Q \to Q : q \mapsto Fq$$

and

$$G : X_0 \to Q : x \mapsto Gx$$

prove that the map δ defined by

$$\delta : Q \oplus X_0 \to Q : (q, x) \mapsto \delta : (q, x) = Fq + Gx$$

is linear.

6.   Verify that $X : \mathcal{S} \to \mathcal{S}$ defined by (15) and (16) is a functor.

7.   In the discussion of tree automata, justify that if $\nu(\omega) = \{1\}$ for each $\omega \in \Omega$, then the case of ordinary automata is obtained.

9–3   Machine Realization

We have already seen how a functor $X : \mathcal{K} \to \mathcal{K}$, which is an input process, may replace the functor $- \times X_0 : \mathcal{S} \to \mathcal{S}$ of "classical" automata theory. In this section we present a way of restating the classical theory of Section 2–5 in categorical terms that have proved to be of sufficient generality for solving the machine realization problem not only for the classical case, but for linear machines, tree automata, and other cases as well (such as the group machines treated in Chapter 8 of Padulo and Arbib). We first divide this section into alternating subsections entitled "Motivation," giving a transmutation of the classical theory, and "Theory," presenting the general categorical statement; and close by applying the general theory to linear machines and tree automata.

MOTIVATION

In the classical case, we are given a behavior $f: X_0^* \to Y$, and we define an equivalence relation $E_f \subset X_0^* \times X_0^*$ by

$$(w_1, w_2) \in E_f \Leftrightarrow f(w_1 w) = f(w_2 w) \text{ for all } w \in X_0^* \tag{1}$$

Clearly,

$$X_0^* = \bigcup_{n \geq 0} X_0^n$$

Thus, we may replace (1) by

$$(w_1, w_2) \in E_f \Leftrightarrow [f(w_1 w) = f(w_2 w) \text{ for all } w \in X_0^n] \text{ for all } n \in \mathbf{N} \tag{2}$$

Recalling from Example 9–2–2 the free dynamics

$$\delta_I: X_0^* \times X_0 \to X_0^*: (w, x) \mapsto wx$$

for the one-element set I (so that $I \times X_0^* \cong X_0^*$), we may extend the map δ_I to the map

$$\delta_I^{(n)}: X_0^* \times X_0^n \to X_0^*: (w, (x_1, x_2, \ldots, x_n)) \mapsto w x_1 x_2 \ldots x_n$$

Note that

$$\delta_I^{(n)}: X_0^* \times X_0^n = (X_0^* \times X_0) \times X_0^{n-1} \xrightarrow{\delta_I \times id_{X_0^{n-1}}}$$
$$X_0^* \times X_0^{n-1} \xrightarrow{\delta_I \times id_{X_0^{n-2}}} \cdots \xrightarrow{\delta_I \times id_{X_0}} X_0^* \times X_0 \xrightarrow{\delta_I} X_0^*$$

so that

$$\delta_I^{(n)}: (w, (x_1, x_2, \ldots, x_n)) \mapsto (wx_1, (x_2, \ldots, x_n)) \mapsto$$
$$(wx_1 x_2, (x_3, \ldots, x_n)) \mapsto \cdots \mapsto w x_1 x_2 \ldots x_n$$

Thus,

$$\delta_I^{(n+1)} = X_0^* \times X_0^{n+1} \xrightarrow{\delta_I \times id_{X_0^n}} X_0^* \times X_0^n \xrightarrow{\delta_I^{(n)}} X_0^* = \delta_I^{(n)} \delta_I X^n \quad \textbf{(3)}$$

where X is the functor $-\times X_0$. This formula for $\delta_I^{(n+1)}$ will prove useful in our categorical treatment.

Using $\delta_I^{(n)}$, we may recast (2) into the form:

$$(w_1, w_2) \in E_f \Leftrightarrow$$
$$[f\delta_I^{(n)}(w_1, w) = f\delta_I^{(n)}(w_2, w) \text{ for all } w \in X_0^n] \text{ for all } n \in \mathbf{N} \quad \textbf{(4)}$$

Now let us define the projections:

$$\alpha : E_f \to X_0^* : (w_1, w_2) \mapsto w_1$$

and

$$\gamma : E_f \to X_0^* : (w_1, w_2) \mapsto w_2$$

Then it should be clear that the "$\Rightarrow$" part of (4) is equivalent to stating that if $(w_1, w_2) \in E_f$, then the diagram

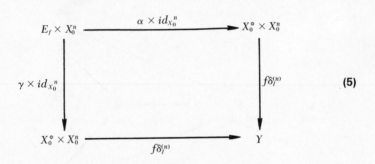

$$\textbf{(5)}$$

commutes for all $n \in \mathbf{N}$.

Suppose that R is a subset of $X_0^* \times X_0^*$ which satisfies the "$\Leftarrow$" part of (4) in place of E_f. Let $p : R \to X_0^*$ and $p' : R \to X_0^*$ be the projections from R such that $r = (p(r), p'(r))$ for each $r \in R$. Then the "$\Leftarrow$" part of (4) says that if

$$f\delta_I^{(n)}(p(r), w) = f\delta_I^{(n)}(p'(r), w) \text{ for all } w \in X_0^n$$

holds for all $n \in \mathbf{N}$, then $r = (p(r), p'(r))$ must be in E_f. Thus, under this circumstance, by defining the map ψ by

$$\psi : R \to E_f : r \mapsto (p(r), p'(r))$$

we can justify the following arrow-theoretic reformulation of (1):

The equivalence relation E_f is defined by the maps

$$E_f \xrightarrow[\gamma]{\alpha} X_0^*$$

(which is just a shorthand way of specifying two maps with the same domain and codomain; we are not, of course, implying that $\alpha = \gamma$) if

(a) for all $n \in \mathbf{N}$ we have that diagram (5) commutes, i.e.,

$$f\delta_I^{(n)}(\alpha \times id_{X_0^n}) = f\delta_I^{(n)}(\gamma \times id_{X_0^n})$$

for all $n \in \mathbf{N}$, and, moreover,
(b) given any pair of maps

$$R \xrightarrow[p']{p} X_0^*$$

for which

$$f\delta_I^{(n)}(p \times id_{X_0^n}) = f\delta_I^{(n)}(p' \times id_{X_0^n})$$

for all $n \in \mathbf{N}$, there exists a unique map $\psi : R \to E_f$ such that the diagram

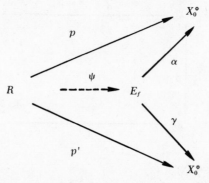

(6)

commutes.

To go to the general case, we simply replace X_0^* by $IX^@$ and $- \times X_0^n$ by X^n. However, whereas in $\mathbf{S}$ we know that diagram (6) always defines an equivalence relation, in our general theory we must *postulate* that the corresponding diagram can indeed be properly formed, just as we had to postulate that $\mathbf{Dyn}(X) \to X$ had a left adjoint.

THEORY

Let $X : \mathcal{K} \to \mathcal{K}$ be an input process, let $\delta_I : (IX^@)X \to IX^@$ be the free dynamics over I in $\mathcal{K}$, and let $f : IX^@ \to Y$ be a response morphism. For any $\delta : QX \to Q$, we define $\delta^{(n)} : QX^n \to Q$ inductively as follows:

Basis Step:

$$\delta^{(0)} = id_Q \text{ (We take } X^0 = \text{ the identity function on } \mathcal{K}.)$$

Induction Step:

$$\delta^{(n+1)} = QX^{n+1} \xrightarrow{\delta X^n} QX^n \xrightarrow{\delta^{(n)}} Q$$

We then have the following:

DEFINITION 1

We say that f **satisfies Postulate 1** if there exists a $\mathcal{K}$-object E_f and a pair of $\mathcal{K}$-morphisms

$$E_f \underset{\gamma}{\overset{\alpha}{\rightrightarrows}} IX^@$$

such that

(a) $\qquad\qquad f\delta_I^{(n)}(\alpha X^n) = f\delta_I^{(n)}(\gamma X^n)$ $\qquad\qquad$ **(7a)**

for all $n \in \mathbf{N}$, and
  (b) given any $\mathcal{K}$-object R and a pair of $\mathcal{K}$-morphisms

$$R \underset{p'}{\overset{p}{\rightrightarrows}} IX^@$$

such that

$$f\delta_I^{(n)}(pX^n) = f\delta_I^{(n)}(p'X^n)$$

for all $n \in \mathbf{N}$, then there exists a unique $\mathcal{K}$-morphism $\psi : R \to E_f$ such that the diagram

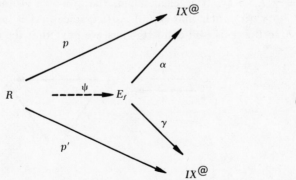

$\qquad\qquad\qquad\qquad\qquad\qquad\qquad\qquad\qquad\qquad$ **(7b)**

commutes.

For any f satisfying Postulate 1, we call $E_f \overset{\alpha}{\underset{\gamma}{\rightrightarrows}} IX^@$ the **Nerode equivalence** for f. The word "the" is justified by the fact that if both $E_f \overset{\alpha}{\underset{\gamma}{\rightrightarrows}} IX^@$ and $E'_f \overset{\alpha'}{\underset{\gamma'}{\rightrightarrows}} IX^@$ are Nerode equivalences for f, then there exists a $\mathcal{K}$-isomorphism $\psi': E'_f \to E_f$ which satisfies $\alpha' = \alpha\psi'$ and $\gamma' = \gamma\psi'$ (Exercise 1).

○

MOTIVATION

After defining the Nerode equivalence, the next step in the classical theory was to form the minimal state set Q_f given by

$$Q_f = X_0^*/E_f = \{[w] \mid w \in X_0^*\}$$

where $[w]$ denotes the equivalence class of w with respect to E_f. We now shall see that we can define the map $r_f: X_0^* \to Q_f: w \mapsto [w]$ arrow-theoretically, instead of by directly specifying that $r_f(w) = [w]$.

We begin by noting that

$$r_f(w_1) = r_f(w_2) \Leftrightarrow [w_1] = [w_2]$$
$$\Leftrightarrow (w_1, w_2) \in E_f$$

Since

and

$$E_f \overset{\alpha}{\to} X_0^* \overset{r_f}{\to} Q_f : (w_1, w_2) \mapsto [w_1]$$

$$E_f \overset{\gamma}{\to} X_0^* \overset{r_f}{\to} Q_f : (w_1, w_2) \mapsto [w_2]$$

then

$$r_f\alpha = r_f\gamma : E_f \to Q_f : (w_1, w_2) \mapsto [w_1] = [w_2]$$

Now suppose that $r: X_0^* \to Q$ is any map which also has the property that $r(w_1) = r(w_2)$ whenever $(w_1, w_2) \in E_f$. In other words, we have that $r\alpha = r\gamma : E_f \to Q$. It is clear, then, that we can define a map $\phi: Q_f \to Q : [w] \mapsto r(w)$, such that $\phi r_f(w) = r(w)$, since $[w_1] = [w_2]$ implies $r(w_1) = r(w_2)$, so that ϕ is well-defined. Thus, we have that the diagram

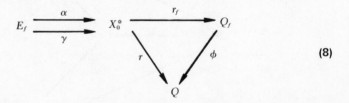

(8)

commutes in the sense that all paths going from one place to another yield the same result, except for the two paths from E_f to X_0^* that are labelled

α and γ. Thus, while we do *not* assert that $\alpha = \gamma$, we do assert that $r_f\alpha = r_f\gamma$, $r\alpha = r\gamma$, $\phi r_f = r$, etc.

In technical jargon, we say that r_f is the *coequalizer* of α and γ, and we write $r_f = \text{coeq}(\alpha, \gamma)$. This discussion then motivates the second postulate of our general theory.

THEORY

With the above in mind, we may make two definitions:

DEFINITION 2

Let $A \overset{h}{\underset{k}{\rightrightarrows}} B$ be a pair of $\mathcal{K}$-morphisms. We say that $B \overset{g}{\to} C$ **is a coequalizer of** $A \overset{h}{\underset{k}{\rightrightarrows}} B$ (or that $A \overset{h}{\underset{k}{\rightrightarrows}} B$ **has coequalizer** $B \overset{g}{\to} C$) and write $g = \text{coeq}(h, k)$ if and only if

(a) $gh = gk$; and
(b) for every $G \quad C'$ such that $g'h = g'k$, there exists a unique $\mathcal{K}$-morphism $C \overset{\phi}{\to} C'$ such that $\phi g = g'$; i.e., such that the diagram

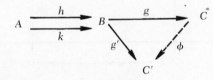

commutes (in the sense explained for (8)).

A $\mathcal{K}$-morphism is called a **coequalizer** iff it is the coequalizer of some pair of $\mathcal{K}$-morphisms. ◯

DEFINITION 3

If f has the Nerode equivalence $E_f \overset{\alpha}{\underset{\gamma}{\rightrightarrows}} IX^{@}$, we say that f **satisfies Postulate 2** if $E_f \overset{\alpha}{\underset{\gamma}{\rightrightarrows}} IX^{@}$ has as coequalizer the $\mathcal{K}$-morphism $IX^{@} \overset{r_f}{\to} Q_f$. ◯

MOTIVATION

In the classical theory $X_0^* \overset{r_f}{\to} Q_f$ is the reachability map of a dynamics $\delta_f : Q_f \times X_0 \to Q_f : ([w], x) \to [wx]$; i.e., the diagram

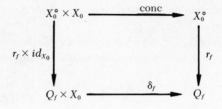

commutes.

THEORY

DEFINITION 4

Suppose that $IX^@ \xrightarrow{r_f} Q_f = \mathrm{coeq}(\alpha, \gamma)$, where $E_f \xrightarrow[\gamma]{\alpha} IX^@$ is the Nerode equivalence of f. Then we say that f **satisfies Postulate 3** if there exists an X-dynamics $\delta_f : Q_f X \to Q_f$ such that r_f is an X-dynamorphism from the free dynamics δ_I to δ_f; i.e., such that the diagram

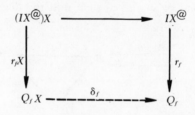

commutes. ○

MOTIVATION

In order to motivate the fourth postulate, we now develop a necessary and sufficient condition for a map in $\mathcal{S}$ to be surjective.

DEFINITION 5

In a category $\mathcal{K}$, we say that a morphism $f : A \to B$ is an **epimorphism** if whenever $gf = hf$ for $\mathcal{K}$-morphisms $g : B \to C$ and $h : B \to C$, it must follow that $g = h$. Furthermore, if $f : A \to B$ is an epimorphism and there exists a $\mathcal{K}$-morphism $f' : B \to A$ such that $ff' = id_B$, then we call f a **split epimorphism**. (See Exercise 2.) ○

LEMMA 1

A map in $\mathcal{S}$ is surjective if and only if it is a split epimorphism iff it is an epimorphism.

Proof

(i) Suppose that $f: A \to B$ is a surjective map. Then for each $b \in B$ there exists some element in A, call it $f'(b)$, such that $f(f'(b)) = b$. In other words, $f': B \to A$ satisfies $ff' = id_B$. Thus,

$$gf = hf \Rightarrow g\,ff' = hff' \Rightarrow g(id_B) = h(id_B) \Rightarrow g = h$$

Hence, f is a split epimorphism, and thus certainly an epimorphism.

(ii) Conversely, suppose that the map $f: A \to B$ is an epimorphism. We assume that f is not surjective. Thus, there exists some b_0 in $B \backslash f(A)$. Let us define the map $g: B \to B$ by:

$$g(b) = \begin{cases} b \text{ if } b \neq b_0 \\ \text{anything but } b_0 \text{ if } b = b_0 \text{ (Exercise 3)} \end{cases}$$

Now

$$g(f(a)) = f(a) = id_B(f(a))$$

for all $a \in A$, since $f(a) \neq b_0$. Therefore,

$$gf = id_B f$$

and since f is an epimorphism, $g = id_B$. However, this contradicts the definition of g. Hence, f is surjective. $\square$

Next let us see that, in any category $\mathcal{K}$, coequalizers are epimorphisms.

LEMMA 2

In any category $\mathcal{K}$, if $g = \text{coeq}(h, k)$, then g is an epimorphism.

Proof

Let $B \xrightarrow{g} C$ be a coequalizer of $A \underset{k}{\overset{h}{\rightrightarrows}} B$. Suppose that there exist $\mathcal{K}$-morphisms $e: C \to C'$ and $f: C \to C'$ such that $eg = fg: B \to C'$. Then from Definition 2,

$$(eg)h = e(gh) = e(gk) = (eg)k$$

and also

$$(fg)h = (fg)k$$

Thus, each of the following two diagrams commutes:

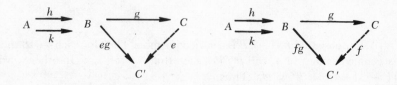

Hence, since $eg = fg$, by the uniqueness property we have that $e = f$; and so g is an epimorphism.   □

Next, let us see what $- \times X_0$ does to a coequalizer in $\mathcal{S}$.

LEMMA 3

In $\mathcal{S}$, if $g = \text{coeq}(h, k)$, then $g \times X_0 = \text{coeq}(h \times X_0, k \times X_0)$.

Proof

Let $F = \mathcal{S}[A \times X_0, B]$, the set of all maps from $A \times X_0$ to B in $\mathcal{S}$, and let $\widehat{F} = \mathcal{S}[A, B^{X_0}]$, the set of all maps from A to $B^{X_0} = \mathcal{S}[X_0, B]$.

Then we may define a map $\widehat{} : F \to \widehat{F} : f \mapsto \widehat{f}$ by the rule:

$$\widehat{f}(a) : X_0 \to B : x \mapsto f(a, x)$$

We note that $\widehat{}$ is a bijection, since the map $\widetilde{} : \widehat{F} \to F : e \mapsto \widetilde{e}$ defined by the rule

$$\widetilde{e} : A \times X_0 \to B : (a, x) \mapsto e(a)(x)$$

(recalling that $e(a) \in B^{X_0}$) is the inverse of $\widehat{}$.

Thus, the diagram

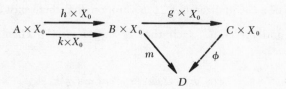

(9)

can be completed by a map ϕ so that it commutes if and only if the diagram

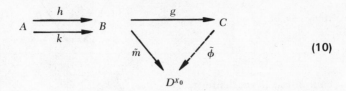

$$(10)$$

can be completed with the corresponding map $\widetilde{\phi}$ so that it commutes. Since $g = \text{coeq}(h, k)$, there is in fact a unique map ψ which completes (10) so that it commutes, whence $\phi = \widehat{\psi}$ is the unique map which completes (9) so that it commutes. But this uniqueness just says that $g \times X_0 = \text{coeq}(h \times X_0, k \times X_0)$. $\qquad\square$

In particular, $g \times X_0$ is an epimorphism for every coequalizer g in $\S$, by Lemma 2. However, we do not require nearly as strong a property as this to hold in $\mathcal{K}$ for our general theory, but only Postulate 4 of the next definition.

THEORY

DEFINITION 6

Suppose that M is a realization of a response morphism $f: IX^@ \to Y$, and the reachability morphism $r: IX^@ \to Q$ of M is a coequalizer. Then we say that f **satisfies Postulate 4** if rX is an epimorphism. $\qquad\bigcirc$

MOTIVATION

In the classical theory, we define

$$\beta_f: Q_f \to Y: [w] \to f(w)$$

so that $\beta_f r_f = f$.

THEORY

From (7a) we have that $f\alpha = f\gamma$ when $n = 0$. Thus, we may define β_f to be the unique $\mathcal{K}$-morphism for which the diagram

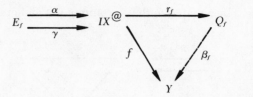

(11)

commutes. If we define τ_f by

$$\tau_f = r_f \eta_I : I \to Q_f$$

we have the following commutative diagrams, of which the second is given by the condition on δ_f in Postulate 3:

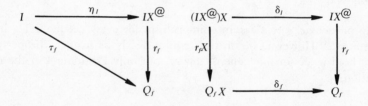

Thus, by Definition 9-2-3, r_f is indeed the reachability morphism of $M_f = (X, Q_f, \delta_f, I, \tau_f, Y, \beta_f)$.

MOTIVATION

In the classical theory, we demonstrated that M_f is minimal by showing that if $M = (X_0, Q, \delta, q_0, Y, \beta)$ is any other realization (where we have altered the classical notation for an initialized machine to conform to our present discussion) of f which is reachable, then the map $Q \to Q_f : \delta^*(q_0, w) \mapsto [w]$ is indeed well-defined and an i/o-homomorphism. The proof in the general case is no harder, except that a little care is required to handle the reachability condition in the form that the reachability morphism of M is a coequalizer.

THEORY

We now prove the following important result.

THEOREM 4: (NERODE REALIZATION THEOREM)

Suppose that $f : IX^@ \to Y$ is a response morphism satisfying Postulates 1, 2, 3, and 4. Then

$$M_f = (X, Q_f, \delta_f, I, \tau_f, Y, \beta_f)$$

is a minimal coequalizer-reachable realization of f in the sense that if $M = (X, Q, \delta, I, \tau, Y, \beta)$ has a coequalizer for its reachability morphism, then there exists a unique X-dynamorphism $\psi : Q \to Q_f$ such that the diagram

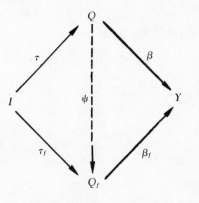

commutes.

Proof

That M_f realizes f is proven by diagram (11); i.e., $f = \beta_f r_f$. The reachability morphism is a coequalizer by its definition (Postulate 2). Thus, it only remains to prove that M_f is minimal.

Let M be a realization of f, so that $\beta r = f$, and let r be a coequalizer, say $r = \mathrm{coeq}(\alpha', \gamma')$, for the pair $E \underset{\gamma'}{\overset{\alpha'}{\rightrightarrows}} IX@$. Now if $Q \overset{\psi}{\to} Q_f$ is an X-dynamorphism satisfying $\psi \tau = \tau_f$, then we have that both ψr and r_f are the unique dynamorphic extension of $\psi \tau = \tau_f$, and hence $\psi r = r_f$, as can be seen from the following two diagrams:

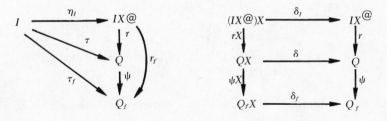

To find a ψ such that $r \psi = r_f$, we solve the coequalizer diagram

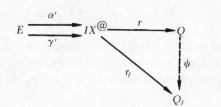

$$(12)$$

for ψ. However, to do this, we must first verify that $r_f \alpha' = r_f \gamma'$. Thus, we will show that $E \underset{\gamma'}{\overset{\alpha'}{\rightrightarrows}} IX^@$ may take the place of $R \underset{p'}{\overset{p}{\rightrightarrows}} IX^@$ in (7b). In other words, we will show that

$$f\delta_I^{(n)}(\alpha'X^n) = f\delta_I^{(n)}(\gamma'X^n)$$

for all $n \in \mathbf{N}$. From $f = \beta r$ and the fact that r is an X-dynamorphism, we can form the following commutative diagram:

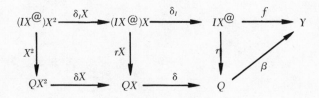

But this just says that

$$f\delta_I^{(2)} = \beta\delta^{(2)}(rX^2)$$

and clearly, this method of proof yields

$$f\delta_I^{(n)} = \beta\delta^{(n)}(rX^n) \tag{13}$$

for all $n \in \mathbf{N}$. Hence,

$$
\begin{aligned}
f\delta_I^{(n)}(\alpha'X^n) &= \beta\delta^{(n)}(rX^n)(\alpha'X^n) && \text{by (13)}\\
&= \beta\delta^{(n)}(r\alpha')X^n && \text{since } X^n \text{ is a functor}\\
&= \beta\delta^{(n)}(r\gamma')X^n && \text{since } r\alpha' = r\gamma'\\
&= \beta\delta^{(n)}(rX^n)(\gamma'X^n) && \text{since } X^n \text{ is a functor}\\
&= f\delta_I^{(n)}(\gamma'X^n) && \text{by (13)}
\end{aligned}
$$

Thus, the conditions for (7) are met, and there exists a unique $E \xrightarrow{\psi'} E_f$ such that

$$\alpha' = \alpha\psi' \qquad \text{and} \qquad \gamma' = \gamma\psi'$$

We thus have that

$$r_f\alpha' = r_f\alpha\psi' = r_f\gamma\psi' \text{ since } r_f\alpha = r_f\gamma$$
$$= r_f\gamma'$$

Thus the condition for using (12) is met, and we do indeed have a unique ψ such that $\psi r = r_f$.

It remains to be checked that

$$\psi\tau = \tau_f \text{ and } \beta_f\psi = \beta$$

and that ψ is an X-dynamorphism, i.e., that $\delta_f(\psi X) = \psi\delta$.

Firstly,

$$\psi\tau = \psi r\eta_I \quad \text{since } \tau = r\eta_I$$
$$= r_f\eta_I \quad \text{since } \psi r = r_f$$
$$= \tau_f$$

Secondly,

$$\beta_f\psi r = \beta_f r_f \quad \text{since } \psi r = r_f$$
$$= f \quad \text{since } M_f \text{ is a realization of } f$$
$$= \beta r \quad \text{since } M \text{ is a realization of } f$$

Thus, $\beta_f\psi = \beta$, since r, being a coequalizer, is an epimorphism. Finally,

$$\delta_f(\psi X)(rX) = \delta_f[(\psi r)X] \quad \text{since } X \text{ is a functor}$$
$$= \delta_f(r_f X) \quad \text{since } \psi r = r_f$$
$$= r_f\delta_I \quad \text{since } r_f \text{ is an } X\text{-dynamorphism}$$
$$= \psi r\delta_I \quad \text{since } \psi r = r_f$$
$$= \psi\delta(rx) \quad \text{since } r \text{ is an } X\text{-dynamorphism}$$

But, by Postulate 4, rX is an epimorphism, and hence $\delta_f(\psi X) = \psi\delta$, so that ψ is indeed an X-dynamorphism. $\square$

APPLICATIONS

We are now done with the motivation/theory alternation that led to the Nerode Realization Theorem, and we turn to applications. By its very construction, this theorem includes the usual theory for $X = -\times X_0 : \mathcal{S} \to \mathcal{S}$ of Section 2–5. To further demonstrate the power of Theorem 4, for $X = -\oplus X_0 : R\text{-}\mathbf{Mod} \to R\text{-}\mathbf{Mod}$, we shall recover the realization theory for linear machines, and follow that with a realization theory for tree automata. But first, we shall make an observation, related to Lemma 3 for $X = -\times X_0$, concerning Postulates 3 and 4.

DEFINITION 7

Suppose $g = \text{coeq}(h, k)$. If $gX = \text{coeq}(hX, kX)$, then we say that X **preserves coequalizers.** ○

LEMMA 5

If f satisfies Postulates 1 and 2, and if X preserves coequalizers, then f satisfies Postulates 3 and 4.

Proof

Postulate 4 is satisfied since coequalizers are epimorphisms. If we can find a dynamics δ_f such that the diagram

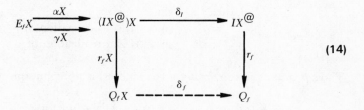

(14)

commutes, then Postulate 3 will be satisfied. Hence, it suffices to prove that

$$r_f \delta_I(\alpha X) = r_f \delta_I(\gamma X) \tag{15}$$

so that we may apply the coequalizer condition.

We wish to show first, that (7) is applicable in the case where $R = (IX^{@})X$, $p = \delta_I(\alpha X)$, and $p' = \delta_I(\gamma X)$. To do this we must verify that

$$f\delta_I^{(n)}(pX^n) = f\delta_I^{(n)}(p'X^n) \text{ for all } n \in \mathbf{N}$$

But

$$\begin{aligned} \delta_I^{(n)}(pX^n) &= \delta_I^{(n)}(\delta_I \cdot (\alpha X))X^n \\ &= \delta_I^{(n)}(\delta_I X^n) \cdot (\alpha X^{n+1}) \quad \text{since } X^n \text{ is a functor} \\ &= \delta_I^{(n+1)}\alpha X^{n+1} \quad\quad\quad \text{by definition of } \delta_I^{(n+1)} \end{aligned}$$

Thus, our condition reduces to

$$\delta_I^{(n+1)}(\alpha X^{n+1}) = \delta_I^{(n+1)}(\gamma X^{n+1}) \text{ for all } n \in \mathbf{N}$$

and this certainly holds by the original conditions on α and γ.

Thus, there exists a unique ψ such that

$$\delta_I(\alpha X) = \alpha\psi$$

and

$$\delta_I(\gamma X) = \gamma\psi$$

Thus,

$$r_f\delta_I(\alpha X) = r_f\alpha\psi = r_f\gamma\psi \quad \text{by the fact that } r_f = \text{coeq}(\alpha, \gamma)$$
$$= r_f\delta_I(\gamma X)$$

Thus, (15) is satisfied, and δ_f is uniquely defined by the coequalizer diagram (14). $\square$

Let us apply this lemma to the theory of linear machines, for, while it is often asking a lot for an arbitrary input process to preserve coequalizers, coequalizers *are* preserved by $X = -\oplus X_0 : R\text{-}\mathbf{Mod} \to R\text{-}\mathbf{Mod}$ (as was also true for $X = -\times X_0 : \mathcal{S} \to \mathcal{S}$ in Lemma 3).

LEMMA 6

In the category $R\text{-}\mathbf{Mod}$, the input process $-\oplus X_0$ preserves coequalizers; i.e., if $g = \text{coeq}(h, k)$, then $g \oplus X_0 = \text{coeq}(h \oplus X_0, k \oplus X_0)$.

Proof

Suppose that the linear map $g : B \to C$ is a coequalizer of $A \underset{k}{\overset{h}{\rightrightarrows}} B$. We verify that the linear map $g \oplus X_0 = B \oplus X_0 \to C \oplus X_0$ is a coequalizer of $A \oplus X_0 \underset{k \oplus X_0}{\overset{h \oplus X_0}{\rightrightarrows}} B \oplus X_0$.

(a) Firstly,

$$
\begin{aligned}
(g \oplus X_0)(h \oplus X_0) &= gh \oplus X_0 && \text{since } -\oplus X_0 \text{ is a functor}\\
&= gk \oplus X_0 && \text{since } g = \text{coeq}(h, k)\\
&= (g \oplus X_0)(k \oplus X_0) && \text{since } -\oplus X_0 \text{ is a functor}
\end{aligned}
$$

(b) Secondly, suppose that there exists a linear map $g' : B \oplus X_0 \to C'$ such that $g'(h \oplus X_0) = g'(k \oplus X_0)$. Consider the diagram

(16)

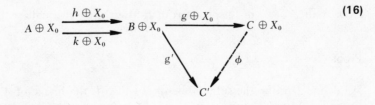

where ϕ is a linear map to be determined. Since ϕ and g' are linear maps, they can be expressed in the form

$$\phi : C \oplus X_0 \rightarrow C' : (c, x) \rightarrow Fc + Gx$$
$$g' : B \oplus X_0 \rightarrow C' : (b, x) \rightarrow F'b + G'x$$

for suitable F, F', G, and G'. Hence, we can separate (16) into the following two diagrams:

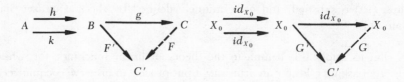

Now, for all a in A and x in X_0, we have

$$g'(h \oplus X_0)(a, x) = g'(h(a), x) = F'h(a) + G'x$$

and

$$g'(k \oplus X_0)(a, x) = g'(k(a), x) = F'k(a) + G'x$$

Thus,

$$g'(h \oplus X_0) = g'(k \oplus X_0)$$
$$F'h(a) + G'x = F'k(a) + G'x$$
$$F'h(a) = F'k(a)$$

for all $a \in A$. Hence, $F'h = F'k$.

Since $g = \text{coeq}(h, k)$, F is the unique linear map such that $F' = Fg$. Furthermore, G is obviously the unique linear map G' such that $G' = id_{X_0} G = G$. Thus, there exists a unique linear map $\phi : (c, x) \mapsto Fc + Gx$ such that (16) commutes. Hence, $-\oplus X_0$ preserves coequalizers. □

We now shall show that any pair of R-**Mod**-morphisms $A \underset{k}{\overset{h}{\rightrightarrows}} B$ has a coequalizer. We leave it for the reader to demonstrate the corresponding result for the category of sets (Exercise 4).

LEMMA 7

Every pair $A \underset{k}{\overset{h}{\rightrightarrows}} B$ of linear maps in R-**Mod** has a coequalizer.

Proof

We define D to be the submodule of B which is the image of A under the linear map $f = h - k : A \rightarrow B : a \mapsto h(a) - k(a)$; that is,

$$D = f(A) = (h - k)(A) = \{b \in B \,|\, b = h(a) - k(a) \text{ for some } a \in A\}$$

We then can form the factor module

$$C = B/D$$

where the elements of C are of the form

$$[b] = \{b + d \,|\, d \in D\} \tag{17}$$

Next we define the linear map

$$g : B \to C : b \mapsto [b]$$

and claim that $g = \mathrm{coeq}(h, k)$.

(a) Firstly,

$$
\begin{aligned}
gk(a) &= [k(a)] && \text{by the definition of } g \\
&= [k(a) + (h - k)(a)] && \text{by the definition of } D \\
&= [k(a) + h(a) - k(a)] && \text{by the definition of } h - k \\
&= [h(a)] && \text{by addition} \\
&= gh(a) && \text{by the definition of } g
\end{aligned}
$$

for all $a \in A$. Thus, $gh = gk$.

(b) Secondly, suppose that there exists a linear map $g' : B \to C'$ such that $g'h = g'k$. Then for all $a \in A$,

$$g'h(a) = g'k(a)$$

or

$$
\begin{aligned}
g'h(a) - g'k(a) &= 0 \\
g'(h(a) - k(a)) &= 0 && \text{by the linearity of } g' \\
g'((h - k)(a)) &= 0 && \text{by the definition of } h - k \tag{18}
\end{aligned}
$$

Consider the following diagram:

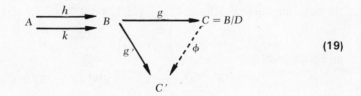

$$\tag{19}$$

Now, the map

$$\phi : C \to C' : [b] \to g'(b)$$

is well defined, since if

$$[b_1] = [b_2]$$

then

$$b_1 = b_2 + h(a) - k(a) \quad \text{for some } a \in A, \text{ by (17)}$$

and so

$$g'(b_1) = g'(b_2) + g'(h(a) - k(a)) \quad \text{by the linearity of } g'$$
$$= g'(b_2) \qquad\qquad\qquad\quad \text{by (18)}$$

Clearly, ϕ is linear and unique (Exercise 5); so we are done. $\qquad\square$

Let us now apply the Nerode realization theorem to a linear response $f: X_0^\S \to Y$. We must first determine that f satisfies Postulate 1 by supplying a Nerode equivalence $E_f \overset{\alpha}{\underset{\gamma}{\rightrightarrows}} X_0^\S$. The satisfaction of Postulates 2, 3, and 4 will then follow, since (by Lemma 7) $E_f \underset{\gamma}{\rightrightarrows} X_0^\S$ must have a coequalizer, and since (by Lemmas 5 and 6) f must then satisfy Postulates 3 and 4.

In the case of a linear behavior $f: X_0^\S \to Y$, diagram (7b) reduces to the diagram:

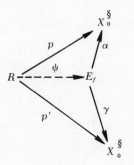

(20)

Let us see that we can take for E_f the choice made in our realization theorem for linear machines (Theorem 7-5-1). There we defined

$$\tilde{f}: X_0^\S \to Y^N : w \to (f(w), f(w0), \dots, f(w0^n), \dots)$$

and took

$$E_f = \{(w_1, w_2) \,|\, w_1, w_2 \in X_0^\S \text{ and } \tilde{f}(w_1) = \tilde{f}(w_2)\}$$

so that, in our present notation, we have

$$\alpha(w_1, w_2) = w_1 \qquad \text{and} \qquad \gamma(w_1, w_2) = w_2$$

But to see that (7*a*) is satisfied

$$f\delta_I^{(n)}(\alpha \oplus X_0^n)((w_1, w_2), w') = f(w_1 w')$$
$$= f(w_1 0^n) + f(w')$$

while

$$f\delta_I^{(n)}(\gamma \oplus X^n)((w_1, w_2), w') = f(w_2 0^n) + f(w')$$

Thus,

$$f\delta_I^{(n)}(\alpha \oplus X_0^n) = f\delta_I^{(n)}(\gamma \oplus X_0^n)$$

since $f(w_1 0^n) = f(w_2 0^n)$ by the definition of E_f.

Finally, we must check that (20) defines ψ uniquely. But, in fact, it is a routine exercise (Exercise 6) to show that the only possible choice is given by $\psi(r) = (p(r), p'(r))$, as in the classical theory of $X = -\times X_0$ in $\mathcal{S}$.

Before we close this section by using the Nerode realization theorem to provide a realization theory for tree automata, let us note one further fact about linear machines. We begin with a lemma.

LEMMA 8

The map $g : B \to C$ is a coequalizer in R-**Mod** iff g is surjective.

Proof

(i) Suppose that $B \xrightarrow{g} C$ is a surjection. We define the R-module

$$B' = \{(b_1, b_2) \,|\, b_1, b_2 \in B \text{ and } g(b_1) = g(b_2)\} \subset B \oplus B,$$

and define p_1 and p_2 by

$$p_1 : B' \to B : (b_1, b_2) \mapsto b_1$$
$$p_2 : B' \to B : (b_1, b_2) \mapsto b_2$$

It is not difficult to prove (Exercise 7) that B' is an R-module and that p_1 and p_2 are linear maps.

Then we claim that $g = \operatorname{coeq}(p_1, p_2)$. It is certainly true that $gp_1 = gp_2$. It only remains to verify that if $g'p_1 = g'p_2$ for $B \xrightarrow{g'} C$, then there exists a unique ϕ such that $\phi g = g'$; i.e., such that the following diagram commutes:

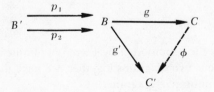

But since g is surjective, every c in C is of the form $g(b)$ for some $b \in B$, and one may then check (Exercise 7) that the map

$$\phi: C \to C': g(b) \mapsto g'(b)$$

is well-defined, linear, and unique. Hence, $g = \text{coeq}(p_1, p_2)$.

(ii) Suppose that the linear map $B \xrightarrow{g} C$ is a coequalizer of $A \overset{h}{\underset{k}{\rightrightarrows}} B$. We define the R-module

$$B' = \{(b_1, b_2) \mid b_1, b_2 \in B \text{ and } g(b_1) = g(b_2)\} \subset B \oplus B$$

It can easily be verified that B' is an equivalence relation on B (Exercise 8). We also define the projections p_1 and p_2 by

$$p_1: B' \to B: (b_1, b_2) \mapsto b_1$$
$$p_2: B' \to B: (b_1, b_2) \mapsto b_2$$

Finally, form the R-module $C' = B/B'$ and the (obviously) linear map $g' = B \to C': b \mapsto [b]$, where g' is clearly surjective.

Since $gh = gk$, it follows that $(h(a), k(a)) \in B'$ for all $a \in A$. Thus we may define $\omega: A \to B': a \to (h(a), k(a))$, and we then have that $p_1 \omega = h$ and $p_2 \omega = k$. Hence $g'h = g'p_1\omega = g'p_2\omega = g'k$. Since $g = \text{coeq}(h, k)$, there exists a unique ϕ such that $\phi g = g'$; i.e., such that the diagram

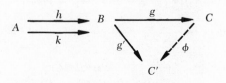

commutes. Now consider the following diagram:

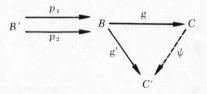

Since $gp_1 = gp_2$ by the definition of B', there is a unique ψ such that $\psi g' = g$. Splicing the previous two diagrams together, we have that the unique completion of the commutative diagram

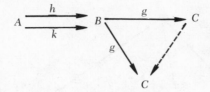

may be taken as $\psi\phi$ or id_C. Thus $\psi\phi = id_C$, and so ψ is surjective. Thus $g = \psi g'$ is surjective, since both ψ and g' are. $\square$

FACT 9

A linear machine $(Q, X_0, Y, \delta, \beta)$ defined by the linear maps $F : Q \to Q$, $G : X_0 \to Q$, and $H : Q \to Y$ is coequalizer-reachable (i.e., the reachability map $r : X_0^\S \to Q$ is a coequalizer) iff every state is of the form:

$$\sum_{j \geq 0} F^j G x_j$$

Proof

Recall that

$$X_0^\S = \{w : \mathbf{N} \to X_0 \,|\, w(\ell) \neq 0 \text{ for finitely many } \ell\}$$

and that r is precisely the map

$$r : X_0^\S \to Q : (\dots, x_n, \dots, x_1, x_0) \mapsto \sum_{j \geq 0} F^j G x_j$$

The result is then immediate from Lemma 8. $\square$

Let us now apply the Nerode realization theorem to tree automata.

To determine E_f for a tree response function $f : IX^@ \to Y$, where $IX^@$ is the set of Ω_I-trees, we must first describe the map:

$$(IX^@)X^n \xrightarrow{\ \delta_I^{(n)}\ } IX^@$$

By equation (15) of Section 9-2, for any Q, we have that

$$QX = \{(q_1, q_2, \dots, q_m, \omega) \,|\, q_1, q_2, \dots, q_m \in Q \text{ and } m \in \nu(\omega)\}$$

Thus, we see that the elements of QX take the form shown in Figure 9-2(a) for $m > 0$ and Figure 9-2(b) for $m = 0$.

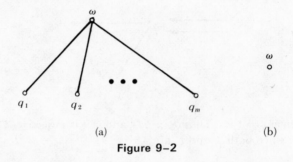

(a)   (b)

Figure 9-2

We may continue in this vein and verify by induction (Exercise 9) that the elements of QX^n can all be represented by trees of height at most n, where any path of length n terminates at a node labelled with an element of Q, while any path of length less than n terminates in a node labelled with an element of Ω_0. For instance, the tree shown in Figure 9–3(a) does not represent an element in QX^2, while the tree in Figure 9–3(b) does.

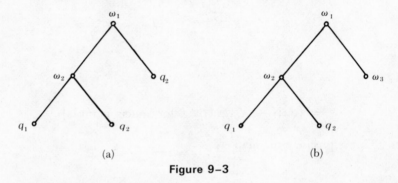

(a)   (b)

Figure 9-3

We may represent any such tree in the form $(q_1, q_2, \ldots, q_m)\Delta$ to stress that the tree Δ has terminal nodes which bear the labels $q_1, q_2, \ldots, q_m$ and elements of Ω_0. Furthermore, different nodes may bear the same label. Then $(q_1', q_2', \ldots, q_m')\Delta$ is the tree obtained by replacing the label q_j by q_j' for $j = 1, 2, \ldots, m$. We call a Δ obtained in this way an m-**ary derived operator,** and we say that Δ is **unary** if $m = 1$.

Now (as mentioned above), the elements of $IX^@$ are Ω_I-trees, so

$$\delta_I^{(n)} : (IX^@)X^n \to IX^@$$

is simply the map which sends an $\Omega_{IX^@}$-tree to the Ω_I-tree obtained by "unfurling" the Ω_I-trees comprising the terminal nodes of the $\Omega_{IX^@}$-tree. For example, if the $\Omega_{IX^@}$-tree shown in Figure 9–4 has as the terminal nodes marked (a) and (b) the Ω_I-trees given in Figure 9–5(a) and (b), respectively, then $\delta_I^{(n)}$ maps the tree of height 2 shown in Figure 9–4 into the tree of height 4 shown in Figure 9–6.

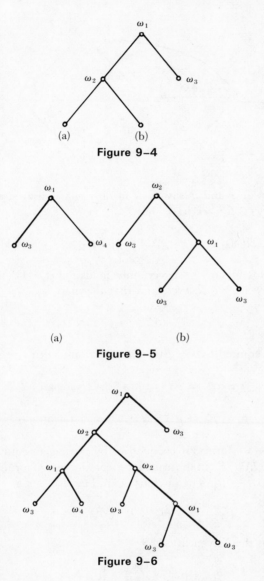

Figure 9-4

(a)   (b)

Figure 9-5

Figure 9-6

Under the circumstances, then, there is little risk of ambiguity if we use the same notation for an $\Omega_{IX}@$-tree and for the Ω_I-tree obtained by applying $\delta_I^{(n)}$ to the $\Omega_{IX}@$-tree.

We now claim that in forming E_f we need only explicitly look at the unary operators, and that we can in fact take E_f to be

$$E_f = \{(t_1, t_2) \in IX@ \mid f[(t_1)\Delta] = f[(t_2)\Delta] \text{ for all unary derived operations } \Delta\}$$

We first recall the combined form of diagrams (7a) and (7b):

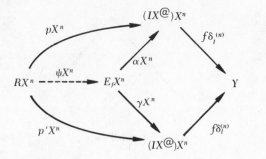

$$(7)$$

The condition on p and p' says that for any m-ary derived operator Δ and any $(r_1, \ldots, r_m) \in R^M$, we have that

$$f[(p(r_1), \ldots, p(r_m))\Delta] = f[(p'(r_1), \ldots, p'(r_m))\Delta]$$

Since this holds for any m, it certainly holds for $m = 1$, and hence $(p(r),$ $p'(r)) \in E_f$ for each $r \in R$. We claim that the map

$$\psi : R \to E_f : r \mapsto (p(r), p'(r))$$

does the job required by (7). But this is obvious, since

$$p = \alpha\psi \Rightarrow pX^n = (\alpha X^n)\psi X^n \quad \text{for all } n \in \mathbf{N}$$

and

$$p' = \gamma\psi \Rightarrow p'X^n = (\gamma X^n)\psi X^n \quad \text{for all } n \in \mathbf{N}$$

As usual in $\mathcal{S}$, we form our coequalizer by passing to equivalence classes:

Let $Q_f = IX^@/E_f$, in the usual set-theoretic sense of forming equivalence classes, with $r_f : t \to [t]$. The obvious definition of

$$(\delta_f)_m^\omega : Q_f^m \to Q_f$$

for $m \in \nu(\omega)$ is then given by

$$(\delta_f)_m^\omega([t_1], \ldots, [t_m]) = [(t_1, \ldots, t_m)\omega]$$

since it is easy (Exercise 10) to verify, using the techniques that justified our definition of E_f, that

$$m \in \nu(\omega) \text{ and } [t_j] = [t_j'] \text{ for } j = 1, 2, \ldots, m \Rightarrow$$
$$[(t_1, \ldots, t_m)\omega] = [(t_1', \ldots, t_m')\omega]$$

Thus, f satisfies Postulates 2 and 3. Postulate 4 is trivial, since coequalizers are split epimorphic in $\mathcal{S}$, and all functors preserve split epimorphisms; i.e., $ff' = id_B \Rightarrow (fX)(f'X) = id_{BX}$.

EXERCISES FOR SECTION 9.3

1. Let $E_f \overset{\alpha}{\underset{\gamma}{\rightrightarrows}} IX^@$ and $E'_f \overset{\alpha'}{\underset{\gamma'}{\rightrightarrows}} IX^@$ be two Nerode equivalences for f. Let $\psi': E'_f \to E_f$ be the ψ defined by (7) on replacing $R \overset{p}{\underset{p}{\rightrightarrows}} IX^@$ by $E'_f \overset{\alpha'}{\underset{\gamma'}{\rightrightarrows}} IX^@$. Let ψ'' be obtained by reversing the roles of E_f and E'_f. Adapt the "splicing trick" of the proof of Theorem 9–1–1(ii) to deduce that $\psi'\psi'' = id_{E_f}$ and $\psi''\psi' = id_{E'_f}$, so that ψ' is a $\mathcal{K}$-isomorphism.

2. Show that a functor X in a category $\mathcal{K}$ preserves split epimorphisms; i.e., show that if $f:A \to B$ is a split epimorphism, then so is $fX:AX \to BX$.

3. The proof of Lemma 1(ii) makes use of the assumption that there exists some $b \in B$ other than b_0. Verify that if $B = \{b_0\}$, then any epimorphism $f:A \to B$ is surjective.

4. Prove that any pair of maps $A \overset{h}{\underset{k}{\rightrightarrows}} B$ in $\mathcal{S}$ has a coequalizer. [Hint: This result is implicit in the way in which we motivated Postulate 2.]

5. Show that the ϕ defined in the proof of Lemma 7 is linear and unique.

6. Show that diagram (20) defines ψ uniquely, and that it is given by $\psi(r) = (p(r), p'(r))$.

7. As defined in the proof of Lemma 8, prove that B' is an R-module and that p_1 and p_2 are linear maps. Also prove that $\phi:g(b) \mapsto g'(b)$ is well-defined, linear, and unique.

8. Prove that the set $B' \subset B \times B$, given in the proof of Lemma 8, is an equivalence relation.

9. For tree automata, prove by induction that the elements of QX^n can all be represented by trees of height at most n, where any path of length n terminates at a node labelled with an element of Q, while any path of length less than n terminates in a node labelled with an element of Ω_0.

10. For tree automata, verify that if $m \in \nu(\omega)$ and $[t_j] = [t'_j]$ for $j = 1, 2, \ldots, m$, then $[(t_1, t_2, \ldots, t_m)\omega] = [(t'_1, t'_2, \ldots, t'_m)\omega]$.

Further Reading for Chapter 9

M. A. ARBIB and E. G. MANES [1973], Machines in a Category, *SIAM Review,* in press.

M. A. ARBIB and E. G. MANES [1974], Foundations of System Theory I, *Automatica,* in press.

E. S. BAINBRIDGE [1973], A Unified Minimal Realization Theory, with Duality, for Machines in a Hyperdoctrine (Ph.D. Dissertation, Univ. of Michigan).

J. A. GOGUEN [1972], Minimal Realization of Machines in Closed Categories, *Bull. Amer. Math. Soc.* 78, 777–783.

S. MACLANE [1972], *Categories for the Working Mathematician,* Springer-Verlag, New York, New York.

L. PADULO and M. A. ARBIB [1974], *System Theory: A Unified, State-Space Approach to Continuous and Discrete Time Systems,* W. B. Saunders Co., Philadelphia, Pennsylvania.

Index